India

Perfect places to stay, eat & explore

Published by Time Out Guides Ltd, a wholly owned subsidiary of Time Out Group Ltd.
Time Out and the Time Out logo are trademarks of Time Out Group Ltd.

10 9 8 7 6 5 4 3 2 1

This edition first published in Great Britain in 2010 by Ebury Publishing
A Random House Group Company
20 Vauxhall Bridge Road, London SW1V 2SA

Random House Australia Pty Limited 20 Alfred Street, Milsons Point, Sydney, New South Wales 2061, Australia
Random House New Zealand Limited 18 Poland Road, Glenfield, Auckland 10, New Zealand
Random House South Africa (Pty) Limited Isle of Houghton, Corner Boundary, Road & Carse O'Gowrie, Houghton 2198, South Africa

Random House UK Limited Reg. No. 954009

Distributed in USA by Publishers Group West
1700 Fourth Street, Berkeley, California 94710

Distributed in Canada by Publishers Group Canada
250A Carlton Street, Toronto, Ontario M5A 2L1

For further distribution details, see www.timeout.com

ISBN: 978184670164-1

A CIP catalogue record for this book is available from the British Library

Printed and bound by Firmengruppe APPL, aprinta druck, Wemding, Germany

The Random House Group Limited supports The Forest Stewardship Council (FSC), the leading international forest certification organisation. All our titles that are printed on Greenpeace approved FSC certified paper carry the FSC logo. Our paper procurement policy can be found at http://www.rbooks.co.uk/environment.

Time Out carbon-offsets all its flights with Trees for Cities (www.treesforcities.org).

Introduction

Welcome to *Time Out India: Perfect places to stay, eat & explore*. We've picked out the most inspiring destinations across the country and taken you straight to the best sights, hotels, restaurants, shops and cultural venues in each, across all price bands. With magazine offices in Mumbai, Delhi and Bengaluru (Bangalore), Time Out is uniquely placed to give you the inside view.

India is a huge country and it would be impossible to capture all of its sights, sounds and colours, but we've tried to reflect its immense diversity by including as wide a range as possible of its cities, towns, historic sites and landscapes. To help with inspiration and planning, we've divided our 26 destinations into seven categories. India's exquisite architectural heritage is represented in **Architectural Treasures**. **The Great Cities** covers the megacities of Mumbai, Delhi and Kolkata, while **Urban Gems** takes in smaller, historically fascinating centres. In **Spiritual Passages**, we give you a glimpse of some of the religious rituals that are part of everyday life here. Our **Wildlife** section reveals the best places to spot tigers and other animals. The remote hill towns and distinctive cultures of North India's mountainous regions feature in **Mountains**; and for those who want a relaxed introduction to India, any of the destinations in our **Alluring Escapes** section can make an ideal holiday – or a peaceful segment of a longer trip. And if you plan to visit more than one destination, our **Itineraries** section shows you how to construct your perfect trip, whether it's a week's holiday or a longer stay.

All the clichés you have heard about India are probably true. For the average visitor it's not an easy country to understand, navigate or sometimes accept. It compels you to alter the way you see the world. It forces you to adjust, to be patient, to negotiate difference. But time spent in India is also certain to leave you with memories that will last a lifetime. So many religions, cultures, cuisines, languages, geographical features and experiences are packed into this vast land that no matter how much you read and plan, chances are that at some point you will feel overwhelmed. But we believe that our careful selections, together with our travel tips and insider knowledge, will help you to experience this fascinating country to the full.

A word about the listings. The $ symbols indicate the price bracket of a venue: $= budget, $$= moderate, $$$=expensive and $$$$=luxury. Unless otherwise stated, hotels, restaurants and shops accept credit cards. However, in general, cheaper establishments and those in more remote locations tend not to accept them, and they can't be used to pay for entry to sites. All our listings are double-checked, but businesses do sometimes close or change their hours and prices. We recommend you check particulars by phone or online before visiting.

Contents

132

181

223

The Great Cities

Urban Gems

Architectural Treasures

Mountains

Spiritual Passages

Wildlife

Alluring Escapes

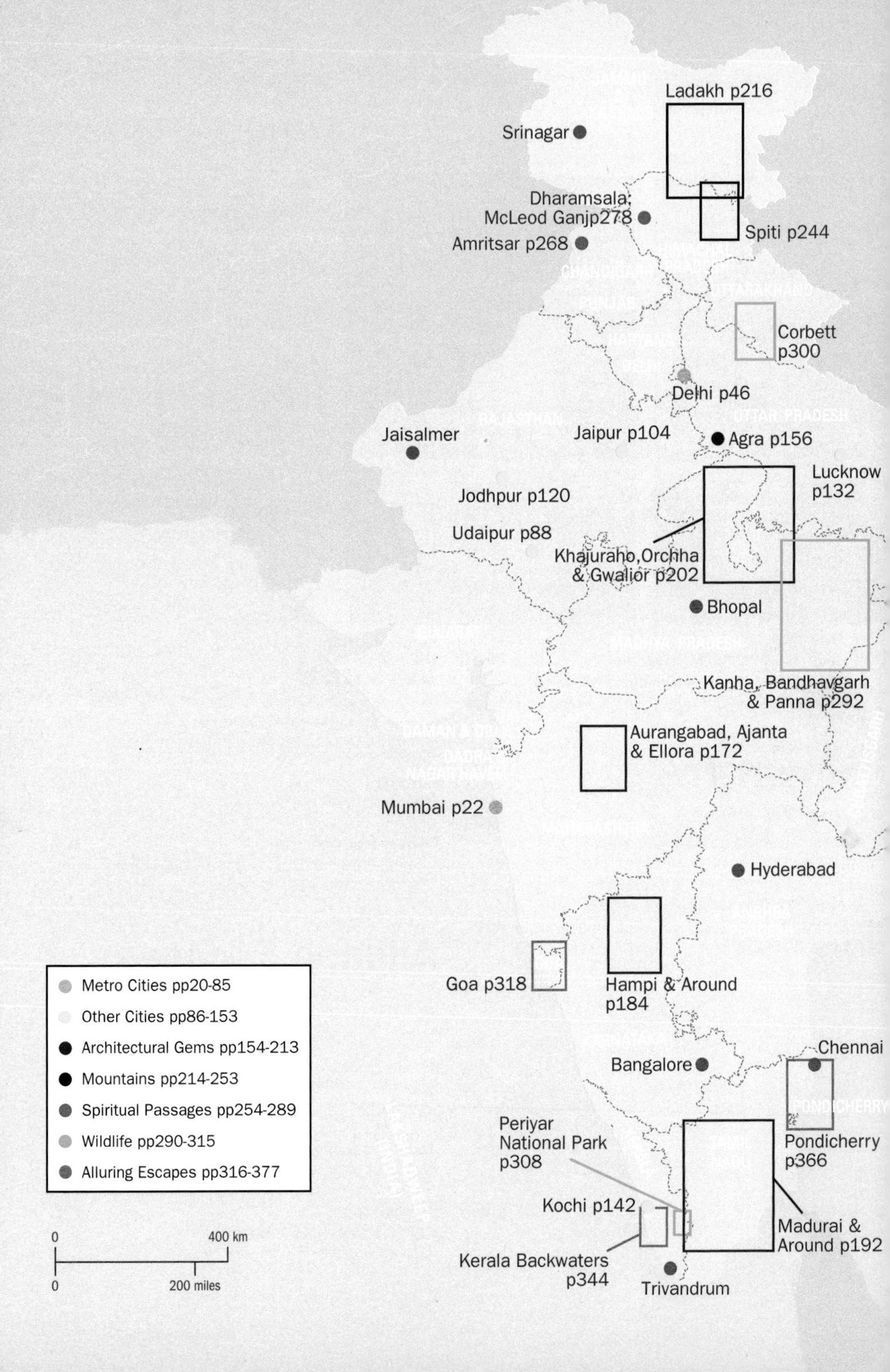
Ladakh p216
Srinagar
Dharamsala:
McLeod Ganjp278
Spiti p244
Amritsar p268
Corbett
p300
Delhi p46
Jaisalmer
Jaipur p104
Agra p156
Lucknow
p132
Jodhpur p120
Udaipur p88
Khajuraho,Orchha
& Gwalior p202
Bhopal
Kanha, Bandhavgarh
& Panna p292
Aurangabad, Ajanta
& Ellora p172
Mumbai p22
Hyderabad
Goa p318
Hampi & Around
p184
Chennai
Bangalore
Periyar
National Park
p308
Pondicherry
p366
Kochi p142
Madurai &
Around p192
Kerala Backwaters
p344
Trivandrum
Metro Cities pp20-85
Other Cities pp86-153
Architectural Gems pp154-213
Mountains pp214-253
Spiritual Passages pp254-289
Wildlife pp290-315
Alluring Escapes pp316-377
0
400 km
0
200 miles

India

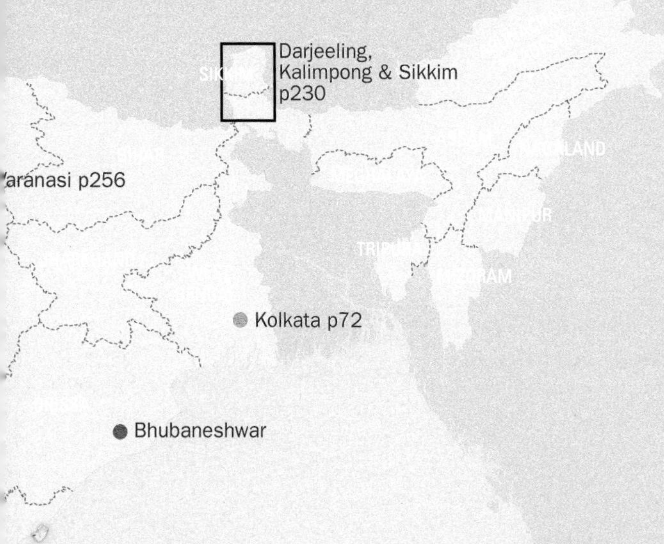

Andaman Islands p354

Editor's Picks

FIVE-STAR DESTINATIONS

Each of our destinations are rated in categories. Here are the best in each:

ART & ARCHITECTURE

EATING & DRINKING

HISTORIC SITES

HOTELS

NIGHTLIFE

OUTDOOR ACTIVITIES

SCENERY

SHOPPING

ACCOMMODATION

LUXURY

Pashan Garh, Panna National Park; Kanha, Bandhavgarh & Panna p298

Raj Vilas, Jaipur p118

Rambagh Palace, Jaipur p118

Taj Lands End, Mumbai p44

Taj Mahal Palace & Tower, Mumbai p44

Umaid Bhawan Palace, Jodhpur p131

HERITAGE

Bangala, Madurai & Around p198

Brunton Boatyard, Kochi p151

Calve WelcomHeritage, Pondicherry p374

Chettinadu Mansion, Madurai & Around p198

Devi Garh, Udaipur p100

Hotel de L'Orient, Pondicherry p374

Maison Perumal, Pondicherry p377

Malabar House, Kochi p153

Old Harbour Hotel, Kochi p153

Raheem Residency, Kerala Backwaters p353

Visalam, Madurai & Around p201

Welcomheritage Ranjit's Svaasa, Amritsar p277

GOOD-VALUE

Amarya Haveli, Delhi p69

Bnineteen, Delhi p69

Bundelkhand Riverside Resort, Orchha; Khajuraho, Orchha & Gwalior p210

Chonor House, Dharamsala/McLeod Ganj p282

The Elgin Mount Pandim, Pelling p240

Hidden Forest Retreat, Kalimpong; Darjeeling, Kalimpong & Sikkim p242

Glenmoor Cottages, Dharamsala/ McLeod Ganj p286

Hotel Diggi Palace, Jaipur p118

Hotel de Pondicherry, Pondicherry p374

Ken River Lodge, Panna National Park; Kanha, Banhavgarh & Panna p296

Kipling Camp, Kanha National Park; Kanha, Banhavgarh & Panna p298

Old Harbour Hotel, Kochi p153

Pooppally's Heritage Homestay, Kerala Backwaters p350

Ratan Vilas, Jodhpur p131

Sheesh Mahal, Orchha p210

Shanti Home, Delhi p70

Thikana, Delhi p71

RESTAURANTS

INTERNATIONAL CUISINE

Bomra's, Goa p331

Diva, Delhi p61

Ernesto's House, Goa p335

La Plage, Goa p335

Thalassa, Goa p335

Tote on the Turf, Mumbai p37

FINE DINING

Blue Potato, Kolkata p79

Indigo & Tote on the Turf, Mumbai p37

Varq, Delhi p61

INDIAN CUISINES

Brittannia, Mumbai p34

Bukhara, Delhi p58

Carte Blanche, Pondicherry p371

Dum Pukht, Kolkata p79; Mumbai p34

Falaknuma, Lucknow p136

The History, Kochi p147

The Malabar Junction, Kochi p147

Oudhyana, Lucknow p138

Peshawari, Agra p164

Sonargaon, Kolkata p81

STREET FOOD (NOT NECESSARILY ON THE STREET)

Bade Miya's, Mumbai p34

Hot Kathi Roll, Kolkata p79

King of Chaat, Lucknow p136

Soam, Mumbai p37

Swati Snacks, Mumbai p37

Tunday Kababi, Lucknow p138

ATMOSPHERE

Britannia, Mumbai p34

Ginger House Restaurant, Kochi p147

The Pillars, Jodhpur p127

Tunday Kababi, Lucknow p138

VIEWS (RESTAURANTS/BARS)

Aurus, Mumbai p39

Le Café, Pondicherry p371

Dome, Mumbai p39

Keventer's Snack Bar, Darjeeling p239

Mehran Terrace, Jodhpur p124

Nine Bar, Goa p339

Shanti Lodge, Agra p164

Sunset Terrace, Udaipur p96

Thalassa, Goa p335

BUILDINGS

COLONIAL BUILDINGS

Delhi p46

Kochi p142

Kolkata p72

Mumbai p22

Old Goa, Goa p327

Pondicherry p366

FORTS

Amer Fort, Jaipur p109

Chittorgarh, around Udaipur p95

Daulatabad Fort; Aurangabad, Ajanta & Ellora p176

Kumbhalgarh Fort, Udaipur p95

Mehrangarh, Jodhpur p122

TEMPLES

Baha'i/Lotus temple, Delhi p57

Chaumukha Temple, Ranakpur, Udaipur p93

Golden Temple, Amritsar p270

Kailashnath temple, Ellora p178

Matrumandir, Pondicherry

Meenakshi Sundareshwar, Madurai & Around p194

Thekchen Chöling Temple Complex p280

Vithala & Virupaksha Temples, Hampi p186

Western group of temples, Khajuraho p204

CHURCHES

Afghan Church, Mumbai p30

St John's Church, Kolkata p76

St John's in the Wilderness, Dharamsala/ McLeod Ganj p281

OTHER RELIGIOUS PLACES

Bara Imambara, Lucknow p134

Jama Masjid, Delhi p53

Lamayuru & Thiksey monasteries, Ladakh p221

PALACES

City Palace, Jaipur p107

City Palace, Udaipur p91

OTHER MONUMENTS

Fatehpur Sikri, Agra p163

Humayun's Tomb, Delhi p53

Itmad-ud-Daulah, Agra p158

Qutb Minar, Delhi p57

Taj Mahal, Agra p159

EXPERIENCES

Audience with the Dalai lama, Dharamsala/ McLeod Ganj p284

Beach number 7, Havelock Island, Andaman Islands p359

The Ghats, Varanasi p258

Homestay, Spiti p247

Lingkor – the Holy Walk, McLeod Ganj/ Dharamsala p281

Manali-Leh road trip, Ladakh p216

Marina: 'You buy we cook', Kochi p148

Monastic festivals, Ladakh p220

Palkhi Sahib and Guru ka langar, Golden Temple, Amritsar p270

Tiger spotting, Corbett p300; Bandhavgarh National Park, Kanha, Banhavgarh & Panna p294

Village backwater cruise, Kottayam, Kerala Backwaters p347

Worship ceremony at Alagar Kovil, Madurai & Around p195

OUTDOOR ACTIVITIES

MOUNTAIN BIKING

Spiti p249

SCUBA DIVING

Andaman Islands p359

TIGER SPOTTING

Bandhavgarh p294

Corbett p300

TREKS

Darjeeling, Kalimpong & Sikkim p236

Dharamsala/McLeod Ganj p281

Ladakh p225

Spiti p247

Periyar National Park p313

WALKING

Andaman Islands p354

Darjeeling, Kalimpong & Sikkim p236

Dharamsala/McLeod Ganj p281

Old Delhi, Delhi p53

Periyar National Park p313

WHITE WATER RAFTING

On the Zanskar, Ladakh p225

VIEWS

Boat ride, Dasaswamedh ghat, Varanasi p258

Daulatabad Fort; Aurangabad, Ajanta & Ellora p176

Dhankar, Spiti p246

Fort Tiracol, Goa p323

Hanuman Temple, Anegundi; Hampi & Around p187

High Bank, Dhikala & Kanda Ridge; Corbett p303

Lamayuru, Ladakh p221

Manali–Leh road trip, Ladakh p218

Mehrangarh Fort, Jodhpur p122

Pangong Tso, Ladakh p222

Pelling and North Sikkim; Darjeeling, Kalimpong & Sikkim p236

Taj Nature Walk, Agra p159

Tiger Hill, Darjeeling; Darjeeling, Kalimpong & Sikkim p232

Vembanad Lake & Kumarakom Bird Sanctuary, Kerala Backwaters p347

Contributors

Rishiraj Ahuja returned to live in Amritsar, the city of his birth, after a decade away, and now runs a photographic equipment manufacturing business. A passion for photography, nature, and travel frequently take him to Punjab's hinterland and the Himalayas. Contributing the Amritsar chapter for this guide led him to a fresh perspective on his home town's sights and sounds.

Naresh Fernandes is editor-in-chief of Time Out's Indian publications. He has reported on crime in Mumbai, right-wing politics in Belgium and low-rider jeans in Italy. He's the co-editor of *Mumbai Meri Jaan* (Penguin India), an anthology of writing about Mumbai, and is the co-author of *Bombay Then and Mumbai Now* (Roli), a coffee-table book.

Amit Gurbaxani can't sing or play an instrument, but his life is a never-ending cycle of gig watching and music article writing. It was somewhat appropriate that the first place he visited in the magnificent city of Hampi was the Vithala Temple, where each of the pillars is said to sound a different musical note. Amit is contributing editor to an indie music blog.

Jaideep VG has spent several sweltering summers crisscrossing Tamil Nadu and Kerala states in search of the finest mutton chops in the country. He is the editor of *Time Out Bangalore* and an unrepentant devotee of beer.

Rachel Lopez is on the staff at *Time Out Mumbai* and has lived in Mumbai all her life, but isn't averse to occasionally and temporarily abandoning her favourite city to take a trip. She contributed to *Time Out Mumbai & Goa* and *Time Out: The World's Greatest Cities* Travelling to north-east India and Madhya Pradesh state for this guide she discovered that she's less of a beach person than she thought she was.

Abhishek Madhukar is a freelance writer and photographer who recently relocated to Dharamsala. He has also worked as a tour guide leading unsuspecting tourists across India and Nepal to quench his own wanderlust. He contributes to a variety of publications, and when he isn't chasing the Dalai Lama or local news stories for Reuters news agency, he tunes into sermons on Buddhist philosophy or contemplates his new life in a curious Himalayan town.

Darshan Manakkal was born in Kerala and spent many holidays freely perspiring in the state's torrid summers. For this book he happily returned to this delightful corner of India to take in the sun, the spicy cuisine and the local brew. He is currently music editor for *Time Out Bangalore.*

Vivek Menezes is a writer and photographer with deep Goan roots, although he was born in Bombay. He left India at the age of 13, and after spending 23 years studying and working in the USA, UK and France, he returned to his homeland in 2004. He now lives in the tiny riverside city of Panjim, Goa with his wife and three young sons.

Kingshuk Niyogy is on the staff at *Time Out Delhi*. As a child, he heard tales of Varanasi from his grandmother and was finally able to travel there for this guide. Though he now lives in Delhi, his heart is in his home town of Kolkata, which he also covered for this guide.

Deepanjana Pal was until recently the art writer for *Time Out Mumbai*. She is the author of *The Painter: A Life of Ravi Varma*, a biography of India's first modern painter, and contributed the chapter on Kolkata for *Time Out: The World's Greatest Cities*. She blames her nomadic childhood for her love of travelling and enjoys the neon of the big city as much as exploring small towns like Aurangabad, which she travelled to for this guide.

Yakuta Poonawalla loves the mountains and their people. She has trekked extensively in the Himalayas, and currently works with an NGO in the Spiti Valley helping create sustainable livelihoods for indigenous communities. Having explored urban and rural landscapes, she has always found the wilderness more appealing. As a lover of adventure and sport, she is constantly planning her next trek.

Roshni Bajaj Sanghvi was, until recently, the editor of the Food & Drink and Shopping & Style sections of *Time Out Mumbai*. She's a city girl who has lived in Mumbai, New York, Pune and Louisville, Kentucky. If she could, she would insure her palate and her passport. For this guide, she went to Pondicherry, a town that fed her passions of food, travel and shopping.

Sonal Shah is a journalist based in New Delhi and New York. She has covered food and art for *Time Out Delhi*, where she was on the staff. She has also worked at a newspaper and freelanced for several publications. She has roamed far and wide in India and the US, but for this guide, went closer home to Agra.

Vijay Jung Thapa is a Delhi-based journalist. The call of Corbett National Park has been ringing in his ears since he was a child, and he has to get a fix of the wild every now and then. He's currently considering settling down outside the park and visiting New Delhi once in a while. Until that happens, he interrupts his work schedule with daydreams of spotting striped predators in Corbett's prime tiger country.

Niloufer Venkatraman, this book's editor, is a cultural anthropologist by training and travel writer and editor by serendipity. She's always ready to put on her hiking boots to meander through wilderness or city, and went to Udaipur, Jodhpur and Ladakh for this guide. She has written for numerous newspapers and magazines and has previously co-authored another international travel guidebook on India.

Contributions by chapter
Delhi Sonal Shah and Avtar Singh; also Jane Mikkelson, Ambika Muttoo and *Time Out Delhi* staff. **Mumbai** Iain Ball & Leo Mirani. **Kolkata** Kingshuk Niyogy; introduction Deepanjana Pal. **Jaipur** Neha Sumitran, *Time Out Mumbai* and *Time Out Delhi* staff. **Jodhpur** Niloufer Venkatraman and *Time Out* staff. **Kochi** Darshan Manakkal; Beyond Performance Raghu Karnad, Dancing Tales Darshan Manakkal. **Lucknow** Kingshuk Niyogy, Arshiya Zaheer; Decadent ruler or people's king? Mahmood Farooqui. **Udaipur** Niloufer Venkatraman, *Time Out* staff. **Aurangabad, Ajanta & Ellora** Deepanjana Pal. **Agra** Sonal Shah. **Hampi & Around** Amit Gurbaxani. **Khajuraho, Orchha & Gwalior** Rachel Lopez. **Darjeeling, Kalimpong & Sikkim** Rachel Lopez. **Madurai & Around** Jaideep VG. **Ladakh** Niloufer Venkatraman. **Spiti** Yakuta Poonawala. **Amritsar** Rishiraj Ahuja. **Dharamsala: McLeod Ganj** Abhishek Madhukar. **Varanasi** Kingshuk Niyogy; Noteworthy Kingshuk Niyogy & Amarendra Dhaneshwar. **Corbett** Vijay Jung Thapa. **Kanha, Bandhavgarh & Panna** Rachel Lopez. **Periyar National Park** Jaideep VG. **Andaman Islands** Naresh Fernandes. **Goa** Vivek Menezes. **Kerala Backwaters** Darshan Manakkal. **Pondicherry** Fiona Fernandez, Roshni Bajaj Sanghvi. **Need to Know**, **Navigating India**, **Festivals & Events**, **Itineraries** Niloufer Venkatraman.

JUNGLE
LODGES & RESORTS

Edited by
Time Out Mumbai
Paprika Media Pvt Ltd
Essar House
11 KK Marg
Mahalaxmi Mumbai 400 034
Tel + 91 (0)22 6660 1111
Email letters@timeoutindia.net
www.timeoutindia.net

For
Time Out Guides Limited
Universal House
251 Tottenham Court Road
London W1T 7AB
Tel + 44 (0)20 7913 3000
Fax + 44 (0)20 7813 6001
Email guides@timeout.com
www.timeout.com

Editorial
Editor Niloufer Venkatraman
Project Manager (India) Neelam Kapoor
Copy Editor Ros Sales
Listings Checker Kamna Malik
Proofreaders James Mathew, Tamsin Shelton
Indexer Ismay Atkins

Managing Director Peter Fiennes
Editorial Director Ruth Jarvis
Business Manager Dan Allen
Editorial Manager Holly Pick
Assistant Management Accountant Ija Krasnikova

Design
Art Director Scott Moore
Art Editor Pinelope Kourmouzoglou
Senior Designer Henry Elphick
Graphic Designers Kei Ishimaru, Nicola Wilson
Advertising Designer Jodi Sher

Picture Desk
Picture Editor Jael Marschner (London), Ashima Narain (India)
Deputy Picture Editor Lynn Chambers
Picture Desk Assistant/Researcher Ben Rowe

Advertising
Commercial Director Mark Phillips
International Advertising Manager Kasimir Berger
International Sales Executive Charlie Sokol
India Advertising Sales Time Out India: Nishit Kumar, Vishwanath Shanbhag, Nagesh Rao

Marketing
Sales & Marketing Director, North America & Latin America Lisa Levinson
Senior Publishing Brand Manager Luthfa Begum
Art Director Anthony Huggins

Production
Group Production Director Mark Lamond
Production Manager Brendan McKeown
Production Controller Damian Bennett

Time Out Group
Chairman Tony Elliott
Chief Executive Officer David King
Group Financial Director Paul Rakkar
Group General Manager/Director Nichola Coulthard
Time Out Communications Ltd MD David Pepper
Time Out International Ltd MD Cathy Runciman
Time Out Magazine Ltd Publisher/MD Mark Elliott
Group IT Director Simon Chappell
Marketing & Circulation Director Catherine Demajo

Maps mapsofindia.com

Back cover photography Nishad Joshi, Vivek M, Ashima Narain.

Photography pages 20/21, 35 (top), 68 (top right), 26, 72, 77, 78, 80, 83, 86/87, 132, 137, 139, 140, 254/255, 256, 261, 262, 265, 266, 367, 375, 376, 391 Amit Chakravarty; pages 22 (top), 38 (bottom) Chirodeep Chaudhuri; pages 22 (centre left), 202, 206, 208, 211, 212, 245, 248, 252, 290/291, 293, 297 Nishad Joshi; pages 22 (bottom), 316/317, 354, 358, 361, 362 Hashim Badani; pages 35 (bottom), 89, 92, 94, 97, 98, 101, 102, 121, 125, 126, 129, 130, 214/215, 173, 177, 178, 181, 182, 217, 220, 223, 224, 227 Ashima Narain; page 38 (top) Poulomi Basu; page 41 (top left) Apoorva Guptay; pages 47 (top), 50 (top left and bottom right), 62 (bottom right), 64, 65 (top), 156, 162, 165, 168, 171, 230, 233, 234, 237, 238, 241 Paroma Mukherjee; pages 47 (bottom), 67 (top) Cherian Thomas; pages 50 (top right), 108 (centre left), 111 (top- and centre left) Dhruba Dutta; pages 50 (bottom left), 59 (top right) Vidyun Sabhaney; pages 59 (top left), 62 (left), 67 (bottom) Anshika Varma; page 59 (centre) Abhinandita Mathur; pages 59 (bottom), 65 (bottom) Sushant Sinha; pages 62 (top right), 104, 108, 111, 112, 115, 116 Taveeshi Singh; pages 143, 146, 149, 152, 154/155, 184, 189, 190, 193, 196, 199, 200, 309 (centre), 312, 314, 345 (bottom left), 348 (centre left), 352 (top and centre right) Vivek M; page 150 S Gautham; page 161 Wildlife SOS/John Wright; page 251 Yakuta Poonawalla; pages 269, 271, 272, 275, 318 (top and bottom left), 329 Rishiraj Ahuja; pages 278, 283, 284, 287, 288, 300 (centre right), 305, 307 (centre) Abhishek Madhukar; pages 300, 306 (top) Hideaway River Lodge; pages 309 (top and bottom), 345, 348, 351, 352 (centre left and bottom) CGH Earth; pages 318 (centre and bottom right), 324, 337 (top right) Vivek Menezes; page 333 Rohan Mukherjee; page 337 (top left and bottom) Parikshit Rao; page 354 (centre left) Vandit Kalia; page 354 (centre right) Qutubuddin Taher; page 373 INTACH Book.

The following images were provided by the featured establishments/artists: pages 41 (top right and bottom) and 42, 68, 306 (top and bottom), 332, 338, 340/341.

The editor would like to thank Smiti Kanodia, Neelam Kapoor, Roopal Soneta, Naresh Fernandes, Kamna Malik, Chirodeep Chaudhuri, Sneha Nair and staff at *Time Out Mumbai*.

The Great Cities

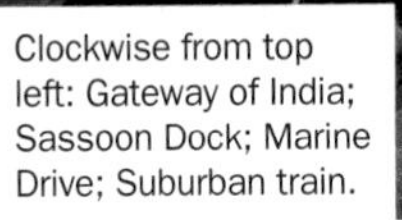

Clockwise from top left: Gateway of India; Sassoon Dock; Marine Drive; Suburban train.

Mumbai

Bollywood, business and beyond.

Visitors often dismiss Mumbai as not being representative enough of 'the real India', accusing the city of being too urban, too Western, too unlike what they want India to be. The fact is that Mumbai is India on steroids: bursting at the seams with the hopes and dreams, cultures and cuisines, languages and races, petty quarrels and disgruntled compromises of 16 million people. Mumbai is the economic engine that drives India's growth. It's home to the country's central bank, two stock exchanges and the commodities markets, and the headquarters of thousands of companies. But it's not just commerce that keeps Mumbai on the move: the city is India's biggest manufacturer of popular culture – film, television, music, dance, fashion. It has dominated the popular Indian imagination through the hundreds of books, movies and songs it has inspired, its headline-grabbing gangsters and supercops, and – surprising for a city with few open spaces – some of the country's greatest cricketing heroes.

But if the 'real' India is supposed to be shocking poverty, appalling living conditions and a gross neglect of basic human rights, then Mumbai is real – disastrously real for the 55 per cent of its residents who live in slums. The city's infrastructure is crumbling, property prices are too high for the lower and middle classes to afford proper housing, the roads are too narrow and battered to handle the exploding traffic and clean water is scarce. Its electric supply is dwindling too, yet, paradoxically, Mumbai is probably the only Indian city with almost no power cuts.

It's hard to remain an observer in Mumbai. This city has a habit of grabbing you by the collar and demanding that you get involved. Mumbai is a noisy, exhilarating, bewildering, enchanting, exasperating, chaotic, smelly and, sometimes, desperately upsetting city. It will insist on getting in your face even – indeed especially – when you don't want it to. Try to just let it wash over you, then dive in and swim.

Explore

Mumbai doesn't have many conventional tourist sights. Its museums are unlikely to have you in raptures and many of its historic buildings are dilapidated, although even the worst still manage a kind of dissipated charm. More often it's the people, the hectic activity of its train stations, its neighbourhoods and streets and their bizarre cheek-by-jowl contrasts that are the city's most compelling spectacles.

Most Mumbaikars divide the city into south and north Mumbai – with the former known as 'town' and the latter as 'the suburbs'. South Mumbai is still where Mumbai's wealthy work and play. Most of the city's sites of architectural and historical interest are located in the south, especially the area known as Fort, named for the long-since-demolished fortress established by the British in the 17th century, which became the nucleus of the city. Meanwhile, the suburbs, once villages, have swelled with new businesses, shops, restaurants and entertainment venues, but possess few places of interest for visitors.

Bombay's name was changed to Mumbai in the mid 1990s amid a controversial political drive to eradicate British Raj-era names from the city. Visitors often assume that it's politically incorrect to use Mumbai's old name, but are surprised to discover that most English-speakers – of whom there are millions – still call the city Bombay. As a visitor, you're unlikely to upset anyone whichever name you use.

TOURS

Bombay Heritage Walks (022-2683-5856, www.bombayheritagewalks.com) organises walking tours of the city's historic areas. Deepa Krishnan of Mumbai Magic (98677-07414, www.mumbaimagic.com) organises customised walks. Reality Tours (022-2283-3872, www.realitytoursandtravel.com) organises sightseeing tours and slum tours (and one that combines the two); it was the first to incorporate a tour of Dharavi, one of the largest slums in India, into its itinerary, and claims that 80 per cent of its profits from these tours go to help NGOs in the area.

Every weekend evening, the city's tourism department arranges hour-long rides on an open-roofed double-decker bus called Nilambari through the heritage precinct of the city. The ride begins at the Gateway of India. Buy tickets at the Gateway of India Tourist Counter (022-2284-1877, open 9am-7pm daily, Rs 150 upper deck, Rs 50 lower deck).

SOUTH MUMBAI

COLABA

Today, Colaba is the main tourist drag of Mumbai, with plenty of street stalls, restaurants and cheap hotels. It's home to the church of

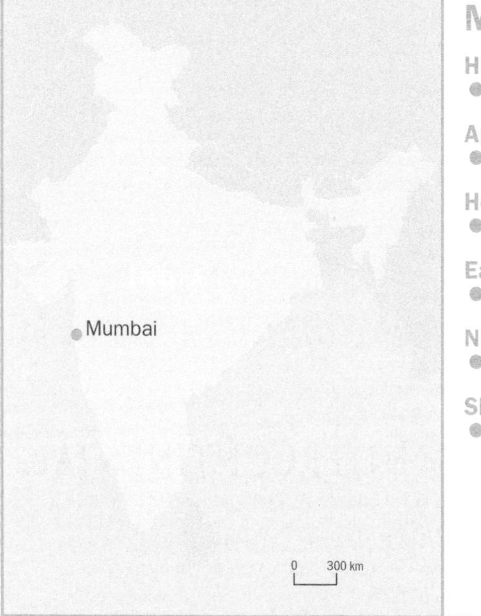

Mumbai

Historic sites
●●●○○

Art & architecture
●●●○○

Hotels
●●●○○

Eating & drinking
●●●●○

Nightlife
●●●●○

Shopping
●●●●●

Let the train take the strain

Whether faced with floods, riots or other disasters, Mumbaikars have one single litmus test to judge the state of their city: 'Are the trains working?'

A vast majority of Mumbai's citizens, allegedly over seven million, spend large chunks of their lives on trains, as a result of which a train-borne culture has evolved. Commuters talk of 'train friends', regular co-commuters with whom they sing songs, exchange life stories and who, most importantly, will 'catch place' for them – keep them a seat, hopefully in a good spot. In the morning, the best seats are on the west side of the train, facing south for the breeze and the direction of travel; in the evening, it's the other side, facing north.

Local trains have two classes: the first class has deodorised padded velour seats; the second class has wooden benches, although in the newer trains the seats are almost identical. Both classes are almost equally crowded, but those who can afford it will shell out up to ten times the price of a second-class ticket for the fractional extra comforts of first class.

The ladies-only compartment is filled with women shopping from train vendors, cleaning vegetables for dinner, and rehashing old arguments about the rival merits of tailors. The 'general compartment' in second class is for anyone at all, but tends to be for the men. Here *bhajans* (religious songs) are sung, *prasad* (food blessed by being offered to the gods) doled out and endless card games played.

Train compartments are scoured by vendors hawking everything from peanuts to mobile phone slipcovers to English courses. Urchins run through with brushes, sweeping the dirt out on to the tracks before begging for tips. On a half-hour journey, you can eat a snack, get your shoes shone, your hair straightened and your soul saved (charity to beggars is good in the eyes of the gods).

The crush in train compartments during rush hours, between 9am and 11am and again between 5pm and 9pm, defies description. Sardines have it easy. Around ten per cent of passengers during these hours aren't even in the train – you'll see them hanging out of the sides, courting death by trackside pole. Some young men even climb on to the roof, partly because there's no room in the train, partly out of sheer bravado. Inside, passengers have to start pushing their way to the door one stop before their station – any later and they'll never make it out in time.

In off-peak hours, there is a little let-up in the crowds, but most visitors will still find train compartments terribly packed. Yet there is no quicker or more efficient way of getting around Mumbai: the trains are fast, generally efficient and cut across the city unmindful of traffic snarls just a few metres away. Travel during peak hours, and you can brag about it for life.

Colaba to Churchgate
Arabian Sea
Back Bay
Harbour
Jai Hind College
Govt Law College
Western Railway Headquarters
Churchgate Station
CROSS MAIDAN
Cathedral School
JB Petit School
Khadi Bhandar
Standard Chartered Bank Building
Universal Building
Monetary Museum
Old RBI
Govt of India Mint
New Custom House
New RBI
VEER NARIMAN ROAD
A Holkar Chowk
Bhika Behram Well
Flora Fountain
Eros Cinema
Brabourne Stadium
Main Gate
R Poddar Chowk
Horniman Circle
Asiatic Society
BALLARD ESTATE
St Thomas Cathedral
FORT
High Court
New India Assurance Building
OVAL MAIDAN
KC & HR College
Advani Chowk
CHURCHGATE
WIAA Chowk
Mumbai University
Rajabai Clock Tower
BSE
KALA GHODA
Collector Central Excise
David Sassoon Library
Kenneseth Eliyahoo
Sessions Court
Elphinstone College
Jehangir Art Gallery
Prince of Wales Museum
St Andrews
Lion's Gate
Mantralaya
Old Secretariat
Institute of Science
NGMA
Bombay Natural History Society
Vidhan Chowk
Vidhan Bhavan
Inox
Nariman Building
Municipal Children's Park
SP Mukherjee Chowk
Anne's School
DOCKYARD
National Centre of the Performing Arts
YB Chavan Auditorium
Campion School
YMCA
Regal Cinema
Nariman Point
NARIMAN POINT
Maker Chamber III
Mittal Tower
Cooperage Maidan
NPA Marker Garden
Raheja Centre
MLA Hostel
MSLTA
J & M Convent
Royal Bombay Yacht Club
Holy Name
Wodehouse Gymkhana
Wesley
Gateway of India
BEST Bhavan
CUSROW BAUG
BADHWAR PARK
PHULE NAGAR
Radio Club
Gita Nagar
Naval Public School
J Maker III
J Maker I
KOLI NAGAR
Colaba Market
J Maker II
Tower
World Trade Centre
CUFFE PARADE
COLABA
Sesoon Dock
Colaba Woods
Dhobi Ghat
St Francis Xavier's Church
Baptist
Mumbai Port Trust Garden
Telegraph Quarters
to Afghan Church
MARINE DRIVE/NETAJI SUBHASH CHANDRA BOSE MARG
JAMSHEDJI TATA ROAD
MAHARISHI KARVE ROAD
KARMAVEER BHAURAO PATIL MARG
MAHATMA GANDHI ROAD
SHAHID BHAGAT SINGH MARG
MADAME CAMA ROAD
VIDHAN BHAVAN MARG
BARRISTER RAJNI PATEL MARG
SIR DORAB TATA ROAD
FREE PRESS JOURNAL
JAGANNATH BHOSLE ROAD
QUEEN'S ROAD
COOPERAGE ROAD
NATHALAL PARIKH ROAD/WODEHOUSE ROAD
SHIVAJI MARG
PJ RAMCHANDANI MARG /STRAND ROAD
ARTHUR BUNDER ROAD
SIR PHEROZESHAH MEHTA ROAD
DN ROAD
MINT ROAD
BALLARD ROAD
GD SOMANI ROAD
PRAKASH PETHE MARG
WODEHOUSE ROAD
NATHALAL PARIKH ROAD/
COLABA CAUSEWAY/SHAHID BHAGAT SINGH MARG
PRAKASH PETHE MARG/CUFFEPARADE ROAD
NANABHAI MOOS MARG
0
300 m
300 yds
© Copyright Time Out Group 2010
D
E
F
G
H
J
1
2
3
4
5
6
7
8

St John the Evangelist, or Afghan Church (Nanabhai Moss Marg, Navy Nagar, open 8am-7pm daily), built to commemorate the soldiers from Bombay who died in the First Afghan War of 1838-43. A little north is Sassoon Dock, a hectic fish market. The local Koli fishermen bring in the night's catch at around 5am; if you can get up that early, it's an experience (and smell) you won't forget in a hurry. From Sassoon Dock, keep going north-west until you hit Colaba Causeway, a thoroughfare crammed with clothes shops, restaurants, bars, cafés, trinket stalls and, of course, tourists. From the Causeway, turning east at Electric House leads to a seaside promenade, at the end of which stands the Gateway of India, an archway of yellow basalt built to commemorate the visit of King George V and Queen Mary to India in 1911.

Bollywood casting agents frequently scour Colaba Causeway for foreign extras, particularly at Leopold's Café (*see p39*). They'll usually pay a few hundred rupees for a day's work; expect to spend a lot of time standing around between shots. Exercise some caution – ask for a business card and call to check the agent's credentials, and opt for safety in numbers.

> "There's a striking contrast between the Victorian Gothic buildings on the Maidan's east side and the art deco apartments on the west."

KALA GHODA

Just north of Colaba Causeway is Kala Ghoda, Mumbai's art district. The largest art galleries in the neighbourhood are the National Gallery of Modern Art and the Jehangir Art Gallery (for both, *see p42*). Artists also display their work on the pavement outside the Jehangir, which stands on one corner of the sprawling compound of the Chhatrapati Shivaji Maharaj Vastu Sangrahalaya, formerly known as the Prince of Wales Museum. On the other side of Mahatma Gandhi Road, and overlooking Kala Ghoda, are the David Sassoon Mechanical Institute and Library and Elphinstone College, Mumbai's oldest college, founded in 1835. Opposite is Rampart Row, where you will find the sky-blue Kenneseth Eliyahoo Synagogue, and the tall spire of St Andrew's and St Columba's Church, built in 1819 and modelled on St Martin-in-the-Fields in London's Trafalgar Square. Every February, Rampart Row is closed to traffic for the two-week Kala Ghoda Arts Festival.

Chhatrapati Shivaji Maharaj Vastu Sangrahalaya

159 MG Road, near Regal Circle (022-2284-4519/ www.bombaymuseum.org). Open 10.15am-6pm Tue-Sun. Admission Rs 25 Indians; Rs 300 others; Rs 150 audio tour in English, French or Japanese.

The city's largest museum was built in 1914, and until the mid 1990s was called the Prince of Wales Museum of Western India. The grand building is a fusion of British, Hindu and Mughal architecture – a style known as Indo-Saracenic – pioneered by British architect George Wittet in the early 1900s. The museum has over 30,000 artefacts, including bronze and stone sculptures, miniature paintings, arms and armour, and Far Eastern art. The explanatory labels are poor, but there is a 45-minute audio tour available.

OVAL MAIDAN

North-west of Kalaghoda, the open space of the Oval Maidan was lapped by the waves of the Arabian Sea until a land reclamation project in the 1920s extended the peninsula nearly half a mile westward to Marine Drive. As a result, there's a striking contrast between the Victorian Gothic buildings on the Maidan's eastern side and the art deco apartments on the west. The Oval is the city's premier venue for impromptu cricket matches.

On the Oval's eastern side is a row of some of the city's most impressive Victorian buildings. Next to the Old Secretariat and the Sessions Court, at the southern end, are the curlicued stones and spiral staircases of the University of Mumbai, built in 1874. Attached to it is the Rajabai Clock Tower. To the left is the Bombay High Court. Visitors are allowed inside; a visit is highly recommended for courtroom scenes straight out of Dickens's *Bleak House*. Westwards along Veer Nariman Road sits the Western Railway Headquarters, built in 1899, with white domes rising above dark stone minarets. The staid concrete structure opposite is the Churchgate Terminus, where the suburban Western Railway line ends. Every weekday, around three million people pass through here (*see p26* **Let the train take the strain**).

Rajabai Clock Tower

Karmaveer Bhaurao Marg, University of Mumbai, next to High Court (www.mu.ac.in). Open 10.30am-6.30pm Mon-Sat. Admission free.

The chimes of Rajabai clock tower, which rises 85m (280ft) above Mumbai University, have been sounding across the Oval Maidan every half-hour since 1880. Modelled on London's Big Ben, the tower was built with a large donation from Mumbai's first share fraudster, Premchand Roychand.

In return, the clock tower was named after his mother, Rajabai. It was designed in Gothic Revivalist style and features stone heads of Shakespeare and Homer peering out from crossed arches under the main spiral staircase. Look out for the pretty stained-glass panels around the staircase, and the arched teak library ceiling.

FORT, FLORA FOUNTAIN & CST

The epicentre of Fort is the 28-storey Bombay Stock Exchange, which stands at the junction of Mumbai Samachar Marg and Dalal Street. This was Mumbai's – and Asia's – first exchange, established in 1875. Nearby is Horniman Circle, a fenced circular garden surrounded by historic buildings, including the imposing neo-classical Asiatic Society of Mumbai (open 10am-7pm Mon-Sat, admission free). Ahead of the Asiatic Society, Ballard Road leads to the business district of Ballard Estate, a neat grid of office buildings in need of restoration.

The hectic Flora Fountain intersection is simply known as 'Fountain', referring to its central ornate fountain mounted with a statue of the Roman goddess Flora, erected in 1864. Its official name is Hutatma Chowk (Martyrs' Square), in remembrance of 105 people shot dead here by police in 1960 during a protest for the creation of Maharashtra state, of which Mumbai is the capital. Nearby is the statue of a martyr with a flame. Just before Horniman Circle, stands the restored St Thomas' Cathedral (open 10am-5.30pm daily, services 7am, 8.45am Sun), the first Anglican church in Mumbai, built in 1718.

"It was declared a UNESCO World Heritage Site for its blend of 'Victorian Italianate Gothic Revival architecture and Indian traditional buildings'."

The road north from Fountain leads to Chhatrapati Shivaji Terminus (CST) and further north is Crawford Market (Dadabhai Naoroji Road, open 9.30am-9pm Mon-Sat), the city's first municipal market, built in 1869 to sell what it still sells today – fresh fruits, vegetables, spices, meats, imported foodstuffs and live animals. Though the market is fraying at the edges, Victorian touches survive intact, the most impressive being two elaborate fountains by J Lockwood Kipling, father of Rudyard Kipling.

Chhatrapati Shivaji Terminus/CST

Nagar Chowk. Open 4.30am-1am daily.

Mumbai's main train station – still known as 'VT' after its old name, Victoria Terminus – is the city's main transport hub and the busiest train station in Asia, with around three million people passing through daily. The building was designed by FW Stevens, who also designed the offices of the Municipal Corporation of Greater Mumbai facing the station. In April 1853 India's first passenger train departed from here; in 2004 it was declared a UNESCO World Heritage Site for its blend of 'Victorian Italianate Gothic Revival architecture and Indian traditional buildings'. The ornate exterior is a jungle in stone, with a life-sized pair of lions guarding the doors to its administration offices, and peacocks, monkeys, owls, chameleons, rams, elephants and other beasts peering down on commuters from the façade.

MARINE DRIVE, CHOWPATTY & MALABAR HILL

Mumbai's most famous boulevard is Marine Drive – a three-kilometre arc sweeping along the western bay from the business district of Nariman Point to the wealthy enclave of Malabar Hill. Also known as the 'Queen's Necklace', after the illuminated curve of the bayfront road at night, Marine Drive is, for most Indians, an iconic shorthand for the city of Mumbai. At the northern end of the promenade is Chowpatty, a broad, curved beach where spectacular idols of the elephant-headed god Ganesha are immersed in the sea during the festival of Ganesh Chaturthi. However, the waters here and everywhere else on Mumbai's long shoreline are too filthy to merit a dip.

The area of Walkeshwar at Malabar Hill is lined with temples and Gujarati-style homes that were rebuilt in the 18th century after being destroyed by the Portuguese in the previous century. The largest temple is Walkeshwar Temple, dedicated to Lord Shiva, which was rebuilt in 1715. Nearby is the holy lake, or 'tank' of Banganga, built some time between the ninth and 13th centuries, and the oldest sacred Hindu site in the city. It's a place of rare serenity, with ducks gliding on the still, green waters and visitors relaxing on the worn basalt steps that lead down to them. Views of the city can be had from Kamala Nehru Park and the Hanging Gardens at the top of Malabar Hill.

Mani Bhavan

19 Laburnum Road, off Ramabai Marg, Gamdevi (022-2380-5864/www.gandhi-manibhavan.org). Open 9.30am-5.30pm daily. Admission free.

A 20-minute walk north-east from Chowpatty is Mani Bhavan, home of Mahatma Gandhi from 1917 to 1934, and base for the civil disobedience movement that helped topple the British Empire in India. The museum contains many photographs, personal belongings and over 50,000 books and documents. It also has a series of tableaux telling the story of Gandhi's life through clay models.

Churchgate to Crawford Market
D
E
F
G
H
J
15
14
13
12
11
10
9
8
7
Arya Samaj
Vithalbhai
Cawasjipatel Tank Road
Swami Narayan
Bhoiwada
JB Shah Road
Merchant Road
Pydhonie
Minara Masjid
Dana Bundar
Ram Mandir
Bhuleshwar
Girgaon
Laxmi Narayan
Bhuleswar Road
Kalbadevi Road
Municipal Market
Mohammed Ali Road
Yusuf Meheral Road
Masjid Bundar Road
Masjid Bunder
Chinch Bundar
Fanas Wadi
B Jaykar Marg/Thakurdwar Road
Panchayat Wadi
Mumbadevi
Anant Wadi
Malhar Wadi
Shaar Harahamim
Balaji
Dena Wadi
Nar Narayan
Mooljl Jetha Market
Jagannath Shankarsheth Marg/Girgaon Road
Poddar College
Dadiseth Agiary
Masjid
Khatri Wadi
Dwarkadeesh
Zaveri Bazaar
Janjikar Street
Dabul
Kalbadevi
Vithal Wadi
SK Patil Udyan
St Xavier
Badam Wadi
Jama Masjid
Shetya Chowk
Carnac Bridge
Thakurdwar
Abdusalam
Princess Street
Crawford Market
Manish Market
Chandan Wadi
Wagh Wadi
Lokmanya Tilak Marg
Ramabai Ambedkar Marg
Hindu Gymkhana
Maharshi Karve Road
Vardhman Chowk
Commissioner of Police
P D Mello Road
Police Gymkhana
Parsee Gymkhana
Gokuldas Tejpal
Dhobi Talao
Haj House
Marine Lines
St Xavier's School
Foreigners Registration Office
Kapadia Chowk
Netaji Subhash Chandra Bose Marg
Islam Gymkhana
Shamlaldas Gandhi Road
Our Lady of Dolours
Rang Bavan
Sir JJ School of Art
0
300 m
300 yds
© Copyright Time Out Group 2010
Framjee Cowasjee Hall & Library
Elphinstone Technical Inst
Metro Cinema
St Xavier's College
Anandilal Podar Road
Cama Albess
Anjuman I-Islam School
Dr Dadabhai Naoroji Road
Central Railway
Port Trust Railway
Liberty Cinema
Esplanade Court
Times of India
RRC Govt Dental College
Pirojsha Godrej Scouts & Guides Pavillion
Mahapalika Marg
Marine Drive/
Mumbai University Grounds
Vithaldas Thackersey Marg
Mahatma Gandhi Road
Chhatrapati Shivaji Terminus
Bombay Hospital
Press Club
Municipal Corporation
Azad Maidan
CST Building
St George
Our Lady of Dolours
Capitol Cinema
General Post Office
Wankhede Stadium
St Andrew's
New Marine Lines
Nagar Chowk
Bedi Chowk
Walchand Hirachand Marg
Deutsche Bank
Bombay Gymkhana
Maharishi Karve Road
SNDT University
New Excelsior
New India Insurance Building
Shahid Bhagat Singh Marg
Back Bay
Mahindra Stadium
Perin Nariman Street
Nirmala Niketan
New Marine Lines Road
Cross Maidan
Siddarth College
Cathedral and John Connon School
Fort House
Churchgate
Aryan Mahal
Sydenham College
Chaphekar Chowk
Parsi Lying In Hospital
Alexandra School
Khadi Bhandar
Jain
Maneckji Nowroji Sett Agiary
Jai Hind College
Govt Law College
JB Petit School
Petit Library
Sir Pheroze Shah Mehta Road
New Customs House
Ballard Road
Cathedral School
Churchgate Station
Western Railway Headquarters
Standard Chartered Bank Building
Universal Building
Monetary Museum
Govt of India Mint
Naval Museum
Veer Nariman Road
Bhikaji Behram Well
Karmaveer Bhaurao Patil Marg
Old RBI
Mint Road
A Holkar Chowk
Flora Fountain
Fort
New RBI
Eros Cinema
R Poddar Chowk
Veer Nariman Road
Horniman Circle
Asiatic Library
Ballard Estate
Braboune Stadium
Jamshedji Tata Road
Oval Maidan
St Thomas Cathedral
Dinshaw Wachha Road
High Court
Mahatma Gandhi Road
Shahid Bhagat Singh Marg

BYCULLA

Byculla was created by the British when they ventured out from the overcrowded walled city of Fort. Today, it is an extremely congested neighbourhood with only two interesting spots: the Bhau Daji Lad Museum, in the compound of the completely avoidable zoo, and the Magen David Synagogue.

Bhau Daji Lad Museum

91 Dr Ambedkar Road, Veermata Jijabai Bhonsale Udyan – City Zoo (022-6556-0394). Open 10am-5pm Mon, Tue, Thur-Sun. Admission Rs 10 Indians, Rs 100 others; children 5-12 yrs Rs 5 Indians, Rs 50 others; free under-5s.

Built in 1872, this was originally named the Victoria and Albert Museum and – like its more famous London counterpart – was intended to showcase industrial skills and craftsmanship. In 2008 the building was reopened after a four-year restoration of its original Renaissance Revival splendour, with intricate iron pillars, ornate chandeliers, exquisite gold railings, and a dramatic painted ceiling. Exhibits include models and maps of the city dating from the late 19th and early 20th centuries, as well as 1,200 original glass negatives that include rare images of the gates of the old Fort.

Magen David Synagogue

340 Sir JJ Road (022-2300-6675). Open 8am-6pm daily. Admission free.

Built in 1861 by the trader David Sassoon, this pillared blue synagogue with an imposing clock tower was enlarged in 1910 to accommodate a growing congregation. Though morning prayers are conducted every day and services held on the Sabbath, the community is occasionally hard pressed to find a *minyan* (quorum). The building is faded but still beautiful, especially when its tall, stained-glass windows cast a rainbow of light across the prayer hall.

NORTH MUMBAI: SUBURBS

The Western, more particularly American, understanding of the term suburb has no place in Mumbai. Here suburbs are merely an extension of the city – just further away and uglier, rather than an American Yet this is where most of Mumbai lives, and parts of it offer a hipper, younger, more chilled-out vibe than the south. Most notable among these areas is the western suburb of Bandra, home to Bollywood stars, loads of bars and restaurants, hidden villages and young professionals with money to burn. Today, Bandra has morphed into the city's hottest area.

Just north of it is Juhu, where the city's busiest sandy beach draws hordes of visitors every day. Juhu is also home to an older generation of Bollywood stars, and is a hub of trendy bars and restaurants. Further north lies an endless list of western suburbs, and in the eastern part of the city, another seemingly never-ending stretch known as the eastern suburbs.

AROUND MUMBAI

Elephanta Caves

Elephanta Island *Boats depart every half-hour from Gateway of India (1hr journey), 9am-2.30pm. Tickets Rs 80-Rs 120. Last return ferry around 5pm. Elephanta Caves admission Rs 10 Indians; Rs 250 others.*

A seventh-century prince from the Chalukya dynasty is supposed to have constructed the breathtaking cave temples at Gharapuri, a small island ten kilometres north-east of the Gateway of India. The island was renamed when it was rediscovered in the 16th century by the Portuguese: they saw an elephant waiting for them as they approached the island.

A highlight of the cave is a six-metre-high full-relief bust of Sadashiva (Eternal Shiva), which shows the three faces of Lord Shiva: the vengeful Aghora Bhairava; the feminine Uma, or Vamadeva; and the central face, which is one of serene contemplation. Many of the sculptures in the 5,575sq m (60,000sq ft) temple have been destroyed, but there still remain several ornate pillars and exquisitely carved sculptures.

If you wander outside, you can see one of the cannons used by the Portuguese when the island was a firing range. Avoid eating near the loitering monkeys, who'll pounce on any food. There is nowhere to stay overnight on the island, so be sure to be in time for the 5pm return ferry.

"The Kanheri Caves are 109 Buddhist caves cut into the rock, with ornate sculpted statues and images of Buddha and the bodhisattvas."

Sanjay Gandhi National Park

Borivali *Western Express Highway (022-2886-0389). Open 7.30am-6.30pm Tue-Sun. Admission Rs 20.*

One of Asia's busiest national parks, with around two million visitors a year. Mumbaikars come here to escape the city, get lost in the greenery with their boyfriend or girlfriend, play cricket, eat vast picnics or just cool off – the average temperatures here are around four degrees cooler than the city. In recent years, the park has been encroached on by slum dwellings, which is bad both for the park and for the slum dwellers, the resident leopards now having acquired a taste for humans. They're mainly nocturnal creatures, though, so there's not too much chance of running into one. There's an information centre near the entrance, with display panels about the park; it also sells books and T-shirts.

From the entrance, there are buses to the **Kanheri Caves** complex. This is a series of 109 Buddhist caves cut into the rock, with ornate sculpted statues and images of Buddha and the bodhisattvas. The caves date back to the first century BC, although the carving continued well into the ninth century AD.

It's easiest to reach the park by taking the Western Railway to Borivali. Buses and rickshaws will take you from the station to the park entrance.

Eat

Mumbai loves food. From the ubiquitous street stalls serving unique Mumbai snacks to rough-and-ready 'lunch homes' to fancy restaurants, every class and ethnic group has its own favourites. For decades, the finest restaurants in Mumbai were confined to the insides of five-star hotels and were out of the reach of all but the city's wealthiest diners. The five-star culture persists, but in recent years it has been challenged by a new breed of high-quality, stand-alone restaurants eager to grab a share of Mumbaikars' skyrocketing disposable incomes.

If you're in the vicinity of the airport, Dum Pukht and Dakshin (at the ITC Maratha hotel, 022-2830-3030) and Stax at the Hyatt Regency (022-6696-1234) are fabulous restaurants.

"The Britannia is famous for its berry pulao, a traditional Iranian dish of boneless mutton or chicken in a sweet, spicy masala, garnished with tart Iranian berries."

Bade Miya's

Colaba *Tulloch Street, off Colaba Causeway (022-2284-8038). Open 7pm-3am daily. $. No credit cards. North Indian.*

Not a restaurant, but a hugely popular streetside stall just off Colaba Causeway, serving fabulous kebabs and rolls (chicken or mutton, with onions and sauces, wrapped in egg-coated parathas) to Colaba's post-party crowd. Bade Miya's started as a single stall, but grew with fame; it now consists of a couple of hard-working skewer-laden grills and a row of plastic chairs and tables. It's not fancy, but it is delicious. Everything's good here, but the top choices have got to be the *baida rotis* (spicy mutton, chicken or beef with egg in a grilled wrap), spicy chicken livers, bhuna mutton and bhuna chicken. The vegetarian seekh kebab is also excellent.

Britannia

2km E of Fountain *Sprott Road, Ballard Estate (022-2261-5264). Open 11.30am-4pm Mon-Sat. $. No credit cards. Parsi.*

Despite the dilapidated wooden interior, complete with wobbly chairs, peeling walls and dusty chandeliers, Britannia manages to exude a homely 1940s charm. Open only for lunch, it's famous for its fabulous berry *pulao*, a traditional Iranian dish of boneless mutton or chicken in a sweet, spicy masala, garnished with tart Iranian berries. If you still have room, follow it with a creamy caramel custard.

Indigo

Colaba *4 Mandlik Road (022-6636-899/www.foodindigo.com). Open 12.30-2.45pm, 7.30-11.45pm Mon-Sat; noon-4pm, 7.30-11.45pm Sun. $$$-$$$$. Modern European.*

Indigo is one of the city's finest stand-alone restaurants, serving – among much else – excellent carpaccio, lobster bisque and goat's cheese on grilled apples. The open terrace upstairs is without doubt the nicest spot in the evenings, but you'll need to book in advance as Indigo is always busy. The all-you-can-eat Sunday champagne brunch is addictive.

Indigo Deli

Colaba *Chhatrapati Shivaji Maharaj Street (022-6655-1010/www.indigodeli.com). Open 9am-11pm daily. $$. Café/deli.*

There's a deli counter with a wide range of imported cheeses, meats, olives, and so on at Indigo's younger sister, plus a wall-full of Indian and imported wines. But the main attraction is the sit-down dining area, smartly decked out in dark woods. A great spot for all-day breakfast, lunch (the eggs benedict is the best in the city) or a snack.

Kebab Korner

Marine Drive *InterContinental, Marine Drive (022-6639-9999/www.mumbai.intercontinental.com). Open 12.30-2.45pm, 7.30-11.45pm daily. $$$$. North Indian.*

Kebab Korner was a Mumbai institution that shut down years ago and was recreated in 2005 with its original chefs and traditional cooking style – the kebabs here are made on a *sigri* (a coal-fired grill) instead of a tandoor oven. The results are amazing – tender and subtly flavoured seekh kebabs, spicy butter chicken and outrageously tasty *kali dal*. The biryani is also fabulous, as is the house special 'Busybee', stuffed chicken kebabs served with burnt onions and yoghurt chutney. Add a sea view and sumptuous wood and marble decor, and you have a Mumbai classic.

Khyber

Kala Ghoda *145 Mahatma Gandhi Road (022-2267-3227/www.khyberrestaurant.com). Open 12.30-3.30pm, 7.30-11.30pm daily. $$$. North Indian.*

A sprawling, two-level restaurant grandly furnished in wood and stone, Khyber is an old favourite of fans of North Indian cuisine, with consistently high standards. Top choices here include the tender Khyber *raan* – a slow-cooked leg of lamb – the biryani and the paneer korma. After dinner, you can waddle through a connecting door into the Red Light nightclub next door.

Top: Khyber.
Bottom: Blue Frog.

Konkan Café

Colaba *Taj President, Cuffe Parade (022-6665-0808/ www.tajhotels.com). Open 12.30-2.45pm, 7-11.45pm daily. $$$. Western Indian.*

Far from actually being a café, this is a beautifully planned and striking restaurant with an interior that mirrors those of village homes along India's Konkan coast, a region that begins in Maharashtra and extends through Goa into Karnataka. Chef Ananda Solomon is a proponent of 'slow food' and prefers traditional seasonings and methods of preparation, including hand-grinding spices. Although the focus is definitely on seafood (including Mangalorean-style *gassi*, steamed fish in turmeric paste and Malwani shrimp curry – all fabulous), Konkan also serves some exquisite lamb chops in East Indian bottle masala, with mustard seeds and curry leaves.

Masala Kraft

Colaba *Taj Mahal Palace & Tower (022-6665-3366/ www.tajhotels.com). Open 12.30-2.45pm, 7-11.45pm daily. $$$$. Modern Indian.*

Contemporary Indian cuisine is delivered with a Western twist – cooking with olive oil, for example, which is unheard of in traditional Indian cooking. It works fabulously: try the tandoori pink salmon dipped in sugarcane vinegar, or paneer in a white sauce (another Western import) with black peppers.

Mahesh Lunch Home

Fort *8B Cawasji Patel Street (022-2287-0938/ www.maheshlunchhome.com). Open 11.30am-4pm, 6-11.30pm daily. $$. Mangalorean.*

Mahesh's walls are dripping with exuberant piscine motifs. But don't let that, or the rather low ceiling, put you off your food. Skip the Chinese-style soups and head straight for the Mangalorean-style seafood dishes, flecked with coconut and chilli. The fish is so fresh you half expect it to wiggle on your plate. With nearby Trishna (*see below*) often too crowded to find a table, Mahesh is increasingly becoming the choice of discerning locals.

Oh! Calcutta

4km N of Chowpatty *Rosewood Hotel, Tulsiwadi Lane, Tardeo (022-2496-3145). Open noon-3pm, 7pm-midnight daily. $$$. Bengali.*

Oh! Calcutta provides a culinary home away from home for misty-eyed Bengali customers. The must-try dish here is *ilish maacher apturi* – lightly spiced boneless hilsa fish from the Ganga, marinated in mustard paste and green chillies, then baked. Don't leave without trying *mishti doi* – a creamy yoghurt dessert that makes Bengalis go weak at the knees.

Soam

Chowpatty *Sadguru Sadan, Babulnath Road (022-2369-8080). Open noon-midnight daily. $$. No AmEx. Street food/Gujarati.*

The true test of a Gujarati snack joint is its *panki chatni* (pancakes steamed in banana leaves, served with chutney), and Soam passes with flying colours. The intense heat makes them hard to touch, but hold up the banana leaf and the pancake falls off in one piece – perfect. If you've ever wondered what the sugarcane juice sold on street stalls tastes like, this is a clean place to try it, and it's delicious. Furnished in dark wood, with ochre-coloured walls, bamboo blinds and comfy seating, Soam is a favourite alternative to south Mumbai's other hugely popular snack joint, Swati Snacks (*see below*).

Swati Snacks

3km N of Chowpatty *Opposite Bhatia Hospital, Tardeo (022-6580-8406). Open 11am-11pm daily. $$. No AmEx. Street food/Gujarati.*

Back in the '60s, Swati Snacks was little more than a street shack serving Gujarati food. Now, it's a swanky, shiny spacecraft of glass and stainless steel. The menu is packed with gorgeous Gujarati staples and some Mumbai street fare like *dahi batata puri* and idlis. Everything on the menu is outstanding, in particular the delectable *panki chatni* (rice pancakes steamed in banana leaves) and the *dal dhokli* – thick cinnamon-flavoured dal with soft squares of chapati. There's also a good selection of fresh juices. Be warned that lunchtimes here are packed; reservations aren't accepted and 40-minute waits are common. Try the delectable sugarcane juice with a hint of ginger while you wait.

"Grill-scarred pork chop comes with a pool of pickled mango reduction and a dollop of apple butter."

Tote on the Turf

6km N of Chowpatty *Mahalaxmi Race Course, opposite Gate nos.4 & 5 (022-6157-7777). Open 7pm-1.30am daily. $$$$. Modern European.*

The latest brainchild of Rahul Akerkar, the chef who owns the hip Indigo restaurants, Tote on the Turf is, as you might expect, on the city's race course. It's huge and the design is breathtaking – triangular and trapezoid panels of wood form jagged planes covering the walls and ceiling. Try the signature Tote Mary cocktail, with balsamic vinegar and crushed cucumber, before moving on to the Tote's version of tiramisu, a non-sweet appetiser with mushrooms and walnuts, with red-wine poached pears and gorgonzola mousse on the side. Grill-scarred pork chop comes with a pool of pickled mango reduction and a dollop of apple butter.

Trishna

Kala Ghoda *7 Sai Baba Marg, behind Rhythm House, (022-2270-1623). Open noon-3.30pm, 6pm-midnight daily. $$$. Mangalorean.*

It's often difficult to get a table at Trishna, but you can be sure that the customers aren't here for the decor. Everyone's so busy tucking into the seafood, cooked Mangalorean-style, that they're willing to forgive the tacky fittings. It did

Top: The Bombay Store.
Bottom: Fabindia.

Trishna's reputation no harm when, a few years ago, the legendary *New York Times*' food critic RW Apple listed it as one of his favourite restaurants in the world. Favourites include butter-pepper-garlic crab, stuffed pomfret and prawn *gassi* or prawns in a coconut-based curry. Of late, some locals have complained that the much-loved icon has turned into an overpriced tourist trap. But that hasn't limited Trishna's popularity. In fact, in November 2008 the owners opened a branch in London.

Nightlife

The older generation of Mumbai's middle class may fret about the damage alcohol is doing to the morals of 'the youth', but there's no doubt that boozing is in Mumbai's blood. British Bombay was founded in an orgy of drunkenness and debauchery, with officials of the East India Company often dying young thanks to their intemperate habits. Boozers of all descriptions cater to every sort: cheap and cheerless 'country liquor' bars; cheap dives; lively white-collar and college-kid hangouts, and expensive cocktail bars for a splash out.

> "Aspiring-to-be-famous children of movie stars and their hangers-on come here, but don't let that dissuade you."

Aurus

Suburbs *Juhu Nichani Kutir, Juhu Tara Road (022-6710-6666/www.dishhospitality.com). Open 8.30pm-1.30am daily.*

There is no finer place to sip a cocktail than leaning against the railings high above the sand, watching the silvery waves beneath. Aspiring-to-be-famous children of movie stars and their hangers-on come here, but don't let that dissuade you. The entrance is so discreet, you'll miss it if you don't know it, so call ahead for directions.

Blue Frog

10km N of Chowpatty *Mathurdas Mills Compound, Tulsi Pipe Road, Lower Parel (022-4033-2300/www.bluefrog.co.in). Open 7pm-1.15am daily. Entry Rs 300.*

Quite simply the best-looking nightspot in Mumbai. Using circular seating 'pods', innovative lighting and an amphitheatre-like design, the architects have attempted to create an opera house-meets-warehouse hybrid. The retro, art deco vibe is offset by the funky visuals projected on the screens. Local bands perform on weekdays, international acts at weekends, and the vibe is always electric.

Dome

Marine Drive *InterContinental, 135 Marine Drive (022-6639-9999/www.mumbai.intercontinental.com). Open 6pm-1.30am daily.*

Undoubtedly south Mumbai's finest hotel bar. Dome is a lounge/grill occupying the InterCon's eighth-floor rooftop terrace, overlooking the fabulous arc of the seafront promenade. The walls are white, the tiled floor is white, and the abundant sofas and armchairs are wrapped in white cotton. A raised platform holds the aqua-blue swimming pool, while a corner rotunda houses a sleek aluminium-and-glass bar counter with matching stools. Drop in before 6.30pm for the glorious pink-orange sunset.

Leopold's Café

Colaba *Colaba Causeway (022-2202-0131). Open 7am-1am daily.*

The default drinking destination for foreign travellers, Leo's is undeniably appealing, with arcaded doors open to the street, a high ceiling and a general similarity to a grand old railway station waiting room. The fruit juices are fresh and the beers cold. Shame about the surly service. It was among the sites attacked by terrorists in November 2008 and it still displays the bullet holes.

Valhalla

Churchgate *First floor, Eros Theatre building (022-6735-3535/www.valhalla.co.in). Open 8-11.30am, noon-1.30am daily.*

Milling around the gorgeous purple and dark wood tapas bar, south Mumbai's finest sip glasses of merlot while munching on miniature starters. A business lounge by day, this place turns into a surprisingly fun tapas bar at sundown. From the rich wood tabletops to the super service, stellar cocktails and killer lounge music, everything works perfectly together.

Zenzi

Suburbs *183 Waterfield Road, Bandra (022-6643-0670/www.zenzi-india.com). Open 7pm-1.30am daily. No AmEx.*

This gorgeous-looking bar/restaurant is a perennial upmarket Bandra favourite. It extends far back off the street into a long bar and dining area split by glass, decked out in natural woods and lit by candlelight. Populated largely by models, musicians, media persons and other assorted folk with what they like to think of as 'boho' jobs, Zenzi treads a fine line between pretentious and truly liberated.

Shop

Most locals still head straight to speciality street markets for everything from kitchen utensils to silk saris to antique chandeliers. But not a day goes by without news of a new 'high-end lifestyle store' catering to the rapidly internationalised tastes of the urban middle class.

Many of the city's markets are worth visiting as much for the spectacle as for the goods they sell. Don't forget to bargain. Fashion Street (Mahatma

Gandhi Road, along Azad Maidan, open 10.30am-7pm daily) is where locals buy all kinds of clothing on the cheap. There's a glorious array of colourful fabric at Mangaldas Market (Sheikh Memon Street, near CST station, open 10am-7pm Mon-Sat). Zaveri Bazaar (Bhuleshwar, open 11am-7pm Mon-Sat) offers customers highly competitive rates for an astonishing variety of gold and silver jewellery. Larger stores sell diamond jewellery as well, making this a one-stop shop for brides-to-be.

Chor Bazaar (Mutton Street, opposite Null Bazaar, open 10.30am-7pm Mon-Thur, Sat, Sun) is where you can find everything from ancient 78 RPM records to elaborately carved cupboards, from ships' wheels to 1950s Bollywood posters and old cameras. 'Chor' means 'Thieves', and it is thought to have its origins as a market where stolen goods were fenced. Though the shops here are shut on Fridays, an informal flea market thrives in the mornings from 7am until 1pm.

Dharavi (Sant Rolida Marg, Sion-Bandra Link Road, open 11am-8pm Tue-Sun) earned global notoriety after the film *Slumdog Millionaire*, but around 125 shops on the edges of the neighbourhood sell high-quality leather products.

Some of the stores listed below have branches in other parts of the city.

Amrapali

Marine Drive *Nos. 39 & 62 Oberoi Shopping Arcade, Nariman Point (022-2281-0978). Open 10.45am-7pm daily.*

This Jaipur institution creates fine gold and silver jewellery, combining Indian tradition and craftsmanship with contemporary design and aesthetics. Naomi Campbell, Jennifer Lopez and the Prince of Morocco seem to like it.

Anokhi

Chowpatty *Rasik Niwas, Metro Motors Lane, off Hughes Road (022-2368-5308/www.anokhi.com). Open 10.30am-7.30pm Mon-Sat.*

Rajasthani prints on fashionable clothing, bed and table linens, easy-to-wash curtains and seat covers.

The Bombay Store

Fort *Western India House, Sir Pherozeshah Mehta Road (022-2288-5048/www.bombaystore.com). Open 10.30am-7.30pm Mon-Sat; 10.30am-6.30pm Sun.*

Plenty of potential for interesting presents and souvenirs – like the modernistic stone Ganesha statues small enough to sit on the palm of your hand. The shop brings together artefacts, home accessories, clothes, jewellery, stationery and more, all proudly bearing a 'Made in India' stamp.

Contemporary Arts & Crafts

4km NW of Chowpatty *19 NG House, near St Stephen's Church, Nepean Sea Road (022-2363-1979). Open 10am-8pm daily.*

Knick-knacks and essentials for the home, ranging from brocade cushions to Christmas lights, candlestands and lampshades. Cool design with Indian influences.

Cotton World Corporation

Colaba *201 Ram Nimi Building, Mandlik Road (022-2285-0060). Open noon-8pm daily.*

Mumbai's answer to Gap, CWC has a host of basics like T-shirts, trousers, capris, shorts and shirts that are perfect for the warm, humid climate.

The Courtyard

Colaba *Minoo Desai Marg, behind Radio Club, Apollo Bunder. Open 11am-8pm daily.*

This chic enclave houses a mix of designer and boutique stores that sell everything from bridalwear to gold jewellery, Aigner handbags and bar accessories. Some top Indian designers also have stand-alone stores here.

Crossword

3km NW of Chowpatty *Mohammed Bhai Mansion, Kemp's Corner (022-2384-2001). Open 11am-8.30pm daily.*

The flagship branch of Mumbai's best-known bookstore chain also sells music and movies, toys and games, and has a great café. There's a good selection of Indian writing in English, but only mainstream international fiction.

"Ensemble was the first store to stock high-profile Indian designers in a luxurious space – at mostly unattainable prices."

Curio Cottage

Colaba *19 Mahakavi Bhushan Marg (022-2202-2607). Open 10.30am-8pm Mon-Sat.*

Curio Cottage sells semi-precious jewellery that fills the pages of fashion magazines, as well as tiny trinkets your friends back home would love.

Dhoop

Suburbs *101 Khar Sheetal Apartments, Dr Ambedkar Road, Union Park, Khar (022-2649-8646). Open 11am-8.30pm Mon-Sat. No AmEx.*

Dhoop's focus is on handicrafts made of natural materials, but this isn't your average jute bag shop – think coconut shells, bamboo, banana, sugarcane, water hyacinth and many more intriguing materials.

Ensemble

Colaba *Great Western Building, 130/132 Colaba Causeway (022-2284-3227). Open 10am-7pm Mon-Sat.*

The pioneer in Indian haute couture retailing, Ensemble was the first store to stock high-profile Indian designers in a luxurious space – at mostly unattainable prices.

Clockwise from top left: Bentley's Hotel; JW Marriott; Taj Lands End.

Top: InterContinental Marine Drive. Bottom: Taj Mahal Palace & Tower (2).

Ensemble carries big-label Indian names such as Monisha Jaisingh, Manish Malhotra and Tarun Tahiliani.

Fabindia

Kala Ghoda *137 MG Road; also other city locations (022-2262-6539/www.fabindia.com). Open 10am-7.45pm daily.*

A very popular store selling stylish, high-quality Indian casualwear – from kurtas to salwar kameez – with a wide range in cotton and silk. It's all made by rural artisans. There's also a home-furnishing section.

Nalanda

Colaba *Taj Mahal Palace & Tower (022-2202-2514). Open 8am-midnight daily.*

The place to go for glossy coffee table books on Rajasthani palaces, Benarasi textiles and the Kama Sutra. It's small but has an India focus, and a strong collection of Indian non-fiction, as well as international magazines and newspapers.

Rhythm House

Kala Ghoda *40 K Dubash Marg (022-4322-2727). Open 10am-8.30pm Mon-Sat; 11am-8.30pm Sun. No AmEx.*

One of Mumbai's oldest music stores, this city institution is the best place to find old Hindi film soundtracks. It also stocks current chart hits, a wide range of Hindustani classical and fusion/lounge music. Best of all, most of the red-jacket-clad shop assistants actually know their music.

Arts

Contemporary Indian art can mostly only be seen in private art galleries, although the National Gallery of Modern Art (Cowasji Jehangir Hall, MG Road, Colaba, 022-2288-1969, www.ngmaindia.gov.in, open 11am-6pm Tue-Sun) has a small collection, albeit not on permanent display. Private galleries with some of the best new work include Chatterjee & Lal (Kamal Mansion, Arthur Bunder Road, Colaba, 022-6521-5105, www.chatterjeeandlal.com, open 11am-7pm Mon-Sat) and Galerie Mirchandani + Steinruecke (16-18 Mereweather Road, Colaba, 022-2202-3030, www.galeriems.com, open 10am-6.30pm Mon-Fri, 10am-4pm Sat).

Older players such as Chemould (Prescott Road, Fort, 022-2200-0212, www.gallerychemould.com, open 11am-7pm Mon-Sat) and Pundole Art Gallery (Flora Fountain, 022-2204-8473, www.pundoleartgallery.in, open 10.30am-6.30pm Mon-Sat) helped nurture the Progressive Artists Movement of the 1940s and still host cutting-edge exhibitions. There are always exhibitions under way at the government-run Jehangir Art Gallery (MG Road, Kala Ghoda, 022-2204-8212, open 11am-7pm Mon-Sat) but it's often a hit-or-miss experience. Check *Time Out Mumbai* for details of the latest art shows.

English-language theatre plays only a minor role in Mumbai's theatre scene. Two venues that host plays are the National Centre for the Performing Arts (Nariman Point, 022-6622-3737, www.ncpamumbai.com), Mumbai's one claim to a world-class performance space, and Prithvi Theatre (20 Janki Kutir, Juhu Church Road, 022-2614-9546, www.prithvitheatre.org), an intimate 200-seater that is partial to Hindi drama but hosts English, Marathi and Gujarati plays as well.

Stay

South Mumbai is the first choice of most foreign travellers, but you won't find yourself spoiled for choice, nor will you feel you are getting value for money. The five-stars have always played an important role in the city's social life, providing restaurants, bars, nightclubs, shopping and private party venues for Mumbai's wealthy. Travellers looking for something cheaper will find mostly characterless and unappetising mid-range 1970s hotels; a better option in this bracket are the 1930s and 1940s hotels, which have some of the period character and sleepy charm of an older Bombay.

> "Bentley's is a strictly no-frills affair, with plenty of period atmosphere, antique furniture, wooden staircases and chequered black-and-white floors."

Ascot Hotel

Colaba *38 Garden Road (022-6638-5566/www.ascothotel.com). $$. No AmEx.*

The Ascot is easily superior to most hotels in the same price range, including all its neighbours on Garden Road. It resides in a charming 1930s building, remodelled from top to bottom to create a contemporary space with ample use of light-wood flooring, mirrors and glass, and a soft, cream colour palette. Rooms are spacious and airy, with plants and glass tables. Most have flat-screen TVs and some have DVD players. Add friendly and efficient staff and you have a top mid-range choice.

Bentley's Hotel

Colaba *17 Oliver Road (022-2288-2890/www.bentleyshotel.com). $. No AmEx.*

On a quiet, tree-lined street just off Colaba Causeway, Bentley's captures the faded elegance of Colaba. Spread over three neighbouring 1930s buildings, it's a strictly no-frills affair, with plenty of period atmosphere, antique furniture, wooden staircases and chequered black-and-white floors. A stay here takes you back to a less frenetic Bombay, with servants cleaning mosaic-tiled floors with floorcloths, sleepy watchmen at the gate and the only noise the clatter of the cage lift door. Oliver Road looks like a suburban London street, lined with 1930s properties, all in desperate need of attention. Superior doubles offer views of a nearby park.

Fariyas Hotel

Colaba *Off Arthur Bunder Road (022-2204-2911/ www.fariyas.com). $$$.*
There's not much to distinguish this standard 1970s-built ten-floor hotel aimed at business travellers, although it does fill a useful mid-range gap in Colaba between the Taj Mahal and the backpacker hotels. Rooms are standard issue, and on the small side – as are the pool and tiny gym. But despite space constraints, there's a perfectly decent sauna and steam room. The position on a dark street off Apollo Bunder means only corner rooms get a slice of sea view.

> "Each room comes with a butler on call, who can be summoned by pressing a large red button."

Gordon House Hotel

Colaba *5 Battery Street, Apollo Bunder (022-2287-1122/ www.ghhotel.com). $$$.*
Mumbai needs more hotels like the Gordon House. It's the city's only real boutique hotel, offering a modern, stylish alternative to the standard five-stars at a competitive price. Smart, cool and beautifully designed, the courtyard atrium at its heart is a sanctuary of calming pine wood, wheatgrain tiles and soothing blues and whites under a high glass roof. Rooms on each of the three floors are themed: vibrant colours and smooth tiles on the 'Mediterranean' floor, cool blues and light woods on the 'Scandinavian' floor, and a homey, warm feel on the 'Country' floor. There's no gym, but a Bullworker is provided in each room, and internet access is free. There are just 29 rooms, so book ahead.

InterContinental Marine Drive

Marine Drive *135 Marine Drive (022-6639-9999/ www.mumbai.intercontinental.com). $$$$.*
With a prime location on the 'Queen's Necklace', as Marine Drive is known, it would be a shame not to fork out the extra cash for a sea-facing room. The view and the plush rooms put the InterCon firmly in the top rank of south Mumbai's five-stars. Rooms are spacious and smart, with wood floors, plasma TVs, Bose music systems and DVD players. Bathrooms have glass partitions that allow you to keep watching TV while you shower; or you could go for a suite, where bathrooms have TVs anyway. The hotel is also home to south Mumbai's coolest rooftop bar, Dome (*see p39*), and a couple of the city's most delectable hotel restaurants.

JW Marriott

Suburbs *Juhu Tara Road, Juhu (022-6693-3000/ www.marriott.com). $$$$.*
The JW Marriott is nothing less than a mini-city of five-star luxury, set back from the mad scramble that is Juhu Tara Road. Behind high walls and the city's toughest hotel security are no fewer than six restaurants, two bars and one of the city's best spas. Ninety per cent of the rooms have sea views. The beds have attractive jute headboards, while the marble bathrooms are prettily stencilled with flower designs. Beach access was closed at the time of writing because of security concerns, but the outside area has three pools: a children's pool with water slide, a large main pool with stone chairs for aquatic lounging and a saline pool.

Oberoi

Marine Drive *Nariman Point (022-6632-5757/ www.oberoimumbai.com. $$$$.*
One of the city's first modern five-stars, the Oberoi has hosted Bill Clinton, Bill Gates, Michael Jackson and numerous visiting heads of state in its fabulously ornate and expensive Kohinoor Suite, which has dramatic sea views. The deluxe ocean-view rooms offer a little taste of that luxury, with broad picture windows and warm wood tones. Each room comes with a butler on call, who can be summoned with the press of a large red button. There's a selection of top-notch restaurants as well. Like the Taj, the Oberoi was devastated by the Mumbai terror attacks of 26 November 2008 and remained closed at the time of writing, slated to reopen by March 2010.

Taj Lands End

Suburbs *Bandra Bandstand (022-6668-1234/ www.tajhotels.com). $$$$.*
Without doubt Bandra's most luxurious hotel, the 18-storey Taj Lands End stands close to the ruins of a 16th-century fort where Portuguese cannons once kept watch over maritime trade routes. It's not uncommon to spot Bollywood stars strolling in for dinner (Shah Rukh Khan lives just down the road) and the restaurants are equipped with private dining rooms for just that purpose. The hotel is so large and self-contained that it's virtually a miniature village, with enough designer shops and restaurants to serve Bandra's elite and keep guests – mostly business travellers – distracted. The vast, plant-festooned central atrium leads through to a large outdoor swimming pool and sprawling landscaped lawns, with fine views of the sea and the nearby fort. Rooms are spacious and, thanks to some cunning design, all offer views of the sea through broad picture windows.

Taj Mahal Palace & Tower

Colaba *Apollo Bunder (022-6665-3366/www.taj hotels.com). $$$$.*
Right in front of the Gateway of India, the Taj Mahal Palace & Tower is the crown prince of Mumbai hotels. It's a tourist

attraction in its own right, admired for its broad, imposing presence, its grand dome, and an architecture that blends Florentine Renaissance and Moorish styles. The legend of the Taj is that its creator, renowned Parsi industrialist Jamsetji Nusserwanji Tata, had it built after being refused entry to the now-defunct European-only Pyrke's Apollo Hotel. When completed in 1903, it was by far the finest hotel in the city. The Tower Wing was added in 1972, but without doubt the Palace Wing offers the original Taj experience, hence the difference in price. Palace rooms are steeped in period feel, with double doors leading from a marbled entranceway into elegant high-ceilinged rooms with antique furnishings and white marble bathrooms, with widescreen plasma TVs. Rooms in the Tower Wing have contemporary, elegant design in soft cream and pastel shades, with fabulous views of the Gateway. The Taj was attacked in the 26 November 2008 terrorist attack, and parts of it were set on fire. It took the hotel less than a month to reopen the undamaged section; the rest is set to reopen in mid 2010. Needless to say, security has since been tightened and there's little evidence of the attack, except for a monument in the lobby.

West End Hotel

1km N of Churchgate *45 New Marine Lines (022-2203-9121/www.westendhotelmumbai.com). $$.*

Built in 1948, the popular West End has retained its mid 20th-century charm, with plenty of dark wood and original features. Scrupulously well maintained, the spacious rooms are very simply and comfortably furnished, but old-fashioned, with whitewashed walls, high ceilings and black marble bathrooms with generously sized bathtubs. Rooms at the front of the hotel have small balconies overlooking the crowded New Marine Lines.

YWCA International Guest House

Colaba *18 Madame Cama Road (022-2202-5053/www.ywcaic.info). $. No AmEx.*

Pay a Rs 50 temporary membership fee – you don't have to be female – and you can stay at the YWCA's International Guest House. Simply, but comfortably furnished, with balconies, the rooms make a great budget option. All meals, served buffet-style in the dining hall, are included. Both air-conditioned rooms and cheaper non-AC rooms are available.

Factfile

When to go

The 'winter', from December to February, is generally considered the most pleasant time to visit Mumbai, when average daytime temperatures may dip to around 24°C with low humidity. April, May and October are the hottest and most humid, when temperatures peak at 35°C. The monsoon (June-September) brings incessant rains and intermittent flooding.

Getting there

Mumbai is well connected by air to cities around the world and to other parts of India. It is also well connected to most parts of India through the country's extensive railway network.

For more on travel within India, *see p378* **Navigating India**.

Getting around

Taxis are a good way to get around, although much of Colaba and Fort can be covered on foot. To travel north into the suburbs, the local train service is far quicker (though more intimidating) than battling Mumbai's notoriously slow and noisy traffic. Beyond Bandra, taxis are harder to find and auto-rickshaws are the main mode of transport.

Tourist information

Maharashtra Tourism Development Corporation Madame Cama Road, opposite LIC Building, Nariman Point (*022*-2202-4627/7762/www.maharashtratourism.gov.in). Open 10am-5.30pm Mon-Fri; 10am-3pm Sat.

Internet

Cybercafés can be found across the city.

Tips

- Note that the international and domestic airports, though several kilometres apart, have the same name: Chhatrapati Shivaji International Airport. Locals refer to the international airport as Sahar and the domestic one as Santa Cruz. Make sure you're in the right place.

- Street names all over the city have changed but locals often still use the old names. In fact, when navigating your way around, you'll find street names are infrequently used, and locals navigate with reference to landmarks.

- Mumbai has perhaps more beggars than any other Indian city, and anyone who can visibly be identified as a foreigner will be accosted repeatedly for hand-outs. Remember that giving to one almost immediately draws a crowd of others, and that you cannot help everyone you see. Learn the art of saying no, and when necessary, to ignore what are no doubt some heart-rending pleas for help. Perhaps also think of contributing to a local charity doing good work; there are many.

Delhi

A modern capital where history runs deep.

Amid the glass and chrome of the modern capital, reminders of the city's millennium-long history are everywhere. Blue-domed tombs serve as traffic roundabouts, the ruins of ancient forts provide the backdrop for rock concerts and a ride up the escalator out of a sparkling new Metro station could deposit you in a warren of lanes that has barely changed since the 17th century.

After negotiating the overstretched infrastructure in the rest of India, many visitors to Delhi are relieved to find a modern metropolis with broad roads, tree-filled parks and swish shops. And there's more to come. The Indian government has spent millions of rupees to spruce up the country's capital for the Commonwealth Games to be held in October 2010. A spanking new Metro system is being built to connect far-flung neighbourhoods in time for the event, the bus service has been improved and hundreds of bed and breakfasts have sprung up.

In the course of a day in Delhi, you could visit a 500-year-old mosque, browse in the upmarket boutiques of local designers, get an Ayurvedic massage, eat sushi and attend a free concert in the park by a living legend of Hindustani classical music. Like India, Delhi's a study in contrasts. But beyond the clichés (or perhaps because of them), Delhi's a fun, vibrant city. Just like India, but smaller.

Clockwise from top left: Jama Masjid; Dilli Haat; Red Fort.

Explore

At the centre of Delhi is Connaught Place, a colonnaded hub of shops and restaurants. Connaught Place lies at the northern edge of central Delhi, a well-planned expanse of Raj-era bungalows that once housed the most senior colonial administrators and are now occupied by government ministers, bureaucrats and judges. To the north lies crowded, colourful Old Delhi, dating back to Mughal times. South Delhi is where the city's affluent live, and where most new restaurants, nightclubs and stores are located. The 1990s witnessed the explosion of two suburbs: Noida, to the east, and Gurgaon, to the south-west. The new Metro system is making many parts of the city easily accessible.

CENTRAL DELHI

Central Delhi was designed by the British architect Edwin Lutyens. It took shape in the first two decades of the 20th century and was officially inaugurated in 1931 as New Delhi. It pulses with political power, containing India's parliament buildings, the president's official residence, and the homes of top politicians and bureaucrats. When the British commissioned the new city, they imagined it would be the capital of an empire that lasted a thousand years. Instead, they enjoyed the splendour of New Delhi for less than two decades.

Connaught Place is the beating heart of central Delhi. CP (as locals know it) is the city's old commercial and retail district, radiating outwards in three concentric circles around a park, under which sits an underground market called Palika Bazaar and the busiest Metro station. (Somewhat confusingly, the Metro station is officially called Rajiv Chowk, though no one uses the name.) Some of the buildings date back to the 1930s, and many of Delhi's most iconic brands have outlets here. The grand old cinema houses, aside from the well-named Regal, are now mostly cineplexes.

Note that New Delhi (Nayi Dilli) and Delhi are used synonymously to refer to the city as a whole.

Cathedral Church of Redemption

1 Church Road, North Avenue (011-2309-4229). Open 11.30am-5pm daily. Admission free.

Just behind Rashtrapati Bhavan (the president's residence) is this neo-classical gem, constructed in 1935. It's an Anglican church, and is now the headquarters of the Church of North India, as the Church of England is known in India. In the Christmas season, Delhi choral groups organise well-attended Christmas concerts.

Humayun's Tomb

Lodhi & Mathura Roads, Nizamuddin East (011-2435-5275). Open sunrise-sunset daily. Admission Rs 10 Indians; Rs 250 others.

This grand structure houses the grave of the second great Mughal, Humayun (Akbar's father). Said to be the model

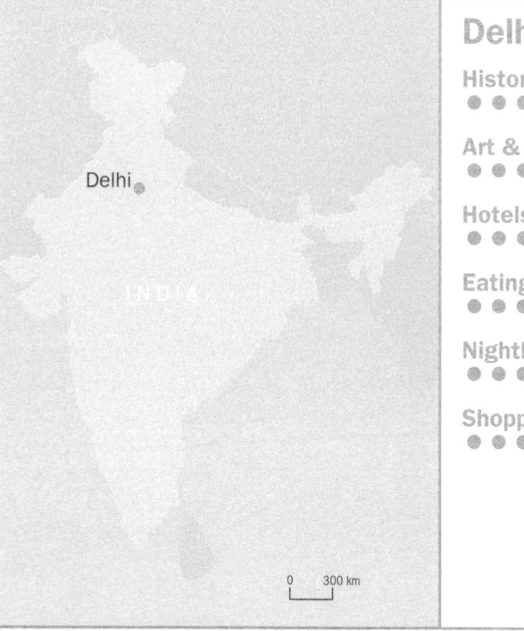

Delhi

Historic sites
●●●●●

Art & architecture
●●●●●

Hotels
●●●●○

Eating & drinking
●●●●●

Nightlife
●●●●●

Shopping
●●●●●

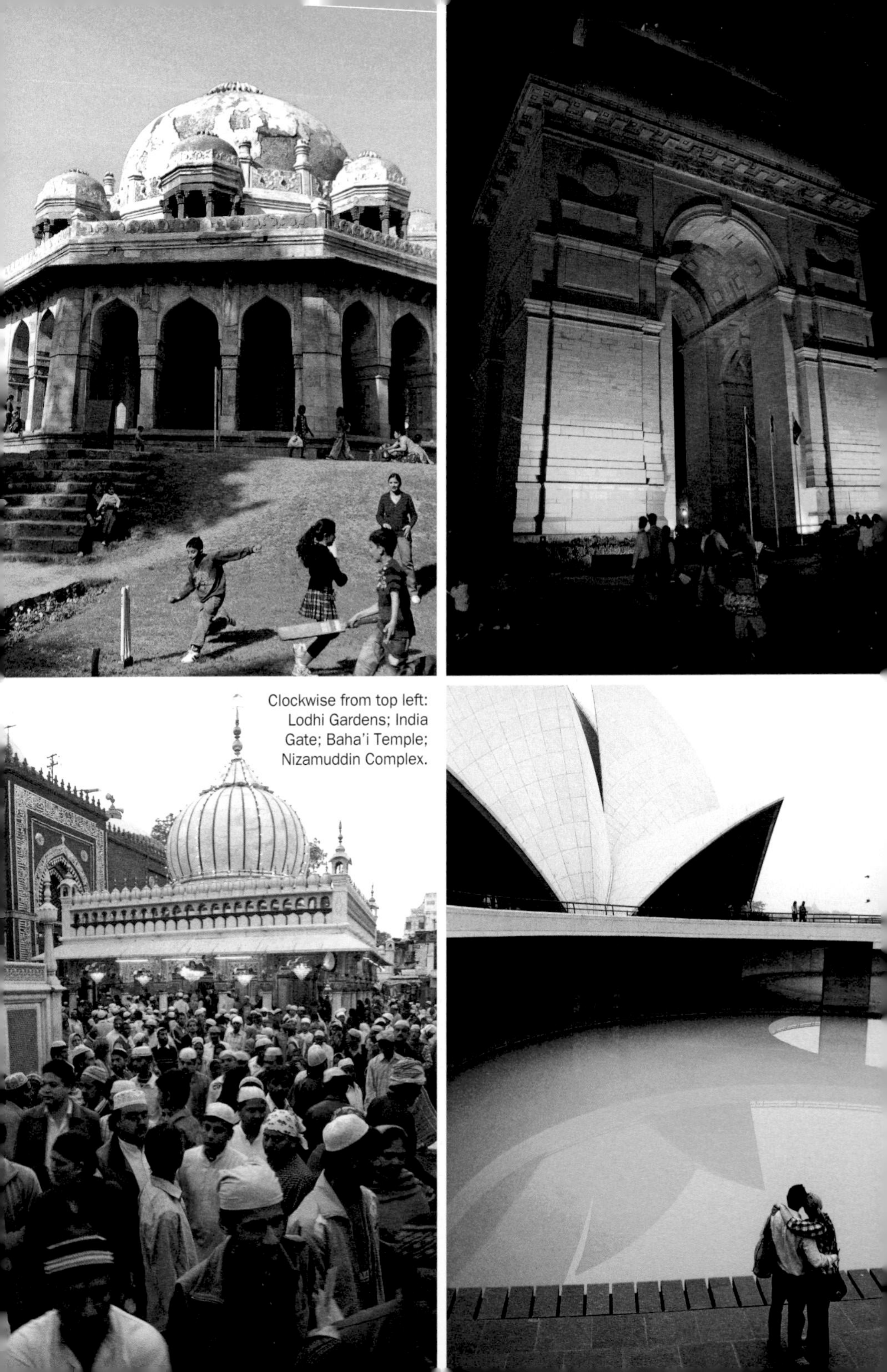

Clockwise from top left: Lodhi Gardens; India Gate; Baha'i Temple; Nizamuddin Complex.

for the Taj Mahal, which was built by Humayun's great-grandson Shah Jahan, this tomb is set among beautifully landscaped gardens, punctuated with water channels. Built in the mid 16th century, it came to define the Mughal style of architecture, with its imaginative melding of Indian motifs with Persian and Central Asian techniques and styles. The structure is built mainly of red sandstone, with white and black marble as highlights. An evening visit here, with the kites wheeling overhead and the river in the background, is memorable. Dotted about the complex are the graves and tombs of various lesser-known Mughals.

India Gate

Rajpath.

Originally called the All India War Memorial, this arch was designed by Edwin Lutyens in memory of the Indian soldiers killed in World War I. At its base is a black marble cenotaph with a rifle, on which sits a soldier's helmet. The Amar Jawan Jyoti, or flame of the immortal soldier, was added in 1971. Lutyens and his colleague Herbert Baker envisaged the broad street that connects India Gate to the Rashtrapati Bhavan – the home of the Indian president that was formerly the viceroy's palace – as the axis of New Delhi and, by extension, of the British Empire in India. It is now the site of the Republic Day parade held on 26 January each year. The monument is lit at night and families like to stroll around eating ice-cream.

Lodhi Gardens

Open 5am-8pm daily. Admission free.

It may have started life as Lady Willingdon Park in the 1930s, but it's definitely Indian. As famous for the privacy-strapped canoodlers who gather here as for the Sayyid- and Lodhi-era tombs on the grounds dating back to the 15th and 16th centuries, this is a delightful urban oasis. In the morning, it's the preferred walking area for the civil service mandarins who live in the government housing close by and for the residents of the outrageously expensive homes next door. Amrita Sher Gill Marg, Delhi's own 'billionaire's row', backs on to this green space. Stop by in the afternoon, when you need a break after a few hectic hours in the nearby plush Khan Market. Or while away time in the evening before catching a performance at the adjoining India International Centre or India Habitat Centre. There's even a bonsai garden.

National Handicrafts & Handloom Museum (Crafts Museum)

Bhairon Road, Pragati Maidan (011-2337-1641/ www.nationalcraftsmuseum.nic.in). Open Galleries 10am-5pm Tue-Sun. Crafts demonstration & Crafts Museum shop 10am-5pm daily. Admission Rs 10 Indians; Rs 150 others; free Mon.

This museum displays textiles, pottery and crafts from all over India. Craftspeople conduct demonstrations, except during the monsoon season (June-Sept) and there's a well-stocked museum shop.

National Museum

Janpath (011-2301-9776/www.nationalmuseum india.gov.ia). Open 10am-5pm Tue-Sun. Admission Rs 10 Indians; Rs 300 others (includes audio tour). Free film shows on India's art heritage 2.30pm Mon-Fri; 11.30am, 2.30pm, 4pm Sat, Sun.

Despite the dilapidated condition of many of the museum's galleries, the collections they hold are quite spectacular. The impressive and newly renovated miniatures gallery, the arms and armaments gallery and the Harappan gallery are recommended.

National Rail Museum

Chanakyapuri (011-2688-1816/www.nationalrail museum.org). Open Apr-Sept 9.30am-7.30pm Tue-Sun. Oct-Mar 10am-6pm Tue-Sun. Admission Rs 10.

Fun for kids, adults and railway enthusiasts. The outdoor gallery is the final resting spot for retired locomotives from around the country dating from the mid 19th century onwards. You'll find broad-gauge, metre-gauge and narrow-gauge locomotives here, including the little specimens from the mountain railroads of India. The Prince of Wales's saloon (1875), with all its fittings and furnishings intact, and the Mysore maharaja's saloon and armoured trains are among the museum's many brilliant exhibits. The indoor gallery features train models, old and new maps and a section for the visually challenged.

Nehru Memorial Museum & Library

Teen Murti Marg (011-2301-5333/www.nehru memorial.com). Open 10am-5pm Tue-Sun. Admission free.

Teen Murti Bhavan, in which the Nehru Memorial Museum and Library is located, was the residence of Jawaharlal Nehru, India's first prime minister. Some rooms have been preserved as they were when Nehru lived here. Displays use photographs and letters to reconstruct Nehru's childhood and youth, including his years at Harrow and Cambridge, his career as a barrister, and his role in the independence movement. The front lawn has a large granite rock inscribed with extracts from Nehru's 'tryst with destiny' speech, delivered at midnight on 15 August 1947, the day India became free of British rule.

Nizamuddin Complex

West of Mathura Road, Nizamuddin. Open sunrise-sunset daily. Qawwalis around sunset Thur. Admission free, donation expected.

The 13th-century Sufi saint Nizamuddin Auliya lived, worked and died in Delhi. His mausoleum has been a place of pilgrimage for 700 years and the surrounding area still carries his name. Within the mausoleum complex, you can also find the graves of Mirza Ghalib, Delhi's patron poet, and Amir Khusrao, poet, musician and all-round Renaissance man, beloved of Nizamuddin and buried close to him. The tank next door actually pre-dates the mausoleum and is in the process of being repaired. There is a lively market around the mausoleum, especially on Thursdays, when *qawwalis* (songs of praise) are sung at sunset. Stop by the shrine, make a wish and tie a string to the filigree screens outside; it is said your wish will be granted. Access to the complex is on foot via the narrow, crowded by-lanes of Nizamuddin. Dress appropriately (cover head and limbs).

Purana Qila

Mathura Road, near Delhi Zoo. Open 10am-5pm daily. Admission free.

This old fort stands across the road from Pragati Maidan. According to legend, this is the site of ancient Indraprastha, the Pandava capital mentioned in the epic *Mahabharata*. While that may not be the case, we do know that this fort served as the principal fort and residence of Sher Shah Suri, who briefly ruled India in the mid 16th century, and later for Emperor Humayun, who died here, after falling down the steps leading to his library. The enclosure is well maintained. Enter through the Bara Darwaza and walk on paths winding through manicured lawns bordered by flowerbeds. Watch for the **Qila-i-Kuna mosque** and the **Sher Mandal**, a two-storey octagonal tower of red sandstone.

Across another road from Purana Qila lies the serene Khairul Masjid complex, while behind the fort is the Delhi zoo. In front of the fort, where the moat would presumably have been, is a bit of a lake, where you can go boating. In winter, concerts and dance recitals are staged here.

"This huge complex is a monument to Safdarjang, the Nawab of Awadh, who played a major role in the court of the declining Mughal Empire."

Rashtrapati Bhavan

Rajpath.

At the western end of Rajpath, on the road that leads from India Gate, lies Rashtrapati Bhavan, now the official residence of India's president. Though it's closed to the public most of the year, you can stop by the gate and admire the imposing classical structure, decorated with elements drawn from Indian architecture. Visitors are allowed into the building's Mughal Gardens in February and March each year, when the flowers are in bloom (open 9.30am-2.30pm Tue-Sun, entry through Gate 35 near North Avenue).

Safdarjang's Tomb

Aurobindo Marg, corner of Lodhi Road. Open sunrise-sunset daily. Admission Rs 5 Indians; Rs 100 others.

This huge complex in the middle of Delhi is a monument to Safdarjang, the Nawab of Awadh (present-day Lucknow), who played a major role in the court of the declining Mughal Empire. Anything within a few kilometres of this enormous landmark eventually came to be named after it, even 250 years after the nawab's demise: Delhi's old airport, a municipal hospital and two housing developments. The tomb itself is a lovely quiet space, surrounded by gardens.

Tibet House Museum

1 Institutional Area, Lodhi Road (011-2461-1515). Open 9.30am-5.30pm Mon-Fri. Admission Rs 10.

Quiet and small, the Tibet House Museum has an extensive range of exquisite *thangka* (Buddhist-themed scroll) paintings and other religious artefacts, including prayer objects and statues. Various items of everyday use, including household objects and jewellery, are also on display.

OLD DELHI

Founded in 1639 by the Mughal emperor Shah Jahan, Old Delhi (or Shahjahanabad) was inspired by the layouts of Central Asian cities such as Samarkand. Its main avenue, Chandni Chowk, originally had a canal leading through it. Most of the elegant homes have long been demolished and those that remain are crumbling. But the congested, labyrinthine lanes still hold many pleasures: delicious food served in small back-street eateries; markets selling spices, saris and sanitaryware; temples and mosques that preserve a flavour of the neighbourhood in its heyday.

Jama Masjid

Off Netaji Subash Road. Open Summer 7am-12.15pm, 1.45pm-sunset daily. Winter 8.30am-12.15pm, 1.45pm-sunset daily. Admission free; Rs 20 rooftop access.

Opposite the Red Fort, Jama Masjid is a huge red sandstone building embellished with black-and-white marble. Perhaps India's most iconic mosque, built by Shah Jahan between 1656 and 1672, it dominates the skyline of the old city. The enormous courtyard can hold 25,000 people, but if you come at a quiet hour, you might see more pigeons than people. Climb the southern minaret for stunning views of the city. The closet in the mosque's north gate preserves a collection of relics said to have belonged to the Prophet Muhammad – a fragment of the Quran written on deerskin, a red hair from his beard, his camelskin sandals and a footprint embedded in a slab of marble.

Raj Ghat Park

Three kilometres east of the Red Fort and Chandni Chowk is the Raj Ghat Park, where a commemorative black marble platform marks the spot where Mahatma Gandhi was cremated in 1948. Nearby is the **National Gandhi Museum** (011-2331-1793, www.gandhimuseum.org, open 9.30am-5.30pm Tue-Sun, admission free), which has several galleries, including a Martyrdom Gallery that displays the clothes he was wearing when assassinated and the bullets he was killed by; it also has a library.

Red Fort/Lal Qila

Netaji Subhash Marg, near Chandni Chowk (011-2327-4580). Open sunrise-sunset Tue-Sun. Admission Rs 15 Indians; Rs 250 others (includes entry to museums); Rs 25 camera. Sound and light show: Hindi 6pm, English 7pm daily. Tickets Rs 60.

Built of red sandstone and embellished with intricate stone-and marble-work, this massive edifice – now a UNESCO World Heritage Site – dominates the eastern view of the old city. It was designed by Shah Jahan's daughter Jahanara

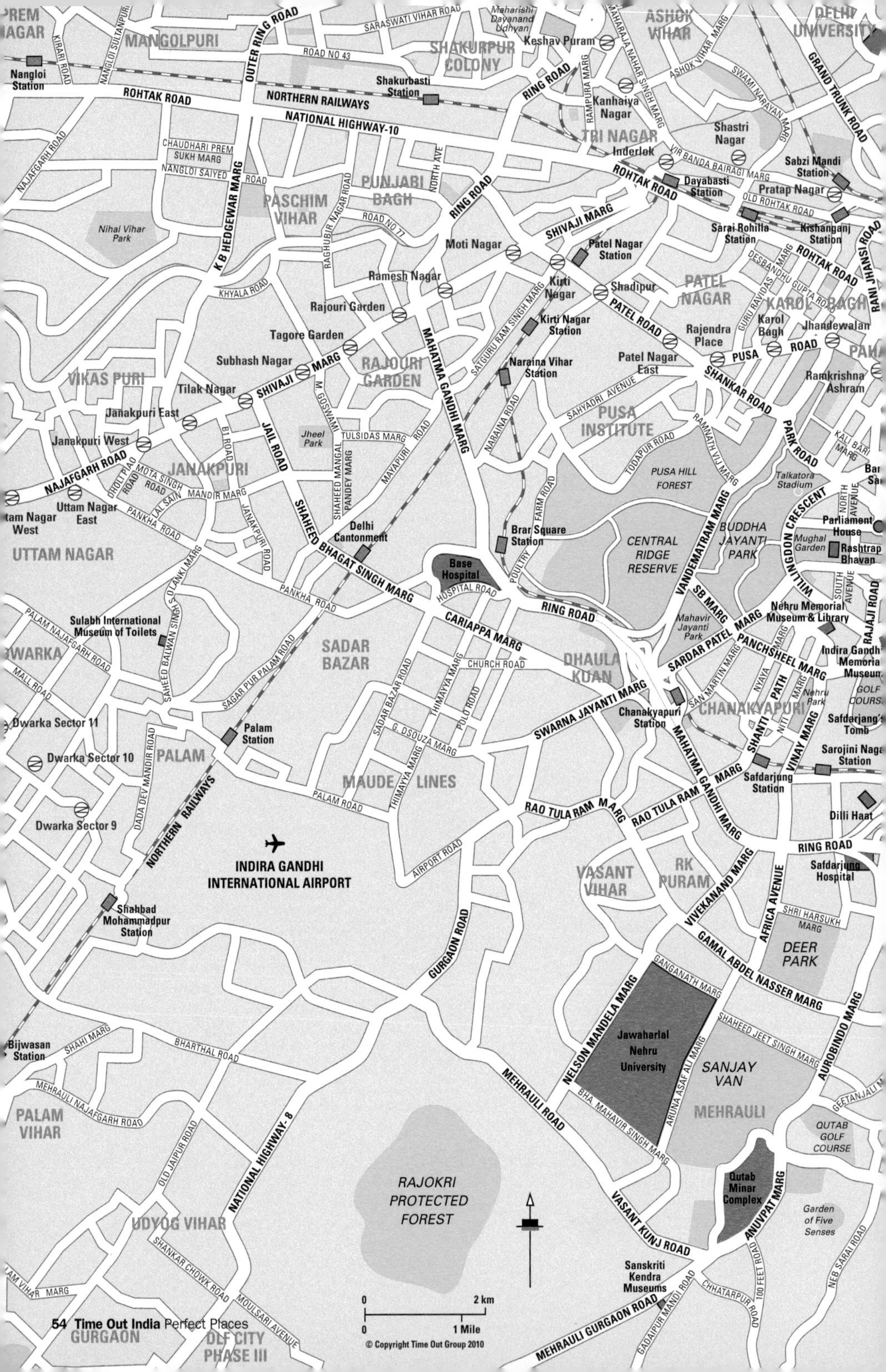

PREM NAGAR
MANGOLPURI
Nangloi Station
KIRARI ROAD
NANGLOI SULTANPURI
OUTER RING ROAD
SARASWATI VIHAR ROAD
Maharishi Dayanand Udhyan
SHAKURPUR COLONY
Keshav Puram
ASHOK VIHAR
DELHI UNIVERSITY
ROAD NO 43
Shakurbasti Station
ROHTAK ROAD
NORTHERN RAILWAYS
NATIONAL HIGHWAY-10
RING ROAD
Kanhaiya Nagar
RAMPURA MARG
MAHARAJA NAHAR SINGH MARG
ASHOK VIHAR MARG
SWAMI NARAYAN MARG
GRAND TRUNK ROAD
Shastri Nagar
TRI NAGAR
Inderlok
VIR BANDA BAIRAGI MARG
Sabzi Mandi Station
Dayabasti Station
Pratap Nagar
OLD ROHTAK ROAD
NAJAFGARH ROAD
CHAUDHARI PREM SUKH MARG
NANGLOI SAIYED ROAD
K B HEDGEWAR MARG
PASCHIM VIHAR
PUNJABI BAGH
NORTH AVE
RAGHUBIR NAGAR ROAD
ROAD NO 77
Nihal Vihar Park
SHIVAJI MARG
Patel Nagar Station
Sarai Rohilla Station
Kishanganj Station
Moti Nagar
Ramesh Nagar
Kirti Nagar
Shadipur
PATEL NAGAR
DESBANDHU GUPTA ROAD
ROHTAK ROAD
RANI JHANSI ROAD
KHYALA ROAD
Rajouri Garden
SATGURU RAM SINGH MARG
Kirti Nagar Station
PATEL ROAD
GURU RAVIDAS MARG
KAROL BAGH
Tagore Garden
Rajendra Place
Karol Bagh
Jhandewalan
Subhash Nagar
RAJOURI GARDEN
Naraina Vihar Station
Patel Nagar East
PUSA ROAD
VIKAS PURI
Tilak Nagar
M. GOSWAMI
MAHATMA GANDHI MARG
SAHYADRI AVENUE
SHANKAR ROAD
Ramkrishna Ashram
Janakpuri East
JAIL ROAD
BI ROAD
Jheel Park
TULSIDAS MARG
MAYAPURI ROAD
NARAINA ROAD
PUSA INSTITUTE
RAMNATH VIJ MARG
Janakpuri West
JANAKPURI
TODAPUR ROAD
PARK ROAD
KALI BARI MARG
NAJAFGARH ROAD
DHOLI PIAO ROAD
MOTA SINGH ROAD
LAL SAIN MANDIR MARG
SHAHEED MANGAL PANDEY MARG
FARM ROAD
PUSA HILL FOREST
Talkatora Stadium
Uttam Nagar West
Uttam Nagar East
PANKHA ROAD
JANAKPURI ROAD
SHAHEED BHAGAT SINGH MARG
Delhi Cantonment
Brar Square Station
POULTRY
CENTRAL RIDGE RESERVE
VANDEMATRAM MARG
BUDDHA JAYANTI PARK
WILLINGDON CRESCENT
NORTH AVENUE
Parliament House
Mughal Garden
Rashtrapati Bhavan
UTTAM NAGAR
S. OLANKI MARG
Base Hospital
HOSPITAL ROAD
RING ROAD
SB MARG
SOUTH AVENUE
RAJAJI ROAD
PANKHA ROAD
Nehru Memorial Museum & Library
PALAM NAJAFGARH ROAD
Sulabh International Museum of Toilets
CARIAPPA MARG
Mahavir Jayanti Park
SARDAR PATEL MARG
PANCHSHEEL MARG
Indira Gandhi Memorial Museum
DWARKA
SADAR BAZAR
DHAULA KUAN
CHURCH ROAD
THIMAYYA MARG
MALL ROAD
SAHEED BALWAN SINGH
SAGAR PUR PALAM ROAD
POLO ROAD
SAN MARTIN MARG
NYAYA MARG
NITI MARG
SHANTI PATH
GOLF COURSE
Nehru Park
CHANAKYAPURI
SADAR BAZAR ROAD
SWARNA JAYANTI MARG
Chanakyapuri Station
Safdarjang's Tomb
Dwarka Sector 11
Palam Station
G. DSOUZA MARG
VINAY MARG
Sarojini Nagar Station
Dwarka Sector 10
DADA DEV MANDIR ROAD
PALAM
Safdarjung Station
MAUDE LINES
MAHATMA GANDHI MARG
RAO TULA RAM MARG
Dilli Haat
PALAM ROAD
Dwarka Sector 9
NORTHERN RAILWAYS
RING ROAD
AIRPORT ROAD
VASANT VIHAR
RK PURAM
VIVEKANAND MARG
AFRICA AVENUE
Safdarjung Hospital
INDIRA GANDHI INTERNATIONAL AIRPORT
SHRI HARSUKH MARG
Shahbad Mohammadpur Station
GURGAON ROAD
DEER PARK
GAMAL ABDEL NASSER MARG
GANGANATH MARG
NELSON MANDELA MARG
AUROBINDO MARG
SHAHEED JEET SINGH MARG
Bijwasan Station
SHAHI MARG
BHARTHAL ROAD
Jawaharlal Nehru University
ARUNA ASAF ALI MARG
SANJAY VAN
MEHRAULI ROAD
MEHRAULI NAJAFGARH ROAD
GEETANJALI MARG
BHA. MAHAVIR SINGH MARG
MEHRAULI
QUTAB GOLF COURSE
PALAM VIHAR
NATIONAL HIGHWAY-8
OLD JAIPUR ROAD
RAJOKRI PROTECTED FOREST
Qutab Minar Complex
ANUVPAT MARG
Garden of Five Senses
VASANT KUNJ ROAD
UDYOG VIHAR
SHANKAR CHOWK ROAD
100 FEET ROAD
NEB SARAI ROAD
Sanskriti Kendra Museums
CHHATARPUR ROAD
GADAIPUR MANDI ROAD
VIHAR MARG
0 2 km
0 1 Mile
MOULSARI AVENUE
MEHRAULI GURGAON ROAD
GURGAON
DLF CITY PHASE III
© Copyright Time Out Group 2010

Delhi
MAHATMA GANDHI ROAD
OUTER RING ROAD
RIVER YAMUNA
Vidhan Sabha
Civil Lines
Kashmere Gate
Tis Hazari
St James Church
ZORAWAR SINGH MARG
Old Delhi Station
Chandni Chowk
CHANDNI CHOWK ROAD
CHANDNI CHOWK
Chawri Bazaar
Jama Masjid
CHURI WALAN ROAD
CHELMSFORD ROAD
New Delhi
New Delhi Station
JLN MARG
Connaught Place
Minto Bridge Station
Barakhamba
DDU MARG
JANPATH
Mandi House
KG MARG
TILAK MARG
ASHOKA RD
Central Secretariat
INDIA GATE
Vigyan Bhavan
SHAHJAHAN ROAD
SB MARG
Khan Market
Sikandar Lodhi's Tomb
LODHI GARDEN
LODHI ROAD
Tibet House Museum
Lodhi Colony Station
Sewa Nagar Station
JANGPURA
DELHI GOLF CLUB
Red Fort
RING ROAD
BAHADUR SHAH ZAFAR MARG
RAJGHAT
Mahatma Gandhi Samadhi
National Gandhi Museum
Doll Museum
ITO
Tilak Bridge Station
Pragati Maidan
Pragati Maidan
Indraprastha
Craft Musuem
National Science Museum
MATHURA ROAD
Purana Quila
DELHI ZOO
SUNDER NAGAR
DR. ZAKIR HUSSAIN ROAD
MAHATMA GANDHI MARG
Humayun's Tomb
Nizamuddin Station
Lajpat Nagar Station
LAJPAT NAGAR
RING ROAD
BHISHAM PITAMAH MARG
LALA LAJPAT RAI MARG
SIRI FORT ROAD
SIRI FORT
HANSRAJ GUPTA ROAD
NEHRU PLACE
Baha'i Temple/ Lotus Temple
HO CHI MINH MARG
Okhla Station
GREATER KAILASH
PRESS ENCLAVE
LAL BAHADUR SHASTRI MARG
DAKSHINPURI
MEHRAULI BADARPUR ROAD
DEOLI ROAD
SAINIK FARM
SANGAM VIHAR
Tughlaqabad Fort
GURU RAVIDAS MARG
MA ANANDMAYEE MARG
OKHLA ESTATE MARG
OKHLA INDUSTRIAL ESTATE
Tughlaqabad Station
NATIONAL HIGHWAY-2
ASOLA WILDLIFE SANCTUARY
BADARPUR
SARITA VIHAR
ROAD NO 13A
KALINDI KUNJ ROAD
MAULANA MOHAMMAD ALI MARG
Jamia University
NEW FRIENDS COLONY
RING ROAD
NOIDA TOLL BRIDGE
RIVER YAMUNA
AMRAPALI MARG
Amity University
GREATER NOIDA EXPRESSWAY
DADRI-ROAD
DADRI-ROAD
Botanical Garden
GOLF COURSE
Noida Sector 18
CAPT VIJYANT THAPAR MARG
Sector 16
Sector 15
New Ashok Nagar
Mayur Vihar
NOIDA LINK ROAD
MAYUR VIHAR
NIZAMUDDIN BRIDGE
Akshardham Temple
Akshardham
Yamuna Bank
PATPARGANJ ROAD
MOTHER DAIRY MARG
GURJAR SAMRAT MIR BOJ MARG
KHICHRIPUR ROAD
GHAZIPUR ROAD
MANDAOLI ROAD
Lakshmi Nagar
VIKAS MARG
LAXMI NAGAR
GEETA COLONY ROAD
Nirman Vihar
Preet Vihar
Karkarduma
Anand Vihar Station
Anand Vihar
GHAZIPUR
HAPUR BYPASS
NOIDA
UDYOG MARG
NARBADA MARG
AMALTASH MARG
JAL VAYU VIHAR ROAD
ASHOK MARG
HAR SINGHAR MARG
VIDYACHAL MARG
ASHOK MARG
CAPT SHASHI KANT SHARMA MARG
Noida City Centre
MAITHALI MARG
VAISHALI
MADAN MOHAN MALVIYA MARG
GOVIND BALLABH PANT MARG
SAHIBABAD
NORTHERN RAILWAYS
NATIONAL HIGHWAY- 24
DILSHAD GARDEN
Dilshad Garden
Vivek Vihar Station
GHAZIPUR ROAD
VISHWAS NAGAR
RD. NO. 71
KARKARI ROAD
VISHWAS NAGAR ROAD
SWAMI DAYANAND MARG
Jhilmil
Shahdara Station
Shahdara
Mansarovar Park
TAHARPUR ROAD
RD. NO. 68
CHOWK NO. 68
MANDOLI ROAD
HANUMAN ROAD
MAIN JAFRABAD ROAD
BRAHMAPURI ROAD
SHAHDARA
Welcome
GRAND TRUNK ROAD
Seelampur
SEELAMPUR
Shastri Park
LALA HARDEV SAHAI MARG
YAMUNA MARGINAL BANDH MARG
Northern India Engineering College

Begum in 1650. With a good guide, preferably arranged through your hotel, it's an interesting walk through the different royal quarters and halls where Shah Jahan held court. It was the headquarters of the Mughal rulers until the First Indian War of Independence in 1857, when the British took it over, converting many of its fine buildings into barracks. The Red Fort is still an important symbol for Indians and each year, on 15 August, the prime minister makes his Independence Day speech from its ramparts.

There are three museums within the complex: the **Indian War Memorial Museum**, with swords, muskets and other ancient armaments; the **Mumtaz Mahal Museum**, with manuscripts and miniature paintings; and the **Swatantrata Senani Museum**, focusing on the Indian National Army, an armed force formed by Indian nationalists that joined with the Axis powers during World War II to fight for Indian independence.

"This area was once a favourite hunting site for the Mughal princes and in the 19th century became a popular weekend retreat for colonial officials."

St James's Church

Lothian Road, Kashmiri Gate. Open 8am-7pm daily. Admission free.

Thought to be Delhi's oldest church in continuous use, St James's was built by James Skinner in 1836. Skinner was a colourful character, and a legend of Raj-era India. Being of mixed English and Indian parentage, he was unable to get a commission in the East India Company's army. He raised his own troop of cavalry, called Skinner's Horse, which later became a regiment in the regular army and still exists as a tank regiment in the Indian Army. The church grounds contain the graves of Skinner and his family, and the church is still known locally as Skinner's Church. Today, it is a quiet retreat amid the bustle of the Kashmiri Gate market, where you can take time to reflect on the strange ways in which race and history intermix in the subcontinent.

SOUTH DELHI

South Delhi is an agglomeration of commercial centres and upmarket residential complexes that Delhiites call 'colonies'. Among the most vibrant shopping areas are South Extension ('South Ex') and the N Block market in the Greater Kailash ('GK') neighbourhood. Further south, Saket has three huge malls with interesting stores, while Vasant Vihar to the south-west is also buzzing.

Baha'i Temple

Nehru Place. Open Apr-Sept 9am-7pm Mon-Sat. Oct-Mar 9.30am-5.30pm daily. Admission free.

Popularly known as the Lotus Temple because of its distinct shape, this beautiful structure is surrounded by manicured lawns and flowerbeds. The temple is open to all. Nine doors open into a large central hall, a quiet and peaceful haven that's perfect for a moment of meditation. The surrounding grounds guarantee an air of tranquillity, even though you're surrounded by tourists. An auditorium in the complex hosts occasional events.

Qutb Minar Complex & Mehrauli Archaeological Park

Aurobindo Marg, 15km S of Connaught Place. Open sunrise-sunset daily. Admission Rs 10 Indians; Rs 250 others.

Delhi's most famous monument is more than 800 years old. This minaret and victory tower is 72.5m (238ft) high, and is named for the 13th-century ruler Qutbuddin Aibak of the Delhi Sultanate, the first Sultan of Delhi. It survived the years and the various pillagings of Delhi, until a stampede in 1981 following a power failure caused the death of 45 and forced the government to declare the interior off-limits. You can still admire its intricately carved bulk, though. Nearby is the fourth- to fifth-century **Iron Pillar**; almost 7m metres tall and weighing more than 6 tonnes, it demonstrates the knowledge of metallurgy of that early era. Other impressive structures in the complex are the **Alai Darwaza (Alai Gate)**, a domed structure of red sandstone with decorated white marble inlay, and the **Quwwat-ul-Islam Mosque**.

Make time to wander through the park that spreads for 100 acres around the complex. This area was once a favourite hunting site for the Mughal princes and in the 19th century became a popular weekend retreat for colonial officials. The park's monuments include **Balban's tomb**, in which Qutb's successor is buried; the **mosque** built by the poet Jamali Kamali, who is also buried here; the 800-year-old fortress-like **Madhi Mosque**; the three-storeyed **Rajon Ki Baoli** step well; and the five-storeyed sulphur-smelling **Gandhak ki Baoli** step well. If nothing else, you'll learn how to compress almost a millennium of built history into one afternoon. For a guided walk, contact INTACH (Indian National Trust for Art and Cultural Heritage, 71 Lodhi Estate, 011-2464-1304, www.intachdelhichapter.org).

Sanskriti Kendra Museums

Mehrauli-Gurgaon Road, Anandgram (011-2650-1796/ www.sanskritifoundation.org). Open 10am-5pm Tue-Sun. Admission free.

Just off the busy Mehrauli-Gurgaon Road are the Sanskriti Kendra's three museums: **Everyday Art**, **Indian Terracotta** and **Textiles**. The Sanskriti Foundation is located in a beautiful estate in the Anandgram farmhouse area. It's a trek of around 20km (12 miles) south of central Delhi, but it's worth it once you get here. Visitors walk through an outdoor gallery made with traditional Indian building materials, such as mud – ideal for the climate – to the Terracotta Museum, which displays more than 1,500 works by master craftspeople from across the country. The Museum of Everyday Art – located in a basement gallery

– displays 2,000 household items used over the past 200 years in India, including toys, cooking utensils, other work tools and even nutcrackers. The Textiles section was being worked on when we visited: call ahead to check if it's open.

EAST DELHI

Akshardham Temple

National Highway 24, near Noida More (011-2201-6688). Open Temple complex Oct-Mar 9am-6pm daily. Apr-Sept 9am-7.30pm daily. Exhibitions 9am-5.30pm daily. Admission temple complex free; exhibitions Rs 125 Indians; Rs 200 others.

A monument to piety or ostentation? You decide. This gigantic temple has swiftly become a must-see on the tourist circuit. Join massive crowds of devotees and daytrippers as they enjoy its Disneyland-like pleasures, including a 'boat ride' through ancient India, animatronic tableaux and a giant-screen film about Swaminarayan, the founder-deity of the sect that built the temple. Or you could simply marvel at the ornately carved sandstone-and-marble structure, and the 326m-long (1,070ft) pink sandstone frieze of massive elephants wrapped around its base.

WEST DELHI

Sulabh International Museum of Toilets

Palam-Dabri Marg, Sulabh Gram, Mahavir Enclave (011-2503-1518/www.sulabhtoiletmuseum.org). Open 10am-5pm Mon-Sat. Admission free.

Visit this unusual museum, set up by the NGO that made public toilets usable in Delhi, to learn about the evolution of toilets and sanitation worldwide. Outdoor and indoor galleries take you through the history of the toilet from the chamber pot to squat toilets to the 'Western' toilets we know today. Displays include ornate porcelain toilets from Austria, a model of a French portable commode that was disguised as a bookcase, and much more. The outdoor gallery takes you through a variety of toilets developed for use across India (especially rural areas), each one customised to make the most of the resources available and the needs of the region. The museum is quirky, fun and informative, and you don't need to spend a penny.

Eat

Delhi has numerous stand-alone and five-star-hotel restaurants serving every imaginable cuisine, but in general eating out here is more expensive than almost anywhere else in the country. Those who want to sample street food can wander around Khan Market, where there are two hole-in-the-wall kebab stalls. Of these, Salim's Kebabs (52A Khan Market, Middle Lane, open noon-11pm daily) is the best – a smoking grill piled with skewers of mutton, chicken and fish. Order a mutton *seekh roomali* roll or the Afghani *burra* (mutton). Another option is Bengali Sweets (Connaught Place, Bengali Market, Tansen Road, near Mandi House, open 9am-11pm daily), a safe place for hygienic street snacks. *Chhola bhatura* is a classic hearty lunch, consisting of spicy chickpeas and huge golden fried breads, speckled with paneer. *Dahi papdi* (fried crisps topped with sweet yoghurt, tamarind, mint and spices) and *golguppas* (crunchy hollow puffs filled with potato and various sweet and sour spices) are typical favourites (ask for *golguppas* made with 'Bisleri', the generic term for bottled water).

Amici

Central Delhi *47 Khan Market, Middle Lane (011-4358-7191). Open 11am-11pm daily. $$$. Italian.*

Amici is the clear pick of the cafés dotting Khan Market. It serves toned-down Italian-style café food, with an emphasis on wood-fired pizzas. It's clean, white, decorated with Italian posters and conducive to light, gossipy lunches or chatty afternoons over coffee.

Andhra Bhawan

Central Delhi *Andhra Pradesh Bhawan, 1 Ashoka Road (011-2338-2031). Open 7.30-10am, noon-3pm, 7.30-10pm daily. $. South Indian: Andhra.*

This Andhra state-government-run canteen serves a staggering amount of thalis at breakneck pace. The set-up is basic: plastic furniture and a pay-before-eating counter. Efficient staff scurry about with pails from which they top up the compartments of your plate with vegetarian food. The unlimited thali is basic but filling. Non-vegetarian add-ons include chicken or mutton fry or curry.

Basil & Thyme

Central Delhi *11 Santushti Shopping Complex, Chanakyapuri (011-2467-4933). Open 10.30am-5.45pm daily. $$$. Western.*

Bhicoo Manekshaw is India's first Cordon Bleu-trained chef, but her restaurant has none of the attendant frippery. The menu changes often to reflect seasonal specialities, new recipes and old favourites, and the sunny establishment pulls in Delhi's most discerning ladies who lunch. A good place to take a break while shopping in the Santushti complex.

Bline

South Delhi *15 Anand Niketan Market, Malviya Nagar (98101-97494). Open noon-11pm Mon, Wed-Sun. $$. No credit cards. Russian.*

When it comes to expat-owned eateries, nothing beats the well-priced Bline. Owner Alexander Melnikov, a big bear of a man in steel-rimmed spectacles and bright blue apron, is the chef: a stern and imposing – but gracious – host, who puts a lot of love into the home-style dishes at his tiny restaurant, which has just four tables. Visit early for the popular beef stroganoff. Otherwise, try cured aubergine salad or a huge bowl of borscht, mutton 'capitan' served with mashed potatoes, or the day's special.

Bukhara

Central Delhi *ITC Maurya, Sardar Patel Marg, Diplomatic Enclave, Chanakyapuri (011-2611-2233). Open 7-11.45pm daily. $$$$. North-west Frontier.*

Top left: Diva (2). Top right: Bukhara. Middle: 1911, Imperial Hotel. Bottom: Navdanya Café (2).

Jewels By
NATASHA UJVAL AHUJA
brainhallcreative.com M: 09891009715

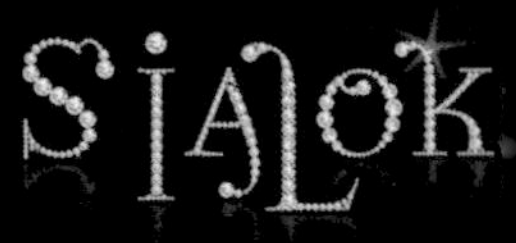
SIALOK

Former United States president Bill Clinton says this is one of his favourite restaurants, and it's hard to find fault with the food. Classics include tandoori *jhinga* (prawns) and *burra* (mutton) kebabs and the famous, buttery dal Bukhara. Mediocre service and epic queues are unavoidable; expect to fork over a small fortune for the luxury of a meal here.

Diva

South Delhi *M-8A Greater Kailash II, M Block Market (011-2921-5673). Open 12.30-3.30pm, 7.30pm-midnight daily. $$$$. Italian.*
Ritu Dalmia left London and Vama, her successful Indian restaurant there, to bring her true love, Italian cuisine, to Delhi. The dim semi-formal dining room is enlivened by lime-green alcoves, an electric-blue bar top and pop art. Dalmia aims for authenticity and uses the freshest ingredients. The daily specials are always good, the swordfish is a city classic and there's an eight- to ten-course tasting menu and an excellent wine list.

Lodi – The Garden Restaurant

Central Delhi *Lodhi Road, opposite Mausam Bhavan (011-2465-2808). Open noon-3pm, 7-11pm daily. $$$$. Mediterranean.*
With its lodge-like indoor seating and enchanting alfresco sections, this is a romantic park restaurant. There's lush greenery, candlelight, and pink rose petals strewn over white pebbles. Lodi is perfect for a post-walk, pre-dinner beer or cocktail. The food is an average mix of Italian and Mediterranean fare.

Mosaic

Central Delhi *M45/1 Connaught Place, Outer Circle (011-2341-6842). Open 11.30am-11.30pm daily. $$. Pan-Indian.*
Mosaic's menu traverses the map of India. The no-frills space is small, low-ceilinged and cosy, and the focus is on the food. Don't miss the classic Bengali snack *mochar* chop (soft, spiced banana flower, covered in mashed potato and breadcrumb-fried), prawns Koliwada, and pork in *til* (sesame) gravy. You'll be stuffed, but the desserts are too exciting to ignore, from *chikoo* mousse to fabulous Bengali *paatti shapta* (rice pancakes filled with grated coconut and palm sugar). During happy hours there's 50% off on Indian drinks.

Navdanya Café

South Delhi *D-26 Hauz Khas (011-2685-4069). Open 11am-7pm Mon-Sat. $. No AmEx. Organic café.*
This organic café is a tiny oasis of calm in the hectic Hauz Khas market, offering shelves of books, lots of light, and guilt-free goodies. The menu changes seasonally but the dosas, amaranth rolls, fresh juices, squashes and teas are all lovely. There's another branch at Dilli Haat.

Nizam's

Central Delhi *H-5/6 Plaza Building, Connaught Place, Middle Circle (011-2332-1953). Open 11am-11pm daily. $. No AmEx. Kebabs.*
Kolkata-style *kathi* kebab rolls are the speciality at this simple, cheap, fluorescent-lit eaterie. Fillings are single or double servings of mutton tikka or seekh, black pepper chicken, paneer and more, rolled up in fried, egg-coated paratha.

Punjabi by Nature

South Delhi *11 Basant Lok, Vasant Vihar (011-4151-6666). Open 12.30-11pm daily. $$$$. Punjabi.*
Punjabi by Nature is most famous for pioneering the vodka *golguppa* – an innocuous sweet-sour street snack turned cocktail conversation piece. Large stone walls with water shimmering down them, a fountain out front and grand tables with majestic silver chalices for water set the tone. Classic dishes include *dal makhani*, *raan-e*-Punjab (lamb), tandoori *jhinga* (prawns) and chicken or *burra* kebabs, and for dessert – *gulab jamuns* flambéed in brandy.

Tamura

South Delhi *8D Block Market, Poorvi Marg, Vasant Vihar (011-2615-4082). Open noon-3pm, 6.30-10.30pm daily. $$$. Japanese.*
Tamura is the closest thing Delhi has to a neighbourhood Japanese restaurant, and a favourite with Japanese expats. Settle into one of the cosy booths and sip your tea while you're choosing from cooked sushi (tempura rolls, California rolls, and so on), raw sushi or sashimi (flown in from Bangkok, only on Fridays and Saturdays), teriyaki fish and many other items. Tamura also stocks shochu, saké and imported beer.

> "UCH, as this institution established at the tail-end of the British Raj is fondly known, oozes retro charm."

United Coffee House

Central Delhi *E-15 Connaught Place, Inner Circle (011-2341-1697). Open 10am-11.30pm daily. $$. Café.*
Ensconced under a high, sky-blue ceiling and within gilt-embellished, peach walls are besuited old men reminiscing about the good old days, raucous families berating the unflappable waiters and tourists poring over guidebooks. UCH, as this institution established at the tail-end of the British Raj is fondly called, oozes retro charm: from the Kona coffee to the double-decker club sandwiches. It's particularly fun during cricket matches and on Friday evenings, when a singer croons old love songs.

Varq

Central Delhi *Taj Mahal Hotel, 1 Mansingh Road (011-2302-6162). Open noon-2.45pm, 7.30pm-midnight daily. $$$$. Modern Indian.*
Varq serves Indian food with Western-style plating. Varqui crab makes a good starter; several main courses are offered in small sizes as well, but you'll want the full serving of *martabaan ka meat*, a surprisingly simple, light lamb dish

Clockwise from top: Janpath (2); Play Clan (2); White.

served in an earthenware pot, which goes well with the mini olive naan or tomato mozzarella *kulcha* breads. *Singada palak* is a cake of spinach, topped with heart-shaped water chestnuts, served with a ricotta-stuffed pickled red pepper.

Shop

Delhi has some of the best shopping in the country, both in terms of markets and individual stores. If you're flying out of Delhi at the end of your Indian holiday, it may be a good idea to stop off for a few days to indulge in some fantastic retail therapy.

In addition to the stores and markets listed below, there's plenty of shopping treasure to be unearthed in Old Delhi. Hop on the Metro in Connaught Place (Rajiv Chowk) and get off two or three stops down, depending on your market of choice. You'll enter a whole new world in Chandni Chowk, Kinari Bazaar, Sadar Bazaar or Pratap Bazaar. Here you'll find silver jewellery, spices, toys from China and a lot more (*see p64* **A walk around Old Delhi**).

Baba Kharak Singh Marg

Central Delhi *Connaught Place. Open (most shops) 10am-6pm Mon-Sat.*
The emporia complex at Baba Kharak Singh Marg is a godsend for travellers who want to do their shopping at the end of their trip, before flying out of Delhi. All the country's crafts heritage is packed into one area; be prepared to do some serious walking. While you will get good prices, as is the case with many government-run establishments, don't expect great service or convenience.

Start at the Gramshilpa end, opposite PVR Rivoli, where the old state emporia are. **Gramshilpa** is a compact version of the massive Khadi Gramodyog Bhavan just across the road; both sell crafts from all over India. Don't miss **Gurjari**, Gujarat's state emporium, which is a colourful place filled with bags, jewellery and fabrics. Further down is **Purbasha**, the Tripura shop, **Lepakshi**, the Andhra Pradesh shop, then **Kairali**, the Kerala shop, and so on. A little further along is the Rajiv Gandhi Handicrafts Bhavan, which is an exciting part of the complex, with a **Cottage Industries Emporium**, the **Rajiv Gandhi Crafts Complex**, the **Export Promotion Council for Handicrafts** and four new state emporia – from Goa (full of shell-adorned objects), Chhattisgarh (packed with *dokra* art), Jharkhand and Uttarakhand. **Tribes India** is a great store stuffed with delightful tribal handicrafts. Beyond the Bhavan, the old emporia complex continues with several more states represented.

Dilli Haat

South Delhi *Sri Aurobindo Marg, opposite INA Market (011-2611-9055). Open 11am-10pm daily. Admission Rs 15. Some stalls accept credit cards.*
This unique open-air bazaar is one of Delhi's most popular shopping venues for handloom and handicraft items. The 200 stalls are rented out to craftspeople from all over India for 15 days at a time, giving them direct access to consumers. The complex also has 25 food stalls representing the different states of India. Themed festivals here often include additional temporary food stalls and lively cultural programmes.

Fabindia

Central Delhi *Connaught Place & Greater Kailash I (CP: 011-4151-3371/GKI: 011-4669-3725/ www.fabindia.com). Open 11am-8pm daily.*
While Fabindia now has stores all over the country, the best collections are often still found in Delhi. There's a great selection of handloom fabric garments, linens, dhurries, home linens and other products, including jewellery and organic foods.

Hauz Khas Village

South Delhi *Haus Khas, next to Deer Park (wwwhauzkahsvillage.in). Open 10am-7pm Mon-Sat.*
This dreamy little village is one of the nicest shopping destinations in town. Take the winding back route and look out for all the vintage poster stores. It's also home to White (*see p66*), Ogaan and lots of other independent fashion and interiors stores.

Janpath

Central Delhi *Janpath Road. Open 11am-8pm daily.*
Pavement shopping at its best. In the prime location of Connaught Place, Janpath is a name everyone in this city knows. Shoes, jewellery, incense, bags, handmade soaps, home decor – all you need to do is bargain, and bargain hard. It's the best place for knock-offs too.

Khan Market

Central Delhi *Open 10am-8pm Mon-Sat.*
This is one of the poshest markets in town, but that's not to say you won't uncover some real finds among the lovely pavement stalls. The Khan is the home of the best interior decor, from Good Earth and Oma to Apartment 9 and FCML, and it's full of fashion stores too (check out the very affordable Bloom).

Play Clan

South Delhi *F-51 Select Citywalk Mall, District Centre, Saket (011-4053-4559/www.theplayclan.com). Open 11am-9pm daily.*
This group of fashion, art and lifestyle designers display its imaginative products with 'India' motifs woven in. Check out its Ambassador car series; there are lamps, notebooks, and a fair amount of graphic art.

Santushti

Central Delhi *Santushti Shopping Arcade, Race Course Road (011-2410-2724). Open 10am-7pm Mon-Sat.*
One of the classiest shopping centres in town, Santushti is made for hours of browsing. Spread over gardens with meandering walkways, each store hawks all sorts of lovely goodies. You'll find Indian designers, household accessories, jewellery, shawls and even cigars.

A walk around Old Delhi

Shah Jahan's city is a retail heaven, an ethnographer's delight and a sensory overload. Its central thoroughfare, Chandni Chowk, branches off into a warren of different neighbourhoods, traditionally divided by religious community, profession or trade. Specialised markets, wholesale shops and old *havelis* (mansions) are punctuated by historic monuments and places to eat. Vendors specialising in street food indigenous to Shahjahanabad enjoy local and even international fame. This walk combines a few historic gems with some culinary delights, which, unfortunately, are not for the weak-stomached (though all can visually appreciate). If you get lost, ask someone, or hail a rickshaw (Rs 10-50 per stretch). You can also pick and choose locales from this itinerary to explore, as the whole walk is a bit ambitious for one day.

From Rajiv Chowk Metro station at Connaught Place, take the yellow line to Chandni Chowk station and follow the crowd out to the main avenue, **Chandni Chowk**. If you're touring the Red Fort in the morning, you can start from the east end of Chandni Chowk, just opposite the fort. Ask for the **Old Famous Jalebiwala** (1795 Chandni Chowk, 011-2325-6973, open 8am-10pm daily), a century-old counter that sells *jalebis* (orange fried sweets). The stall is on the corner of Chandni Chowk and Dariba Kalan (Incomparable Pearl Street) – a jewellers' and gem merchants' area.

The surrounding area, called **Dharampura**, is home to the Old City's Jain population and is dotted with Jain temples. The most famous, the early 18th-century **Lal Mandir**, at the eastern end of Chandni Chowk, opposite the Red Fort), is just as well known for its bird hospital as for the temple itself. Browse antique silver jewellery as you walk down **Dariba Kalan** – keep asking for the right turn to the **Kinari Bazaar**. Walk down that colourful haberdashers' street, festooned with tinsel, embellishments for clothing, beads and ribbons, keeping an eye on an opening into a cul-de-sac on your left. **Naugharana** (Nine Houses) is a little enclave of jewellers' *havelis*, some of them remarkably well maintained. The enclave gives you an idea of what the area may have looked like decades ago. At the end of the street, on the right, is the **Jauhri Temple**, a Jain 'jeweller's temple'. Take a look inside the two-level building, which was built in the late 18th century and renovated later. The paintings seem to be

influenced by a synthesis of various traditions, including Mughal miniature painting.

Exit the cul-de-sac and continue down Kinari Bazaar until you reach **Parathewali Gali** on your right. Keep an eye out for a man with a big basket of white and yellow milk foam. This delicate confection, known as *daulat ki chaat*, is built up of layers of whipped, sweetened milk, sprinkled with brown sugar and pistachios and topped with thin edible silver foil. The street is named for the several paratha specialists here – some of whom have served prime ministers and film stars. If you do want to eat, stop at the cramped eaterie of **Pandit Babu Ram Devi Dayal** (Parathewali Gali, 098116-02460, open 9am-midnight daily). Eventually, you'll emerge on to Chandni Chowk.

Cross the street and turn right, and you'll come to **Ghantewala Sweets** (1862 Chandni Chowk, 011-2328-0490, open 8am-9pm daily)

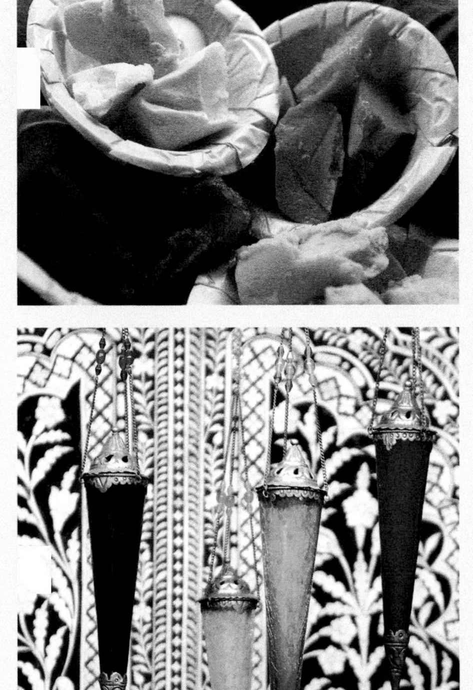

on your right. This sweet shop, established in 1790 and said to have catered to Mughal emperors, sells delicious *sohan halwa* – hard, saccharine-sweet roundels of brown sugar and ghee. A little further ahead, at the fountain, is **Gurudwara Sisganj**, an important Sikh place of worship, built on the site of the martyrdom of one of the Sikh spiritual leaders, Guru Tegh Bahadur.

Double back on Chandni Chowk or take a green minibus to the western end of the street at **Fatehpuri** (keep an eye out for the Town Hall, built in 1866, on your right). In front of you, at the intersection, is **Fatehpuri Masjid**, built in 1650 by Fatehpuri Begum, one of Shah Jahan's wives. The large mosque and madrasa complex is worth a visit. If you're facing the complex, take a right and then a left on to **Khari Baoli**, the wholesale spice market. Straight past the left turn is **Giani's** (Church Mission Road, Fatehpuri, 011-2393-6174, open 11am-midnight daily) – famous since 1951 for the *kulfi falooda* (traditional ice-cream topped with sweet vermicelli).

From Fatehpuri, walk down Khari Baoli, past sneeze-inducing piles of ground and whole chillis, turmeric, peppers, home-made soaps, sweet drink concentrates and *murabbas* (fruit pickles). From here, take a rickshaw and ask for **Hamdard Dawakhana**. You'll go down **Naya Bans Street**, passing the *paan* (areca nut, betel leaf and tobacco) wholesale market. Continue via rickshaw, keeping an eye out for the first-floor **Masjid Mubarak Begum**, built in 1823 by one of the wives of Sir David Ochterlony, the first British Resident of Delhi, down to **Hauz Qazi Chowk**, the intersection where the Chawri Bazaar Metro station is located. Walk a little bit down **Bazaar Sita Ram** and turn right at Kucha Pati Ram, a narrow, quiet street that leads to **Lala Dulli Chand Naresh Gupta** (934 Kucha Pati Ram, Bazaar Sita Ram; 011-2323-7085, open noon-8pm daily), who sells fruit kulfis in flavours from pomegranate to mango. Back out on Bazaar Sita Ram, take a longish rickshaw ride down to the **Kalan Masjid**, which was one of seven identical mosques built in 1387 by Khan-i-Jehan Jujan Shah, prime minister to the Tughlak ruler Feroze Shah. The mosque is gaudily painted in bright blue, purple, turquoise and green, has a marble courtyard fountain with goldfish swimming in the green water and a marvellous view from the roof (ask the imam if you can climb up).

From here, it's another long but interesting rickshaw ride via a wholesale paper market to **Jama Masjid**, India's largest mosque, built in 1656 by Shah Jahan. Nearby is **Bazaar Matia Mahal**, which houses the famous **Karim Hotel**, which claims to have been founded by imperial Mughal cooks (16 Gali Kababian, Bazaar Matia Mahal, opposite Gate 1, Jama Masjid, 011-2326-9880, www.karimhoteldelhi.com, open 7am-midnight daily). Try the mutton *burra* kebabs or a korma with *sheermal*, a sweetish bread. Opposite Karim's you'll see a few stalls selling *shahi tukda*, Delhi's most unholy bread pudding, loaded with sugar, heavy cream and a pool of ghee. Take a rickshaw via a shorter route through Chawri Bazaar to the Chawri Bazaar Metro station to bring you back to Connaught Place.

For a guided walk of Chandni Chowk contact INTACH at 011-2463-2267/www.intachdelhi chapter.org.

Shahpur Jat

South Delhi. *2km E of Haus Khaz.*

Truly a treasure trove for shopping, the Shahpur Jat area invites you to get lost in its many maze-like alleyways and by-lanes. It's also a fantastic place for bags and little ethnic design stores. Amaatra (right next to Slice of Italy) has lovely innovative jewellery.

White

South Delhi *31 Hauz Khas Village (011-4605-4817). Open 10.30am-7.30pm Mon-Sat; 11.30am-6.30pm Sun.*

This newish store stocking Western-style womenswear is worth looking at because it's one of the few places in Delhi to stock innovative, young Indian fashion designers.

Arts

Art galleries and exhibitions abound in Delhi and interested visitors will find no dearth of events to attend. Grab a copy of *Time Out Delhi* for the latest information on what's on at all the places listed below, as well as at Delhi's many art galleries.

Some Delhi institutions can't be missed. The India International Centre (40 Max Mueller Marg, 011-2461-9431, open 11am-7pm daily), for instance, offers an immense variety of cultural events all year round. It plays host to an annual film festival, art shows, Indian classical dance and music recitals, talks and conferences. Events are usually free.

One of the most important cultural institutions in the capital is the India Habitat Centre (Lodhi Road, 011-2468-2005, open 10am-8pm daily). There's a great variety of events here, ranging from art exhibitions, plays and Indian classical dance and music recitals, to panel discussions, lectures and film screenings.

The revamped, government-run Lalit Kala Akademi (Rabindra Bhavan, 35 Feroze Shah Road, Mandi Circle, 011-2338-6626, open 11am-7pm Mon-Sat) now has multiple renovated display rooms that host exciting shows of traditional and contemporary Indian art.

The National Gallery of Modern Art or NGMA (Jaipur House, India Gate, 011-2338-6111, open 10am-5pm Tue-Sun, admission Rs 10 Indians, Rs 150 others) was opened in 1954 to house art dating from the 1850s onwards. Though shows are few and far between, the gallery houses some fine pieces by Indian (and some international) artists. The permanent collection is occasionally rotated, but works by Raja Ravi Varma, Amrita Sher Gil and other well-known artists are often on view.

Aside from the NGMA, Delhi Art Gallery (11 Hauz Khas Village, 011-4600-5300, open 11am-7pm daily) probably has the best permanent collection in town.

The Devi Art Foundation (Sirpur House, Sector 44, Plot 39, near Epicentre, 011-4166-7474, open 11am-7pm Tue-Sun) is an initiative by well-known art collector Anupam Poddar. It's the latest addition to the capital's list of fantastic cultural institutes. Its aim is to bring art to the public and Devi does this through a spectacular warehouse-style exhibition space as well as by talks, guided tours and open days where the public can meet and interact with artists and curators.

At the Triveni Kala Sangam (205 Tansen Marg, Mandi House, 011-2371-8833, open 11am-7pm Mon-Sat) you'll find four excellent art galleries. It also organises Indian classical dance recitals. When you need a break, stop by at the quaint Triveni Tea Terrace for tea and snacks.

The Academy of Fine Arts & Literature (4/6 Siri Fort Institutional Area, 011-2649-6289, open 9am-7pm daily) has a well-presented gallery with over 200 miniature paintings from the Mughal, Sikh, Pahari and Rajasthani schools. Several unique and rare works are on display. The Museum of Folk Art – part of the Academy – has an expansive collection of paintings and sculpture from across India. Part of this specially commissioned collection includes provocative renderings of contemporary issues in traditional styles.

Nightlife

Most of Delhi's clubs require patrons to be semi-formally dressed, which usually means no jeans, sneakers or T-shirts. Some levy a cover charge on some nights of the week, always redeemable against the purchase of drinks.

ai

South Delhi *MGF Metropolitan Mall, Second Floor, District Centre, Saket (011-4065-4567). Open 7.30pm-midnight daily.*

ai has a separate dining area, jazz lounge and bar, and they're all posh. The Love Hotel is the breezy, Mediterranean-style terrace bar, with little cabanas and plush cushioned seats. Music is mainly house.

Aqua

Central Delhi *The Park, 15 Parliament Street, Connaught Place (011-2374-3000). Open 7pm-1am daily.*

This bar has a strict dress code. It's a massive outdoor space, with the bar beside a pool. Friday is retro night, while Saturday features loud thumping trance; the rest of the week has up-tempo house music.

Baci

Central Delhi *23 Sundar Nagar (011-4150-7445). Open 7.30-11.45pm daily.*

This spot has a charming Italian bistro vibe. Popular with expats and the local 'it' crowd, it morphs from a relaxed restaurant into a loud electronica club on Saturday.

Clockwise from top: ai; Urban Pind; Manré; F Bar & Lounge.

Top left: Shangri-La – Eros Hotel (2). Top right: Bnineteen. Middle: Maidens Hotel (2). Bottom: The Manor (2).

F Bar & Lounge

Central Delhi *Ashok Hotel, 50B Diplomatic Enclave, Chanakyapuri (011-2611-1066). Open 10.30pm-4am Mon-Thur, Sun; 10.30pm-5.30am Fri, Sat.*

It's all about partying at this cavernous central Delhi club. A king-sized console and a terrific laser display complement the very strong cocktails. Ask the bartender for the Ronella – it's delicious, with vodka, ginger, lemon and orange chunks. Unlike other bars in this city, this place stays open late. Expect loud techno, house and other club-happy genres. The hefty cover charge is Rs 1,000-Rs 2,500 per couple.

"Weekends are packed, so get here early. Expect anything from loud retro nights to cutting-edge local house music, complete with visuals."

Magique

South Delhi *The Garden Village, Gate No.3, Garden of Five Senses, Said-ul-Ajaib (011-3271-6767). Open 7.30pm-1am daily.*

This upmarket bar and restaurant is within the Garden of Five Senses in South Delhi. Frangipani trees and bushes outline its perimeter. The outdoor area is gorgeous, with tables set with candles and white carnations. Staff are friendly and the drinks menu top-notch, including a comprehensive martini menu.

Manré

South Delhi *MGF Metropolitan Mall, fourth floor, A Wing, District Centre, Saket (011-4066-8888). Open 8pm-1am daily.*

In 2009 this was the most popular spot in town, with separate areas for dining and clubbing and two large terraces. Weekends are packed, so get here early. Expect anything from loud retro nights to cutting-edge local house music, complete with visuals.

Q'BA

Central Delhi *E 42-43 Connaught Place, Inner Circle (011-4151-2888). Open noon-midnight daily.*

This huge restaurant and bar takes up an entire corner of a Connaught Place block. It's spread over two floors: downstairs is loud, with comfortable couches and little tables spread around a central bar; the dining section upstairs is slightly quieter and more sedate. A lovely terrace looks out over the green centre of Connaught Place circle and is the main draw of this place. The mojitos are faultless too, and the atmosphere relaxed. Q'BA's kitchen produces competent Western dishes and above-average Indian food.

Urban Pind

South Delhi *N-4 GK-I, N Block Market (011-3251-4646). Open 12.30pm-midnight daily.*

By day Urban Pind is a relaxed restaurant, frequented by college kids and middle-aged ladies who lunch. At sundown, the windows are covered, the music morphs into chilled electronica and the Khajuraho-esque figures on the wall come alive. Voilà, you're in a lounge bar, with a dancefloor upstairs.

Yum Yum Tree

South Delhi *Community Centre, New Friends Colony (011-4260-2020). Open 7pm-midnight daily.*

This lovely large bar-cum-restaurant has a separate section devoted to dancing. The peaceful vibe and reasonable prices attract a youngish, cosmopolitan crowd. This is a great place to come with a large group of friends, dress up or down (depending on your mood), and have an affordable, fun night out. Try the wildberry sour from the cocktail menu.

Stay

Amarya Haveli

South Delhi *P-5 Hauz Khas Enclave (011-4175-9268/ www.amaryagroup.com). $$.*

The Amarya Haveli is owned by Alexandre Lieury and Mathieu Chanard, two Frenchmen who have made it their mission to combine Western comfort with oriental opulence. Each of the six rooms has a different theme and colour; the Jodhpuri Room is decorated entirely with blue motifs and designs from Jodhpur, while the Cochin Room is painted all in white with a golden Tree of Life emblazoned on the wall. There's a nice upstairs terrace, and a Japanese-themed common lounge and dining area. Located in a quiet, safe neighbourhood in south Delhi, it's the perfect distance from the noise of the city centre.

Bed & Breakfast at Eleven

Central Delhi *Area 11, Nizamuddin East (011-2435-1225/www.elevendelhi.com). $$. No credit cards.*

A five-minute walk from Humayun's Tomb and a 20-minute drive from Central Delhi, this bed and breakfast occupies a colonial bungalow with a nice lawn and swing and a pleasant front patio. It's surrounded by greenery, lending a secluded, peaceful ambience. Decor is not particularly elegant, but all the rooms are comfortably furnished. What the Eleven lacks in high-end hotel luxury, it makes up for with simple domestic comfort.

Bnineteen

South Delhi *B-19 Nizamuddin East (011-4182-5500/ www.bnineteen.com). $$.*

Bnineteen is luxury with a personalised touch from hosts Rajive and Janis. Rooms are decorated with objets d'art and antiques, the linen and upholstery are tasteful, and the bathrooms large. The terrace has great views of Humayun's Tomb, especially breathtaking at night when the monument is lit up. Meals on the candlelit terrace are delightful, as is the service at this stylish home away from home.

Colonel's Retreat

South Delhi *D-418 Defence Colony (99997-20024/ www.colonelsretreat.com). $$. No AmEx.*

Located in the posh residential Defence Colony neighbourhood – loved by tourists, business travellers and diplomats alike – the Colonel's rooms are simply furnished. Common areas comprise a dining room and a lounge with leather couch, armchairs, TV and a fully stocked bookshelf for guests who want to read up on Delhi or just lose themselves in a novel. There's no kitschy oriental opulence here, but the simplicity of the Colonel's Retreat is a treat.

"High ceilings, huge windows, faded paintings all lend an old-fashioned charm – you can almost see the ghosts of imperial officers."

Imperial

Central Delhi *Janpath (011-2334-1234/ www.theimperialindia.com). $$$$.*

The fragrance of jasmine wafts around you, there's soothing piano music in the background and opulence is everywhere: in the marble floors, the cisterns full of flower petals, the fountains and the chandeliers. It all adds up to an air of luxury harking back to a different era. Most of the lobbies and restaurants in the Imperial are furnished in a colonial British style, with white couches and armchairs, plush carpets, and old sepia-toned photographs from the days of the Raj. Tea and coffee are taken in the Atrium, which seems more like the set of a Henry James novel than a modern-day hotel. In the midst of all that Indo-British luxury, guests will also find more modern amenities, from a Chanel store to a beauty salon and barbershop. The Imperial's magnificent restaurant, 1911, extends over three connected areas: bar, formal dining area and turquoise-pillared veranda, overlooking a lawn. If the imperial architecture, wicker chairs, impeccable collection of photos and prints and unusual floral arrangements aren't impressive enough, 1911's 15-page wine list should keep you occupied.

Inn at Delhi

South Delhi *C-34 Anand Niketan (98681-40243/ www.innatdelhi.com). $$.*

Surrounded by parks and nestled in the pleasantly quiet and posh neighbourhood of Anand Niketan (also a diplomatic enclave), this inn is set in a three-storey mansion typical of the neighbourhood. It's run by Mr and Mrs Subhash Chander, an amiable retired couple (he is a former professor, she used to be a doctor) who also live on the premises. They have taken pains to create a comfortable and pleasant space for guests and tailor the menu to suit their tastes. Bathrooms come with bathtubs; half of them have jacuzzis. Every room has a mini fridge, Indian paintings on the walls, embroidered pillows and bedspreads and cosy desk lamps, all of which make one feel right at home.

Maidens Hotel

Old Delhi *7 Sham Nath Marg (011-2397-5464/ www.maidenshotel.com). $$-$$$.*

This Civil Lines landmark has been around since 1903. The grandeur of the building has survived, while the amenities have been updated. High ceilings, huge windows, faded paintings all lend an old-fashioned charm – you can almost see the ghosts of imperial officers. Start with a drink at the Cavalry Bar, hop across to the Old City or Delhi University by cycle-rickshaw, return and take a swim in the quiet pool. Suites (regular rooms aren't as nice) are spotless and modern, with enormous bathrooms, but note that windows are frosted and overlook a communal veranda. By Delhi standards, for what you're getting, the Maidens is pretty affordable; service is outstanding too.

The Manor

South Delhi *77 Friends Colony, West (011-2692-5151/ www.themanordelhi.com). $$$.*

With the mansions of media moguls, pharmaceutical millionaires and old-time oil industry executives as its neighbours, the Manor certainly has an impeccable address. Some of these magnates can occasionally be found on the hotel's large lawn, having discreet meetings or simply enjoying a cocktail or two. The hotel has been around since the 1950s, but it has had an international-style makeover: The decor is minimalist with just a flash of marigold. The 15 rooms are spacious, with wood-panelled floors and walls, large beds and writing tables. Make sure to eat at the restaurant, Indian Accent, which has been winning enthusiastic reviews for its innovative Indian fusion cuisine. The menu includes the likes of tamarind-glazed lamb shanks, masala morels and Indian breads stuffed with mushrooms and drizzled with truffle oil.

Shangri-La – Eros Hotel

Central Delhi *19 Ashoka Road, Connaught Place (011-4119-1220/www.shangri-la.com). $$$$.*

Located bang in the middle of Central Delhi, the view from any side of the Shangri-La is spectacular: India Gate and Rashtrapati Bhavan are always in sight, and on a clear day, you can even see the Qutb Minar in the distance. Luxurious rooms are tastefully furnished, with wood-panelled closets, desk, chair, couch and many mirrors. A glass partition separates the bathroom from the bedroom, making rooms appear more spacious. The East Asian cuisine restaurant 19 Oriental Avenue is one of the best Asian food places in Delhi. The spa, lit by candles, has running water flowing through every room; it's a wonderful place to relax and indulge.

Shanti Home

West Delhi *A-1/300 Janakpuri (011-4157-3366/ www.shantihome.com). $$. No AmEx.*

Close to the international airport and five minutes from the closest Metro station, this boutique hotel is a bit far from the main sights, though some may not find this a bad thing. Decor is a fusion of styles, but high-backed carved benches, *urulis* of flower petals, statues of Ganesha, other Hindu figurines and oriental carpets adorn the foyer and common areas. Wi-Fi and breakfast are included in the room charge, and there's also a lounge with desktop computer. 'Shanti' means inner peace in Hindi, and the hotel makes every effort to help their guests attain such a state of bliss. On the rooftop is a 24-hour restaurant and bar.

Thikana

South Delhi *A-7 Gulmohar Park (011-4604-1569/ www.thikanadelhi.com). $$. No AmEx.*

Tiny photos of four generations of the family that runs this airy B&B hang from twigs stuck into a glass bowl in the dining room: just Sheetal and Atul Bhalla's many little touches. There's also tasteful Indian art on the walls and traditional home-cooked meals available on request. Though Thikana is located on a busy street, its eight rooms are strangely quiet. They're also elegantly furnished, with large beds and inviting armchairs. Bathrooms are spotless, and are supplied with handmade soap. The living room has TV, free internet and photocopying facilities. Thikana is around a 25-minute taxi ride away from the Connaught Place tourist hub, and is popular with expat journalists and NGO workers. Guests are made to feel welcome.

Factfile

When to go

Mid October to mid March sees crisp, cool nights (close to freezing in December and January) and warm sunny days. The fine weather makes this the city's busiest time in cultural terms, with lots of outdoor activities. April to September is uncomfortably hot.

Getting there

Indira Gandhi International Airport is connected to most international and domestic destinations. Delhi has three major railway stations: Delhi Railway Station in the Old City, New Delhi Railway Station just off Connaught Place and Nizamuddin Station in south Delhi. The Inter State Bus Terminals service millions of travellers every day.

For more on travel within India, *see p378* **Navigating India**.

Getting around

Visitors intending to cover a lot of ground should hire a private taxi for the day. While still not covering the whole city, the new Metro is a safe and quick way to get around much of town (www.delhimetrorail.com, from Rs 6). Avoid the buses. Taxis can't be hailed on the street; most neighbourhoods have stands where you can get one. Alternatively, call Meru Cabs (011-4422-4422) or Easy Cabs (011-4343-4343). If you take an auto-rickshaw or a taxi from a local stand, negotiate the price in advance. Cycle-rickshaws in congested areas like Old Delhi are a good option; negotiate a price and hop on.

Tourist information

Delhi Tourism has an office at Baba Kharak Singh Marg (Coffee Home, 011-2336-5358, open 10am-7pm Mon-Sat). Its Travel Division, responsibile for organising car hire, guided tours and so on, is in Connaught Place (N-36, Bombay Life Building, Middle Circle, New Delhi (011-2331-5322, www.delhitourism.nic.in, open 10am-7pm Mon-Sat).

The tourist Helpline numbers are 011 2336-5358/3607.

Internet

Internet cafés can be found all over the city.

Tips

- Delhi's Metro is still under construction, with some lines open at the time of writing. Much of the central and southern parts of the city will be covered by the Metro by October 2010.

- When visiting the crowded lanes of Old Delhi carry only what you need and have it in your front pocket and close to your body. Pickpocketing is not uncommon in congested areas such as Chandni Chowk.

- Delhi is full of tourist scams and traps. The most common of these are agencies and offices that pretend to be 'government-run' or tourist offices. It's hard to tell them apart from the real thing, so it's best to take a private taxi and the recommendations of a reliable hotel or reputable agent. Anything that seems too good to be true is usually just that.

- Between mid December and the end of January, Delhi suffers severe morning fog that hampers flight arrivals and departures. During this period, try to book yourself on flights arriving or leaving Delhi after noon, and still expect weather-related delays.

Top: Victoria Memorial.
Bottom: Hooghly river.

Kolkata

A colonial creation, now proudly Bengali.

Kolkata comes with a cautionary note: don't be put off by first impressions. This city is something of a kaleidoscope. Take the time to look into it, and its diverse neighbourhoods and histories begin to fall into myriad interesting patterns.

Despite the mushrooming malls and neon lights, Kolkata teeters between quaint and passé. Some argue that it has been in a time warp since the 1970s, losing the polish and edge that had made it India's cultural capital. And while the new India is certainly encroaching on this city, there are still many nooks and corners – the bookshops on College Street, the wrought-iron and green-shuttered windows of north Kolkata among them – that resonate with the past.

From three swampy villages on the Ganga delta, bought by the East India Company in the late 17th century, Kolkata grew to become the first British capital of India 100 years later; it was from here that the British ruled a large part of south-east Asia for around 200 years. Following in British footsteps, the Bengali aristocracy and ambitious middle class came to settle in the then-wealthy, now-crumbling neighbourhoods of north Kolkata, with their palatial bungalows. The Armenians came too, as did the Jews and the Chinese. And, from the other end of India, Marwaris from Rajasthan migrated here and made it their home. All of them left their imprint. Perhaps it's this historical layer cake of cultures that makes Kolkata – the anglicised name of Calcutta was officially dropped in 2001, but continues to linger in English conversations – both friendly and welcoming of outsiders and, at the same time, fiercely proud of its Bengali identity. It won't be long before any visitor discovers that Kolkata has birthed greats like Nobel laureate Rabindranath Tagore, filmmaker Satyajit Ray and economist Amartya Sen. Or that *adda,* a Bengali word for chatter, debate and conversation, whose central purpose is to waste time, is a well-established tradition here – along with left-liberal politics, eating well and partying hard.

Explore

Kolkata has some of the finest colonial architecture in India. Early British settlers put up magnificent buildings, perhaps to remind them of home. Rich locals soon followed suit, building mansions, temples and so on.

Kolkata is not a sprawling city. It's mostly concentrated around the east bank of the River Hooghly, and locals use the extensive river transport system to get around. The Howrah Bridge – linking to the industrial city of Howrah – is the principal connecter between the two sides of the river, and marks the line between north and central Kolkata.

The area south of the bridge is central Kolkata, at the core of which is BBD Bagh (formerly known as Dalhousie Square). South of BBD Bagh is the sprawling open space of the Maidan. On the east of the Maidan is the Chowringhee Road (now Jawaharlal Nehru Road), perhaps Kolkata's most famous street, filled with Raj-era buildings. South of Chowringhee Road is Park Street, the hub of much activity, with lots of restaurants and shopping. South of the Maidan lie the posh residential neighbourhoods of Kolkata. One of the oldest of south Kolkata's neighbourhoods is Kalighat, where you'll find Kolkata's famous Kalighat Temple.

The city has a quaint electric tram system that dates back to 1902; an early morning ride across the Maidan is recommended. Kolkata is also the first Indian city with a metro system, which runs from Dum Dum in the north to Garia in the south.

NORTH KOLKATA

North Kolkata is one of the oldest parts of the city, marked by narrow lanes and old mansions and buildings. This area of the city has several temples. In its far north, ten kilometres from the Howrah Bridge, near Nivedita Bridge, is Dakshineshwar Kali Temple (open 6.45am-noon, 3.30-8.30pm daily), which also has 12 adjoining shrines. On the opposite bank of the river is the Belur Math (open 6.30-11am, 3.30-7pm daily), headquarters of the Ramakrishna Mission, whose philosopher-founder preached the oneness of all religions.

Jorasanko Thakurbari

286 Rabindra Sarani (033-2269-5242). Open 10am-5pm Tue-Sun. Admission Rs 10 West Bengal residents; Rs 30 other Indians; Rs 50 other nationalities. Photography prohibited.

A little beyond the crossing of Chitpore Road and Muktaram Babu Street stands Jorasanko Thakurbari, home of the Tagores. This is where the city's greatest son, the poet and Nobel laureate Rabindranath Tagore, was born. The mansion was built by his grandfather, Prince Dwarakanath Tagore, in the late 18th century, and was used as a meeting place for the Bengali literati in the 19th century. It now houses the Rabindra Bharati University, named after

the poet, and a museum that contains priceless memorabilia and paintings by Rabindranath and his artist nephew Abanindranath Tagore. On the poet's birthday, thousands gather at this ancestral home to celebrate his contributions to Bengali art and culture.

Marble Palace

46 Muktaram Babu Street (033-2269-3310). Open 10am-4pm Tue-Wed, Fri-Sun; prior permission (24hrs in advance) required from West Bengal state government tourist office (see p85). Photography prohibited. Admission free.

This has got to be one of the weirdest museums around – a grand mansion that gets its name from the 100 varieties of marble used in its construction. Two kilometres east of the Howrah Bridge, the building was put up by Raja Rajendra Mullick, a wealthy local landlord, in 1835, and part of it is still a residence for some of his descendants. The museum is filled with artefacts, antique clocks, mirrors and other bric-a-brac from the family's collections. There are many paintings, some of which are allegedly by old masters such as Rembrandt, Rubens and Reynolds, though chances are that you will be unable to spot them. There is a small menagerie in the grounds – which, incidentally, are scattered with statues of lions, Hindu gods, the Virgin Mary, Jesus Christ, Lord Buddha and even Christopher Columbus; there's also a fountain that wouldn't look out of place in Rome.

"Bright orange and yellow marigolds, roses and other flowers are seen on people's heads, in baskets, on display, on the ground, on carts and in trucks."

CENTRAL KOLKATA

Just south of Howrah Bridge lies all of central Kolkata. The BBD Bagh area, named after three freedom fighters – Benoy, Badal and Dinesh – who were hanged in 1905 for taking up arms against the British in protest at the division of Bengal, is full of grand colonial buildings set around the water of Lal Dighi (locals call it a tank; really it is a small lake). Once called Dalhousie Square, this historical zone has some prominent buildings. Most remarkable is the huge Writer's Building on the north of the square, which now houses government offices. Opposite it, to its east, is St Andrew's Church, with its towering spire. South of the square is Raj Bhawan, the governor's residence, and St John's Church, one of the city's oldest. West of the square is the GPO building and beyond (further west), on the riverfront, is Millennium Park, a good place to wander around and observe life along the river.

About a kilometre south of BBD Bagh is Shahid Minar (Martyr's Column) and just a short distance south of that is the vast green, open space of the Maidan.

The beautiful Paresnath Jain temple (Badridas Temple Street, open 6am-noon, 3-7pm daily), four kilometres east of the bridge, is a quiet temple, with stained glass and elaborate mirror-work in its ornate interior; outside is a peaceful garden. The unusual Nakhoda Mosque in the busy market area of Rabindra Sarani is also worth a stop.

GPO

BBD Bagh. Open 10am-6pm Mon-Sat. Admission free.

The imposing dome of the General Post Office (GPO) is easily visible if you're in the BBD Bagh area. Inside the imposing building is a philatelic museum. The building is the site of the original Fort William; its guard room became infamous as the 'Black Hole of Calcutta' where, it was alleged, numerous British prisoners were imprisoned in the small room with no ventilation by the troops of Nawab Siraj-ud-Daulah in 1756 after they had overrun Fort William, causing the death of many of them.

Howrah Bridge/Rabindra Setu

Gateway to Kolkata, this cantilever bridge greets visitors – wealthy tourists and migrant workers alike – when they disembark at one of the city's two major railway stations. The bridge dominates the western skyline of the city. It is to new arrivals here what the Statue of Liberty was to immigrants to the US: a symbol of hope and new beginnings. It's no surprise that it is one of the busiest bridges in the world and that chaos is a way of life here. The bridge itself is a marvel of engineering. It was built in 1943, without using nuts and bolts – the various parts are riveted together.

Indian Museum

27 Jawaharlal Nehru Road (033-2286-1699/www.indianmuseumkolkata.org). Open Mar-Nov 10am-5pm Tue-Sun; Dec-Feb 10am-4.30pm Tue-Sun. Admission Rs 10 Indians; Rs 150 others.

One of the oldest museums in the world, the Indian Museum was founded by a Danish botanist in 1814. Though not very well maintained (lighting in some galleries is so poor that you would be lucky if you saw anything worthwhile), it is still worth visiting. Over 60 galleries cover archaeology, anthropology, geology, zoology and botany; there are also some fine works of art, as well as ancient coins and even an Egyptian mummy. Recently, a flyover has been built in front of the museum, spoiling the view of the façade.

The Maidan

Visit this vast green expanse on a wintry afternoon or a balmy summer evening for a slice of local life. Towards the east you can see the skyline of Chowringhee Road, while in the north is the Raj Bhawan, the governor's residence. You can also catch a glimpse of the famous Victoria Memorial (*see below*) at the southern end of the park. The Maidan is thought of as Kolkata's lungs, and there's a lot going on here: youngsters play football or cricket; walkers and joggers take their exercise; lovers cosy up together; hawkers sell street food; street performers entertain the public, while mounted police exercise their horses. There are some quirky things to see, such as a Patton tank captured from the Pakistani forces during the war in 1965; there's also a memorial to Indian soldiers who died during World War I. Besides its many public spaces and sports clubs, race course and football fields, the Maidan is also home to the famous Eden Gardens cricket ground and the second incarnation of Fort William, built by the British when the original fort was taken over in the 18th century.

Mullickghat Flower Market

Early morning at Howrah Bridge can be sweetened if you pay a visit to its 126-year-old flower market, which lies almost directly underneath the bridge. Thousands gather daily to buy and sell all kinds of flowers and plants. Bright orange and yellow marigolds, roses and other flowers are seen on people's heads, in baskets, on display, on the ground, on carts and in trucks. Around 2,000 sellers come here each day and the number doubles during major festivals. The market winds down by around 8am; try visiting between 5am and 6am.

Nakhoda Mosque

Chitpore Avenue, Rabindra Sarani. Open 6am-8pm daily.
Nakhoda is the city's largest mosque, built in 1926 in Indo-Saracenic style. It is modelled after Mughal emperor Akbar's mausoleum in Sikandra, near Agra, and its granite gateway is a copy of Fatehpur Sikri's Buland Darwaza. The dome and pair of minarets are 46m (151ft) high, and there are 25 tall pillars as well. The mosque is close to Mahatma Gandhi Road metro station.

St John's Church

Kiran Shankar Roy Road (033-2243-6098). Open 9am-5.30pm daily. Admission Rs 10.
This is one of the city's most beautiful churches, and also one of its oldest. Modelled on St Martin in the Fields in London, it is also known as the Stone Church, and was the first Anglican church in Kolkata, dating to 1787. There's a beautiful altar inside and many rare drawings of various archbishops of Canterbury, along with the centre of attraction – a painting of the Last Supper by German artist Johann Zoffani. The tombstones in the churchyard make interesting reading. Many come here to visit the octagonal mausoleum of Job Charnok, the 'founder' of Kolkata, in one corner.

Shahid Minar

Park Street, behind Dharmtala Bus Stand (near Esplanade metro station). Open 10am-6pm daily.
Shahid Minar (the Martyrs' Column) rises 48m (157ft) in the southern corner of the Maidan. It was originally known as the Ochterlony Monument after Sir David Ochterlony, who built it in 1848 to commemorate his victory in the Nepal War (1814-16). A blend of Turkish, Syrian and Egyptian architecture, it contains an internal staircase that goes up to its top. It used to be possible to walk up for a breathtaking view of the city, but after several suicide attempts it is now closed to the public. On the ground below, all manner of meetings, political and otherwise are held; street performers regale people who hang around.

SOUTH KOLKATA

The expanse of the Maidan stretches from central Kolkata into the city's southern area. Its classic colonial monument, the Victoria Memorial, is at the Maidan's southern end. St Paul's Cathedral is a short walk away and South Park Street Cemetery is four kilometres to the east. The Kalighat Temple lies four kilometres to the south; nearby is Nirmal Hriday, the first of Mother Teresa's homes for the dying.

Kalighat Temple

Kalighat Road. Open 7am-8pm daily; inner sanctum closes 6pm (only Hindus admitted to inner sanctum). Admission free.
Considered by many to be the most sacred temple in the city, thousands of devotees (some from far-flung corners of the country) throng the shrine to pay obeisance to the goddess Kali, Kolkata's patron deity. The idol of the goddess is striking, with a massive tongue made of gold sticking out. Though a temple has been here for over 400 years, the current temple was built in 1809.

St Paul's Cathedral

Cathedral Road. Open 9am-noon, 3-6pm daily.
Located east of the Victoria Memorial, this Gothic structure was rebuilt after being severely damaged by an earthquake in 1934. The present tower is modelled after the Bell Harry tower of Canterbury Cathedral. Inside the catherdral you will find ornate carved pews, splendid stained glass, intricate designs on the walls and many murals and paintings.

South Park Street Cemetery

Park Street, near Mullick Bazaar. Open sunrise-sunset daily.
This cemetery is poorly maintained, but there are some beautiful mausoleums, cenotaphs, obelisks and the like here, some dating as far back as 1767. Graves include those of firebrand poet Henry Louis Vivian Derozio; Lieutenant Colonel Robert Kyd, the botanist and founder of the East India Company's Botanical Gardens; Sir William Jones, the founder of the Royal Asiatic Society of Bengal; and even sons of Captain Cook and Charles Dickens. One of the most interesting tombs is that of Major General Charles Stuart, popularly known as 'Hindu Stuart' after he went native. When he died in 1828, he was buried with Hindu idols that he had collected. His tomb looks like a Hindu temple, surmounted by an elaborate edifice, with stone carvings of a Hindu goddess.

Victoria Memorial

Queen's Way (033-2223-5142). Open 10am-5pm Tue-Sun. Admission Rs 10 Indians; Rs 150 others.
One of Kolkata's iconic buildings, the memorial was built in honour of Queen Victoria following her death in 1901.

Clockwise from top: tram; Jorasanko Thakurbari; Indian Museum; St Paul's Cathedral.

The god-makers

Durga Puja is eastern India's biggest and most elaborate religious festival, and everyone's favourite. During the five days of festivities, idols of the goddess Durga are set up at *pandals* (temporary pavilions) around the city for the public to come and worship. On the final day of the festival, the idols must be immersed in a body of water. The idols used range from small foot-tall statues to towering effigies that can be up to 12 metres (40 feet) high.

Hundreds of artisans are involved in making these clay idols, and the best place to find them is in the Kumartuli neighbourhood of north Kolkata. Although Durga Puja is usually celebrated in September or October, depending on the Hindu lunar calendar, the artisans of Kumartuli begin their work seven months in advance. The most interesting time to visit is from around two months before Durga Puja, when the idols are taking their final shape, or in the process of being painted.

Kumartuli gets its name from its workers in clay, the potters and idol-makers – called *kumars*. The *kumars* are commissioned by *puja* (worship) committees and households to create the clay idols of the ten-armed goddess Durga, portrayed slaying the demon Mahishasura, and her four children – Saraswati, Laxmi, Ganesh and Kartik. Durga is a demon-fighting manifestation of Parvati, wife of Lord Shiva.

It is said that the Pals, as this particular community of clay artisans are known, were in this area even before the birth of the city, and that they moved into Kumartuli when the East India Company took over their land to build Fort William.

The area of Kumartuli, with its narrow, crowded, dirty lanes, is dotted with studios; artisans' entire families pitch in to make the clay models. The artisans start off by making a skeleton of the figure with small wooden sticks and bamboo, which form the basic structure on a wooden pedestal. The deity's torso is roughly shaped with straw and tied with jute rope. The final shape of the image depends on how well the straw dummy was conceived. A thick coat of blackish clay mixed with rice husk is applied over the dummy and left to dry in the sun. It is followed by a compound of sand, clay and jute fibre smeared over the first coating, and then smoothed with a wet cloth. Between each layer of this modelling procedure, the figure is dried completely. The head and fingers, made separately from master moulds, are fixed on with clay paste. After this has dried, a base colour is painted. Specialists paint the elaborate brows and lips; the dresses the statues wear are made of satin (silk for more expensive idols) and brocade, while gold foil and silver filigree is used to create ornaments. The final touches are added on the eve of the festival when the most senior artisan paints the eyes, in a part of the process called Chokkhu Daan – which literally means the 'gifting the eyes'.

To satisfy the demand from expat Bengali populations around the world, artisans innovate by making lighter idols that are easily exported abroad from Kumartuli to London, New York, Toronto, Sydney, Sao Paolo and so on. For Bengalis this festival is huge; it's the highlight of the year – a time for renewing bonds with friends and relatives and for remembering the gods.

Kolkata is at its most vibrant during Durga Puja and visitors can join locals hopping from one *pandal* to the next, and observe all the accompanying merriment while seeking the goddess's blessings. When the festival comes to an end after five days, and the idols are immersed in the Hooghly river, it's both a festive and sombre occasion as the artisans and worshippers watch these creations disappear into the waters – until the next year comes around.

A massive edifice of white marble, a blend of European and Mughal architecture, it houses a large museum of paintings, life-sized statues and other Raj-era relics. The Angel of Victory, bugle in her hand, stands on top of the huge central dome; at one time, the black bronze figure rotated on its pedestal according to the time of day, but it stopped moving long ago. The monument also has extensive grounds.

Eat

Bengalis are passionate about food; if you are lucky enough to be invited to a home for a meal, don't miss the chance. Bengalis love mustard in its many forms – if you can handle that, you will enjoy your meal.

Kolkata has plenty of restaurants and cafés where you can find a reasonably priced, satisfactory meal. Locals may be besotted with Indian-Chinese food, and there's lots of Western fare available too, but you'll find great Bengali cuisine at restaurants such as Oh! Calcutta or Sonargaon (for both, *see p81*). For more economical Bengali food, try Aaheli (Peerless Inn, 12 Jawaharlal Nehru Road, 033-2228-0301, open 12.20-3pm, 7.30-10.30pm daily), Kewpie's (2 Elgin Lane, 033-2474-8962, open 12.30-2.30pm, 7.30-10.30pm daily) or Bhojohari Manna (9/18 Ekdalia Road, 033-2440-1933, open 7.30am-10pm daily). The city is also famous for its street food (it's wise to be cautious, though, as its cleanliness is questionable).

Given that Kolkata lies right on the delta of the Ganga, freshwater fish is naturally a Bengali staple. *Ilish* or *hilsa* is the favourite and *bekti* and *rui* come close runners-up. Bengal is also famous for its sweets (*mishtis*). Most of these are made from curdled milk (*channa*) and *sandeshes* are the most popular. If there's one speciality you cannot leave without tasting, though, it's *mishti doi*, caramelised-sugar-sweetened yoghurt, served in an earthenware pot.

Blue Potato

Central Kolkata *27 Shakespeare Sarani (033-3259-7833/www.thebluepotato.co.in). Open 12.30-3pm, 7-11pm daily. $$$$. French-Italian.*

Blue Potato is a sensational fine-dining restaurant in the heart of the city. The menu changes often, and dishes use the best fresh and seasonal ingredients. If you can't decide between butter-poached chunks of east coast lobster and pan-fried breast of duck, ask chef Shaun Kenworthy to make a recommendation.

Dum Pukht

South Kolkata *The Sonar, JBS Haldane Avenue, opposite Science City (033-2345-4545/www.itcwelcom group.in). Open 7.30-11.45pm daily. $$$$. Awadhi.*

Dum Pukht is one of the Sonar's flagship restaurants and the best place to eat Awadhi and Lucknavi cuisine outside Lucknow. Signature dishes include the Dum Pukht *kakori* kebab, *jhinga dum nisha* and Dum Pukht biryani.

Flurys

Central Kolkata *18 Park Street (033-4000-7453/www.flurysindia.com). Open 7am-10pm daily. $$. Western.*

Founded in 1927, this Kolkata landmark, with wood panelling and chandeliers, is famous for its all-day breakfasts. It's the ideal place to hang out and enjoy super-sized sandwiches washed down with coffee or Darjeeling tea. Lunches are also available, and there's an extensive choice of cakes and pastries.

"Kebabs are garnished with onions and various sauces, and wrapped up in egg-coated parathas to make one of the most popular fast-food eats in the city."

Hot Kati Roll

Central Kolkata *1B Park Street (033-2217-7308). Open 10.30am-11pm daily. $. No credit cards. Kolkata rolls.*

Kolkata's rolls are famous around the country. They come in various forms and go by many names, but residents of Kolkata insist that they are a Kolkata creation. Kebabs, both chicken and mutton, are garnished with onions and various sauces, and wrapped up in egg-coated parathas to make one of the most popular fast-food eats in the city. This little joint has been serving up rolls for around 25 years, and is one of the most reliable.

Indian Coffee House

Central Kolkata *Bankim Chatterjee Street (033-2241-4869). Open 9am-9pm Mon-Sat; 9am-12.30pm, 5-9pm Sun. No credit cards. $. Café.*

This 50-year-old coffee house, run by the Indian Coffee Workers Co-operative Society, was once abuzz with literary figures and intellectual conversations. Today, it's still animated, though the *adda* (conversational) culture it was famous for has declined with the times. For coffee, conversation and cheap eats, though, this is still the place to head. It's also known as the College Street Coffee House, and is quite popular with students due to its proximity to educational establishments and low prices. There are several other branches around the city.

Mocambo

Central Kolkata *25B Park Street (033-2229-0095). Open 11am-midnight daily. $. No AmEx. Multi-cuisine.*

Clockwise from top left: On Track; Hot Kati Roll; Dum Pukht; New Market; Flurys.

With its quiet ambience, dim lights and comfortable leather upholstery, Mocambo has a 1950s feel. It is, after all, one of the city's oldest surviving restaurants, along with Flurys. Service is prompt, there are a number of Western dishes to choose from, and the food is superb. Pepper devilled crab – crabmeat in a cheese, mustard and pepper sauce served in the crab shell – is recommended, as is fish à la Diana, which is local *bekti* fish stuffed with prawns and cooked in a cream sauce, and chicken tetrazzini (strips of chicken cooked with pasta, green peppers and mushrooms in sherry sauce).

Oh! Calcutta

South Kolkata *10/3, Elgin Road, Fourth Floor, Forum Mall (033-2283-7161). Open 12.30-3pm, 7.30-11pm daily. $$$. No AmEx. Bengali.*

This stylish restaurant has the decor of an upper-crust club and specialises in food from some of the communities that have had a lasting influence over Kolkata's taste buds. Traditional Bengali dishes such as *malai chingri* and *bhapa ilish* (mustard-flavoured steamed hilsa fish) are the staples here, but you'll also find colonial dishes such as railway mutton curry and food from further away such as Lucknavi biryani and mutton *rezala*.

On Track

Central Kolkata *25B Park Street (033-2227-3955). Open noon-3.30pm, 7-11pm daily. $$. No AmEx. Indian/Chinese.*

This restaurant has a replica of an old steam engine inside the premises – and if you're lucky you can find a table inside the locomotive, the Indo-China Express. Prices are reasonable and children will have a great time exploring the driver's cabin, which is equipped with video games. Indian starters include a tasty fish masala kebab; the Chinese dishes pass muster as well.

Peter Cat

Central Kolkata *7 J & M Park Street (033-2229-8841). Open 11am-midnight daily. $$. No AmEx. Kebabs/Western.*

Peter Cat is popular with locals and tourists for its good food and reasonable prices, even if service is slow. The excellent *chello* kebab, made with an unusual blend of spices and Persian herbs and served on a bed of buttered rice topped with an egg, is perhaps the most popular dish. Other favourites include Chicken Marakesh, chicken and mutton kebabs served with rice, and Shah Nawaz, a spring chicken stuffed with mutton *kheema* (spiced ground meat) and chicken liver.

Sonargaon

South Kolkata *Taj Bengal, 34B Belvedere Road, Alipore (033-6612-3321/www.tajhotels.com). Open 12.30pm-2.45pm, 7.30-11.45pm daily. $$$$. Bengali/ North-west Frontier.*

One of the finest restaurants in the city, Sonargaon's faux-rustic decor is eye-catching: there's a traditional village well, stone steps lead up to another level, hibiscus flowers hang from some of the walls and the ceilings have wooden beams with hanging ceramic pots. Signature dishes include *lasooni jhinga*, fresh prawns marinated in garlic and charcoal-grilled; kebab Sonargaon, star anise-flavoured chicken legs baked in a charcoal-fired clay oven; the Bengali favourite *chingri malai* curry, fresh river prawns cooked in coconut cream; Pabnar *murgi*, home-style chicken curry from Pabna (now in Bangladesh), flavoured with *radooni*, a local herb; and *mochar ghonto*, a dry Bengali fish dish with banana flowers, coconuts and potatoes.

Waldorf

Central Kolkata *13D Russell Street (033-4001-1424). Open 11am-midnight daily. $$. No AmEx. Chinese/Thai.*

One of the oldest Chinese restaurants in the city, Waldorf is over 50. The interior is pretty typical, with Chinese lanterns and fans on the walls. Established by a Chinese couple and later taken over by a Swiss, the restaurant claims to serve Szechuan cuisine (the Indianised version, of course), characterised by pungent flavours and extensive use of chillies. Try the twice-cooked lamb in sweet bean sauce, the seafood sizzler, or, if you're in luck, the Waldorf special stuffed duck.

Zaranj & Jong's

Central Kolkata *26 Jawaharlal Nehru Road (033-2249-5572). Open noon-3pm, 7.30-11pm Mon, Wed-Sun. $$. North-west Frontier/pan-Asian.*

Though this opulent restaurant opened in 1991, it looks as if it dates back to the Raj era, with solid, dark leather chairs and waiters dressed as footmen. The food prepared behind the glass-fronted kitchen is superb; there's a mix of North-west Frontier cuisine (Zaranj) and oriental (Jong's) to choose from. The former is probably best; try the special Zaranj *raan*, or the *murg nawabi*, *dahi ke* kebab, *machli begum bahar* or *bhuna gosht* – they're all good.

Shop

At one time, Kolkata's shops of note were nearly all in the heart of the city, in and around the Park Street area and Esplanade, and near Gariahat in the southern part of the city. These continue to be thriving shopping areas, but there are now glittering malls in Garia in the extreme south of Kolkata and along the Eastern Metropolitan Bypass on the way to the airport in the north.

Artisana

Central Kolkata *First floor, 13 Chowringhee Terrace (033-2223-9422). Open 11am-7pm Mon-Sat. No AmEx.*

Artisana is a centre for crafts and textiles established by the Crafts Council of West Bengal, a voluntary non-profit organisation working to promote the work and livelihood of craftspeople and weavers. You'll find metal castings made using the 'lost wax' process, *sholapith* crafts – carved pieces made from an ivory-coloured softwood, traditional paintings of Bengal, pottery, tribal jewellery, jute items, home linens, silver filigree saris, scarves and traditional *kantha* embroidery of West Bengal.

Bengal Home Industries Association (check correct name)

Central Kolkata *11 Camac Street (033-2282-1562). Open 10am-6.30pm Mon-Fri; 10am-2pm Sat. No credit cards.*

A good place for local (Bengali) handicrafts as well as silks, cottons, home linens, shawls, metalwork, and assorted pieces made from bamboo, cane and paper.

Central Cottage Industries Emporium

Central Kolkata *Jawaharlal Nehru Road (033-2228-4139). Open 10am-7pm Mon-Fri; 10am-2pm Sat. No credit cards.*

Like its namesake stores around the country, this outlet stocks a range of Indian handicraft items as well as fabrics and carpets.

Curio Emporium

Central Kolkata *16/2 Jawaharlal Nehru Road (033-2249-2299). Open 11am-8pm Mon-Sat. No AmEx.*

A striking collection of copper and bronze objects, plus carpets, silver and gold jewellery, wood carvings, paintings and other Indian crafts.

"Run by tea writer and researcher Dolly Roy, this is a fantastic place to sip fine Darjeeling and Assam tea, and buy it too."

Dakshinapan Shopping Complex

South Kolkata *2 Gariahat Road (South). Open 2-7.30pm Mon; 11am-7.30pm Tue-Sat.*

At this open-air shopping complex set around a large courtyard you can pick up handloom fabric and handicrafts from all over India. Each store is run by its respective state government and so prices are reasonable. There are also numerous privately owned shops here, selling footwear, ethnic clothing and fabric.

Dolly's Tea Shop

South Kolkata *G-62 Dakshinapan Shopping Complex, 2 Gariahat Road (South) (033-2423-7838). Open 10am-8pm Mon-Sat. No AmEx.*

Run by tea writer and researcher Dolly Roy, this is a fantastic place to sip fine Darjeeling and Assam tea and buy it too. Dolly is often around and can answer tea-related questions.

New Market

Central Kolkata *Lindsay Street. Open 10am-7.30pm Mon-Sat.*

Opened in 1874, this market was originally called Hogg Market, and was the place where you could find all kinds of Western-style and imported goods. Now you can buy household items, clothes, curios, luggage, books, processed food and confectionery, meat, fruit and vegetables. It's fun to wander through.

Sasha

Central Kolkata *27 Mirza Ghalib Street (033-2252-1586/www.sashaworld.com). Open 10am-7pm Mon-Sat; 10am-1pm Sun. No AmEx.*

The non-profit organisation that runs this shop supports craftspeople from all over the country. Pick up crafts and handloom fabric products made by disadvantaged artisans; you'll find lots of great gifts and items for decorating your home, and you'll know you're supporting fair trade practices.

Arts

Contemporary art is best seen in private galleries such as Birla Academy of Art and Culture (108 Southern Avenue, 033-2466-6802, www.birlaart.com, open noon-8pm Tue-Sat, 3-8pm Sun) Chitrakoot Art Gallery (5 Ballygunge Gariahat Road, 033-2475-2275, www.chitrakoot.com, open 3-8pm daily), Chemould Art Gallery (12F Park Street, opposite the Park Hotel, 033- 2229-8641, open 2-7pm daily) and CIMA Art Gallery (Sunny Towers, 43 Ashutosh Chowdhury Avenue, 033-2485-8717, www.cimaartindia.com, open 3-7pm Mon, 2-7pm Tue-Sat). The government-run Academy of Fine Arts (Cathedral Road, 033-2223-4302, open 3-8pm daily) is one of the oldest societies of its kind in India and houses works by Rabindranath Tagore.

Kolkata has a culture of hosting the best talent in the country for Hindustani classical music performances. The annual Dover Lane Music Conference, usually held in January or February, is a week-long affair that features some of the finest Hindustani classical music performers.

The coming of spring and the anniversary of the birth of legendary poet Rabindranath Tagore bring a host of cultural programmes to the city, especially at Rabindra Bharati University and Jorasanko Thakurbari (*see p75*).

Ever since the filmmakers Satyajit Ray and Ritwik Ghatak made their mark in the 1950s, Bengali cinema has been at the vanguard of art-house films in India, and Bengalis are justifiably proud of the Nandan Complex. Nearby is Birla Academy of Art and Culture (*see above*), which hosts both exhibitions and varied cultural events.

Nandan Complex

South Kolkata *1/1 AJC Bose Road, SE end of Maidan, near Park Street (033-2223-1210).*

This cinema complex shows art-house films and runs other cultural programmes. It hosts the annual Kolkata Film Festival in November, which screens contemporary

Clockwise from top: Oberoi Grand (2); Taj Bengal; The Sonar, Kolkata (3); The Park.

international and Indian cinema, as well as retrospectives of past masters. Within the complex, the Sisir Mancha (033-2223-5317) is an excellent spot for musical performances.

Nightlife

Kolkata's well-heeled like to party hard. There are a handful of good nightspots and these are buzzing almost every day of the week. Every large hotel has a bar or nightclub that's open late. The Park's venues are the hottest of these and have been for years. Call ahead to find out rules about singles and cover charges for men, as many clubs have couples-only policies. For a relaxed atmospheric garden in which to chill with a beer, look no further than Fairlawn Hotel (*see below*).

The Park

Central Kolkata *17 Park Street (033-2249-9000/ www.theparkhotels.com). Someplace Else Open 6pm-midnight Mon, Tue, Thur, Sun; 6pm-4am Wed, Fri, Sat. Tantra Open 6pm-midnight Tue, Thur, Sun; 6pm-4am Wed, Fri, Sat. Roxy Open 6pm-midnight Mon, Tue, Thur, Sun; 6pm-4am Wed, Fri, Sat. Aqua Open noon-midnight Mon, Tue, Thur, Sun; 6pm-4am Wed, Fri, Sat.*

Four nightlife destinations under one roof make the Park very busy indeed, even though it's expensive to party here. Someplace Else is a smallish pub that hosts live bands; Tantra is the rocking nightclub; Roxy is the chic cocktail bar and lounge that's designed to resemble an old factory; and Aqua is the alfresco bar beside the pool.

Shisha, the Hookah Bar

Central Kolkata *Block D, Fifth Floor, 22 Camac Street (033-2281-1313). Open 6pm-midnight daily. No credit cards.*

As the name suggests, this is a place for hookah smoking, but there's also music and dancing with the city's trendy crowd, as DJs spin Bollywood, house and some hip hop sounds.

Venom

Central Kolkata *6 Camac Street, near Shantiniktean Building (033-3252-2900). Open 7pm-midnight Mon, Wed-Sun. No AmEx.*

Venom's best features are a glass wall that overlooks the Victoria Memorial and a superb sound system. The cocktails are satisfactory, the dancefloor larger than you'll find in most Kolkata nightclubs and the music is Bollywood, remix and trance – making it a hit with the partying kind.

Underground

South Kolkata *235/1 AJC Bose `Road, opposite Nizam Palace (033-2280-2323/www.hhihotels.com). Open 7pm-2am daily.*

This club is themed to imitate the London Underground. Wooden stairs lead underground to the basement, where you'll find areas marked 'Leicester Square', 'Trafalgar Square' and 'Oxford Street', as well as a large dancefloor. The club is rather popular and busy almost every night.

Stay

Hotel Aston

South Kolkata *3 Aston Road, opposite Lakshmi Narayan Mandir (033-2486-3145). $. No AmEx.*

This is a good budget spot to rest your head if you're planning to hotfoot it around Kolkata: proximity to the centre and the markets in the south of the city make this a convenient location. Rooms are comfortable and clean and have wooden floors and TVs; bathrooms are better than basic.

Chrome

Central Kolkata *226 AJC Bose Road (033-3096-3096/www.chromehotel.in). $$-$$$.*

From its unique façade and lobby to the rooftop lounge, this ultra-modern hotel is sleek, chic and good value. Upper floors have hip rooms with wooden floors and modern bathrooms with TVs and great amenities; suites are particularly striking. Khana Sutra, the nouvelle Indian cuisine restaurant, serves exceptional food and even has two gazebos in case you want to dine alone. There's a thematic touch to the interiors with coloured circles of varying sizes throughout (even the windows are circular); it's rather soothing.

"Many theatre-world celebrities make this their home when in Kolkata, attracted by its quaint charm and history."

Fairlawn

Central Kolkata *13A Sudder Street (033-2252-1510/ www.fairlawnhotel.com). $$. No AmEx.*

Centrally located on the corner of Sudder Street and Madge Lane in the Park Street area, the Fairlawn building dates back to 1783. Originally run by a feisty Armenian, Rosie Sarkies, it passed to her daughter, Violet Smith, whose own daughter, Jennifer Flower, is now managing director. Staying here can feel like being in someone's home. There is a lovely garden attached to the building; the lunch spread is simple but good, and regular local patrons swear by this place. In keeping with the colonial feel, don't be surprised to find spotted dick on the menu. Many theatre-world celebrities make this their home when in Kolkata, attracted by its quaint charm and history. It was undergoing renovation at the time of writing, which is scheduled to be completed by the end of 2010.

Floatel

Central Kolkata *9/10 Kolkata Jetty, Strand Road (033-2213-7777/www.floatelhotel.com). $$$.*

If you're looking for something different, try this floating hotel that provides a good mid-range option very close to the centre of town: the vessel is moored at the Kolkata jetty on the bank of the Hooghly. Maritime instruments serve as decoration; staff wear seamen's uniforms; the Compass Room is actually a banqueting hall; the Bridge is the coffee shop, and so on. The hotel's eco-friendly claim is slightly questionable, but the USP of this venture is the spectacular sunrise and sunset views over the Hooghly; if you book a suite, you can enjoy both.

Oberoi Grand

Central Kolkata *15 Jawaharlal Nehru Road (033-2249-2323/www.oberoikolkata.com). $$$$.*
Superbly located in the heart of Kolkata, this was originally home to a certain Colonel Grand, who modelled the building after a Sussex country seat he had admired in his younger days; the hotel is probably the last remnant of the era when Kolkata was second city of the British Empire. Rooms are opulent and there is great deal of attention to detail. Everything from the pillared entrance to the old-style bathtubs and taps transport you to a bygone era. The pool and central courtyard area, with tall palms, is a peaceful spot where you can escape the crowded city after a long day. Service is perhaps the best you can get in all of Kolkata.

The Park

Central Kolkata *17 Park Street (033-2249-9000/ www.theparkhotels.com). $$$$.*
The Park's design is strikingly contemporary throughout. Room decor is urban chic with local touches, such as the indigenous terracotta and *kantha*-stitch work displayed on the walls. All have LCD TVs, and the bathrooms are space-age new. Best of all is the location, at one end of Park Street, with some of the best restaurants, cinemas and the New Market shopping district all within walking distance. As Kolkata's hottest nightspot, the hotel throbs with energy emanating from its various clubs and bars (*see pxxx*). Those who want peace and quiet should ensure they get a room far from this nightlife.

The Sonar, Kolkata

South Kolkata *JBS Haldane Avenue, opposite Science City (033-2345-4545/www.itcwelcomgroup.in). $$$$.*
The Sonar may look banal on the outside, but it's pretty eye-popping inside: big is beautiful is the theme here. Rooms vary a lot so make sure you get an ITC One room, with indulgent leather massage chairs. The restaurants, and there are many, are some of the city's finest; and the spa, Kaya Kalp, is lovely. The most striking feature is the way the artificially created bodies of water, filled with water-lilies and other exotic plant life, mesh with the surrounding concrete. The only drawback, if you want to call it that, is the distance from the city centre, though some may find it handy to have the airport nearby.

Taj Bengal

South Kolkata *34B Belvedere Road, Alipore (033-2223-3939/www.tajhotels.com). $$$$.*
The first thing you notice on entering the Taj Bengal is the interesting atrium, lovely antiques and art. There's live music in the lobby, which you can hear piped into your room as well. Rooms are great, and many have pleasant views of the city's sites; to make things even better, guests experience some of the best service in town. More than seven restaurants offer top-quality cuisine. The French windows of the fabulous Chinese restaurant Chinoiserie overlook the pool, while the superb Bengali restaurant Sonargaon (*see pxxx*) is set up like an ethnic village. The hotel's central location only adds to its overall appeal.

Factfile

When to go

Summers are oppressive in Kolkata and while the monsoon is a little better, the humidity is high. The best time to visit is during winter (early Dec-Feb).

Getting there

Kolkata, which is the eastern hub of the country, has two major railway stations, Howrah and Sealdah. Of these, Howrah is busier. There is also a 'new' Howrah station that caters to arrivals from South India. Sealdah station handles some north-bound traffic, and local trains arrive and depart from here.

Netaji Subhash Chandra Bose International Airport, popularly known as Dum Dum Airport, connects the city to all major destinations in the country and many international locations. For more on travel, *see p378* **Navigating India**.

Getting around

Taxis are cheap and unlike other Indian cities, drivers will almost always go by the meter (ask the cabbie for the rate chart when it's time to pay). Trams are available in some parts of the city. Kolkata is also home to the first underground metro service in the country and it is a fast, cheap and efficient way to travel from the southern part of the city to the tourist and shopping areas in central and north Kolkata.

Tourist information

The India Tourism office Shakespeare Sarani (033-2282-5813). Open 9am-6pm Mon-Fri; 9am-1pm Sat.
West Bengal Tourism Centre BBD Bagh (033-2248-271/www.wbtourism.com). Open 10.30am-4pm Mon-Fri; 10.30am-1pm Sat.

Urban Gems

Udaipur

City of romantic lakes and palaces.

Venice of the East; city of lakes and palaces; India's most romantic city: Udaipur has never been short on compliments. Built around the shimmering Lake Pichola, home to haunting marble palaces and surrounded by the undulating Aravalli Hills, it's hard to remember that it's actually in the middle of a desert.

The royal family of Sisodia Rajputs that ruled over the historical area of Mewar – of which Udaipur is part – lays claim to an unbroken line of descent that can be traced back to AD 734. The towering City Palace, where family members still reside, is a spectacularly beautiful sight during the day – soft yellow and pretty, yet monumental, rising slowly from a windowless base to a baroque profusion of *chhatris* and balconies. At night, lit in a warm glow, it is magnificent: a golden masterpiece set against the night sky, with an ethereal reflection in the waters of Lake Pichola.

Within the narrow, winding streets of the Old City, rooftop cafés promise Western-style meals and exotic cocktails, stores sell handicrafts made in Kashmir and knock-offs of miniature paintings. And the Bond film *Octopussy* continues to be screened every night in at least one of the city's countless terrace restaurants, 27 years after it was shot here.

When the magic of this city has been explored, getting to the temples of Eklingji, Nagda and Nathdwara requires just a short drive north. And there are other wonderful sites in the region: Ranakpur, Kumbhalgarh and – further away – Chittor and Dungarpur. The drives through the Rajasthani countryside to find them are a treat in themselves; you'll pass trains of camels, fields of swaying mustard flowers, and tractors piled high with bales of hay.

Top: Lake Palace Hotel.
Middle: Old City (2).
Bottom: City Palace.

Explore

Udaipur's Old City, which is the area around the City Palace, has streets that are narrow and winding and not very conducive to travel by car. Many sights can be covered on foot, or by hired auto-rickshaw. To properly appreciate Udaipur city, plan on spending at least three days here. After that, the temples of Eklingji (22 kilometres/14 miles north), Nagda (two kilometres from Eklingji) and Nathdwara (48 kilometres/30 miles north-east), can be covered in a day, and Kumbhalgarh and Ranakpur in another.

LAKE PICHOLA & THE OLD CITY

So long as Udaipur gets its annual share of rainfall, Lake Pichola stands out as the shining centrepiece of this lovely Rajasthani city. While out on a hunt in 1559, Maharana Udai Singh II came upon the lake, known then (as now) as Pichola Talao. Years later he decided to move here, had the City Palace built and the lake widened. Today, the shores alongside the City Palace, which are lined with ghats (steps), temples, *havelis* (mansions) and palaces, form part of the Old City. In the last five years, Lake Pichola has dried up entirely on several occasions. The lake bed then becomes the local cricket field, and four-wheel drives can be seen steering across it, trying to avoid dry-docked boats.

Lake Pichola has two island palaces: Jag Niwas and Jag Mandir. Jag Niwas, the summer residence of the kings of Udaipur, was converted into the Lake Palace Hotel in the 1970s, and is closed to the public. The only way you can peep inside its legendary marble and mosaic walls is if you stay there. Jag Mandir, once a pleasure palace, is the older of the two, now called Jagmandir Island Palace (0294-242-4186, open 9.30am-5pm daily, admission Rs 25), and visitors are welcome. Once past the eight marble elephants raising their trunks in salute, you reach a large landscaped courtyard surrounded by a marble two-storey palace. It was on this island, at the Gol Mahal – a domed structure at the north-eastern end of the palace complex – that Prince Khurram (later to become Shah Jahan) once took refuge from his father, Emperor Jehangir. According to legend, this palace was his design inspiration for the Taj Mahal. Dinner at the colonnaded restaurant on the island, with the sound of rippling lake waters and a view of the lights of the city, can be quite romantic.

The Old City lies on the east side of the lake. Along the lake shore, north of the City Palace, are a series of ghats (steps leading to the water). Here you will find the area of Lal ghat, and just beyond it Gangaur ghat. North-east of Gangaur ghat is Chetak Circle, home to a lively bazaar. Behind (east of) the City Palace is City Palace Road, where you'll find numerous shops as well as the Sajjan Niwas Garden.

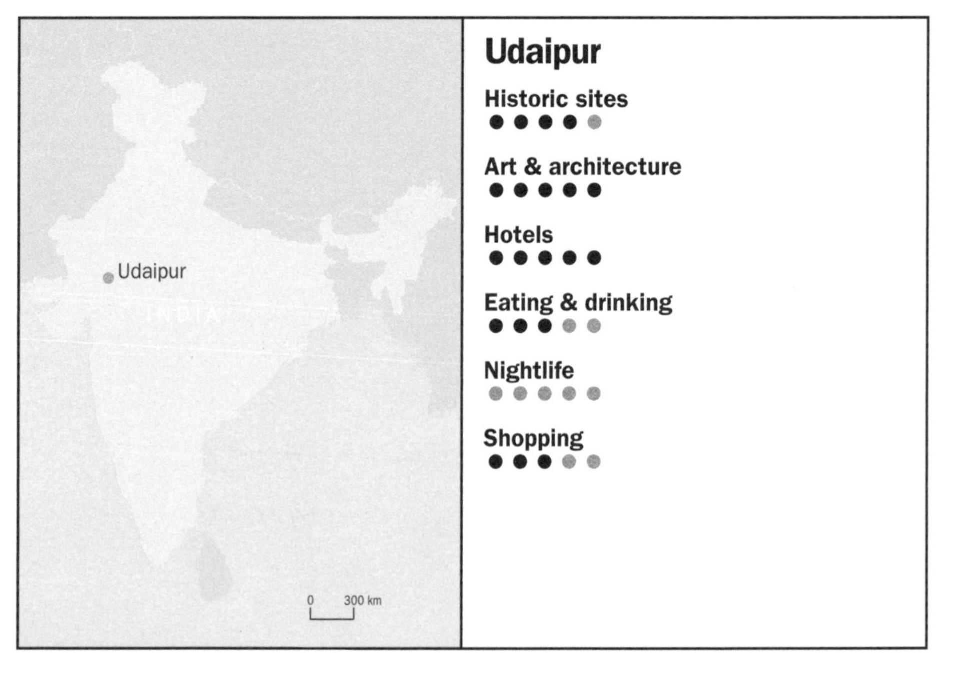

Not far from the entrance to the City Palace is the Jagdish Temple (open 5am-2pm, 4-10pm daily), where a black stone image of Jaganath (an avatar of Vishnu) is enshrined.

Across the lake from the City Palace, which can be crossed on foot via a bridge, is the area of Hanuman ghat, which is quieter, but where, slowly, every *haveli* is being transformed into a guesthouse. The rest of Udaipur city radiates quietly in every direction from the lake's shores.

Bagore ki Haveli

Gangaur ghat (0294-242-2567). Open 10am-5.30pm daily. Admission Rs 35 Indians; Rs 60 others.

This 18th-century *haveli* on Gangaur ghat is a museum of traditional Rajasthani arts and crafts. At 7pm every evening (Oct-Feb only) traditional Rajasthani dance performances are held.

City Palace Complex

0294-241-9023/www.eternalmewar.in. Open 9.30am-5.30pm daily. Admission Rs 50; Rs 30 5-12s; Rs 200 camera; Rs 150 guide; Rs 500 Crystal Gallery; Rs 850 combination ticket for museum, Crystal Gallery, boat ride & beverage.

Mewar sound-and-light-show (0294-252-8016). Shows 7-8pm daily (in English Oct-Mar, in Hindi Apr-Sept). Tickets Rs 300; Rs 100 8-12s.

On the eastern shore of Lake Pichola, the imposing City Palace is every bit as beautiful inside as it is impressive outside. Built in yellow stone, it is the largest palace complex in Rajasthan. Maharana Udai Singh II began this palace in 1570. Around it, the court nobility and subjects established their own dwellings, merchants set up markets, and a huge city wall with imposing gateways was erected; the maharana named the burgeoning city after himself. The original edifice of the City Palace has been added to by over 20 successive maharanas over 400 years, but still looks remarkably uniform in both design and age. Today, the palace is part museum, part royal residence and part two luxury hotels.

The City Palace has a windowless base with ornate turrets and canopies. Inside, there are 11 separate palaces. Enter the **City Palace Museum** through the Ganesh Deori (door of Lord Ganesh), which opens on to the Raja Angan Chowk (courtyard). Down a flight of steps, and part of the **Mardana Mahal** is devoted to the museum's armoury section, which has a collection of old weapons. Look out too for a collection of palanquins with intriguing motifs. In this part of the museum is the **Mor Chowk**, with beautiful mosaics of enamelled peacocks, carved during the reign of Sajjan Singh. Each of the peacocks, with a stunning intricacy of design, is made with 5,000 pieces of green, blue and gold glass and convex mirrors. **Krishna Vilas**, a small room next to this, has a remarkable collection of miniature paintings depicting royal processions, festivals and royal games.

In quick succession come the **Manek Mahal** or Ruby Palace with its glass- and mirror-work; the **Bari Mahal** (Big Palace), which has a central garden and some great views of the city; the **Moti Mahal**, with ornamental mirror-work; and the **Chini Mahal**, with Chinese and Dutch ornamental tiles. The **Surya Chopar** has a huge, ornamental sun that symbolises the origins of the Mewar dynasty, whose members claim descent from the Sun God. In many ways, this image has become iconic and represents Mewar, the City Palace and Udaipur itself. Move on then to the **Zenana Mahal**, the area for the women of the palace, to examine its delicately painted windows, alcoves and floors.

At the sound-and-light show held each evening, the story of Udaipur and the Mewar dynasty unfolds with all the gravitas of a Greek play, taking in the span of centuries from Bappa Rawal through Maharana Pratap, and from the arrival of the British to the present. Many of the stories belong to other locations, but it's all part of the long glorious tradition of the Mewars, and quite enjoyable in the splendid setting.

Part of the palace, against the lake shore, is converted into two luxury hotels – the **Shiv Niwas Palace** and the **Fateh Prakash Palace** (*see p100*). You can see some parts of them for a fee (Rs 850). Fateh Prakash's *darbar* hall is most impressive – huge crystal chandeliers grace the ceilings, there's grim weaponry on the walls and distinguished portraits of former rulers stare down at you.

The palace's **Crystal Gallery**, in the main wing of the Fateh Prakash Hotel, holds a breathtaking and rare collection of Osler's crystal, ordered from England by Maharana Sajjan Singh in 1877. Exhibits include crystal dressing tables, lamps, chairs, crockery, table fountains and even beds. There is also a beautiful antique jewel-studded carpet, which you obviously can't walk on.

You can easily spend a day exploring the City Palace if you intend to take in every bit of its history; otherwise half a day is enough. Out of bounds is Shambhu Niwas, residence of the current Maharana Arvind Singh and his family. The City Palace Complex also organises regular hour-long boat rides around the Jag Niwas, which allows a glimpse into life around the lake, and halts at Jag Mandir.

Karni Mata Mandir

Machchla Hill; cable car from Lake Pichola shore.

At the top of Machchla Hill on the south side of Udaipur city is the little-known (at least to tourists) Karni Mata Temple, also called Rat Temple, because it is home to numerous red-eyed white mice. The mice are believed to house the souls of Karni Mata's departed devotees. Karni Mata is considered an incarnation of the goddess Durga, and is the patron deity of Udaipur. The hill is a scenic spot for sunrise or sunset views over Lake Pichola, the City Palace and Udaipur city, and the surrounding hills.

A Swiss-style cable car with six-seater gondolas (0294-241-6316, open 8am-9pm, Rs 60 round-trip) runs to the top from the shore of Lake Pichola in under five minutes. Alternatively, take a vehicle to the parking lot ten minutes from the temple.

Vintage & Classic Car Collection

Garden Hotel, opposite Sajjan Niwas Garden (0294-241-8881). Open 9am-9pm daily. Admission Rs 100.

Though run by the City Palace administration, this museum is located a little distance away, at the Garden Hotel. A semi-circular garage displays a large collection of vintage cars owned by the royal family, including some priceless classics. Of particular interest is the Rolls-Royce collection, including the Rolls-Royce Phantom II (1934) used in the Bond film *Octopussy*, and a Rolls-Royce Jeep converted into a hunting

Clockwise from top: Saheliyon ki Baari; Kumbhalgarh Fort; Fateh Sagar; Ranakpur.

vehicle with all kinds of slots and compartments for hunting paraphernalia. The cars bear the crest of the Maharana of Mewar and some have screens to protect the maharanis from prying eyes. All the cars are kept in working order and are driven around the palace once a week. Alongside the vintage cars is an interesting set of solar-powered vehicles. The current Maharana Arvind Singh Mewar, through his charitable foundation, is trying to foster development of solar bicycles, rickshaws and motorbikes. Slightly ironic for a man who owns so many gas guzzlers. Still, they are a great idea, though they haven't made it to the streets of Udaipur yet.

UDAIPUR OUTSKIRTS

To the north of Lake Pichola is Udaipur's second lake, the Fateh Sagar. On a hill (Moti Magri) overlooking it is a statue of Maharana Udai Singh's son, Rana Pratap, on his horse, Chetak. Rana Pratap went down in the pages of history for defying, to the very end, the greatest Mughal ruler, Emperor Akbar, at a time when the rest of Rajasthan had surrendered.

Further north is the garden of Saheliyon ki Baari; the Sajangarh or Monsoon Palace lies five kilometres west of the main city.

Fateh Sagar

An artificial lake created in 1678, Fateh Sagar lies barely a kilometre north of Lake Pichola, is fringed by hills and connected to Lake Pichola by a canal built in the early 20th century. You can get a ferry to take you to Nehru Park, a little island in the lake (open 8am-6pm daily, admission Rs 3, pedal boats Rs 40 for 30mins). The park was constructed in 1937 as famine relief employment, and while its setting is peaceful, it could do with some upkeep.

Saheliyon ki Baari

This pleasant garden, two kilometres north of the Old City, was created in the 18th century and has been a location for scenes in many a Hindi film. It has a shaded courtyard with a row of defunct fountains, marble elephants and kiosks. There's a wide range of trees and flowers. During the monsoon the pool (filled with colourful lotuses) is nice. It's not much of a stopover, though, and certainly not worth going out of your way to visit.

Sajangarh/Monsoon Palace

Bansdara Hill. Open 10am-6pm daily. Admission Rs 25 Indians; Rs 150 others.

A steep and winding road leads up Bansdara Hill to Sajjangarh, a serene palace five kilometres west of the main city. It's surrounded by forested hills that are a protected area for wildlife. The palace itself is nothing more than a few bare walls, but the tranquil setting, the greenery and the views all around make it a lovely spot to come and enjoy the sunset. Entry gates close one hour before sundown, so visitors need to enter before then. The Laxmi Vilas Palace Hotel (*see p103*) runs an alfresco café here, which serves snacks (sandwiches and pakoras) and drinks as well as lunch and high tea. Guests of the hotel get special access to a set of lounging rooms beside the café; a great spot for a relaxed day away from the tourist circuit.

AROUND UDAIPUR

EKLINGJI, NAGDA & NATHDWARA

These temples to the north-east of Udaipur can be seen in a day. After visiting Eklingi, 22 kilometres (14 miles) out of the city, head for Nagda, two kilometres to its south. Here are ruins of the 10th- to 11th-century Saas-Bahu temples (mother-in-law and daughter-in-law; Vishnu temples) and Adbudji Temple (a Jain temple), all with elaborate sculptures.

Forty-eight kilometres north-east of Udaipur is Nathdwara (Gateway to the Gods), one of the principal places of pilgrimage in Rajasthan, attracting devotees from all over India. Nathdwara village has the flavour of an old hamlet, with narrow cobbled streets and small bazaars. The famous *meenakari* jewellery can be found here, as can artists making *pichhwais*, cloth paintings with vegetable dyes, depicting stories from the life of Lord Krishna. Shrinathji Temple was established here because a chariot carrying a black stone statue of Lord Krishna (as a child) got stuck in the mud here, while being smuggled away from Mathura, to escape the intemperate Mughal emperor Aurangazeb. Considering this to be the will of Krishna, a temple was built at the spot. The temple is only open to Hindus.

Eklingji Temple

22km N of Udaipur. Open 4.15-6.45am, 10.30am-1.30pm, 5.15-7.45pm daily; aarti 5.30-7.30am.

Lord Shiva is worshipped here as his incarnation Eklingji, the generative force of the universe, and the deity of Mewar's rulers since the eighth century. The walled boundary of the temple complex has 108 shrines. The 16th-century main temple has a double-storeyed porch and sanctuary, an elaborate pillared hall, and a flat, pyramidal roof adorned with hundreds of circular knobs and is crowned by a tall tower. A four-faced black marble idol of Lord Eklingji is in the inner sanctuary. Traditionally, the maharanas of Mewar have worshipped at the temple each Monday night (Shiva's day).

RANAKPUR

Ranakpur is a little off the beaten track, tucked away in a valley in the Aravalli Hills, 65 kilometres (40 miles) north-west of Udaipur. It is home to an exquisitely carved temple, the Chaumukha Temple, considered one of five key places of pilgrimage for followers of the Jain faith.

Chaumukha Temple (Adinath Temple)

65km NW of Udaipur. Admission free; Rs 40 camera; Rs 150 video camera. No leather, mobile phones, or photographs of deities.

Built in 1439, the temple is dedicated to Adinath, the first Jain *tirthankara* (holy person who has gained enlightenment and passes their knowledge on to others). The marble temple's exterior is not carved, leading to quite a surprise

Mewar art

While most historians agree that the art of miniature painting did not flourish in India until the Mughal era, it actually dates back to the ninth century as an art form here. Early miniature art was done on palm leaves, but the introduction of paper in the 12th century brought about changes in style, allowing for more elaboration and a larger scale of production. The first school of miniature painting was set up during the Lodi period of the 15th to 16th centuries, but it was under the Mughal Empire that professional studios were established.

As the Mughal Empire declined, Rajput artists took over the craft, and to this day Rajasthan remains the stronghold of miniature painting. Talented artists worked out different styles, leading to the development of various schools of miniature art. The Mewar school is one of the most popular, with many artists working in Udaipur and its neighbouring villages. This school is known for using simple, bright colours to evoke an emotional response.

The first step in creating a miniature is to get the right kind of brush. For this, squirrel hair is softened and then attached to a pigeon feather, making a quill. Of course, many of the paintings in the shops of Udaipur are mass produced, made using normal paintbrushes and synthetic paints such as acrylics. However, the traditional production of miniatures relies on natural colours obtained from plant and mineral sources that are ground in a mortar with *chaar gund* (gum arabic), which acts as a binding agent. Water is then added to the mixture, turning it into usable paint that binds to various surfaces. Gold leaf is often used to highlight the paintings. Besides paper, paintings were traditionally done on bone panels, wooden tablets, leather, marble and cloth, and even the interior walls of houses and palaces.

City scenes and Hindu religious themes are among the most popular subjects, though you can also find portraits and scenes from the lives of Rajput rulers. Animals are also common motifs, particularly the elephant, though horses, camels and elephants marching together in a line are also often found; these three animals represent the cities of Udaipur, Jaisalmer and Jodhpur respectively. Note the rolling clouds that decorate many of the paintings: they probably represent a yearning for rain.

Exquisite miniatures can be found in the souvenir shops in the lanes behind Udaipur's Jagdish Temple. Or head to a workshop or to Shilpgram, the government-sponsored arts village, where you can buy miniatures directly from artists, often at a fraction of prices in the city centre. If you are lucky enough to buy a piece directly from an artist, you can also ask him to paint a little elephant on your fingernail; you will be impressed at the precision with which these skilled artists create mini nail art.

inside. A carved image of Adinath, shown with four faces, is enshrined in the main sanctum. The temple is three storeys high, with about 84 underground chambers, once used for hiding enshrined deities from invaders, but not accessible to the public. One of the two most interesting features of this temple is its 1,444 pillars, each one unique and an ornamental masterpiece of relief carving. The second is the magnificent, intricate filigree work in concentric circles done on the ceilings. Friezes on the walls depict the life of Adinath; but don't miss the plaque dedicated to Parsvanath, the 23rd Jain *tirthankara*, at the far end of the temple.

Get one of the young priests at the entrance to act as guide, which they will do willingly; afterwards they request a small donation to the temple. Several of them speak English and can point out intricate details to you. You can also wander around on your own watching the routine temple rituals taking place. Also within the temple complex are two other Jain temples and one Hindu temple – all are beautiful.

KUMBHALGARH FORT

Kumbhalgarh, 90 kilometres (56 miles) north of Udaipur, is where the rulers of Mewar sought protection in times of danger. The fort (open 8.30am-6pm daily, admission Rs 5 Indians, Rs 100 others) was built by Maharana Kumbha of Mewar in the 15th century and is the most formidable of the 32 forts constructed by him. Built at an altitude of 1,100 metres (3,600 feet) on the crest of the Aravalli range between the kingdoms of Marwar and Mewar, the massive fort walls sprawl impressively and impregnably over 36 kilometres (22 miles), making it the second-longest wall in the world. The fort is protected by seven gates, several encrusted with huge spikes meant to deter even an elephant.

A fully functioning village with 5,000 residents sits inside the first gate of the fort. When you enter, the smaller fort of Kartargarh (a fort within the fort) is to your left; to the right and beyond are innumerable ruins of temples, palaces, gardens and water storage tanks.

Crowning the fort is the Badal Mahal (Cloud Palace), an elegantly painted and airy palace restored in the 19th century, where the legendary warrior king Rana Pratap was born. Not only is the trudge to the top worth it for the views of the surrounding countryside, but you can also check out the use of vents that provide a superb natural cooling system for the palace.

If you are staying nearby (the Aodhi Hotel is a short distance away and is a good breakfast stop) you can come back at 7pm for the sound-and-light show.

Around the fort is the Kumbhalgarh Wildlife Sanctuary. Summers are very hot, but the dry waterholes make it the best time to see animals. Permission for entry from the forest department at Kelwara or from the deputy chief wildlife warden in Udaipur is necessary; this is best done through a travel agent.

FURTHER AFIELD

CHITTORGARH

A significant detour, 115 kilometres/72 miles or three hours' drive north-east from Udaipur, Chittorgarh is one of the oldest cities in Rajasthan and once the seat of power of the Mewar dynasty.

Chittorgarh Fort (open 10am-4.30pm daily, admission Rs 5 Indians, Rs 100 others) sits on a massive hilltop, enclosed in a five-kilometre-long wall. There has been a fort on this site since the seventh century. What remains are mainly ruins, but the place has a magnificent, if tragic, history, associated with the Rajput ethos that death is preferable to dishonour. It was here that Rajput rulers under siege, and a breath away from certain defeat, marched out to approaching enemies, while their women (and some say children as well) committed *jauhar*, or immolation, in a massive funeral pyre in 1303.

"Padmini's Palace is the subject of legend: it is said that Alauddin Khilji caught a glimpse of the beautiful Rani Padmini in a mirror here."

The ascent to the fort is marked by seven gates that defended it from invaders. Near the second gate are *chhatris* (cenotaphs) of Rajput martyrs who died in the second sacking of Chittorgarh. Ram Pol, the final gate, takes you to the ruins and a deer park; it also houses a small community.

Rana Kumbha Palace is the first building you come across, a classic example of Rajput architecture. The Jaya Stambha (Tower of Victory) is a nine-storey monument erected by Rana Kumbha to commemorate his victory over Alauddin Khilji in 1440. The Gaumukh Kund (Cow's Mouth Tank) features spring water gushing out of a carved cow's mouth into a tank below. Padmini's Palace, beside a lotus pool and with a pavilion in the centre, is the subject of legend: it is said that Alauddin Khilji caught a glimpse of the beautiful Rani Padmini in a mirror here. However, these days the palace is run-down and no reflection of its former glory. The most modern construction in the fort complex is the 20th-century Kumbha Shyama Temple.

DUNGARPUR

Three hours' drive south of Udaipur is the somnolent town of Dungarpur, where two lovely palaces stand, Juna Mahal and the Udai Bilas Palace. The latter, on the shore of Gaibsagar Lake, is now a heritage hotel and a superb example of the architecture and art of the region; its one-pillared palace, in particular, is a fantasia in stone.

Juna Mahal

Open 8am-1pm, 3-5pm daily. Admission Rs 150 for guests of Udai Bilas Palace or tip for caretaker.

The 13th-century fort-palace of Juna Mahal looks rather uninspiring externally, but its inteior is packed with art. Every room of its seven levels has well-preserved miniature paintings and murals in a riot of colours. Scenes from the epic *Mahabharata*, battle scenes and religious themes abound. The queen's room is studded with coloured glass and paintings, while Shiv Niwas, the king's room, has 54 illustrated scenes from the *Kama Sutra* discreetly behind closed doors.

Eat

The Old City is filled with rooftop restaurants with tourist menus so similar that it's hard to distinguish one from another. In peak tourist season most restaurants are crowded, and diners may sometimes have to wait half an hour for a table.

Ambrai

Lake Pichola *Hanuman ghat side, opposite Lal ghat, (0294-243-1085). Open 7.30-11.30pm daily. $$. Multi-cuisine. No AmEx. North Indian.*

Undoubtedly Udaipur's most well-known restaurant, Ambrai is busy, crowded and serves fairly good tandoori kebabs and North Indian fare. There are also some Western and Asian items on the menu, but if you stick to naans, *dal makhani* and the tandoori dishes you can't go wrong. As it is an alfresco restaurant set in a garden on the shores of Lake Pichola, opposite the Lake Palace Hotel and City Palace, the view at night is superb and the shady trees provide a comfortable setting for a leisurely lunch as well. There's live Rajasthani music most nights.

Jagat Niwas

Lake Pichola *23-25 Lal ghat (0294-242-2860/ 0133/www.jagatniwaspalace.com). Open 6am-10pm daily. $$. No AmEx. North Indian.*

Right next door to the Kankarwa (*see below*), this is a popular rooftop restaurant with splendid views over the lake. Particularly comfortable are the little cushioned *jharokhas* (balconies). The menu has standard North Indian dishes, such as paneer in thick gravies and assorted biryanis. Service is laid-back so don't come here if you are in a hurry; conversely, if you want to linger, no one will rush you out.

Kankarwa

Lake Pichola *26 Lal ghat (0294-241-1457). Open 7.30-9am, noon-3pm, 7-9pm daily. $$. Rajasthani.*

It's another rooftop restaurant, but the real blessing here is that you won't get barbecued chicken or paneer masala. Come if you are willing to eat what the family eats: wholesome, vegetarian Rajasthani food, served in a thali. Breakfast is home-made parathas, or, for those who can't do without, toast and cereal. You're welcome to walk into the family's kitchen at any time, where manager Janardhan Singh's mother Indira and sister-in-law Suchana personally cook everything. If you are not staying at the *haveli* (*see p100*), call ahead, or come in before 7pm for dinner. For those who don't want Rajasthani food, some Western meals can be prepared.

Savage Garden

Old City *22 Chandpol (0294-242-5440/94142-96958/ www.savagegardenindia.com) Open 11am-10.30pm daily. $$. Western.*

Just follow the numerous signs to this part German-owned restaurant in an 18th-century *haveli* in a tiny lane in Chandpol. The high-walled courtyard opens to striking Mediterranean blue walls. Upstairs is quieter, with open rooms providing semi-private areas for dining. Savage Garden serves standard Western and Mediterranean tourist fare – the likes of chicken breast with rosemary potatoes (order the creamy sauce on the side) – which hits the spot if you're weary of spicy food and fancy a change. Pastas are also well made – try the home-made ravioli stuffed with aubergine and mozzarella. This is also a safe place to consume fresh juices, salads and fruit salads. Those looking for a snack will find a decent meze platter, and bruschetta, among other choices. Service is pleasant and laid-back, but not inefficient.

Sunset Terrace

Old City *Outside City Palace (0294-252-8016). Open 7-10.30am, noon-3pm, 7.30-10.30pm daily. $$. Multi-cuisine.*

Come here for the location – Sunset Terrace is just outside the City Palace, overlooking the City Palace and the rest of Udaipur. At night the tables are candlelit, making the setting even more romantic. Food, however, is hit or miss. It's best to either chat with the chef about what's popular and fresh, or stick to common North Indian or Rajasthani dishes (or the barbecue, if there is one) rather than ordering Western food, or anything that requires exotic ingredients.

Udai Kothi

Lake Pichola *Hanuman Ghat Road, opposite Lal ghat (0294-243-2810/www.udaikothi.com). Open 7-11am, 1-4pm, 7.30-10.30pm daily. $$. No AmEx.*

The setting for this rooftop restaurant is utterly romantic, if you can bag the open-air poolside floor seating in one of the cushioned little alcoves, which get full quite early during peak season. Tables in the adjoining alfresco restaurant section are a tad too close. The menu is limited; avoid Western food entirely and go for Indian basics – the setting is the main event here.

Kumbhalgarh Fort.

Clockwise from top: Udai Kothi Rooftop Restaurant; Kankarwa Haveli; Devi Garh (3).

Shop

One of the joys of Udaipur is roaming the streets, looking at the wares on display. Near the Jagdish Temple (*see p90*), for instance, the streets are lined with little shops selling all kinds of goods, from handmade paper diaries to wooden toys, from embroidery to prints of miniature paintings. Scarves, stoles, bags, tie-dyed and block-printed clothes and fabrics, and leather goods can be found in stores all along Palace Road. Udaipur is also famous for *meenakari* (enamel-work) and *kundan* jewellery. For window- and gift-shopping there are numerous shops around Hathi Pol, Chetak Circle and Bada Bazaar. Inside the City Palace are stores that sell clothing, jewellery and souvenirs, invariably more expensive than those on the outside; but they are worth a browse because their merchandise is of good quality. Silver Stone (0294-241-4146, open 9.30am-5.30pm daily) sells interesting traditional jewellery as well as marble and other handicrafts. Anokhi (0294-252-9881, www.anokhi.com, open 10am-7pm daily), the popular chain store from Jaipur, also has a branch here that sells its beautiful hand-block-printed clothing and home accessories.

Mewar Art Gallery

Saheliyon ki baari *10A Saheliyon ki baari, New Fatehpura (0294-242-2309/www.mewarartgallery.com). Open 9am-8pm daily.*

Most of the artists at work here come from a long line of artists, who pass down the skills and techniques of miniature painting to each successive generation. Owner Jagdish is always on hand and willing to describe the intricacies of the art. Pieces are painted on silk, paper, marble, camel bone and other surfaces and you can see the vibrant colours being extracted in-house from natural stones. Each work is priced according to the amount of labour put in and the skill of the artist. Expect to pay anything from Rs 500 for a tiny painting on cloth to tens of thousands for large pieces. The store also stocks a variety of sculptures and other artefacts.

Sadhana

Near Saheliyon ki bari *Seva Mandir Road, Old Fatehpura, near Fatehpura Police Station Circle (0294-245-1041/www.sadhna.org). Open 10am-6pm Mon-Sat. No credit cards.*

Sadhana employs and supports over 625 local rural women and helps them on the road to becoming self-sufficient. The women produce an array of embroidery, appliqué and other crafts, and make clothes, linens and other homewares, all of which are sold here. You'll also find quilts, bedspreads, other home furnishings and a variety of colourful accessories. This simple store is a bit off the main road, but easy enough to find once you are in the Old Fatehpura neighbourhood.

Shilpgram

7km W of Udaipur *Rani Road, Havala village (0294-143-1304). Open 10am-6pm daily. No credit cards.*

Part of the series of rural arts and crafts villages set up by the government around the country, Shilpgram is a good place to meet and interact with local artists and artisans. Dancers and puppeteers perform to the tune of traditional instruments and visitors can roam the rustic grounds and buy arts and crafts directly from those who create them. Wooden crafts, miniature paintings and various other arts and crafts of Rajasthan are showcased here.

Silver Art Palace

Saheliyon ki bari *Road 135, near IDBI Bank (0294-241-4334). Open 9.30-8pm daily. No AmEx.*

This 30-year-old family-run shop has a variety of traditional jewellery, such as *kundan*, *meenakari*, and silver *rawa* work. Pieces use precious and semi-precious stones, and there are many contemporary designs, something that's hard to come by in the average store. Besides jewellery, there are silver candlesticks, photo frames, cutlery and other silver pieces made with excellent craftsmanship.

Arts

The Bharatiya Lok Kala Mandal

Old City *NN Acharya Marg, near Mohta Park/Chetak Circle (0294-252-5077). Open 9am-6pm Mon-Sat. Admission Rs 35.*

This centre comprises an amphitheatre where folk dances and dramas are performed, and galleries where tribal life, arts and customs are brought to wider audiences. The museum was set up by Devilal Samar, a schoolteacher turned puppeteer, who dedicated his life to saving folk arts from imminent death after they lost royal patronage after Independence. Puppetry finds a special place in the museum, with puppets from around the globe on display. The museum also organises puppetry classes every summer, and puppet shows throughout the year.

Stay

Apart from the upmarket options on Lake Pichola, there is also accommodation on the quiet Fateh Sagar Lake. *Havelis*, right on the waterfront, can come at a fraction of the cost, naturally without the same amenities. *Havelis* are usually ancestral homes that have been converted into guesthouses, though some, like Udai Kothi (*see p103*), are newly built. We have also included some outstanding accommodation in rural Rajasthan, from the area around Udaipur.

Deogarh Mahal & Fort Seengh Sagar

135km N of Udaipur *Deogarh Madaria, Rajsamund District (02904-252-777/www.deogarhmahal.com). $$$-$$$$. No AmEx.*

On top of a hill, in the heart of tiny Deogarh village, this 17th-century fort-palace hotel is managed by the family of Nahar Singh, the Rawat of Deogarh (rawats were feudal landlords, and are still treated like royalty). The ochre palace looks stunning from the outside. Inside, rooms and suites are large and personalised with family heirlooms, portraits, antiques, mirrors and paintings; each is different (older ones are nicer). Lounges, terraces, turrets and balconies mean there are innumerable cosy nooks to hang out in and there's also a pleasant pool that's heated in winter. This is an old palace converted into a hotel, in the middle of rural Rajasthan, so expect small issues with plumbing/hot water and laid-back service. Beyond those limitations, this is a superb rural idyll with opportunities to explore off-the-beaten-track Rajasthan, including a 24km (15-mile) heritage train ride along a metre-gauge track.

The family also has a former hunting lodge five kilometres away in the heart of panther country, converted into a four-room hotel. Fort Seengh Sagar is a little fort with a moat around it (sometimes dry, like Lake Pichola) in a wilderness setting: balconies and open spaces overlook desert countryside and the Aravalli Hills. Rooms are decorated in vibrant Rajasthani colours and furnished with antiques; bathrooms are modern.

At both properties the Rawat's family take pains to meet and chat with their guests, and offer courteous, old-fashioned hospitality – all of which makes for a fine detour from the cities of Rajasthan.

Devi Garh

28km NE of Udaipur *Near Eklingji, Delwara village, Rajsamund (02953-304-211/www.deviresorts.com). $$$$.*

This 18th-century fort-palace turned boutique hotel is utterly atmospheric, overlooking rolling hills and striking countryside. Each suite is unique, a streamlined modern take on an Indian aesthetic. Beds are raised marble plinths with thick comfortable mattresses. Furniture is mostly carved out of marble blocks and white predominates, with splashes of colour. Bathrooms are modern, with aromatic Forest Essentials toiletries. However, some rooms are showing signs of age (with a broken temperature control panel or mould-stained marble), and garden suites, in the annexe area, lack the ambience of the rest of the place. Still, this highly acclaimed award-winning hotel is one of the most stunning properties in Rajasthan and its outdoor and indoor spaces are a design sensation. Food is good contemporary Indian and Western fare, and some of the private dining areas in the fort are supremely romantic.

Fateh Prakash & Shiv Niwas Palaces

City Palace *(0294-252-8016/www.eternalmewar.com). $$$$.*

These two palaces are part of the City Palace complex. The Fateh Prakash Palace Hotel has two wings: the Dovecote wing where interiors are staid, but have brilliant views of the lake, and the main wing, where few rooms have views, but all have an old-fashioned charm. Neither offers real value for money.

Shiv Niwas Palace was built as a royal guesthouse and visitors have included Queen Elizabeth II. Suites are arranged in a semicircle around the pool; lake-facing on one side, city-facing on the other. Suites are themed; one, for example, has red crystal everywhere and bedspread and furnishings to match. Nice window seating areas and a movable stand with plasma TV are the positives. Bathrooms are large, but fixtures basic and functional.

Unfortunately, everything about these two hotels, from the rooms and public spaces to the service, is looking a bit tired these days, and where modern elements have been added it hasn't been done well. For all that, the uniqueness and charm of the location – right inside the City Palace – is hard to beat. How can you match the thrill of staying in a palace, surrounded by beautiful 17th-century Mewar art, Moreno crystal chandeliers, semi-precious stone and glass inlay work on the pillars and, if you can bag it, some of the best lake views in Udaipur?

Jagat Niwas Palace

Lake Pichola *23-25 Lal ghat (0294-242-2860/0133/www.jagatniwaspalace.com). $$. No AmEx.*

Jagat Niwas is a large 17th-century *haveli*, with rooms built around a central courtyard scattered with benches and potted plants. Few are lake-facing, all are spotless and homely. Lake-facing rooms, like the Raj room, are rather compact, but comfortable and quaint, with cosy *jharokha* windows. Larger rooms tend not to be lake-facing, though most have traditional teak furniture and block-print furnishings. Amenities like TVs and phones are also present, making this good value.

Kankarwa Haveli

Lake Pichola *26 Lal ghat (0294-241-1457/khaveli@yahoo.com). $. No AmEx.*

Kankarwa is a charming family-run *haveli* with a superb location, right by the lake on Lal ghat, offering a real Rajasthani experience. Owner-manager Janardhan is a friendly, obliging sort who is happy to discuss everything from your travel plans to the state of the nation. Each room is different, decorated in ethnic fabrics, but all are atmospheric and homely. Some have extra-large attached bathrooms, but no fancy fittings or water pressure. You won't find any luxuries here in the form of electronics, or even a phone in your room. There are no alternatives if there is a power failure, even in the summer, and no heaters in the winter. Anything you want, you have to go down to reception for. But at such a budget price, and with such a lovely atmosphere, this place is great value.

Lalit Laxmi Vilas Palace

Fateh Sagar *(0294-252-9711/www.thelalit.com). $$$.*

This former guesthouse of Maharana Bhupal Singh was built in 1911, and is on a hill with fantastic views over Fateh Sagar Lake. Suites in the Heritage wing are nicer than the rooms in the Srinathji wing, and many were upgraded in 2009. They are modern and spacious but without any real heritage feel: the hotel's best feature is undoubtedly its view (make sure to get a lake-facing room). Staff are friendly, courteous and helpful, but though the kitchen tries hard, the food is mediocre. Its location is ten minutes' drive into the city: an advantage or disadvantage, depending on your point of view.

Taj Lake Palace.

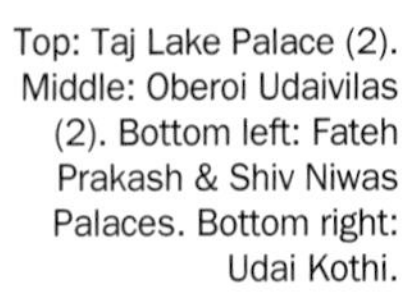

Top: Taj Lake Palace (2). Middle: Oberoi Udaivilas (2). Bottom left: Fateh Prakash & Shiv Niwas Palaces. Bottom right: Udai Kothi.

Oberoi Udaivilas

Lake Pichola *Mulla Talai Haridasji ki Magri (0294-243-3300/www.oberoihotels.com). $$$$.*

This is the cluster of grand domes, arches, turrets and sprawling lawns that you can see across the lake from the Old City, about four kilometres away. An enormous pool runs along the hotel's periphery, making for a serene setting. A large part of the property is an animal sanctuary where deer and peacock can be spotted. Regularly featured as one of the world's top hotels by the likes of Condé Nast, Forbes, and Zagat, this is a truly luxurious space, although one without traditional Rajasthani ambience. Rooms have comfortable beds with appliqué bedspreads, there are separate changing areas outside modern bathrooms (with free-standing bathtubs), window seating beside large windows, a small outdoor seating area and access to either a private or semi-private pool. Lake views are few; exceptions are the Chandni terrace restaurant and some therapy rooms at the swish Banyan Tree spa. This hotel is sometimes a venue for big fat Indian weddings, so if you value tranquillity, make sure you're not booked alongside a loud wedding party.

Taj Lake Palace

Lake Pichola *Jag Niwas Island (0294-242-8800/ www.tajhotels.com). $$$$.*

The Taj Lake Palace is easily one of the most beautiful and romantic palace hotels in all India. Not just opulent, it offers exceptional service guaranteed to make you feel like royalty. From the rose and cardamom welcome drink to the discreet oil-diffusers in hallways and fresh-cut oriental lilies with stamens removed, every detail is taken care of here. Rooms are actually on the small side, but they have rich furnishings and every conceivable amenity. Suite bathrooms have free-standing Jacob Dalafon bathtubs and use slick local granite to create a feeling of luxury; toiletries are from Molton Brown. Particularly lavish and romantic is the Khush Mahal suite, from where the lit-up City Palace is visible at night. In the morning its stained-glass windows catch the sun's rays: the effect is magical. The central courtyard, with its lily pond, and the dreamy and serene poolside are both incredibly romantic spots. For exclusive dining, too, the Lake Palace is unsurpassed, with its many private dining spaces, from a moonlit lily pond and breezy terraces, to boats and floating platforms. From here, Udaipur city seems so near and yet so far.

Udai Kothi

Lake Pichola *Hanuman ghat Road, opposite Lal ghat (0294-243-2810/www.udaikothi.com). $$. No AmEx.*

The azure rooftop pool is the best feature of this hotel, built in the style of a *haveli*. The painted entrance archway sets the tone for the interior of the new, well-maintained premises. The reception, hallways, poolside and rooms are filled with colonial-style furniture and assorted artefacts from around India. Lake-facing rooms, which are the ones to get, have comfortable *jharokha* window seating and canopied four-poster beds. Vivid floral curtains and matching bedspreads give the rooms a bright look, though some do feel ever-so-slightly cramped with all the furniture, cushions, window mattresses and objets d'art. Service is prompt and good, and because this isn't really an old *haveli*, there is a lift.

Factfile

When to go

Mid September to March is peak season here. The monsoon starts receding by early September, which is the time the lakes are most likely to have water. In summer lake waters are at their lowest, and sometimes the lakes are bone dry.

Getting there

Udaipur is connected to Mumbai, Delhi, Jaipur and Jodhpur by several daily direct flights. It's also well-connected by train services to Jaipur and other major cities in and outside Rajasthan.

For more on travel within India, *see p378* **Navigating India**.

Getting around

Auto-rickshaws are the most convenient mode of transport within the city, as the streets are narrow. A car with driver is useful to cover more distant sights.

Tourist information

A Tourist Reception Centre can be found at Surajpol (Fateh Memorial, 0294-241¬1535, 241-1364, open 9am-6.30pm Mon-Sat). There's also a tourist counter at the airport (0294-265-5433, open from 9am-7pm Mon-Sat).

Tips

● It's a good idea to check whether Lake Pichola or any of the surrounding lakes have any water in them before you come, so you're not disappointed.

● The *havelis*, forts and ex-palaces of Rajasthan are often old structures with a lot of stairs, so they're not a good choice for those with limited mobility.

● If you dine alfresco in Udaipur, especially by the lake, expect mosquitoes. Carry mosquito repellent and put it on even before you sit down.

Clockwise from top: Jaigarh Fort; City Palace; Museum; City Palace gate; Hawa Mahal.

Jaipur

Rajasthan's colourful, chaotic pink city.

In Jaipur, palaces aren't just monuments, they're homes too. A seven-course meal isn't a feast, it's just dinner, and anything that's less than a century old is modern. Jaipur was founded by Maharaja Jai Singh II, a Kachwaha Rajput, who moved his capital here from Amer, some 11 kilometres away. After years of meticulous planning, the construction of Jaipur – the City of Victory – began in 1727. Today, the past remains very visible in the city's dusty, bustling streets, its filigreed windows and majestic forts.

The old or walled city is often referred to as the Pink City, because that's the colour of the Hawa Mahal and many of the other buildings. But that doesn't mean everything's rosy here. Despite the overwhelming scent of history and some of the country's most vibrant bazaars, modern Jaipur is a crowded, polluted, heaving metropolis, brimming with traffic, painted hoardings and diesel-thirsty rickshaws.

In the midst of all this, though, many buildings have been preserved. The opulent palaces, magnificent forts and formidable gates of Jaipur are testament to two of the most important characteristics of the Rajputs: self-indulgence and strategic planning. On the one hand, you can't fail to appreciate the decadence and extravagance of Rajasthan's royals when you walk through their palaces, but you'll also discover that most of these sandstone monuments were designed on such awe-inspiringly large scales to offer vital vantage points for defence purposes. Centuries after they were laid in stone, their visual impact remains the same.

Explore

The main attractions – the City Palace, Jantar Mantar and Hawa Mahal – are all in the old walled city in the north-eastern section of Jaipur, though few of the original city walls actually remain. Besides these, it is the clamour of the bazaars, the endless procession of people, animals, bargains and deals, that make up the total experience of the Old City.

Jaipur's other chief attraction is Amer (or Amber) Fort, 11 kilometres north of the city; two other outlying forts – Nahargarh and Jaigarh (nine kilometres and 12 kilometres to the north-west) – are also of interest. Set aside at least four days to experience Jaipur.

OLD CITY

City Palace

0141-260-8055. Open 9.30am-5pm daily. Admission Rs 40 Indians; Rs 300 others; Rs 25 under-12s; Rs 50 camera; Rs 200 video camera.

Built by Maharaja Jai Singh II, this huge palace is a blend of Rajput and Mughal architecture and houses numerous courtyards, gardens and the **Maharaja Sawai Man Singh II Museum**. The museum has three galleries that showcase the collections built up by the rulers of Amber and Jaipur.

The first structure, the **Mubarak Mahal** (Welcome Palace), was once a reception and guesthouse for the Maharaja's visitors. It now houses a textile and costume museum (on the first floor) and has pieces like the *atamsukh*, a luxurious Banaras brocade quilted cloak, rich 17th- and 18th-century fabrics and fine Dacca muslin, and a maharani's elaborate black ensemble, richly embellished with gold embroidery, estimated to weigh 30kg (66lbs).

In an adjacent building that was once the queen's palace is the museum's Sileh Khana (armoury suite), which houses the biggest collection of Indian weapons in the world. On display are swords of Mughal emperors Jehangir and Shah Jahan, Sawai Jai Singh's pistol, 17th-century matchlock guns, and shields made of tough crocodile and rhinoceros hide, embossed or lacquered and studded with precious stones.

Also worth reflecting over at the City Palace is the intricately carved **Diwan-i-Am** (Hall of Public Audience) and the **Diwan-i-Khas** (Hall of Private Audience), which has a marble paved gallery. The dimly lit **Art Museum** in the Diwan-i-Am is full of lovely miniatures and intricately woven carpets, and has some rather unusual paintings like the one depicting the birth of Christ (to the left of the entrance near the Gopinathji painting). There are also displays of *howdahs* (palanquins) used by the royal family, and a treasure trove of miniature books. From the Peacock courtyard, you can take a look at the seven-storey Chandra Mahal, where the royal descendants of Sawai Man Singh still reside.

Jantar Mantar

Next to City Palace. Open 9am-4.30pm daily. Admission Rs 20 Indians; Rs 100 others; Rs 20-Rs 50 camera; Rs 50-Rs 100 video camera.

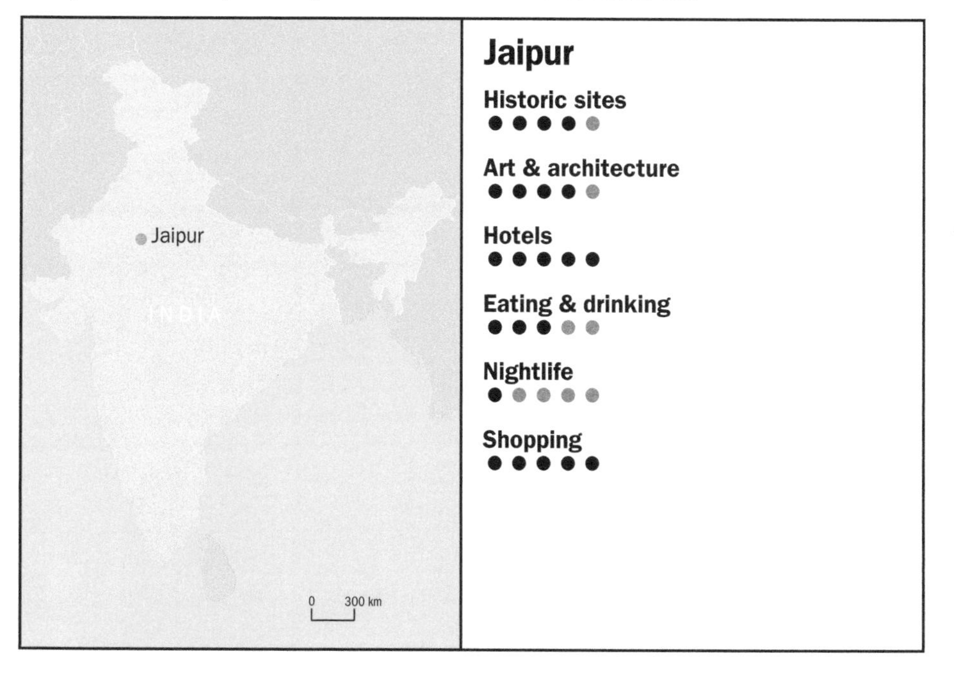

Clockwise from top left: Anokhi Museum of Hand Printing (3); Amer (Amber) Fort; Jantar Mantar.

Jaipur's Jantar Mantar is said to be the largest open-air observatory in the world. Built in 1728 by Maharaja Jai Singh, who had a passion for astronomy, Jantar Mantar is full of curious-looking instruments that were once used to measure the position of stars and calculate the time of eclipses. The most striking of these is the sundial, with its 27m (89ft) gnomon (rod), which still provides accurate time. The observatory has 18 large instruments, but unless you have a solid knowledge of astronomy or an excellent guide, their use remains a mystery.

Hawa Mahal

Next to City Palace (0141-261-8862). Open 9am-4.30pm daily. Admission Rs 10 Indians; Rs 30 others.

The 'Palace of Winds' was built in 1799 by Maharaja Sawai Pratap Singh, for the royal ladies to watch and enjoy the processions on the street below. The five-storey structure, with its pink façade, is Jaipur's most popular landmark. It was designed to resemble the *mukut* (crown) that Lord Krishna wears and each of its 953 windows has intricately carved filigree work. The structure now houses a museum and visitors can walk the corridors and take in the sights of shoppers swarming in the market beneath.

AMER FORT & AROUND

Amer (Amber) Fort

11km N of Jaipur, Delhi–Jaipur Highway (0141-253-0293). Open 9.30am-5pm daily. Admission Rs 25 Indians; Rs 150 others; Rs 50-Rs 100 camera; Rs 70-Rs 150 video camera. Elephant ride Rs 550 for 2 people. Sound-and-light show 7.30pm English, Rs 200; 8.30pm Hindi, Rs 100.

It's worth coming to Jaipur just to see the Amer Fort. Work on the former capital stronghold of the Kachwaha Rajput clan, crowning the top of a hill overlooking Maotha Lake, was begun in 1592 by Raja Man Singh I, a Rajput commander in Emperor Akbar's army; it was continued by the next two generations of rulers.

Amer Fort is awe-inspiring both on account of its sheer scale, and for the quantity and detailing of the decoration and artwork in its many halls and courtyards. It is a classic fusion of Mughal and Hindu architecture, built in red sandstone and white marble. It's best approached systematically, and a local licensed guide will help you make the most of your visit.

Suraj Pol (Sun Gate), the eastern gate, is the main entrance. Visitors can drive here, trek uphill or indulge in a 20-minute elephant ride. Admittedly, the latter is a little touristy, but it provides spectacular views of the ruins and manicured gardens – the perfectly geometrical Dil-Aram Bagh and Kesarkyari Bagh (Saffron Garden).

Towards the right, after going through the Singh Pol, is the **Shila Devi Temple**, flanked on either side by two large silver lions. The temple is dedicated to the goddess Kali, family deity of the Kachwaha clan (photography is prohibited here). Further up is the **Diwan-i-Am** or the court for commoners and public audiences. Built in Mughal architectural style, the public hall is supported by numerous columns made of red sandstone; the inner ones are made of snow-white marble.

The magnificent three-storey **Ganesh Pol** (gate) leads to the splendid **Sheesh Mahal**. This structure has two exquisitely decorated halls with low arched entrances with intricate floral patterns etched into the stone; elaborate mirror-work adorns the walls and ceilings. It is said that when a candle is lit inside the inner hall, the flame is reflected in every single mirror on the ceiling and wall, giving the appearance of a star-spangled sky. Above the Sheesh Mahal is the **Jas Mandir** (Hall of Glory), a rectangular chamber with elaborate *jali* (filigree work) windows that look down on the terraced gardens. The **Man Singh Palace** is to the rear of the fort and is the oldest part of the palace. The mural-painted **Zenana Mahal** is the best-preserved section, built to accommodate Man Singh's wives.

Also within the Amber Palace is **Gallery Artchill**, an art gallery that gives special focus to Jaipur's up-and-coming artists (0141-253-0015, open 8am-6pm daily, www.artchill.com). Said to house up to 2,500 paintings at any given time, it is one of the largest art galleries in the country.

Those with time can take a detour to the ruins of **Pracheen Mahal**, where the founders of Amer once lived.

Anokhi Museum of Hand Printing

Amber Anokhi Haveli, near Biharji Temple, Kheri Gate (0141-253-0226/www.anokhimuseum.com). Open 10.30am-5pm Tue-Sat; 11am-4.30pm Sun. Museum shop & café 11am-4.30pm Tue-Sun. Admission Rs 30; Rs 15 children; Rs 50 camera; Rs 150 video camera.

Housed in a renovated *haveli* near Amer Fort, this museum displays the craft of block printing, emphasising the revival of this traditional craft from the 1970s onwards. Each of the rooms is devoted to a certain style of fabric block printing. Glass cases exhibit artisan tools, and the different dyes used to achieve colours like indigo, rust and ochre that are characteristic of hand-printed fabrics. Don't miss the display that traces the process of creating a vest from simple bleached cloth to intricately printed finished product. This innovative museum is an arm of the chain of boutique stores of the same name. Visitors can participate in day-long block printing workshops (Rs 800; prior registration required), or make their own block-printed T-shirts for Rs 150. There's a museum shop, and a small café.

Jaigarh Fort

Above Amer Fort, Delhi–Jaipur Highway (0141-263-0848). Open 9am-4.45pm daily. Admission (free with City Palace admission) Rs 20 Indians; Rs 35 others; Rs 50 camera; Rs 150 video camera.

Located 120m (400ft) higher than Amer, on the same hill, the Jaigarh Fort was constructed in 1726 for the security of Amer and Jaipur. Jaigarh (House of Victory) was also believed to be where gold, silver, jewels and other war booty was hoarded. Jaivan, believed to be the world's largest cannon on wheels, is also here. There are fantastic views of the surrounding hills and countryside from the fort.

Nahargarh Fort

6km NW of Jaipur (0141-514-8044). Open 10am-5pm daily. Admission Rs 25 Indians; Rs 45 others; Rs 20 vehicles; Rs 10-Rs 30 camera; Rs 20-Rs 70 video camera.

Nahargarh Fort, which acted as a sentinel for the Amber Fort and Jaipur, offers some breathtaking views of both. Built by Sawai Jai Singh II as a retreat for his wives, the fort was originally called Sudarshangarh, and was later known as Nahargarh, as the ghost of one Prince Nahar Singh had to be appeased. The palace complex has terraces, courtyards and colourful chambers and looks particularly beautiful at night.

MIRZA ISMAIL ROAD, BANI PARK & RAM NIWAS BAGH AREA

Running just south of the Old City is Mirza Ismail Road (MI) Road, a noisy, busy street where many of the city's eating and shopping places are clustered. One kilometre north-west of MI Road is the Bani Park area, where many government offices are located. Ram Niwas Bagh lies immediately south of MI Road and the Old City's Chaura Rasta junction. It consists of large tracts of manicured gardens that are popular with families at weekends, and is also home to the magnificent Albert Hall. South and west of it are the broad avenues of the expanding new city.

Albert Hall/Central Museum

Ram Niwas Bagh, Ashok Nagar (0141-257-0099). Open 10am-4.30pm Tue-Sun. Admission Rs 15 Indians; Rs 100 others.

Housed in the architecturally impressive Albert Hall, the Central Museum was designed by the British architect Sir Swinton Jacob in 1867. The structure of the building draws heavily from existing British models, but the arched verandas and domed pavilions hint at Mughal inspiration. Inside there is an interesting collections of miniatures, clothes and ornamental wooden boxes, in addition to unusual exhibits like old-style dioramas of Rajasthani tribespeople, dances and customs, and tiny clay models of yogis executing *asanas* (yoga poses). There's also an Egyptian collection (including a mummy) and a doll museum on the premises.

Museum of Indology

Ram Niwas Bagh, Ashok Nagar, off Jawaharlal Nehru Marg (0141-260-7455). Open 10am-5pm daily. Admission Rs 20 Indians; Rs 40 others; Rs 9 over-5s; Rs 15 students. No photography allowed.

The Museum of Indology houses the private collection of Acharya Vyakul, a poet and painter. Situated in the Ram Niwas Public Gardens of Jaipur, the collection includes fossils, tribal ornaments, manuscripts (including one written by Emperor Aurangzeb), clocks, old currency, a map of India painted on a grain of rice, 20,000 buttons and the quaint marriage contract of the last Mughal emperor, Bahadurshah Zafar. It also has the largest collection of tantric art in the world. The sheer volume and range of these extraordinary oddities make this place worth a visit. Due to lack of display space, many of the artefacts are crammed into cupboards, until the planned move to larger premises takes place.

Eat

All over Jaipur, restaurants offer Italian, Chinese and Punjabi food. But you're in Japiur, so this is the time to try Rajasthani food. Be warned: it is generally spicy and heavy on ghee. Most restaurants will turn down the heat a few notches for foreigners, but it's better to let staff know just how spicy is too spicy.

Many of the city's best eating places are to be found on MI Road (Mirza Ismail Road), just south of the walled old city.

Chokhi Dhani

19km S of Jaipur *Tonk Road (0141-222-5001/ www.chokhidhani.com). Open noon-3pm, 7-11pm daily. $$. No AmEx. Rajasthani.*

Mention Rajasthani food and you are likely to be directed to Chokhi Dhani, which is essentially a fake village designed to provide tourists with a crash course on Rajasthan. Dinner is a thali meal served in a rural hut by waiters in ethnic Rajasthani garb. Guests sit on the floor, though a few chairs are available. Speak up if you want to prevent the server from dousing your meal with lavish quantities of ghee and powdered sugar. Music and dance performances are also held here; there's a Rs 200 cover charge to enter.

"Visit Dasaprakash for South Indian cuisine that's as easy on your stomach as it is on your wallet."

Dasaprakash

Mirza Ismail Road *Kamal Mansion (0141-237-1313). Open 11am-11pm daily. $. No AmEx. South Indian.*

Visit Dasaprakash for South Indian cuisine that's as easy on your stomach as it is on your wallet. This hygienic little restaurant on MI Road offers popular favourites like *idli* (steamed rice cakes), dosa (rice pancakes) and thalis, as well as unusual variations like *gulliapa*, shallow-fried rice balls with green chillies and onions served with a tasty coconut chutney.

Gulab Mahal

2km SW of Mirza Ismail Road *Taj Jai Mahal Palace, Jacob Road, Civil Lines (0141-222-3636). Open 11.30am-3.30pm, 7-11.30pm daily. $$$$. North Indian/Rajasthani.*

Gulab Mahal's extensive menu and decor are impressive. Tuck into *pyaaz aur boondi ki kadhi* (onion and gram flour-flavoured spicy yoghurt sauce), *murg methi ki bhajia* (chicken rolled in fenugreek leaves and deep fried) and

Clockwise from top left: Lassiwalla; Om Revolving Restaurant; Chokhi Dhani; LMB (2).

Rambagh Palace.

mouth-watering *maas ka soyeta* (lamb on the bone). Expect to feel a strong wave of inertia after a meal here.

Handi Restaurant

Mirza Ismail Road *Opposite General Post Office, Panch Batti (0141-236-4839). Open 11.30am-3.30pm, 7-11.30pm daily. $. No credit cards. North Indian/Rajasthani.*

Handi is about good food and little else, and its menu is the best in town in the budget price bracket. Meats are tender and rotis fresh. Try the *handi maas* (mutton cooked in a clay pot) or *kathi* kebabs.

"At Suvarna Mahal you get to sample old-school cooking, made with the two most important ingredients of Indian cuisine: pure ghee and infinite patience."

Lassiwalla

Mirza Ismail Road *Opposite Niro's (no phone). Open 10am-7pm daily. $. No credit cards.*

Lassiwala is not a restaurant, but something of a Jaipur institution. Decision-making is limited to large or small servings of the sweet, frothy beaten yoghurt drink, served with a dollop of cream in a cone-shaped terracotta container. There are three Lassiwallas opposite Niro's (two of them are parvenus); look for the one with the board that says Kishan Lal Govind Narain Agarwal.

LMB

Old City *Johari Bazaar (0141-256-5844). Open 11.30am-11pm daily. $. Rajasthani.*

LMB (once called Laxmi Mishtan Bhandar) is where locals and tourists crowd on to small tables to gorge on vegetarian Rajasthani food: the *gulab churma* and *bhatti* are particularly famous here. The Rajasthani thali starts off with a *papad mangori* soup (with a slightly sour tang). The thali includes desert classics like *ker sangri* (capers and desert beans), *bela* Rajasthani (dumplings of gram flour in a yoghurt gravy) and *panchmela* (five vegetables of the chef's choice). Three kinds of flat bread are served and the meal is rounded off with *ghewar*, a delicious dessert made from paneer. Schedule nothing but deep sleep afterwards.

Niro's

Mirza Ismail Road *(0141-221-8520). Open 10am-11pm daily. $. Multi-cuisine.*

Don't be fooled into thinking that the extensive Western section on Niro's menu means it serves up a good stroganoff or a decent club sandwich. It doesn't. But it is one of the few places along MI Road where women can swing by for a pint of beer, minus judgemental stares, which is why it's so popular. Stick to kebabs and other Indian fare.

Om Revolving Restaurant

Mirza Ismail Road *Hotel Om Tower, 3 Church Road (0141-236-6683). Open noon-11.30pm daily. $$. No AmEx. North Indian vegetarian.*

Try it simply because it revolves 54m (177ft) above ground, and that's something of a novelty. The food is strictly average Punjabi fare and the ride can get the tiniest bit bumpy, but you do get a magic-carpet view of Jaipur by night. It takes about an hour to complete a revolution, which is about how long it will take you to complete your meal.

Suvarna Mahal

3.5km S of Ram Niwas Bagh *Taj Rambagh Palace, Bhawani Singh Road (0141-221-1919). Open 11.30am-3.30pm, 7-11.30pm daily. $$$$. North Indian.*

Suvarna Mahal comes with all the royal trappings, and then some. Under its Renaissance-frescoed ceilings, liveried waiters present feasts on gold-plated plates, with silver engraved glasses and the finest crystal and china throughout. This fine-dining restaurant at the Taj Rambagh has stellar food from Jaipur as well as Awadh, Mewar, Punjab and Hyderabad. *Koh-e-Awadh* is a mouth-watering preparation of lamb shanks; *maas ke sule* (skewered meat marinated in Rajasthani spices and *kachri* – a berry that's a tenderising agent) is outstanding. Here you get to sample old-school cooking, made with the two most important ingredients of Indian cuisine: pure ghee and infinite patience.

Spice Court

2km SW of MI Road *Jacob Road, Civil Lines (0141-222-0202). Open noon-3.30pm, 7-11pm daily. $$. No AmEx. North Indian/Rajasthani.*

Spice Court serves North Indian food in an alfresco setting accompanied by live music, puppet shows and dance performances. The service is a bit slow, but the food and setting make up for it. There's also an air-conditioned dining room on the premises.

Shopping

Jaipur's bazaars are its USP. A chaotic riot of colour, crowded and loud, they are quintessentially Jaipur. Bargain hunters and those looking to experience a slice of local flavour should walk through Bapu, Johari and Hawa Mahal bazaars. Each sells an assortment of goods, ranging from embroidered leather shoes and silver jewellery to block-printed materials and handicrafts, and are best tackled with comfortable shoes, lots of time and plenty of patience. When planning a shopping trip there are a couple of tips to bear in mind: arrange your retail excursions by neighbourhood; and never go with a guide.

At Bapu Bazaar (Old City, near Chaura Rasta, open 10am-8pm Mon-Sat) multicoloured sheer materials, funky camel-leather *jootis* (traditional flat slip-on sandals) and earthy block-printed materials vie for your attention, as do vendors who are up for a good haggle. This place is an explosion of colour but products don't differ much from store to store. The embroidered camel-skin *jootis*, quilted jackets and belts are good buys.

Hawa Mahal Bazaar (Hawa Mahal, open 10.30am-8pm Mon-Sat) is alive with the possibility of stumbling upon something exquisite at half the price you would pay in a boutique – if you're prepared to spend the better part of your day bargaining. Popular for its fabrics, glass and *lac* (insect resin) bangles, *cholis* (blouses), *lehenga* skirts (long skirts, worn with a *choli*), jewellery and salwar suits, the market also has home furnishings.

A trip to Jaipur would be incomplete without a visit to Johari Bazaar (Old City, near Sanganeri Gate, open 10.30am-8pm Mon-Sat), known for the scores of match box-sized jewellery stores that line its streets. Pieces range from super-sized diamond-, emerald- and ruby-studded *kundan* jewellery (a traditional style, set in precious metals with *lac* and popular as wedding sets) to more modest gold and silver *meenakari* (enamel-work) pieces. Beware of touts trying to sell worthless gems they claim can be resold for many times their price abroad. Bling apart, the stalls hawk fabrics, saris and assorted bric-a-brac.

Those who prefer to shop in boutiques should investigate the shops on Jacob Road, while MI Road has scores of handicraft stores.

"Bunkar is a treasure trove of traditional Rajasthani fabrics. Among the saris and textiles are delicate block-printed cottons and indigo-dyed batik silks."

Anokhi

3km S of MI Road *Second Floor, KK Square, C-11 Prithviraj Road, C-Scheme (0141-400-7244/ www.anokhi.com). Open 9.30am-8pm daily.*

Contemporary design aesthetic meets traditional block-printing textile technique. The look is muted colours, intensive detailing and earthy tones; the garments include *kurtas*, tops, kaftans, trousers and sun dresses for men and women. There are also home furnishings and a limited but exquisite range of ethnic jewellery.

Bunkar

Mirza Ismail Road *Opposite Ajmeri Gate (0141-274-4577). Open 11am-7.30pm Mon-Sat. No AmEx.*

Bunkar (which means weaver) is a treasure trove of traditional Rajasthani fabrics. Among the saris and textiles are delicate block-printed cottons, indigo-dyed batik silks and striped tassar silk weaves, all made using only natural dyes. There is also a reasonably priced range of handbags made from jute and dhurries in earthy colours.

Cottons

3km SW of MI Road *Main Achrol House, Jacob Road (0141-222-3870). Open 10am-8pm Mon-Sat; 10am-6pm Sun. No AmEx.*

All things ethnic get tastefully refined and slightly funkier here. Garments include basic *kurtas*, tunics, tops, skirts and pants in colourful prints embellished with sequins and beads.

Gobindram Ramchand Handicraft Emporium

Mirza Ismail Road *(0141-237-3079). Open 10.30am-8.30pm Mon-Sat. No credit cards*

There's an exhaustive collection of wares on offer at this dusty store. It lacks finesse (no air-conditioning and a grouchy soul behind the counter), but makes up for it with an extensive stash of cheap goodies: trinkets, brass, wooden and beaded jewellery, wind chimes, foot stools, tiffany lamps, vases, blue-pottery doorknobs and ceramic coasters.

Handloom Corporation

Mirza Ismail Road *Opposite Ajmeri Gate (0141-237-1109). Open 10am-5pm Mon-Sat. No credit cards.*

Come here for the superb selection of *ajrakh* (block prints) with sharply etched motifs, in vibrant colours, and *masuriya*, a highly textured sheer cotton fabric woven with designs that mingle geometrical figures, fruits and flowers.

Jaipur Blue Pottery Art Centre

Amer Fort & Around *Amer Fort Road, near Jain Mandir (0141-263-5375). Open 10am-7.30 daily.*

Though Persian in origin, blue pottery is seen as one of Jaipur's traditional crafts. The intricately hand-painted products on offer range from doorknobs, bowls, plates and glasses to 1m-high vases and lamps. Classic designs include deep indigo and cream floral and arabesque patterns.

Kadar Bux

Mirza Ismail Road *Near Rajmandir Cinema, Mall 21. Open 11am-8pm daily. No credit cards.*

This is the store for lightweight yet ultra-warm Jaipur quilts in gorgeous block prints of traditional paisleys or florals, as well as snazzier velvets with bold prints.

Neerja Pottery

3.5km S of MI Road *Shop 19, Bhawani Singh, C Scheme Extension (0141-222-3511). Open 10am-6.30pm Mon-Sat. No AmEx.*

Clockwise from top left: Hawa Mahal bazaar; Johari bazaar; Bapu Bazaar; Neerja Pottery.

Clockwise from top left: Raj Vilas (3); Alsisar Haveli Hotel; Hotel Dera Rawatsar; Hotel Narain Niwas Palace; Rambagh Palace (2).

This garage-store isn't easy to find, but it's worth the search because it puts the traditional art of blue pottery to innovative uses. There are coasters, ashtrays, picture holders, jewellery, frames and mugs in contemporary designs and more unusual colour combinations. Nothing at Neerja Pottery is churned out in a factory; all the pieces are handcrafted by artisans from surrounding villages.

Rajasthali

Mirza Ismail Road *Opposite Ajmeri Gate (0141-510-3329). Open 11am-5pm Mon-Sat. No AmEx.*

This multi-storey handicraft store (one of the better-maintained government initiatives) has a vast collection of bric-a-brac, with pieces ranging from pricey *kundan-*, *meenakari-* and *jadau-*style jewellery to ornamental boxes with Mughal floral motifs that are easier on the wallet. The hand-painted furniture (coffee tables, small cupboards and so on), with depictions of deities and scenes from great Indian epics, is quite lovely; not very travel-friendly, but more than worth the price.

Soma

2km SW of MI Road *5 Jacob Road (0141-222-2778/www.somashop.com). Open 10am-8pm Mon-Sat; 10am-6pm Sun.*

It is with good reason that Soma once made it to the *Forbes* list of the world's top shops. It stocks everything from lamps with shades in floral chintz to photo frames to clothing and bags. Most pieces are one of a kind.

Tholia Kuber

Mirza Ismail Road *Opposite Niro's (0141-237-7416). Open 10.30am-7.30pm Mon-Sat.*

Silver jewellery enthusiasts, be warned: the chances of walking out of this store without a purchase are slim. Very slim. Tholia Kuber is brimming with pieces that range from heavy tribal-influenced necklaces to show-stopping beaten-silver cocktail rings. For those with more contemporary taste, there are armbands, pendants and earrings studded with turquoise, chalcedony, amethyst and rose quartz.

Stay

In Jaipur, lodgings are often old, family-run *havelis* (mansions) of varying levels of upkeep. But even the most run-down of Jaipur's *haveli*-hotels boasts of an impressive driveway, an intimidating dining room filled with pictures of royal princes, and sizeable lawns.

Most accommodation is spread out across Bani Park and Jacob Road, which are bustling residential suburbs in the north-western part of Jaipur. Avoid staying along MI Road; it's noisy and lacks charm.

Alsisar Haveli Hotel

1km NE of Bani Park *Sansar Chandra Road (0141-368-290/www.alsisar.com). $$.*

It's easy to miss the entrance of Alsisar Haveli if you aren't paying attention. The large, fort-like wooden door that leads to this charming *haveli* sits on a noisy main road flanked by stores selling metalware. It doesn't look like the ideal location, but it's peaceful inside. Rooms, most of which overlook the large garden, are clean, airy and filled with wooden antiques such as four-poster beds and armoires. The frangipani-scented courtyards with wrought-iron furniture are great for a lazy breakfast, while the garden, which in season has a carpet of flaming-orange gulmohar flowers, is a nice place to lounge over drinks in the evening.

Barwara Kothi

2km SW of MI Road *5 Jacob Road, Civil Lines (0141-222-2796/www.barwarakothi.com). $$. No AmEx.*

This colonial villa was once the home of Raja Man Singh of Barwara, polo player extraordinaire whose claim-to-fame in Jaipur was that he was the cousin of the maharaja. Evidence of this relationship dot Barwara Kothi's walls in the form of framed, handwritten letters and old black-and-white pictures. That, and a few battle shields and swords in the dining room, add a heritage element to this otherwise sparse family-run homestay. Rooms, which overlook gardens, are large and functionally furnished with all the basic necessities required for a comfortable stay, but not much more. Beverages and meals, served at specific times in the dining room, are strictly average.

"Peacocks play hide-and-seek among Diggi Palace's many gulmohar trees, pigeons flutter about its corridors, and cows placidly chew the cud beside a stable of polo ponies."

Hotel Dera Rawatsar

Bani Park *D194/C, Vijay Path, behind Central Bus Stand (0141-220-6559/www.derarawatsar.com). $$. No AmEx.*

One of the most tasteful budget hotels in Jaipur, Dera Rawatsar falls somewhere between a homestay and a boutique hotel. Suites have comfortable double beds with ethnic linens, large bathrooms with bathtubs, two-seater sofas and leftover space. Most rooms also have private balconies with views of bustling Bani Park. The more expensive rooms replace cotton duvets and drapes with richer silks. Especially nice is the sun-lit lounge area overlooking the pool. It's filled with old leather-bound books, sepia-toned family pictures and curios like an antique brass telephone and treasure chests. Home-style food is available. No room service except for beverages.

Hotel Diggi Palace

2.5km S of MI Road *C Scheme, Shivaji Marg (0141-237-3091/www.hoteldiggipalace.com). $$.*

The largest property in Jaipur, after the Rambagh, is also among its most unpretentious. Peacocks play hide-and-seek among Diggi Palace's many gulmohar trees, pigeons flutter about its painted corridors, while cows placidly chew the cud by a stable of polo ponies. The owners, a charming family who live on the property, grow their own veggies and have a mini-dairy that supplies raw materials for their manure-to-methane gas plant. Accommodation is divided into basic rooms and larger colonial-style cottages that are furnished with ethnic prints and earthy cotton drapes. Deluxe suites have two double beds and a private porch area. In January every year, the peaceful hotel becomes a cultural hub when it plays host to the UNESCO-endorsed international literature festival. For the rest of the year, it remains a peaceful haven where the only sounds one hears are bird calls and the occasional moo of a cow.

"The Taj's Rambagh Palace hotel assaults the senses. Built in 1835 on a modest scale, and later refurbished as a royal guesthouse and hunting lodge, it was given its final opulent makeover in 1925."

Hotel Narain Niwas Palace

1km W of Ram Niwas Bagh *Kanota Bagh, Narain Singh Road (0141-256-1291/www.hotel narainniwas.com). $$. No AmEx.*

Narain Niwas's biggest draw is its charming 1850s feel. The central hall, which was once the dining room, has century-old chandeliers, life-sized portraits of generations past and a runway-like wooden table where large family dinners were once held. More modern additions include a lemon-grass scented spa, a large swimming pool and flat-screen TVs in deluxe suites. Most have brass-studded wooden doors, slightly weathered ceiling paintings and old furniture. Bathrooms are tiled in white with glass shower cabins and bathtubs. It's better to opt for a suite than the now slightly run-down standard rooms. Much of Narain Niwas has the air of an abandoned mansion, which may explain the slight mustiness in some corridors.

Jas Vilas

Bani Park *Jai Singh Highway (0141-220-4638/ www.jasvilas.com). $$. No AmEx.*

Jas Vilas is owned and run by a warm, friendly couple, Mahendra Singh and his wife Lily, who also live here. The reception looks like an airy living room, the kitchen serves home-style meals, and the library – a single glass-fronted wooden cupboard – is full of books with notes left by former residents. Accommodation consists of one suite and 11 pool- and garden-facing rooms that line the paisley-painted corridors. The suite isn't much larger than the standard room but has an enormous bathroom with a turquoise- and indigo-tiled bathtub, an antique brass fan and fountain. Jas Vilas is far from fancy, but it has a rare kind of comfort that comes only from personalised attention and constant care.

Khasa Kothi

Mirza Ismail Road *(0141-237-5151). $$. No AmEx.*

Khasa Kothi has a lovely laid-back atmosphere that is reminiscent of Merchant Ivory films. It's hard to believe that it's on the bustling MI Road. Rooms are basic, clean and frills-free. Along with large verandas, there's also a swimming pool with blue tiles, across a small patch of garden, and a health club on the premises.

Raj Vilas

8km S of Old City *Gonar Road (0141-268-0101/ www.oberoirajvilas.com). $$$$.*

It might look like one of Rajasthan's sprawling historic fort-palaces, but most of it is recently built. Rooms, villas and luxury canvas tents are spread across manicured lawns so getting anywhere is a few minutes' walk or a golf-cart ride away. While rooms aren't decked in bright traditional textiles, there are some nods to the local aesthetic: a flat-screen TV sits on an antique wooden treasure chest that doubles as a table; soap dishes are beaten-brass bowls; and bathrobes have paisley prints on them. High ceilings, dim lighting, intricate Mughal-style murals and ornate embellishments are restricted to the main reception area and restaurants. For the most part, Raj Vilas's friendly rather than formal service and serene surroundings give it a Zen feel.

Rambagh Palace

3.5km S of Ram Niwas Bagh *Taj Rambagh Palace, Bhawani Singh Road (0141-221-1919/ www.tajhotels.com). $$$$.*

The Taj's Rambagh Palace hotel assaults the senses. Built in 1835 on a modest scale, and later refurbished as a royal guesthouse and hunting lodge, it was given its final opulent makeover in 1925 when it became the residence of the Maharaja of Jaipur. From perfectly manicured gardens and two-storey-high Renaissance-style ceilings to games of elephant polo and dinners under many-tiered crystal chandeliers, it is the epitome of indulgence. Attentive service recreates the feeling of Rajputana royalty, with staff attending to guests' every whim and fancy. Its 79 rooms range from suites swathed in silk overlooking the central courtyard, to even more decadent lodgings that boast of domed, gold-flecked ceilings, pink marble bathtubs and armoires laden with mother of pearl. It's hard to imagine that this is a toned-down version of what the palace used to be.

Samode Haveli

Old City *Gangapole (0141-263-2407/ www.samode.com). $$-$$$.*
The urban child of the Samode family of hotels is not as opulent as its other properties, but still manages to retain much of the old-world charm its siblings are known for. The spacious rooms are a mix of old and new. So you're likely to find a leather-and-chrome lamp sitting beside an antique rosewood four-poster bed. Particularly noteworthy is the hand-painted dining hall, with an airy veranda, which serves good Indian and Western fare.

Samode Palace

42km NW of Jaipur *Samode District (01423-240-014/ www.samode.com). $$$.*
In the Aravalli Hills outside Jaipur, Samode Palace is all about old-school luxury. Unlike most other five-star hotels, it does not cut itself off from its surroundings, but makes the most of them. Within its stately walls, the normal five-star formula of ornate drapes, frigid 18-degrees-temperatures and sealed windows are done away with in favour of delicate cotton curtains gently fluttering in the breeze of its corridors. The understated furnishings only bring out the exquisite detailing of its architecture. There are century-old halls full of intricate Mughal mirror-work and terrace and porch areas that make the most of the palace's wonderful views. The infinity pool, which is one of the northernmost points of the palace, is a lovely place to catch the sunset. But what sets Samode apart is that its employees seem genuinely happy and proud to be there. It's a 90-minute drive from Jaipur city, but it's elaborate enough to give the city's monuments a run for their money. A visit here, even simply for a meal, is highly recommended.

Shahpura House

Bani Park *Devi Marg (0141-220-3392/ www.shahpurahouse.com). $$.*
'Heritage' borders on kitsch at Shahpura House. Think silver sofas on century-old carpets surrounded by multi-coloured stained-glass windows, and a *durbar* hall, and you've got a fair idea of what the place is like. The over-the-top decor extends to the hotel's rooms as well, which are done out in vivid green and magenta faux-silk linens and drapes. The older wing showcases the original owner's love for weaponry and polo paraphernalia, while the corridors of the newer wing have frescos that depict scenes from the *Mahabharata* and *Ramayana*.

Factfile

When to go

October to March is the best period to visit Jaipur. It's winter and can get cold, but at night temperatures rarely fall below 8°C. In peak summer months (Apr-July), temperatures can get as high as 40°C, making sightseeing uncomfortable.

Getting there

Jaipur is four hours from Delhi by road, and four and a half hours by the Ajmer Shatabdi train. There are also plenty of direct flights connecting Jaipur to Delhi, Mumbai and other cities in Rajasthan.

Getting around

Auto-rickshaws are available, as are cycle-rickshaws (for short distances within the main city). Private taxis, booked for the day, are the most convenient way of negotiating all the sights.

Tourist information

The Rajasthan Tourist Information Office is on MI Road (Tourist Hotel, 0141-511-0598, open 9am-6pm Mon-Fri). There's also a Tourist Counter at the airport (0141-272-2647, open 6am-7pm Mon-Sat) and at the railway station (0141-231-5714, open 7am-10pm daily).

Internet

It's easy to find an internet café almost anywhere in Jaipur city.

Tips

- It may sometimes seem as if everyone is out to part you from your money in Jaipur. It is one of the Rajasthan destinations where tourists get most harassed. Keep calm and learn to say a firm 'no' to services that you don't want.
- To avoid the stress of constantly haggling for everything, hire a car and driver, and a guide from a reputable operator, instead of picking up auto-rickshaws and guides from outside monuments.
- Unless you don't mind paying a lot more than you should for your purchases, venture out shopping on your own.
- At least six major festivals are celebrated in Jaipur; particularly interesting is the Elephant Festival usually held in March.

Jodhpur

A walled city at the foot of a magnificent fort.

Jodhpur epitomises all that is royal about Rajasthan. From the massive, recently restored hilltop fort of Mehrangarh on one side, to the majestic and opulent Umaid Bhawan Palace on the other, the city exemplifies the spirit of the Marwar region, a spirit forged in the heat of the desert and on a thousand bloody battlefields. In between these sandstone edifices is the sprawling Blue City, with its innumerable alleyways, bazaars and indigo-tinted houses. Founded as a fortress by Rao Jodha, chief of the Rathore clan, in 1459, Jodphur lies in the heart of the Thar desert. His original fort witnessed the growth and prosperity of the clan, and the expansion of its territory.

Modern Jodhpur, Rajasthan's second-largest city, lives in the present, but its past is never far away. It's home to a thriving and vibrant culture. Here, every turban tells a story – there's meaning in their colour, or the way they're worn. In its markets, streets of fruits and vegetables give way to others full of spices, textiles, bangles and jewellery. And if you should get lost – which is easy enough to do in a place where every street winds and turns and street signs are few and far between – just look for the immense Mehrangarh Fort and the Clock Tower. These city landmarks can be used to make logistical sense of a complex and confusing urban space.

Middle: Umaid Bhawan Palace. Bottom left: Old City Bazaar. Bottom right: Mandore Gardens.

Explore

Mehrangarh Fort, north of the city, towers over Jodhpur. At its base lies Brahmapuri, the Old City. Here, winding narrow streets without street signs make navigation and getting to your destination a feat. The walled Old City has eight gates, of which Jalori Gate and Sojati Gate in the south are the most important; the busiest commercial centres surround them. The new city expands to the south and east of the Old City, while Umaid Bhawan lies further off in the east, and Mandore and Balsamand are on the northern outskirts.

MEHRANGARH FORT

This rugged, burnished red sandstone fortress, standing on sheer cliffs rising 122 metres (400 feet) above Jodhpur city, was built in 1459 by the founder of Jodhpur, Rao Jodha. It was added on to and modified by successive Rathore kings. Recent and still-ongoing restoration on a massive scale has ensured that the fort remains Rajasthan's most stunning. Along the winding road that leads up to the fort are seven gates (pols). Jai Pol is the main entrance and Suraj Pol leads to the palace, now a museum run by the Mehrangarh Museum Trust.

Walking along the battlements connecting the main fort to its southernmost tip gives one a bird's eye view of the Blue City. Old cannons dot the battlements, and at the fort's southernmost end lies the Chamunda Devi Temple, dedicated to the Goddess Durga.

Mehrangarh Fort Palace & Museum

0291-254-8790/www.mehrangarh.org. Open 9am-5.15pm daily. Admission Rs 30 Indians, Rs 150 audio guide; Rs 300 others, includes audio guide; Rs 15 elevator; Rs 75 camera; Rs 200 video camera.

For over 500 years, until the Umaid Bhawan Palace was built in the 20th century, Mehrangarh was home to the Rathore royal family. As rugged as the fort is on the outside, the palace is elegant inside; in particular, notice the exquisitely carved *jharokhas* (balconies), with *jali* (lattice-work) screens. The lattice openings on the *jali* windows point downward to the courtyard, to make it difficult for anyone to look up at the maharanis, who could look out from above. The room known as the **Moti Mahal** (Pearl Palace) has a majestic marble coronation seat upon which all the rulers of Jodhpur have been crowned, and 19th-century carved woodwork. Alcoves on the walls once held oil lamps – their lights would be reflected in the mirrored ceiling. Ceilings and walls still retain glass tiles, along with gold paint.

The **Phool Mahal** (Flower Palace) is one of the most opulent rooms in the palace. It was a dancing hall for the maharajas' entertainment and, at times, a durbar (royal court). All the outstanding paintings on the walls are the work of one artist. All the stained glass in the windows is Belgian, and the ceiling is lined with gold – 80 kilogrammes (177 pounds) of it.

The palace galleries display a fine collection of palanquins, *howdahs* (carriages that sit on top of an

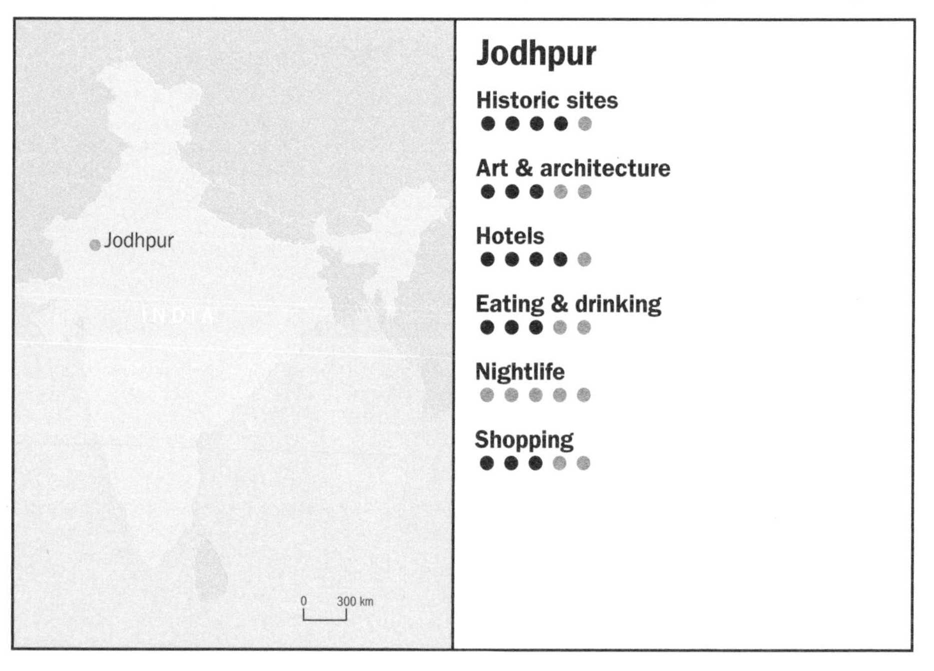

elephant) and royal cradles (including the one that current Maharaja of Jodhpur, HH Gaj Singh, slept in and the only motorised one). There are also small collections of traditional Rajasthani jewellery, weapons (in the *sileh khana* or armoury), paintings and other treasures. **Takhat Vilas**, the heavily decorated private room of Maharaja Takhat Singh (1843-73), is filled with intricate Ras Leela miniatures; notice the Christmas balls hanging from the ceiling.

The Mehrangarh audio guide (1 hour 20 minutes) gives visitors a chance to listen to the voices of three generations of Marwar's royalty. Chances are that the royal eulogies will get to you, but the guide is well organised so you can easily skip the extras and return to the main narrative. The museum shop is probably the best in India, and the small café (Café Mehran) is where you can relax and hydrate after all that walking.

Each year the fort hosts the Rajasthan International Folk Festival (www.jodhpurfolkfestival.org), a five-day music festival that showcases traditional Rajasthani musicians alongside folk musicians from around the world. It's promoted by the current maharaja, has Mick Jagger as patron, and a line-up that is usually pretty impressive; performances are often held in the fort's Zenana Courtyard.

Jaswant Thada

Open 9am-5.30pm daily. Admission Rs 15 Indians; Rs 30 others; Rs 25 camera; Rs 50 video camera.

On the way up the winding road to Mehrangarh Fort is a white marble cenotaph, a memorial to Maharaja Jaswant Singh II (1878-95). Jaswant Thada, also known as the 'Taj Mahal of Marwar', is a marble memorial to the king who was credited with purging Jodhpur of dacoits (bandits), initiating and developing irrigation systems and boosting the economy. Ashes of the royal family from his time onwards also rest here. Like the fort, this cenotaph has been restored to its former splendour. Inside, the marble is translucent and so fine in places that it admits a diffused yellow sunlight.

CHITTAR HILL AND UMAID BHAWAN PALACE

Perched on the top of Chittar Hill, the Umaid Bhawan Palace can be divided into three distinct parts. Most of it houses the super-luxury hotel run by the Taj group (*see p130*); then there's the residence of HH Gaj Singh; and, finally, a small palace museum, the only area open to the public.

Built as part of a 15-year-long famine-relief exercise that kept over 3,000 employed, this over-the-top palace is at once awesome, magnificent and breathtaking. Made of yellow sandstone (*chittar*), it was commissioned in 1929 by Maharaja Umaid Singh of Jodhpur, and initially called Chittar Palace. Originally with 347 rooms, it's one of the largest residences ever built. It was designed by Edwardian architect Henry Lanchester and the interior artwork, including Throne Room frescoes and murals near the subterranean swimming pool, were painted by Stefan Norblin, an expat Polish artist. Umaid Bhawan's architecture displays some varied influences – from ancient Indian temples and Buddhist *chaityas* (prayer halls) to the European Renaissance (there's a Renaissance-style cupola at its centre). Interiors are fashioned in the dominant art deco style of the period. Most impressive is the subterranean swimming pool with its striking mosaic of the 12 signs of the zodiac. Ostensibly, it was built underground so the maharanis could take a swim in privacy. Acres of lawns, where a large number of resident peacocks roam, are well maintained.

Unfortunately, members of the public can only gain access to the super-exclusive palace hotel if they are staying here, or if they shell out Rs 3,000 to enter the premises and dine at one of the restaurants (the entry fee is set against your bill).

Umaid Bhawan Palace Museum

Open 9am-5pm daily. Admission Rs 15 Indians; Rs 50 others.

The palace museum has numerous family portraits and photographs of royals, a selection of their crockery, clocks and watches, and a model of the palace.

BRAHMAPURI – THE BLUE CITY

From the Mehrangarh Fort, the sprawl of blue houses at the foot of the hill looks picture-postcard perfect. Stories about why the city is blue are numerous. Some say indigo acts as a mosquito repellent, others believe it was originally a caste marker for Brahmin families. It is also argued that indigo was used because it retains its fresh colour longer than whitewash; another theory is that indigo was used simply as it's soothing to the eye.

Brahmapuri – the Old City or Blue City – has eight gates and around 100 bastions. You definitely need a good guide to take you around. Along the way you may spot the Taleti Mahal, a 17th-century palace that was built for concubines, and Raikabagh Palace and Jubilee buildings, used as public offices. The latter two draw elements from traditional Hindu and Islamic architecture, and combine it with the Gothic-revival style favoured in Victorian England, intended, perhaps, both to convey a sense of royal power and to intimidate subjects into submission. If you really want to stretch those calf muscles, you can seek out the 19th-century Kunjebehari Temple, a Vaishnava temple built of Makrana stone with some interesting sculpture, huge pillars and paintings. It's close to the Raj Mahal garden palace, near Gulab Sagar to the east of the fort.

The Clock Tower is one of the city's most well-known structures; use it as a landmark when you get lost among the winding lanes. All the little alleys radiating from the Clock Tower are packed with stores selling everything from rice to jewellery. It's where the locals shop, and most of it is a dense mêlée of bodies, bicycles, motorbikes, auto-rickshaws, cars and animal-drawn carts.

MANDORE

Mandore, nine kilometres north of Jodhpur, is the former capital of Marwar. Mandore Gardens (open 8am-8pm) are somewhat spoiled by the detritus of its many Indian visitors, and also overrun by *langurs* (black-faced monkeys),which are enthusiastically and regularly fed by visitors. Set around the former cremation ground of Rathore rulers, its main attraction is the dark red sandstone *chhatris* (cenotaphs), whose size and grandeur are proportionate to the prosperity of the kingdom. Largest is Maharajadhiraj Ajit Singh's *chhatri*, which looks almost like a Shaivite temple, with its towering roof crowned by the four faces of Shiva. The 17th-century chhatri of Maharajadhiraj Jaswant Singh is also impressive, with an octagonal pavilion, vast dome and huge pillars with sculptures of Krishna and the gopis (cowherd girls).

Near to the Mandore Gardens is the Hall of Heroes and Divinities, a series of life-sized gods and local heroes hewn out of rock in the early 18th century. It has all the merits of spectacular kitsch, from which one can comfortably abstain.

Relatively unknown are the Panch Kund cenotaphs (near Mandore Goofa and the Bal Samand Lake Palace Hotel, *see p128*). These are often considered less important than the Mandore centotaphs, but are in fact absolutely fabulous. Set in a remote location, there are dozens of unmarked domed tombs with none of the crowds associated with Mandore Gardens. They are especially beautiful just before sunset. Visitors can wander through the cenotaphs, sit, meditate or just watch the light change the colour of the sandstone monuments as the sun slowly disappears.

Bal Samand Lake Palace Garden

Mandore Road. Open 9am-5pm daily. Admission Rs 500.

This serene lake and garden on the outskirts of the city is a peaceful oasis if you want a little time away from the hustle of Indian towns. Enter via a long, tree-lined driveway leading to the *chhatris* overlooking the delightful Bal Samand Lake, created over a thousand years ago. Guava, lime, pomegranate, *amla* (Indian gooseberry) and spice orchards cover large parts of the extensive property. These gardens are a magnet for a variety of birds, many of which, like the very vocal peacocks, are permanent residents. Countless varieties of flowers and large banyan, gulmohur and laburnum trees are another part of the appeal here. There's also a dog cemetery, an aqueduct and an abandoned and overgrown stepwell (wells reached via a series of steps) on the premises. Only guests at the hotel (*see p128*) are allowed to visit the stable of gorgeous Marwari horses, which have distinct ears that curve inwards so the tips almost touch. This hardy, indigenous breed of horse holds pride of place in Rajasthan, was used in royal battles and more recently in that favourite royal sport, polo.

Eat

While the high-end Umaid Bhawan Hotel (*see p130*) is the only place you'll find anything approaching haute cuisine, there are plenty of places to sample traditional Rajasthani or North Indian food – although they may offer little in the way of ambience. Others that offer atmosphere and service fall short with the food.

Jodhpur is famous for its speciality snacks such as *mirchi vada* (a disembowelled chilli covered in mashed potato, dipped in gram flour and deep fried), sweets like *mawa kachori* (deep-fried flour balls stuffed with sweetened cardamom-infused evaporated milk solids), other desserts and lassis. Shri Mishrilal (0291-254-0049) at the Clock Tower is where you can get many of these sweet and savoury specialities. Agra Sweet Home (0291-325-3238) on C Road in Paota and Rawat Mishtan Bhandar (0291–262-2903) on Station Road are also good choices.

Green Court Garden restaurant

2km S of Mehrangarh Fort *Nimhera House, Mandore Road, Paota (0291-255-6654/www.marvelumed.com). Open 7am-11pm daily. $. No AmEx. Multi-cuisine.*

Located in the Marvel Umed hotel, this restaurant has garden seating in the evening (after 7pm). In the daytime when it's too hot to sit outside, food is served in the banquet room at the rear of the property. Ignore the characterless decor and get to the food, which is good. Service is attentive and while most dishes aren't really spicy, the kitchen will cut the level of chilli on request. For a simple meal nothing beats the *palak paneer* (spinach with Indian cottage cheese) and dal, mopped up with delicious rotis or naans hot off the tandoor.

Kebabs Korner

Mandore *Bal Samand Palace Hotel, Mandore Road (0291-257-2321). Open 7.30-11.45pm daily. $$. Indian barbeque.*

In the sprawling grounds of the Bal Samand Palace, Kebabs Korner has a great outdoor location and ambience. Live kebab counters are set up each evening and guests can watch the chefs at work a few feet from their tables. Service is attentive and prompt. However, the kebabs tend to be rather dry and mediocre, which is sad given the atmospheric setting.

Mehran Terrace

Mehrangarh Fort *(0291-254-9790). Open 7-10.30pm daily (reservations required). $$. Rajasthani and North Indian kebabs.*

With a spectacular location on the ramparts of Mehrangarh Fort, this outdoor restaurant has only one drawback: you have to stand up to take in the fabulous views of Jodhpur city. The limited but adequate menu includes a small selection of kebabs and Rajasthani thalis, beer and wine. The vegetarian or non-vegetarian thalis are the best bet if you want variety, and the kebabs make good starters or

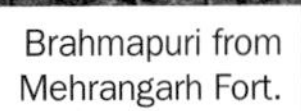

Brahmapuri from Mehrangarh Fort.

Clockwise from top: Kebabs Korner; The Pillars; Mehran Terrace.

light meals. Dining under the stars in this magnificently restored fort is a delight, service is good and prompt and the food well made and quite delicious.

Mid Town

4km S of Mehrangarh Fort *Shanti Bhawan Lodge, opposite railway station (0291-263-7001). Open 7am-10.30pm daily. $$. No credit cards. Rajasthani.*
Mid Town is well known for its Rajasthani fare. Try the Rajasthani Maharaja thali with *chakki ki sabzi* (steamed balls of wholewheat dough cooked in a spicy gravy), *panchkuta* (a mixture of five desert berries, leaves and spices cooked together), *mirchi vada* and a variety of other traditional foods. For those willing to experiment, there is also a Rajasthani paneer pizza, with a base made from millet flour.

On the Rocks

4km SE of Mehrangarh Fort *Outside Ajit Bhawan, Circuit House Road (0291-510-2701/510-7880). Open noon-11pm daily. $$. Visa only. Multi-cuisine.*
On the Rocks is not just one restaurant, but a clutch of them. Besides OTR, there's Rocktails – a part-enclosed, part open-air bar and nightclub – and a small bakery section as well. The main restaurant has a nice outdoor garden setting, even if it's a little worn around the edges. Food is hit and miss, but you probably won't go wrong if you order dal *makhani,* any one of the chicken kebabs or the chicken with cashew and saffron with *misi* rotis or garlic naans. Be aware that it can get quite loud at night.

Pal Haveli Terrace restaurant

Brahmapuri *Gulab Sagar (0291-329-3328/www.palhaveli.com). Open 7-10.30am, 5-11pm daily. $$. Rajasthani.*
The terrace restaurant in this 180-year-old *haveli* in the Blue City overlooks Gulab Sagar Lake (a pond really), which is rather dull by day, but has 30m (100ft) fountains and is lit at night. More than anything, this is a fine place from which to watch busy streetlife and the sun disappearing behind Mehrangarh Fort, while you sip a Kingfisher beer. Food is mostly unexceptional North Indian fare, though the kitchen sometimes does Rajasthani specials from old heirloom recipes.

The Pillars

Umaid Bhawan Palace *(0291-251-0101/www.tajhotels.com). Open 6.30am-11pm daily. $$$. Multi-cuisine coffee shop.*
The Pillars has far the best ambience for a sumptuous breakfast or coffee in all Jodhpur, and is certainly the spot to be at sunset. Peacocks walk right up to your table if you are there early enough in the morning, or you can see them dance in the distance as you gaze out on to the manicured lawns and the city and fort beyond. Note that there is a stiff cover charge of Rs 3,000 for non-guests to eat here (this amount is set against your food bill), which staff are careful to mention before seating you or when you make a reservation. Ask for the unusual smoked *chaas* (thin, savoury yoghurt drink); it's a tasty and super-refreshing beverage, particularly on a hot day. You will find all sorts of sandwiches, pasta and snacks on the menu, and, after 7pm, dinner as well. But it's really all about the romantic and regal setting.

Priya

2km S of Mehrangarh Fort *Just outside Blue City's Sojati Gate, 181-182 Nai Sarak (0291-254-7463). Open 6am-midnight daily. $. No credit cards. North Indian.*
This corner restaurant is where the locals eat, and if you're in the neighbourhood, stop by for a yummy paratha. They make a filling breakfast or snack, served with yoghurt and a spicy Indian *achaar* (a heavily spiced relish).

Shop

Jodhpuri *jootis* (flat camel or sheepskin slip-on sandals), colourful textiles and clothing, jewellery and metal artefacts are just some of the vast array of Jodhpur's consumables. Nai Sarak (New Road) leads through Sojati Gate to the biggest shopping thoroughfare and then to the market area, Sadar Bazaar, at the base of the Clock Tower that marks the centre of Jodhpur. While exploring the streets of the Old City radiating out from the Clock Tower, you will come across all kinds of goods on sale. For spices (most of them acquired from out of the state) walk the streets to the west of the Clock Tower; for bangles, head to the Lakhara area.

"Silk embroidery, appliqué and filigree work, zardozi bedspreads, wall hangings and silver artefacts – the selection is mind-boggling."

Two other areas of the city are marked by shops that cater specially to tourists, often with prices to match. Along the road leading up to the Umaid Bhawan Palace are several large warehouse-like stores such as Maharani (*see p128*), selling everything from tiny souvenirs to antiques, oversized statues and furniture. Outside the Ajit Bhawan hotel (*see p128*), several upmarket stores sell better-quality goods than you'll find in Sadar Bazaar, no doubt for a price that's significantly higher. Anokhi and Tulsi for clothing and Amrapali and Gems and Art for jewellery are all worth a look. Throughout Jodhpur, very few stores have fixed prices and price tags, and bargaining is a way of life.

Maharani Art Exporters

Brahmapuri *Tambaku Bazaar, near Clock Tower (0291-325-5943). Open 9.30am-8.30pm daily.*

Fabric-lovers will be bowled over by the variety of rich fabrics in this multi-level store. Silk embroidery, appliqué and filigree work, zardozi bedspreads, wall hangings, as well as some silver artefacts – the selection is mind-boggling. Little wonder, then, that this is a favourite among Western designers, who sometimes come and spend a whole day here. Those who bring their own designs can have garments stitched for a fraction of what it costs at home. Having said that, nothing in the store has a marked price and the attending salesman quotes what he thinks he can get out of a customer. They are savvy about prices overseas and shoppers need to bargain hard. Maharani also has a massive store near Umaid Bhawan, rather messily stacked with wooden, marble and brass artefacts, furniture and a smaller selection of fabric.

Mehrangarh Museum Shop

Mehrangarh Fort *(0291-255-0410). Open 9am-8pm daily.*

This trendy little museum shop has nice Mehrangarh Fort souvenir T-shirts and playing cards and an assortment of gift items. There's an interesting selection of books and some modish jewellery on sale. Best of all is the collection of intricate miniature paintings available in two price ranges, those done by students (Rs 1,000-Rs 10,000) and by skilled artists (Rs 5,000-Rs 75,000).

Rajasthan Textile Development Corporation

4km S of Mehrangarh Fort *Maharaha Gah Sigh Vishram Bhawan, Rai Ka Bagh. Open 9am-8pm daily.*

One of the few stores in Jodhpur where prices are not flexible. It's stocked with colourful wall hangings, Indian garments and saris, block-printed bed sheets, quilts, carpets and handicrafts. All of this is of variable quality, so select carefully. The sheepskin *jootis* are softer on the feet than the normal camel-hide ones, but they do smell pretty strong. There's also some jewellery, *lac* bangles and numerous other reasonably priced knick-knacks that make good gifts.

Stay

Ajit Bhawan

4.5km SE of Mehrangarh Fort *Circuit House Road (0291-251-3333/251-0410/www.ajitbhawan.com). $$$.*

Though touted as a palace hotel, none of the guestrooms are actually in the palace, which is next door. Rooms, which were renovated in 2008, are in a village-style block of cottages, each featuring a heritage element in its decor. These range from peacock-carved wooden headboards to bedside lamps made from real battle helmets. The heavily textured walls and colour co-ordination go a bit too far sometimes. Rooms have enormous, gleaming modern bathrooms with top-notch fittings and aromatic Forest Essentials toiletries. Silk furnishings are courtesy of the owner's designer son Raghavendra Rathore. There are plenty of sitting areas, large well-kept lawns with pretty, trimmed bougainvillea, a nice, if noisy, pool and a garage full of vintage cars to gawk at. Service, however, can be a bit on the rough side, especially given the price.

Bal Samand Palace & Bal Samand Garden Retreat

Mandore *Mandore Road (0291-257-2321-27/ www.welcomheritagehotels.com). $$-$$$.*

Bal Samand Palace and Bal Samand Garden Retreat occupy the same amazing property, but offer distinctly different accommodation. Palace suites, in the Bal Samand Palace, overlooking the lake, have massive rooms with colonial furniture and exquisite furnishings. Pick a room that opens on to the attractive garden, where you can be served breakfast. The lake-facing terrace is a perfect spot to catch the sunset. Garden rooms at the Garden Retreat, previously the palace stables, cost half the money and are unexceptional, with small, cramped bathrooms. The real USP of this place, however, is the serene lake, the orchard-filled grounds and the stable of handsome Marwari horses. Guests can also enjoy a ride in a horse-drawn carriage, putting and pitching on the nine-hole golf course and much peace and quiet – except for the regular wailing call of the grounds' numerous peacocks. A little-known path leads from the palace to Mehrangarh Fort, along which riding enthusiasts can take one of the hotel's horses.

Devi Bhawan

2.5km south of Mehrangarh Fort *Ratanada Circle, Defence Laboratory Road (0291-251-2215/ 98280-35359/www.devibhawan.com). $.*

This quiet *haveli* is an extension to an old residence and is worth staying at if only for the lush, atmospheric garden with a lotus pond and small, inviting pool. Manager Rakesh takes the business of hospitality seriously and it's hard to believe the personalised service that comes at such economical rates. Clean, basic rooms (semi-deluxe are nicer than the deluxe) and comfortable outdoor sitting areas in the serene well-kept garden, which attracts much bird life, make this a good choice if you're on a budget.

Raas Haveli

Brahmapuri *Tanwarji Ka Jhalra, Makrana Mohalla, Umed Chowk Road (96942-37859/ www.raasjodhpur.com). $$$. No AmEx.*

Though this brand new boutique hotel was a few months from opening at the time of going to press, it deserves a mention because of its fabulous location in the heart of the Blue City, and its unrivalled views. Carved out of an original *haveli*, Raas is a sophisticated blend of traditional Jodhpuri and contemporary design. Judging from the attention to detail in the design and decor, owner Nikhilendra Singh looks set to create a classy operation, something missing in Jodhpur's accommodation scene. Particularly impressive are the hand-chiselled stone panels that adorn the walls in each room and the attractive black

Top: Old City bazaar.
Bottom: Maharani Art Exporters (2).

Top: Ajit Bhawan (3). Middle: Umaid Bhawan Palace (3). Bottom: Devi Bhawan (3).

terrazzo floor tiles. Best of all is the fact that all but four of the 39 rooms and suites overlook Mehrangarh Fort. It also forms the backdrop for the alfresco poolside restaurant. Refurbished auto-rickshaws have been painted blue and specially remodelled to take guests around the Blue City – an excellent idea since it's impossible to drive a car through many of the walled city's lanes.

Ratan Vilas

4km S of Mehrangarh Fort *Loco Shed Road, near Bhaskar Circle, Ratanada (0291-261-4418/ www.ratanvilas.com). $-$$. No AmEx.*

Ten minutes from the bustling centre of town, just off a busy street, a long driveway leads to the surprisingly tranquil Ratan Vilas *haveli*. This is a very well-maintained, value-for-money option, with highly personalised service. It's owned and run by the friendly, welcoming Brijraj Singh and his wife Namrata. Ratan Vilas received a makeover in mid 2009 and there are plans for other upgrades and extensions. Rooms have old colonial teak furniture. Deluxe rooms, which cost only a little more, have large bathrooms with tubs and strong showers. Rooms are comfortable and pleasant, but neither luxurious nor high on amenities, though some do have televisions. If you like peace and quiet it's a good idea to ask for a room on a higher floor, or away from the very pleasant but busy courtyard restaurant, which is a great place to hang out. Home-style Indian food with toned-down spiciness is served buffet-style either indoors or outdoors. There's a well-kept garden and cosy sitting areas where the family's friendly dog Mallet may keep you company. The free airport or station pick-up is a nice plus.

Umaid Bhawan Palace

Umaid Bhawan Palace *(0291-251-0101/www.taj hotels.com). $$$$.*

If you want to experience royal life in a royal residence, look no further than this opulent art deco palace. Its romantic ambience has attracted celebrities from Liz Hurley, who was famously married here in 2007, to Madonna, who occupied the Maharani suite and dined in the Baradari pavilion at the far end of the bougainvillea-filled gardens. Unmatched service is provided by red-turbaned staff who treat guests as if they are the personal company of the maharaja: they'll anticipate your every move and call ahead to wherever you're headed in the hotel, so members of the staff are waiting to attend to your needs. All the historical suites have balconies with lovely views, impeccable bathrooms with Molton Brown toiletries, and many little luxuries and thoughtful touches. The opulent Maharaja and Maharani suites are humungous multi-room art deco residences, which come with a personal butler and a first-class list of amenities. The indoor pool is visually stunning if a little cold; it's intentionally kept at that temperature, as heating it damages the heritage art on the walls. The outdoor pool has views of Mehrangarh Fort. This multi award-winning hotel is at the top of the scale for an over-the-top regal, formal experience.

Factfile

When to go

November to February is the best and coolest time to visit Jodphur, though visitors tend to flock here from early October onward. The summer months (March to July) are blisteringly hot; Jodphur is in the middle of the Thar Desert, after all.

Getting there

Jodhpur is conveniently connected by air to Delhi, Mumbai, Udaipur and Jaipur. There are also good train connections from Jaipur, Delhi and Mumbai.

For more on travel within India, *see p378* **Navigating India**.

Getting around

Much of the Old City can only be traversed on foot or by auto-rickshaw. Mehrangarh Fort can be reached by car, as well as on foot. To reach most other places, and for travel outside the city to Mandore and other destinations, it's best to hire a private taxi.

Tourist information

Rajasthan Tourism Development Corporation Hotel Ghoomar, High Court Road (0291-254-5083). Open 10am-5pm Mon-Fri.

Travel tips

- **Guides and drivers** may try to get you to shop at stores that give them a hefty commission. While some recommendations can be good, be wary and compare prices before you buy.

- **Touts and other con artists** tend to hang around the road leading up to Mehrangarh Fort during peak season, so be wary of any 'free' services that you may be offered.

- **Most shops don't have marked prices** and quoted prices will vary according to how much the salesman thinks he can extract from you. Don't let fast-talking salesmen avoid giving you prices until you have spent so much time and energy looking at his wares that you feel obliged to buy. If the price isn't right, don't hesitate to bargain or to leave if you think you are being had.

Clockwise from top: Bara Imambara Complex (2); Chhota Imambara; the Residency; tomb of Saadat Ali.

Lucknow

Cultural refinement and sophisticated Awadhi cuisine.

Lucknow's residents favour three words to describe their local culture: *tehzeeb* (etiquette), *nafasat* (refinement) and *nazakat* (delicacy). *Pehle aap* (you first) is a way of life for the well-mannered citizens of this city, where Hindus and Muslims have lived side by side for centuries, sharing common cultural traits and customs.

Lucknow's status reaches far beyond that earned as capital of India's most populous state, Uttar Pradesh. It built a lofty reputation for itself during the era of the Mughal nawabs – the mid 18th to mid 19th centuries – as a place of sophistication and refinement, a centre of Indo-Persian art and culture. It was during the reign of Nawab Asaf-ud-Daulah that some of Lucknow's most striking monuments, such as the magnificent *imambaras*, were built. Succeeding nawabs ignored prosaic matters such as administration and focused instead on promoting art, music, calligraphy, Urdu literature and poetry, and cuisine. The nawabs considered their kitchens the crowning glory of their palaces. When the deposed nawab Wajid Ali Shah was exiled by the British to Calcutta in 1856, it is said that he took an entourage of cooks numbering in the hundreds with him. To this day, Lucknavis are devoted to food, and no visitor can leave without sampling the city's extraordinary cuisine.

The weight of modern life has taken its toll on Lucknow. Yet remnants of its former grandeur remain, both in physical form in its monuments and in its old-fashioned charm.

Explore

Lucknow is built along the Gomti river, and is an easy city to explore. The Husainabad area in the north-west houses most of the city's monuments and historic buildings, many now crumbling. East of this is the Residency area, along with Qaiserbagh and the busy Hazratganj area. South-east of these is where you will find La Martinière and the Dilkusha Gardens. Though the city is spread out, all these areas are easily accessible and don't require too much travel time.

OLD LUCKNOW

Numerous monuments are scattered around Old Lucknow, many in need of restoration and repair. The most important are the *imambaras*, built by Shiite Muslims as places to congregate and, especially, to commemorate the death of Imam Hussain, son-in-law of the Prophet Muhammad, during Muharram. Most *imambaras* were also used as burial places for the nobility.

A short distance to the north-west of the imposing Bara Imambara is the breathtaking arched Rumi Darwaza (Turkish Gate), said to be modelled on a gateway in old Constantinople. This 18-metre (60-foot) arched gateway has ornate designs, with stylised flower buds projecting outwards, through which little fountains of water once flowed. It was built by Asaf-ud-Daulah in 1784 under a charitable food-for-work programme, instituted at a time of famine that had driven people from the countryside into the city. East of the Rumi Darwaza is the Husainabad Clock Tower, a 67-metre (221-foot) Victorian tower erected in 1887. Nearby is the Picture Gallery (open sunrise-sunset, admission RS 100 or free with Bara Imambara entry), which displays life-sized portraits of all the nawabs of Awadh. To the west is the Chhota Imambara or Husainabad Imambara. Next to it is the sandstone Jami Masjid (mosque) begun by Muhammad Ali Shah in 1839. It stands on a square terrace and is decorated with coloured stucco motifs and two minarets. Three pear-shaped high double-domes top the prayer hall. Unfortunately, unless you are Muslim you can only admire the building from the outside.

Bara Imambara Complex

Husainabad *Open 7.30am-5.30pm daily. Admission Rs 25 Indians; Rs 300 others. Guide for Bhul Bhulaiya Rs 75.*

The **Bara Imambara** is the central monument of the complex, and Lucknow's grandest. Construction was begun by Nawab Asaf-ud-Daulah as a relief measure during the famine of 1784, and continued for 15 years. It is said that after workers had toiled during the day, noblemen would be hired to undo their work at night, so that the work could continue for longer than necessary. Workers were paid in food, cooked in community kitchens, from where – it is believed – the *dum pukht* (slow-oven) style of cooking emerged.

Two triple-arched gateways lead to the main courtyard. To the east is the **Asafi Mosque**, which is a grand building in its own right, capped with three domes and two minarets.

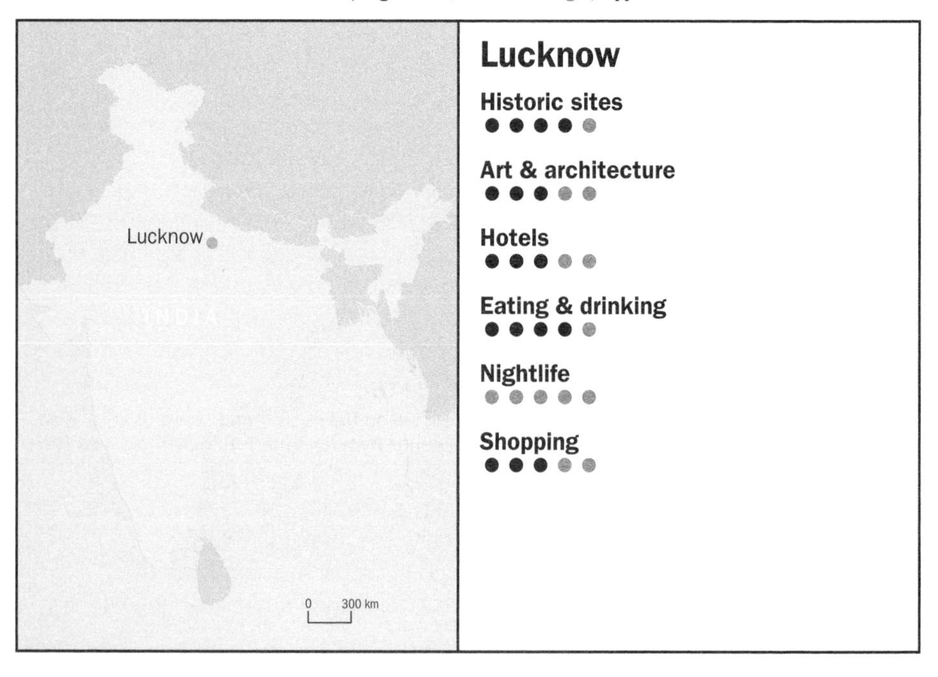

The exterior of the Imambara is decorated with calligraphy and adorned with latticework parapets and *chhatris* (canopied pavilions); the interior contains chandeliers, *tazias* (miniature mausoleums) and other objects. The three-storey main building is constructed on a raised platform and has three halls – the central hall flanked on either side by the Chinese and Indian halls. The huge central hall is a stupendous feat of engineering. It is totally unsupported by pillars, and the 15m (49ft) arched roof has neither beams nor girders for support. The tomb of Asaf-ud-Daulah and that of the monument's architect, Kifayatullah, lie here.

A hidden staircase leads to the top floor **Bhul-Bhulaiya**, a labyrinth of passages with 489 identical balconies. A guide is essential to explore this maze and its unique acoustics. Originally built to support the massive weight of the vaulted roof of the halls below it, it is now mainly associated with the mystery surrounding the lost treasures of the nawabs.

Another intriguing part of the complex is a five-storey *baoli* (step well – two storeys are above the water, three below), also known as the *shahi-hammam* (royal bath), which lies at the western end.

Chhota Imambara/ Husainabad Imambara

Husainabad *Open 7.30am-5.30pm daily. Admission Rs 10.*

Husainabad Imambara, also known as the Chhota Imambara, is much smaller and more tranquil than the Bara Imambara, which lies to its south. In front of the main gateway is a crumbling ornate building, the Naqqar Khana or Naubat Khana, where musicians and other performers would welcome the nawab as he entered. Like the Bara Imambara, the Chhota Imambara was also built under a food-for-work programme, by Muhammad Ali Shah (1837-42), under the supervision of architect Azim-ud-Daulah. It contains the graves of Muhammad Ali Shah and his mother Malqah-e-Alia. Its vaulted roof is capped by a gilded dome in the centre and two cupolas on either side. The main hall is embellished with ornamented writing. Interiors are decorated with *zari* (brocade), *tazias*, chandeliers, a silver pulpit, ornate gilded Belgian mirrors and paintings. Facing the main building is a canal with a small wooden bridge. To the east of the mausoleum is the tomb of the princess Maqbara Shahzadi Saheba, with a replica of the Taj Mahal. To the west is its *jawab* or copy, another Taj replica, where her husband is buried. The Chhota Imambara complex also has a *shahi-hammam* (royal bath), *langarkhana* (kitchen) and a mosque.

THE RESIDENCY, QAISERBAGH AND HAZRATGANJ

As you enter the vast grounds of the Residency (open 10am-4.30pm daily, admission Rs 5 Indians, Rs 100 others, free under-15s), an eerie silence greets you. The tranquillity of the place belies the tremendous bloodshed it witnessed during the uprising of 1857 against British rule, when – as the British Residency – it was under siege for months. Once you examine the demolished buildings, the scars become apparent. Heavy damage was caused by shelling and some buildings were razed to the ground. Since the complex has been left untouched, you get a sense of the ferocity of the fighting. During the Siege of Lucknow, 3,000 Europeans took shelter at the Residency and close to 2,000 died, some from gunshot and cannonball injuries, others from disease; they are buried in the cemetery nearby. Those unfamiliar with the history of the period should come with a guide. There's a museum (open 10am-4.30pm Tue-Sun, admission Rs 5) in the main building, with lithographs, documents, artillery, a model of the Residency and artefacts relating to the struggle.

Wajid Ali Shah, the last of the nawabs, built the Qaiserbagh Palace, a little east of the Residency complex, between 1848 and 1850, at great cost. Some of the buildings were residences of his favourite begums, while many of the pavilions were for dance and music performances. In the centre was the Safed Baradari (White Court Palace). Much of the palace complex was destroyed in the uprising of 1857, and streets now run through former courtyards. With a guide and a little imagination, though, one can still visualise its former splendour. Some of the *baradaris* (garden palaces), for instance, are still in use as official buildings. The Safed Baradari has a magnificent hall that is often a venue for lavish weddings and other functions, while the Lal Baradari houses a government museum. Close by are two imposing tombs, that of Nawab Saadat Ali Khan and his wife Mushir Zadi (also known as Khurshid Zadi).

The Tomb of Saadat Ali Khan (entry into the building is not permitted) was built by his son Ghaziuddin Haider. The nawab is buried in an underground vault that also contains graves of some of his brothers, begums and daughters. Nearby is the Tomb of Mushir Zadi, also built by Ghaziuddin Haider, for his mother, the queen. Similar in design to her husband's tomb, the vault contains two graves – that of the queen, and another believed to be a daughter. The grounds outside are now used by kids to play cricket.

Directly east of Qaiserbagh is the area of Hazratganj, or, as Lucknavis like to call it, 'Ganj'. It's the busiest shopping and business district of the city, a place where locals come to eat and for entertainment – hence the term 'Ganjing', meaning aimlessly ambling through the area.

SIKANDAR BAGH

Perched on the banks of the Gomti river, a short distance from the busy Hazratganj area, is the magnificent edifice of the Imambara Shah Najaf commissioned by Nawab Ghaziuddin Haider (1814-27). Built in memory of Hazrat Ali, the son-in-law of the Prophet Muhammad, the Imambara is said to resemble the shrine to Hazrat Ali in Najaf, Iraq. Its central chamber is adorned with *zari*, *alams* (symbolic flags), *tazias*, chandeliers, mirrors, glass, portraits and other paintings. The hall also has tombs of the nawab and his three wives, Sarfaraz Mahal, Mubarak Mahal and Mumtaz Mahal. This building was one of the strongholds of freedom fighters during the uprising against the British in 1857.

Sikandar Bagh was built by Wajid Ali Shah in memory of his favourite queen, Sikandar Mahal, at a cost of Rs 500,000. All that remains of this once-beautiful building is a fortified wall, a small mosque and an imposing gateway. One side of the gateway is adorned with the Awadhi emblem of the twin fishes, while on top are perched two peacocks facing each other. A fierce battle was fought here on 16 November 1857, marking the beginning of the end of the Seige of Lucknow.

SOUTH-EAST LUCKNOW

Dilkhusha Palace constructed during the reign of Saadat Ali Khan, is now in ruins. It was originally a hunting lodge, but later used as a summer resort. Its architecture was that of an English manor with Awadhi touches. During the early part of Wajid Ali Shah's reign, he used the grounds to hold military exercises but was ordered to stop by the British. During the First Indian War of Independence in 1857, many British soldiers died here and the building suffered great damage, though its extensive gardens remain.

North of Dilkhusha Palace is La Martinière College, named after Claude Martin, a French adventurer and one-time soldier. Construction of the palatial house known as Constantia was begun by Martin in 1785. After his death, through a bequest, a boys' college was established here, and then a girls' college. The palace is probably the most bizarre monument in Lucknow. It's a hodge-podge of various Indian and European architectural styles, its façade adorned with angels, gargoyles and other sundry creatures. In front of the building are two massive cannons. Martin is buried in an underground vault. The long front steps, made of stone, are etched with names of old boys. Since it is a working college, you'll need prior permission from the principal (0522-223 5415) to gain access to the grounds.

Eat

Get past the crummy locations and seemingly unhygienic conditions, and you'll find a gustatory heaven of Awadhi cuisine. Awadhi cooking was refined to an art form under the nawabs, who historically paid vast sums of money to, and put up with the various idiosyncrasies of, their chefs.

Besides its famous kebabs, Lucknow is known for street food (specially chaat), drinks (like *thandai, garam doodh* and *kashmiri chai*) and desserts (like the famous *shahi tukda*). In winter *nimish*, a frothy milk that's been left to catch the dew is available only very early in the morning.

Visitors do need to be careful where they eat. Desserts, at least, can be consumed with relative impunity; try Prem Sweets (Nishatganj Pul, Faizabad Road) and Prakash Kulfi (Aminabad, 0522-262-6737); finally, you can buy Lucknow's famous gajak (a sesame seed praline-like sweet snack) just about anywhere.

Cappuccino Blast/Ultra Violet

3km S of Hazratganj *12 Mall Avenue (0522-223-6238/93352-15414). Open noon-4.30pm, 7.30-11.30pm daily. $$$. No AmEx. Multi-cuisine.*

Young entrepreneur Puja Vaid has created much more than a coffee shop. Multiple spaces offer a coffee shop, restaurant and an art/craft gift shop. Both the outdoor coffee shop, with tropical foliage, and the hip interior of Ultra Violet, with comfortable sofas, are good places to relax. You can order just about anything from the extensive menu, but as is often the case with long menus, nothing really stands out.

Chhote Nawab

1km E of Sikandar Bagh *Sagar International Hotel, 14A Jopling Road (0522-220-6601). Open noon-3.30pm, 7.30-11.30pm daily. $$. Awadhi.*

This Awadhi restaurant serves some of the best kebabs in the city and it comes as no surprise that it was established by chef Ishtiyaque Qureishi, whose culinary bloodline goes back to the time of the nawabs. Kebabs aside, signature dishes include *dum gosht* and an awesome Lucknavi biryani. The breads are an art form in themselves, especially the *warq-e-sada*, which is so thin and soft, it's hard to imagine how it can have been handled as it was made. Traditional desserts rule; the *shahi tukda* (saffron-scented bread pudding) is a classic.

Falaknuma

Hazratganj *Hotel Clarks Avadh, MG Road (0522-262-0231/www.clarksavadh.com). Open 1-3pm, 8-11.30pm daily. $$$$. Awadhi.*

From vantage point on the ninth floor of the Hotel Clarks Avadh, guests at Falaknuma enjoy a bird's eye view of Lucknow; try and get a table overlooking the Gomti river. Most evenings there's live music (*ghazals*). The kebab platter and *bhuna ghost* are recommended, though almost everything is well made. For those missing their alcohol, this place has a well-stocked bar.

King of Chaat

Hazratganj *Opposite D Magistrate's house (0522-225-3841). Open 5-10pm daily. $. No AmEx. Street food.*

Street food in a relatively hygienic setting. *Alu tikki* (potato patties) with yoghurt and chutney is the star of the show.

Naushijaan

Hazratganj *Tulsi Theatre Building, Rani Laxmi Bai Marg (0522-228-0294/www.naushijaan.com). Open 5.30-9.30pm Mon, Wed-Sun. $$. No AmEx. Awadhi.*

A little away from the centre of the busy Hazratganj area, this air-conditioned restaurant has a vast menu. It's a good place for the uninitiated, since the curries are milder and less oily than at Tunday or Rahim's (for both, *see p138*). The chicken biryani and mutton korma are good bets.

Clockwise from top left: Oudhyana; Tunday Kababi; Falaknuma.

Oudhyana

8km E of Hazratganj *Taj Residency Hotel, Gomti Nagar (0522-671-1053/www.tajhotels.com). Open 12.30-3pm, 7.30-11.30pm daily. $$$. Awadhi.*

Some of the city's finest food is served here. Try the *kawab e tashkari* (kebab platter) or *kakori* or *shammi* kebabs and a sultani dal, teamed with your favourite kind of naan (or ask for a basket of assorted naans). At Oudhyana it's about luxury, with excellent service, ambience and food. Vegetarians too will find hearty Awadhi dishes they can enjoy, such as *bhindi til wali* (okra flavoured with sesame) and *lasuni palak* (garlicky spinach). While the standard remains high, star chef Ghulam Rasool has moved on, and with him the superlative quality of food.

Rahim's

Old Lucknow *Akbari Gate, Chowk (no phone). Open 11am-11pm daily. $. No credit cards. Awadhi.*

Hidden in the by-lanes of Chowk, this local eaterie is often missed, but it's one of the most authentic places for Lucknavi food. Get here by 7pm, before the awesome *boti* kebabs sell out. Eat your kebab with *sheermal* or any of the breads available. During Ramzan (Ramadan), the top pick is the *nahari kulcha* (curry made with sheep, goat or cow's feet or tongues, with *kulcha* bread). Like other eating places, Rahim's is open nearly all night during Ramzan.

Tunday Kababi

Old Lucknow *Akbari Gate, Chowk (no phone). Open 11am-11pm daily. $-$$. No credit cards. Awadhi.*

Every visitor to Lucknow stops at Tunday for a legendary, mouth-watering *galawat* kebab (they supposedly contain a secret 160-spice mixture), along with translucent parathas made on a *tawa* (iron hotplate). True Lucknavis will insist that the original Tunday in the narrow lanes of Chowk, near the Akbari Gate in Old Lucknow, is the superior branch. To them, an air-conditioned, characterless restaurant just can't compare to standing on the street and eating a kebab to the accompaniment of the rhythmic tak-tak hammering of *varq* (edible silver sheets) next door. Visitors, on the other hand, may find the other branches (Nazirabad-Aminabad 168-166, Naaz Cinema Road and the Sahara Ganj Mall Food Court) more appetising, if somewhat sanitised. Aside from the superb kebabs, biryani, roast chicken and *phirni* dessert (not available at the Chowk branch) are all outstanding.

Shopping

Lucknow is best known for its *chikankari*, a style of exquisite hand embroidery. Traditionally done with white thread on white cotton fabric, it's now found in a variety of fabrics and designs, including *zari* (using silver or gold brocade), *mokaish* (with silver-thread embroidery) and *zardozi* (with gold-thread embroidery). Work comes in different qualities, and prices vary accordingly. You'll find low-end stuff being sold on the streets of Chowk pretty cheaply. Mid-range chikan work is available at Janpath Market (off Hazratganj), but note that sizes aren't standardised. High-quality *chikan* clothing is sold at Habibulah Market (also in Hazratganj) and at Sewa (for both, *see below*).

Other areas that offer congested lane upon lane of interesting knick-knacks and local flavour are the market areas of Aminabad and Gadbadjhala.

Ram Advani Bookseller

Hazratganj *Mayfair Building (0522-262-3511). Open 10am-9pm Mon-Sat. No credit cards.*

Ram Advani's non-fiction bookshop – still presided over by the genial 88-year-old owner – is a longstanding Lucknow institution. The store is stacked with books on Lucknow and the knowledgeable Ram is happy to chat with visitors.

Sanatkada

Qaiserbagh *130 JC Bose Road (0522-407-7698). Open 11am-8pm daily. No AmEx.*

Sanatkada is Urdu for 'house of crafts' and this fine store and cultural centre, with attached café (the Adda), has created a space for crafts and craftspeople. All the merchandise is sourced from NGOs that direct profits to the artisans. Top-quality *chikankari* work, dhurries, kites and all kinds of other crafts can be found here. The centre is also involved in reviving traditional crafts; artisans are invited to talk about their work and there are occasional film shows.

Sewa

Hazratganj *11 AC Market, Habibullah Estate (0522-261-5907). Open 10.30am-7pm Mon-Sat. No AmEx.*

Before Sewa came along, *chikan* workers were exploited and the intricate art was dying. With the effort of activist Runa Banerjee, Sewa has transformed the lives of these women, as well as reviving the intricacies of *chikankari*. With design inputs from a range of good designers, Sewa produces and sells some of the best-quality *chikan* work you will find in Lucknow. Kids' clothes, fabric, home linens and clothes for men and women are among the top buys.

Sugandhco

Hazratganj *Janpath Market (0522-262-1748). Open noon-7.30pm daily. No AmEx.*

Anyone who likes exotic fragrances should visit this superb store to buy *ittar* (perfume); its manufacturing process is an art form handed down over two centuries. Aromatic essential oils and agarbatties (incense or joss sticks) are also sold.

Stay

Lucknow isn't bogged down by traffic jams and congestion, so wherever you stay, whether it's the busy Hazratganj area or a quiet residential neighbourhood like Gomti Nagar, it will not take you too long to get to the main sites.

Hotel Clarks Avadh

1.5km NW of Hazratganj *8 Mahatma Gandhi Marg (0522-262-0231/www.clarksavadh.com). $$.*

Lucknow's first upmarket hotel passes muster as far as decor goes, but it's definitely not in the top class. Junior staff

Decadent ruler or people's king?

Wajid Ali Shah was the last nawab to rule Awadh before the East India Company annexed the kingdom in 1856. The deposing of the nawab and its aftermath became a public spectacle: after the takeover, Wajid Ali Shah planned to travel to London to meet Queen Victoria to protest the annexation in person. To this end he first made a months-long journey to Calcutta on foot, palanquin and by steamer. It is said he fell ill in the city, after which he was held there by the British, more or less in exile. The full repercussions of the anger caused by the annexation would emerge a year later, in 1857, with the greatest uprising against the British Empire, when proclamations, pamphlets and newspapers joined in the condemnation of this 'perfidious act' on the part of the British.

Contemporary British accounts viewed Wajid Ali Shah as an artistically inclined, debauched and self-indulgent king. Effete and cowardly rulers like him – so the story went – were the main reason the British needed to step in and take over India. Decadence, extravagance and irresponsibility became bywords not just for Wajid Ali Shah, but for the whole 100-year-old kingdom of Awadh. It was a contradictory and double-edged narrative: Awadhi splendour and Indian emasculation seemed to be two sides of the same coin.

Modern historians now concur, however, that Wajid Ali Shah was no pusillanimous tyrant. By the time he ascended the throne in 1847, his kingdom was already tightly in the grip of British officials. British representatives controlled the army, finance and administration. His initial attempts to reform the administration and expand the army were stopped by them. The famous report from Sleeman, the British Resident, about Wajid Ali Shah's tyranny and the misery of his subjects, was to rebound later on the British during the uprising of 1857, when Awadh became the fiercest and toughest theatre for that uprising, with the most protracted battle. Events proved how badly the annexation of Awadh had been taken by Indians at large. This was truly a 'people's war' against the British, and Wajid Ali Shah had become an immensely popular, almost legendary figure, the subject of innumerable folk songs. As late as 1911, a full 60 years after he was deposed, the British ethnographer William Crooke was still able to find and collect songs about him.

The buildings, spectacles, plays, music and dance that abounded in Awadh, all of which were enthusiastically patronised by Wajid Ali Shah, served to enhance the kingdom's reputation for refinement, sophistication, art and culture. And the king was an artist as well as a patron. Not only was he the writer of 32 works, in four different languages, but he was also an accomplished dancer, singer and poet. *Kathak*, the North Indian dance form, received a huge fillip from his attention, as did the semi-classical singing form known as *thumri*. He was among the pioneers of Indian theatre through his *rahas*, devotional plays about Hindu gods, especially Krishna, and the *Indersabha*, the first Urdu dance-drama, written by Sayed Hassan Agha Amanat, a poet in his court, which he produced and performed in. All this was undertaken by a king who was a devout Muslim who prayed five times a day and was – for all his indulgence in other areas – a lifetime teetotaller.

Wajid Ali Shah's personality and his personal achievements have much to do with the way Indians today look back at the kingdom of Awadh: as a mythical repository of all the good things in life.

Taj Residency.

provide good service, but don't expect anything from the management, especially if you have a problem. Falaknuma, the restaurant on the top floor, is popular and serves great food along with breathtaking views of the city.

Gemini Continental

Hazratganj *10 Rani Laxmibai Marg (0522-401-1111/ www.geminicontinental.com). $$.*
Although located in the heart of the city, in Hazratganj, the hotel is actually a little removed from the chaos of the market. Its glass façade looks a bit boring, but the rooms are satisfactory; they are spotless, with flat-screen TVs, nice showers, and all the usual business hotel amenities: mini-bar, safe and Wi-Fi connectivity. Some rooms overlook the famous KD Singh Babu cricket stadium, others the Residency. A reasonable option if you bag a good deal.

La Place Sarovar Portico

Hazratganj *6 Shahnajaf Road (0522-400-4040/ www.sarovarhotels.com). $$.*
Formerly La Place Park Inn, this hotel pleases both business travellers and tourists, but it's not luxurious by any stretch of the imagination. Rooms are simple and clean, and offer the standard amenities for this class of hotel, including Wi-Fi connectivity. A rooftop restaurant serves tandoori, grilled and barbecue food, but it's generally deserted during the oppressive summers.

Lucknow Homestay

2km S of Hazratganj *110-D Mall Avenue (0522-301-0481/www.lucknowhomestay.wordpress.com). $. No credit cards.*
It would be hard to find a more cheerful budget place to stay in Lucknow. Owned and efficiently run by Naheed Varma, it has a lounge area with bright yellow furniture, as well as a small library with books donated by visitors. Make reservations well in advance as there are only 12 rooms; not all have attached bathrooms. If you need someone to take you around, ask for the services of auto-rickshaw driver Gautam, who knows the city inside out and offers reasonable rates.

Taj Residency, Lucknow

8km E of Hazratganj *Gomti Nagar (0522-671-1000/ www.tajhotels.com). $$$.*
Tucked away in a posh neighbourhood, far from the traffic and noise of the main town, the Taj nevertheless has easy access to the sites. The hotel attempts to recreate the era of the nawabs with its architecture and service. Its splendid dome can be seen from afar, and the columns, arches and interiors are all quite grand and elegant. Rooms are smart, spacious and comfortable and face either the pool or the garden; the pool is gorgeous, and lawns are huge and well maintained. The Oudhyana restaurant serves authentic Awadhi cuisine, while the Mehfil bar presents Hindustani classical music along with its drinks.

Factfile

When to go

Winter runs from October to March and is the best time to visit. Summers (Apr-June) are oppressive. The monsoon (July-Sept) is humid, but otherwise not a bad time to visit.

Getting there

Lucknow is connected by direct flights to Delhi, Patna, Kolkata, Mumbai, Varanasi and many other Indian cities. Dozens of trains connect Lucknow's Charbagh station (and Lucknow Junction) to the rest of the country, including the super-fast Shatabdi from Delhi, which covers the 490km (340 miles) distance in seven hours.

For more on travel within India, *see p378* **Navigating India**.

Getting around

For the journey from the airport or railway station it's best to take a pre-paid taxi to your hotel. For travelling around the city, auto-rickshaws or cycle-rickshaws are easily available. They don't have meters or fixed prices, but rates are generally reasonable and can be negotiated. You could also hire a car for Rs 1,000 to Rs 1,500 a day, or an auto-rickshaw for half that amount.

Tourist information

The Directorate of Tourism, Uttar Pradesh, is at Tandon Paryatan Bhavan, C-13 Vipin Khand, Gomti Nagar (0522-230-8916, upstdc@up-tourism.com). **The Regional Tourist Office** is at 10 Station Road (0522-263-8105).

Internet

Internet cafés can be found all over Lucknow.

Tips

- Local people are usually polite and helpful. Do stop someone and ask if you are unsure of directions or feel as if your agent, driver or guide is trying to take you for a ride.

- Street-food stalls may sell some of the tastiest food in Lucknow, but it can be spicy, and food stalls won't tone down spice levels to suit your taste. Don't expect very hygienic conditions either; visitors should exercise caution.

Kochi

Kerala's ancient trading centre and a modern melting pot.

Kerala state and Kochi have been welcoming travellers for over 3,000 years. Traders from ancient Arabia and China who made the journey to the 'Queen of the Arabian Sea' would have gawked in amazement at entire bazaars filled with pepper – a commodity treated on a par with gold. This ancient crossroads for traders, said also to be known to the ancient Romans and Egyptians, as well as to later envoys, adventurers and battling European empires, was to liberally borrow cultural attributes from its many visitors and settlers and mingle these with indigenous flavours over the years. Its kings even welcomed European colonists, bestowing gifts and trade concessions in return for protection from their rivals, the Zamorins of north Kerala.

The pepper markets may be long gone, but modern-day visitors continue to flock to Kochi to admire its pleasantly incongruous mix of cultures, epitomised by its famous Chinese fishing nets – just a stone's throw from a Portuguese church and Dutch cemetery – pulling up bucket-loads of shrimp to be consumed within hours in traditional Keralan homes.

Kochi has managed to preserve much of its old-world charm and the architectural legacies of its colonists. At the same time, as Kerala state's commercial centre, the town is brimming with shopping malls, apartment complexes and luxury hotels. In its older neighbourhoods, the remaining members of an ancient Jewish community hang on to their customs. In swankier suburbs, young men and women turn out in their modish best to dine at fancy restaurants overlooking the bay. But no matter how 'modern' they are, Keralites, also called Malayalis, are immensely proud of their state, culture, language (Malayalam) and the beauty of their land. When you arrive in Kochi, prepare for a warm welcome; Malayalis are as gracious as hosts today as they have been for centuries.

Clockwise from top left: Dutch Cemetery; Jew Town Road; Chinese fishing nets at Fort Kochi; Mattancherry Palace Museum.

Explore

Kochi's history is closely linked to that of pepper and other spices. But it was a flood in the 14th century, following a storm surge in the Arabian Sea, that converted its lazy lagoon into one of the world's finest and busiest natural harbours; until then the nearby port of Cranganore had been the leading port of the region.

Today, the city of Kochi (once called Cochin) consists of mainland **Ernakulam** with its suburbs, the peninsula occupied by **Fort Kochi** and **Mattancherry**, as well as a cluster of islands including the larger Willingdon, Bolgatty and Vypeen islands. All of these are well connected by road and regular ferry services to the mainland.

Most of Kochi's tourist attractions are concentrated in Mattancherry and Fort Kochi, and can be visited over two days. While these are best explored on foot or by bicycle, you can also hire an auto-rickshaw or taxi for the day to take in the sights without breaking a sweat. However, there's more to Kochi than its handful of churches and monuments; it's well worth a longer stay for a more insightful and rewarding experience.

FORT KOCHI

Originally a fishing village in pre-colonial Kerala, this stretch of land was given to the Portuguese by the king of Kochi to build a fort. Few remnants of the battlements the Portuguese built here remain. Later European colonists, including the Dutch and the British, also settled here, leaving behind a curious grid of streets lined with old bungalows and churches built in different European styles.

Chinese Fishing Nets

River Road. Open sunrise-sunset daily.

Perched on the waterfront near Vasco da Gama Square are the much photographed Chinese fishing nets that greet all visitors to Fort Kochi. These huge mechanical contraptions consist of a large net suspended from a wooden cantilever by a complex system of ropes and rocks used as counterweights. The nets are lowered into the water by a team of fishermen who leave it there for a few minutes, while they take a cigarette break, before hauling it up and gathering the fish trapped inside. Visit early in the morning, before the busloads of day trippers arrive, and the fish market is stirring to life.

Dutch Cemetery

Fort Kochi Beach. Open on request.

The oldest European cemetery in India, the Dutch cemetery is a short walk from the lighthouse near the beach at Fort Kochi. Established in 1724, it has 100-odd tombs; the last burial took place in 1913. The cemetery gates are locked most of the time but you can ask the authorities at St Francis Church nearby, who now look after the cemetery, to open them for a visit.

Indo-Portuguese Museum

Bishop's House (0484-221-5400). Open 9am-6pm Tue-Sun. Admission Rs10 Indians, Rs 25 others.

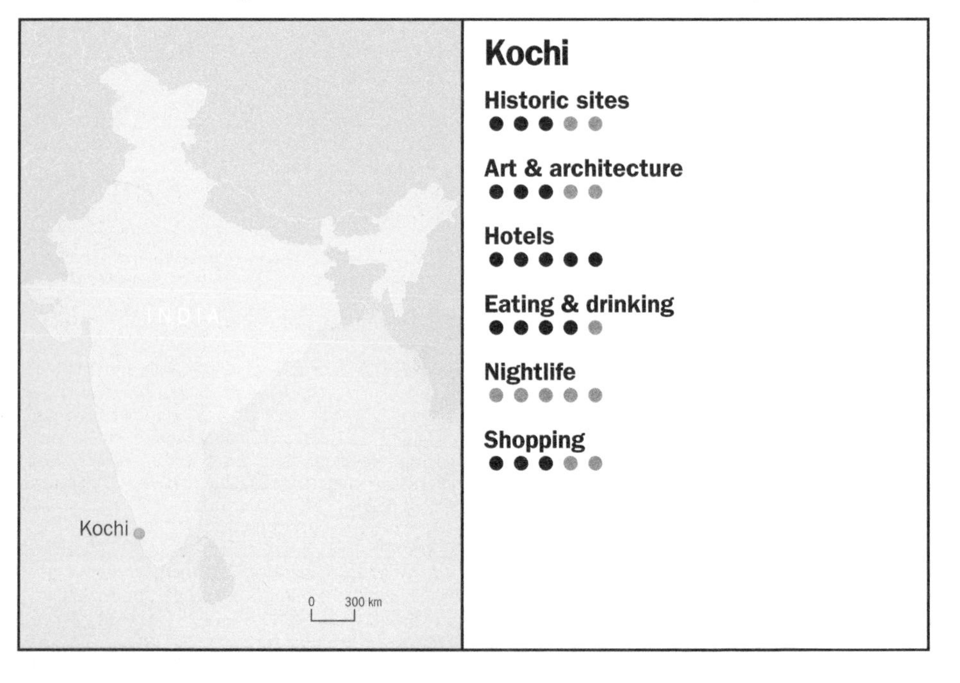

The Indo-Portuguese Museum is attached to Bishop's House, a large mansion with Gothic arches, formerly the residence of the Portuguese governor in India. It's now the home of the bishop of the diocese of Cochin. The museum has a collection of sculptures, precious metal objects and vestments from the Santa Cruz Basilica and other churches of the diocese. Apart from entire altars, altar decorations, candlesticks, chalices and priests' robes, it also houses old maps of Kochi and a book detailing marriage and funeral ceremonies dating back to 1663.

Princess Street

A walk along Princess Street takes you past a series of stately mansions built in British, Dutch, Portuguese and even French colonial styles, with flowerpots on their wrought-iron window sills and stucco walls. These old homes are protected by local heritage laws that permit only minor renovations and no major facelifts. Many of them are now hotels.

"Jew Town Road was once the hub of a thriving Jewish community, and the world's only international pepper exchange operated from here."

St Francis Church

Church Road (0484-22-7505). Open 6am-7pm daily.

The oldest European church in India, St Francis was originally built in 1503 by the Portuguese, and rebuilt in around 1562. Much of the original structure has survived four centuries and three warring European empires and is a rich storehouse of history. Vasco da Gama was buried here from 1534 to 1538; his body was later moved to Lisbon, though there's still a gravestone in the grounds south of the church. A record of baptisms and marriages from the 18th century, and original title deeds written on palm leaves and signed by the king of Kochi, are carefully preserved here; photocopies are kept outside the vestry. This is now an active Anglican church.

Santa Cruz Basilica

KB Jacob Road. Open 9am-1pm, 3-5pm daily.

Built in 1505 by the Portuguese, this was one of two churches spared by the Dutch when they wrested control of Fort Kochi from the Portuguese, and then set about destroying all the Catholic churches they found here. Perhaps this basilical was spared because the Dutch were overawed by its imposing beauty, with its stained-glass windows, Gothic spires and huge caryatids (supporting columns carved in the shape of people). The present structure, rebuilt in 1905 after the church was destroyed by the British in the 18th century, has a high ceiling with teak rafters, which – along with the walls and pillars – are painted with scenes from the life of Christ. One caryatid that survived the British demolition is kept as a monument in the basilica.

MATTANCHERRY

South of Fort Kochi is Mattancherry, an ancient trading centre and home to the last of the Malabar Yehudan, descendants of the original Jewish immigrants to India. This Jewish community controlled the spice trade routes for centuries before the Portuguese and other European colonists arrived, and they were once a prosperous and thriving community. Mattancherry today has few survivors from that past, and the great spice warehouses have been converted to shops selling antiques and curios.

Mattancherry Palace Museum

Palace Road. Open 10am-5pm Mon-Thur, Sat, Sun. Admission Rs 2. No photography.

The Mattancherry Palace was constructed by the Portuguese and given to the king of Kochi, Veera Kerala Varma, in 1555, to appease him after the Portuguese had pillaged a temple in the vicinity. Built in traditional Keralan Nalukettu style, with a central courtyard, the two-storey palace was later renovated by the Dutch. Exhibits include portraits of royals, umbrellas, palanquins, costumes, coins, stamps and a selection of arms including ceremonial spears, daggers, axes and swords. All over the museum are well-preserved traditional Keralan murals, depicting scenes from Hindu epics.

Paradesi Synagogue

Jew Town Road. Open 10am-noon, 3-5pm Mon-Thur, Sun. Closed Jewish holidays. Admission Rs 5. Dress code: no shorts, short skirts or sleeveless shirts; appropriate clothing available to hire.

Jews were among Kerala's earliest settlers, building their first synagogue in Cranganore in the fourth century AD. Paradesi is the last of the functioning synagogues in Kochi. It was built in 1568 by the Malabar Yehudan. An inordinate number of Belgian glass chandeliers hang from the ceiling, and the floor is covered in 18th-century hand-painted Chinese porcelain tiles. Outside is the synagogue's most distinctive feature – an 18th-century clock tower with four dials with numerals in Arabic, Hebrew, Latin and Malayalam. Jew Town Road, the thoroughfare leading to the synagogue, was once the hub of a thriving Jewish community, and the world's only International Pepper Exchange operated from here. Today, most Jewish families have migrated to Israel, and the pepper exchange has gone online.

ERNAKULAM

On the mainland, east of Mattancherry, is Ernakulam, the most urbanised part of Kochi. It is the financial capital of Kerala, a bustling business centre with hotels, restaurants,

Dancing tales

In the court of Marthanda Varma, the 18th-century king of the Indian princely state of Travancore (South Kerala), the great Malayalam poet Kalakkaththu Kunchan Nambiar once dozed off while playing the *mizhavu*, a copper percussion instrument, during a *chakyar koothu* dance performance. He was insulted in public for his carelessness, and decided to avenge his humiliation by devising his own art form – *ottamthullal*, a performance art that combines dance and drama to deride cultural and political practices and prejudices.

Kerala has many other traditional dance and martial arts forms besides these, ranging from those with roots in classical and religious texts, to other, less-restrained forms that rely heavily on satire and ridicule. Kerala's kings and rulers were enthusiastic patrons of the arts and they continued to thrive through the years, guided by practitioners who were willing to constantly improvise and adapt.

Chakyar koothu is one of Kerala's oldest performance arts. With pronounced use of facial expressions, the artist narrates episodes from Hindu epics like the *Mahabharata* and the *Ramayana* in Sanskrit. *Kathakali* is the most widely recognised of Kerala's dance forms, with detailed make-up and elaborate costumes. *Kathakali* artists use no words, only hand gestures and a series of nine facial expressions, to enact stories, most of which are composed to last an entire night. Another Keralan classical dance form, *mohiniyattam*, is performed exclusively by women.

Kalaripayattu, believed to be the world's oldest martial art, is still practised in Kerala, and choreographed sparring sequences from *kalaripayattu* are sometimes applied to contemporary dance.

An art form with a particular spiritual dimension is *theyyam*, a possession ritual that involves elaborate costuming and a few dance steps. This form of worship is practised extensively in north Kerala; as it moves further south, it takes on different forms. *Theyyam* is also a cult and when in full costume, its artists are treated on a par with God.

Artists adaptability and refusal to be boxed in by tradition, constantly adding contemporary social and political commentary to their performances, is largely responsible for keeping many of Kerala's performing arts genres alive. In a *chakyar koothu* performance, for example, it's not uncommon for the artist to direct comments at members of the audience, with some remarks even bordering on obscene.

Today, traditional *kathakali* performances have been distilled into more concise and palatable versions. It's interesting to note, however, that even these performances seldom play out according to the script.

Kochi has many centres promoting traditional performances for tourists with daily shows. Of the two daily shows at Greenix Village (*see p151*), one is a *kathakali* performance; in the other, artists perform short segments from different dance forms before coming together for a grand finale. At the Cochin Cultural Centre (*see p148*) the daily performances focus on *kathakali*. Both centres allow visitors to see the artists putting on their elaborate make-up, costumes and headgear, and all the finer nuances of the dance forms are explained in English before performances commence. Performances, especially forms like *theyyam*, are far less frenzied than they normally are, but they still offer visitors a convenient and exciting introduction to a fascinating aspect of Kerala's culture.

cinemas and malls. Gold Centre, the name given to a long stretch along MG Road in the heart of Ernakulam, with large showrooms selling gold jewellery, is a bracing testimony to the average Keralite's appetite for the precious metal. Gold apart, Ernakulam has few other attractions, but for tourists it remains an important transit hub because of its excellent connections. A few kilometres south of Ernakulam is Kumbalanghi Kallancherry Island (0484-224-0329, www.kumbalanghivillagetours.com), a tourist village where visitors can get a pre-packaged Keralan village experience, including the chance to witness coir rope making, shellfish processing, toddy tapping (collecting sap from palm-tree flowers) and fishing.

Eat

Kochi has liberally drawn inspiration from the many cultures that have visited Kerala in the last three centuries. Its culinary scene, like its architecture, is a vibrant mish-mash of Arab, Dutch, English, Jewish, Keralan, Portuguese and Syrian-Christian influences, all generously enhanced by Kerala's triad of spices – cardamom, ginger and pepper. Most interesting restaurants are concentrated in the Fort Kochi area.

Fort Cochin

E of Fort Kochi *Casino Hotel, Willingdon Island (0484-301-1516/www.cghearth.com). Open 7-10.30am, 12.30-3pm, 7.30-11pm daily. $$$$. Multi-cuisine.*
The Casino Hotel started out as a local eaterie serving spicy fare to itinerant sailors and port workers. It has risen from these humble beginnings to become part of CGH Earth, a green hotel chain with numerous upmarket properties. Its current seafood restaurant, Fort Cochin, continues to dish up sumptuous fare, in keeping with the establishment's 50-year tradition. There's no regular menu, so look out for a blackboard listing the catch of the day. A trolley carrying the day's haul of fresh fish is pushed around at lunch and dinner. Pick from an assortment of fish and crustaceans and choose to have it flambéed, grilled with lime and butter, curried with local spices or prepared in a variety of other ways.

Ginger House Restaurant

Mattancherry *Jew Town Road (0484-221-1145). Open 8am-8pm daily. $$. No AmEx. Keralan.*
Ginger House is a curious mix of antique store and waterfront restaurant. The premises were once a ginger warehouse and the theme – predictably – is ginger. Begin with a zesty ginger lime soda, and then ask for the house special – ginger prawns served with chapatis, *appams* (bowl-shaped rice-batter crêpes) or rice, before finishing with ginger ice-cream. While you wait for your meal, you can explore the vast antique store, watch the chef at work in the open kitchen, or laze in one of the long-armed wooden lounge chairs (oddly named Bombay fornicators), facing Kochi port.

Grande Residencia

Fort Kochi *Abad Grande Residencia, Princess Street (0484-221-8981/www.abadhotels.com). Open 7-10.30am, noon-3pm, 7-10.30pm daily. $$. No AmEx. Multi-cuisine.*
This poolside restaurant offers a colonial ambience and spicy menu selections. The house special is alleppey fish curry, cooked with raw mango in a mildly spiced coconut gravy, and *naadan* (traditional) chicken curry made with coconut paste and spices. For starters, the batter-fried squid rings are recommended. Stick to the Keralan dishes, and definitely give the Punjabi menu a miss.

Grand Pavilion

Ernakulam *Grand Hotel, MG Road (0484-238-2061/www.grandhotelkerala.com). Open 7am-11pm, lunch noon-3pm, daily. $$. Multi-cuisine.*
Authentic Keralan cuisine is the way to go at this Ernakulam restaurant, which is very popular with locals – a popularity it richly deserves. Try the thalis for lunch. At dinner, sample the famous pearl spot fish dishes, especially *meen pollichatu*, fish marinated with spices, wrapped in a banana leaf and slow-roasted. Also try *ammachi's* (grandmother's) special chicken curry, a very spicy affair, not recommended for the faint-hearted.

The History

Fort Kochi *Brunton Boatyard (0484-221-5461/www.cghearth.com). Open 7.30-10pm daily. $$$. Multi-cuisine.*
If you can't stay at the Brunton Boatyard, try to visit this lovely restaurant. Like the rest of the hotel, it exudes a warm, woody feel, with massive teak crossbeams holding up the roof. Before the Brunton Boatyard opened, its chefs spent a few months in the kitchens of local housewives, learning their recipes. The menu pays tribute to Kochi's historical influences and a meal here allows you to sample all those different cuisines in one evening. Its Syrian *konju* curry, tiger prawns cooked in a simple coconut milk gravy, and *kozhi mappas*, spicy chicken curry served with Kerala *parottas* (parathas) or rice are classics. Those looking for a break from seafood can try the cocoa- and honey-glazed ham served with tossed vegetables.

Kashi Art Café

Fort Kochi *Burgher Street (0484-221-5769/www.kashiartgallery.com). Open 8.30am-7.30pm daily. $. Western. No credit cards.*
Set around a tropical garden, Kashi Art Café combines an art gallery experience with healthy eating. There's no fixed menu here: you get whatever is fresh in the markets. There's a lot of fresh fruit and an assortment of cakes and pies.

Malabar Junction

Fort Kochi *Malabar House, Parade Road (0484-221-6666/www.malabarhouse.com). Open 7am-11pm daily. $$$. Multi-cuisine.*
At lunch, the chef conjures up superb vegetarian and seafood thalis, served on brass plates. For dinner, go with the *dégustation* menu: tapioca tarts filled with *thoran* (minced vegetables), steamed or stir-fried and served with

a coconut gravy; tiger prawns in ginger or garlic sauce and served with *appams* (bowl-shaped rice-batter crêpes); fish biryani and *vattayappam*, a baked dessert of caramelised fruit layers served with coconut sorbet.

Marina: 'You buy we cook'

Fort Kochi *River Road (99471-35264/99959-91278). Open 9am-10pm daily. No credit cards. $. Multi-cuisine.*
'You buy we cook' is an essential Kochi experience. Get to the Fort Kochi waterfront early in the day, when the local fishermen are just returning from a night out at sea. Stand around as the first catch of the day arrives and is quickly auctioned off to merchants at the makeshift fish market, just behind the Chinese fishing nets. At one of the stalls, choose from a wide array of fish including shark, crab and prawns, and drive a hard bargain. Prices vary daily, so ask a local shopper for approximate rates. Next, select an establishment with a 'You buy we cook' signboard. Recommended is Marina, just a few minutes' walk from the Chinese fishing nets, with a competent chef and a great view of the harbour.

Poovath Heritage Hotel

Fort Kochi *DC Road (0484-221-5241/www.poovath.com). Open 7am-10pm daily. $$. No AmEx. Multi-cuisine.*
There are Indian, Italian, Chinese and Punjabi choices to go with the lovely views of Fort Kochi Beach from this hotel restaurant, but the best bet is the Keralan cuisine. Ask for the fish *moily*, cooked in mildly spiced coconut milk and accompanied by *appams* (bowl-shaped rice-batter crêpes) or rice, or get the Syrian-Christian staple, beef *ularthiyathu*, beef fried in an open pan with spices and coconut pieces.

Shop

Many former Jewish homes and spice warehouses in Mattancherry have now been converted to shops selling antiques, curios, handicrafts and spices. Avoid the makeshift stalls at the entrance to Jew Town, as most sell inferior-quality reproductions; also steer clear of guides who promise to show you around.

Cochin Spice Market

Mattancherry *Jew Town (0484-229-829/93888-84300). Open 9.30am-6.30pm Mon-Sat. No credit cards.*
None of the fabled spice shops that overawed visitors to Jew Town in centuries past exist any more. Cochin Spice Market is but a small store with a selection of packaged spices (black and green cardamom, coriander, mace, nutmeg, pepper and turmeric) as well as vanilla bean, natural oils, massage oils and traditional wooden spice storage boxes.

Crafters

Mattancherry *Jew Town (0484-222-3346/www.crafters.in). Open 9am-6pm Mon-Sat. No AmEx.*
Crafters is a huge emporium selling antiques, curios, handicrafts, jewellery and furniture sourced from all over India. On display is the world's largest *varpu*, a metal vessel used to cook food during traditional feasts, and a giant-sized chessboard.

Fabindia

Fort Kochi *Napier Street, near Parade Ground (0484-221-7077/www.fabindia.com). Open 10am-8pm daily.*
Ethnic-chic clothes made with handlooms and natural dyes, plus furnishings, organic food and everything that's typical of a Fabindia store. Call in if you're not going to visit the Delhi branch.

Heritage Arts

Mattancherry *Jew Town Road (0484-221-1145). Open 8am-8pm Mon-Sat. No AmEx.*
A large snake boat is the centrepiece of this former ginger warehouse that now sells antiques and furniture that the affable owner NB Majnu, a former tourist guide, sources from all over India.

Niraamaya

Mattancherry *AB Salam Road, Jew Town (0484-327-3388/www.ayurvastraonline.com). Open 10am-5.30pm Mon-Sat. No AmEx.*
Niraamaya offers organic, eco-friendly cotton apparel with a twist: its collection of clothes for men and women, Ayur Vastra, is handmade using herbal dyes and infused with Ayurvedic medicines that promise to help diabetes, arthritis, high blood pressure and skin conditions.

Arts

Traditional performing arts, from *kathakali* to *mohiniattam*, *kalaripayattu* to *theyyam*, and many others, have thrived in Kerala, and Kochi has a vibrant arts scene featuring these traditional forms (*see p146* **Dancing tales**). In addition, Fort Kochi has a few galleries dedicated to contemporary art. Select venues and a few hotels host traditional dance and dance-drama performances every evening.

Cochin Cultural Centre

Fort Kochi *KB Jacob Road (0484-221-6911/www.cochinculturalcentre.com). Show 6.30pm daily. Tickets Rs 150.*
Kathakali performances are held daily. Visitors can also watch and photograph the artists as they put on their elaborate make-up and costumes., (*see p146* **Dancing tales**).

David Hall

Fort Kochi *Opposite Parade Ground (0484-221-8298/www.davidhall.in). Open 11am-7pm Tue-Sun.*
A 17th-century bungalow built by the Dutch, this was home to David Koder, a prominent Jewish businessman. It's now part of the CGH Earth initiative and showcases contemporary art sourced from all over India.

Clockwise from top left: Kashi Art Café (2); Poovath Heritage Hotel; shops on Jew Town Road (2).

Beyond performance

While staying in India to research his new book, *Nine Lives: In Search of the Sacred in Modern India* (Bloomsbury 2009), author William Dalrymple found himself spending more time in Kerala than any other part of the country. The book's most acclaimed chapter is the story of Hari Das, a Keralan labourer and a Dalit – a member of a low-caste, oppressed community traditionally considered as untouchable. For nine months of each year Hari Das works as a prison warden and well-digger, but for the remaining three months he channels the gods in fearsome *theyyam* performances. We interviewed William Dalrymple about his experience of Kerala and its many fascinating stories.

Had you spent much time in Kerala before you went there in pursuit of the story of Hari Das?
I'd spent a lot of time in Kerala, and I love Kerala – I'm thinking about writing an entire Kerala book. For *Nine Lives*, right until the last minute there were two Kerala stories. The one I had to reject was the story of a Christian exorcist in a village called Mannarkad, near Kottayam, where the Devi Bhagawati and the Virgin Mary are supposed to be twin sisters. I made six visits to Mannarkad, trying to get that story to work.

But I'd never been to northern Kerala, to Kannur or Tellicherry, before I began working on *Nine Lives*. It was intriguingly different from the south.

Given the darkness of the caste institutions you examined, and the darkness of *theyyam* itself, have you changed how you think about the state?
I have, but it only makes it more intriguing to me. My eye on Kerala has lost its innocence, I think. The Kerala caste thing, which I was totally unaware of before [investigating] the *theyyam*, led me in there, although it's there in the literature. British travellers in the 18th and 19th centuries talk of caste barriers being far more rigorous than anywhere else.

But it's such a beautiful and complicated and interesting place. There are so many institutions there that I'd be interested to write about. The Christian bards of Kerala I investigated for a long time: they speak of the Margam Kalipattu – the hymn of St Thomas, the mythology of his travels in India. All this is passed on orally; it's fascinating.

The end of the Hari Das chapter, when the goddess Chamundi appears, is definitely the most thrilling, unnerving and extreme moment in a book that is packed with extreme episodes.
It was, for me also, the most exciting. In the night performance we saw, these guys were dancing in front of a bonfire at four in the morning, sparks flying up, this huge crowd gathered in the middle of nowhere. It was an extraordinary moment.

Can you think of any other event you've witnessed in India to rival it?
Significantly, another one in Kerala, which I wrote about in *The Age of Kali*. It's the Chottanikkara festival, near Kochi, with one of the wildest Devi cults I've ever seen. All these possessed people knock nails into a tree with their foreheads. It happens in the middle of the night, and they cover themselves with *guruthi* [red liquid used in religious ritual: a mixture of lime and turmeric], so that they all look as if they're covered in blood even before they begin. So it can be a different world out there.

Greenix Village

Fort Kochi *Calvathy Road (0484-221-7000/www.greenix.in). Open 7am-8pm daily. Make-up 5.30pm, shows 6.30pm daily. Tickets from Rs 150.*
Dance performances are held here every day, and Greenix Village is also home to many artists. The former spice warehouse also has a curio shop, cultural museum and restaurant (*see p148* **Dancing tales**).

Kashi Art Gallery

Mattancherry *Bazaar Road (0484-221-5769/www.kashiartgallery.com). Open 10am-5pm daily.*
Anoop Skaria and Dorrie Younger set out to create Kochi's first contemporary art space in 1997, opening the Kashi Art Gallery. The couple continue to host budding artists and offer residency programmes with stipends.

Stay

Most heritage stay options in Kochi are concentrated in the Fort Kochi area, where colonial mansions and trade houses have been restored and re-opened as boutique hotels. Most are a short walk from each other and the Fort Kochi waterfront. Willingdon Island, the man-made island created by the British while dredging Kochi's port, has a few five-star accommodation options, while Ernakulam on the mainland has many large business hotels to choose from.

Brunton Boatyard

Fort Kochi *Calvathy Road (0484-221-5461/www.cghearth.com). $$$$.*
Brunton Boatyard is an impressive hotel, resurrected from an 18th-century shipbuilding yard. It's large, yet intimate, and teak is its overriding theme. From the prints depicting old Kochi in the reception area to the *punkahs* (old-fashioned fans) and rafters in the long passageways, Brunton Boatyard has carefully preserved its colonial past. All 22 rooms have great views of the harbour and are furnished with four-poster beds, footstools and other colonial artefacts.

Dream Cochin

Ernakulam *SA Road, Kadavanthara (0484-412-9999/www.dreamcochin.com). $$-$$$.*
On the mainland, far removed from Fort Kochi's heritage hotels, Dream Cochin, opened in 2009, is set in a very different, modern, mould. Like other Vikram Chatwal properties around the world, it promises 'whimsical decadence'. Rooms are lit with blue indirect lighting, (changeable to red and other colours), which takes a while to get used to. Bewildering choice of lighting apart, the club suites also come with a plush leather massage chair, two flat-screen TVs and – you'd better believe it – an automatic ironing machine. Very much in the proprietor's trademark style, Dream Cochin defies convention; its in-house nightclub, Ava Lounge, with its expensive entry charge for single men, is creating ripples in Kochi's conservative circles.

Fort House Hotel

Fort Kochi *Calvathy Road (0484-221-7103/www.hotelforthouse.com). $$. No AmEx.*
Fort House Hotel offers a refreshing change from the sterility of many Fort Kochi hotels. Its 16 modest and clean rooms are built in traditional Keralan style around an overgrown tropical garden with mango trees, herbs and flowering plants, interspersed with clay and granite sculptures. There's a lovely waterfront restaurant serving traditional Keralan cuisine and a competent Ayurvedic centre. An excellent option for those willing to compromise on amenities.

Koder House

Fort Kochi *Tower Road (0484-221-8485/www.koderhouse.com). $$$$. No AmEx.*
The distinct red façade of Koder House has been a Fort Kochi landmark since it was built by Samuel Koder in the early 19th century. The Koders, a prominent Jewish family that migrated to Kochi from Iraq, resurrected it as a boutique hotel in 2004. Two large, creaky wooden staircases on either side of a lobby, with a chessboard floor, connect the three floors and six suites. Each suite has a curious selection of antiques and traditional Keralan furniture, spread over a huge bedroom, living room and bathroom with jacuzzi. Four suites also have a small balcony overlooking the waterfront. An inviting plunge pool, set in a central courtyard adjacent to the seafood speciality restaurant, is the other attraction.

"Rooms have brightly painted walls adorned with Madhubani, Kalamkari and Tanjore paintings; antiques are placed in little recesses all around."

Le Colonial

Fort Kochi *1/315 Church Road, Vasco de Gama Square (0484-221-7181/7182/www.neemranahotels.com). $$$-$$$$.*
Vasco da Gama and his ilk are said to have stayed at this exquisitely restored 500-year-old house. It's a stunning residence that's more like a museum than a hotel, located right beside the Chinese fishing nets, owned by French businessman John Persenda and his wife Marie Jose-Frankel, and looked after by the Neemrana group. It's stacked to the hilt with the couple's personal art collection, photographs and artefacts. Rooms are tastefully decorated and bathrooms are lovely, with top-notch fittings. The experience here is luxurious, rather than luxury-hotel. Nearby is the 17th-century Tower House (320-321 Tower Road, 0484-221-6960),

Clockwise from top left: Brunton Boatyard; Malabar House; Koder House; Poovath Heritage Hotel; Taj Malabar.

a charming, high-ceilinged colonial heritage property that's very reasonably priced, also managed by the Neemrana group, and also overlooking the Chinese fishing nets.

Malabar House

Fort Kochi *Parade Road (0484-221-6666/ www.malabarhouse.com). $$$$.*

From Dutch settlers to spice traders, tea firms to bankers, the Malabar House has changed hands many times. Joerg Dreschel bought it in 1996 and turned it into Fort Kochi's first boutique heritage hotel. A passionate collector of art and antiques, he was also creating a space for his art collection. The hotel is a pleasant mix of understated elegance and vibrant traditional art from around India. An oddly proportioned wooden horse greets you as you enter. A lone frangipani tree droops over a swimming pool in the courtyard, beyond which are 17 rooms. All have brightly painted walls adorned with Madhubani, Kalamkari and Tanjore paintings; antiques are placed in little recesses all around. As the many celebrities who've stayed here will testify, this is not only Kochi's first boutique heritage hotel, it's also its best.

Old Harbour Hotel

Fort Kochi *Tower Road (0484-221-8006/ www.oldharbourhotel.com). $$-$$$.*

This 300-year-old mansion was the first hotel in Kochi, hosting visiting envoys and traders in colonial times. Present owner Edgar Pinto, along with Karl Damschen, a long-time resident of Kochi and an architect who specialises in restoration, has painstakingly resurrected this building to its former glorious state and transformed it into a boutique hotel. All 13 suites are large, airy, high-ceilinged and filled with handpicked antiques and red-oxide window seats. Large windows open on to a central courtyard, lush garden or waterfront. You'll find organic soaps and lotions in the bathrooms, and flower oils are used for the spa's massages.

Poovath Heritage Hotel

Fort Kochi *DC Road (/0484-221-5241/93497-62975/ www.poovath.com). $$. No AmEx.*

This grand old Dutch mansion has been restored with a few colourful liberties taken in the process. The main building is bedecked in vibrant blue-and-white paint and overlooks Fort Kochi Beach. Rooms are simple and elegant, with wooden floors, bathtubs and decor that is a blend of traditional and art deco. Most rooms have generous views of the Arabian Sea, while others look either on to a garden or the Dutch cemetery next door. There's a swimming pool, with deckchairs, and a steady sea breeze keeps you perennially comfortable.

Taj Malabar

E of Fort Kochi *Willingdon Island (0484-266-6811/ www.tajhotels.com). $$$$.*

For 65 years, the Taj Malabar has been the defining feature on the horizon when you're standing on Marine Drive on the mainland, and looking out towards the Arabian Sea. Both the modern Tower Wing and the older Heritage Wing offer great views of the harbour. Rooms are opulent, with teak panelling and creature comforts aplenty. The Sunset Room in the Tower Wing, glass-fronted on two sides, is easily the best room in the hotel, commanding astounding views. Service is exemplary.

Factfile

When to go

Mid September to March is the best time to visit Kochi, as the weather is at its coolest. However, the monsoon (June to mid September, and again in mid October) has a special charm in Kerala. If you don't mind lots of rain, hotels and tour operators often offer deals from June to mid September.

Getting there

Kochi is well connected by air, rail and road to the rest of the country, with regular flights from major Indian cities, as well as to Singapore, Colombo and the Middle East.

For more information on travel within Inida, *see p378* **Navigating India**.

Getting around

Short distances can be covered on foot or by auto-rickshaw. Private taxis can be found for longer trips. You can also hire a motorboat to explore the harbour from either the Sea Lord boat jetty or from near the main Ernakulam boat jetty.

Tourist information

The District Tourism Promotion Council office is at Kanayannur, in Ernakulam (0484-236-7334, open 10am-5pm Mon-Sat).

There's also a tourist desk at Ernakulam's main boat jetty, opposite Kochin Corporation (0484-237-1761, open 8am-6pm daily) and another in Fort Kochi (Kamalakadavu, 0484-221-6567, open 10am-5pm Mon-Sat, closed 2nd Sat of month).

Tips

- Mosquitoes are going to bother you in Kochi, especially if you're drinking or dining alfresco at dusk. Carry some mosquito repellent with you at all times.

Architectural Treasures

Taj Mahal.

Agra

The Taj Mahal, and more Mughal magnificence.

The Taj Mahal is the jewel in India's crown. But it is just one – albeit the most exquisite – of Agra's wonderful, if indifferently preserved, Mughal buildings. That the magnificence of Agra's monuments manages to transcend the city's bad reputation for pollution, commercialism and aggressive touts says something about just how fascinating a repository of Mughal architecture and history it is.

Shah Jahan, the architect Mughal emperor, built the Taj Mahal as a memorial for his second and favourite wife, Mumtaz Mahal, who died in childbirth. Although Shah Jahan built a new capital in Delhi, and though his son, Aurangzeb, abandoned Agra to wage war further south, the elegant fort, the mysterious ghost town of Fatehpur Sikri, and the many tombs, gardens and mosques within the city limits ensure Agra's place in Indian history. It was an important centre during British colonial rule as well, and many colonnaded white buildings, imperial courts, offices and a large military quarter survive from this period.

Agra's glorious monuments – particularly its magnum opus, the Taj – leave all visitors in a state of awe and admiration, but taking a little time to understand their history makes a visit much more enthralling. Unfortunately, Agra city doesn't inspire prolonged visits, catering to day trippers and overnighters rather than encouraging visitors to explore its colourful older areas or discover its lesser-known monuments. Frustratingly, it's hard to get away from package prices and set itineraries, but though you can see all the major sites in a day, the city rewards a little time and patience.

Explore

Contrary to popular belief, there is more to Agra than the Taj. South of the Taj Mahal is the backpacker area of Taj Ganj. Curving around this is Fatehabad Road. The Yamuna river runs north of the Taj and there are several interesting sites clustered on the opposite bank. Agra Fort lies to the north-west. A little further north-west of the fort is the Jama Masjid and, beyond this, the old city of Agra. Most visitors won't get a chance to explore the old city, and locals will try to discourage you from its tangle of streets and speciality bazaars. But if you have a few days to spare, it's worth lingering here to wander and lose one's way in the rambling lanes. Sikandra (Akbar's tomb) is just west of of Agra city and the ruined Mughal city of Fatehpur Sikri a 40-kilometre (25-mile), one-hour drive away.

It is possible to cram in all the major monuments in a day, though you'll probably get more out of the experience if you are able to linger at some of the less popular sights and avoid high temperatures in the summer and crowds in the winter. But whether you are seeing the sights in a day or taking a bit longer, it'll make life easier to hire a taxi or auto-rickshaw for the day at a fixed price.

Admission to most monuments is Rs 5-Rs 10 for Indians, Rs 100- Rs 250 for other nationalities (Rs 500-Rs 750 for the Taj Mahal); children under 15 can enter for free. A somewhat complicated admission fee structure exists for Agra's monuments depending on one's nationality (see details at www.uptourism.com/destination/agra/toll_tax.htm), with some monuments offering minor discounts when you show your Taj ticket. Note also that Friday tends to be the busiest day at most monuments (except the Taj, which is closed) because of free or reduced admission prices.

YAMUNA RIVERFRONT MONUMENTS, TAJ GANJ & AROUND

During Mughal times, the waterfront played a central role in Agra life, with many noblemen's homes, tombs and gardens flanking the Yamuna river. Of these the most famous is, of course, the Taj Mahal on the west bank. Several monuments on the east bank of the river opposite the Taj Mahal are worth a visit as well – Itmad-ud-Daulah's tomb in particular. You can get to these monuments by crossing the Yamuna river via a very busy bridge. South of the Taj Mahal is the area of Taj Ganj and the busy Fatehabad Road, a heavy tourist enclave.

Chini ka Rauza

E bank of Yamuna, 1km N of Itmad-ud-Daulah. Open sunrise-sunset daily. Admission Rs 5 Indians; Rs 105 others.

This early 17th-century mausoleum houses the tomb of Afzal Khan, prime minister in Shah Jahan's court and

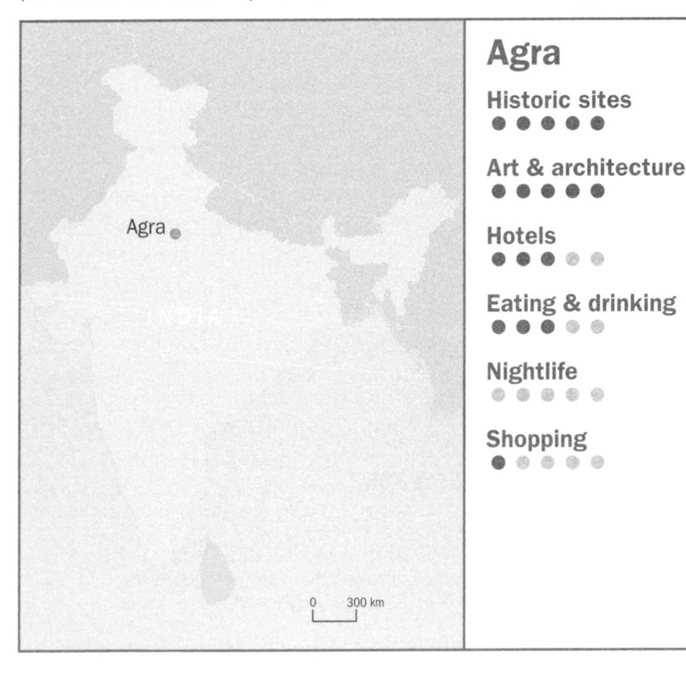

Agra

Historic sites
●●●●●

Art & architecture
●●●●●

Hotels
●●●○○

Eating & drinking
●●●○○

Nightlife
○○○○○

Shopping
●○○○○

brother of the calligrapher of the Taj Mahal. The tomb gets its popular name 'China tomb' from the colourful, complicated glazed tilework that adorns it.

Itmad-ud-Daulah

E bank of Yamuna. Open sunrise-sunset daily. Admission Rs 5 Indians; Rs 105 others.

Affectionately (but not very accurately) known as the Baby Taj, this diminutive tomb makes up for in beauty what it lacks in size. The squat marble mausoleum was built by Emperor Jehangir's wife Nur Jahan, for her father Mirza Ghiyath Beg, a prominent Persian courtier. The Persian influence is evident in the gorgeous, fine inlaid carvings on the exteriors. Botanically accurate representations of Persian flowers, intricate geometric designs and a staggering variety of semi-precious stones adorn the outside of the building, while the interior chambers have fine paintings and inlaid bouquets and vases. Keep an eye out for an unusual eye-level painting in an alcove on the far side of the tomb: a vase composed of several grinning fishes may be the result of some mischievous restoration work.

Mehtab Bagh

E bank of Yamuna, opposite Taj Mahal. Open sunrise-sunset daily. Admission Rs 5 Indians; Rs 105 others.

Mehtab Bagh (Moonlit Garden) was built by Shah Jahan and faces the Taj across the river. Woefully devoid of the reflecting pools and fountains that existed in its heyday, Mehtab Bagh is still a pleasant place for a walk and provides an uncrowded view of the Taj. If you have time, visit the village of Kachhpura just to the north, to see a mosque built by Humayun in 1520. Some five-star hotels arrange moonlight viewings or private dinners from nearby Mehtabgarh village – for a price, of course.

Taj Mahal

0562-233-0489/www.asi.nic.in. Open 6am-7pm Mon-Thur, Sat, Sun. Admission Rs 20 Indians; Rs 750 others.

Despite the droves of tourists and inevitable hassling by touts that surrounds a visit to this iconic mausoleum, the experience is still breathtaking, and you'll be left in no doubt that the Taj is truly deserving of its World Heritage Site status. Travellers have been journeying to Agra to see the Taj since it was built by the grief-stricken Mughal emperor Shah Jahan as the final resting place for his beloved wife, Mumtaz Mahal, who died in 1631. The tomb took 12 years to complete and has many myths and legends associated with it. Some even debate the emperor's real motive for building this monument, but in all likelihood, after a visit you'll believe the romantic version of history – that this is indeed one of the world's most luminous and dazzling monuments to love. It's impossible to come here and not be moved by the staggering beauty of the marble building, which poet Rabindranath Tagore called 'a teardrop on the cheek of time'. With every nuance of light, it changes, yet remains an eternal icon of India and a symbol of love and life after death.

There is no better time to see the Taj than at sunrise, when the monument opens. Otherwise you'll have to queue up for tickets, the bag deposit and entry, not to mention the obligatory photograph at the benches in front of the tomb. Night viewing is possible on full moon nights, but requires advance planning and permission.

Enter the forecourt from any one of the tall, red sandstone archways. Once through the imposing double-arched main gateway surmounted by marble domes, the Taj is in front of you, the grand vanishing point at the end of the parallel lines of the gardens and reflecting pool. Divided into the typical Mughal *charbagh* (four gardens) layout, these gardens are well maintained, though the streams and fountains often run dry. You have to take your shoes off or put on the shoe-covers (provided with a 'foreigner ticket') before climbing up to the marble plinth that supports the mausoleum and its four minarets.

The large domed central chamber, with its replica or public tombs, is surrounded by octagonal, flower lattice-work marble screens encrusted with jewels. Mumtaz Mahal's tomb, inscribed with the 99 Islamic names of God, lies in the centre beneath the dome; a good guide will point out the perfect symmetry with which the tomb is lined up to the main entrance. Shah Jahan's tomb was added here later, and its presence actually mars the symmetry. Mumtaz Mahal and Shah Jahan's real graves lie in a crypt beneath the chamber. Four corner rooms were built to house graves of other royal family members, but these remain empty. Inside, the acoustics are brilliant, the magnificent dome designed to echo the recitation of Quranic verses. The beauty of the wide, even stones of pearly white marble, the walls inlaid with delicate, coloured floral designs and precious and semi-precious gemstones and the swirling Quranic calligraphy create an effect that is ethereal, dreamlike and guaranteed to melt the most cynical heart.

Left of the garden is the Taj Museum (Admission Rs 5), which houses (in various stages of dilapidation) some interesting documents pertaining to the Taj Mahal as well as numerous Mughal artefacts, Mughal miniatures and British paintings. To the west of the Taj is the main mosque of the complex, and to the east an identical pavilion that once functioned as a rest house, built for the sake of architectural symmetry. The Yamuna river lies to the north.

Taj Nature Walk

600m NE of the Taj East Gate, near Shilpgram parking (www.tajnaturewalk.in). Open 6.15am-7pm daily. Admission Rs 10 Indians; Rs 50 others.

When the going gets tough in Agra, take time off for a walk on the quiet side at the peaceful green sanctuary of the Taj Nature Walk. You can catch glimpses of the Taj from behind trees and several 'viewing mounds'.

AGRA FORT

Around two and a half kilometres to the north-west of the Taj Mahal, Agra Fort, the second of Agra's top tourist spots and also a UNESCO World Heritage Site, was built between 1565 and 1574 by the Mughal emperor Akbar. Covering a large area, it is like a walled, fortified town. Constructed on the site of an earlier fort,

it took over 3,000 labourers eight years to complete. From the rounded red sandstone fortified entrance to the elegant marble domes of the Moti Masjid (closed to the public) inside, the architecture of the fort is awe-inspiring.

Entry is through the spectacular southern Amar Singh Gate, which opens out into an outer courtyard. A series of courtyards and pavilions built by various emperors for various purposes in varying styles, follows. The largest courtyard leads to the Jehangiri Mahal, which has several brilliantly carved rooms, each with a different style of ornamentation. To its left are Shah Jahan's pavilions, built in white marble, where he is said to have spent the last years of his life gazing at the Taj while incarcerated by his son Aurangzeb. A passage takes you to the next courtyard, Anguri Bagh, which is thought to have been the site of a weekly bazaar for the women of the court. Notice the torch holders set into the sandstone above the courtyard. Shah Burj, the pavilion overlooking the Yamuna river, has unforgettable inlay work. Unfortunately the domed edifice is fenced off.

Next is the Macchhi Bhawan (Fish Enclosure, an area that probably contained fishponds, and was intended for harem functions) above which is the Diwan-i-Khas (private audience room), and a wide marble veranda with a good view of the Taj Mahal. Exit through the marble-pillared Diwan-i-Am, where Shah Jahan held public audiences. Nagina Masjid just beyond this is one of two mosques in the complex, this one a private mosque for women.

Agra Fort

Yamuna Kinara Road (0562-236-4557). Open sunrise-sunset daily. Admission Rs 20 Indians; Rs 250-Rs 300 others.

Wildlife SOS

One rather furry feature of Mughal court entertainment was a reluctant participant. Trained by a nomadic community called the Qalandars, sloth bears became popular in the Mughal courts and, unfortunately, continue to be used as 'dancing bears' even up to the present day. Until fairly recently, a man leading a shaggy black bear by its nose was a common sight on the road from Delhi to Agra.

Through the use of a stick, bears are made to 'dance' for public amusement. This particularly cruel form of entertainment (more so because the nose ring requires making a painful, often unhealable piercing through the cub's muzzle) was banned in 1972. However, the ban was hard to enforce, partly because the Qalandar community had no alternative source of livelihood. Poachers continued to steal sloth bear cubs from their mothers, and the animals continued to be psychologically and physically tortured. Young bears' canines are knocked out, their muzzles pierced with hot nails and the males are brutally castrated. Many go blind due to malnutrition.

In 1995, Kartick Satyanarayan and Geeta Seshamani decided to do something about the plight of the bears. They formed Wildlife SOS, an organisation that focuses on wildlife rescue and rehabilitation. At the same time, they realised the need to provide alternative sources of income to those communities that were reliant on the animals. By creating incentives for Qalandars to give up their bears and pursue other types of sustainable trade, Wildlife SOS has managed to rescue more

and more animals. At last count, 518 sloth bears had been saved – many of them through undercover anti-poaching operations – and taken to three bear rescue facilities across India.

The first of these rescue centres is located just off the highway between Delhi and Agra, about 30 kilometres (19 miles) from the Taj Mahal. Here bears are quarantined, given medical treatment and the chance to live comfortably in a natural (though fenced) environment. They climb trees, eat fruit and begin to get over the trauma they have experienced at the hands of humans. Donors and other visitors interested in furthering their welfare can call on the bears with a prior appointment (011-2462-1939, www.wildlifesos.org).

Clockwise from top:
Sikandra; Agra Fort;
Fatehpur Sikri.

AROUND AGRA

SIKANDRA

Around eight kilometres to the north-west of Agra, in Sikandra, are a pair of notable Mughal tombs: that of the Mughal emperor Akbar and another believed to be that of his wife.

Akbar's Tomb

Open sunrise-sunset daily. Admission Rs 10 Indians; Rs 100 others.

A splendid red sandstone structure, designed and begun by Akbar (1542-1605) – widely considered the greatest Mughal emperor – during his lifetime. Entry to the walled square grounds of the tomb is from the striking south gate, decorated with geometric patterns, stars and stripes in yellow, black and white, as well as some contrasting delicate floral patterns. There are three other 'false gates' surrounding the tomb – the western gate in particular has an outstandingly well-preserved sculptural façade. Blackbuck antelopes roam the gardens surrounding the central mausoleum, which is topped by numerous white marble domes and walkways. Look up as you enter; the decorated ceiling is stunning blue and gold, in stark contrast with the underground burial chamber.

Mariyam's Tomb

Open sunrise-sunset daily. Admission Rs 5 Indians; Rs 100 others.

To the west of Akbar's tomb is Mariyam's tomb, a square tomb believed to be the mausoleum of one of the emperor's wives, Mariyam al-Zamani, mother of Jehangir. According to popular belief, the site originally housed a Lodhi pleasure garden. The red sandstone building is in relatively good condition, with geometrical relief carvings and delicate ornamental towers.

FATEHPUR SIKRI

Fatehpur Sikri – some 40 kilometres (25 miles) west of Agra – is the source of much of the fantasy and myth surrounding the Mughals. Rarely is one place the wellspring for so much legend, more or less defining the character of a historical era. Countless Bollywood film sequences have been shot here, striving to capture the romance, grandeur and mystery of the Mughals.

Construction of the 'City of Victory' was begun by Akbar in 1571 but it was only capital of the Mughal Empire until 1585; it's said that it was abandoned because of lack of water, eventually turning into a ghost town. The site is surrounded by a crumbling city wall. If you have the time and a good guide, it's worth exploring the city ruins between these outer limits and the palace walls. Otherwise, the highlights are the palace and adjacent mosque.

Fatehpur Sikri's **Palace** lies on top of a hill (take a natural gas-powered auto-rickshaw if you don't feel like walking). There are two entrances. The western entrance opens out into the Diwan-i-Am or public audience hall. Beyond this are the inner living quarters of Akbar and his retinue. While helpful signboards describe the architecture in detail, the actual historical importance of most of the buildings is up for debate; guides have a field day telling visitors fantastic stories with little historical verity.

Wander through the Diwan-i-Khas or private audience hall, with central pillar and overhead walkways. Beyond this is the Ankh Michauli or 'blind man's bluff room', probably a treasury, with an adjacent astrologer's pavilion. Note the large parcheesi board pattern in the main courtyard flooring – apparently games were once played using human pieces. On the other side of the courtyard, the Anup Talao is a green pool with an elevated stage in the centre – legendary as the performance area of Akbar's court musicians and immortalised in many a Bollywood song-and-dance scene. Beyond the Anup Talao on the south side of the courtyard is the many-pillared Khwabgah, where Akbar slept. A passage leads into the area, said to have been used by his wives to visit him.

Other areas of interest include the Turkish Sultana's House, with its lush relief carvings of fruit and flowers, Jodhabai's Palace, allegedly belonging to Akbar's Hindu wife, and the House of Birbal, said to have accommodated the emperor's famously clever courtier.

Adjacent to the palace is the spectacular **Jama Masjid** (also called Jami Masjid), where the Sufi saint Sheikh Salim al-Din Chishti lies buried in the white marble tomb towards the rear of the complex. Chishti moved to Sikri from Delhi in the late 15th century. Famously, he foretold the birth of Akbar's son Jehangir and the emperor built his new city around the religious leader's tomb. Chishti's dargah (tomb) is a lovely lattice-shrouded marble enclosure. Crowds perambulate around the grave; thousands of red strings are tied around the intricately carved lattice screens by pilgrims who come with prayer requests for the saint. Outside the tomb, Pir Mohammad Qawwal, who says he is descended from the original bards of the tomb, sings *qawwalis* (songs of tribute), accompanied by his harmonium. The spacious courtyard has the magnificent Buland Darwaza (Victory Gate) on one side, with a view of the surrounding countryside, as well as the large red sandstone tomb of Nawab Islam Khan (Chishti's grandson), and the Badshahi or Emperor's Gate.

Fatehpur Sikri

40km W of Agra. Open Site sunrise-sunset daily; Dargah complex (religious area) 5.30am-8pm or after prayers. Admission Rs 10 Indians; Rs 260 others; free under-15s.

Eat

With the exception of a few upmarket restaurants in five-star hotels, there's not a lot to rave about in Agra's culinary scene, though a couple of budget eateries manage to make up for uninspiring food with winsome ambience or Taj views. Locals may also direct you to a few notable street-food options, but it's wise to be wary about these.

Dasaprakash

1km S of Agra Fort *Meher Theatre Complex, Gwalior Road, Balu Ganj (0562-246-3535). Open 11am-10.45pm daily. $. No credit cards. South Indian.*

This famous no-frills South Indian diner is a hit with locals and visitors. Service is efficient and polite, and the list of dosas is long and appealing. If you've had South Indian food in South India, you'll be disappointed by the quality, but this is still the right place in Agra for a tasty, filling vegetarian meal.

Esphahan

Taj Ganj *Oberoi Amarvilas, Taj East Gate Road (0562-223-1515/www.amarvilas.com). Two seatings daily 7pm & 9pm. $$$$. Indian.*

If you can't stay at the Amarvilas, you may want to get a taste of its opulence at its Awadhi restaurant. Given the magnificence of the rest of the hotel, Esphahan is actually slightly underwhelming: located on the lower ground floor, it has no Taj views and is a bit dark. You may find it difficult to get a reservation but if you manage it, and you don't mind a little splurge, get here early for a cocktail in the lobby bar, which has a lovely view of the Taj. The menu is short but interesting; signature dishes include quail stuffed with minced chicken in saffron gravy and tandoori prawns marinated in citrus and yoghurt. There's live Indian classical music to accompany dinner.

Hotel Maya

Taj Ganj *18/184 Purani Mandi Circle, Fatehabad Road (0562-233-2109/97191-07691/www.mayainmagic.com). Open 7am-10pm daily. $. No credit cards. Multi-cuisine.*

With tables set on a mosaic-tiled floor and ground-level seating on cushions, Hotel Maya's terrace is the spot for an enchanting – and cheap – meal. A generously shady wild fig tree spreads over a part of the terrace and a couple of fans do the rest of the work. The menu includes filling, fresh and completely inauthentic Indian, Chinese and Western dishes. Guests typically order from different cuisines, getting garlic naan to accompany the fresh home-made pasta with tomato sauce and tuna, say, while the hotel's skinny cat looks out for friendly patrons.

Mughal Room

3km SW of Taj Mahal *Hotel Clarks Shiraz, 54 Taj Road (0562-222-6121/www.hotelclarksshiraz.com). Open 12.30-2.45pm, 7-11.30pm daily. $$$. No AmEx. Multi-cuisine.*

Locals have been eating at the plush Mughal Room on the top floor of the Hotel Clarks for decades. Star-shaped lanterns, slender wooden archways and big picture windows pull together nicely and the borderline kitsch decor is endearing, not offensive. At dinner, a capable music troupe plays atmospheric Hindi film favourites and takes requests. Old-hand waiting staff know the menu inside out and the bartender is generous. At sunset, the outdoor terrace is the perfect spot for a drink and some tender *galawat* kebabs, chicken malai tikkas (chicken cream kebabs), or vegetarian yoghurt kebabs.

Paatra

Taj Ganj *Jaypee Palace Hotel, Fatehabad Road (0562-233-0800/www.jaypeehotels.com). Open 7.30-11.45pm daily. $$$. Punjabi.*

Jaypee Palace's new dining venue offers food 'from Amritsar to Lahore' (in other words, the cuisine of undivided Punjab). Tastefully decorated in dull gold tones, Paatra is only open for dinner. Savour excellent kebabs, spicy curries, crisp-yet-fluffy breads and a gorgeously simple yellow dal and end the meal with local Madhu brand kulfi. A musical troupe featuring a guitarist and tabla player accompanying the accomplished *ghazal* singer performs most nights.

Peshawari

Taj Ganj *ITC Mughal, Fatehabad Road (0562-233-1701/www.itcwelcomgroup.in/itcmughal/). Open 12.30-2.45pm, 7.30-11.30pm daily. $$$$. North-west Frontier.*

Peshawari is the sister restaurant (same look and North-west Frontier Province menu) to Bill Clinton's favourite, the Bukhara in Delhi. The protocol is simple: guests pull up a wooden bench, strap on a red-checked bib, and commune, caveman-like, with meat. The tandoori *jhinga* (prawns) are popular, coming second only to the *burra* (mutton) kebabs. The buttery dal Bukhara is justly famous and must be accompanied by the delicious creamy raita.

Shanti Lodge

Taj Ganj *nr Taj South Gate (0562-223-1973). Open 6am-10pm daily. $. No credit cards. Multi-cuisine.*

A rooftop restaurant with a particularly lovely view, Shanti is a backpacker favourite – especially for parathas and pancakes after morning sightseeing. The roof has a direct view of the Taj Mahal and the clutter of lesser Taj Ganj rooftops.

Zorba the Buddha

4km SW of Agra Fort *E-19, Shopping Arcade, Sadar Bazaar, Agra Cantonment (0562-222-6091). Open noon-10pm daily. Closed 1 June-5 July. $. No credit cards. Indian & vegetarian fusion.*

Sameer Wahi's family runs this quirky café as an extension of their belief in the Osho philosophy of the 'ideal man', who is equal parts Gautam Buddha and Zorba the Greek. Vegetarian and very clean, the creative 27-year-old eaterie has pretty marble panels with pietra dura (inlaid) flowers. Pineapple, potato and paneer are primary ingredients in the Indian and Western offerings. Cheese naan is a yummy fusion option, and those with a sweet tooth may like the *rassila* kofta, a potato dumpling in banana sauce. If Zorba's 'new heights of vegetarian delights' make you dizzy, choose from the set menu.

Taj Ganj.

Shop

While Agra is known for its marble work, rugs, leather and brass, shopping here is invariably more a headache than a pleasure. Most taxi and auto-rickshaw drivers insist on taking you to shops where they can earn a commission, while hotel shopping arcades generally have reliable, quality goods, but are overpriced. Very few stand-alone shops are worth visiting in Agra. If you are travelling on to Jaipur or Delhi, keep your shopping for later. Shilpgram (*see below*) and the various state government-run handicraft emporiums such as Gangotri, Rajasthali and Kairali inside the Taj Mahal complex are good places to shop; the latter has a variety of marble, leather and brass knick-knacks at reasonable prices. Marble mementos are heavy, but the best bet as souvenirs.

Ganeshi Lall Emporium

2km W of Agra Fort *MG Road (0562-246-4842/ http://gle845.com). Open 8.30am-7.30pm daily. No credit cards.*

The family that owns this shop claims to have been in business since 1845; famous visitors have included Queen Elizabeth and Prince Philip, and Jacqueline Kennedy. Besides lavish jewellery, the shop also specialises in jewelled carpets. You do get treated like royalty here, with prices to match.

Kalakriti

Taj Ganj *41/142, A/1 VIP Road to Taj, Taj East Gate (0562-223-1011/www.kalakritionline.com). Open 9am-8pm daily. No AmEx.*

This cultural centre includes a crafts showroom with good quality (if slightly expensive) items: the marble work is particularly notable. The shop is owned by the same company that created the largest Taj replica in the world.

Shilpgram

Taj Ganj *Telipara (no phone). Open Oct-Mar 10am-10pm daily.*

An open-air crafts complex, Shilpgram is most lively in February, when it hosts the Taj Mahotsav (festival). Shopping here is a relatively quiet and hassle-free experience, where you can interact directly with craftspeople.

Arts

Kalakriti

Taj Ganj *41/142, A/1 VIP Road to Taj, off Fatehabad Road, Taj East Gate (0562-404-5370)/www.kalakriti online.com). Open Box office 9am-8pm daily. Shows Aug-Mar 6.30pm daily. Tickets Rs 250-Rs 750.*

Agra's only cultural centre stages a Bollywood-meets-biopic show entitled *Mohabbat The Taj: The Saga of Love* daily for a mix of local and foreign tourists. The kitschy show is surprisingly well produced, even if Kalakriti's three-metre-high Taj replica does rise out of the ground, courtesy of a hydraulic lift. Dancers are decked out in bright costume jewellery, there's song and dance, and translation via headsets in eight languages.

Stay

New to Agra's accommodation scene are business-style hotels and homestays, which are popping up as alternatives to the two standard ends of the accommodation spectrum – luxury hotels and backpacker places.

Most of the city's larger hotels are strung along Fatehabad Road, which curves around the Taj Ganj area, just a short distance from the Taj. Parallel to and south of Fatehabad Road is Shamsabad Road.

Prices fluctuate a lot depending on the season; most hotels hike rates at the start of the autumn.

"Guests love Mrs Lamba's home-style vegetarian fare and cooking demos."

Clarks Shiraz

3km SW of Taj Mahal *54 Taj Road (0562-222-6121/www.hotelclarksshiraz.com). $$. No AmEx.*

From the glowing 'C' logo on top of its main tower to the kidney-shaped pool, Agra's first five-star hotel has a definite 1960s air. While basic rooms are carpeted and slightly stuffy, newer rooms are modish, with green marble flooring and Taj views. This is a comfortably casual, family-friendly hotel, with many old hands among the staff making the service a plus. The top-floor Mughal Room restaurant (*see p164*) is a local favourite and the adjacent rooftop terrace is a good spot for sundowners.

Col Lamba Homestay

2km W of Agra Fort *58, 71 Gulmohar Enclave, off Shamsabad Road (0562-329-8921/93198-42921/ www.agra-indianhomestay.com). $. No credit cards.*

Colonel Inderjeet Singh Lamba, an affable, retired army man, and his wife run this endearing if slightly cramped seven-room homestay just 3.5km from the Taj. Rooms vary, especially in terms of natural light, but they are all air-conditioned, comfortable and very clean. Bedrooms in the main building and the annexe across the road are built in suite-like clusters with common lounges and small kitchens. Top-floor rooms in the annexe, in particular, are nice, with a large attached terrace and a stairway to the roof. This has a (distant) Taj view and a tiny but welcome plunge pool. Little touches make this place special: a chessboard built

Top & middle:
Oberoi Amarvilas.
Bottom : ITC Mughal (2).

into a patio floor; wine bottles overflowing with plants; a cosy central dining room; and plenty of reading material. Guests love Mrs Lamba's home-style vegetarian fare and cooking demos. Breakfast is included; lunch, dinner and classes are a bit extra.

Garden Villa

2km W of Agra Fort *11 Kaveri Vihar, Phase III, Chamrauli, off Shamsabad Road (97191-13626/97600-21665/www.gardenvillahomestay.com). $. No credit cards.*
Garden Villa is a bit tricky to get to – it's off the beaten track in a residential block – though it isn't far from Taj Ganj. It's best to arrange a pick-up as auto-rickshaws will probably refuse to ferry you here. Owner NN Rajbansh, a loquacious architect by training, and his green-fingered wife Madhu are constantly upgrading their pleasant, if slightly impersonal, guesthouse. Comfortable and clean air-conditioned rooms are in two buildings, separated by a patch of lawn. Rooms in the additional building, particularly the Lily Room, have a more modern aesthetic than the functional ones in the main house.

Gateway Hotel

Taj Ganj *Fatehabad Road (0562-223-2400/ www.thegatewayhotels.com). $$.*
The former Taj View hotel may seem a little worn around the edges, but the experienced service balances things out. Rooms are very comfortable, with plenty of amenities and little local touches (red sandstone headboards with pietra dura inlay work, for instance). The Gateway has a comprehensive shopping arcade and two restaurants: Aashiyaana, a catch-all greenhouse-like coffee shop, and Jhankar, which serves Indian and Chinese food. The poolside grill and bar is a good place to relax at the end of a tiring day. Numerous cultural activities, including palm reading, biking, kite flying, are available to guests. There's also the Taj Jiva spa, a gym and salon.

Hotel Sheela/Sheela Inn

Taj Ganj *Taj East Gate (0562-233-3074/ www.hotelsheelaagra.com). $. No credit cards.*
Built over 20 years ago on the grounds of a school near the Taj East Gate, this family-owned guesthouse has capitalised on its location within the pollution-free Taj zone. Lawns are shaded by trees and the Green View restaurant is a charming, relaxed space. Rooms are on the superior side of budget: clean, marble-floored, relatively spacious and good value for money. Down the road is a sister property, the newer Sheela Inn, which has three levels of clean, sunny rooms. These rooms have less atmosphere, but there is a pretty garden terrace restaurant cooled by fans and potted plants.

ITC Mughal

Taj Ganj *Fatehabad Road (0562-233-1701/www.itc welcomgroup.in/itcmughal/). $$$.*
Roughly inspired by the layout of Fatehpur Sikri, this hotel has won architectural awards. However, it has an institutional feel, with tons of sandstone and marble, sprawling red brick wings, an enormous lobby chandelier and expanses of lawn (including a maze). There's a lovely observation tower, matching Sikri's Ankh Michauli, where you can toast the Taj at sunset. The Kaya Kalp spa is India's largest, with its luscious pomegranate theme and jacuzzis, outdoor showers, hammams and swimming lagoon. Warm service, a range of good restaurants and a sense of (1970s) style are further pluses.

Jaypee Palace

Taj Ganj *Fatehabad Road (0562-233-0800/ www.jaypeehotels.com). $$-$$$.*
The Jaypee Palace is a red sandstone behemoth set on a hill, with a reputation for catering to large tour groups and business conventions. Designed by the same firm that built the ITC Mughal and located in a quiet area, this huge hotel features hallway upon hallway, various restaurants and banqueting halls – including the excellent Paatra (*see p164*) – and dozens of entertainment options, including shops, a cinema, bowling alley, nightclub and an Ayurvedic spa. But it somehow manages to achieve a warm elegance despite its size. Softening all the stone and marble are acres of surrounding lawn, two inner courtyard gardens, a reflecting pool and eco-friendly water features. Rooms are spacious, with austere wooden flooring and furniture; each looks out over a garden or courtyard. Nicer and pricier Palace rooms are housed in an exclusive wing with its own reception.

Maya Hotel

Taj Ganj *18/184 Purani Mandi Circle, Fatehabad Road (0562-233-2109/97191-07691/www.mayainmagic.com). $. No credit cards.*
Israel seems to be the theme for this cheery blue-and-white hotel, with a Star of David motif repeated in the latticework banisters, wrought-iron window grilles and pretty much everything else (the management insists it welcomes all nationalities, however). The three-storey building is constructed around an open stairwell, which keeps things cool in the summer. Fairly spacious rooms include lots of marble (even marble bed-stands in some cases) and tie-dye. There's an enchanting terrace restaurant and a rooftop with a Taj view. Located on the edge of Taj Ganj, Maya feels a bit more peaceful than other backpacker hotels. Room 7 is particularly nice; rooms 6, 11 and 12 are second choices.

Oberoi Amarvilas

Taj Mahal *East Gate Road (0562-223-1515/ www.amarvilas.com). $$$$.*
The Monument of Love looks jaw-droppingly close from the Amarvilas's Mughal-baroque check-in tea lounge: its marble domes rise unimpeded from the stretch of green protected forest – the only thing that lies between the Taj and the Amarvilas. That view is shared by all 102 rooms and suites of this luxury hotel. Just in case the Taj isn't close enough, the presidential Kohinoor suite has an old-fashioned telescope as its central furnishing (and a shower with a view). Indian textile accents and crafts adorn all the rooms, which have plenty of space and top amenities. The pool, with its Moorish arcade and adjacent gardens and terraces (perfect for private dining), is stunning. Non-guests can drink in the view at the lobby bar, though access to the tiny outdoor balcony is for residents only.

The Bellevue coffee shop and Indian restaurant Esphahan (*see p164*, neither has a Taj view) are open to outside reservations. There's a fully equipped spa and guests are encouraged to while away hours under the hands of experienced imported masseurs.

Trident

Taj Ganj *Fatehabad Road (0562-223-5000/ www.tridenthotels.com). $$.*
Built around a large courtyard garden and pool, this relaxed business-chain hotel has modern, serviceable rooms, with a bright yellow-and-purple colour theme. It's laid-back and quiet on the whole, and while you may not see the Taj from here, you're not far away, and it's certainly removed from the bustle of Taj Ganj.

Welcomheritage Grand Imperial

3km W of Agra fort *MG Road (0562-225-1190/ www.hotelgrandimperial.com). $$. No AmEx.*
About four kilometres west of the Taj area, this is an ideal place to stay if you want to be away from the flurry of the city centre. The hotel has a grand history. Recently refurbished, it was originally a British building, functioning as a hotel until the mid 1960s and hosting distinguished princes and politicians. High archways and ceilings, wrap-around verandas, a big lawn and pool all contribute to its considerable charm. Ground-floor rooms that open out on to the pool are among the nicest; most have four-poster beds, antique furniture and vintage photographs. Because of the age of the building there are small imperfections, but the hotel's quaintness and history make up for them.

Factfile

When to go

November to February is coolest and also the most crowded time. From March to October, the searing daytime heat makes sightseeing difficult. However, good hotel deals can be had during the low season.

Getting there

Agra is best reached by road or train from Delhi. Agra's biggest train station is Agra Cantonment. Several trains run between Delhi and Agra daily. The fastest and most convenient is the Shatabdi Express (two hours). Others include the Taj Express (three hours) and the Intercity Express (four hours).

Buses run from Delhi, Jaipur, Mathura and Khajuraho to Agra's Idgah station, near the Agra Cantonment railway station. Delhi Tourism also runs day tour buses to Agra (011-2336-5358).

Hiring a car and driver from a travel agent is the best bet for those short of time or requiring flexibility (the drive from Delhi to Agra takes three or four hours).

Several airlines have introduced and then dropped flights to Agra in recent years; check with airlines if you want to fly.

For more on travel within India, *see p378* **Navigating India**.

Getting around

Prepaid auto-rickshaw and taxi booths at Agra Cantonment railway station have published rates for various lengths of hire, distances and destinations. Be advised that full day rates only include certain monuments. If you want to go off the beaten track, you'll have to bargain or pay extra. Auto-rickshaws and cycle-rickshaws also park outside most Fatehabad Road hotels, so finding one is never difficult. Air-conditioned cars cost from Rs 1,400 per day, and auto-rickshaws from Rs 500 per day. Auto-rickshaws charge at least Rs 50 per journey, no matter how short.

Tourist information

Agra Cantonment Railway Station
Open 8am-8pm daily.
India Tourism Office 191 Mall Road (0562-222-6378). Open 9am-5.30pm Mon-Fri; 9am-4.30pm Sat.
UP Tourism Office 64 Taj Road, near Hotel Clarks Shiraz (0562-222-6431). Open 10am-5pm Mon-Sat (closed 3rd & 4th Sat of month).

Travel tips

● **Touts selling everything** from package tours to miniature Taj Mahals are a constant and unavoidable aspect of Agra. Sidestep some of this hassling by prepaying for transport (clarify your itinerary though), refusing to shop or eat where your driver takes you, and fixing a price for all services beforehand.

● **Guides at monuments** may charge anything from Rs 30 to Rs 300, depending on the season and the tourist. If you must hire a guide at a monument, try to wait until you're past ticket collection and ask to see accreditation if possible. You'll have a better experience if you get your hotel to arrange a good English-speaking guide well in advance; the best ones get booked up months ahead. Expect to pay up to Rs 1,000 for an eight-hour day.

Top & bottom left: Welcomheritage Grand Imperial. Right: Trident (2).

Aurangabad, Ajanta & Ellora

India's most exquisite rock-cut architecture.

Buddhist monks made their way through dense jungle to the rocky hills here as long ago as the second century BC. They began chipping away at the rock with immense skill to craft the cave monasteries of Ajanta, adorning them with murals and sculptures. Over six centuries, more huge Buddhist, Hindu and Jain cave temples were hewn out of the volcanic rock to create Ellora. And years later, an expansionist medieval emperor shifted his capital here, taking over and strengthening the old fortress city of Daulatabad, only to abandon it soon afterwards, when the land proved too arid.

This whole area is part of the Deccan Plateau, the oldest land mass on the Indian subcontinent, and its long human history is written on these monuments. Today's Aurangabad brings you up to date with a bang. With its shiny buildings, it represents the new India. Home to assembly plants for international car companies and a thriving spare parts industry, it's a prosperous small town with ambition to become a big city. It is also the obvious base for exploring the fort at Daulatabad and the UNESCO World Heritage Sites of Ajanta and Ellora.

Appreciate these important works of art and faith while you can. With each passing year, a little more of the rock-cut architectural creations crumble, and a little of India's past is lost.

Clockwise from top left: Ellora Caves; Daulatabad Fort; Ajanta Caves; Bibi ka Maqbara.

Explore

Though **Aurangabad** has few tourist sites of its own, it is where most of the hotels and tourist infrastructure is, making it a convenient hub from which to visit the **Ajanta Caves**, **Ellora**, **Daulatabad Fort** and **Khuldabad**. Ajanta is 107 kilometres (66 miles) to the north-east of Aurangabad. Ellora lies 30 kilometres (19 miles) to the north-west of the city, and Daulatabad is about halfway between the two. Khuldabad lies between Daulatabad and Ellora, around three kilometres from Ellora, 27 kilometres (17 miles) from Aurangabad.

It's best to set aside at least one day each for Aurangabad, Ajanta and Ellora, and another for Daulatabad and Khuldabad – even though they are on the way to Ellora.

AURANGABAD

Today, Aurangabad is a dusty industrial city whose residents are keen to fast-forward into a metropolitan future, an aspiration evident from the numerous malls, pizza outlets and bizarre public art. Little of the city's historic architecture is easily visible. What has survived are the 52 gates that let travellers into the city, fragments of the boundary wall that once encircled it, and a few minarets and domes. These gates appear unexpectedly while travelling through the city, still imposing despite the surrounding modern buildings.

Locals say it's possible to see all of Aurangabad in around 25 minutes, though half a day is probably better. Tourism is an important part of the city's economy, and camera-toting visitors are greeted warmly – and often fleeced with certain affection. It isn't unusual to be given a few freebies by a smiling shop owner who hopes you will be goaded into buying something blatantly overpriced.

Gul Mandi is the old market area. Doors are brightly painted, vendors sell flowers (fresh and fake), shiny sari borders and various knick-knacks – including, for some reason, a lot of trumpets and drums – all piled cheek-by-jowl in little shops.

Around five kilometres north of the railway station is the Bibi ka Maqbara mausoleum and just a little further north are the Aurangabad Caves.

Aurangabad Caves

8km N of Aurangabad. Open 9am-5.30pm daily. Admission Rs 5 Indians; Rs 100 others.

The Aurangabad Caves are really two sets of Buddhist caves that date to around the sixth to seventh centuries. It's a steep climb up to the caves, which are in two groups, about a kilometre apart. The Western group is believed to be the older set. Cave 4 has a *chaitya-griha*, or prayer hall with a *stupa*, while carvings in Cave 3 relate tales of the Buddha's many incarnations. In the Eastern group, Caves 6 and 7 get a lot of attention not only because of the idols of Buddha and Ganesha, but also because the walls are adorned with sculptures of voluptuous scantily clad women. No official guides are available here.

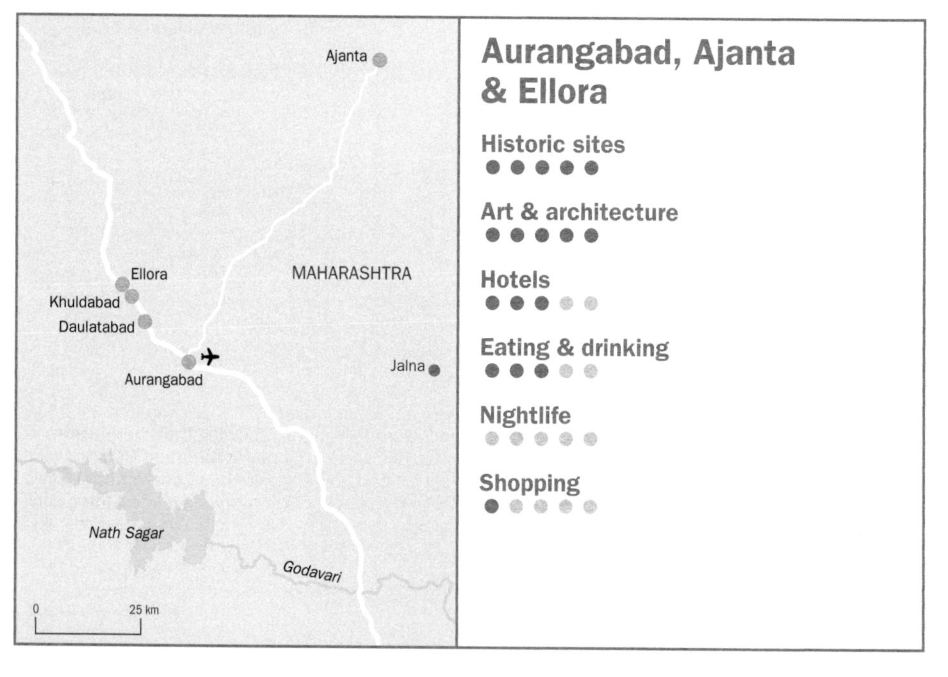

Bibi ka Maqbara

6km N of Aurangabad. Open 7am-9pm daily. Admission Rs 5 Indians; Rs 100 others.

Rather unjustly known as the 'poor man's Taj Mahal', this mausoleum to Emperor Aurangzeb's wife Rabia ul Durani is pretty enough in its own right. Built over a ten-year period by Prince Azam Shah in memory of his mother, it looks particularly lovely in the evening light (try to ignore the ugly cement supports that have been erected in parts). The mausoleum is made partly of marble, and is covered with fine plaster adorned with stucco work and floral motifs. It's a relatively simple affair, surrounded by marble screens that turn the harshest sunlight into a rather romantic glow. The surrounding gardens are attractive and a favourite picnic spot for Aurangabad's residents. Guides are available outside, but you don't really need one.

AJANTA CAVES

The Ajanta Caves represent the most spectacular ancient Buddhist art and rock-cut architecture in India. Unfortunately, ever since a British cavalryman out on a hunt spotted these caves in 1819, the rate of decay of the murals has been rapid, despite serious efforts at preservation and restoration.

In its heyday Ajanta was probably a Buddhist college monastery. In a horseshoe-shaped rocky hill just above the Waghora river, 30 caves were carved by monks who were also outstanding artists and brilliant architects. Five of these are *chaitya-grihas*, or prayer halls, and the rest are *viharas* (monasteries). The oldest cave dates to the second century BC, but construction in this hill went on, with interruptions, until about the ninth century AD. The most lavish caves were created between the fifth and sixth centuries AD. No one knows why they were later abandoned, but it's likely that work stopped when the religious activity lost royal patronage.

Today, the wall murals that these caves are so famous for have faded to the point of being indecipherable in many parts. The architecture and carving will still amaze you, though. It's worth dedicating a whole day to Ajanta, so you can take the time to pop into every cave. But if your time is limited, some of the favourites are Caves 1, 2, 6, 9, 10, 16, 17 and 19.

Though not the oldest, **Cave 1** is certainly one of the finest examples of a *vihara* at Ajanta. Dating from the sixth century AD, it's a virtual museum of Buddhist art, with intricately carved panels and superlative paintings. Few other caves are so extensively covered with sculpture: from the bodhisattva gatekeepers at the entrance to the enormous Buddha in the antechamber, it is full of detailing, and its painted panels add to the decorative effect. Since the paintings are not divided into frames, they blend into each other to create a single seamless story from the Jataka (a collection of moral tales of the former lives of Buddha). Special features include panels showing how the Buddha was tempted by Mara, the embodiment of evil; Boddhisattva Padmapani, who seems to face you no matter where you are in the cave; cavorting drunks and visiting foreigners; and the miracle at the old city of Shravasti, by which the Buddha multiplied himself so that every citizen had their own personal Buddha.

Cave 2 is smaller and not as extensively worked on as Cave 1, but still very impressive and somewhat better preserved. Dating from the sixth century, its ceiling is decorated with canoodling couples, jugglers, wrestlers and fantastical scenes. The antechamber (or shrine) has a thousand Buddhas painted on it. The story of Gautama Buddha's birth, complete with the white elephant his mother dreamed of while she was pregnant, are painted on the walls.

Also dating from the sixth century AD, **Cave 4** is the largest *vihara* in Ajanta, but remains unfinished. The main hall has 28 pillars and just outside the antechamber are six enormous standing Buddhas.

The double-storeyed monastery of **Cave 6** must have been quite elaborate in the fifth century AD, but much of the decoration has crumbled. The antechamber has beautifully carved couples on the doorjambs and the Buddha on the chamber's left wall looks as if it's made of marble, but is actually coated with a fine lime plaster. An upper storey looks incomplete, even though at some point monks took the trouble of crafting musical pillars – they were carved in such a way that tapping them at different points produces different musical notes.

Dating to the first century BC, **Cave 9** is the second oldest in Ajanta. Its murals appear to have been touched up in the fifth century AD. An echo bounces off the pillars and arched ceiling.

Cave 10 was the first cave to be dug out at Ajanta, and is believed to be the oldest, dating back to the second century BC. It has a big *stupa* in its large main hall, which must have been an impressive space when resonating with the chants of gathered monks. Barely perceptible is the painted story of Shyama Jataka, a poor Brahmin boy who was accidentally killed by a king. This version of the story shows the boy being restored to life.

Cave 12 shows how the monks lived, in cells with stone beds and little else. The holes in the wall were for hinges, showing that there were once doors here. Some of the most frequently reproduced paintings of Ajanta come from **Cave 16** and the next cave. Monks sculpted the ceiling in this *vihara* to look as if it had wooden beams and rafters. Tubby figures seem to hold up the beams. The famous mural of Princess Sundari portrayed as she swoons with shock upon hearing that her husband Nanda has joined the order of monks is also here.

Similar to the previous cave, **Cave 17** is also beautifully decorated with paintings and sculptures. There's an amorous tone to the art here, though the love stories don't seem to have happy endings. One complete wall tells the story of a virtuous merchant shipwrecked on an island of ogresses who assumed the form of beautiful women by day, but turned into cannibals by night. Other notable features include the painting of Buddha in monk's garb visiting his wife and son, the sculpture of the Naga king at the entrance, and the *apsara* whose hair and neck ornaments appear to gleam when light hits them at a certain angle.

One of the most perfect examples of Buddhist art in India is in **Cave 19**. With none of the austerity of the *chaitya* (hall) in Cave 9, it dates from the late fifth century AD and marks a change in Buddhist symbolism. The cave is full of ornamentation and images of Buddha, and the façade shows many Buddhas, including two with ornate crowns. It also has remarkable panels showing interwoven animals, birds and humans, and a notable one with two elephants fighting.

For a spectacular end (or beginning) to your day out at Ajanta, drive up to Viewpoint to get a panoramic view of the horseshoe-shaped hill in which the caves lie. There's also a path down the hill (which takes approximately 30 minutes to walk); a slight detour will bring you to a bench perched on the edge of the cliff facing the caves.

Ajanta Caves

107km N of Aurangabad. Open 7am-6pm Tue-Sun. Admission Rs 10 Indians, citizens of SAARC countries, Thailand and Myanmar; Rs 250 others; free under-15s. CNG buses take visitors from the foot of the hill to the caves. Last bus leaves the caves for the parking lot at 5.30pm; tickets Rs 24 air-conditioned bus; Rs 14 non-air-conditioned bus.

DAULATABAD FORT

Thirteen kilometres (eight miles) north of Aurangabad, on a conical hill whose sides have been cut away into vertical cliffs at its base, stands the fortress city of Daulatabad. At the bottom of the hill there were once two moats filled with poisonous snakes and crocodiles. Breaching one boundary wall brought invaders to another (with four layers of fortification), finally leading to endless secret passages where hidden soldiers lay in wait, ready to repel incursions with brutality. Within the walls was a bustling city.

Once a fortress of great strategic importance, today Daulatabad lies abandoned. At its base is an interesting mosque that was allegedly built by Delhi Sultanate ruler Mubarak Khilji in 1318 from relics plundered from Jain temples. Nearby is the Chand Minar, a 63-metre (207-foot) tower with Persian inscriptions, believed to have been built as a symbol of victory by the rulers of the Bahmani Sultanate.

Originally called Deogiri (Mountain of the Gods), the city fort was built by the Yadava dynasty in the 11th century. It was annexed to the Delhi Sultanate in the 14th century. In 1328, the part-mad, part-visionary king, Muhammad bin Tughlaq, decided to shift his capital from Delhi to Deogiri because of its strategic strength. The fort city was rechristened Daulatabad, meaning Abode of Prosperity, and the entire citizenry of Delhi forced to march southwards. It proved to be a monumental blunder; the land was too arid despite the many wells that Tughlaq had built. A few years later he ordered everyone to trudge back to Delhi. Over the years, the fort changed hands repeatedly, from Tughlaq to the Bahmani Sultanate, from Akbar to Ahmad Nizah Shah of Ahmednagar, and back to Shah Jahan.

The fort has an awesome labyrinth of rock-hewn passages called *andheri* (not recommended to anyone afraid of the dark) that are both interesting and eerie to walk through. Even with a guide lighting the way, you need to walk cautiously.

Hiring a guide to explore this site is highly recommended. It's impossible to fully appreciate the cleverness and ruthlessness of the fort's design without a guide pointing out how the structure was used in warfare: for instance, the spot from where hot oil was poured on the enemy, or where decapitated bodies were flung down a cliff to feed hungry crocodiles.

A white pillared *baradari* (Mughal pavilion) at the top of the fort can be seen from miles away. It's a climb of 400-odd steps up to this pavilion, built by Shah Jahan; you are rewarded by a superb panorama of the area. At the very summit of the hill is a large cannon with a ram's head.

Daulatabad Fort

13km N of Aurangabad. Augrangabad–Ellora road. Open 7am-6pm Tue-Sun. Admission Rs 5 Indians; Rs 100 others.

KHULDABAD

Next to the splendours of Ajanta, Ellora and Daulatabad, all this modest village – 43 kilometres (27 miles) north of Aurangabad – has to offer is a couple of tombs: no architectural or artistic flourishes here, just a few simple graves. Significant among them is the tomb of Mughal Emperor Aurangzeb (open sunrise to sunset), in the courtyard of the Alamgir Dargah. Aurangzeb had wanted to be buried here, near the tomb of Moinuddin Chisti, his spiritual guide, and had left very specific instructions about the simplicity of his tomb. Its austerity is in stark contrast to the opulence of his father, Shah Jahan's, creations. In view of the fact that Aurangzeb was a ruler who was driven to extend his empire relentlessly, the lack of pretension and ornamentation is perhaps surprising. The marble screens around the tomb were erected about 300 years later on the

Clockwise from left: Ellora Caves; Aurangabad Caves; Khuldabad.

Clockwise from top: Lemon Tree (2); Buddhi Lane; Aurangabad Himroo Industry; Gul Mandi market.

instruction of the viceroy of India, Lord Curzon. There is a wonderful tranquillity in this little compound that makes it worth the stopover, and you will want to linger, particularly after the bustle of the other, more touristy spots in the area.

ELLORA CAVES

Ellora is unique for two reasons. First, because it attracts pilgrims of three different religions: Buddhism, Hinduism and Jainism. And second, because its cave temples are hewn out of a single, solid mountainside rock. Ellora's cave temples date from the sixth or seventh century AD to the 11th or 12th century, and though there are over 100 caves in the area, 34 cave temples form the main Ellora complex. Caves 1 to 12 are Buddhist, Caves 13 to 29 Hindu and Caves 30 to 34 Jain. The years have not been kind to this UNESCO World Heritage Site: too many visitors have touched the beautifully carved rock, causing significant wear. Even so, the beauty of Ellora's sculptures is breathtaking. We strongly recommend hiring a guide to explain the wealth of detail in the sculpture and architecture.

The masterpiece of the Ellora complex is the awe-inspiring **Kailashnath Temple** (cave 16) begun by Krishna I of the Rashtrakuta dynasty around AD 750, and completed over 150 years later. Built to represent Mount Kailash, the mythical abode of Shiva, the temple's façade and ceilings were once both carved and painted. Today, very little of the painting remains and the carving is losing its detail, despite the efforts of the Archaeological Survey of India. The temple walls show Shiva and Vishnu in various avatars, panels with episodes from the epic *Mahabharata*, and many other elements from Hindu mythology. It is estimated that almost 56,600 cubic metres of rock was excavated to build this single monolithic temple alone. Curiously, this temple was constructed from front to rear and from ceiling to floor.

Other outstanding caves include nos. 10, 14, 30 and 32. Cave 10 is the **Vishwakarma Cave**, named after the patron deity of artisans. It features hunting scenes, decorations on the pillar, and a ceiling supported by male and female figures. **Cave 14** has a four-armed goddess Durga, goddess Laxmi seated on a lotus and a sculpture of Vishnu in the avatar of a boar. It also contains a shrine guarded by representations of the holy rivers Ganga and Yamuna, the former mounted on a crocodile and the latter on a turtle. Some panels are devoted to Shiva, including one that shows Ravana, the villain of the epic *Ramayana*, shaking the mythical Mount Kailash as Shiva and his wife Parvati sit on it. Cave 30 is the **Chhota Kailash** (mini Kailash), considered to be a copy of the Kailashnath Temple. **Cave 32** is one of the most beautiful of the Jain caves, with a miniature temple constructed in the Dravidian style, complete with flagpole.

Ellora Caves

30km NW of Aurangabad. Open sunrise-sunset Mon, Wed-Sun. Admission Rs 10 Indians, citizens of SAARC countries, Thailand & Myanmar; Rs 250 others; free under-15s.

Eat

It is inexplicable how a city with as much tourist activity as Aurangabad can have such unimpressive eateries. Our advice: stick to Indian fare and ignore culinary experiments along the lines of chop suey dosa (Chinese food, albeit in its Indian avatar, is popular with locals). If you have the stomach for street food, Buddhi Lane is the place where Aurangabad's youth converge for snacks and dinner (after 7pm). Here you'll find kebabs and garlic-heavy Indian Chinese. Even if you don't want to risk trying the street food, it's an interesting walk along the tiny stretch to see assorted shops and stall fronts with tandoori chickens hanging in a row.

Angeethi

Aurangabad *6 Meher Chambers, Jalna Road (0240-244-1988). Open 11am-10.30pm daily. $$. North Indian.*
The waiters are surly, the service slow, the tablecloths look worn and the air-conditioners rattle. But there's a reason why, even on a weekday, the restaurant is full: it serves some of the best Indian food in Aurangabad, outside of the big hotels.

Bhoj

Aurangabad *Kamgar Bhavan, Bhav Pathik Smriti (0240-235-9438). Open 11am-3pm, 7-11pm daily. $. Indian vegetarian.*
Thali is king at this little establishment, and there's nothing for those who crave meat. If you're willing to go vegetarian, there's a homely quality to the food here. Best for quick lunches.

The Garden Café

Aurangabad *Taj Residency, 8-N-12 CIDCO, Rauza Bagh (0240-238-1106). Open 7am-11pm daily. $$$. Coffee shop/multi-cuisine for dinner.*
If you're craving a quiet coffee and snack, or just pasta and salad, this is the place; it also serves soups, sandwiches and other standard fare. Barbecue dinners are held most nights. Not a bad place to unwind after a day spent ruin hopping.

Kaffe – Coffees and More

Aurangabad *CIDCO Town Centre, Jalna Road, next to Hotel Riviera (0240-248-0123/www.kaffeaurangabad.com). Open noon-9pm daily. $. Coffee shop/Italian.*
This little café had the first espresso machine in Aurangabad and coffee is what it's known for. There's also a restaurant section serving pungent Indo-Italian cuisine. A small gift shop sells knick-knacks.

Madhuban

Aurangabad *Rama International Hotel, R 3 Chikalthana, Airport Road (0240-248-5441). Open 10am-2pm, 3-11pm daily. $$$. Multi-cuisine.*

This restaurant often has a *ghazal* singer performing live in the evenings. It's pricier than most places in Aurangabad, but has a prettier setting, overlooking a leafy garden on one side. Locals tend to go for the Chinese section of the menu, but the standard Indian fare is well worth trying.

Tandoor

Aurangabad *Shyam Chamber, Station Road (0240-645-2444). Open 11am-10.30pm daily. $$. North Indian.*

True to its name, the best thing to eat in this restaurant are the kebabs. There seems to be a mother gravy that spawns all the other main courses, which come in varying shades of red.

VITS Coffee Shop

Aurangabad *VITS Hotel, Station Road (0240-235-0701). Open 24hrs daily. $$$. Multi-cuisine.*

VITS' 24-hour coffee shop has an expansive menu that runs the whole gamut from tandoori starters, burgers and sandwiches to full meals, which range from biryanis to pastas and Thai curry. Food is tasty and staff are attentive.

Shop

Aurangabad is famous for three things: Paithani saris, himroo shawls and bidri work. Paithani is a centuries-old weaving tradition that has, like all such crafts, been in decline. However, here in Aurangabad you can still see weavers work at their old-fashioned looms. Himroo weaving has its roots in Persia, as is evident from the delicate floral designs. Bidri work is a kind of metalwork, with intricate silver inlaying and engraving on zinc alloy; once popular in Aurangabad, it's now only seen in a few places. Bidriware's distinctive silver patterns on black are unusual in a country that loves gold, but it is still desirable and expensive.

Aurangabad Himroo Industry

Aurangabad *Zaffar Gate, Mondha Road (0240-235-5416). Open 11am-7pm daily.*

The Qureishi family has been in the weaving trade for generations now and have done their bit to preserve the 2,000-year-old Paithani art form. They're so used to people asking about the Paithani sari that they go into tour guide mode the moment a visitor arrives. Old looms from the early 1900s are still on the premises for visitors to see, gathering cobwebs and dust. If you're not particularly enamoured with the loud colours of the Paithani, there are a range of other textiles and more modern designs, including some fabulous scarves.

Silver & Art Palace

Aurangabad *Plot No.1, beside Taj Residency, N-11, Sector L, Rauza Bagh (0240-238-0020). Open 11am-6.30pm daily.*

This well-known shop sells bidri work, Ajanta and Ellora souvenir paintings and assorted jewellery, including pieces studded with semi-precious gemstones, and of course silver jewellery. No innovative designs here, but it does have fake miniatures and other gift shop goodies.

Madhu Bidri Works

Aurangabad *Taj Residency, Rauza Bagh (92262-17864/madhubidri@yahoo.co.in). Open noon-6pm Mon-Sat.*

Tucked away in a corner near the Garden Café of the Taj Residency is a small cabinet of bidri items. This little shop is run by Vijay and Mukesh Gawai, two brothers who learnt this painstaking craft from their artisan father. Though they hav college degrees, the brothers gave up the opportunity to pursue regular jobs to preserve a dying tradition. Their bidri work is quite lovely and delicate, and their attempt to bring in modern designs to the traditional patterns impressive. It's painstaking work to create bidriware so even small pieces are not cheap.

Stay

In Aurangabad most budget hotels are too basic to be conducive to relaxation or unwinding after a long day trip. Room rates change according to season and most listed hotels include breakfast and transfers in their rates. Many hotels are concentrated in the area near the station; the rest tend to be spread on the outskirts of town.

Hotel Kailas

Ellora *Next to Ellora Caves (02437-244-446/ www.hotelkailas.com). $$. No credit cards.*

This is the only respectable, if basic, hotel in Ellora. Barely five minutes' walk from the Ellora Caves, it's a good spot to spend the night if you want to return to the caves the next day. Kailas has a clutch of no-frills cottages, some overlooking the caves. Only some rooms have air-conditioning; other facilities are basic. Bring your own soap, shampoo and towels. Since all the cottages are on the ground floor and surrounded by greenery, you will inevitably have some insect company. The hotel cafeteria serves satisfactory home-style Indian food.

Lemon Tree Hotel

Aurangabad *R 7/2, Chikalthana, Airport Road (0240-660-3030/www.lemontreehotels.com). $$.*

Located three kilometres from the airport, Lemon Tree is both convenient and modestly priced. It takes the 'lemon' theme rather seriously: you smell citrus as you step in; all the pony-tailed men male staff tie their hair with little yellow bows, and rooms have lemon teabags. The hotel was recently renovated so everything is new and smells – well – lemon fresh. Nice little touches include room towels wrapped up like Lord Ganesh. A fitness centre overlooks the biggest swimming pool in Aurangabad, surrounded by frangipani and coconut palms, where guests gather in the evening. The hotel staff are some of the friendliest in the city.

Taj Residency.

Top: The Meadows.
Middle: Taj Residency.
Bottom: Lemon Tree.

The Meadows

Aurangabad–Nasik Highway *Gates 135 & 136, Mitmita (0240-267-7412/www.themeadowsresort.com). $$.*

When the Meadows opened in the mid 1990s it must have been a pretty resort. It's a short distance out of the city of Aurangabad and made up of cottages surrounded by landscaped gardens and greenery. It is still charming on first appearance, particularly at night. Unfortunately, the charm doesn't extend to the interiors. The signs and stains of age are everywhere – cracks in the bathtub, rickety furniture, malfunctioning telephones. The hotel has a pool, a small gym and steam room. In late 2009, plans for renovation were afoot.

Taj Residency, Aurangabad

Aurangabad *8-N-12 CIDCO, Rauza Bagh (0240-238-1106/www.tajhotels.com). $$$.*

Though this hotel looks like a lovely old palace, especially when lit up at night, it was actually built in 1993. It's a cocoon of comfort, service is charming and the food excellent. All rooms are spacious, and executive rooms have their own balconies. Guests gather by the pool and bar in the evening for barbecue dinners and, occasionally, concerts. Young trainees from the Taj's hotel management school next door often work here, and are always eager to please. A disadvantage to some is the location on the city outskirts.

VITS

Aurangabad *Station Road (0240-235-0701/660-4444/www.vitshotelaurangabad.com). $$$.*

One of the newest arrivals on the Aurangabad hotel scene, it's hard to miss VITS' large signage, especially if you arrive in the city by train. Guest rooms are spotless, spacious, modern and comfortable. Families may like their one-bedroom apartments, which have a sofa-cum-bed for the kids. All the usual amenities, including a pool and health club, are available. Like the Lemon Tree, VITS' major advantage is its location. Most of the city's restaurants are close by, though you're probably better off in its coffee shop.

WelcomHotel Rama International

Aurangabad *R-3 Chikalthana (0240-248-5441/ www.itcwelcomgroup.in). $$-$$$.*

An uninspiring façade, but this is one of the most popular hotels in Aurangabad with business travellers. The advantage of the WelcomHotel is that it tends not to be noisy like the Ajanta Ambassador nearby. And while it may have taken a hit in recent times with the arrival of the newer, cheaper Lemon Tree next door, service standards remain good. Overall it's a pretty enough hotel, offering the usual amenities, though the pool is rather small. Rooms have undergone a much needed recent renovation.

Factfile

When to go

The best time is straight after the monsoon (June-mid Sept), when the countryside is at its greenest. November to February is also good, and though you can go almost any time, it's pretty hot the rest of the year. The peak heat kicks in at the end of April and lasts until June.

Getting there

Daily flights and trains connect Aurangabad to Mumbai and Delhi. From Mumbai it's a one-hour flight or a fairly convenient eight-hour overnight train ride.

For more information on travel within India, *see p378* **Navigating India**.

Getting around

Auto-rickshaws are easily available for travel within the city. For travel beyond the city, it makes the most sense to hire a private taxi for the day. Most hotels have a tie-up with a taxi service.

Tourist information

Both the MTDC-Maharashtra Tourism Development Corporation (0240-233-1198, www.maharashtratourism.gov.in, open 10am-6pm Mon-Sat, closed 2nd and 4th Sat of every month) and the India Tourism Offices (0240-236-4999, 233-1217, open 9am-6pm Mon-Sat) are on Station Road.

Internet

Cyber cafés can be found all over Aurangabad and most hotels have both internet access and Wi-Fi connectivity.

Tips

- **Taxi drivers** will try to take you to shops where they can hope to get a commission. The good news is that the shops are pretty much all the same – they'll all try and get as much as they can out of you. Haggle hard and almost everywhere.
- **Most sites require a lot of walking** and at a few of the caves you may need to take off your footwear, so make sure you wear comfortable and appropriate shoes.
- **Even in the winter**, carry a hat and at least one bottle of water.

Clockwise from top left: river crossing to Anegundi; Pattadakal; Badami Caves; Vithala Temple.

Hampi & Around

A boulder-strewn landscape and millennia-old temple architecture.

The natural landscape of Hampi, on the southern bank of the River Tungabhadra in Karnataka state, is liberally studded with huge boulders. Man added temples, now mostly sprawling ruins. They meld together to create a unique, rather otherworldly place. The fact that what's known of Hampi's past is a mix of history and legend only adds to its aura of mysticism. It was once the capital of the prosperous Vijayanagar Empire, which ruled over a large part of Central India from the 14th to the 16th century. But it is also said to be the mythological Kishkinda, which features in the epic *Ramayana* as the city where Rama and Lakshman met Hanuman while on their search for Sita.

The abundance of historic temples, their elaborate architecture and their striking natural setting make Hampi's UNESCO World Heritage Site status well deserved. Today, visitors from around the world join pilgrims from across India and the site has become an international tourist hub. Hampi has joined Goa and Gokarna as part of the Western India backpacker trail, and it's this group that has brought parties and full-moon raves to the once-sleepy town and its surrounds.

A few hours' drive north-west of Hampi, Aihole, Badami and Pattadakal have magnificent cave temples, examples of the architecture of the Chalukyan Empire. Aihole and Badami reveal the experimental and emerging style of South Indian temples, while the reddish gold sandstone of Pattadakal's temples represents the finessed result. Despite their attractions, these sites draw only about a third of the numbers who visit Hampi. All the better, perhaps, to enjoy their serene majesty.

Explore

Hampi is best accessed through the gateway town of **Hospet**, 13 kilometres (eight miles) away, where the better hotels are located. The journey from Hampi/Hospet to **Badami**, 175 kilometres (109 miles) away, takes around four hours. A good plan is to start early in the morning, detouring for **Aihole** (120 kilometres/75 miles from Hampi, 46 kilometres/28 miles from Badami) and **Pattadakal** (20 kilometres/12 miles from Aihole) along the way. Guides (Rs 750) can be hired outside the temple complexes in each place; your hotel can also arrange for one to meet you there. Remember though, that even if you spend just an hour and a half at each site, you'll have an exhausting day.

HAMPI

Hampi's ruins are spread over approximately 25 square kilometres (ten square miles). You could easily spend several days exploring with a car, map and a good guide – your hotel can arrange a licensed guide for you. The ruins are broadly divided into the sacred centre, comprising temples and religious sites, the royal centre of regal residences and recreational centres, and a few civic structures.

The Hampi bus stand is in an area called Kamalapur, just north of which is the royal centre. A short walk further north is the Hampi Bazaar, the busy street leading up to the Virupaksha Temple, its tall *gopuram* (tower) visible from afar; to its immediate south is the sacred centre. Across the Tungabhadra river from here, on the north bank, is Virupapura Gaddi (*see p189* **Hampi's hippie island**). On a hill a couple of kilometres from Hampi Bazaar is the awe-inspiring Vithala Temple.

Elephant Stables

Kamalapur (royal centre). Open 10am-5pm Mon-Thur, Sat, Sun. Admission with ticket to Vithala Temple.

All the king's elephants were housed here in 11 domed chambers. Each dome is different – you'll see circular, octagonal, ribbed and fluted varieties.

Lotus Mahal & Zenana Enclosure

Kamalapur (royal centre). Open 10am-5pm Mon-Thur, Sat, Sun. Admission with ticket to Vithala Temple.

Housed within the Zenana Enclosure is the Indo-Islamic Lotus Mahal. The pyramid-like spires are inspired by Hindu temple designs while the arches and domes on the inside are typically Islamic. Palaces of Krishnadevaraya's two main queens Chinnadevi and Tirumaladevi were located here.

Virupaksha Temple Complex

Hampi Bazaar (sacred centre). Open 6.30am-12.30pm, 2-8pm daily. Admission Rs 2; Rs 50 camera; Rs 500 video camera.

Hampi's oldest temple, parts of which were built in the seventh century, is the only active shrine in the ruined city. Dedicated to Lord Shiva in the form of Virupaksha or Pampapati, his consort Pampa and other deities, the Virupaksha has an 11-tier, 50m (164ft) *gopuram* (entrance

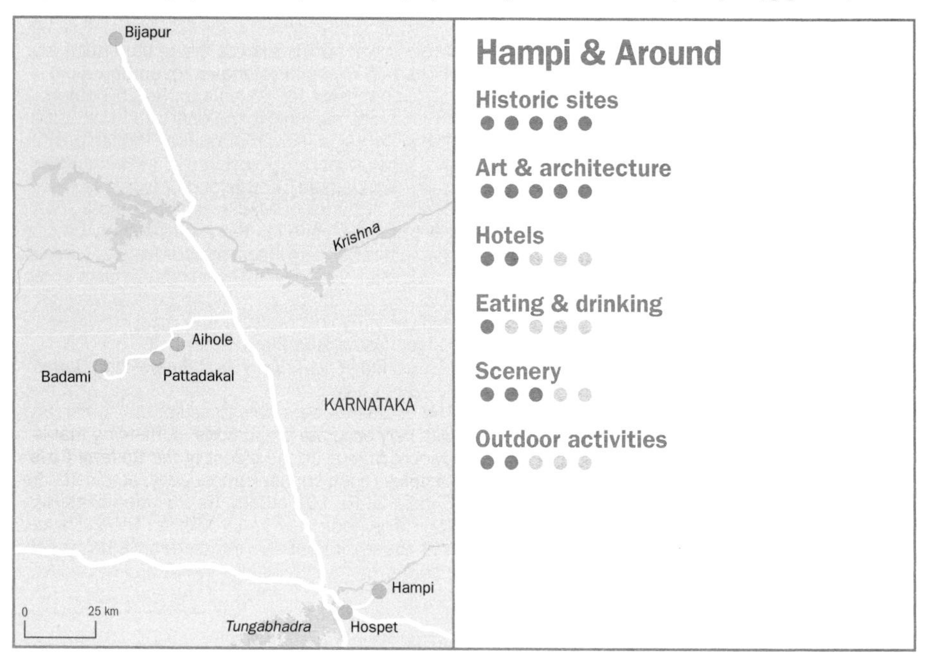

tower), the tallest among Hampi's temples. The rectangular tiers are characteristic of South Indian temples, while their pyramid-like formation is characteristic of those in North India. Beware of touts who escort you to a dark room at the back of the temple complex to see an inverted image of the *gopuram* on a wall and then ask for a tip.

Vithala Temple

2km NE of Hampi Bazaar. Open 6.30am-6.30pm daily. Admission Rs 10 Indians; Rs 250 others; free under-15s; Rs 25 video camera. Ticket also valid for entry to the Zenana Enclosure & Elephant Stables.

Dedicated to Vithala (an incarnation of Lord Vishnu), this temple was commissioned by King Krishnadevaraya, under whose reign Hampi enjoyed its Golden Age. It was never completed, but the finished parts are magnificent enough to make it one of the grandest in Hampi. Highlights include the elaborately carved pillared hall, the columns, said to produce different musical notes, and the stone chariot at the entrance, modelled on the famous Sun temple in Orissa. Friezes on the base of the pillared hall include images of what look like traders from China, Turkey and Portugal who came to Vijayanagar to sell horses.

Ugra Narasimha & Badavilinga

Halfway between royal centre & sacred centre. Open sunrise-sunset daily. Admission free.

One of the last architectural contributions made by Krishnadevaraya, this imposing monolithic sculpture depicting the half-man, half-lion avatar of Vishnu (Narasimha) sitting on a snake is the most photographed of Hampi's sites. Right next to it is another monolithic sculpture, the Badavi Lingam, a 3.7m (12ft) granite *lingam* (representation of Shiva), the tallest in Hampi, always partially covered in water.

ANEGUNDI

Sparsely populated Anegundi is believed to be Kishkinda, the birthplace of Hindu monkey god Hanuman. Located on the northern bank of the Tungabhadra river, the 14th-century capital of the Vijayanagar Empire has its share of temples and ruins. To reach **Hanuman Temple**, at the top of Anjanadri Hill, you must climb approximately 500 steps. There's a panoramic view of Hampi from the top: ask the priest to point out the Vithala and Virupaksha temples in the distance. Since this is Hanuman territory the hill is surrounded by his earthly counterparts, so guard food closely.

DAROJI BEAR SANCTUARY

Daroji Bear Sanctuary (open 6am-6pm daily) lies just 15 kilometres (nine miles) south-east of Hampi, along a well-marked road. It's a protected natural habitat for the highly endangered wild Indian sloth bear, about 120 of which are believed to live here, feeding on termites, wild fruits and honey. Between 4pm and 5pm each evening, forest guards place jaggery to lure the animals to the base of a viewing tower inside the sanctuary. Visitors can then watch the bears as they consume the food and play or fight with each other. It's a fascinating sight to see these creatures in their natural environment – albeit attracted by man-laid bait.

AIHOLE, BADAMI & PATTADAKAL

The Chalukyas of Badami, who ruled over South India between the sixth and eighth centuries, laid the blueprint for temple architecture in the region by experimenting with the structural design of the shrines they built in the cities of **Aihole**, **Badami** and **Pattadakal**.

Most day trips only allow time for the highlights, and tend to begin in Aihole, the first capital of the Chalukyas kingdom, on the banks of the Malaprabha river. It has temples built in both the South Indian style, with tiered *shikaras* (the superstructure above the sanctum), and North Indian style, with curvilinear *shikaras*. Aihole's architects were clearly given a lot of space to practice as is evident from over 120 temples visible in the village, on hilltops and by the river.

The **Durga Temple Complex** (open 6am-6pm daily, admission Rs 5 Indians, Rs 100 others, museum open 10am-5pm Mon-Thur, Sat, admission Rs 2), noted for its semicircular Buddhist prayer hall-like design, is the largest and grandest of Aihole's temples. The **Lad Khan Temple** (open sunrise-sunset daily, admission free) also has an interesting history. A Shiva temple initially used as an assembly hall, it is named after the Muslim man found living inside it by British archaeologists in the 19th century.

Located between Aihole and Badami, Pattadakal was the chief coronation centre of the Chalukyas. Along with Hampi, Pattadakal (open 6am-6pm daily; admission Rs 10 Indians; Rs 250 others; Rs 25 video camera) is the only other UNESCO World Heritage site in Karnataka. The largest and most elaborately sculpted of its 10 temples is the **Virupaksha Temple** and beside it is the similar, but smaller **Mallikarajuna Temple**. They were commissioned in the eighth century by King Vikramaditya II's two queens, sisters Lokadevi and Trilokadevi. Lokadevi's Virupaksha Temple is the only one in Pattadakal in which both the *lingam* and the *nandi* bull sculpture (a massive work carved from granite) are intact.

Founded in AD 540 by King Pulakeshi I, Badami was the Chalukyas' capital until the eighth century. The Chalukyas were able to sculpt the human body with very accurate proportions, something that is evident from even the oldest of the **Badami Cave temples** (open sunrise-sunset daily, admission Rs 5 Indians, Rs 100 others, Rs 25 video camera). **Cave 1** is dedicated to Lord Shiva. The entrance hall houses impressive larger-than-life bas reliefs of his avatars. The highlight here is a Nataraja carving; different pairings of the sculpture's 18 arms combine to depict 81 *mudras* of the classical dance form *bharatanatyam*.

Cave 2 and **3** are dedicated to Lord Vishnu. The former has a striking carving of Varaha, the half-boar, half-human avatar that was the royal emblem of the Chalukyas. The latter, the only one bearing an inscription (AD 578), has an imposing carving of Vishnu sitting on Adishesha, the multi-headed serpent who forms both his seat and crown. **Cave 4**, situated some 200 steps above Cave 1, is a symbol of Chalukyan religious tolerance: a Jain temple. It has sculptures of each of Jainism's 24 *tirthankaras* or spiritual guides. It looks out on to some Shiva temples on the hill across and the **Bhutanatha Temple** below. Both are worth visiting as is the **Archaeological Museum** (open 10am-5pm Mon-Thur, Sat, Sun; admission Rs 10 Indians; Rs 100 others).

Eat

Hampi is a desert as far as good restaurants go. At least for dinner, it's best to eat at your hotel. All the cafés along Hampi Bazaar road look alike and serve a mish-mash of cuisines, getting little right. Step inside only to replenish fluids. Hotel Mayura Bhuvaneshwari (Kamalapur, 08394-241-574) is an unremarkable government-run hotel with one advantage – it serves beer, useful if you don't fancy hopping across the river to Virupapura Gadd. Skip the dull South Indian buffet, though. For good food you have to go to the big hotels in Hospet.

Fiesta

Hospet *Krishna Palace Hotel (see below). Open 7am-midnight daily. $$. No AmEx.*

North Indian food in South India. While almost every restaurant serves up butter chicken, this is the only one where you'll get a decent bhuna gosht or chicken biryani.

Laughing Buddha

Virupapura Gaddi *Open 7am-11pm daily. No phone. $. No credit cards.*

Laughing Buddha is the only restaurant in Virupapura Gaddi that's open all 365 days of the year; and perhaps that's why they don't get around to changing the tablecloths. More hippie than hip, everything is designed for the perfect stoner vibe – psychedelic banners of Hindu deities, chillums, large mattresses and standard fare. Pair your butter chicken with a bottle of beer.

Mango Tree

Hampi *River Side Drive (94487-65213/94488-77420). Open noon-10pm daily. $. No credit cards.*

It's undisputedly the most popular restaurant in Hampi, and visitors flock here for the pastoral ambience. Walk past banana plantations to reach this secluded spot, take your shoes off before you enter, sit on a *chatai* (mat), and eat on a low bench under a mango tree overlooking the river. If you're willing, get the vegetarian thali, if not, stick to Nutella pancakes and crescent-shaped cheese samosas. Don't forget mosquito repellent if you're there in the evening.

Stay

Accommodation options in Hampi town proper are geared towards the backpacker, but thanks to its proximity to Hampi, and the fact that UNESCO guidelines prevent the building of new structures there, Hospet, 13 kilometres (eight miles) away, is where the better hotels are located. Anegundi is best if you want a quiet tourist-free space immersed in the life of the region, or wish to benefit local communities.

Hotel Badami Court

Badami *17/3 Station Road (08357-220-230/ www.hotelbadamicourt.com). $$. No AmEx.*

Each of the 26 marble-floored rooms at this two-storey hotel has accoutrements such as flatscreen TVs and electric kettles. While it's all rather characterless, it's the cleanest option you'll find in Badami, a couple of kilometres from the Badami caves.

Hampi's Boulders – The Wilderness Resort

Hampi *Narayanpet (94497-58666). $$. No credit cards.*

Located on the other side of the river (you have to cross by boat), Boulders comprises 13 cottages (six of them air-conditioned) built quite literally on boulders. The rocks jut into bedrooms and bathrooms, suggesting what home life might have been like for the Flintstones. Each cottage has a different theme: the castle-like Star Cottage, the homely Sun Cottage or kid-friendly Gayan cottages. Book one of six rooms with a patio beside the Tungabhadra river; after a long day of sightseeing, they're the perfect spot to sit and enjoy a sundowner.

The Kishkinda Trust

Anegundi *Heritage House, Royal Street (08533-267-777/94483-33191/www.thekishkindatrust.org). $. No credit cards.*

To put money into the local community, book a room at one of the restored traditional homes run by the Kishkinda Trust. They contain little more than a bed and side table, but the stone floors, mud walls and wooden doors have a charm you won't find in the sanitised confines of a proper hotel. At meals you'll sample authentic Anegundi cuisine. The downside? Detached toilets without flowing water.

Krishna Palace

Hospet *Station Road (0839-429-4300/ www.krishnapalacehospet.com). $$. No AmEx.*

Krishna Palace looks and feels like any other starred hotel in India. It has a large, ornate lobby – with muzak soundtrack – rooms with massage showers and electronic safes, and an English pub-like bar. It also has some of the best service around: not only do staff pay attention, they're almost too eager to please, which can be refreshing in a town where high standards in hospitality are all but unknown.

Hotel Malligi

Hospet *6/143 JN Road (0839-422-8101/www.malligi hotels.com). $-$$.*

Hampi's hippie island

Interchangeably referred to as Hampi Island, Israeli Island and Hippie Island, **Virupapura Gaddi**, not actually an island, was once an isolated green patch on the other side of the Tungabhadra river from town. These days it's a backpacker hub and site of occasional raves during the peak season.

The possible disadvantage of staying here is that you must leave Hampi by 6pm, when the boats and coracles make their last trip across the river from Hampi Bazaar. However, the advantage is that the island's guesthouses, both in terms of pricing and comfort, are a welcome alternative to the dingy quarters in Hampi Bazaar and the mainly characterless lodgings of Hospet. They are also home to the only nightlife Hampi has. Most guesthouses have restaurants attached, which turn into hippie haunts post-sunset, when music and marijuana flow freely.

However, getting stoned is not the only way to get high in Hampi. Bouldering has become an increasingly popular adventure sport on Hampi's extremely challenging hard granite rocks. Bouldering guru Chris Sharma's 2003 film *The Pilgrimage* was shot here, bringing cult status to Hampi's difficult boulders. These days, Virupapura Gaddi is a meeting place for bouldering enthusiasts from around the world, who come here to worship at their own sites – rocks with names like Cosmic Cave, Sunrise Boulder and Psycobloc – by day, and discuss their passion by night. The caretaker at **Begum's**, in the lane opposite Shanthi Guesthouse, rents out climbing equipment (crash pads, chalk bags and some rock-climbing shoes) and sells bouldering route maps.

If you decide to base yourself in Virupapura Gaddi, be sure to survey the properties before renting a room. The quality of the accommodation varies, and though there may not seem to be much difference between rooms, it's the views that give one place an edge over another. **Shanthi Guesthouse** (08394-325-352, shanthi.hampi@gmail.com, open Sept-Apr), for instance, has ten rooms with a swing-equipped patio looking out to paddy fields. **Hema Guest House** (94491-03008, 08533-387-074, open mid Sept-Mar) is not too bad either if you can bag a cottage with attached bath.

Clockwises from top:
Hampi Old Bazaar;
Mango Tree; Kishkinda
Trust, Anegundi (2);
Hampi Boulders.

Rooms at Hospet's oldest hotel are efficient if not particularly inspired. But the management scores by adding little touches: each room has a small map with Hampi's major sites marked on it; and in November and December, George Michell and John M Fritz, authors of authoritative books on Hampi, conduct audio-visual presentations in the conference hall. It also has an Ayurvedic spa, a car rental service, and two restaurants, of which the zodiac-themed Temptations (open 6.30am-3pm, 6.30-11pm) is a fine place to fuel up before a hot day of traipsing around Hampi.

Shama's Cottages

Anegundi *Kishkinda Trust (08533-267-777/ 94483-33191/www.thekishkindatrust.org). $. No credit cards.*

Owned by Shama Pawar, the founder of the Kishkinda Trust, but operated as a separate entity, this group of cottages offers an experience midway between homestay and hotel. The non-air-conditioned rooms are similar to those run by TKT, but come with Fabindia furnishings, attached bathrooms, and thatched grass roofs that keep them cool.

Factfile

When to go

Hampi is hot all year round. From mid October to February, temperatures (particularly in the evening) are most tolerable. Summers (Mar-May) are the hottest. Mid June to August is the monsoon season, when the Tungabhadra sometimes floods.

Getting there

The easiest way to get to Hampi is to fly to Bangalore and take the overnight Hampi Express train to Hospet, 13km (eight miles) from Hampi.

There's also a popular (but nightmarish) overnight bus from Goa. More comfortable, if you can make an advance reservation, is the Vasco da Gama Howrah Express train that runs the eight-hour journey between Vasco da Gama and Hospet four times a week.

For more information on travel within India, *see p378* **Navigating India**.

Getting around

Hiring a chauffer-driven, air-conditioned car from your hotel to ferry you around (Rs 1,000-1,500 per day) is the most comfortable way to see Hampi and the surrounding area. You can also walk to the sites or hire a bicycle, motorcycle or auto-rickshaw from Hampi Bazaar, but keep in mind the scorching sun. Shuttle buses (Rs 10) run to and from Hospet station to Hampi Bazaar every half-hour (6.30am-8.30pm).

The quickest (albeit precarious) way to get to Anegundi is on a boat or coracle (a small circular craft made of wickerwork and tar) from near Hampi Bazaar; it's a ten-minute ride as opposed to an hour-long drive by road. Within Anegundi, auto-rickshaws (Rs 500-Rs 800 per day) are readily available.

Hiring a car is the best way to travel to the towns of Aihole, Pattadakal and Badami. These destinations, and their temples, can be covered in a long day trip. You need to plan to leave quite early, though, to have time to see everything.

Tourist information

In Hampi, the Karnataka State Tourism Development Corporation (KSTDC) Information Counter is near the bus stand in Hampi Bazaar (08394-241-339, open 10am-1pm, 2-5pm Mon-Thur, Sat, Sun). Tourists can board the shuttle bus here.

Hospet's KSTDC office is on College Road (08394-221-008, open from 8am-8pm daily).

Badami's KSTDC Information Counter is at Hotel Mayura Chalukya (Ramdurg Road, 08357-220-414, open 10am-1pm, 2-5pm daily). Staff can organise tour guides for Badami, Aihole and Pattadakal on request.

A good website for all Hampi-related tourist information is www.hampi.in.

Internet & phone

Hampi Bazaar has a number of cheap internet cafés, but don't expect much in terms of speed.

Bharat Sanchar Nigam Ltd (BSNL) is the only mobile phone service that works throughout North Karnataka. It's possible to buy a connection in Hampi Bazaar.

Tips

- **The best times to go sightseeing** are from early morning to noon and late afternoon to sunset. It's best not to hang around deserted sites after dark.

- **Foreigners visiting Hampi** are advised to register at the police outpost close to the Virupakhsa Temple.

- **An annual cultural festival,** the Hampi Utsav, which includes dance, music and theatre events, is held in the first week of November.

Madurai & Around

A temple town, opulent old mansions, and quiet hill retreats.

In South India's most prominent temple town of Madurai, the goddess Meenakshi wields irrefutable power. Everything and everyone here – townsfolk, travellers, traffic, temple priests and livestock – are subservient to the desires of this consort of the Hindu god Shiva. Each day, priests anoint her with milk, butter, diamonds, gold and perfumed potions, and prepare her for visits from the faithful in the inner sanctum of the temple complex.

Madurai may be a repository of India's spiritual heritage, but it's no historical theme park. As peninsula India's oldest city, it traditionally served as a trading hub for farmers, fishermen, floriculturists, textile merchants and jewellers. Commerce still thrives, and can create some surreal contrasts. There's nothing unusual in spotting a set of medieval stone pillars to which palace elephants were once tethered while wandering past a shop selling knock-off Nikes. But if you wander enough, and observe enough, Madurai can offer a vibrant spiritual and cultural experience.

The area around Madurai has plenty to complement the city's attractions, with splendid examples of distinctive Chettiyar architecture to the west in Karaikudi, and the delights of Athoor, with the serene beauty of Kamarajar Lake and the Cardamom Hills, to the north. For more peace, head to the undulating Pandari Hills around Kodaikanal, where an abundance of wildlife makes its home.

Clockwise from top: Meenakshi Temple Complex (2); Thirumalai Nayakar Palace; Kodaikanal Lake.

Explore

The Meenakshi Temple Complex is the spiritual centre of the city of **Madurai** in the South Indian state of Tamil Nadu. Wildflower-laden **Alagar Kovil** is 21 kilometres (13 miles) away. Eighty-five kilometres (52 miles) due east are the 19th- and early 20th-century Chettiyar mansions of **Karaikudi**. Leave the plains around Madurai and head north for the Palani foothills around **Athoor**, a distance of 60 kilometres (37 miles). West of Athoor are the balmy hills around **Kodaikanal**, 98 kilometres (61 miles) from Madurai, 62 kilometres (38 miles) from Athoor.

MADURAI

The Meenakshi Temple is on the south side of the Vagai river. Immediately to its north is the Madurai market, where mountains of fragrant jasmine are sold each day. Around the east of the temple you can also buy curios and Madurai's famous silks, and get bespoke garments made at the Pudumandapam or Tailor Market. The small Gandhi Memorial Museum (www.gandhimmm.org) is around five kilometres to the south-east.

Meenakshi Temple Complex

0452-234-4360. Open 5am-12.30pm-4-9.30pm daily; Aarti at 8.30pm. Admission Rs 5 Indians; Rs 50 others; Rs 2 under-5s; Rs 50 camera; Rs 250 video camera; Rs 2 footwear locker; Rs 10 golf-cart for circuit.

Like the city around it, the Meenakshi Sundareswarar Temple (also known as the Meenakshi Amman temple) is constructed like a lotus: a series of concentric, descending levels lead to the innermost reaches of the temple where the deity is housed. The Pandian kings who ordered its construction over two millennia ago followed ancient norms in building it this way – each set of petals of the flower forming one row of corridors housing the various deities, and at the core or bud, the temple pond. As with many South Indian temples, there is a reason to everything. For instance, these descending levels have porous connecting sections, channelling rainwater down to the central temple pond, in which sits a golden lotus. If you're flying into town, it's hard to miss the temple's 14 colourful *gopurams* (towers) rising into the sky. They symbolically guard the structure and are as imposing as they are magnificent. The tallest one rises 52m (170ft) and, like the others, is covered in carved images of gods, demons, animals and mythological creatures.

Sundareswarar is the incarnation that Shiva assumed to wed Meenakshi, who is herself an incarnation of Shiva's celestial wife, Parvati. The grandest festivities at the temple occur in April. As crippling heat sweeps across the plains, the goddess is led and given away to her betrothed.

Take in the astonishing Pandian sculptures – they are marked by an intricacy you're unlikely to encounter in other parts of the state. Though priests here will tell you that much of the temple's splendour was either sullied or destroyed by the Muslim invader Malik Gafur in 1310, what remains is amazing. The best time to visit is early in the morning, when everything is swept clean, the first Vedic chants rise into the air, and the resident temple elephant, just-scrubbed, is ready to place his trunk on your head to bestow blessings.

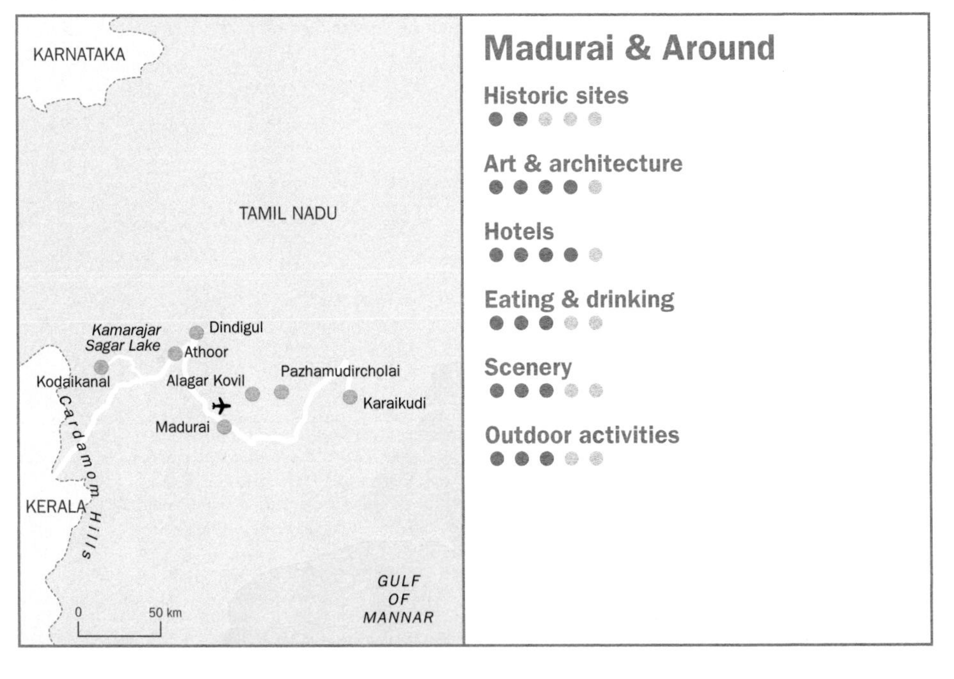

Of the four entrances to the temple, the best approach is through the portal guarded by the tallest tower, facing south. As you enter, walk due east, towards the rising sun, past the other shrines housed in the complex, and continue until you complete the circle to return where you began. However, if you prefer not to walk, a fleet of golf carts can whizz you around the temple for a fee.

Inside the temple complex lies the **1,000 Pillar Museum** (open 7am-8pm, admission Rs 5). It's basically a hall at the end of which stands the statue of King Ariyanatha Mudaliar astride his steed. At first glance the place appears to be overrun with stalls selling cheap, Chinese-made toys and baubles. Deeper within, amid 985 (not 1,000) sculpted pillars, lie reclaimed temple statues, historic memorabilia, and large canvases that record the lives of the kings. Unfortunately, almost everything is either unlabelled or labelled in Tamil.

A good guide, arranged through your hotel, will cost Rs 750 and help you get the best out of this site.

Thirumalai Nayakar Palace

2km SE of Meenakshi Temple Complex (0452-233-8992). Open 9am-5pm daily. Admission Rs 10 Indians; Rs 50 others; Rs 5 under-10s; Rs 30 camera; Rs 100 video camera.

Approach this palace from Ten Pillar Street. Walk down the winding street, past shops selling children's clothing, to the ten megaliths bordering the palace, once employed to tether royal elephants. Once past the pillars, turn left, back towards the palace, and enter through the large portal in front.

Built in 1636 by King Thirumalai Nayakar, the palace's façade is rather unprepossessing. But once you enter, there is an overwhelming sense of space and grandeur. Light streams into the central courtyard, illuminating the massive columns and casting shadows. (The best time to visit is just after noon, when the light is just right.) There are 248 pillars holding up this massive structure and as you follow them from their base to their top, where they spread out to form the vast dome, you sense the majesty of Nayakar's vision.

Of the palace's two parts – Swarga Vilasa (heavenly abode) and Ranga Vilasa (abode of arts) – only the former remains. In its heyday, the latter played host to classical dance and music performances, royal weddings and funerals, sacred rituals and – if the caretakers are to be believed – insidious plotting. Tales of Thirumalai Nayakar smuggling beautiful women into his royal bed via underground tunnels abound. This, locals say, proved to be his undoing when a band of enraged cuckolded subjects reportedly sealed him in one of his own tunnels. The Archaeological Department's signage however, says nothing of secret affairs or irate citizenry. It merely dates the structure and states that Nayakar's grandson, Chockanatha Naik, was responsible for tearing down large sections of it. Restoration work, which began in 2007, continues, and everything – floors, windows, pillars and walls – is covered in a fine layer of dust.

There's also a museum of sorts inside, where glass cases containing retrieved sculptures and statues, undated and inadequately categorised, line the walls. Outside, more statues and sculptures rest on a raised stone platform, open to the elements.

ALAGAR KOVIL & PAZHAMUDIRCHOLAI

Early evening, when the fragrance of the forest seems to rise in the fading light, is the best time to visit these temples (open 5am-12.30pm, 4-10pm daily, admission free), 21 kilometres (13 miles) north-east of Madurai. **Pazhamudircholai**, 15 minutes' drive uphill from Alagar, is dedicated to Lord Murugan, god of war and victory. The temple itself is unremarkable, but the surrounding unblemished forest is spectacular and, as one watches the thronging devotees, one gets a sense of the whole experience of worshipping at a temple in the jungle. Much of the surrounding area is a restricted-access herbal garden and as you drive down the mountain, the sweet, exotic fragrance of hundreds of wildflowers fills the air.

The **Alagar (or Azhagar) Kovil** (temple) is a distinctive shrine at the base of the hill. According to Hindu mythology, Alagar is an incarnation of the god Vishnu. Legend has it that he descended from the heavens to give away his sister Meenakshi as a wife to Shiva. Insulted that the townsfolk did not offer him a welcome befitting his status, he stormed away in anger; this event is re-enacted in April every year during the Chitirai festival.

Though his sister is worshipped in Madurai predominantly by Brahmins, Alagar finds favour with local tribal people. Ceremonies are colourful and raucous, with pushing, jostling, yelling, loud chanting and the use of ornamental materials and flowers. You have to be pretty hardy to endure it; otherwise it's probably best to observe from a distance. The statues guarding the temple and the figures that stare at you from the walls include winged lions, with fangs bared, beckoning buxom maidens, mighty horses taking flight and armed demons ready to defend Alagar's life. All of the incredible sculpture of Alagar Kovil looks best in the bronze shade of twilight.

KARAIKUDI

The once-palatial family mansions of the Chettinad region are today mostly uninhabited and in disrepair. They were built between 1850 and 1940 by the Nattukottai Chettiyars, a community of shrewd bankers who travelled to south-east Asia and amassed fortunes. Much of their wealth was poured into these fantastic homes, filled with Burma teak pillars, beams and furniture, exquisite Belgian glass and mirrors, and paintings and artefacts from around the world. Houses can be seen in **Karaikudi** and its surrounding villages, 80 kilometres (50 miles) east of Madurai.

KM Ramanathan (Ramu) is the man to talk to about all things Chettinad. His home, **APL House** (64, KM Street, Kanadukathan; Ramu c/o Visalam 04565-273-301), is a typical example of the architecture of the Chettiyar merchants. Although the house is in need of repair, Ramu has no hesitation in opening his 63-room home to visitors and walking them around. Before leaving,

A Chettiyar house.

look up at the first-floor façade. From the belly of the goddess protrudes a dull, egg-sized scarlet sphere, purportedly a Burmese ruby brought to Karaikudi by his great, great grandfather.

Among the other houses in Kanadukathan, the **Chettinad Palace**, constructed by SA Ramaswamy Chettiyar in 1912, is the finest example of this architectural style. Its specially plastered walls, Spanish roof tiles, intricate floor tiles, and wealth of art are all well preserved. Inside is a curious mix of objects collected over the years. Tanjore-style paintings, for instance, hang next to black-and-white photographs of a Chettiyar scion in breeches. Caretakers take visitors around to all but a few private sections, unless the owners are in residence, in which case the palace is closed (check with Ramu above). There's also a museum next door that has valuable information on the heritage of the area.

The neighbouring villages of Devakottai and Pallathur also contain Chettiyar homes. Excellent examples of homes converted into hotels in the area include the Chettinadu Mansion (*see p198*), the Bangala (*see p198*) and Visalam (*see p201*).

Shops in Karaikudi's antique street (Muniswaran Kovil Street) stock everything from ornate windows to painted wooden columns, all obtained from crumbling Chettiyar houses. It's not clear if objects have been stolen or salvaged, but most are genuine antiques. Shops also sell a variety of bric a brac: ink wells, bronze pots, enamel mugs, lacquer jewellery boxes, Tanjore-style paintings and old family portraits. Shops are manned by friendly locals open to bargaining.

KAMARAJAR LAKE, CARDAMOM HILLS & ATHOOR

Athoor village in the Dindigul district, an hour and a half's drive north of Madurai, is a quiet area unfrequented by tourists that's perfect for rest and relaxation. The village is small; the approach road to Kamarajar Lake, a large, scenic, monsoon-fed body of water, is narrow and a bit scary. There are only three small guesthouses here, so it's best to book ahead. There are opportunities for birdwatching, walking and trekking, horseback riding in the Cardamom Hills with a guide, a ride to the vineyards of Chinalapatti, or a day trip to visit the Dandayudhapani Temple in Palani, where visitors can ride a cable car to the top or join devotees on the long trudge uphill.

Chauffeured motorcycles and cars are available for exploring the Athoor area. All guided trips can be organised by the guesthouses.

PALANI HILLS

Three hours drive from the heat of the plains are the cool, shady, water-laden jungles of the Western Ghats, of which the Palani Hills is a section. Though **Kodaikanal** was once a quiet, sleepy hill town, it is now overrun with tourists, and barring a couple of places such as Cinnabar (*see p198*), is generally best avoided.

The area around the Elephant Valley Hotel (*see p198*), on the other hand, is home to bison, panthers, elephants, black eagles and Malabar whistlers, as well as many other species of animals small and large, rare plant life, waterfalls and even a few prehistoric dolmens. The hotel offers facilities to saddle up (Rs 250 per hour) and trot out into the foliage with a guide. Staff know the area well and are more than happy to get off the trail if there's an elephant or bison around. Be cautious and follow the lead and instructions of the guide; elephants in the area that have been steadily losing their habitat have been known to charge when provoked. Guided treks are also available (Rs 250 for up to four).

Eat

The Madurai area is almost as famous for its mutton as it is for its divinity. The meat is usually steeped in fiery spices, but chefs are generally willing to cut down the chilli on request, while preserving delicate flavours.

Though Madurai, Karaikudi, Dindigul and Kodaikanal all have small local restaurants that are good, visitors might prefer to play safe and stick to local cuisine from their hotel restaurants. Two essential dishes to try are local versions of mutton biryani and *nandu* (crab) masala.

In Madurai, the View at the **Gateway Hotel** (*see p198*) has an expansive local and international menu. At the Madura Club Restaurant, overlooking the pool at the **Heritance** (*see p198*), food is uniformly good. The menu is multi-cuisine but it's the local fare that wins out.

Murugan Idli Shop (196 West Masi Street, 0452-234-1379, open 7.30am-3pm, 7-11pm daily, $, no credit cards) started as a small local eaterie but now has branches in Chennai, Singapore and the Middle East. It's almost always crowded and chaotic, and you have to wait your turn (especially if you're here for breakfast). When you do find a seat, rattle off your order quickly; the waiters have little patience. Once the banana leaf is set down before you, give it a quick wipe down with a moistened tissue before two *idlis* and five different chutneys are rapidly placed on it; the flavours are hard to beat.

All of the heritage hotels in and around Karaikudi serve authentic and delicious Chettinad cuisine and they do it in style, whether with fancy heirloom crockery or on banana leaves. Chettinad cuisine is generally spicy, but its flavours and aroma are distinctively different from others in South India. And it's better known for its non-vegetarian dishes in an area of the country dominated by vegetarian cooking. The **Bangala** (*see below*) has a well-deserved reputation for outstanding Chettinad home-style food, albeit slightly toned down for tourist taste buds. **Visalam** (*see p201*) also deserves special mention because of its focus on procuring ingredients locally and the unusual fusion elements in some of its dishes. Everything from the *vazhapoo vada* (banana flower blended with lentils and spices and deep fried) to the drumstick leaves soup to the wonderfully marinated Pallathoor mutton masala reveals attention to detail and delicately paired flavours. Neither of these restaurants is cheap, but the meals are worth every rupee. Advance reservations are required at both.

Stay

Bangala

Karaikudi *Senjai Devakottai Road (04565-220-221/ www.thebangala.com). $$. No AmEx.*
Named after the Tamil pronunciation of the word bungalow, this converted Chettiyar house has 12 elegant, airy rooms that are spotless and well furnished with teak pieces. Fifteen more rooms are to be added by mid 2010. The hotel is a family-run affair, and staff are helpful. Interiors are old-world and tasteful, though not as ornate as that found in some of the other houses. Food is authentic Chettinad home-style, and not overly spicy. Tours of other Chettinad homes can be organised here. Owner Meenakshi Meyyappan can proffer advice if you want to buy antiques, or require information about Chettinad.

Chettinadu Mansion

Kanadukathan *TKR Street (04565-273-080/ www.chettinadumansion.com). $$. No AmEx.*
This rambling 106-year-old house was built by RM Ramasami Chettiar according to exacting architectural principles. Unlike Visalam (*see p201*), Chettinadu Mansion sticks to traditional motifs, and though not as opulent as Visalam, it retains the charm of old-world hospitality and offers a truly authentic experience. Staff members, all locals, are graceful and friendly and offer valuable tips on exploring the village. The 12 rooms are fitted with all the comforts you could ask for, but are not as large as those in other houses nearby. Every room is named after a woman who lived here.

Cinnabar House

Kodaikanal *Chettiar Road (04542-240-220/ www.cinnabar.in). $$. No credit cards.*
Kodaikanal is best avoided in the holiday season, with the exception of K Balakrishnan's Cinnabar House, an island of peace located in a quiet lane off the busy main street. Bala takes great pride in his cooking, his cheese and his garden, and runs a small, well-managed operation, renting out two rooms and cooking for guests. Vegetables are grown organically, and Bala's excellent cheese is made from milk produced by his two cows. The kitchen produces everything from Italian to Lebanese food, and can cater to any dietary habit; guests are encouraged to indicate likes and dislikes before arrival. Guests can spend evenings in the living room being regaled with stories about the nearby hills over a round of postprandial drinks.

Double Dutch Cottage

Athoor *Holland House (0451-255-6763/gajmol@ eth.net). $. No credit cards.*
Dutch couple Gé Mol and Gemma CJ den Boer came to India in the 1990s and established this guesthouse overlooking Kamarajar Lake. There are five large rooms, and visitors are treated like members of an extended family. The couple can either accompany you on treks in the area, or send a guide along. Visitors can also explore on motorcycles that they rent out with riders (they drive, you ride). The couple have incorporated various cuisines, ranging from Indian to Indonesian, into the menu at the Cottage. They also run a charitable organisation that educates underprivileged children and welcome travellers to volunteer their time.

Elephant Valley

Palani Hills *Ganesh Puram, Perumal Malai, 22km from Kodaikanal (0413-265-5751/www.elephant valleyhotel.com). $$. No AmEx.*
Eco-friendly Elephant Valley Eco Farm Hotel is part of a coffee plantation in the Palani Hills. Though just 20km (13 miles) from Kodaikanal, it's a picture of tranquillity and sustainable living. Vegetables, coffee and spices are organically grown and restaurant toilets use sawdust instead of a flush. Water in the rooms is heated using reclaimed wood chips and solar power. A small clearing outside each room is perfect for sitting out in the evening to enjoy the sounds of the jungle. There's carom and Scrabble in the restaurant, and a campfire at night. By day there's plenty to do, from horseback riding to relaxing with a book from their eccentric collection. Helpful staff can also take you on guided walks of the plantation or arrange a traditional Ayurvedic treatment.

Gateway

Madurai *40 TPK Road (0452-237-1601/ www.thegatewayhotels.com). $$.*
Up in the Pasumalai Hills, this fine hotel is immaculately maintained and exudes old-world charm. The hotel is set in extensive grounds, covered in greenery. Rooms overlook the tropical foliage and are connected by winding pathways that weave in and out of trees. The View, the hotel's well-regarded all-day restaurant, offers vistas of the temples below and the hills around.

Hotel Germanus

Madurai *28 Bypass Road (0452-435-6999/ www.hotelgermanus.com). $$.*
A mid-priced hotel close to the temples in Madurai. It has none of the luxuries of the Gateway and Heritance, but it's clean and practical. Its 85 air-conditioned rooms are adequate, bathrooms are basic and functional, and staff are competent.

Heritance

Madurai *11 Melakkal Main Road, Kochadai (0452-238-5455/www.heritancehotels.com). $$$.*
Close to the temples in Madurai, the Heritance has a history that can be traced to the British Raj, though stylistically it

Top: Pudumandapam Market (2). Middle: Elephant Valley (2). Bottom: roadside coconut seller.

Clockwise from top left: Heritance; Chettinadu Mansion; Double Dutch; Elephant Valley; Taj Gateway; Visalam.

remains firmly Indian, or, more particularly, Chettinad. Vinod Jayasinghe, the young Sri Lankan architect who designed it, took his cues from the Chettiyar homes in nearby Karaikudi, using materials from the area and dotting the landscape with fragrant frangipani trees. All the villas bear the stamp of the Chettiyar lifestyle and offer quiet comfort and sophistication. Rooms have large beds, wooden pillars, high ceilings, open-plan bathrooms, and, in the case of the luxury villas, a private plunge pool. If this proves too small, head for the coffee shop that overlooks a luxurious temple tank-style pool. Among Madurai's hotels, the Heritance is best for service and luxury.

Lakeside

Athoor *(0451-320-2817/www.lakeside.co.in). $. No credit cards.*

Peter and Dorinda Balchin came from Swindon in the winter of 2008 and never left. Charmed by Lakeside, set up by English charity worker Joe Homan in 1965, they bought the place. They now rent out four rooms and cottages. Rooms are not air-conditioned, but the cool air blowing over Kamarajar Lake obviates the need for electrical cooling. The Balchins (accompanied by dog Loki) run an efficient operation and are splendid company. They provide helpful tips on things to do, can set you up to explore the lake that fronts your cottage, guide you on treks, walks, visits to villages nearby, and can even arrange a round of golf at Kodaikanal Club. Set meals with both Indian and Western cuisine are served using fresh ingredients.

Visalam

Kanadukathan *7/143 Local Fund Road (04565-273-301/0484-301-1711/www.cghearth.com). $$$.*

Visalam is a Chettiyar house converted into a heritage hotel by boutique hospitality chain CGH Earth. It's architecturally outstanding: Chettiyar but with many art deco elements. Its grandeur, seen in the large doorways, sunlit courtyard surrounded by teak columns, massive four-poster beds and the performance space, bear testament to a lavish lifestyle. Everyone who works here is local, produce is grown locally and organically, and the food served is completely Chettinad and utterly delectable. It's the most authentic local experience you can get with comfort and luxury thrown in. Friendly staff are conversant with the house's history and the front desk will happily arrange for cycles or a guide with which to explore the area. At the end of the day, head to the cooling waters of the pool, which has a jacuzzi at the deep end.

YMCA International Guest House

Madurai *Main Guard Square, Netaji Road (0452-234-6649/www.ymcamadurai.com). $. No credit cards.*

While Madurai is loaded with budget accommodation catering to pilgrims, most of it isn't suited to travellers. The YMCA International Guesthouse is easily the best budget option in the city. Conveniently located at the fringe of the temple and in the city centre, it's an ideal base for the culture-hungry visitor. It's housed in an old, well-maintained stone building. Rooms are clean and functional and breakfast is complimentary, but you get nothing in the way of luxury.

Factfile

When to go

It's hot all year round in Madurai. From September to February, the temperature hovers around 30°, and this is the best time to visit Madurai and its surrounding areas.

Getting there

Madurai is connected by air to Bangalore, Mumbai, Chennai and Cochin. Convenient trains from Bangalore, Chennai and Pondicherry (Villipuram) bring you to Madurai Junction.

See also p378 **Navigating India**.

Getting around

A car with driver is the only reliable means of transport. Ask your hotel to arrange one for you.

Tourist information

The Tamil Nadu Tourism office is located close to the Meenakshi Temple (1 West Veli Street, 0452-233-4757, www.tamilnadutourism.org, open 10am-5.45pm Mon-Fri).

Internet

Sify I-Way (9 RB Complex, KK Nagar, opposite Wakf Board College, 80-Foot Road; other branches throughout the city) is open 8.30am-10pm daily. The Heritance and Germanus offer guests free Wi-Fi.

Tips

- **Non-Hindus are not allowed** complete access to the Meenakshi Temple. Everyone can wander about most parts of the complex except for the inner sanctum. The temples of tribal gods like Alagar, however, impose no such restrictions.

- **Photography is not permitted** in all areas of the Meenakshi Temple; signs let you know where it's not allowed.

- **Footwear of any kind and immodesty** of all kinds is prohibited at the Meenakshi Temple.

- **Winter temperatures** at Athoor and Elephant Valley can dip below 10°C and rooms have plenty of insects; bring warm clothing and insect repellent.

Clockwise from top left: Ram Raja Temple, Orchha; Laxminarayan Temple, Khajuraho; Kandariya Mahadeo Temple, Khajuraho; Gwalior Fort (2).

Khajuraho, Orchha & Gwalior

Erotic temple art, royal palaces and grand medieval forts.

Home to the pre-Mughal forts and temples of the Chandela and Tomara dynasties, and the exquisite weathered palaces and cenotaphs of the Mughal era, this part of northern Madhya Pradesh is full of intricately embellished structures – slabs of stone and marble turned into enduring (if unsigned) works of art. Magical leogryph-like beasts hold up ceilings at the Raja Man Singh palace complex in Gwalior. Peacocks spread their tail feathers on Orchha Fort's walls and vaulted archways. Corners of Orchha's royal enclave are covered with ancient murals and religious paintings, and couples copulate on Khajuraho's temple walls, alongside friezes of leering monkeys and prudish servant girls.

In the towns, meanwhile, life goes on pretty much as usual. While Khajuraho seems to revel in the attention it attracts, tourism is concentrated only around a wide avenue leading to the western block of temples. A few streets away, neighbourhoods look relatively untouched by the onslaught of visitors, and resemble any other Indian town. Orchha has only a handful of souvenir shops and no trendy cafés, and seems almost embarrassed to be the object of so much curiosity. And Gwalior's residents, almost all of whom gravitate towards Gwalior Fort on summer weekends, tend to view their historic surroundings more as a picnic spot than a grand monument. Indeed, in the streets it can seem that the intricate temples are pretty much ignored. It's not because residents are blind to their beauty; rather, they're among the lucky few for whom the fantastic has become familiar.

Explore

Khajuraho, **Orchha** and **Gwalior** are all in northern Madhya Pradesh state, but they lie a fair distance from each other. Khajuraho is the easternmost of the three; Orchha is roughly 170 kilometres (106 miles), or five hours, west of Khajuraho. Gwalior lies 120 kilometres (75 miles) or three hours north of Orchha.

While most forts, temples and monuments in all three towns are open throughout the day, it's a good idea to start early to allow enough time to linger over the structures you find interesting. English-speaking guides mill around the entrances of the bigger, more important sights such as Khajuraho's temples and Gwalior's Man Singh Palace.

Stick around for the sound-and-light shows at Khajuraho and Orchha and Gwalior forts after sunset, for a history lesson that has more than dry dates and dynasties. Admittedly a little corny, they are actually a great way to see the past recreated with coloured halogens, a soundtrack of swordfights and staged dialogue – and a voiceover by Bollywood star Amitabh Bachchan.

KHAJURAHO

Khajuraho's temples are roughly grouped around three locations: Western, Eastern and Southern. The Western group lies immediately west of the main road, where the main bazaar is located. Khajuraho village lies a kilometre to the east, and around and to the south of it are the temples of the Eastern group. Southern group temples are a kilometre further south.

Khajuraho Temple Complex

Open sunrise-sunset daily. Admission Rs 10 Indians, Rs 250 others; Rs 50 audio guide.

Khajuraho's group of temples is a UNESCO World Heritage Site. They contain some of the finest temple craftsmanship anywhere. In Khajuraho, to err may be human, but, apparently, to fornicate divine: scores of carved figures indulging in wildly varied and experimental sexual activity cover temple walls and roofs. Though Khajuraho's temples are most famous for their display of erotic activity, they actually depict and celebrate all aspects of life. The temples were built between AD 950 and 1050 by the Chandela Rajput kings, who claimed descent from the moon. In the absence of any proper written records of their origins or function, their history has often been intermingled with myth or legend. Of the town's original 85 temples, only 22 survive. They're grouped roughly on the basis of their location: Western, Eastern and Southern.

The **Western group**, which features passionate embraces, impossibly buxom women and limber lovers most prominently, sees the most traffic. But erotica is not all there is to admire. Stone panels depicting the Chandela people at work, at war and at prayer are astonishingly well crafted, appearing to stand free of the rock into which they are carved. Most prominent of the group is the **Kandariya Mahadeo Temple**, dedicated to Lord Shiva, which depicts 872 magnificent deities, winged maidens, couples,

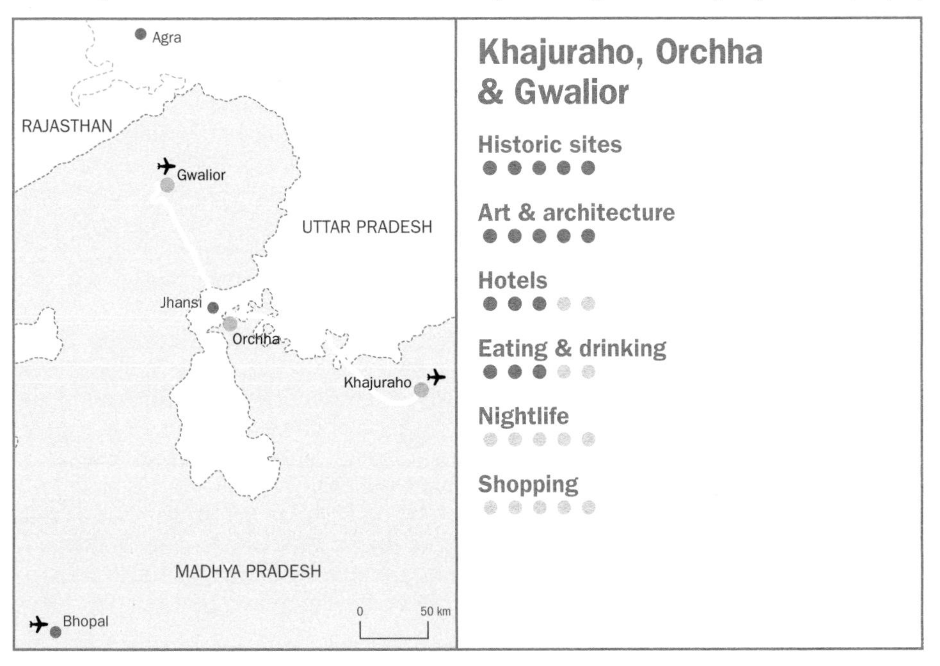

gods and goddesses. **Lakshmana Temple** is not only one of the better preserved of Khajuraho's large temples, but also receives the most visitors because of its location as the first temple you come to as you enter the Western group. Heavily detailed carved pillars, with representations of *apsaras* (divine nymphs), hunters and musicians flank the four corners of its central raised platform. The **Chaunsath Yogini Temple**, possibly the oldest surviving structure of the group, is dedicated to the goddess Kali, while the east-facing **Chitragupta Temple** is dedicated to the Sun god and depicts the deity on a horse-drawn chariot. Other structures include the **Vishwanatha Temple**, consecrated to Lord Brahma, with massive stone elephants guarding its steps.

Even if you only have a couple of hours to spend at Khajuraho, a quick spin around the Western group is enough to make you feel as if would have had a lot more fun if you'd been born around here a thousand years ago. Ditch the droning audio guide, but follow the stone signs indicating its route. It's the best way to see the temples. Each evening there's a **sound-and-light show** (Rs 90 Indians, Rs 300 other nationalities, in English 7.30pm summer, 6.30pm winter).

The temples of the **Eastern group**, perhaps less visited because they contain fewer sexy stone figures, are usually categorised as Hindu and Jain, depending on the gods in whose honour they were built. Largest of the Jain group is the **Parsvanath Temple**, consecrated to the Jain saint Parsvanath. Its northern wall bursts with ornate stone depictions of winged celestial beings. The **Adinath Temple** is dedicated to Adinatha, the first Jain Tirthankara (saviour who has attained enlightenment). It has detailed carvings of *yakshis*, female spirits said to offer fertility and wealth. Stone sculptures retelling the 16 dreams of the mother of Mahavira, the 24th and last *tirthankara*, and depicting a goddess seated on the wings of the mythical bird Garuda, are the most remarkable features of the **Ghantai Temple**.

Oldest among the Hindu temples of the **Eastern group** are the ones built to honour **Brahma** and **Hanuman**. Initially devoted to Lord Vishnu, the granite and sandstone structures now house Brahma's familiar four-faced depiction and a 2.4m (8ft) statue of Hanuman. Equally stunning is the **Javari Temple**, dedicated to Lord Vishnu, which features an elaborately decorated doorway and wall sculptures of men and women in different postures.

Attractions in the least-visited **Southern group** include the **Duladeo** and **Chaturbhuja** temples, which feature richly ornamented celestial women and an intricately carved image of Lord Vishnu in the stonework.

There's a small **Archaeological Museum** (open 10am-5pm Mon-Thur, Sat, Sun, admission Rs 5, free under-15s) opposite the Western group temples, which has some fine sculptures retrieved from ruins in the early part of the 20th century.

Adivart Museum

Chandela Cultural Centre, near Western group of temples Link Rd No.1 (07686-272-721). Open 10am-5pm Mon-Thur, Sat, Sun. Admission Rs 10 Indians; Rs 50 others.

A visit to Adivart, the Madhya Pradesh state museum of tribal and folk art, makes a nice change from temple viewing. Located about half a kilometre from the Western group of temples, it sees little traffic, so it's possible to take in the folk paintings, masks and terracotta, woodcraft and metal artefacts in a calm uncrowded environment. The museum is best visited in the afternoon, leaving the cooler mornings and evenings for Khajuraho's alfresco sights.

ORCHHA

All Orchha's sites are a short walk from the main market area. The fort complex lies on an island in the Betwa river, reached by a small bridge, just east of the market. Rama Raja and Chaturbhuj temples and Phool Bagh are all adjacent to the market, on its west side; a kilometre-long pathway links Rama Raja to the Laxminarayan Temple.

"Its architecture is characterised by projected balconies, elaborate terraces and filigreed jali windows."

Orchha Fort Complex

Near Orchha Market. Open 9am-5pm daily. Admission Rs 30; Rs 20 camera; Rs 50 video camera. Sound-and-light show (English) Rs 75 Indians; Rs 250 others; summer 7.30pm, winter 6.30pm. Archaeological museum Rs 10 Indians; Rs 250 others.

A walk around Orchha's fort-palace complex is both rewarding and slightly taxing on the knees. There are three main palaces within the complex. **Raja Mahal**, built by Orchha's founder, the Bundela Rajput king Rudra Pratap, in the early 16th century, has a simple exterior that hides lavish interior architecture. Its windows, arched walkways and layout play with sunlight and shadow to create areas of different moods and temperatures throughout the day. Ask the resident caretaker to point out the wall panels covered with vibrant paintings depicting religious scenes.

The 17th-century multi-level **Jahangir Mahal** just opposite was built by later king Bir Singh Ju Deo, ostensibly to honour the Mughal emperor Jahangir. Its architecture is characterised by projected balconies, elaborate terraces, filigreed *jali* windows and fabulous views of the temples and city just outside. There's a tiny archaeological museum inside.

Rai Parveen Mahal, adjacent, was built by the 17th-century Raja Indramani to honour his concubine Rai Parveen. Legend has it that the courtesan had captured the attentions of the Mughal emperor Akbar, who took her with him to his kingdom but failed to win her heart. The loyal dancer was returned to Orchha to be reunited with the Bundela king, who built the palace in her honour. Top-floor

Top: Chhatris, Orchha.
Bottom: Gwalior Fort Complex.

windows offer lovely views of the Anand Mahal gardens nearby. While the palace isn't as tall or as opulent as its neighbours, it has surprisingly airy underground chambers, possibly used to escape the heat during the summer months.

Ram Raja Temple

Near Orchha Market. Open 8am-noon, 7-10.30pm daily. Aarti ritual at about 7pm. Admission free.

Ram Raja Temple's claim to fame is that it is the only temple in the country in which Lord Rama (he who defeated the ten-headed king of Lanka and rescued Sita from his lascivious clutches) is worshipped as a mortal king – it is said he visits Orchha at night. Originally the queen's palace, the temple has a beautiful ornamental façade, rarely seen on religious structures, with intricately decorated domes, windows and archways. Legend goes that Lord Rama's statue was temporarily housed here while the nearby Chaturbhuj Temple was being built to honour him. When the temple was ready, the idols refused to move and so the queen's palace became a temple. As with many places of worship in India, the sacred and profane overlap at Orchha, with a bustling marketplace just outside the temple's entrance. Shops here sell garlands, sweets and religious paraphernalia, or brass knick-knacks visitors can take back home.

> **"The mammoth palace garden is a memorial to Dinman Hardaul, a local Bundela prince who killed himself to prove his innocence to his older brother."**

Laxminarayan Temple

Near Orchha Market. Open 8am-noon, 8-10.30pm daily. Aarti ritual at sunset. Admission free.

Located adjacent to the Ram Raja Temple, and accessed along a charming stone pathway, the Laxminarayan Temple is almost fortress-like in its profile. Most popular for its frescoes, which feature violent battle scenes (beheaded demons and horses crushed under carriage wheels) alongside depictions of popular Indian myths (Lord Krishna serenely wooing a group of *gopis* or cowgirls), the paintings are well preserved and still retain their vivid colours.

Phool Bagh

Near Palki Mahal. Open 9am-6pm daily. Admission free.

Take a break from the monuments to visit Phool Bagh, the mammoth palace garden that is a memorial to Dinman Hardaul, a local Bundela prince who killed himself to prove his innocence to his older brother. It is home to several rare plants and trees and is especially beautiful in the spring, when it also hosts several flower festivals. Other attractions include an underground pipe system, which supplies water to the Chandan Katora, a fountain in the centre of the garden, and the Badgir Sawan Bahdon Towers, expressly built to ventilate the palace by creating wind tunnels to supply cool breezes. More than 300 years on, they still do a fine job of providing respite from the blazing heat.

TARAgram

Tegela More 17/7, Bavedi Jungle.

One of Orchha's newest sights is also one of its proudest accomplishments. TARAgram, an industrial village that houses paper-making plants, weaving looms, tile and brick kilns, biomass energy units and dung fertiliser works, has been in operation since 2006, offering employment opportunities for local tribal women. A tour of the area includes a visit to TARAgram's paper and construction materials sectors. Villagers sell souvenirs, though a fly-ash brick may be too cumbersome to carry home. The paper, however, handmade using recycled cloth and wood pulp, makes a great gift.

GWALIOR

The city of Gwalior, a political, cultural and industrial centre with a population of over a million, takes its name from the fort complex that dominates its centre.

Gwalior Fort Complex

Open 8am-6pm daily. Admission Rs 5 Indians, Rs 100 others. Sound-and-light show (English) tickets Rs 50 Indians; Rs 250 others. Shows 7.30pm summer, 6.30pm winter. Archaeological Museum Open 10am-5pm Tue-Sun. Admission Rs 10 Indians; Rs 100 others.

Gwalior Fort sits on top of a tall sandstone hill. Within its walls are several palaces, a sculpture museum, a modern residential school, a pond older than the city, temples and plenty of stories of battles, imprisonment and love. The winding road up to the fort passes giant rock-cut statues of various Jain saints dating from the seventh to the 15th century. Once inside the complex, start with the magnificent **Man Mandir Palace**. Now stripped of its detailed exterior tiles and inlaid jewels, the architecture is still more elaborate than any other in the region. Filigree stone screens (*jali*), which let in breezes at the same time as shielding women from the court, border on long corridors and wrap around courtyards. Sunlight was once directed into the underground chambers via a vast system of tunnels and cleverly aligned mirrors. A primitive 'telephone', a long tube drilled between the king's and queen's apartments, can still carry private messages today. The bat-filled basement rooms, built to house princesses and later turned into dungeons for prisoners, are decidedly creepy.

At **Gujari Mahal**, built by Raja Man Singh for his fearless queen, the vibe is more romantic. Now converted into an archaeological museum, it houses several statues depicting Maheshwar, an avatar of Lord Shiva, lovingly embracing his consort Uma. The museum's gem, an anatomically correct miniature statue of the tree goddess Shalbhanjika, can be viewed on request.

It's all rai

In the last few years, *rai* music and dance has been making headlines for all the wrong reasons. Local ministers have sullied their reputations after being caught drunk, in compromising positions with women, at *rai* performances. Political parties have expressed self-righteous concern over the more raunchy *rai* dance moves, Meanwhile, government-organised cultural programmes meant to showcase central Indian folk forms have conspicuously excluded *rai* from their repertoire.

Rai is music and dance with a bad reputation. This is partly because it has traditionally been performed by the women of Bundelkhand's Bedia caste, the sole breadwinners in a community that counts prostitution as a traditional occupation. Then there is the innate suggestiveness of the dance itself: usually performed to love songs and accompanied by the flute, harmonium and drums, it features quick, graceful movements, and sexy little thrusts. In short, the dance is everything that India's conservative contemporary society finds hard to swallow.

While many hotels in Orchha will readily organise *rai* performance evenings for tourists, don't expect innuendo in the lyrics or raunchy moves on stage. Most performance troupes are all-male. The idea seems to be that getting sweet-faced clean-shaven boys to don wigs, belled anklets and swirling skirts will do something to legitimise and sanitise the form. And the songs are squeaky clean. Most vocalists do line-by-line translations of their songs to reveal lyrics about new love, competitive lovers, women looking to keep their lovers close and the little stings associated with first love. Dances are simple if ever-so-slightly weird (bearing in mind that it's a man doing the suggestive thrusts). That's not to say it's not worth watching: the instrumentalists are energetic despite the obvious toning down of the content and the music is melodic and hummable.

The attractive **Saas-bahu temples**, dedicated to mothers- and daughters-in-law, about 500m (1,640ft) from the Urwahi gate, and the 30m (100ft) **Teli Temple** (near the gate and the oldest in the fort), complete the tour.

A walkway runs along the fort's walls, and the ancient viewing podiums offer spectacular views of the city. The concave fortifications trap in all the city sounds, letting people eavesdrop on honking cars, mooing cows and the collective buzz of thousands of people living out their daily lives below. It's a pretty kingly experience.

Jai Vilas Palace & Museum

Jayandra Ganj (0751-232-1101). Open 10am-5.30pm Mon, Tue; Thur-Sun. Admission Rs 30 Indians; Rs 200 others; Rs 30 camera; Rs 80 video camera.

In a perfect world, we'd all have parking spaces for our vintage Rolls-Royces outside the sweeping driveway of our dazzling white palaces. But then, there would be no reason to visit Jai Vilas Palace, the home of local royals the Scindias. The current generation of the family retains much of the palace, giving over one wing to a public museum. Suspended from the ceiling are giant crystal chandeliers so over the top they've been billed as the world's largest and no one's had reason to believe otherwise. Occupying one gigantic wall is Asia's largest carpet, which depicts famous kings and leaders from history (Jesus is there, so are Napoleon, Akbar, Xerxes, Caesar and the Scindia maharaja in a prominent corner). The chambers of one queen, who was too short for regular furniture and had everything made to child-size dimensions, are decorated as if she might drop by any minute. Stately halls display everything from silverware and chinoiserie to arms and lithographs of battle-scenes.

Eat

Khajuraho is the only one of these three towns with anything close to a restaurant scene. The tourist area around the temples is dotted with casual and inexpensive terrace restaurants serving everything from Indian dishes to a local take on European food. Breakfast of toast, eggs and hash browns is served all day at most places and, apart from sandwiches and pizza, offers the best value for money. Korean writing can be found on many restaurant walls, but the authenticity of the script may not translate into the meal. The in-house restaurants of the area's hotels are open to walk-in diners, but get there early: Khajuraho shuts down at 10.30pm – even if the hotel restaurants stay open longer – and the streets are dark at night.

Gwalior's eating options are dull. However, some locations with satisfactory food include the restaurants in the Landmark (0751-401-1271), India (0751-234-1983) and Central Park (0751-223-2440) hotels. The Silver Saloon (indoor) and the Court (outdoor) restaurants at the Usha Kiran Palace serve excellent food.

Orchha's eating-out options are virtually non-existent so it's best to eat at your hotel.

Bella Italia

Khajuraho *Jain Temple Road, near Surya Hotel (98934-54795). Open 7.30am-10.30pm daily. $$. No credit cards. Italian.*

Brothers Manoj and Kallu Khan, who run this terrace restaurant, like to tell guests that their chef was trained by a woman in Rome. While nothing on the menu would urge you to take the first flight out to Italy to shake her hand, the Khan brothers do manage to turn out decent pizzas and sandwiches. Watch the world go by over a beer, some Italian food and candlelight.

Blue Sky

Khajuraho *Opposite entrance to the Western group temples (0768-627-2246). Open 7.30am-10pm daily. $. No credit cards. Multi-cuisine.*

The best seats in the house at Blue Sky are those that are part of the projecting balcony at the edge of the terrace. Great for catching the sun setting behind the temples and for North Indian food.

Raja Café

Khajuraho *Near Western group temples entrance. Open 7am-10.30pm daily. $-$$. No credit cards. Multi-cuisine.*

A souvenir shop, informal resource centre, restaurant and cyber café all rolled into one, Raja Café is a split-level property, with an air-conditioned ground floor and alfresco terrace. The menu runs through a host of European and Asian staples, none of which are specially noteworthy, and rush hour is usually at breakfast. It's a great place to a cool drink through the evening watching the light change over the temples; Raja Café is made for idling and the staff don't mind.

Stay

It's easy to live like a king in these parts. In Gwalior, the former residence of the local Scindia rulers is now the city's finest hotel. Orchha has two hotels that formerly housed royalty and plans are under way to convert Khajuraho's 19th-century Rajgarh Palace into the city's first heritage hotel. Most palace hotels come with all the royal trappings one would expect: liveried waiters whose families served generations of kings; portraits of princely families on the walls; royal recipes on the menu and suites named 'Maharaja' and 'Maharani'. Tours of palace hotels are usually free, even though they're not advertised by the management; hotels are also open to non-residents for lunch and dinner if they book in advance. These palaces are definitely worth visiting: they can be nearly as overwhelming as the tourist sights.

Amar Mahal

Orchha *(07680-252-102/www.amarmahal.com). $$. No AmEx.*

Designed to resemble a heritage palace hotel, Amar Mahal was actually built in 2004, and somehow manages to fuse Western minimalism with Indian opulence. The 46-room hotel has a separate area to house large families, a pool, a massage room and a Mughal-style manicured garden that hosts cultural programmes in the evening. But its most outstanding feature is its ceilings: a team of painters have mimicked Mughal inlay decoration with gilt, watercolours and fine brushwork; the crowning glory is a procession scene in the dining room. They're employed year-round to keep the place looking spanking new.

Bundelkhand Riverside Resort

Orchha *(07680-252-612/www.bundelkhand riverside.com). $$. No AmEx.*

A one-time summer retreat-cum-hunting house for the Maharaja of Orchha, the Bundelkhand Riverside Resort is now one of Orchha's prettiest tourist addresses. The hotel, surrounded by forest and with the Betwa river on one side, makes the most of its kingly past. Guns and swords are on display in the lobby, as is a map of the Bundelkhand region to which Orchha belongs. The architecture is a blend of local, Mughal and colonial styles, producing blue tiled roofs, walls in ochre and terracotta, gilt work around a landscaped quadrangle and a dining room that is an explosion of indigo and chintz. The hotel arranges for massages, rooftop sunrise viewings, regional music demonstrations and river rafting to complete the maharaja experience.

"A Hindu *aarti* at the in-house temple at sunset is accompanied by a flautist, flickering lamps and a priest who chants mantras."

Hotel Chandela

Khajuraho *Airport Road (07686-272-355/ www.tajhotels.com). $$.*

Don't look now but the Chandela is changing. The 94-room Taj hotel – it's been around since 1968 and is Khajuraho's oldest – had started to look its age. But a room-by-room upgrade should mean that the hotel will be rid of its dim lights, low ceilings and dated furnishings by the end of 2010. What will remain are the old-world brass switch panels, chandeliers, pool parlour, spa, croquet lawn and excellent service. The best rooms are the ones facing the pool and lawns.

Lalit Temple View

Khajuraho *Opposite Circuit House, near Western Group (07686-272-111/www.thelalit.com). $$$.*

Khajuraho's newest hotel – a 1973 property refurbished, rebranded and relaunched in 2007 – is the closest to the temples. Crisp ivory walls, simple dark wood furniture and amber lighting lend a slight business-hotel look to the 40-room property. Still it's a pretty enough place to return to after a day of observing copulating stone figures. Bright, large rooms are nothing to write home about, decor-wise, but they are immaculately maintained. Some overlook a badminton court, a pool and a mahua tree – under which candlelit dinners can be organised. Pool-facing rooms are particularly nice as they also have views of the temples in the distance. Service is extremely attentive. An *aarti* (prayer ritual that includes offering a lit lamp or incense to deities) at the in-house temple at sunset is accompanied by a flautist, flickering lamps and a priest who chants mantras. Guests may find that the candlelit poolside or spa offer more immediate blessings.

Orchha Resort

Orchha *Kanchanghat (07680-252-677/www.orchha resort.com). $-$$.*

An atypical Orchha hotel on many counts – it's built along a single level, has modern architecture and includes tented accommodation – Orchha Resort caters mainly to wealthy, conservative Hindus. This means bright murals of the Ramayana and the life of Krishna in the lobby and corridor, and all-vegetarian meals. Rooms are rather characterless and pokey. However, the property has a great view of some of Orchha's cenotaphs, there's a tennis court, a swimming pool near which musical performances are held every night, and a spa. Air-cooled tents (if the weather's not too hot) make a refreshing change from the opulent palace rooms elsewhere in town.

Sheesh Mahal

Orchha *Inside Orchha Fort, near Jahangir Mahal (07680-252-624/www.mptourism.com). $$. No AmEx.*

Orchha rooms don't come any more regal than the suites at Sheesh Mahal. The palace-turned-hotel (the only one inside Orchha Fort, with landmarks like the Jahangir Mahal and the Raja Mahal for neighbours) was initially intended as lodgings for local king Udait Singh. A hotel since Independence, it may have been stripped of its expensive finery but it still looks every bit as old-worldly and intimidating as the abandoned palaces next door. The entrance leads into a jaw-droppingly gorgeous high-ceilinged dining hall – and it manages to remain striking despite the fact that some of the restoration work has been done in ugly coloured laminate. However, it's the view of Orchha from the terraces of the two suites that will really make guests feel like a king (or queen) for a day.

Hotel Usha Bundela

Khajuraho *Temple Road (07686-272-386/www.usha lexushotels.com). $$.*

The 68-room Usha Bundela promises newly renovated lodgings for guests in 2010. It makes sense, since the rooms currently resemble film sets from 1980s Bollywood blockbusters. Long, carpeted and fluorescent-lit hallways bring to mind horror-movie chase sequences; the Maharaja portraits, antique letter bureaux and princely bric-a-brac

Usha Kiran Palace.

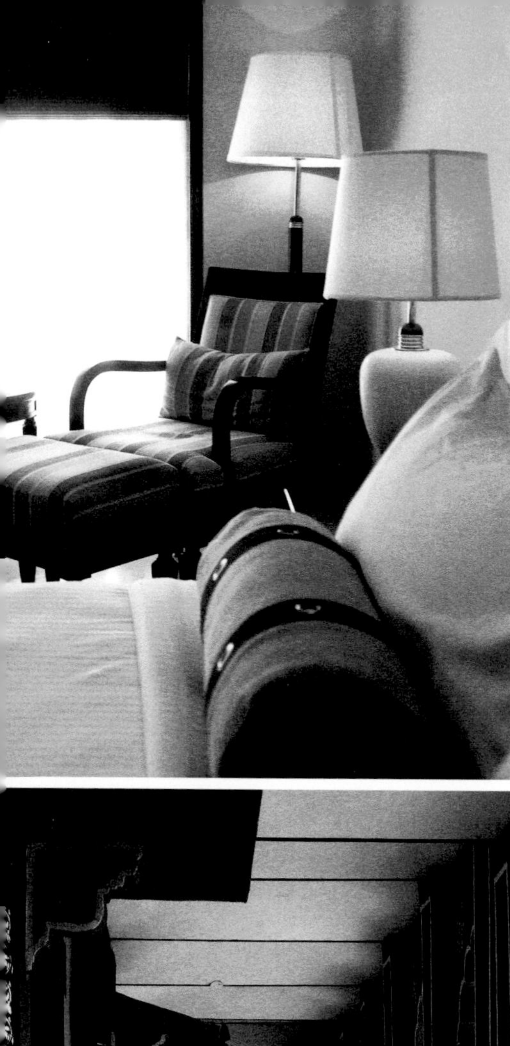

Clockwise from top left: Lalit Temple View (2); Orchha Resort; Bundelkhand Riverside Resort.

seem a bit disorganised. It is, however, a beautiful property. Rooms look out to the pool and the lobby has a high ceiling that makes the most of natural light. Get a deluxe room; the wood floors are much nicer than the carpets.

Usha Kiran Palace

Gwalior *Jayandraganj, Lashkar (0751-244-4000/ www.tajhotels.com). $$$.*

Everyone in Gwalior knows where the Usha Kiran Palace is, but most cannot give correct directions to it. Gwalior's best hotel is accessed only by a little by-lane. Usha Kiran has one of the most fabulous driveways of any hotel in India. Dazzlingly white, and incorporating a landscaped courtyard and fountains, the entrance leads to a 120-year-old palace with 30 rooms, eight suites, and private villas. The Taj group, which manages the hotel, has retained the place's century-old elements – including an old-style lift – while discreetly replacing old plumbing and wiring. Images of the much-photographed Maharaja of Gwalior and his family are everywhere, as is the royal crest (it's even tiled into the swimming-pool floor). The larger suites offer a view of the fort (although the panorama is marred by a giant supermarket billboard), and the largest suite, a modern villa some distance from the palace, has its own pool, dining nook and waiting staff. But no luxury matches up to a Mangan Snan treatment at the award-winning Jiva spa, which sets a rare oil and herb massage, saffron bath and henna hand design session to live music played by a team of musicians from behind a jali screen. The only fine dining with service to match in Gwalior is found in the

Factfile

When to go

October to March is the best period to visit Khajuraho, Orchha and Gwalior; the season peaks in December and January.

Getting there

Khajuraho is linked by direct flights to Delhi and Varanasi. Jhansi, 175km (109 miles) south on the two-lane National Highway 76, is the nearest railway station for both Khajuraho and Orchha. Orchha is roughly 170km (106 miles) from Khajuraho, a five-hour eastward drive. Gwalior is connected by air and train to Delhi, Bhopal and other major Indian cities and is 120km (75 miles) north of Orchha and 320km (199 miles) south of Delhi. Most hotels offer pick-ups from the airport or railway station for a fee.

For more on travel within India, *see p378* **Navigating India**.

Getting around

Most hotels offer full- or half-day sightseeing tours in hotel vehicles. In Khajuraho and Orchha, the monuments are walking distance from the hotels, while Gwalior is best explored by hiring a car with driver.

Tourist information

The Madhya Pradesh State Tourism Development Corporation (www.mptourism.com) has offices in Khajuraho, Orchha and Gwalior.
Khajuraho bus stand and airport (07686-274-051) both have tourist offices.
Orchha Sheesh Mahal Hotel, inside Orchha Fort (07680-252-624).
Gwalior Railway Station (0751-404-0777). All tourist offices are open 11am-5pm Monday to Saturday; closed on government holidays and the second and third Saturday of the month.

Internet

Most big hotels in Khajuraho offer in-house internet facilities and there are internet cafés along the main avenue; Raja Café also has internet access. There are no internet cafés in Orchha, though some hotels may let guests use their internet facilities. In Gwalior internet access is easily available in the city centre.

Tips

- **When hiring a guide**, either insist on a government-approved one or be prepared to take their monologues with a pinch of salt.

- **Temples and monuments** in smaller towns and places don't always open exactly when they are supposed to. Times sometimes vary with the season or daylight hours so it's always best to double-check with your guide or the tourist office.

- **Comfortable easy-to-remove shoes go a long way** in helping you to appreciate the sights, since most structures have steep stairways or require that inner sanctums be entered barefoot.

- **Archaeological museums** located near the main attractions in each of the towns are a far better resource for history buffs than the state-run Interpretation Centres, which often do little more than stock a few brochures and house indifferent tour operators.

Mountains

Ladakh

Mountains and monasteries in India's far north.

Adrenalin addicts, culture enthusiasts, backpackers and spiritual seekers will all find what they're looking for in Ladakh. Isolated from the world for decades, today Ladakh is the hot new destination for travellers seeking something out of the ordinary. From the valleys of the blue-green River Indus to the gorges of the raging muddy Zanskar, this northernmost region of Jammu and Kashmir state is visually stunning and culturally absorbing. And yet, at heights well over 3,000 metres (10,000 feet), you can still enjoy balmy weather and drive on tarmac roads far superior to those in many Indian cities.

As you journey from the pine forests of Manali through high mountain passes to reach this high-altitude plateau, much more changes than the scenery. In Ladakh, the influence of Tibetan Buddhism is everywhere, and it can be experienced first-hand through visits to centuries-old monasteries or just by chatting with locals. Though not as visible, Ladakh also has a strong Muslim population and a number of indigenous peoples, with distinct cultures and customs.

There's just one drawback to this glorious region of Mediterranean-blue high-altitude lakes, snow-covered peaks, rivers and glaciers: Ladakh is only fully accessible from June to September. Just as well, some would say, as it prevents it from being overrun and choking on its own beauty and success.

Clockwise from top left: Thiksey Gompa; Baracha Pass; Lamayuru Gompa; Basgo.

Explore

Ladakh is a high-altitude desert plateau that lies in the rainshadow of the Himalayas, in the eastern part of Jammu and Kashmir state. Its capital city, **Leh**, is in central Ladakh, with the Indus river flowing just south of it. The hard-to-reach **Zanskar** region lies to the south-west, the picturesque and flower-laden Nubra Valley is to the north of Leh, and the militarily significant town of **Kargil** is to the north-west. The road from Manali (in Himachal Pradesh state) crosses over into Ladakh just beyond Sarchu, south of Leh.

MANALI–LEH ROAD TRIP

The journey from Manali to Leh is lauded as the mother of all Indian road trips, and with good reason. It's an exhausting 473-kilometre (294-mile) stretch that is sometimes road, sometimes mere widened path, a trans-Himalayan journey through streams and glacial moraine, crossing four high-altitude passes. It's only open from June to mid September, and neither the back-breaking roads nor the incredible scenery are for the faint-hearted.

This is one road trip that proves that the journey is as important as the destination; it should ideally be undertaken over three days and two nights. Tour operators in Manali promise to do the route in one day; believe it or not, they do a 25-hour ride, with just one driver. But doing that won't allow proper acclimatisation, and you miss out on most of the views: the two primary reasons for undertaking this journey in the first place.

Just beyond Manali, you leave the Beas river behind and start the climb towards the Rohtang Pass. It's best to do this part of the journey really early in the morning, around 5am, as the narrow road often gets jammed for hours, and if there has been a landslide, vehicles will be backed up for the whole day. Rohtang Pass is a heavily touristed spot where visitors from Manali come to frolic in the snow, many for the first time in their lives.

Beyond Rohtang, there's still traffic until the dusty, stark Lahaul Valley. Past the turn-off for Kaza, it gets calmer and you can begin to appreciate your surroundings. Much of the road then runs alongside the Chandra river, which has cut its way deep into the earth. It's best to make the first overnight halt two hours beyond Rohtang, at one of several lodges or campsites in **Tandi** (or nearby Tupchilling) or **Keylang**.

Beyond Keylang, the road continues to twist and turn beside the Bhaga river with the arid land occasionally relieved by small patches of green. At **Jispa** and **Darcha**, numerous private lodges or Himachal Pradesh government guesthouses have basic facilities to spend the night, the last comfort until Leh. Many travellers, however, prefer to journey along further to **Sarchu** to overnight there.

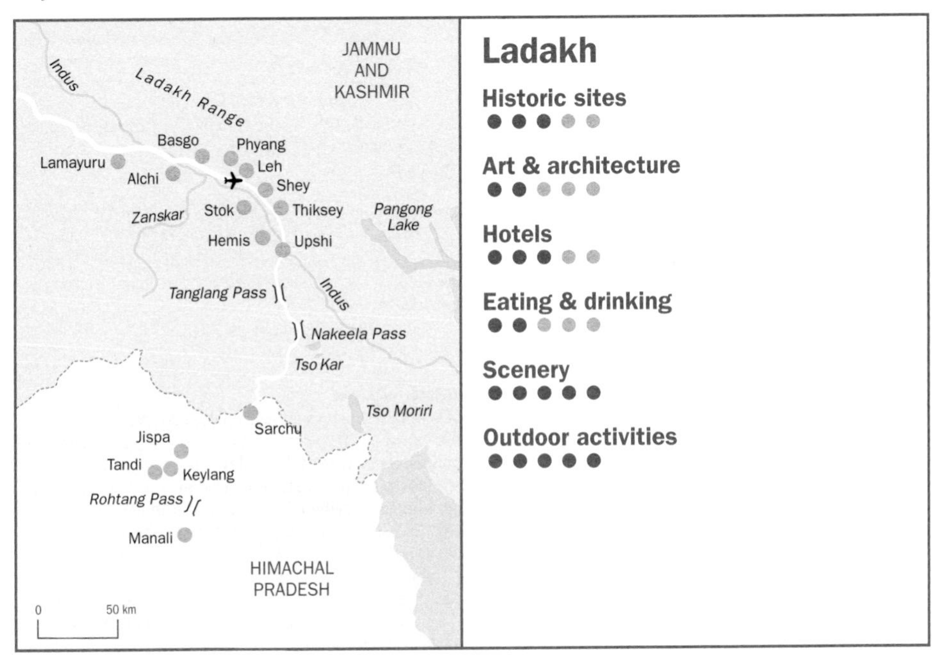

Beyond Jispa it's a long uphill trudge across spectacular Trans-Himalayan mountain scenery until you cross the Baracha La (Baracha Pass, 4,830 metres/15,845 feet). Sarchu is downhill beyond the pass – a flat, empty nothingness, interspersed by the occasional tented camp, set up to cater to those passing through.

The third day's journey is a long one whether you're coming from Jispa or Sarchu. Once you cross the Lachung La (pass), suddenly, as if from nowhere, you reach a huge plateau. At 4,267 metres (14,000 feet), the Moreh Plains, a 40-kilometre (25-mile) stretch of flat land, seems oddly misplaced. This is one of the surreal stretches of the journey, and it's fascinating to watch the Changpa nomads, whose little settlement is on this plain, wandering around grazing their sheep on its sparse vegetation.

"An hour beyond Sarchu are the dramatic Gata Loops, a series of 21 hairpin bends that climb about 500 metres over a short stretch to take you to the Nakeela Pass."

Along the route, mountain streams run across the road, eroding it further. At dozens of places there are earthmovers at work, moving mud, rock or ice, to clear the way for vehicles. The Indian government would normally not care to spend this kind of money to fix roads for just four months of the year, but it's the army presence and the movement of army vehicles and supplies that is the chief motivation. Tourists are just passers-by on a road maintained to assist military deployment on the India–Pakistan border, an area of extreme conflict and sensitivity.

An hour beyond Sarchu are the dramatic Gata Loops, a series of 21 hairpin bends that climb about 500 metres (1,640 feet) over a short seven-kilometre stretch to take you to the Nakeela Pass. Downhill again, at **Paang**, is a temporary encampment where a series of tented stalls serves travellers hot meals. Finally, the journey crosses the Tanglang La (the world's second-highest pass accessible to motorised vehicles at 5,328 metres, 17,480 feet) and descends to **Upshi**. Near to the pass, sections of the road are in a terrible state, having been washed away by melting snow that leaves behind stones and loose rock, and huge potholes.

No matter how tired you are, the last two hours of the journey to Leh are awe-inspiringly beautiful, winding for long stretches on the banks of the Indus river, with mustard and barley fields and tiny villages all around. There's a huge military presence in this border area, not to mention all kinds of quirky messages on road signs meant to promote road safety. Trucks in endless convoys are the main vehicles in these parts, although the whole Maneli–Leh road has become a classic motorbike trip too. It's not easy and definitely not comfortable, but the journey has a mythic quality and the rewards of travelling this high-altitude, ancient trading route can only be fully grasped when you've achieved it.

LEH CITY

Leh is a bit of a surprise. At an altitude of 3,350 metres (11,000 feet) one expects a sleepy village, but Leh is bustling. While most of the small city's attractions can be covered in a day, it will also be the base from which you visit Ladakh's different regions. And its very pleasant vibe is thoroughly conducive to a relaxing week-long stay doing very little. All of its attractions are in the centre of town.

Leh Palace

Open 8am-5pm daily. Admission Rs 20 Indians; Rs 100 others.

This nine-storey palace, built by the Ladakhi king Sengge Namgyal in the early 17th century, is undergoing extensive renovation. The terrace offers views of the city and there are a few faded murals inside. It's said to be built on similar lines as Lhasa's Potala Palace, but though it looks majestic on the outside and must have been remarkable in its day, there is currently little evidence of that in the maze of empty rooms. The palace will probably look more striking once renovations are complete.

Namgyal Tsemo Gompa & Namgyal Fort

Open sunrise-sunset daily. Admission Rs 20.

Namgyal Tsemo gompa (monastery), with a three-metre-high gold Maitreya (future Buddha) and colourful murals, is perched on a hillside behind Leh Palace. A winding path leads from it to the ruins of a mud fort, a good spot to take in panoramas of the Leh Valley.

Shanti Stupa

Open sunrise to sunset daily. Admission free.

This *stupa* is a recent addition to the centuries-old Buddhist structures of the valley. Only opened in 1985, it's also known as the Japanese Peace Pagoda. You can see it from almost anywhere in Leh city. It's an ideal spot to go to at sunset for marvellous views of the surrounding mountains and Leh city. Vehicles can drive up, or you can climb the rigorous 554 steps from the bottom of Changspa Road. Walk around the *stupa* to view the brightly painted modern-looking Buddhas, very different from anything in Ladakh's monasteries.

Monastery festivals

All of Ladakh's *gompas* (monasteries) hold an annual festival. They're important social occasions, as well as religious ones, for local Buddhists. Stalls selling food and other wares spring up inside and outside the monastery gates, and the atmosphere is festive.

Central to the festivities is the performance of *chhams*, or masked dances: ritualised steps performed as an offering to the monastery's deities, and to dramatise philosophies for the audience. They tend to focus on the soul's journey and the victory of good over evil, with darker human emotions seen as an aspect of evil.

Most festivals end with the ritual destruction of a human figure made of dough. There are many interpretations for *dao tulva* (killing of the enemy). Some say it represents the symbolic removal of all enemies of Buddhism; others that it's a re-enactment of the assassination of the Tibetan king, Lang Darma, persecutor of Buddhists, by a monk.

The most famous of Ladakh's monastic festivals is undoubtedly the **Hemis Tse-Chu**, celebrated at the Hemis *gompa* on the tenth day of the Tibetan calendar, the anniversary of the birth of Guru Padmasambhava (usually in June or July). Once every 12 years, the enormous *thangka* of Guru Padmasmbhava, which is exquisitely embroidered and studded with semi-precious stones, is lowered from one of the high windows for display. People come from around the world to experience this festival; when crowding is too intense, visitors can even be found on the rooftops outside, overlooking the monastery's courtyard.

At the Phyang monastery, the **Phyang Tsedup** is held in the main courtyard, which gets packed with locals and lamas from around Ladakh, who crowd on to the walls and balconies to watch lamas in terrifying masks dancing around the courtyard to the tune of drums and pipes. Another huge attraction of the festival is the display of the *thangka* of Skyabje Jigten Gombo, founder of the Drigungpa monastic order.

Thiksey's festival is called the **Thiksey Gustor**. While performing the mystic *chhams* at Thiksey, resident lamas wear masks of various divinities as well as of guardians of law (*dharmapalas*), and other patron saints of the Gelugpa order. Thiksey's festival is particularly popular and well attended by Tibetan Buddhists of the region.

Lamayuru's annual monastic festival is the **Yuru Kabgyat**, usually held in July. It begins with a procession of lamas in their maroon robes and big hats. Later, lamas wearing masks topped with skulls perform traditional *chhams* in the large central courtyard.

A seven-year (2008-2014) calendar of all Ladakh's monastery festivals is available on the government website http://india.gov.in/allimpfrms/allannouncements/4549.pdf.

NORTH-WEST OF LEH: PHYANG, BASGO, ALCHI AND LAMAYURU

A short distance out of Leh, **Phyang Gompa** (monastery) is roughly four kilometres off the main highway. After a stopover you can proceed to **Alchi**, stopping at **Basgo** on the way. En route to Basgo is the Sikh place of worship, the Pathar Sahib Gurdwara, 25 kilometres (15 miles) and an hour's drive north-west of Leh, built primarily for the large population of Sikhs in the Indian army. The area around Alchi is lovely, speckled with streams and apricot and apple trees; if you're not in a hurry, stop here for a picnic.

Once on the Srinagar–Leh highway, the landscape changes dramatically as the road climbs up to the Fatu La (pass, 4,108 metres/ 13,478 feet). As the road descends to **Lamayuru**, the high desert moonscape is awe-inspiring; you'll probably want to make several stops to take in the surreal beauty.

Alchi Gompa

70km W of Leh *Open sunrise-sunset daily. Admission Rs 20.*

The pretty path leading from the main road to the ruins of the Alchi monastery has numerous hotels, shops and stalls selling souvenirs. Alchi is an early 12th-century monastery that is unlike any other in Ladakh. It's not perched on a mountainside, it's not a functioning monastery (it's said that it hasn't been used for worship for over 500 years) and its religious art is heavily influenced by Kashmiri characters, mixed with Tibetan Buddhist styles. You'll need to stoop low to enter each of the five shrine rooms through low doors. The Dukhang (assembly hall) and Sumstek (three-storey shrine) have the most intricate paintings and murals. The latter holds a huge statue of Avalokiteswara that spans three floors, and is covered in intricate paintings; you cannot go to the higher floors. Many of Alchi's murals are badly damaged and restoration work was in progress in 2009. But it's impossible to fully appreciate Alchi monastery without the help of a good guide and sturdy flashlight; you may miss most of what makes Alchi unique, such as the Green Tara hidden in a quiet corner. We hope the site will be a little more visitor-friendly once the restoration is complete.

Basgo

40km W of Leh *Open sunrise-sunset daily. Admission Rs 20.*

En route from Leh to Alchi, a slight detour takes you to the ruins of the 15th-century castle-fort of Basgo, at the top of a heavily eroded hill. There's a functioning Buddhist temple within the ruins at the top of the fort, dedicated to Maitreya (future Buddha), containing original murals dating from the 16th century. The pleasant resident monk will be happy to open the locked doors, if you make the request. From the fort, you can watch daily life going on in the picturesque village below.

Lamayuru Gompa

130km NW of Leh *Open sunrise-sunset daily. Admission free but donation expected.*

Perched dramatically in a moon-like mountain landscape, Lamayuru has perhaps the most beautiful setting of all Ladakh's *gompas* (monasteries). This 11th- century monastery is Ladakh's oldest and a spectacular one at that. It takes around four and a half hours to drive here on the mountain roads from Leh. The road up to the monastery is lined with whitewashed *chortens* (stupas), prayer flags flutter furiously in the wind, and amid the stark barrenness of the mountains are patches of green fields. Just below the main monastery building, the ruins of the old *gompa* can be seen from above, and on the other side, the village of Lamayuru. If you go early you can catch the calming chanting of morning prayers. In the large courtyard you can sometimes watch young monks at play. Inside the prayer hall, monks and other devotees prostrate themselves in front of the shrine and light oil lamps. Besides the main Vairocana (luminous Buddha) statue, there are numerous other interesting statues, murals, and even a cave where the founding lama, Naropa, is thought to have meditated.

Phyang Gompa

17km NW of Leh *Open sunrise-sunset daily. Admission free.*

Like the Lamayuru monastery, this 16th-century monastery is a significant *gompa* of the Drigungpa Order. It's an active centre of learning and you can see the friendly resident monks go about their daily religious affairs. Each year the monastery holds a two-day festival that attracts vast crowds from around the region (*see left* **Monastery Festivals**).

SOUTH-EAST OF LEH: SHEY, STOK, THIKSEY & HEMIS

All of these sites can be covered in a day. But that can make you a bit monastery-weary, so try to split the visits over two days, beginning, perhaps, with Shey and Thiksey, and venturing to Stok and Hemis another day. When arriving from Leh, scattered white *chortens* (stupas) indicate that you are almost at Shey. At the base of the hill where Shey Palace is located is a large, fenced pond that was once the royal fishing lagoon.

Shey Palace & Monastery

15km SE of Leh *Open sunrise-sunset daily. Admission Rs 20.*

Five hundred years ago Shey was the royal summer capital. Today, its crumbling fort walls don't offer much insight into the past, but some restoration work is in progress. There are two temples at the 17th-century monastery. The larger one enshrines Shey's centrepiece, a 12m (39ft) gilded copper statue of Shakyamuni Buddha that spans three storeys; all around it are beautiful murals of the 16 *arahats* (enlightened disciples) and at the rear are the protector deities.

Thiksey Gompa

18km SE of Leh *Open sunrise-sunset daily. Admission Rs 20.*

A large red gateway leads into the mid 15th-century Thiksey monastery, which is impressive even before you enter. Stretched out over a cliff, its buildings, on multiple levels, are a dramatic sight that you encounter every time you travel this route into or out of Leh city. The large complex has many ruins and splendid murals, but also a new Maitreya (future Buddha) temple, where a 15m (49ft) statue of Maitreya Buddha, seated on the ground in the meditation position, rises over two floors. The statue's golden face and intricate colourful paintings are worth examining. This representation of Maitreya is considered unusual since Maitreya is usually depicted on a throne or standing. The monastery also has a collection of Tibetan *thangkas* (banners) and other shrines.

Most interesting of all are the young lamas in training, going about their daily life; visitors may stop off at the communal dining hall and kitchen for a quick glimpse without being too intrusive.

Stok Palace

17km S of Leh *Open 8am-1pm, 2-6pm daily. Admission Rs 30.*

Stok is the 19th-century residence of Ladakh's erstwhile royal family, the Namgyals, and the queen mother, Deskit Wangmo, is still often in residence. Visitors can stop at the museum containing various artefacts from the king's collections of heirlooms, weaponry, *thangkas* and jewellery. The imposing 77-room hilltop structure has splendid views of the Indus Valley.

Hemis Gompa

44km SE of Leh *Open 10am-1pm, 2-6pm daily. Admission free; museum Rs 50.*

Of all Ladakh's monasteries, this is the best known, not because it is in any way better than the others in the region, but because it is the largest, the richest, has had greater patronage, and its annual festival has become a major tourist attraction. Hidden from view until you are almost right upon it, it's seven kilometres off the main road. The monastery was established in the 11th century, but it is believed to have been revived in the 17th century under royal aegis. The various assembly halls display an interesting array of Buddha images and other artefacts, including a large silver statue of Buddha embedded with turquoise, well-preserved murals and an impressive three-storey statue of Guru Padmasambhava, who took Buddhism from India to Tibet. Hemis's annual festival is dedicated to him (*see p220* **Monastery festivals**). Every 12 years there is the unveiling of the monastery's greatest treasure – an 11m (36ft) *thangka*.

At the far left end of the courtyard you pass through a shop to go down to a lower level, where the Sku-rten Khang (Hemis Museum) is filled with glass cases holding sacred objects, gold statues and dozens of *thangkas* depicting the life of the Buddha.

PANGONG TSO

From Leh, Pangong Tso (Pangong Lake) in eastern Ladakh is a 150-kilometre (93-mile), five-hour drive through dramatic landscape. Day trippers need to start early in the morning. For the most part, the route is a narrow road chiselled into the sides of steep brown mountainsides. As you climb higher and look back towards Leh, you can see a range of silvery mountain peaks that look as if they're suspended from the sky.

At the halfway point the road goes across the Chang La (pass) at 5,360 metres (17,585 feet), also an army checkpost, with a *chorten* (stupa) heaving with countless Buddhist prayer flags. Just after that, in the distance, the distinct patch of Pangong Lake's blue becomes visible for a while. After snowy sections, the road descends into a green valley, where wild horses and innumerable marmots can be spotted; the latter appear and disappear from their homes in the ground. On the road you are also likely to encounter a settlement of Changpas, an indigenous people who herd yaks and live a tough nomadic life.

Before too long, the awesome expanse of Pangong Tso sprawls ahead of you. This saltwater lake, 140 kilometres (87 miles) long and three kilometres wide, is the largest in Asia; 60 per cent of it is in Tibet. You can drive along its shore right up to the village of **Spangmik**, just seven kilometres from the Indo-China border, where local Khampas live all year round in some of the world's harshest conditions. In summer, many of these tough individuals work in the tourist facilities that spring up around the lake.

"The lake is much smaller than Pangong, but its altitude, remoteness and the surrounding panorama of mountains make it just as stupendous."

As the day wears on, and the sun and clouds play games with each other, the colour of the lake changes repeatedly: at any given time some parts can be light blue, others a deep purple and others all shades in between. You could linger here forever, but by noon day trippers need to turn back for Leh because as the day warms up and glaciers and ice melt, some of the streams swell (one in particular dubbed *paagal nala* or 'mad stream'), and become too large for vehicles to cross. Vehicles must pass these areas before this happens at around 2pm. For those who have the time, an overnight halt at the tented camp on the banks of the lake is highly recommended.

TSO MORIRI

Tso Moriri is even more inaccessible than Pangong. At 240 kilometres (150 miles) south-east of Leh, a visit to the lake generally requires

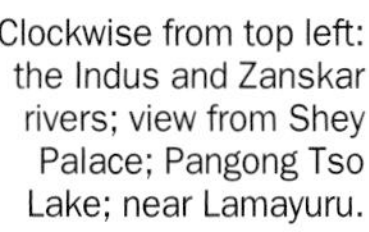

Clockwise from top left: the Indus and Zanskar rivers; view from Shey Palace; Pangong Tso Lake; near Lamayuru.

Clockwise from top: Leh Market; Summer Harvest; Useless Wali.

an overnight stay midway at Korzok village or at Tso Moriri Camps and Resorts. The lake is much smaller than Pangong, but its altitude, remoteness and the surrounding panorama of mountains make it just as stupendous.

On the journey to or from Tso Moriri, visitors can also detour to visit the saltwater lake of Tso Kar and the freshwater Tsartsapuk Lake, both quite stunning and home to migratory birdlife.

OUTDOOR ACTIVITIES

Ladakh is popular for outdoor activities both in the summer and – surprisingly – in the freezing winter months as well. Trekking is the most popular, with options ranging from one-day hikes for novices to six-week-long expeditions. Some treks begin in Ladakh and end a week later in Spiti. Others, like the tough Lamayuru to Darcha trek via the Zanskar Valley take 19 days. Average costs for shorter four- to five-day treks such as the Lamayuru to Alchi stretch or the Stok to Hemis trek are around Rs 3,500 per person per day. In winter, the most famous and strenuous route is the Chadar trek, which involves walking on the partly frozen Zanskar river.

White-water rafting on the Indus and Zanskar rivers is also available, with expeditions of one to five days. The rapids on the Zanskar are regarded as some of the world's best. Some common rafting journeys are the tame Hemis to Choglamsar route, or the slightly more challenging Nimmu to Khalsi route. Short trips (three hours) include Nimmu to Alchi and Spituk to the confluence of the Indus and Zanskar at Nimmu and cost approximately Rs 1,500.

Leh's main market area has travel agents lined up cheek-by-jowl. By far the most reliable local agent is Rimo Expeditions (Hotel Kanglachhen Complex, opposite police station, 01982-253-348). You can also contact Mountain Trails (2 Hemis Complex, 01982 254855, 011-6466-3444), and most hotels will make arrangements for you; just make sure you spell out what level of adventure you are looking for, to ensure you are not disappointed. For the more adventurous, who have two or more weeks to spare, a superb option is Project Himalaya (www.project-himalaya.com, www.project-himalaya.com), which runs intimate, friendly expeditions on less popular routes in Ladakh.

Shop

Every street and corner of Leh's Main Bazaar area is packed with shops selling jewellery, books and a variety of clothing (including traditional Ladakhi *gonchas* or gowns) and Tibetan and Kashmiri handicrafts. On the street, women sell local produce ranging from super-fresh greens to golden apricots; buy the fantastic juicy fresh apricots for a healthy snack while travelling.

From handheld prayer wheels and little Buddha statues, to large *thangkas* (and replicas) and hand-knotted carpets, shopping in Ladakh can be quite rewarding – if you've mastered the fine art of bargaining. At the top of Fort Road is the Tibetan Refugee market, where stalls are set up each day to sell much the same wares you will find all over Leh, including lots of silver jewellery. Note that much of the merchandise here comes from everywhere else but Ladakh, from Srinagar to Rajasthan. Much of it, while attractive enough, is now mass-produced.

Some interesting stores selling organic mountain produce include the Ecological Shop of Organic Products (Old Fort Road, near Hemis Complex), where you can buy apricot jam, dried apricots, dried Himalayan apples, fragrant Himalayan soaps, apricot face scrubs and moisturisers. Next door is Dzomsa (also at Changspa Road, 01982-250-699, open 8am-9pm daily), an eco-friendly shop selling a variety of organic produce as well as plastic-free drinking water (bring your own water bottle) and delicious, locally made seabuckthorn berry or apricot juice. Ledeg (north end of Old Fort Road, 01982-253-221, open 10am-5pm Mon-Sat) is another eco-friendly store selling organic foods and Ladakh-made goods such as silver jewellery, woodwork, handicrafts and T-shirts.

Jewellery fans should visit the Ladakh Art Palace on Main Bazaar Road (01982-252-116, second floor, Akbar Shopping Complex, open 9am-8pm daily), where staff will clearly tell you what's real and what's fake. The Evergreen Arts Emporium (01982-250-452, Main Bazaar Road, near Post Office, open 9.30am-9pm daily) is a Kashmiri-owned store that moves to Goa off-season; here you can get lots of traditional designs in jewellery at relatively reasonable rates. For really unusual jewellery from Ladakh and Kashmir a little store called Useless Wali (yes, that's its name) on the corner of Main Bazaar Road and Old Fort Road (opposite Ladakh Book Shop) is a find. The store owner, Azad, may be slightly pushy, but his unkempt store has many unique pieces of jewellery rarely found anywhere else in Ladakh.

Both the Ladakh Book Shop on Main Bazaar Road and Bookworm on Fort Road (beside Hotel Lingzi) have interesting Ladakh-related books.

Eat

Leh's eating-out scene is unexceptional, not because of a shortage of restaurants, but because there's not much to differentiate one from another. Because most of the visitors here are Western, bakeries abound and menus include lots of pizzas and pastas of varying quality. The German Bakery (Fort Road) and Pumpernickel Bakery (Old Fort Road) are also to be found here among countless other cafés, including the Leh Café (opposite Hotel Lingzi), Café Jeevan (bottom of Changspa Road) and Orange Sky World Garden Café (Changspa Road).

It is also possible to get Tibetan and Chinese food, and some Kashmiri and North Indian dishes as well. Countless restaurants and cafés on Main Bazaar Road, Old Fort Road and Changspa Road are open during the summer to cater to visitors (they are generally closed in winter).

Meals in hotels are invariably served buffet-style. There's usually enough variety to satisfy hungry diners; Indian-Chinese dishes are particularly prevalent.

Budshah Inn

Leh *Lal Chowk, opposite Leh taxi stand (01982-252-813). Open noon-11pm daily. No credit cards. Kashmiri/North Indian.*

The no-frills Budshah Inn is favoured by locals looking for large portions of meat and non-touristy fare. Mutton *yakhni* (it's huge, ask for half a helping), with a yoghurt-based sauce, is tasty but not as mildly flavoured as it looks. Vegetable dishes include Kashmiri *saag alu,* a mix of greens and potatoes in a gravy. Everything can be mopped up with regular rotis, or rich *churi* naan, a delicious butter naan so loaded with cashews and raisins that it could pass as dessert.

Dreamland

Leh *next door to Summer Harvest, Fort Road (01982-258-899). Open 7am-10pm daily. No credit cards. Multi-cuisine.*

Popular from breakfast to dinner, and serving an international variety of dishes, Dreamland gets particularly packed at night, especially when fresh river trout (shallow fried with garlic and butter) is on the menu.

La Pizzeria

Leh *Changspa Road. Open 6-10pm daily. No credit cards. Multi-cuisine.*

The open-air section has a pleasant ambience at night, with a bonfire going. The menu spans many cuisines. Pizzas are satisfactory, the 'Thai' food is really Chinese, and the service is seriously laid-back. This might just be the reason to come, though, as you can spend several relaxing hours over drinks and conversation without being bothered.

Summer Harvest

Leh *Off the corner of Fort Road & Old Fort Road (01982-252-226). Open 11am-10.30pm daily. No credit cards. Tibetan/Indian.*

A simple, family-run restaurant serving Tibetan, Indian and Kashmiri food, though the Tibetan dishes are best. Staples like *momos* (mutton or vegetarian) and *thukpa* (noodle soup) are served in decent, filling portions and pass muster. Service is prompt and efficient and meals are good value.

Tibetan Kitchen

Leh *Hotel Tso Kar, Fort Road (01982-253-071). Open 11am-10.30pm daily. Tibetan.*

This place is famous for its Tibetan food, and it's often difficult to find a table. The mutton and vegetarian *momos* aren't very different from those in other restaurants, though.

Stay

Undertaking the Manali–Leh road trip requires visitors to spend at least one night in Manali. The town is brimming with accommodation, but few places let you shut out the din and madness. Three options are an exception to this rule. The Mayflower Hotel (Old Manali Road, 01902-252-104, www.mayflowermanali.com, $-$$) is set in a lovely wooden building and furnished with walnut furniture. Spacious verandas have comfy chairs to lounge in, and food is excellent. Chuki and Raj Mahant run Retreat Cottages (Log Huts Area, 98160-42360, www.retreatcottages.com, $$) across the river from the Mall, above the mountaineering institute compound. Each pretty, self-contained cottage has a sit-out and garden attached, and a cook is provided on request. Out of the main tourist area, the cottages are high on ambience, and Chuki (who, by the way, is the Dalai Lama's niece), maintains it as a tranquil, modest haven. Back in the thick of Manali's action, and yet still managing to provide a quiet refuge, is Johnson's Hotel & Café (Circuit House Road, 01902-253-023, 98162-73023, www.johnsonshotel.in, $-$$), which has rooms in a variety of settings. Those in the early 20th-century stone house or the self-contained cottages amid apple orchards are especially charming. Johnson's also has a restaurant, serving Western food that's very popular with tourists, and for good reason.

Given Ladakh's remote location, extreme climate and super-short tourist season, the quality of the accommodation available in Leh is surprisingly good. Many hotels welcome guests all year round, though July to September is peak tourist season. There's also good accommodation available at Alchi, but staying at the more remote Lamayuru makes for an even more dramatic experience.

Camp Watermark

Pangong Tso *(www.mountaintrails.in). $. No credit cards.*

On the southern bank of the ethereal lake Pangong Tso, this is a well-kept, cosy camp. Tents, all facing the lake, have attached bathrooms, with flushes and running water – all quite luxurious for this remote region. Each has two beds covered in floral orange sheets and a jute carpet to keep feet warm when the temperature dips. Blue camp chairs on the small sit-out are perfect for enjoying the views. A spacious

Clockwise from top left: The Kaal; Lha-ri-mo; Camp Watermark; Grand Dragon; Mayflower Hotel.

dining tent sits almost at the water's edge and serves good, hot meals. The manager, Captain Vaidya, an ex-army man, tries hard to make guests comfortable. The sound of water lapping the bank, the clear blue sky and surrounding barren mountains make this setting unbeatable and unforgettable.

Eco Poplar Resort

Leh *Fort Road, Sheynam (01982-253-518/www.poplar-ecoresort.com). $-$$.*
This hotel has huge appeal for nature lovers. Sitting amid acres of poplars, apple and apricot trees, and flowerbeds brimming with colours, it's hard to believe it's just five minutes from Leh's main tourist drag. Appropriately placed hammocks and swings are very welcoming, as is the friendly young owner, Rinchen Namgyal, who lives on the premises with his family. Simple tiled-roof cottages house basic rooms that are clean and comfortable. An organic kitchen garden provides produce for meals. There is also a focus on yoga and meditation for those who want to extend that serene feeling.

"The double-ceilinged lobby, with large glass panes, is bright, airy and stylish. Unusual interconnected wooden walkways add warmth to the property."

Grand Dragon

Leh *Old Road, Sheynam (01982-250-786/ www.thegranddragonladakh.com). $$-$$$.*
The 53-room Grand Dragon is something of an aberration on Ladakh's hotel scene. It's a modern luxury hotel with all the usual trappings and no surprises. Large lobby, marble floors, fancy marble bathrooms, large wall-mounted LCD TVs, all of which would be unexceptional elsewhere, are found nowhere else in Ladakh. It caters for those seeking to cocoon themselves in comfort after enjoying the outdoors, free from worry over plumbing or hot water. There's a small but nice outdoor seating area, though meals, the average multi-cuisine buffet, are served in the somewhat over-decorated dining room. South-facing rooms have large picture windows with mountain views. A swimming pool and health club are in the pipeline. Its nearby older sibling, the Dragon, is more atmospheric, but if it's standardised efficiency you're after, the Grand Dragon hits the spot.

The Kaal

Leh *Skara (01982-250-333/hotelkaal@gmail.com). $$.*
In a quiet part of Leh, less than two kilometres from the Main Bazaar, this family-run hotel exudes warmth and serenity. In traditional Ladakhi woodwork, the building encloses a very pleasant flower-bedecked garden-courtyard, with views of the surrounding mountains. Interiors, too, are warm, with lots of wood, Tibetan carpets, verandas, lounge and a quiet prayer room. Service is attentive and friendly. A good choice for a leisurely stay.

Lha-ri-mo

Leh *Old Fort Road (01982-252-101/ lharimo@yahoo.com). $$.*
Though only a few minutes from the busy Changspa area, this hotel manages to give the impression of being in a rural setting. It overlooks magnificent mountains and, following a renovation in 2008, its 27 rooms are all neat, well maintained and comfortable. Bathrooms are large and modern. Traditional Ladakhi ceilings, painted wooden pillars, a sunny central courtyard and the pervading scent of poplar all contribute to a warm atmosphere. Staff are efficient and attentive and the food is better than that generally found in Leh. Meals are served buffet-style and consist mostly of Indian and Chinese dishes, served hot and prepared with care. The hotel also has a set of 21 budget rooms, off the main area, that are best avoided.

Lha-Ri-Sa Resort

Leh *Skara (01982-252-000/www.ladakh-lharisa.com). $$.*
Built, owned and run by the soft-spoken Tashi Motup Kau, this is a modern hotel with elements of traditional Ladakhi architecture – Tashi went to great lengths to get local artisans to replicate architectural and ornamental features from Leh Palace and other buildings. The double-ceilinged lobby, with large glass panes, is bright, airy and stylish. Unusual interconnected wooden walkways add warmth to the property. Rooms are simple but efficient and colour-themed, with balconies. This is perhaps the only hotel in all Ladakh with a disabled-access room. The hotel is surrounded by poplars, and has mountain views, and a tree-house-like lounge area that's great for sitting out. Meals, with Indian, Tibetan and Chinese dishes, are served in the Ladakhi-style dining room. Although it's just ten minutes from the Main Bazaar/Changspa area, this is a peaceful retreat that's very Ladakhi in essence.

Moonland Hotel

Lamayuru *(no phone, book through a Leh travel agent). $. No credit cards.*
It's astonishing that at this altitude, so far from any resources, a hotel even exists. Moonland is a quaint family-run place that's one kilometre from the Lamayuru *gompa*. Some rooms have attached bathrooms, but even those that don't are functional and pleasant enough. All are clean, warm, private and comfortable, with a bed, chairs and some shelves. Rooms without en suite are in a separate lower section overlooking the valley, with two clean bathrooms for guests to share. Good buffet-style meals, with Indian and Chinese dishes, are served in the pleasant dining room.

Omasila

Leh *Changspa (01982-252-119/www.hotelomasila.com). $-$$.*
As this hotel grew out of a family home, with extensions and modifications made over decades, it has its quirks.

These are quickly forgotten, though, when you encounter the rose bushes sprouting giant blooms and the friendly owner, Nawang Tsering. The guest rooms aren't fancy, with slightly worn wooden floors and pretty basic bathrooms. Only some have mountain views. (It's best to avoid those rooms with a wall of glass overlooking a hallway, and the suites don't quite cut it either.) The sunny terrace, overlooking an organic vegetable patch and the mountains, is a pleasant place to hang out; snacks and beer are served here. Meals are served buffet-style in the dining room, with cuisines alternating between Chinese and Indian. The place has tons of warmth and charm, and everyone is courteous and helpful. Nawang is a gracious host, and the staff will make sure your needs are met. Whatever this hotel lacks in style, it makes up for in warm, personalised service.

Factfile

When to go

Mid June to September is the time to visit Ladakh and the only months the Manali–Leh road is open. Winters are brutal in these high mountains and most tourist facilities, with the exception of hotels, are closed.

Getting there

You can take the direct flight over the Zanskar mountain range to Leh from Delhi. But you'll need to set aside two days for doing nothing as you will suffer from altitude sickness, which generally lasts for 48 hours. Alternatively, make the tiring but inspiring journey from Manali. There's also a less-frequented road from Srinagar into Ladakh, open from June to mid November, traversing some of the world's highest passes accessible to motor vehicles.

For more on travel within India, *see p378* **Navigating India**.

Getting around

The best (and perhaps only way) for tourists without their own vehicles to get around is to hire a car and driver from Leh's taxi stand. Taxis from other states are not allowed to work within Ladakh, except to bring visitors in or out from or to Himachal Pradesh. Rates are governed by the taxi union in Leh and while they may seem expensive, the pricing structure is intended to make driving economically viable for locals, considering the short length of the tourist season.

Internet

Internet cafés are all over Leh's Main Bazaar Road, Fort Road and Old Fort Road. Try Get Connected Cyber Café in Main Bazaar Road or Dream Cyber Internet Café in the Dreamland Hotel on Fort Road.

Tips

- Most sites, restaurants and shops are open only from June to September, though many hotels now stay open all year round. Winter visitors come to a completely different land. This chapter covers Ladakh during the summer months of June to September.

- Everyone, regardless of nationality, requires an Inner Line Permit to visit Pangong Tso, Tso Moriri and numerous other places in Ladakh. Check with local travel agents, who can arrange permits, but require 24 hours to do so. The fee is Rs 100.

- On the Manali–Leh journey you will lose mobile phone reception just before you hit the Rohtang Pass, and only recover it once you reach Leh's outskirts.

- All travellers should read up on the signs and symptoms of Acute Mountain Sickness, caused by high altitude, and understand its dangers. It's best not to pop diuretic pills without proper medical advice.

- Carry a flashlight and extra batteries even within Leh city as power cuts are common and streets can be dark.

- There are no places to eat on the journey to Pangong Tso and many other locations, so take food with you.

- Carry plenty of cash as ATMs in Leh sometimes run out of money, or there can be hour-long queues to access them.

- While monks in all the monasteries are friendly and accommodating, visitors need to dress modestly, talk softly and not use their camera flash within the prayer halls.

- No restaurants or shops accept credit cards, though some hotels do.

- Sometimes monks are assigned by travel agents as guides for monastery trips. They often know little to nothing of the places you are visiting, or even about Buddhism and some speak inadequate English. Try and chat to them before committing to a tour.

Clockwise from top left:
Yumthang Valley;
Pemayangtse Monastery
(2); Pineview Nursery.

Darjeeling, Kalimpong & Sikkim

Beauty at altitude.

High in the eastern Himalayas, in the far-flung north-east of India, where tea plantations spill over mountainsides and a Buddhist monastery is only a hairpin bend away, are the towns of Darjeeling and Kalimpong. Here, brightly painted cottages jut out from valleys of terraced fields. Waterfalls spill over sheer drops, then disappear under thin slivers of roads. An astonishing variety of orchids are nurtured in nurseries and gardens, or grow wild among oaks and pine. Steam trains chug alongside cars and – once in a while – the clouds part, the mists clear, and a blind curve opens on to a view of the five-peaked Mount Kanchenjunga: at 8,598 metres (28,200 feet), it's the world's third-highest mountain, less than a hundred kilometres away on the India–Nepal border. Locals say that as you climb higher, the roads get worse and the tea gets better. But the quality of the beverage is not the only thing that benefits from elevation. These hill towns are calmer, greener and cooler than the land below.

As you go higher up the mountains into the state of Sikkim – once an independent kingdom, which became part of India after a referendum in 1975 – you come upon an ethereal, unspoiled and isolated landscape of high peaks, lakes and ravines, home to peoples of different and distinctive culture and ethnicity.

Explore

Distances are great and towns at varying altitudes, so it's best to start lower and proceed to higher altitudes to acclimatise properly. **Darjeeling**, with its tea gardens and colonial houses, is a great start, from which a two-hour drive leads to the quieter, more bucolic **Kalimpong**. **Pelling** is five hours by road from Kalimpong, and Sikkim's capital city, **Gangtok**, another six hours beyond. Those going directly to Gangtok can get there from Kalimpong in under three hours. From Gangtok, **Lachung** (the nearest town to Yumthang Valley) is a five-hour journey.

In the mountains, judge distances in time rather than kilometres. Steep cliffs, single-lane winding roads, sharp bends and landslides (especially during the monsoon season) make the destination that's just beyond the next mountain several hours away. All-terrain vehicles, 4X4s or sturdy SUVs are most suited for the steep ascents and slow crawls.

DARJEELING

Most of Darjeeling's attractions can be explored on foot or on bicycle. Chowrasta – literally 'four roads' or crossroads – is part town square, part boardwalk and a popular meeting point. Young monks amble around in maroon robes, as do young fashionistas. Schoolchildren, tourists, and locals congregate here to watch the world go by. Scores of stores, cafés, pony stables and other establishments cater for visitors.

The Bhutia Busty *gompa* (monastery) is a colourful structure, just a short walk downhill from Chowrasta (open 10am-5pm daily, admission free but donation expected).

Darjeeling Himalayan Railway

http://203.176.113.182/DHR/.

Often called the 'toy train', this railway connects Darjeeling with New Jalpaiguri in the plains, along a narrow-gauge track using steam locomotives. The UNESCO World Heritage railway runs the 86km (54-mile) journey in eight to nine hours, but the railway also runs a two-hour, 12km joyride (Mar-May, Oct-Dec, Rs 240) from Darjeeling to Ghoom, the highest point on the railway, and back, with a brief halt at the Batasia Loop, where passengers can admire views of Darjeeling town and the mountains around.

Immaculate Heart of Mary Church

Takda. Open 7am-9pm daily. Admission free.

This interesting Roman Catholic Church in Takda, not far from the Yogachoeling Monastery, was built in 1975. Its architecture is more typical of eastern pagodas than Christian churches: Tibetan-style murals cover its side walls; one even depicts Jesus and his disciples as angels from Tibetan mythology. Sunday masses (at 7am, 8am and 9am) are accompanied by tabla and cymbals.

Tiger Hill

Admission Rs 5 Indians; Rs 15 others; viewing tower Rs 40.

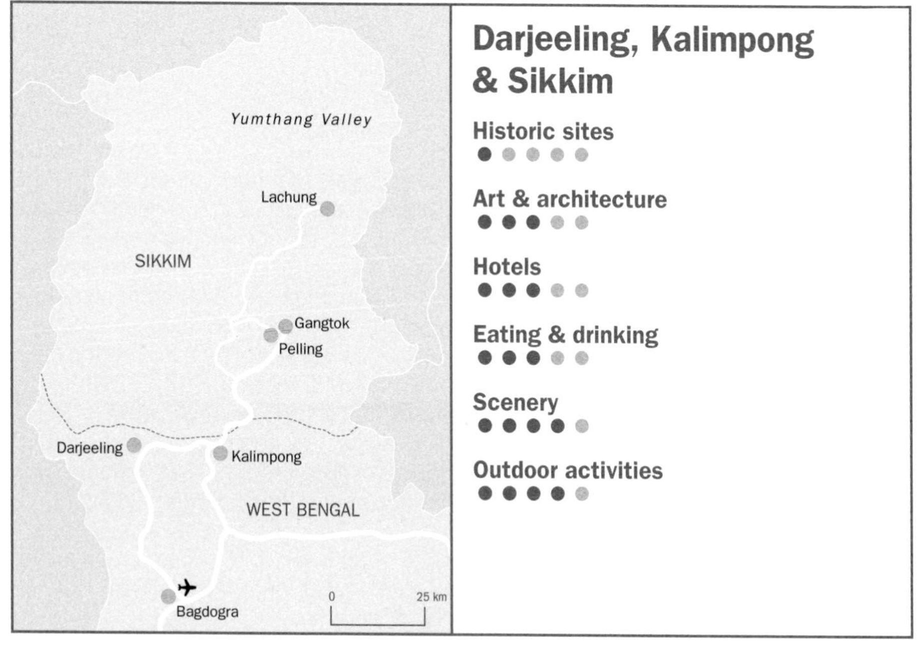

Mayfair Darjeeling.

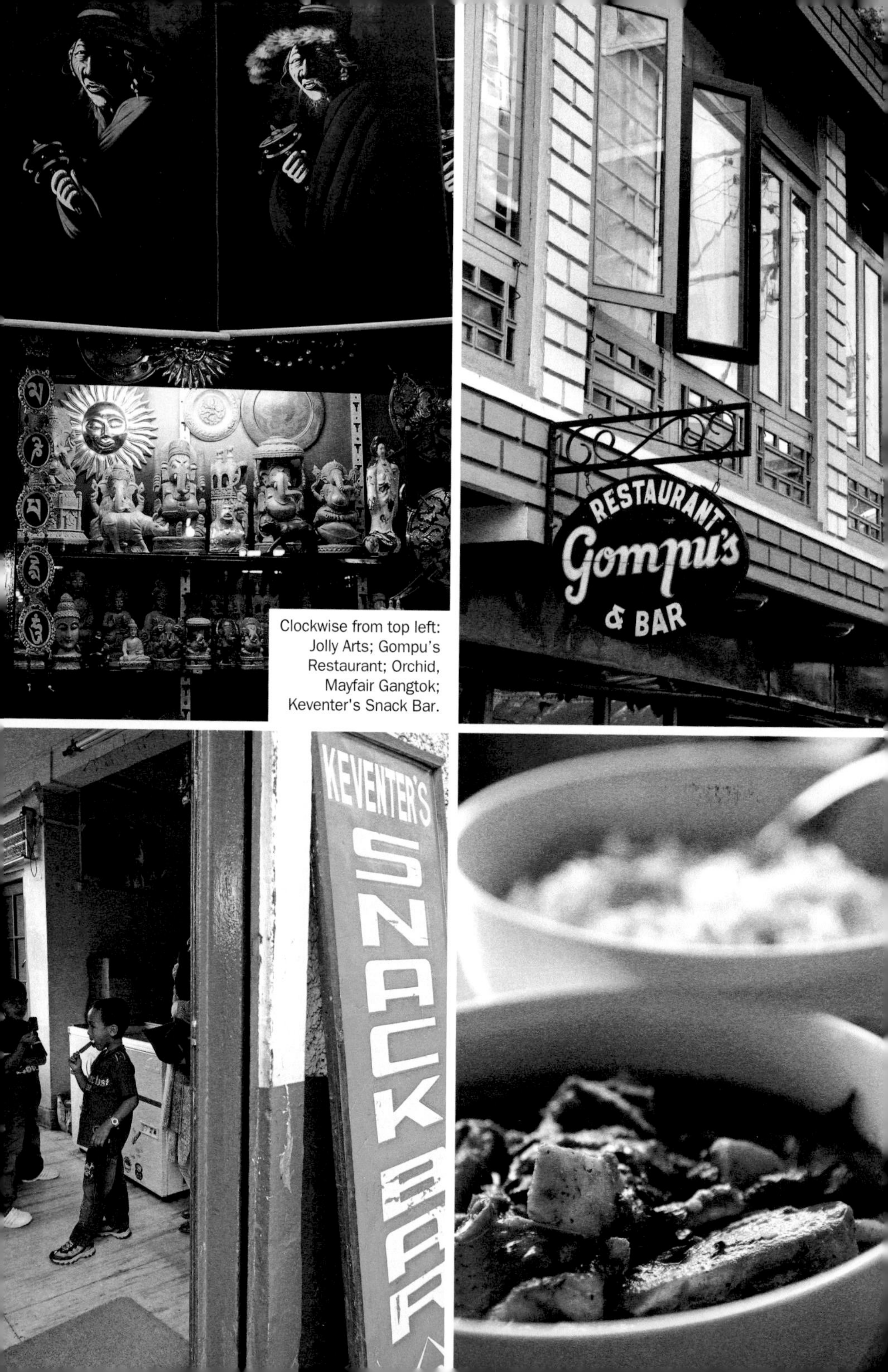

Clockwise from top left: Jolly Arts; Gompu's Restaurant; Orchid, Mayfair Gangtok; Keventer's Snack Bar.

Twelve kilometres from Darjeeling is Tiger Hill, where tourists head at 4am, to catch the sunrise over Mount Kanchenjunga. If you're lucky, you'll be treated to one of the most spectacular scenes in the Himalayas, including a peek at Mount Everest, albeit in the company of hundreds of other tourists. If a haze blocks out the mountains, be prepared to return disappointed. Dress warmly as it is freezing at the top of Tiger Hill, and though there is a viewing tower, the best views are from the outside.

Yogachoeling Monastery (Ghoom Gompa)

Ghoom. Open 10am-5pm daily. Admission free but donation expected.

This monastery in Ghoom, eight kilometres south of Darjeeling, is the town's oldest and best-known. Built in 1875, it is home to a five-metre statue of the seated Maitreya Buddha. Devotees circumambulate the monastery, spinning prayer wheels built alongside the exterior walls. Dimly illuminated interiors reveal colourful murals and *thangkas* (banners), countless offerings of silk, and cash in recessed bowls of rice.

KALIMPONG

About two hours (56 kilometres/35 miles) from Darjeeling, Kalimpong is what Darjeeling would look like it if had fewer people, a slower pace of life and twice as many plants. It's filled with British-era bungalows, epitomised in the buildings of Dr Graham's Homes School, with its sprawling campus. This little town, with only one main street, is a tranquil setting for a rest and a good starting point for walks along winding trails and up misty mountains. Visits to plant nurseries, lookout points and hikes to Deola Hill and Durpin Dara are among the popular activities.

Pineview Nursery

Atisha Road (03552-255-843/www.pineviewcactus.com). Open Summer 8am-5pm Mon-Sat. Winter 8.30am-4.30pm Mon-Sat. Admission Rs 5.

Established in 1971, Pineview Nursery houses over 1,500 species of cactus, giving it the prickly distinction of having Asia's largest collection. All growing in rows of hothouses, the collection also includes rare species from Africa and South America. Other flowering plants are also grown here, and yes, there's a view of a pine-covered valley at the far end.

SIKKIM

PELLING

Tiny little Pelling is famous because it's home to the most important monastery in Sikkim. It isn't much more than a village – a cluster of hotels and a hub for backpackers headed to west Sikkim's mountains – but for those seeking a little quiet, it has views of ancient forests and Kanchenjunga without the intrusive chatter of crowds. While the Dubdi Monastery in west Sikkim is the state's oldest, the Pemayangtse Monastery is the most important from a religious point of view. The Sangachoeling Monastery (open 7am-4pm daily, admission Rs 5), two kilometres away, requires some uphill walking. Built in 1697 and renovated in 1965, the monastery only admits Buddhists of the local Bhutia and Lepcha communities as monks. It's worth a visit for the views from its fabulous mountaintop location.

Pemayangtse Monastery

Pelling. Open 7am-4pm daily. Admission Rs 5.

Built in 1705, this monastery is the hub of all Buddhist religious activity in the state. Murals on its walls depict themes and scenes from Buddhist philosophy and mythology. The top floor holds an assortment of ancient (and rare) statues, carvings and texts, including the monastery's highlight, a sculpted illustration of *sang-tho-palri* (heaven). There are murals too; the more graphic ones (particularly of nude gods and demons) are prudishly covered up with paper.

GANGTOK

Sikkim, with its dramatic landscapes and distinctive culture, is one of this region's great attractions. Gangtok, its capital, is its most urbanised and best-planned city, and the base from which to explore the state. There's a ceiling on the number of tourist establishments permitted here, so the valleys around aren't likely to be taken over by concrete buildings any time soon. Deorali Orchid Sanctuary (Deorali, open 10am-4pm, admission Rs 15), an easy walk from central Gangtok, has a wonderful collection of orchids – some 200 of the 454 species found in Sikkim. Animal-lovers will find much to like at the Fambong La Wildlife Sanctuary, 20 kilometres (12 miles) north of Gangtok, and home to rare varieties of orchid and rhododendron. Sightings of the civet cat, bear cat and Himalayan black bear are common, sightings of the red panda very rare.

Namgyal Institute of Tibetology

Deorali, near central Gangtok (www.tibetology.net). Open 10am-4pm Mon-Sat; closed 2nd Sat of mth. Admission museum/library Rs 5.

Tibetan culture and the study of Buddhist philosophy and religion is the focus at the institute, often considered the highest seat of learning for followers of the Mahayana sect. Inside its hallowed walls are rare manuscripts on Mahayana Buddhism. The museum also has Buddhist icons, xylographs, antique paintings, *thangkas*, shrines, tapestries, masks and other religious art.

Rumtek Monastery

www.rumtek.org. Open 6am-6pm daily. Admission Rs 5.

The region's most important attraction. This grand and imposing monastery complex, Sikkim's largest, is perched on top of a hill 24km (15 miles) from Gangtok, and contains a four-storey main temple, a golden *stupa* (dome), monks' quarters and a learning centre around a spacious courtyard. The temple's roof holds the Ghanzira, a golden sculpture symbolising the five Buddha families through a lotus, wheel, bell, vase and jewel. Several sacred objects are housed within the monastery, the most important of which is the golden *stupa*, containing relics of the 16th *karmapa*, Rangjung Rigpe Dorje, who died in 1981. Climb up to the terrace to see a gazebo-like room filled with illuminated butter lamps. Lucky visitors may even be able to catch an animated monks' debate in progress.

NORTH SIKKIM

As you follow the Teesta river north from Gangtok and head deeper into the mountains, you pass little settlements like Phodong, Namok, Singhik, some of which are no more than a few tea stalls. Both Phodong and Labrang monasteries along the way are well worth stopping to see, as are the numerous waterfalls along the way, including the famous Seven Sisters waterfall, which gets its name from the seven levels it cascades down. From the Lepcha village of **Chumthang**, the road splits: one fork leads to **Lachung** (21 kilometres/13 miles), and the other to **Lachen** (28 kilometres/17 miles); both are bases for venturing further up the mountains.

From Lachen, you need to leave at the crack of dawn to make the gruelling three-hour journey to the sacred, high-altitude, glacier-fed **Gurudongmar Lake** at 5,242 metres (17,200 feet) – a trip that is only advisable for the very fit. Of course, it's freezing cold, and you'll have climbed 2,450 metres (8,000 feet) in just a few hours. But if it's a clear day, the views are awe-inspiring and make the journey worthwhile. Because of the altitude, you cannot stay long; in any case, the checkposts, army trucks and bunkers indicate proximity to the Sino-Indian border, where you cannot linger.

From Lachung, an insignificant town with basic tourist facilities, visitors can travel to the wonderful **Yumthang Valley** (open Apr-Nov, a 90-minute drive north). At 3,600 metres (11,800 feet) above sea level, it's chilly even in the summer, but has a unique topography and breathtaking scenery. Yumthang marks the end of the tree cover, but the rhododendron, the state flower, thrives at the Shingba Rhododendron sanctuary, which is home to some 24 species. They bloom in April and May, a season when alpine flowers of all varieties blossom on the slopes. Long used as a grazing ground for cattle, the valley is a good viewing point for the Himalayan peaks of Pauhunri and Shundu Tsen. Though the roads are in bad shape, and landslides and rain often make matters worse, the magnificent vistas of snow-capped Himalayan peaks and isolated mountain settlements, dotted with secluded monasteries, grazing yaks and fluttering prayer flags, are captivating and unforgettable. On the return journey to Lachung, take the time to visit the natural sulphur hot springs.

OUTDOOR ACTIVITIES

Adventurers and vicarious thrill-seekers should head to Darjeeling's Himalayan Mountaineering Institute and visit its interesting Mountaineering Museum (Jawahar Road, West, 0354-225-4083, www.himalayanmountaineeringinstitute.com, open 8am-4pm Mon-Wed, Fri-Sun, admission Rs 30 Indians, Rs 100 others). The Everest section is particularly informative, as is the telescope in the main museum.

It goes without saying that the Himalayas are a prime destination for lovers of the great outdoors. From Darjeeling to Sikkim and beyond, opportunities for trekking abound. Not only are the vistas breathtaking, there's also the added bonus of experiencing the region's cultures. Some popular routes include the Darjeeling to Sandakphu trek, or the longer Darjeeling to Singalila route. In Sikkim, short treks can take you through brilliant rhododendron forests, others go through the Fambong La Wildlife Sanctuary. Sikkim's most famous trek, however, is the eight- to ten-day Dzongri route. Other excellent, longer (ten or more days) treks are the Shangri-la trek and Goecha La trek. For the inexperienced, a short day trip from Darjeeling to Tiger Hill and back, or walks in the Yumthang Valley in north Sikkim, can be very rewarding and not too taxing.

White-water rafting on the Teesta and Rangit rivers is also available, with programmes covering everything from a relaxing day on the water to exciting rapids of grades two to four. Overnight trips set up camp on the sandy banks of the river.

The rugged mountains of Darjeeling and north and west Sikkim also offer an extremely challenging terrain for mountain biking. Numerous operators arrange bikes, logistical support, guides and customised mountain-biking trips, varying in length from one to 21 days.

For any of these activities contact a reputable operator to organise logistics and permits.

Eat

All three towns serve plenty of local food, in addition to generic Indian and Chinese dishes, and an insipid version of old-fashioned Raj-style Western cuisine. When it comes to local food, a plateful of *momos* (steamed dumplings) and *thukpa* (noodle soup) are as pleasing to the palate as to the digestive system. Local vegetables like mustard greens, stinging nettles and bamboo shoots are liberally used. In Sikkim, try *tongba* (also called *chaang* and *thumba*), the local millet beer. Served with a straw in a thick hollowed-out bamboo container, with hot water poured over millet, yeast, rice and a few herbs, it is warm, earthy and deceptively mild.

Top tea

While the rest of India enjoys its tea with milk and sugar, and while sophisticated urban youngsters are just learning the term 'chai latte', in Darjeeling, noses are turned up at such philistine behaviour. The region produces some of the best tea in the world – leaves so fine that adding anything other than hot water is considered not only an insult to their flavour, but also to the painstaking hours of labour required to produce it.

Some 87 tea plantations in Darjeeling have been accorded the Geographical Indication status for their produce, which means that, just as only sparkling wine from Champagne can be called champagne, only tea from a Darjeeling estate can be called Darjeeling. The estates collectively cover about 175 square kilometres (68 square miles), and produce nine million kilogrammes of tea annually, just one per cent of India's total. But tea is the backbone of the region's economy, employing just under half the population, on plantations that can cover large areas and house homes, schools, hospitals and day-care centres.

Plantations are everywhere here, but the ones in higher altitudes, with plants set on steep inclines so that rainwater quickly drains downhill, generally produce the best tea.

Estates such as Glenburn (www.glenburntea estate.com), Goomtee (www.goomteeresorts.com), Tumsong (www.chiabari.com) and Makaibari (www.makaibari.com) have accommodation for visitors, and several others offer tea tours that can last from an hour to a day. Typically, visitors are taken through the process of tea-making 'from leaf to cup'. This involves explanations on what makes the two-leaf-and-bud so prized, how the delicate nature of the job means leaves can only be hand-picked, how Darjeeling's 'orthodox' process is different from the more commercial 'CTC' (curling, tearing, crushing) and why tea bushes are only grown up to chest level. The sessions take visitors through the tea factory, where the leaves are cleaned, dried and sometimes fermented to produce different tastes and flavour profiles. Tea-tasting sessions with the estate's head taster, antique weighing scales and an assortment of little teapots and cups complete the tour.

It's easy to think that tea has always been grown in Darjeeling, but the first trial planting was actually made in 1845 by a Dr A Campbell. Darjeeling's teas have come a long way since then. Today, its plantations produce black,

green, white, oolong, blended, scented and flavoured teas, with special editions in particularly good seasons. The picking season starts in March and April with new leaves, referred to as the first flush. A second flush is picked from May to June. The months between July and September yield a monsoon flush or a green tea harvest, and the autumn flush is picked in October and November.

Top-grade teas from the first and second flushes fetch the best prices: a single kilogramme of tea can contain more than 9,000 hand-plucked leaves, worth Rs 50,000. Plantation owners warn that the market is flooded with lookalikes from Bhutan and Sri Lanka. but real Darjeeling tea can be identified by its logo: the profile of an Indian woman with two leaves and a bud in her hand.

Top & middle: Elgin Mount Pandim. Bottom left: The Elgin Silver Oaks. Bottom right: Orchid Retreat.

Baker's Café

Gangtok *MG Road (03592-220-195). Open 8am-8pm daily. $. No credit cards.*

The decor takes the cooking and baking theme a bit too far: the place is cheery, but bursting with posters, fridge magnets, ceramic whatnots, and cutesy slogans on the walls, tables and counter. It's empty in the afternoons, the perfect time to while away hours over a book, sandwich and crème de chocolat. By evening, it's packed with locals, hastily ordering awful pastas, passable pizzas and heavily iced pastries.

Fiesta

Darjeeling *Chowrasta, near Jolly Arts (no phone). Open 9am-6pm daily. $. No credit cards.*

A table by the window is hard to find on a regular evening, since Fiesta is a great place to pass the time with a hot chocolate, while people-watching at Darjeeling's central square. It's packed with local teens and backpackers tucking into Indian snacks, tandoori, baked savouries and pastries, though the food is secondary to the ambience. The small alfresco area is nice for summer evenings.

Glenary's

Darjeeling *Nehru Road, opposite Chandulal's Shawls (03542-257-554). Open 8am-8pm daily. $. No credit cards.*

Like many structures built on mountain slopes, it's difficult to tell which floor Glenary's is on. Turns out that this Darjeeling institution's basement is a pub, it's first floor a bakery and pastry shop and second floor a café and multi-cuisine restaurant. Each floor is accessible separately along the inclined road. The ubiquitous *momo* soup is on the menu – as are macaroni cheese and kebabs; adventurous visitors may want to try the Chinese-style crispy fried pork.

Gompu's Restaurant

Kalimpong *Damber Chowk (03552-255-818). Open 9am-3pm,6-9pm daily. $. No AmEx.*

On a cold day – and it's often a cold day in Kalimpong – nothing beats a good *pishi* (wonton soup). Gompu's, a dimly lit restaurant just off the main crossroads, serves one that is large, steaming hot and peppery enough to warm you up. Try the pork *momos* and the huge steamed-bread dumplings. Avoid the Chinese fare.

Indulge

Gangtok *Off MG Road, opposite old Children's Park (03592-204-534). Open 8am-11pm daily. Karaoke 7pm. $$. No AmEx.*

A nice change from Gangtok's touristy cafés and Sikkimese restaurants, Indulge can come across as a little bizarre at first glance. With white walls, sailcloth-covered ceilings, green leather couches and mirror-work mosaic on the walls, it's a bar, lounge and restaurant all in one. It tends to be filled with groups of Gangtok's young hip kids enjoying beer, snacks and karaoke; with participants from North-east India winning talent and singing shows on TV, it's not hard to figure out why every wannabe crooner makes a beeline for the microphone. The well-stocked bar and a menu that covers pizzas, *thukpas* and everything in between ensure a sense of camaraderie, and fun evenings for locals and visitors.

Keventer's Snack Bar

Darjeeling end of Nehru Road (03542-254-026/256-542). Open 7.30am-7pm daily. $. No credit cards.

Better for a quiet breakfast than a full meal, Keventer's is a popular meeting place. Drop in for piping hot chocolate and coffee, or sausages and bacon rolls, all of which can be eaten in the first-floor dining area. Windows open out to a view of Kanchenjunga peak, which is part of the draw.

Little Italy

Gangtok *SNOD Complex, near Petrol Pump, Deorali (03592-281-980). Open noon-3pm, 7-11pm daily. Live bands Wed-Sun. $$. No AmEx.*

This restaurant is Gangtok's best-loved watering hole and performance space for bands and visiting musicians. Among the mish-mash of junk memorabilia that forms the decor is a rubber chicken dangling from the window, a sign that says 'Karma is Karma, Baby' and vinyl disc covers on the walls. Locals strum Guns'n'Roses and Bob Dylan songs or play their own music to an audience enjoying a cocktail or a plate of Little Italy's top-selling spaghetti. Pizza and pasta, as well as Chinese and Indian food, are also on the menu.

Orchid

Gangtok *Mayfair Gangtok, Lower Saamdur Block, Ranipool (03592-250-128/www.mayfairhotels.com). Open 8-10.30am, 12.30-3pm, 7.30-10.30pm daily. $$$. No AmEx.*

To feast like a king, head to Gangtok's newest hotel. Orchid, the Mayfair Gangtok's enormous restaurant, features huge wall panels hand-painted with giant orchid blooms and a pleasant veranda section. There are Indian, Chinese, European and some Sikkimese dishes on the menu. Try the local version of prawn curry, made using Sikkimese herbs. Restaurant staff are efficient, but the kitchen is slow.

Shangri-La

Gangtok *Nor-Khill Hotel, Paljor Stadium Road (03592-205-637/220-064/www.elginhotels.com). Open 7-10am, noon-3pm, 7-10pm daily. $$. No AmEx.*

You'll need to be hungry to make the best of the four-course Sikkimese menu at the Nor-Khill. It starts off with *tongba* (millet beer). *Thukpa* comes next, followed by chicken *momos* with chutney. The main course includes pork cooked with mustard greens, capsicum in cottage cheese, stir-fried potatoes and bamboo shoots, local vegetables and a dal made with nettles and eaten with rice. Dessert is a milky *kheer* (like rice pudding). Dishes change according to the season and availability of ingredients, but food on the menu is all prepared in home-cooking style, unlike the greasy buffets.

Shop

Darjeeling's famous tea, silk *thangka* paintings and Tibetan handicrafts are the top buys from the region. Nathmulls (Laden La Road, 03542-256-437, www.nathmullstea.com, open 9am-9pm Mon-Sat, no AmEx) stocks over 50 varieties of Darjeeling tea, along with tea accessories. Jolly

Arts (Chowrasta, 03542-254-059, 94341-51101, open 10am-8pm Mon-Sat, no AmEx) is a tiny one-stop shop for silver trinkets, Tibetan crafts, prayer flags, papier-mâché work and wooden masks; staff are open to a little bargaining. But at Life and Leaf (Ajit Mansion Annexe, 94349-84644, www.lifeandleaf.org, open 10am-7pm Mon-Sat, no credit cards), a fair-trade shop along Nehru Road's market, all prices are fixed. It stocks inexpensive woven baskets, linens, light tunics, incense and furniture and proceeds support marginalised communities in the eastern Himalayas. Pick up wraps and woollens down the road at Chandulal (opposite Glenary's, 03542-256-939, open 9am-8pm Mon-Sat). And if possible, visit Glenburn Tea Estate (Glenburn Valley, 98300-70213, www.glenburnteaestate.com, open 9am-4pm daily, no AmEx) to buy the estate's fine tea, honey, jams and chocolates.

The pedestrian-only MG Road is Gangtok's shopping hub. Souvenir (03592-201-324, open 9am-8.30pm Mon, Wed-Sun), one of the area's oldest stores, has a wide assortment of prayer wheels, charms, *thangkas*, folding fans and more elaborate metal statuettes. The Sikkim branch of the Charitrust Tibetan Handicraft Emporium (Hotel Tibet, 03542-223-468, open 10am-5pm Mon-Sat, no credit cards) is a short walk away and is good for massage oils, messenger bags and T-shirts, all of which generate income for Tibetans. For books, book-related events, art shows and screenings, visit Rachna (Development Area, 03592-204-336, www.rachnabooks.com, open 9.30am-6pm daily, no AmEx). It's a ten-minute walk from the main market and is quickly becoming as much a hub for local artists and culturati as a store that stocks more than just mountaineering books.

Stay

In the Darjeeling area you can choose to stay in the town itself or further out, in quieter Kurseong, 30 kilometres (19 miles) to the south, or on one of the nearby tea estates. Similarly, in Sikkim, there is good accommodation both in Gangtok and in homestays and farms in towns and villages in the surrounding area.

The region's heritage hotels are straight out of a Regency romance novel or colonial-era film. Smaller hotels, even ones with ornamental exteriors, tend to have simple rooms. Homestays are generally no-frills establishments, neat and functional. Many hotels have spectacular views.

Cochrane Place

Kurseong *132 Pankhabari Road, Fatak (03542-330-703/999320-35660/www.imperialchai.com). $$. No AmEx.*
Kurseong's most popular hotel is full of quirks such as stuffed teddy bears on beds and a vintage Beetle car perched on top of the office entrance. It's lit using solar energy and has a vegetable garden whose produce goes into the Raj-style Western, Chinese and Indian meals. Tours of the surrounding tea plantations, forests and villages can be arranged. Less adventurous types can relax at the spa. Local musicians play the piano, *sarangi* or violin in the evening. Each wood-panelled room is named after a mountain peak: Kanchenjunga, with its view of the eponymous peak, is undoubtedly the best in the house. By 2010, some new dormitory-style lodgings will be ready, allowing those with budget constraints to enjoy the same superb views.

Elgin Mount Pandim

Pelling *Near Pemayangtse Monastery (03595-250-756/250-273/www.elginhotels.com). $$. No AmEx.*
Rising out of eight acres of forest and painstakingly maintained gardens, the Elgin group's Pelling property seems almost regal, which is fitting, since it once belonged to Sikkim's royal family. Rooms are furnished in a kind of nouveau-vintage style, with Tibetan motifs, shiny wood floors, brass fittings and plaster mouldings sharing space with bathtubs, electric heaters and televisions. The centre of activity is the colonial-themed lobby, the picture-window of which opens out to a beautiful view of the forest and Mount Kanchenjunga. As with other Elgin hotels, give the buffet a miss: steamed vegetables and Anglo-Indian cuisine make up the European menu and dessert is giant bowls of jelly and custard. Still, Mount Pandim is stylish, luxurious and comfortable, and having a 300-year-old monastery for a neighbour has obviously boosted its popularity.

Elgin Silver Oaks

Kalimpong *Ringkingpong Road (03552-255-296/766/www.elginhotels.com). $$. No AmEx.*
The Elgin group's properties are characterised by the same old-world colonial façades, bright amber lighting, ivory walls, period furniture, multitude of framed pictures and unexciting buffets. The one at Kalimpong may be smaller than its counterparts, but it looks no different. Built in the 1930s by a jute trader as a single-storey home, it was converted in the 1980s into a two-level hotel that overlooks a beautiful garden, complete with gazebo, fish pond and fluttering butterflies. The lobby's card tables, the tiny bar that looks more like a cigar room at a gentleman's club and the long dining hall all seem ready to welcome a batch of time-travelling Company officers. But it's the rooms – particularly the rocking chair, old-fashioned dressing table and clear view of the mountains in Room 23 – that really send guests back in time.

Glenburn

30km E of Darjeeling *Glenburn Valley (97350-02036/www.glenburnteaestate.com). $$$$. No AmEx.*
It's a rocky 3km stretch of road that finally lands you at the region's poshest address. But it's a small price to pay for what Glenburn offers: grand planter-style colonial bungalows, bright spacious suites, a view of the Himalayas against the estate's tea plantations, and staff that spoil you. It's easy to give in to the good life at Glenburn: claw-foot bathtubs and Darjeeling green tea-scented soaps, four-poster beds, bay windows and sit-outs. Glenburn organises tea tours, camping at its riverside log cabin, river rafting

Top & middle left: Mayfair Gangtok. Middle right & bottom: Glenburn.

and hikes. It also funds welfare programmes for plantation workers and sources much of its food and seasoning from its own garden. So meals – which might include Indonesian-style soups with Darjeeling rice, a spicy fish salad with glass noodles, steamed and fried dumplings and green tea ice-cream – are not only outstanding, they're good for the earth and local community.

The Hidden Forest Retreat

Gangtok *Middle Sichey Busty (03592-205-197/ 94341-37409/www.hiddenforestretreat.org). $$. No credit cards.*

The Hidden Forest Retreat is aptly named. The Lachungpa family's green thumbs have gone into overdrive at their property, planting vegetables and flowering plants on every available patch of land. Meanwhile, Kesang Lachungpa's smiling manner makes guests feel as if they're staying in a friend's home. There are 12 rustic but comfortable double rooms, and a dining area that serves garden-fresh produce cooked according to Kesang's delicious recipes. Each room opens out to a little balcony, has a television, mosquito net and insect repellent. Walk around the lovely grounds, complete with nursery, before heading out to the city for the day.

Himalayan Hotel

Kalimpong *Upper Cart Road (03552-255-248/258-602/www.himalayanhotel.com). $$.*

The historic Himalayan Hotel's old section, a huge stone cottage, is pretty on the outside, and thick with plants and foliage. Indoor public spaces, however, are marked by thin red carpets, murky windowpanes, cloudy glass lamps and dim lighting. Rooms are less depressing. They're clean and simple, and most have a fireplace. The newer section is better, with brighter, airier corridors and modern furnishings. Make the best of the lawns and the foliage and take the opportunity to sip tea in the courtyard.

Mayfair Darjeeling

Darjeeling *The Mall, opposite Governor's House (03542-256-376/92339-04009/www.mayfair hotels.com). $$$. No AmEx.*

Though it has 44 rooms scattered across the side of a mountain slope, this big hotel successfully achieves the cosy small-hotel feel. A heritage property dominated by browns and yellows, it has plenty of little alcoves and landscaped corners at which to quietly take in a cup of tea and forget that the hotel is in Darjeeling's most bustling quarter. The decor features a little bit of everything: Regency mouldings, cupid statuettes, Dutch-style façades, dark polished wood furniture and chintzy furnishings – and they all seem to co-exist rather than clash. Rooms are bright and modern, with Orchid Villa having the roomiest bathrooms and a dressing area that overlooks a valley full of modest houses. Photos of maharaja families, indigenous peoples and mountaineer Tenzing Norgay's family, as well as army uniforms and railway signs, make sure no wall is left unadorned, and the intimidating leather-bound books in the library actually include John Grisham and Harry Potter. Less atmospheric is the ceramic menagerie of farm animals in the gardens.

Mayfair Gangtok

Gangtok *Lower Saamdur Block, Ranipool (03592-250-555/92328-55007/www.mayfairhotels.com). $$$. No AmEx.*

Not only is this the first five-star luxury spa and resort in the eastern Himalayas, it's also the hippest, most opulent address in Sikkim. Sprawled over 45 acres, golf carts are needed to transfer guests from the reception area to their rooms. This is a no-expense-spared kind of place, with plush furnishings, flat-screen TVs, enormous bathrooms and gigantic fountains in the courtyard fighting for attention. It is full of wide walkways, sculpted greenery and abstract oil paintings of the Buddha's limpid eyes, long-fingered hands and other emblems of new age Buddhism. The spa section, a three-storey affair with a heated pool and separate rooms for high-end therapies, has massage chairs from car-manufacturer Porsche and spa products by luxury brand Pevonia Botanica. The best rooms are those in the Imperial Villa, which come with two butlers. And the best seats are at the new casino, where big spenders can become high rollers.

Modern Residency/Taagsing Retreat

Lachung *(03592-204-670/205-131/www.modern residency.com). $$. No credit cards.*

Lachung's biggest hotel is a multi-storey 24-room affair with a museum of Sikkimese and Tibetan artefacts on one floor. Walls are decorated with images of traditional instruments and people in traditional costume. Rooms are simple and better furnished than others in town and also offer room heaters and hot-water bottles on request (essential in all seasons). Get a corner room that faces east to make the most of the day's sunlight and heat.

Norbu Ghang Resort

Pelling *(03595-258-245/272/ www.norbughangresort.com). $$$. No AmEx.*

Norbu Ghang was Pelling's best address before Mount Pandim opened a few years ago. Today, it ranks a distant, but competent second. Its lobby is decorated like a monastery: hand-painted murals and Tibetan motifs cover the lintel, beams, front desk and much of the furniture. The rest of the 40-room hotel is starkly simple. The walls, floors and ceilings of the bedrooms are wood-panelled and contain rustic-looking furniture. Forget the suites and book Room 101, which catches the light better than the larger rooms. Stop by the gift shop to stock up on tea and Tibetan souvenirs.

The Nor-Khill

Gangtok *Paljor Stadium Road (03592-205-637/ 220-064/www.elginhotels.com). $$-$$$. No AmEx.*

Nor-Khill, which means House of Jewels in Sikkimese, refers to the natural beauty of Sikkim. While the Nor-Khill's immediate surroundings don't offer much evidence of these gems (being situated a hairpin bend away from a long line of smaller hotels and overlooking a football field) it is still elegant enough for visiting dignitaries and holidaying ministers to make this their hotel of choice. There's a grand piano in the lobby, driftwood art on every landing and the rooms are elegantly decorated. The Sikkimese set meal at its restaurant distinguishes it from other Elgin properties.

Orchid Retreat

Kalimpong *Ganesh Villa (03552-274-517/www.theorchidretreat.com). $$. No credit cards.*

The Pradhan family, owners of this 14-year-old homestay, have put their personal touch into every corner of the property. The cottages and single duplex building that provide accommodation are built in the garden area of the family's flower nursery. Hand-sewn embroidery by Honey Pradhan brightens up each of the ten rooms. Her recipes for Indian, Western and local dishes dominate the meals. Her father-in-law, Ganesh, an avid birdwatcher and photographer, leads nature tours of the property, the surrounding forest and Lava, a birdwatching hotspot some 30km (19 miles) away. Their dog Laboo III, a shiny black Labrador, comes out to greet new guests. This kind of warmth does much to gloss over the Orchid Retreat's basic accommodation and slow water heater. The best room is at the very bottom of the mountain-slope property; it offers the most privacy, even if it means an uphill climb for every meal.

Factfile

When to go

Darjeeling, Kalimpong and Sikkim March to mid June and October to November are the best times to visit. The area has a different kind of charm during the winter months.

Getting there

Darjeeeling is 600km (373 miles) north of Kolkata. The nearest airport is Bagdogra, with flights from Delhi or Kolkata; Darjeeling is a two-hour drive away. Kalimpong is a further two hours from Darjeeling. From Kalimpong, Gangtok is 78km/48 miles or a 2.5-hour drive and Pelling 115km/71 miles or a five-hour drive on mountain roads. New Jalpaiguri railway station, about 88km (55 miles) from Darjeeling, is the nearest railhead; from there a narrow-gauge mountain railway runs to Darjeeling (*see p235*).

For more on travel within India, *see p378* **Navigating India**.

Getting around

All-terrain vehicles or 4X4s with local drivers (from Rs 2,000 per day) are essential for negotiating the region's steep winding roads and blind curves. In Gangtok, only tourist vehicles with valid Sikkim licence plates and drivers with Sikkim licences are allowed on the roads, so tourists need to switch vehicles in the city or hire separate taxis for the day.

Tourist information

In Darjeeling, the Tourist Bureau is at Nehru Road (03542-256-020, www.wbgov.com, www.darjeeling.gov.in, open 9am-7pm daily).

Sikkim Tourism's Gangtok office is on MG Road (03592-221-634, www.sikkimtournet.com, open 8am-8pm daily).

There's also a West Bengal Tourism Office (0353-269-8025, open 10am-6pm Mon-Sat) and a Sikkim Tourist Information Centre (0353-269-8030, open 10am-8pm daily) at Bagdogra airport, but both of these offer limited information.

Internet

Darjeeling's Chowrasta and Nehru road and MG Road in Gangtok have lots of internet cafés, but internet access is unreliable or non-existent in smaller towns; in general expect to browse on sluggish speeds.

Mobile phone connectivity is strongest in Darjeeling, Gangtok, Pelling and Kalimpong. Reception is weakest on the mountain roads, between cities and is non-existent in Lachung and other remote areas.

Tips

● Special Inner Line Permits are required to visit some areas of Sikkim. Most travel agents will arrange these for a fee; you will need two photographs and a photocopy of your passport. The process usually takes one working day.

● Temperatures drop sharply just before dusk, so carry adequate warm clothing, including a hat and thick socks. In Lachung and beyond, it's freezing most of the time. Trekking boots with good soles are advised for this mountainous region.

● Dawn, which is around 5-5.30am, is the best time to spot Mount Kanchenjunga, provided there is no cloud cover or mist. Early mornings are also the best time to start tours since market areas, tea-processing units and roads tend to get crowded as the day warms up, and road navigation is tougher after sunset.

● It's not always possible to find bottled water in remote areas, so stocking up for long journeys or carrying a water purifying system may be a good idea.

Spiti

A remote mountain valley steeped in Tibetan Buddhist culture.

Buddhist prayer flags flutter in the strong winds at Kunzum Pass, welcoming visitors to the stark, beautiful Spiti Valley – a cold, high-altitude desert tucked away in the Trans-Himalayan belt of Himachal Pradesh state. Like its better-known neighbour Ladakh, Spiti was part of the Western Tibetan Zhang-Zhung civilisation, and retains a strong Tibetan influence. Most locals are Buddhists and followers of the Dalai Lama. With large-scale commercialisation yet to taint this valley, a visit here can be a soul-stirring experience.

Isolated, hard-to-reach Spiti is home to rare flora and fauna – the endangered snow leopard roams the Pin Valley area, along with the Himalayan wolf, blue sheep and ibex. And while Spiti's geography and climate attract adventure seekers, the stunning landscapes and panoramic views appeal to all. Above all, though, Spiti is a destination that offers outsiders a valuable opportunity to sample a distinctive heritage and culture at first hand. In addition to the many trekking and biking trails, there are millennia-old paintings at atmospheric *gompas* (monasteries) and beguiling Buddhist architecture. Everyday life in some of Asia's highest villages can be experienced at homestays with local families: aware of the valley's fragile ecology, Spitians are making a concerted effort to find green ways to earn a livelihood, and the homestay system is part of this drive.

Tibetan and Buddhist culture is at Spiti's heart. Here, you can be welcomed in a monastery and join the monks in prayer. Or help your hosts bring in pea or barley crops on their isolated farmstead; or entertain their children. The warmth of this valley's people is in direct contrast to its chilly climate.

Dhankar.

Explore

At a height of 3,810 metres (12,500 feet), **Kaza** is the rather uninspiring administrative headquarters of the Spiti Valley, a necessary base for treks to villages, day trips to monasteries, safaris and so on. Since spending some time here is inevitable, it's worth taking an evening walk to the brand new Kaza Monastery. The monasteries of **Dhankar** and **Tabo** lie to Kaza's south-east, while **Kee** and **Kibber** are directly to the north. Spiti is a cold, harsh desert environment, but during the tourist season (May-October) plenty of welcoming guesthouses and tiny wayside restaurants open up. In the third week of August each year the Ladarcha Mela festival is held in Kaza to mark the end of summer; it's a good time to visit.

TABO

Fifty kilometres (31 miles) south-east of Kaza, along the banks of the Spiti river, sits the ancient and magnificent **Tabo Chogskar Gompa** (monastery, open 6am-6pm daily). Unlike other monasteries that are located at much higher altitudes, Tabo is at the relatively modest height of 3,050 metres (10,000 feet). Surrounded by mountains and lush pastures, this area of lower Spiti is ideal for acclimatisation to the region.

The relatively plain exterior of the monastery, founded in AD 996, belies the fact that Tabo is one of the oldest Gelugpa Buddhist monasteries in India and a treasure trove of religious paintings and scriptures. So significant is it within the Buddhist faith that the Dalai Lama has suggested that he may retire here.

The monastery's ancient mud and clay architecture is not elaborate, but it is considered to be as fine as that of Tibet's famous Tholing Monastery. The temple complex consists of nine temples and 23 *stupas* (structures containing symbolic objects).

The main hall of the Tsuglag Khang (Temple of Enlightened Gods) has a total of 36 striking statues; 33 of these are life-size figures on the walls, surrounding the central figure of Vairocana, regarded as one of the five spiritual sons of Adi-buddha, the first Buddha. However, the real treasure here is the collection of painstakingly detailed paintings depicting the different stages of the past, present and future Buddha, as well as the priceless *thangkas* (painted banners) and religious manuscripts. Bring a good flashlight to fully appreciate the intricate motifs on the 1,000-year-old murals.

DHANKAR

Making the steep and winding eight-kilometre climb from Shichling (24 kilometres/39 miles from Kaza) to Dhankar, you can truly appreciate the surreal beauty of this region. The traditional homes of **Dhankar village** are somewhat like those of Tibet's holy city of Lhasa many years

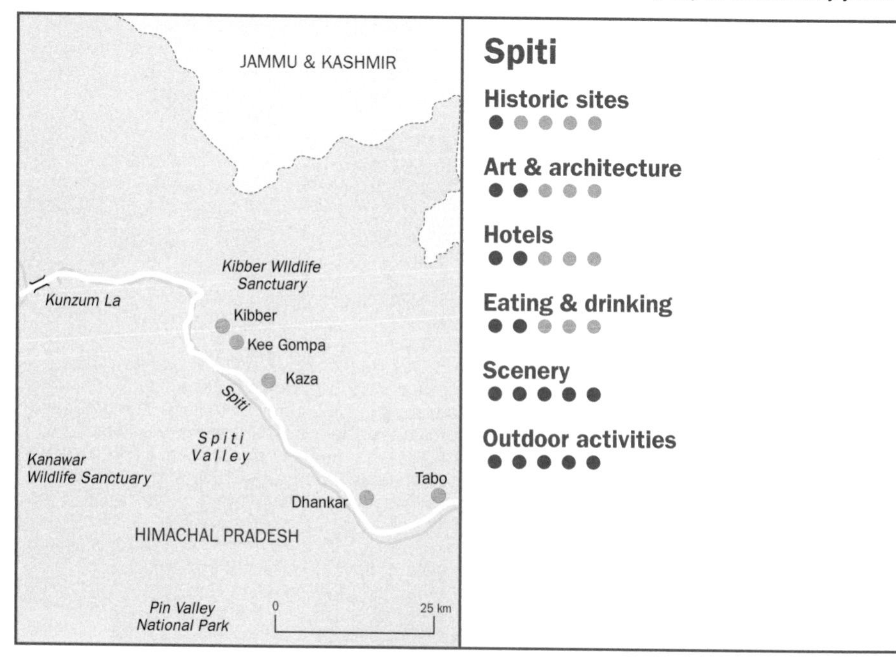

ago – simple square houses of mud and stone. Situated at an altitude of 3,870 metres (12,700 feet) the old and beautifully dilapidated **Dhankar Tashi Choling Monastery** (open 6am-6pm daily, admission Rs 25) clings precariously to the top of a mountain. Dhankar was once the capital of Spiti, and although this monastery isn't used regularly any more by monks, it still houses a beautiful collection of ancient Buddhist art. Efforts are currently under way to restore the monastery and preserve its treasures.

The rooftop (not for those prone to vertigo) looks on to some of the most spectacular views of the Spiti Valley, including the confluence of the Spiti and Pin rivers. Sunsets are other-worldly.

Close to the old monastery, on an adjoining outcrop, sits the ancient **Dhankar Fort**. The views it offers are similar to those from the monastery, but, being long abandoned, there isn't much to see at the fort itself.

At the new monastery, right at the entrance to the village, visitors can join monks in prayer at 7am or 4.30pm every day. Not only is this a spiritual sojourn, it also provides an insight into monastic life. Resident monks are extremely friendly and don't mind being photographed.

An hour's climb from the new monastery leads to **Dhankar Lake**. It's a bit of a hike to get to this high-altitude stretch of water, but the sight of the still blue waters reflecting the surrounding mountains is worth every breath. There's usually no one around, so it's not just scenic but extremely tranquil. The best option is to leave for the lake just after lunchtime to enjoy the late afternoon sky and nip in the air. Adventurous visitors can linger until just before sunset, when flocks of sheep returning home from their pastures stop by for a drink. On the walk back down, the view of Dhankar village and the monasteries against the backdrop of a striking pink and purple sky is stunning.

KEE MONASTERY AND KIBBER

Kee Gompa (open 6am-6pm daily) was first built as a fort in the 11th century, and lies perched precariously on top of an imposing mountain, 12 kilometres (seven miles) north of Kaza. Today, the monastery, the largest in Spiti, is an important centre for Buddhist learning, and can house over 250 monks and pilgrims. It is at this monastery that the Dalai Lama performed the first Kalachakra (Wheel of Time, one of the most sacred Tibetan Buddhist rituals) ceremony of the new millennium in August 2000.

Rotate the customary prayer wheels with your right hand at the entrance to the monastery. Inside, monks welcome visitors with a cup of Tibetan butter tea followed by a tour of the dark and mystical interiors. Beautiful *thangkas*, sacred scriptures and some ancient musical instruments are among Kee's many treasures.

Each year in June or July the monasteries of Spiti hold their annual Cham religious festival. Kee Monastery has the most elaborate and fervent celebrations, which attract the faithful from near and far.

Eight kilometres beyond Kee is the village of **Kibber,** one of the largest in Spiti. At an altitude of 4,205 metres (13,800 feet) it offers breathtaking 360-degree views. It's a popular hub for trekkers, owing to the numerous surrounding peaks and the nearby **Kibber Wildlife Sanctuary**, famous for snow leopard activity. It's also a good base for scenic day walks to villages such as **Gette**, **Tashigang** and **Chichim**. Kibber also has a little monastery called **Yaktin Chuling**, though it may seem a little underwhelming if you've already visited Kee Monastery.

OUTDOOR ACTIVITIES

TREKS AND HOMESTAY TRAILS

Himalayan Homestays (*www.himalayan homestays.com*) aims at promoting and preserving Spiti's rich cultural heritage, while fostering income-generating tourism. The organisation offers various trails, focusing on themes such as local culture or wildlife, each involving stays with host families. A typical trail begins at **Langza** (eight kilometres from Kaza), and proceeds to **Komic**, **Demul**, **Lahlung** and **Dhankar**. Homestay trails are best experienced on foot over a period of five days, with overnight stays in each of the villages. Each day's walk between villages takes five hours on average, allowing for a relaxed start in the morning and time to socialise with the host family on arrival.

By staying in local homes, it's possible to experience the way of life in some of the world's highest and most isolated villages. Built in traditional style with mud and stone, village homes are similar to those found a generation ago in old Tibet. A wood- (or dung-) burning stove doubles up as cooking range and fireplace, and the whole family gathers around as the women prepare the evening meal. It's an opportunity to sample authentic local cooking and home-made *arak* (barley wine) or *chang* (barley beer). Drinking water provided is boiled and therefore relatively safe, but some travellers may still prefer to carry a water-purifying pump or tablets. Some homes provide regular beds; others have traditional mattresses on the floor. Both are clean and comfortable (and warm). Toilets are outside the main home and are built in the traditional Spitian manner – squat-style, they recycle all waste as manure for the fields. Although there are no bathrooms, homes have an all-purpose area (*charhi*) designated for washing everything from clothes to faces, and the families will happily provide hot water and towels.

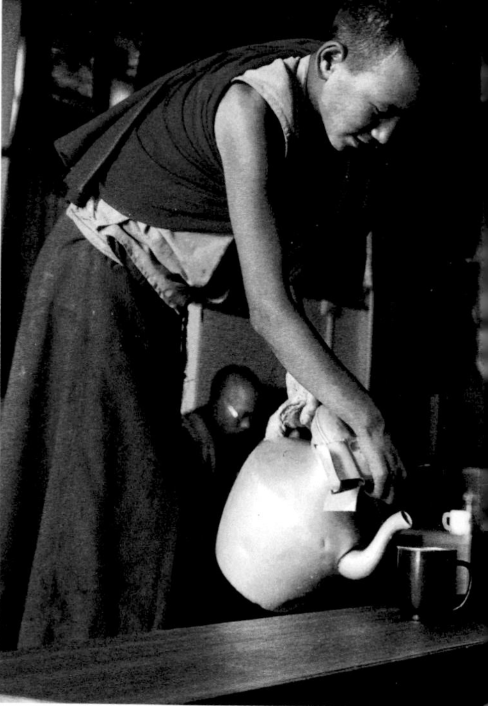

Clockwise from top left: Dhankar Lake; new Dhankar Monastery; Tabo Monastery.

There's plenty to do to supplement your daily trek, from attending prayer sessions at monasteries and temples to leisurely early morning walks in the barley or pea fields, inspecting mud crafts in Langza, or watching cultural performances in Demul. Demul is also home to one of the most popular *amchis* (traditional doctors) in Spiti, and it's fascinating to check out his collection of ancient healing plants and paraphernalia.

For those who enjoy truly immersing themselves in new environments, any help in the fields or home is likely to be appreciated by hosts. Summer is a busy time, with a lot of work to do in the fields (for this reason it's important to book ahead).

An alternative homestay trekking itinerary is the **Kee–Kibber–Gette–Tashigang–Chichim** route, which cuts across the **Kibber Wildlife Reserve** on its way to Tashigang. For a short trek, the **Kaza–Komic** route is a two- to three-hour walk, allowing some of the best views of Kaza and its surroundings.

Pin Valley is another area of Spiti that's popular with trekkers. There are a number of routes that lead from its main village of **Mudh**. Pin Valley is a different environment from Spiti, particularly during the summer when it has green pastures and abundant wildflowers. Pin Valley National Park is home to some rare medicinal flora, as well as wildlife such as the ibex and blue sheep; it's also one of the last refuges of the snow leopard. Performances by the **Bhuchen** (a tribe known for their sword dances), native to Khar village, are sometimes organised locally for a fee when a significant number of tourists are around.

Note that Pin Valley is even more remote than the Kaza area, with fewer tourist amenities.

MOUNTAIN BIKING

With roads that vary from freshly laid asphalt to loose rock, as well as spectacular vistas, Spiti has a lot to offer adventurous mountain bikers. Those who come without their own bikes can find them for hire (Ecosphere, for instance, has Trek and Firefox mountain bikes available at Rs 400-500 per day; guides, if required, are Rs 500 per day). One moderately difficult cycle route leads from Kaza to Kee (12 kilometres/ 7.5 miles) and then on to Kibber (another eight kilometres). Though mostly uphill, the road is in good condition and the route has striking views of Kee Monastery. The return journey down to Kaza is a great ride.

Another good option for a day's ride is the route from Kaza to Dhankar. Start early and stop off at Lingti or Shichling for breakfast and chai. From Shichling you leave the main road to begin a steep, winding eight-kilometre ascent to Dhankar.

YAK SAFARIS

The stretch between the villages of Komic and Demul is famous for yak safaris. Since the distance between these villages is considerable (six to seven hours on foot) and gains serious altitude (Komic is the highest village in the Spiti Valley at 4,513 metres/14,800 feet), riding a yak is a viable alternative to walking. The yaks are locally owned, clean (as far as yaks can be!) and well looked after. Although the ride is comfortable and slow, occasional breaks to stretch one's legs are necessary.

Pin Valley's Mudh area is another starting point for yak safaris. Since yaks are available only at Demul and Langza, and have other duties in addition to ferrying tourists, safaris need to be planned and booked in advance.

OPERATORS

Recommended operators for all outdoor activities and guided excursions in Spiti are **Ecosphere** and **Spiti Holiday Adventures**. For both, *see p253* **Factfile**.

Eat & Stay

As you'd expect, restaurants in Spiti aren't exactly gourmet standard. This is not due to lack of effort, but scarcity of ingredients and lack of a restaurant tradition. However, portions are large and food is served with a smile, and most visitors find it satisfying.

In Kaza, wayside restaurants pop up during the summer serving Chinese, Italian and other international cuisines, as well as local Tibetan dishes. Most of the chefs spend the off-season working in places like Goa. For breakfast, the hot delicious *aloo parathas* at **Khyoma** (near the taxi stand) are best enjoyed with a cup of strong *chai*. Khyoma is run by two energetic young women from Manipur and the atmosphere here is friendly and lively. The **German Bakery** in the main market is best in the morning, when the aroma of fresh baked goods entices you to step inside. The croissants and apple crumble are as close to the real thing as you will get in these parts. The **Lotus Café** (also known as the Hasty Tasty Café, or simply Tom's) is the place for lunch or dinner. Chef Tom is often willing to cook beyond the menu: his mutton *momos* and risotto (available on request only) are worth a try.

In Kibber village, you can get a mean *shakshuka* (a quick Middle Eastern dish of eggs cooked with peppers, onions and spices) in restaurants like **Norling**. A cup of tea on the **Serkong Guest House** terrace is a great way to pass the time in the evening, as it allows a beautiful view of all the village cattle returning home.

Local cuisine at homestays includes staples such as *thentuk* (noodle soup with spinach and potatoes), *thukpa* (noodle soup with vegetables) and *momos* (stuffed and steamed rice flour dumplings). Guests sit on carpets on the floor and eat at low wooden tables.

While in Spiti, try the nutritious and energy-boosting seabuckthorn fruit, native to the valley. Eat it whole or sample refreshing seabuckthorn juice or tea.

Although Spiti does not have any fancy or luxury accommodation, the warmth of the service and the homeliness of the hotels more than make up for the lack of facilities. Electricity is not a given in many areas and phone lines are often out of service, though these days mobile phones have become a better communication option. Spitians are truly helpful, so don't hesitate to ask for anything; they just may be able to organise it.

"Views from room balconies are stupendous, with fields of barley dancing in the foreground and Tabo Monastery in the background."

Delek House & Restaurant

New Kaza *Near Post Office (01906-222-348/ 94184-48485). $.*

This small hotel, with a line of trees on one side and Spitian mountains on the other, is new and slick. Located in New Kaza, away from the hustle and bustle of the market, Delek House is ideal for peace and quiet. Owner Phunchog Negi has designed the rooms in warm rust, orange and red, and there are great views of the Spiti river. The dining area is simple and near to the entrance and reception area, so room service may be a better bet for a quiet meal. The menu lists local dishes like *thentuk*, *momos*, and chow mein and even a vegetarian thali, which is reliably hearty and tasty.

Dewachen Retreat

Tabo *(01906-223-301/223-318/94183-63999/ 94182-08975/ashok80_thakur@yahoo.co.in). $-$$.*

Modern style sits side by side with old-world ethnic Indian decor at the Dewachen Retreat. Views from room balconies are stupendous, with fields of barley dancing in the foreground and Tabo Monastery in the background. The hotel has a small library where guests can exchange a book with something from the collection. Instead of carpets, *chataais* (mats) made from banana leaves cover the floors. A laundry service (a rarity in Spiti) is also available. Guests can also enjoy good buffet meals in the professionally laid-out dining area. The family suite is the best room in the house.

Dhankar Monastery Guesthouse

Dhankar *Dhankar Monastery. No phone. $.*

Friendly, genial monks run the show here with the help of locals. Their guesthouse is new, with fresh upholstery and simple furniture. Besides the rooms, there is a spacious dormitory on the top floor with large windows facing the valley. The chef is chatty and well travelled and makes anything from Chinese to European food, depending on the availability of supplies. A small monastery shop sells basic snack foods.

Sakya Abode

New Kaza *(01906-222-256/94185-56213/ 94187-57496). $.*

Situated just 50m (164ft) from the Kaza Monastery, this is the only hotel in Kaza built in the local architectural style. The warm dining room is vibrant (painted in local designs), and a good place to catch up on some reading while sipping hot tea. Rooms are clean and have basic furniture. Attached bathrooms are reasonably well equipped, with shower and hot water geyser. The main attraction is the green lawn, with its seasonal yellow and pink flowers; a good spot to sit and soak in the sun. Sakya is famous for its delicious *kyu* (vegetable barley stew).

Hotel Spiti Sarai

Rangrik *(94184-39247/www.spitiholiday adventure.com). $.*

Eight kilometres outside Kaza, in Rangrik, Spiti Sarai is known for its excellent hospitality, accommodation and food. The hotel is set amid green fields and is pleasingly atmospheric. Owner Ramesh Lotey is extremely resourceful and always around to chat and help out, and staff are knowledgeable and helpful too. Rooms are spacious and well furnished with a wardrobe, tables and chairs; some come with lovely balconies as well. Breakfast can be hot *aloo parathas* or toasted brown bread and eggs made to order. Feel free to ask for a dollop of peanut butter on your toast.

Hotel Trojan (Parasol Camps & Retreats)

Tabo *(94182-08975/94188-44772/ www.himalayantrailsindia.com). $.*

Part of a chain of hotels and restaurants in Himachal, the Trojan has pleasant views of Tabo Monastery and village life from the rooms' balconies. Built in traditional style, the hotel tries to be eco-friendly and has solar-powered lights. Beautiful Tibetan carpets adorn the floors of all rooms, which are tastefully decorated with souvenirs from different parts of India. Food includes both Tibetan and European meals; the minestrone, and mashed potatoes with fried onions are considered house specials. Spiti T-shirts and postcards are sold at reception. Helpful manager Lama Dechan is also a monastery guide and a fount of information on the monastery.

Tread softly

The ecology of Spiti, a harsh, arid valley with scarce vegetation and a cold six-month-long winter, is extremely fragile. In the face of recent development and a burgeoning tourist industry, the valley is already facing environmental degradation. It is also beginning to feel the ill-effects of climate change, with the arrival of rainfall during the summer months – unknown in this region before.

To prevent further deterioration, locals have formed welfare committees in collaboration with the Ecosphere group (*see p253*) to create a system of garbage management, protect flora and fauna, address sewage problems, protect the region's rare fossils and introduce efficient water management systems. Ecosphere, winner of the 2009 Sierra Club Green Energy and Green Livelihoods Achievement Award among others, also works with local communities to promote and create sustainable livelihoods; all its projects are linked to conservation and protection of the environment. Local handicrafts, including pottery and mud crafts, are being revived. And efforts are under way to harness the area's natural resources – particularly the local seabuckthorn plant – and make products like seabuckthorn tea, jams and juices. Seabuckthorn is a wild, hardy deciduous plant, high in minerals and Vitamins C, E and K. Besides serving as a nitrogen-fixing plant, its highly developed root system is excellent for soil conservation.

Tourism is growing rapidly and tourist behaviour will have a long-term impact on the sustainability of the fledgling industry. Some suggestions for visitors may seem obvious, but even small actions help the environmental effort. For example, tourists can begin by not using plastic at all, not buying fossils, trekking or mountain biking instead of hiring taxis, not picking flowers or medicinal plants, and using water efficiently (having bucket baths instead of showers).

Spiti's homestay owners, too, are constantly looking for new ways to help the environment. The use of solar power is catching on, with many homes installing solar geysers, solar cookers and passive solar houses (an energy-efficient building made with local mud brick to retain heat) instead of burning wood, and the building of greenhouses is increasing. Homestays follow a standardised rotational system for bookings so each homestay in the village benefits. For its hospitality and services, Himalayan Homestays won a Travel and Leisure 2005 Global Vision Award for Community Outreach. Look out for the Sustainable Tourism Initiatives boards outside each of the homes.

Spiti hotels also follow an eco-rating system. Ratings depend mainly on the optimum use of available resources; this can be related to accommodation, electricity or heating systems, drinking water facilities and the like. (Tourists can contribute to the ecological balance by carrying water-filtering systems or iodine tablets instead of buying mineral water.)

Five tips for responsible travelling:

1. Use water efficiently and do not dispose of waste like detergents, toothpaste etc in rivers or lakes.

2. Stay on the trails even if they're rough and muddy. Walking on trail edges and cutting corners on zigzagging paths increase damage and soil erosion.

3. Don't buy animal products, skins, furs, plants or fossils.

4. Don't give local children gifts, especially sweets. Sweets damage their teeth in an area where dental care isn't easily available, and gifts encourage them to expect handouts and beg from other tourists.

5. Take photographs of people if you want to, but be courteous and ask permission.

Visitors who want to volunteer or contribute in any way can contact Spiti Ecosphere (www.spitiecosphere.com).

Clockwise from top left: German Bakery; shop at Kaza; Sakya Abode; homestay in Komic; Dhankar Monastery Guesthouse; Hotel Spiti Sarai.

Factfile

When to go
May to October is ideal. This is when the sun shines most. Although this is the monsoon season in most of India, this region receives scanty rainfall.

Getting there
Spiti is accessible by two road routes, from Shimla and from Manali. The former is ten hours or 351km (218 miles) from Delhi, while Manali is 15 hours or 570km (354 miles) by road from Delhi, and also has an airport nearby in Kullu.

From Manali the road to Kaza opens only in May and closes by mid October. Himalayan Road Transport Corporation (HRTC) buses and shared taxis ply the rough 12-hour/210km (130-mile) journey. For a more comfortable journey, take a private taxi from Manali's Taxi Union office. Altitude sickness is common due to steep climbs and rapid height gain.

The road from Shimla to Kaza is open throughout the year, though heavy monsoon rain can sometimes disrupt movement. The 421km (262-mile) journey along the famous Hindustan-Tibet Road can be strenuous and tiring if covered in just two days, especially if you choose to travel by an HRTC bus or shared taxi. It's a much more pleasant journey if spread over a week with stops in hill towns and villages such as Narkanda, Sarahan, Sangla (Chikul) and Reckong Peo/Kalpa, until you get to Tabo.

For more on travel within India, *see p378* **Navigating India**.

Getting around
While local buses and shared taxis are available, it's most comfortable to hire a car and a driver. All local buses to surrounding villages in the valley depart from Kaza in the evening and return the next morning.

Taxis to nearby monasteries cost between Rs 700 and Rs 2,000 for a day trip or drop-off. Jeep safaris can also be organised and cost Rs 2,000 for the first 90km (56 miles) and Rs 12 per kilometre thereafter. Check all rates at the Taxi Union office opposite the Kaza bus stand.

Tourist information
No government-run tourism office has yet been set up in Spiti. Get information and bookings for accommodation (hotels and homestays), food, treks, safaris, bicycle rentals and other conservation and development-related projects in Spiti from the social enterprise **Ecosphere** (Main market, Kaza, 94184-39294, 01906-222-652, 98994-92417, 94188-60099, www.spitiecosphere.com. www.himalayan-homestays.com). It also has a water purifying system where visitors can refill their water bottles for free. **Spiti Holiday Adventure** is a travel agency (Main market, Kaza, 94184-39247, 01906-222-711, 01906-222-634, www.spitiholidayadventure.com) that can provide information and book guided tours and accommodation.

Internet
The area's only internet café is in Kaza's main market; it's simply marked 'Internet'. Internet access is provided via a satellite connection and costs Rs 80 per hour. Public phone facilities are available in Kaza and Tabo; mobile phones don't work unless you have acquired a local sim card and number.

Tips
● **Get fit** before travelling to Spiti.

● **Spiti is a high-altitude desert** with nothing more than simple medical facilities. Adequate time for acclimatisation is absolutely essential. Read up on signs, symptoms and how to avoid high-altitude sickness. Seabuckthorn tea (available at the Ecosphere office) is reputed to help acclimatisation.

● **Keep hydrated**. This is a high-altitude area where you may not feel thirsty, but you do need a lot of water.

● **An Inner Line Permit** (ILP) is required for all foreign tourists travelling to or from Spiti via the Kinnaur Valley from or to Shimla. This can be obtained from the Deputy Commissioner's offices in Kaza, Shimla or Reckong Peo. Documents required: passport, visa, photocopy of passport and visa, passport-sized photographs. It's an easy process but can sometimes take up to two hours depending on the number of tourists and the availability of the Commissioner. No permits are required for travelling via Manali.

● **Carry Indian rupees in cash.** There are no ATM facilities in Spiti, no credit cards are accepted anywhere and money exchange is difficult. Some shops and hotels may unofficially exchange foreign currency.

Spiritual Passages

The ghats.

Varanasi

Sacred city on the River Ganga.

On the banks of the holy River Ganga sits the sacred city of Varanasi. At sunrise every morning thousands come to the river to take a dip, perform rituals, wash away their sins, meditate and pray. Away from the ghats – the steps leading into the waters – the city's labyrinthine alleyways are crowded with people, most of them pilgrims. They come from around the country to the city of Lord Shiva to spend time; some come to die. Hindu scriptures tell us that Shiva dwells in Varanasi and excludes from his realm Yama, the all-prevalent god of death. To be cremated in Varanasi and have one's ashes sprinkled in the mother river is said to ensure *moksha,* liberation from the cycle of death and rebirth. Therefore, Varanasi and its river are the ultimate sources of redemption.

Love it or hate it, Varanasi evokes strong feelings. This holiest of Indian cities supports a seething mass of humanity, out to celebrate both life and death. It can be confounding and disorienting, a place of sensory overload. At every step, the senses are assailed by sights, colours, smells, sounds and tastes; the aromas of spices, incense, perfume and food meet the odours of human sweat, cows and funeral pyres. The chanting of sacred texts, often at ear-splitting volume, can have a hypnotic effect, known to drive people into a trance. It takes perseverance, luck and a somewhat sturdy constitution to come to understand and enjoy the city's many facets: the temples, the river, the pilgrims, the rituals and sadhus. This place holds a million secrets, and each visitor can discover but a few of them. For some, then, it's a mysterious city, but for many it represents the quintessential India.

Just ten kilometres from Varanasi is another major pilgrimage site, this time for Buddhists. Sarnath, where the newly enlightened Buddha delivered his first sermon, has *stupas*, ruined monasteries and modern temples.

Explore

Varanasi has been known by many names: Anandavana ('the forest of bliss'); Kashi ('the city of light'); Benaras or Banaras, which is an Anglicised corruption of the word Varanasi – which is itself derived from the names of the two tributaries of the Ganga, Varuna and Assi.

The most conspicuous elements of this holy city are its many ghats (steps leading down to water) and its innumerable temples. The ghats punctuate the riverbank for a stretch of around five kilometres, with Manikarnika and Dasaswamedh ghats lying at the centre. Next to the river is a maze of tiny alleys and crowded lanes.

Most of the city's temples and shrines are dedicated to Lord Shiva. They number in the thousands and vary in size from small boxes on the road to grand temple complexes. Kashi Vishwanath Temple is one of the most important. Others worth a visit include the Sankat Mochan Temple, Durga Temple, Kal Bhairav Temple and the new Vishwanath Temple.

While Varanasi is an ancient city, most of the crumbling buildings are actually no more than 300 years old; most pre-existing structures were demolished by Muslim invaders and rebuilt after the 18th century. Take the time to wander through the old city, adjacent to the ghats, on foot at least once. You're sure to get lost in the warren of twisting lanes, tiny shops and shrines, but it's worth the effort to be able to feel the pulse of this vibrant, thriving culture.

THE GHATS

Varanasi's nerve centre is its collection of 80-odd ghats, the steps leading down to the water dotted along the river banks from north to south. This is where all the religious activity that Varanasi is famous for takes place. Any visitor who has made the effort to visit Varanasi should make two trips: one on foot from the southern end to the northernmost ghat (at least part of the way), the other, a pre-dawn (and repeat at dusk) boat ride from near Dasaswamedh ghat to watch life unfold on the banks of this, the holiest of Hindu cities.

Dasaswamedh ghat is the most centrally located, and popular with both pilgrims and tourists. It's especially celebrated because of the grand Ganga *aarti* (prayer ritual that includes offering a lit lamp or incense to deities) that takes place here every evening. Young Brahmin priests blow conch shells, make fire offerings and invoke ancient Vedic verses amid the dizzy beating of drums, blaring klaxons and the frenetic chanting of devotees. Pilgrims and tourists throw garlands and set afloat *diyas* (oil lamps) as offerings to the Ganga. Dasaswamedh is one of the five key pilgrimage spots in Varanasi.

Next to Dasaswamedh, as you walk up the steps, is a squat rectangular building, a temple

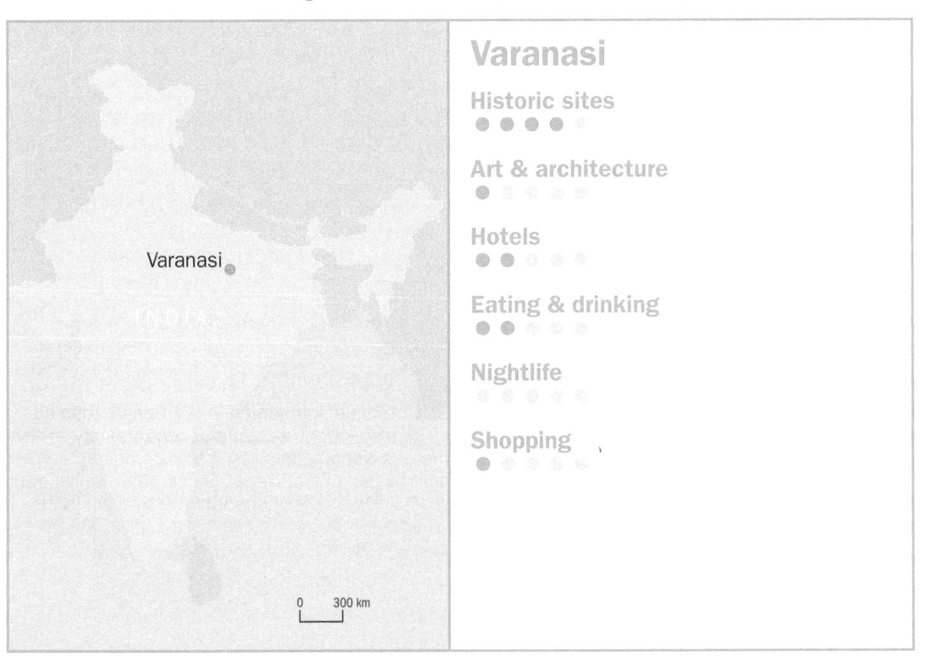

dedicated to Ma Shitala, goddess of smallpox. The goddess and the *lingam* inside attract large numbers of women pilgrims.

Assi ghat is the southernmost and only ghat with an ordinary mud bank going down to the river (as opposed to stone steps). All the ghats probably looked like this 200-300 years ago. The ghat gets its name from the Assi river that flows into the Ganga here. Assi is the starting point for those who make the *panchtirth (*five-point pilgrimage) in Varanasi, touching five of the holiest ghats: Assi, Panchganga, Manikarnika, Dasaswamedh and Adi Keshava. A few ghats away is **Tulsi ghat**, named after the great poet Tulsidas, who translated the *Ramayana* into Hindi. A temple stands on the spot where the poet apparently wrote his opus.

"Hindus consider Manikarnika ghat the most sacred place in Varanasi and the primary port of call on the pilgrimage circuit."

Another of the five pilgrimage spots, **Panchganga ghat** on the northern end of the river, is one of the most beautiful. From the riverfront, you can see the steep steps growing narrower as they go up, finally disappearing into the lanes. Here the bank is at its highest and from the riverfront you can see crumbling houses overlooking the steps. Panchganga is believed to be one of the most sacred ghats, and a prime bathing spot for pilgrims, because it is considered to be the confluence of the five sacred rivers – Ganga, Yamuna, Saraswati, Kirana and Dhupapa (which is how the ghat gets its name). There was once a Vishnu temple here, but it was demolished by the Mughal emperor Aurangzeb, who built the Alamgir Mosque in its place (one of two mosques in Varanasi built on the sites of former temples; the other is the Jnana Vapi Mosque).

Hindus consider **Manikarnika ghat** the most sacred place in Varanasi and the primary port of call on the pilgrimage circuit of five ghats (or *panchtirths*). Hindu scriptures state that the world was created here and will be destroyed here too. Manikarnika means 'precious stone of the earring', and legend attributes the origin of the *kund* (pool) near the ghat to Lord Vishnu, who dug the pool with his discus and filled it with his sweat. So delighted was Shiva at Vishnu's asceticism that he dropped an earring into the pool while dancing – hence the ghat's name. This is also a burning ghat, one of two cremation sites in Varanasi (the other is Harishchandra, *see p259*). It is one of the easiest ghats to spot from afar as you can see the pyres burning at night, while during the day a blueish haze of smoke hovers above it. An old temple that is no longer in use also sits here, blackened by smoke. It is said that the funeral pyres never stop burning here – and, indeed, there are always scores of men (women generally do not visit cremation grounds) queuing up to cremate their dead relatives. The bodies are cremated by Doms, or Untouchables, who are in charge of the ghat. The palace of the Dom Raja (king of the Doms), who is said to be very rich, is close by. Note that photography is prohibited; you're expected to observe silence and to pay due respect to the dead, and it is advisable (especially for the squeamish) to observe the proceedings from a boat at a safe distance.

Next to Dasaswamedh ghat, **Manmandir ghat** was built by Raja Man Singh (a trusted general of Mughal emperor Akbar) in 1600. A beautiful palace that belonged to the king overlooks its steps. The ornate exterior leads to what was converted into an observatory (usually open 7am-5.30pm daily, admission Rs 5 Indians, Rs 100 others) inside by Maharaja Sawai Jai Singh, the founder of Jaipur, in 1710. Known as the Jantar Mantar, it is similar to (though smaller than) the Jantar Mantars built by him in Delhi and Jaipur. The observatory has several stone instruments, including a large sundial, that were used to record the motion, speed and patterns of the planets and stars. Inside the observatory is a shrine to Someshwar, the moon god.

There are, of course, many other ghats that are worth visiting. The last of the *panchtirths* (places on the traditional pilgrimage circuit), the **Adi Keshava ghat**, is the northernmost ghat. Since, it is a little out of the way, it is visited by few tourists. Elevated above the confluence of the Varuna and Ganga, it is the site of the Adi Keshava temple, dedicated to Vishnu. Until the Muslim invasions, starting in the 12th century, this was the centre of Varanasi. **Kedar ghat** is brightly painted, a ghat where devotees take an early morning dip. There's a Shiva temple here (styled like a South Indian temple) and a pool that is said to have healing properties. **Scindia ghat** has several temples and is identified by a tilted Shiva temple submerged in the Ganga, toppled by its own weight a couple of centuries ago. Then there is **Nepali ghat**, which has a wooden temple built by the king of Nepal. Some other well-known ghats include **Harishchandra ghat**, which is the other burning ghat – though it is not as popular as Manikarnika, because it uses an electric crematorium. **Dhobi ghat** is where local washermen and women come to do their work. A pleasant time to visit this place is either early in the morning or in the afternoon.

Besides walking, hiring a boat is probably the best way to see the many ghats: not only the crumbling buildings overlooking the steps but also the people gathered along them. Generally, boats can be hired from Dasaswamedh ghat and you can either go north towards Adi Keshava or travel south to Assi. The best time to take these rides is early in the morning (between 5am and 7am in summer, 6am and 9am in winter). You can hire the boat outright, which costs Rs 150 an hour, or share with other tourists, in which case rates may vary.

Kashi Vishwanath Temple

Vishwanath Gali. Open 4am-10pm daily. Mobile phones, handbags and cameras are prohibited inside the temple complex; non-Hindus are not allowed inside the temple but can access the compound.

The most important temple in Varanasi, it is dedicated to Vishveshwara (Lord of the Universe), an avatar of Shiva. The original temple which was located nearby was destroyed by Muslim invaders. In Varanasi's history temples have repeatedly been erected only to be demolished, the last being the handiwork of Aurangzeb. He built a mosque, called the Jnana Vapi Mosque, which is inside the current temple complex. The current Kashi Vishwanath temple was built by Ahilyabai Holkar, the queen of Indore, in about 1777. The temple complex is home to several smaller shrines as well. It is often referred to as the 'golden temple' because its huge spire is covered in gold, donated by Maharaja Ranjit Singh of Punjab in 1839. Next to the temple is the famous Jnana Vapi Well (well of knowledge); drinking its waters is said to take one to a higher spiritual plane, but with heavy security in and around the temple complex it is no longer possible to partake of its waters.

CHOWK AND GODAULIA

Also part of the old city, along with the ghats, Chowk and Godaulia are located in Varanasi's centre, to the east of the central Dasaswamedh ghat. Most of the city's shops selling goods that appeal to visitors are here.

CANTONMENT

Around five kilometres to the north-west of the old city, near the Varanasi railway station, is the Cantonment district. Quiet and with plenty of space, it has a very different feel to the noise and hustle of the old city, and is home to many of Varanasi's luxury hotels.

BANARAS HINDU UNIVERSITY

Located on the huge campus of Banaras Hindu University, on the southern outskirts of the city and one of the premier centres of learning in India, is the Bharatiya Kala Bhavan Museum.

Also within the university is the New Kashi Vishwananth Temple, supposedly built as a replica of the Kashi Temple that was destroyed by Aurangzeb in the 18th century. It's also called the Birla Temple after the well-known business family that built it, and unlike its namesake in the old city, this temple welcomes visitors of all religious persuasions (open 5.30-noon, 3.30-9pm daily).

Bharatiya Kala Bhavan Museum

0542-230-7621. Open 11am-4.30pm Mon-Sat. Admission Rs 10 Indians; Rs 40 others; Rs 20 camera.

This on-campus museum houses a fantastic collection of miniature paintings. There are also Hindu and Buddhist sculptures, manuscripts and Mughal artefacts. Its only problem is that it is poorly maintained.

SARNATH

It was in Sarnath's Deer Park, ten kilometres north of Varanasi, that the newly enlightened Buddha delivered his first sermon in 528 BC. Slightly to the south of the Deer Park is the Dhamekh *stupa*, built roughly 1,000 years later. Around this *stupa* (domed monument) are the ruins of Buddhist monasteries and other sites, many built by the Mauryan emperor, Ashoka, and later destroyed by Turkish invaders in the 12th century. Samples from these ruins are now in the fine Sarnath Archaeological Museum (open 10am-5pm; admission Rs 5, free under-15s), worth a visit despite the fact that exhibits aren't displayed in the most visitor-friendly manner. The museum contains the famous Lion Capital of the Ashoka Pillar, along with other superb sculptures excavated on the site. The red sandstone four-sided lion head was once on top of the 14-metre (45-foot) pillar. This capital is particularly significant since it has been adopted as the emblem of India, while the Ashoka Chakra or *dharma chakra* (wheel) on which the lions sit has been incorporated into the national flag, its 24 spokes representing the teachings of Buddha. The pillar itself, now headless, has inscriptions in Brahmi and can still be found in its original spot near the Dhamekh *stupa*.

Close to the Deer Park is the Mulagandhakuti Vihara (open 4-11.30am, 1.30-8pm daily, chanting 6.30pm Mar-May, 7pm June-Oct, 6pm Nov-Feb, admission free, Rs 5 camera, Rs 30 video camera), a temple built by Sri Lankan Buddhists in 1930, containing interesting murals and Buddha statues. For a more modern temple, visit the bright red temple of the Tibetan community.

Buddhists also regard with reverence the Chaukhandi *stupa*, built in the Gupta period, but added to by successive dynasties. Finally, a little south-west of Dhamekh *stupa* is a Jain temple built in 1824, where the 11th Jain *tirthankara* (spiritual guide) is believed to have been born. This Digambara Jain temple's murals depict the life of Mahavira, the 24th and last *tirthankara*.

Sarnath Deer Park

10km north-east of Varanasi. Ruins open sunrise-sunset. Admission Rs 5 Indians; Rs 100 others.

Clockwise from top left:
Dasaswamedh ghat;
sadhu; Assi ghat;
Chowk; oil lamps.

Tabla tales

Varanasi has been a cultural crucible for centuries, and its musical legacy has been integral to its identity. It is believed that Mian Tansen, the legendary musician of Mughal emperor Akbar's court, was born in Varanasi, where his father sang in the temples. Two of India's famous musicians have their roots here. The world's foremost sitar virtuoso, Ravi Shankar, was born here; and Bismillah Khan, the *shehnai* (wind instrument) maestro, learnt his art here in the early part of the 20th century, from an uncle attached to the Vishwanath Temple.

Even those with a casual interest in Hindustani classical music will hear the term 'Banaras *gharana*' (Banaras is an alternative name for Varanasi; *gharana* means school). Developed by Pandit Ram Sahai 200 years ago, the Banaras *gharana* of the tabla is one of six common styles of tabla playing. Some of the greatest tabla maestros of the country have emerged from the Banaras *gharana*: Kishan Maharaj, Samta Prasad and, more recently, Kumar Bose and Samar Saha. The Banaras style of tabla playing is characterised by bold and resounding strokes.

The accompanying vocal side of the Banaras school has not had the same success in finding acceptance among musical purists, who tend to associate it with lighter, semi-classical forms of singing, such as *thumri, kajri, chaiti* and *dadra*. However, not all performers use these styles. Brothers Rajan and Sajan Mishra are perhaps the best-known contemporary exponents of the Banaras *gharana*, and they perform *khayal* – colloquially referred to as 'pure classical' music. The Benaras style of *khayal* is known for its characteristic lilting quality, with an emphasis on song lyrics and the emotional content of the compositions rather than on virtuosity of performance.

However, the most popular genre of the Banaras *gharana* remains *thumri* – known as the Purab Ang style – with exponents like the late Rasoolan Bai and Girija Devi, known for their heart-wrenching performances of love songs.

Varanasi has regular music festivals that aim to preserve these traditional styles of classical and folk music, often drawing masters from around the world: the Sankat Mochan Sangeet Samaroh festival is held in April and May; and the Dhrupad Mela festival is in February. Those seriously interested can contact Dr Ritwick Sanyal, Music Department, BHU, 0542-231-4375, dhruvapada@gmail.com.

Music festivals are also held alongside religious festivals such as Kartik Purnima in November (Ganga Festival), Buddha Purnima in May (Buddha Festival) and Shivaratri in March (Shivaratri Mahotsav).

Shashank Singh of the Hotel Ganges View (*see p264*) organises music performances for tourists at his hotel during peak tourist season, from November to January. And Varanasi is full of places that offer music lessons and sell musical instruments. Be warned though: many of them are quite dodgy. The International Music Centre Ashram (D 33/81 Khalishpura, near Dasaswamedh ghat, 0542-2452302, open 7am-8pm daily) is one of the more reliable ones. It offers sitar and tabla lessons and organises concerts on most Wednesdays and Saturdays.

Eat

Varanasi is not a gourmet destination. Because it is a holy town and a very prominent Hindu pilgrimage spot, most of the food is simple and vegetarian. Resourceful restaurant owners, however, do try to create an array of vegetarian dishes that they think will appeal to overseas tourists, including Western, Chinese, Japanese, Italian and Middle Eastern dishes. Very few places, especially near the ghats, offer meat. Restaurants in the fancier hotels in the Cantonment area, on the other hand, offer elaborate menus with everything you may crave, and top-quality service – with prices to match, naturally.

Vishwanath Gali is an alley very near the Kashi Vishwanath temple, where you can sample street food Banarasi-style (if you're confident your constitution is up to it). Favourites here include *puri-sabzi* (deep-fried flat bread with spicy vegetables); follow it up with *rabri* (sweetened, thickened milk flavoured with cardamom and pistachio). End with the famous Banarasi *paan* (betel leaf, areca nut and other ingredients), which is a good digestive, but an acquired taste for most.

There's also a long tradition here of lassis and Indian desserts such as *kalakand*, *lalpeda*, kulfi, *rabri* and *rasmalai*. Most unusual is *malaiyo* (similar to Lucknow's *nimish*), a sweet, mousse-like dessert that can be bought from little shops only very early in the morning in the winter. Note that most restaurants don't accept credit cards.

Bread of Life Bakery

The ghats *Shivala, near Agrawal Radio (0542-227-5012). Open 7am-10pm daily. $. Multi-cuisine. No credit cards.*

On the main road parallel to Shivala ghat, this eaterie was established by an American (though it's now owned by locals), which explains the presence of American pancakes with 'pure' maple syrup and bean burritos on the menu. The Chinese spring rolls (both vegetarian and non-vegetarian) and chicken with cashew nut pass muster. Stuff yourself and feel good that a part of the profits goes to charity. There's an art gallery and shop selling handicrafts upstairs.

Haifa Restaurant

The ghats *Assi ghat B 1/107 (0542-231-2960/ www.hotelhaifa.com). Open 8.30am-10pm daily. $. Multi-cuisine. No credit cards.*

While there is a range of cuisine served here, your best bet for a change is to try out the Middle Eastern thali (Rs 80), which includes pita bread, salad and any three of the following items of your choice: houmous, baba ghanoush, labaneh, falafel and chips. Service is prompt and the food quite filling.

I:ba

The ghats *Shivala B3/335B (0542 227-7523). Open 7am-10pm daily. Multi-cuisine. No credit cards.*

I:ba takes the prize for being the most unusual restaurant in Varanasi. It's a comfortable, almost fashionable space and the Japanese owner takes pains to ensure the quality of food is good. Choose from an eclectic menu that includes Japanese, Thai and Indian dishes.

Keshari Restaurant

Godaulia *D 14/8 (0542-240-1472). Open 9am-10.30pm daily. $. Mainly North Indian. No credit cards.*

During peak season this restaurant crams in more patrons than it should, and is choc-a-bloc with foreigners rubbing shoulders with blasé locals and Hindu pilgrims, all here for the authentic local vegetarian fare. There's a vast menu, which includes some of the ubiquitous Chinese and Western fare you find in these parts. Stick to Indian food; order a lassi and one of the authentic North Indian thalis: Punjabi, Rajasthani or Marwari, all of which will include curry, rice, roti, vegetable, salad and dessert.

Vaatika Café

The ghats *Assi ghat (98380-94111). Open 7am-10.30pm daily. $. Continental. No credit cards.*

Located on Assi ghat, this quiet place is ideal for all-day breakfasts. It has its own wood-fired oven and you can watch your bread being baked. Relax amid potted plants in the small alfresco area and watch boats go by on the river. Pizzas are well made and the home-made muesli makes for good comfort food (as does the apple pie topped with ice- cream).

Shop

While most people don't visit Varanasi for the shopping, touristy stuff such as clothing, miniature stoneware, brasswork and Indian musical instruments like the tabla and the sitar are all on sale here. Textile-lovers will find it hard to resist buying a Banarasi silk sari, made of silk intertwined with gold brocade. After spirituality, the Banarasi silk sari – coveted by women around India – is Varanasi's most famous export. Most shops are in the Chowk and Godaulia areas in the old city, though some assorted shops are also in the old city at the ghats.

Jaharlall & Pannalall

Chowk-Godaulia *D 36/267 Dasaswamedh Road (0542-245-0071). Open 11am-7.30pm Mon-Sat.*

This shop has been around for close to a century and is a fine place to buy Banarasi silk saris; the fabric makes for stunning soft furnishings too. Staff are helpful and well-informed and you are unlikely to be cheated. Prices can range from Rs 500 to Rs 10,000 (the low-end varieties are a mix of silk and cheaper fabrics) and some can be priced even higher. The value of the garment depends on the quality of the silk and brocade work and is higher for garments with more weaves.

Sangram Art Galerie & Raj Vijay Murtikar Shop

The ghats *Assi ghat B 1/154 (0542-236-8437). Open 10am-8pm daily.*

Miniatures of animals, gods and famous Indians made of various kinds of stone are sold here. The proprietor is obsessed with Lord Ganesha and, if asked, will demonstrate how he draws a figure of the god blindfolded.

Kashi Annapurna Book House

The ghats *Assi ghat B 1/185 (0542-231-5992). Open 8am-8pm daily.*

This small bookshop on Assi ghat (next to Tulsi ghat) is a good place to buy books on India. These include Indian fiction, books on religion and philosophy, and a nice selection of coffee-table books as well. You can also find Indian films on DVD and CDs of Indian classical music.

Stay

Varanasi is one of the most visited places in India. Summer (mid April to mid July) is the only relatively quiet period as far as tourists go, and the time when hotels offer discounts. Book your accommodation well in advance, especially if you want to stay in a riverfront guestfhouse near the ghats; the best rooms get booked months in advance. The other hub for accommodation, mostly more upmarket chain hotels, is in the Cantonment area, far from the central ritual activity. Hotels here can be peaceful, and an ideal end-of-day retreat for those who find the pulsating ghats a bit overwhelming. But while it may be a relief to cocoon oneself in a faraway hotel to escape the intensity of Varanasi, the Cantonment area may prove too far out if you are in Varanasi to immerse yourself in the ritual of daily life. Depending on traffic, it takes 20 to 40 minutes to get there from the ghats.

Ganges View

The ghats *Assi ghat (0542-231-3218/www.hotelgangesview.com). $$. No credit cards.*

Located on the southernmost ghat, far from the madness of Dasaswamedh, this pleasant and rather quaint hotel looks familiar, the kind of place that must surely have featured in a Bollywood film or two. All rooms are furnished with Rajasthani paintings and antiques, including four-poster beds, marble-top tables and brass lamps. Doors with glass panels and walls with rose motifs painted on are just some of the little touches that make this guesthouse different. The veranda overlooking the river offers breathtaking views. You can either while away your time here or pore over books from the well-stocked collection. An added bonus is the tasty home-cooked vegetarian food.

Hotel Haifa

The ghats *Assi ghat B 1/107 (0542-231-2960/www.hotelhaifa.com). $. No credit cards.*

If you're looking for a beautiful place to stay, then skip this one. But if you want clean rooms and toilets on the cheap, then Haifa is a good bet because it's so close to the Assi ghat. You can drink in the sunrise and sunset over the Ganga from the hotel's rooftop and enjoy the yogic meditation sessions that are held here.

> "The best part of the property is its extensive grounds, where peacocks roam among the orchards and fragrant jasmine bushes."

Nadesar Palace & Gateway Hotel, Ganges Varanasi

Cantonment *Nadesar Palace grounds (0542-250-3001/www.tajhotels.com). Nadesar Palace $$$$; Gateway Hotel, Ganges Varanasi $$.*

Live like a maharaja at Nadesar Palace, Varanasi's swankiest hotel, far from the ghats in the Cantonment area. The ten rooms and suites are named after famous visitors who stayed here, including King George V, Queen Mary, Queen Elizabeth II and the Shah of Iran. While the fabric canopied four-poster beds, clawfoot bathtubs and marigold or pink blinds are all quite luxurious, the best part of the property is its extensive grounds, where peacocks roam among orchards and fragrant jasmine bushes. Guests can hire a bicycle to explore the 40-acre property, ride the maharaja's horse-driven buggy, or just walk. A five-hole mini golf course was due to open soon at the time of writing.

Adjacent to and sharing the same grounds as the Nadesar Palace, and also run by the Taj group, is the Gateway Hotel, Ganges Varanasi, at a third of the price. The Gateway has had a pleasant facelift in recent years and rooms are more contemporary in decor, though the lobby is a throwback to the Raj, with a huge central dome adorned with chandeliers, and large French windows on all sides looking out on to the garden. Both hotels have exceptional service and similar amenities, but the Nadesar is tops in old-world charm and heritage feel.

Palace on Ganges

The ghats *Assi ghat B 1/158 (0542-231-5050/www.palaceonganges.com). $$. No credit cards.*

Located in an older building, this hotel has a multicultural theme and its decor attempts to recreate aspects of various Indian states. It doesn't quite work and the result is a kitschy mish-mash of styles. If you can bag a room with a balcony overlooking the ghats, you'll have done very well. Walls are adorned with photographs of well-known Hindustani classical musicians, and paintings and photographs of Varanasi, and curiously enough, old buildings of Kolkata. Staff are courteous, though service is

Top: street food. Middle: Bread of Life Bakery. Bottom left: Sangram Art Galerie. Bottom right: Jaharlall & Pannalall.

Top & bottom left: Nadesar Palace. Bottom right: Radisson Hotel Varanasi.

a bit slow. This hotel gets recommended mostly because of the paucity of satisfactory rooms on Varanasi's ghats.

Radisson Hotel Varanasi

Cantonment *The Mall (0542-250-1515/ www.radisson.com). $$$.*
One of Varanasi's few modern hotels, with a grand double-ceilinged lobby. Before the opening of the Nadesar Palace it was a strong contender for the top slot, mostly because it offers excellent service. Rooms are archetypal chain hotel, though some of the furnishings are in attractive gold-infused pastels. The spacious, impeccable bathrooms are a luxury in a city where the overwhelming feeling is one of being cramped. Those starved of meat should head straight to the Great Kebab Factory for sumptuous kebabs and other meat dishes for dinner; the Oakwood Bar is well stocked too. One drawback (shared by the Nadesar Palace) is its distance from the riverfront, though some may like being away from the hustle of the ghats.

Rashmi Guest House

The ghats *Manmandir ghat D16/28A (0542-240-2778/www.rashmiguesthouse.com). $$.*
Overlooking the nerve-centre of Varanasi, the Dasaswamedh ghat, this guesthouse (also sometimes called A Palace on River) is a big hit with tourists. Rooms are standard issue, clean and air-conditioned, and service is prompt. Dolphin, the Rashmi's rooftop restaurant, is great for early-morning breakfasts. The guesthouse's prime ghat location is boosted further by proximity to the Dom Raja's palace on one side and the 17th-century Man Singh observatory on the other on Manmandir ghat.

Factfile

When to go

November to March is the best time to visit Varanasi. But no matter when you visit, it will be crowded. Summer (Apr-mid June) is oppressively hot and humid, with temperatures soaring to 40°C and upwards. Avoid the monsoon (mid June-Sept).

Getting there

There are numerous flights connecting Varanasi with Delhi and other cities. Varanasi airport is 18km (11 miles) from the city.

Varanasi Cantonment railway station is conveniently connected by overnight trains to Delhi and many other cities, including Kolkata.

For more on travel within India, *see p378* **Navigating India**.

Getting around

Cycle-rickshaws and auto-rickshaws are the best way to travel around the city, though the latter cannot enter many of the small lanes of the old city. Since there are no fixed rates, tourists have to bargain. You can hire a car for a day or half-day, but a car will not be able to travel through much of the old city, though it's useful to get to or from the airport and Sarnath.

Tourist information

The India Tourism Office is in the Cantonment area (15B The Mall, 0542-250-1784, open 9am-5pm Mon-Fri, 9am-2pm Sat).
UP Tourism's Office (Tourist Bungalow, Parade Kothi; 0542-220-6638) is open 10am-5pm Mon-Sat. There's also a branch at Varanasi railway station (0542-234-6370, open 9am-7pm daily).

Internet

Though there are numerous internet cafés all over Varanasi, finding one with decent speed is a problem. Prices vary from Rs 25-Rs 50 per hour.

Tips

- **Be prepared for a dirty, dusty city**, as much of Varanasi and the Ganga are filthy. You'll need to suspend worries about hygiene, and find interest in religious practice, to get the most out of your visit.

- **Whether you're walking** through Varanasi's narrow lanes or travelling by cycle- or auto-rickshaws, expect to encounter pollution, especially during winter. Most establishments run on generators that spew out vast quantities of diesel fumes.

- **Book accommodation** in advance and avoid taxis where the driver promises to take you to the 'best' hotels or 'best' anything. Auto-rickshaw drivers are known to lie blatantly to tourists being picked up at the train station, stating their pre-booked hotel doesn't exist or has caught fire. If you want to go to a particular hotel or shop ask to be dropped off at the nearest ghat or for shopping, at Goudalia Chowk, never letting on where you really want to go. Find your destination on foot once you get to the general area.

- **Bhang lassi, commonly sold** in the old city, is marijuana-infused and intoxicating (don't mistake it for regular lassi). The effects creep up on you slowly, but you'll feel them suddenly.

Amritsar

Symbolic heart of the Sikh faith.

Amritsar's raison d'être is its Golden Temple. In fact, the city gets its name from the Golden Temple's Amrit Sarovar or Pool of Nectar, the man-made lake surrounding the temple. This temple is a place so magical, peaceful and spiritually moving that it's worth the schlep to this far-flung north-western border of India, in the state of Punjab, just to see it. Since its construction, the Golden Temple has been sacked, desecrated and destroyed repeatedly, but each time it has been rebuilt and restored, with the sacred tenet at its core – a belief in the oneness of humanity – retained. Every local devotee at the temple has a story to tell: for some it's a place where wishes come true, for others it's where they come to connect their soul to God.

The city of Amritsar became an important trading centre along one of the old silk routes from Central Asia to India. Its walled city consists of a warren of old alleyways, but just a few minutes away are the city's newer tree-lined residential boulevards. A religious centre, a bustling wholesale market, a burgeoning tourist destination with hundreds of hotel rooms under construction: Amritsar is a city on the move, but one that appears comfortable mixing the old with the new, where old *akharas* (traditional wrestling gymnasiums) sit a stone's throw from state-of-the-art air-conditioned health spas.

Punjabis have a reputation for being loud and ostentatious. Yet you only have to ask a stranger for directions and it's quite likely that he will insist on escorting you to your destination. Punjabis also love food, and more than that, they love feeding people. Don't be surprised if you are invited to a stranger's home for a meal. In any case, no one need ever go hungry in this city. So long as they can make their way to the Golden Temple, a meal is always guaranteed.

Golden Temple.

Explore

In Amritsar all roads lead to the Golden Temple, and nothing is too far away from anywhere else. A short walk from the Golden Temple leads to Jallianwala Bagh. Just two kilometres north is the bustling Lawrence Road. The rest of the sights in this chapter are a half-day trip from the city. Additionally, enthusiastic birders can head to the freshwater wetlands of Harike Pattan, a little-known birder's paradise 60 kilometres (37 miles) to the south of the city.

During the 15th century, the basin of fertile plains lying between the arid Sindh in the south-east and the Himalayas in the north, the region now called Punjab, was a favourite entry point for invaders drawn by reports of India's wealth and riches. Guru Nanak, later to become the first Sikh guru, was born here in 1469. He studied Muslim and Hindu scriptures, travelled far and wide, including to Mecca and the deep Himalayas, and experienced teachings of Sufi and Bhakti saints. Guru Nanak then began preaching with a simple statement: 'there is no Hindu, there is no Mussulman.' His simple teachings appealed to many who felt badgered by iconoclastic Islam on one side and ritualistic Hinduism on the other. His disciples were called *shish* (Sanskrit for disciple), which later became Sikh.

Guru Nanak was followed by nine gurus over the next two centuries, all dynamic leaders, under whom Sikhism emerged as a separate religion. Its base was further strengthened by the formulation of the *Gurmukhi* script (from which today's Punjabi language has evolved), the compilation of the *Adi Granth* (*Granth Sahib,* the Sikh holy book) and the laying of the foundation of the Golden Temple, the holiest of Sikh shrines.

Golden Temple

Temple complex open 24hrs. Sanctum sanctorum open 4am-10pm daily. Langar open 7am-11pm (though anyone who requests food will be fed outside those times).

It was in the 16th century that the fifth Sikh guru, Guru Arjan Dev, began construction of this magnificent temple, and assured the establishment of a settlement around it. Additions to the temple complex continued over several centuries, and there were phases when it was destroyed and rebuilt. Finally, the temple's lotus-shaped domes were gilded by Sikh ruler Maharaja Ranjit Singh in the 19th century.

Visitors get their first view of the Golden Temple through the massive arches of the main entrance, the north gateway. At the centre of a square sacred pool lies the shiny marble and gold structure, a temple of part-Hindu and part-Islamic architecture.

Once you enter, a staircase leads down (symbolising humility while approaching God) to the spotless marble *parikrama* (pathway) that circles the large **Amrit Sarovar** (Pool of Nectar). In the middle of the pool is the sanctum sanctorum or **Harmandir Sahib** (also **Hari Mandir** or **Darbar Sahib**), shimmering ethereally both in sunlight

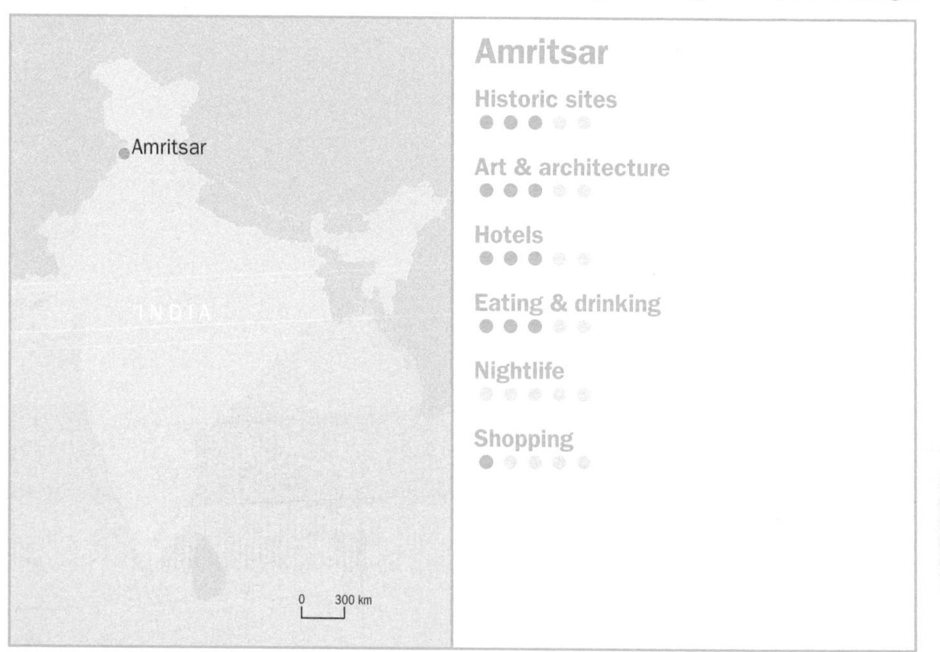

Top left: Serai Amanat Khan. Right: bangle seller. Bottom: Golden Temple.

Street food.

and at night. Devotees circumnavigate the pool in a clockwise direction along the *parikrama*, to reach the entrance to the marble causeway that leads to the sanctum. The gateway to the bridge supports massive silver doors (Darshani Deori), which face a large five-storey building, the Akal Takht.

The Golden Temple welcomes people of all castes and creeds. Visitors wait their turn to enter the Hari Mandir, which may take anything from a few seconds to hours if there are long queues, depending on the time of day and whether you are there on the day of a religious festival. Once inside, worshippers touch their forehead to the ground in front of the *Adi Granth*, the Sikh holy book, placed on a bed under a bejewelled silk canopy. A *granthi* (priest who recites the holy texts) intones the scriptures, all of it broadcast live to Sikhs across the world. Look up when inside – the Hari Mandir's ceiling is inlaid with semi-precious stones, mirror-work and gold leaf.

"Worshippers touch their forehead to the ground in front of the Adi Granth, the Sikh holy book, placed on a bed under a bejewelled silk canopy."

To view the domes up close, climb a narrow staircase that connects the terrace to the temple's upper storey. This upper storey also has nooks and vantage points along windows that open out to views of the Amrit Sarovar and *parikrama*. Devotees and visitors can meditate here or simply gaze out; few are left untouched by the all-pervading spirituality.

The **Akal Takht** is a five-storey structure across the courtyard facing the Darshani Deori. Built by Guru Hargobind in 1609, it is the seat of Sikh religious authority, and serves as the resting place for the *Adi Granth* at night. After the last prayers each night (9.45pm in winter, later in summer), the holy book is carried in a large silver palanquin across the causeway and courtyard to the Akal Takht. Devotees take turns shouldering the enormous palanquin on its journey from the Hari Mandir to the Akal Takht, amid the beating of the *nagada* (large kettledrum) and religious chants, and the showering of flower petals, while the scent of sprinkled rosewater fills the air. This nightly ceremony (Palki Sahib) is a great time to visit the temple to witness a truly devotionally charged atmosphere. (As you've come this far, it's a good idea to visit the temple several times, at different times of day.)

Before entering the temple complex visitors must cover their head, take off footwear and socks, and rinse their feet in the small pool near the steps. A variety of scarves are available for devotees and visitors at the entrance. Although there is absolutely no pressure or necessity, those who wish to make an offering can drop some cash into one of the many donation boxes. Alternatively, counters along the *parikrama*, just before the Darshani Deori, accept cash and issue a receipt and some *kadah-parshad* (sweet offering) in leaf bowls or steel trays (the quantity you receive is based on the size of your donation). Deliver this *kadah* to one of the *granthis* stationed within the Hari Mandir, who will then return a small quantity that has been blessed. The rest is added to a common vat, from which it is doled out to others. On the way out, stop to view the large fish swimming in the pool close to the marble causeway, no doubt fattened on morsels of *kadah* dropped by enthusiastic pilgrims (a practice discouraged by the temple administration). Once your palate is sweetened by *kadah* and soul infused with the heady spiritual atmosphere, you can head out; it's a visit that is quite unforgettable.

Those who want to experience a little more of this faith should take part in the **guru ka langar** (guru's kitchen). Every Sikh temple has a *langar* or community kitchen where anyone who wants to can sit and eat a simple – and free – vegetarian meal. The community kitchen was started by Guru Nanak to emphasise the oneness of all human beings. It's a lesson in humility and devotion as everyone, irrespective of social status or position, sits together in orderly rows on the floor to eat at the *langar*. They are served by a rota of volunteers, who have also cooked the food and will clean up afterwards, all part of their *sewa*, or service, an essential aspect of the faith. At the Golden Temple the *guru ka langar* takes on another form altogether, as the mammoth task of feeding 40,000 people every day gets under way. No matter what time of day or night, anyone who asks will be served a free meal here. Visitors who have the time should partake of this communal meal, as part of the total experience of equality and spirituality of this holy place.

Jallianwala Bagh

0.5km E of Golden Temple. Summer open 6am-9pm daily. Winter open 7am-8pm daily. Admission free.

On 13 April 1919, around 10,000 men, women and children congregated at the Jallianwala Bagh (garden) for a peaceful protest against the imposition of the draconian Rowlatt Act, a law that allowed their leaders to be imprisoned by the British government, without trial. Since it was also the day of Baisakhi (the first day of spring) and a Sunday, several hundred visitors had come to Amritsar from surrounding villages to visit the Golden Temple. Many of them then moved to the Jallianwala Bagh for the nationalist meeting. British brigadier general Reginald Dyer, in charge of law and order, arrived later when the park was full and positioned his troops to block the sole narrow passageway into it. The park boundary, formed by the brick walls of the surrounding buildings, offered no other exit. Without warning, Dyer ordered his troops to open indiscriminate fire. Around 1,650 rounds were fired on an unarmed crowd that panicked; many jumped into a deep well in the park to escape the hail of bullets, only to drown or be crushed by others who jumped in after them. Others were trampled in the stampede. The 15 minutes of continuous firing resulted in the death of at least 379 people and another 1,200 were wounded (these were official figures; no one knows how many really died). An unrepentant Dyer was quoted as saying that he would have ordered his men to continue firing had they not run out of ammunition. The Jallianwala Bagh massacre proved to be a turning point in the Indian struggle for independence. Many moderate leaders, shocked at the cruel act, turned nationalist, giving a fillip to the efforts of other freedom fighters. Today, a memorial marks the spot where the innocent were gunned down. Plaques and bullet marks around the well (now barricaded with mesh) are a poignant reminder of those who were butchered simply for being there.

FURTHER AFIELD

WAGAH BORDER

The closest city to Amritsar is not in India, but 45 kilometres (28 miles) to its west in neighbouring Pakistan. Lahore is the administrative capital of the Pakistani province of Punjab, while Amritsar is the cultural capital of the Indian state of Punjab. About midway between the two cities, along the famous Grand Trunk Road, lies the India–Pakistan border at Wagah.

Each evening this border checkpoint witnesses what can be described as a rather ridiculous display of military bravado. Foot-stomping, moustache-twirling guards on both sides glare malevolently at each other while slamming the metal gates of the border shut. Each knee-high kick in the air by a bristling sentry is greeted by cheers from the spectator galleries.

Stands for spectators erected on the Indian and Pakistani sides are usually packed with spectators who rent the air with jingoistic slogans. On the Indian side, popular Hindi songs blaring through loudspeakers add to the cacophony. Don't be too surprised if an over-enthusiastic spectator jumps down from the stands on to the road to perform a body-twisting dance straight out of a Bollywood blockbuster. Such revellers are usually quickly shooed back to the stands by security, only to be welcomed back by applause from onlookers.

Just before sundown, the flags of both countries are slowly lowered to the sound of bugles. Each flag is then reverently folded and marched off to the respective barracks, signalling an end to the day's proceedings. People then rush to the gates for photographs. Early birds at the border get seats closer to the gates where the ceremony takes place.

PUL KANJARI

The villages of Daoke and Dhanao Kalan, 35 kilometres (22 miles) from Amritsar, near the Wagah border, lie along a traditional trade route. Once they served as a resting place for weary travellers. Troupes of dancing girls accompanied by *mirasis* (professional ballad singers) would congregate here for an evening of dance, song and music. Bards and minstrels, who have been part of Punjab and its folklore for centuries (and still exist today), would join them.

Maharaja Ranjit Singh (1780-1839) is eulogised as the greatest ruler of the Punjab and believed to have freed northern India from the Afghans, and built a secular empire. At the height of his reign his empire stretched across the Punjab up to the borders of modern-day China (including Lahore, Multan and Peshawar).

According to legend, he met and fell in love with a *nautch* (dancing) girl called Moran. Since their relationship was frowned upon, Ranjit Singh would meet her at her village, Makhanpur, between Amritsar and Lahore. On one occasion Moran is said to have slipped and lost her slipper while crossing a canal near her village. The maharaja had a bridge constructed there and the place came to be known as Pul Kanjari (*pul* means bridge, *kanjari* is a derogatory term for a dancing girl).

> "A sheltered enclosure on one side served as the bathing ghat for women; a ramp leading down to the water was used for mounts and packhorses."

It's a legend, but one that has attached itself to the real Pul Kanjari, a site with an interesting *baoli* (step well) and a temple, near to Daoke and Dhanao Kalan. *Baolis* served as a resting place for travellers during the time of the silk trade. Steps on all four sides lead to the bottom. A sheltered enclosure on one side served as the bathing *ghat* for women, and a ramp leading down to the water was used for mounts and packhorses. A Vishnu temple with murals stands on the eastern side. The process of rebuilding the crumbling brickwork is on, and plans to refill the ancient *baoli* by channelling water from a nearby canal are in progress.

SERAI AMANAT KHAN

As chief calligrapher of the Quranic inscriptions of the Taj Mahal, Abd-ul-Haq was conferred the title of Amanat Khan (Lord of Trust) by Shah Jahan in 1632. In 1640-41 he built a *serai* (a resting place for travellers and animals, also called a caravan serai) along the ancient trade route between Central Asia and India, on a site

Top: Ista (2). Bottom: WelcomHeritage Ranjit's Svaasa (2).

39 kilometres (24 miles) south-west of Amritsar. The Archaeological Survey of India has recently begun restoration and repair work here.

Two arched gateways encompass a sleepy village that has progressively occupied what was once a massive complex with rooms for travellers, stables for their mounts and food stalls. A central cobbled street leads across the breadth of the village from one massive gateway to another. Glazed tile work adorns the arches of the gateways; the eastern gate is called Dilli Darwaza (Gateway to Delhi) and the western gate Lahori Darwaza (Gateway to Lahore). In spite of serious neglect, the beautiful calligraphy on the blue tiles is still visible. The ruined mosque in the heart of the village is bereft of worshippers. The tomb of Amanat Khan is nearby, surrounded by four minarets.

Serai Amanat Khan enjoys the pastoral calm typical of a Punjabi village. It's a good place to reflect on history, and the transformation of a bustling inn complex of the Mughal period into a somnolent village.

Eat

Amritsar is often called the food capital of the Punjab. Famous for vegetarian and non-vegetarian fare, its cuisine borrows heavily from Mughal cuisine, as well as from the peasant fare of the region's farmlands. The passion for milk, butter and ghee is evident in most dishes, and even the rotis (flat breads) are liberally doused in ghee or cream. Amritsar's food is delicious, but to enjoy it, you need to banish all thoughts of clogged arteries and counting calories. All three hotels listed below serve excellent food, but Amritsar's street food and *dhaba* (small local restaurant) food is its culinary delight. Locals throng **Kulcha Land** (opposite Hotel MK, Ranjit Avenue, 99159-07482) for crispy *aloo kulchas* (tandoor-roasted breads with potato stuffing), while the *poori chana* (deep-fried flat bread and spicy chickpea curry) from **Kanha Sweets** (opposite Bijli Pehlwan Temple, Lawrence Road, 0183-222-2855) are regular fare for Sunday brunch in many households. Amritsar has a serious sweet tooth – a bustling sweet shop can be found on almost every street. Sweets like *jalebis* (bright orange, deep-fried flour batter; looks a bit like funnel cake) are eaten any time; get some at **Sharma Jalebiwala** (on Lawrence Road). Whatever you do, don't leave without sampling Amritsar's lassi, thick and delicious with a massive blob of butter and cream.

Crystal Restaurant

2.5km N of Golden Temple *Crystal Chowk (0183-222-5555). Open 11am-11.30pm daily. $$. No AmEx. Multi-cuisine.*

This 75-year-old restaurant provides delectable North Indian fare. Try the chicken *tawa* frontier or the superb tandoori fish (freshwater sole roasted in an earthen oven). Be prepared to wait for a table even on weekdays, though a request to affable owner Gagan Khanna can speed things up.

Kesar da Dhabha

500m N of Golden Temple *Chowk Passian (0183-255-2193). Open noon-midnight daily. $. No credit cards. Punjabi.*

This legendary eating place traces its humble origins to a small eaterie selling dal and roti set up by Lala Kesar Mal in Lahore in 1916. The establishment moved to Amritsar with the partition of the subcontinent, and it has flourished in this narrow backstreet ever since. Kesar's simple but delicious Punjabi food brings tourists and locals in droves. Servers rush from table to table amid the clatter of steel plates and cutlery. Recipes for the flavourful *maa ki* or *kaali dal* (black lentils), *paneer palak* (cottage cheese with spinach) and *chana* (chickpeas) are family secrets handed down over generations. Ask for the thali, which consists of *maa ki dal, chana* or *rajma*, yoghurt, pickle and two large tandoori parathas (layered breads cooked in an earthen oven) dripping with ghee, followed by dessert: *phirni* (rice pudding) served in shallow earthen bowls cooled over blocks of ice placed at the entrance of the restaurant.

> **"A milkman calls in twice a day to milk the buffaloes in the in-house dairy."**

Oka

5.5km NW of Golden Temple *SCO38 District Shopping Centre, Ranjit Avenue (0183-250-5722). $$. No AmEx. Multi-cuisine.*

Oka is a pleasant alternative to the heavy, ghee-laden local fare. Run by Navneet Singh and his wife Lindsay, this charming restaurant offers a varied menu consisting of steaming woks of savoury vegetables and meat, fresh salads, blended yoghurts and sumptuous burgers. Winter afternoons are especially enjoyable, spent relaxing at Oka's cosy terrace with hot coffee.

Stay

Ista

5km E of Golden Temple *Alpha One City Centre, MBM Farms, Grand Trunk Road (0183-270-8888/ www.istahotels.com). $$$.*

A warm smile and *namaste* greet guests at Amritsar's newest five-star hotel, opened in 2009. Central to the hotel is its large open-air glass-walled lobby space. Each evening, this atrium is the venue for a display; flames shoot up from pools of water, shimmering in three large brass lotuses surrounded by a profusion of green plants. Each of the 248 well-furnished, compact rooms are bathed in natural light filtered through a large wall of windows. An azure pool on the first-floor terrace is inviting, while more energetic guests can jog their calories away in the gym overlooking the city. Ananda, the hotel's spa, has Ayurvedic treatments, Swedish massages (using sunflower and wheatgerm oils) and various other options – and they are uniformly good.

Guests can dine on Thai or Chinese food at Thai-Chi, or at Collage, the multi-cuisine restaurant with wide windows, teppanyaki counter and enormous pizza oven. Chef Arvind Sharma's smoked salmon platter and miso soup are not to be missed.

Mrs Bhandari's Guesthouse

7km NW of Golden Temple *10 Cantonment (0183-222-2390/bhandari_guesthouse.tripod.com). $. No AmEx.*

Set amid the old trees and sprawling colonial bungalows of the Cantonment area, Mrs Bhandari's Guesthouse is a lovely red-brick ivy-covered building that has witnessed the changing face of Amritsar since its construction in 1930. Mrs Bhandari herself passed away at the age of 101 in 2007, but the house exudes the spirit of her life and times. A cast-iron wood-burning stove in the spotless kitchen still heats kettles as it has done over the decades. A Frigidaire from 1956 chugs along efficiently while the old Arthur-Martin enamelled gas grill ensures piping hot food. Mrs Bhandari's youngest daughter Ratan now runs the guesthouse, and with steely efficiency. An advocate of environmentally friendly living, Ratan grows spinach, potatoes and pulses on the sprawling grounds, supplying the kitchen with fresh ingredients. A milkman calls in twice a day to milk the buffaloes in the in-house dairy. The communal dining area, the Thicket, is an inviting space, always stocked with beer and non-alcoholic drinks. Dinner must be ordered at least an hour in advance, but whether it's spicy mutton curry, or spaghetti with tomato and basil sauce, you can be sure the food is freshly prepared and tasty. Stewed guavas with fresh cream for dessert are a house special. Rooms are simply furnished and comfortable. Handmade painted tiles adorn floors and fireplaces provide warmth during the chilly winter months. Mrs. Bhandari's transports guests to back to an age when life was simpler and slower.

WelcomHeritage Ranjit's Svaasa

3.5km N of Golden Temple *47A Mall Road (0183-256-6618, 329-8840/www.svaasa.com). $$$. No AmEx.*

As you enter the lobby of this 250-year-old *haveli* turned boutique hotel, you'll notice the fragrance of incense and aromatic oils. Tucked away in a leafy by-lane off the bustling Mall Road, Svaasa (Sanskrit for 'breath of life') makes a comfortable and tranquil retreat. Its well-furnished rooms, filled with colonial furniture and family memorabilia, reflect the owners' – brothers Abhimanyu and Vishal Mehra – for their cherished heritage. There's a serious focus on wellness here: Svaasa is a haven for those looking to relax, whether with an Ayurvedic massage at the outstanding in-house spa or simply by lounging on comfortable sofas in leafy nooks. Personalised service is the norm. Guided tours of the city in a *tanga* (traditional horse-drawn carriage) are arranged on request. Evenings spent enjoying Svaasa's eclectic cuisine, or sipping flavourful organic tea accompanied by Vishal's renditions on the piano, are a perfect way to end the day after a serene visit to the Golden Temple.

Factfile

When to go

October to March is the coolest period of the year, and the best time to visit Amritsar. During the summer months – between April and August – the heat and humidity levels are enervating and debilitating, making sightseeing rather tiring and onerous.

Getting there

Amritsar is well connected to Delhi by train services, with several trains running between the two every day. The fastest and most convenient is the twice-daily Shatabdi Express service (journey time five hours). Amritsar is also connected by several daily non-stop flights to Delhi; the airport is 15 minutes from the city.

For more on travel within the country, *see p378* **Navigating India**.

Getting around

Cycle-rickshaws can be hailed just about anywhere in the city. Though slow and bumpy, they're a great way to see the sights. Radio taxis are available from Mega Cab (0183-515-1515); though they are not very prompt to arrive, the taxis are clean and air-conditioned. For travel to Wagah, Serai Amanat Khan and beyond it's best to hire a car and driver (usually Rs 600 round trip for one destination). Auto-rickshaws can also be found, but they are unmetered and charge unreasonable rates; it's usually not worth the trouble of haggling and arguing.

Tourist information

The Golden Temple's Tourist Information Centre is located outside the main entrance to the Golden Temple (0183-255-3954, open 8am-8pm daily).

Top: Norbulingka Institute (2). Bottom: Thekchen Chöling Temple Complex.

Dharamsala: McLeod Ganj

Tibet recreated in India.

Surrounded by pine, oak, deodar and rhododendron forests, the small, shabby town of Dharamsala – tucked into the snow-capped Dhauladhar range of the Himalayas in Himachal Pradesh state – is refuge and home to the Dalai Lama and 10,000 exiled Tibetans. It's also where thousands of others, from nations around the globe, come to find spiritual peace or a new perspective on life. Dharamsala's Buddhist epicentre is actually the small settlement of McLeod Ganj, nine kilometres uphill from the main town. It is here that is the centre of pilgrimage for Tibetans (many cross the treacherous high Himalayan passes every year to reach here), and place of interest for the thousands of Westerners who come for more than a quick breeze-through. Here they can meditate at the temple or monasteries, walk the mountain paths, or watch the sun go down over a cappuccino at one of the numerous cafés that dot the town.

In this small enclave, over the 50 years that the Dalai Lama has been here since fleeing Tibet, the Tibetan way of life has been reborn, creating a Little Lhasa alongside the daily routine of Indian life. Buddhist chants echo up and down the valley in the pre-dawn hours, the sound of long horns emanates from the temple complex during the day, and quiet candlelit vigils are held at twilight. It is a cultural mish-mash of sorts, but in the temples, institutes and cultural centres, Tibetan culture is preserved and lived in a way that is impossible in Tibet today.

Explore

Lower Dharamsala, the town at the base of the mountain, a nine-kilometre road journey from McLeod Ganj, holds no interest for the traveller. Further uphill, past McLeod Ganj town, are a few accommodation options and meditation centres; just beyond them is Dharamkot.

For locations outside the main town, don't judge walking times by kilometres: in the mountains it can take over an hour to cover a two-kilometre stretch. Dharamkot, for instance, is just one and a half kilometres from McLeod Ganj but it's a 45-minute walk.

MCLEOD GANJ TOWN

McLeod Ganj town is a colourful, buzzing place, filled all year round with visitors. The sound of chanting comes from stores and restaurants, all possibly from the same soothing CD. Most evenings a candlelit procession winds its way down the narrow streets – a simple gathering meant as a prayer for the Tibetan struggle and way of life, and perhaps for a return to the homeland.

Two long, parallel streets (Temple Road and Jogibara/Jogiwara Road) run along the mountain ridge, southwards from the main square and bus stand, covering most of McLeod Ganj. Forking out from these are Bhagsu Road and Hotel Bhagsu Road (at different ends of Temple Road), and other smaller roads.

Thekchen Chöling Temple Complex

Temple Road. Open sunrise-sunset daily. Admission free. Shoes must be removed before entering the temple.

This complex at the south end of Temple Road is the centre of Tibetan spiritual activity in Dharamsala, and consists of the Main Temple (also called the Dalai Lama's temple), a *gompa* (monastery), the Dalai Lama's residence, a café, bookshop and museum. Tibetans refer to the temple as Tsuglagkhang (or main cathedral). The complex is simple in construction, unlike its grand original counterpart in Lhasa. On regular days, mornings and evenings are the best times to visit the complex, as this is when most Tibetans come to pray. Monks, nuns, locals and other visitors rotate the brass and copper prayer wheels heavily inscribed with Tibetan mantras, and then circumambulate the two large halls that house Buddhist deities. On the right is the hall where the Dalai Lama usually sits on his throne and delivers his teachings. Surrounding his throne are three large sculptures: of Guru Padmasambhava (the scholar who introduced Buddhism to Tibet, popularly called Guru Rinpoche by Tibetans); of the Avalokiteshvara (the Buddha of Compassion of whom the Dalai Lama is considered a reincarnation), and behind the throne, a large gold statue of Shakyamuni (Gautam) Buddha.

The second hall, mostly used by the monks for prayers and teaching sessions, has on its interior walls a large, intricate and colourful mural of the *kalachakra* (wheel of time) mandala, representing the Shambhala War (the epic Buddhist war between good and evil), and another with a life-size image of Shakyamuni Buddha and other mythical Tibetan creatures. The hall also houses a few small antiques and rare sculptures of Buddha that were brought

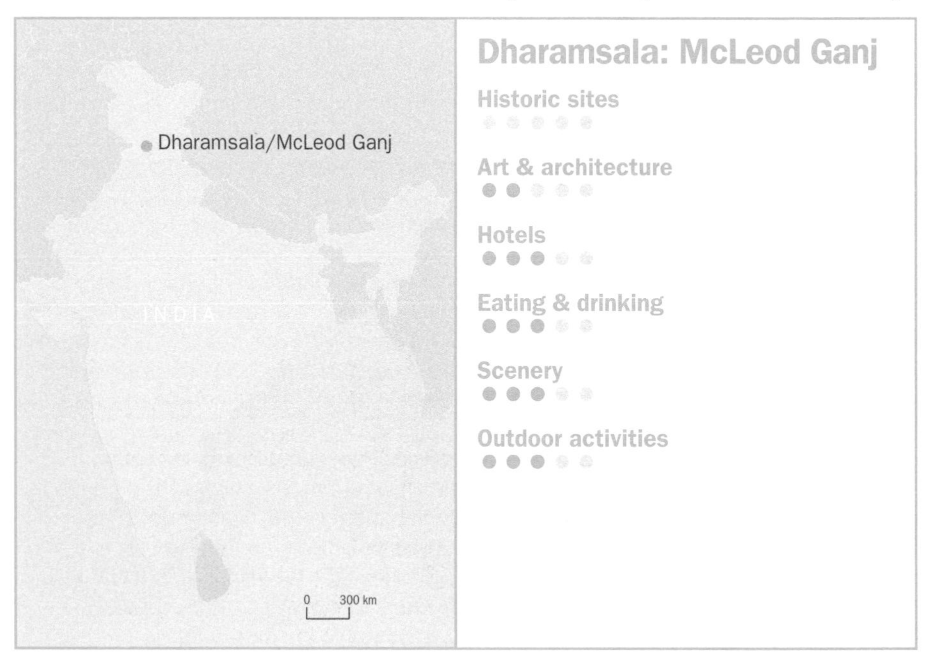

secretly from Tibet, and three life-sized brass sculptures, one of them of Green Tara (the goddess of compassion).

The vibrantly painted Namgyal *gompa* (monastery) is home to hundreds of monks, who study and practise meditation techniques and prostrations, and participate in Buddhist academic debates at the temple complex. The **Tibet Museum** (www.thetibetmuseum.org, open 9am-5pm Tue-Sun, admission Rs 5) is a memorial museum with visuals on the Chinese occupation of Tibet and heart-rending stories of atrocities, the persecution of former political prisoners and refugees who made it (or did not) to India. It sends a powerful, moving message of the Tibetan struggle. Also inside the complex is the **Namgyal Book Store**, where you can buy books on Tibetan art, history, culture and religion. Finally, you can walk up to the gate of the simple, though sprawling, 'palace' of the Dalai Lama, with its heavy security.

You can undertake a spiritual journey along with the local Tibetans and other pilgrims who circumambulate the two-kilometre path around the Dalai Lama's temple and residence every morning and evening in a ritual known as the **Lingkor, the Holy Walk**. Starting at the gate of the Main Temple, follow the railed path on the left stepping down, and join devotees as they chant prayers and rotate prayer wheels while walking along the path, which has a spectacular view of the valley.

AROUND DHARAMSALA

Church of St John in the Wilderness

1.5km from McLeod Ganj towards Lower Dharamsala. Open 10am-5pm daily. Admission free.

The pleasant 20-minute walk from McLeod Ganj is good enough reason to visit this church, surrounded by pine trees and deodars. However, the building is of interest in itself, constructed in 1852 with local stone in neo-Gothic style. Most of it survived a major earthquake that flattened much of the region in 1905: the beautiful, original Belgian stained glass remains intact. Memorial plaques line the walls, recording intriguing stories of the lives and deaths of military officers, one of whom was killed by a Himalayan black bear. The British governor general and viceroy of India, Lord Elgin, who was said to love this area, died here in 1863 and is buried in the churchyard.

Norbulingka Institute

15km downhill from McLeod Ganj *PO Sidhpur, near Lower Dharamsala (01892-246-405). Open Workshops 9am-5.30pm Mon-Sat; closed 2nd Sat of month. Temple, Doll Museum, shop 9am-5.30pm daily.*

Norbulingka, west of Lhasa, was the summer palace of the Dalai Lama. This institute, named after that palace, is built in traditional Tibetan style, in a picturesque setting of lush gardens and stone pathways, against the backdrop of green fields and lofty mountains, about a 30-minute drive from McLeod Ganj. The institute is a haven for Tibetan artists and their ancient (and dying) art and culture. New arrivals from Tibet are provided with training (and many are given employment) in the process of preserving these traditional and sacred art forms in a sustainable way. The large complex houses the artists' workshops, a temple, a doll museum, garden, café, guesthouse and store. The landscaping of the complex aptly incorporates rock, trees, pools and flowing water, and the natural terracing of the land to create a serene, Japanese-garden-like space.

Deden Tsuglagkhang, the temple, is an elegant stone structure with a four-metre (14ft) gilded copper statue of the Buddha, surrounded by elaborate paintings and murals created by in-house *thangka* (scroll-painting) artists. The **Losel Doll Museum** displays 150 costumed dolls depicting the regional, official and monastic costumes of Tibet.

The **artists' workshops** are open to visitors, and are the best place to watch skilled sculptors, craftsmen, *thangka* artists, appliqué workers, wood carvers, carpenters, metal crafters and statue makers (and their students) create pieces from scratch using traditional styles and methods. *Thangkas* are considered much more than an art form; they are religious objects used by Buddhists in their practice, to assist them on their spiritual journey. Most are individually commissioned and custom-made. They follow strict standards and use the best natural minerals and plant materials. *Thangka* appliqué work with silk and brocade is also done here. Skilled master statue makers at the institute teach their apprentices the art over ten to 12 years. Students learn a traditional 'lost wax process' for creating small statues, while larger statues are hammered from sheets of copper and are hollow inside. All Tibetan monasteries and temples use these statues, depicting Buddha in various forms and positions.

DHARAMKOT

Three kilometres north of McLeod Ganj, heading up the mountain, is the town of Dharamkot. The main street, largely the preserve of Israeli backpackers, is entirely missable, though the surrounding area is pretty. Those looking for something beyond the tourist circuit may like to attend a serious meditation workshop here. The Dhamma Sikhara, Himachal Vipassana Centre (www.sikhara.dhamma.org) offers a ten-day course in meditation. This course is not easy; you have to maintain complete silence, read nothing, and are provided with just two basic meals a day.

Tushita Meditation Centre (www.tushita.info), set in a lovely forest, is focused specifically on teaching Tibetan Mahayana Buddhism. It offers a ten-day residential course as well as shorter, more relaxed, programmes. Tushita's courses are taught by Western teachers, and include discussions. Students are allowed to eat more than twice a day and to read relevant texts.

Courses at both centres are said to be free, but while Vipassana accepts voluntary donations, Tushita requires a donation to participate.

OUTDOOR ACTIVITIES

There are many opportunities for trekking in this region and McLeod Ganj is full of trekking companies that can set up a route, guide and other facilities for you. The most popular trek from McLeod Ganj is the route to Triund, which can be undertaken as a day trip or an overnighter, on your own. It involves a climb of over 1,000 metres: the fit can achieve it in about three hours, others take longer. Triund has fantastic views of the snow-capped Dhauladhars. The more ambitious (and better prepared) can carry on further up the mountain to the snowline. There are no accommodation facilities further up the mountain, but at Triund there is a small run-down forest guesthouse, along with camps and tea shops that rent out tents and basic rooms. Triund's high ground is a popular picnic spot for locals and visitors at weekends.

Note that this route is not a stroll, so carry water and a snack, though at most times of the year you can buy all the basics at tea shops along the way. Also bring along something warm, even during the summer months, as the temperature can drop suddenly.

Eat

McLeod Ganj is packed with restaurants. Most are clustered on Temple, Jogibara and Bhagsu roads and serve tourist fare over a range of cuisines. Bakeries and Italian restaurants are particularly popular; most are pretty decent.

Carpe Diem

McLeod Ganj *Opposite Tibetan Reception Centre, Jogibara Road (no phone). Open 7am-10.30pm daily. $$. No credit cards. Multi-cuisine.*

You can order just about anything from a garden salad to tandoori chicken at this Nepali-run restaurant, and some of the dishes are pretty good. All food is said to be cooked in extra virgin olive oil, and the fruit and veg are washed in sterilised water. Service is friendly and very attentive.

Chonor Terrace Restaurant

McLeod Ganj *Temple Road, near Main Temple (01892-221-468/94180-31468/www.norbulingka.org). Open 7am-10pm daily. $$. No AmEx. Tibetan.*

With an extensive menu of Tibetan dishes, Chonor House's Tibetan restaurant and café is a cut above the other Tibetan places in town. The dining area has indoor as well as outdoor seating. Indoors, you are surrounded by beautiful Tibetan paintings, while the outdoor terrace overlooks the Main Temple and valley. Apart from standard Tibetan dishes like *thenthuk* (noodle soup), *thukpa* (noodle soup with vegetables) and *gyathuk* (egg noodle soup with tofu and mushrooms), the restaurant serves possibly the best *shabalay* (large fried dumplings stuffed with meat and served with a soup of fresh veggies and tofu) that you'll find outside Tibet.

Common Grounds Café & Restaurant

200m uphill from McLeod Ganj *Behind Hotel Asian Plaza (98162-73240/www.commongroundsproject.org). Open 10.30am-9pm Tue-Sun. $. No credit cards.*

The first Chinese restaurant in Dharamsala, Common Grounds serves good, traditional Taiwanese, Chinese and Tibetan food in a cheerful and homely environment. There's an interesting library filled with books related to Tibet and China, and the Tibetan issue. The restaurant's Taiwanese-American owner's aim is to create a space where Chinese and Tibetans can share common ground in a relaxed, friendly and informal atmosphere, enjoying conversations over Chinese and Tibetan food. Popular dishes include Cantonese wok-fried noodles and Hakka drunken chicken with shitake mushrooms. An all-day favourite with regulars is the pork stew rice – a popular Taiwanese street food. The place also has excellent coffee. Common Grounds also has a centre where Tibet-related programmes, talks and film screenings are held every Saturday at 5.30pm.

Dokebi

McLeod Ganj *Off Jogibara Road, near Lung Ta (98169-84199). Open 10am-10pm daily; closed alternate Mon. $$. No credit cards. Korean.*

It's not easy to find this Korean restaurant, but it's worth the effort. Dokebi's low lighting, fireplace and classical music make it an ideal venue for a romantic evening. The extensive vegetarian and non-vegetarian menu has a range of traditional Korean dishes that can be spiced to your taste. Try *bee bim bab* (a combination of rice and vegetables), served with a hot pepper sauce in a hot stone bowl, or spicy stir-fried chicken with mixed vegetables. The superb ginger lemon honey tea or coffee with Bailey's Irish Cream are indulgent ways to finish off your meal.

Hotel Tibet

McLeod Ganj *Bhagsu Road, near Main Square (01892-221-587/426). Open 9am-9.30pm daily. $. No credit cards. Tibetan.*

Now in the hands of a Tibetan co-operative society, Hotel Tibet was once run by the Tibetan government in exile. It still has a bureaucratic, somewhat shabby look and slow service, but it's one of the places that offers authentic (and cheap) Tibetan food and alcoholic drinks. It's patronised by Tibetan government officials and is considered a venerable establishment. Though the Tibetan dishes are limited in number, they are authentic. This is the only place in town to serve *gyakho* (chicken, mutton, eggs, tofu, pork, button mushrooms, seasonal vegetables and rice noodles, served over a flaming hotpot with a clear soup), with steamed rice or *tingmo* (Tibetan bread). It's a dish for special occasions and the most expensive item on the menu at Rs 600; you'll need to order it 24 hours in advance, for a group of at least four people. Other Tibetan dishes include meat and vegetarian versions of *gyathuk* (spicy noodle soup). If you appreciate strong spices and want to sample non-Tibetan dishes, try the braised pork cubes in hot pepper sauce or the pepper chicken.

Lung Ta

McLeod Ganj *Next to Gu-Chu-Sum, southern end of Jogibara Road (01892-220-689). Open noon-8.30pm Mon-Sat. $. No credit cards. Japanese.*

Lung Ta is the name of the Japanese NGO that founded this restaurant, and supports Tibetan prisoners of conscience. Located in a quieter part of town, this all-vegetarian eaterie

Top: Common Grounds Café & Restaurant.
Middle: Moon Peak Café.
Bottom: Dokebi.

Learning from the Dalai Lama

Tenzin Gyatso (the name means 'ocean of wisdom') or the living reincarnation of Avalokiteshvara (the Buddha of Compassion): both are names for the spiritual and temporal head of the Tibetans, more often known as His Holiness the 14th Dalai Lama. The man himself considers that he is just a 'simple Buddhist monk', but for millions of admirers and devotees he is a god-like figure to be treated with deep respect and reverence. To outsiders there may seem some incongruity here, when you consider that Buddhism does not subscribe to the concept of 'God' as master/creator of the universe, emphasising instead 'karma', or one's own actions and deeds, and a belief in afterlife and rebirth. But the Dalai Lama is considered to be a reincarnation of a bodhisattva, who manifests a physical form to help others, and is reborn according to his wish and will.

The belief system of bodhisattvas and Avalokiteshvara is played out every time the Dalai Lama appears publicly in Dharamasala, his home for five decades, in front of his thousands of devotees. The gatherings are simple affairs, but the displays of devotion and faith are amazing; even the strictest rationalist would be challenged not to be moved. Perhaps it is the charisma and charm of the man, and his powerful presence, or perhaps it is the message he brings – of peace, simplicity and compassion – and his very personal way of transmitting it, which make his audiences so special.

In many countries people pay hundreds of dollars to attend such events, and tickets are sold out months in advance. If the gathering is free, it can draw crowds larger than the most popular rock bands. For instance, his free address in Central Park in New York in 1999 drew over 90,000 visitors; reports claimed you could hear a pin drop when he spoke.

When the Dalai Lama gives a public audience at the Main Temple in Dharamsala, the atmosphere is calm in spite of the crowds. On 10 March every year (anniversary of the Tibetan uprising), close to 10,000 followers congregate in and around the temple, to hear their leader speak. Visitors can also attend.

If you are in Dharamsala, you may be fortunate enough to catch one of his teaching sessions or prayer ceremonies. Audiences are in Tibetan, but the organisers arrange for simultaneous translations in numerous languages. When the Dalai Lama, ('Kundun' to Tibetans) walks in, he greets as many people in the audience as he can before sitting on his elaborate throne. His teaching session usually begins with a joke or two, and then continues into a discourse that mixes anecdotes and religious teachings.

Interested visitors must register at the Tibetan Branch Security Office (near Hotel Tibet), preferably three to four days before the audience, with a photocopy of their passport and two passport-sized photos. When you attend, you can take a cup, bowl and spoon so you can partake of the simple vegetarian meal that is served free at all his audiences. These days, due to stringent security checks, no mobile phones, cameras, cigarettes or lighters are allowed in.

Details of the Dalai Lama's public teaching sessions and prayer ceremonies in Dharamsala (and across the world) are available at the official website (www.dalailama.com); visitors can check schedules, dates and get practical advice on what to bring and when to turn up.

offers snap-worthy mountain views from its terrace, and floor seating. The menu, which changes daily, includes hearty dishes such as Japanese rice omelette with salad and batter-fried veggies in noodle soup. The chefs are former Tibetan political prisoners, who sing folk songs while they work. For dessert, try their famous lemon curd squares. Sushi days are Tuesdays and Thursdays. All vegetables served here are washed in germicide, so salad is a safe option.

Moon Peak Café

McLeod Ganj *Temple Road (98160-69746). Open 8am-8pm daily. $. No credit cards. Café food.*
This tiny, often-crowded café at a prime spot halfway down Temple Road has an outdoor space right next to the road as well as indoor seating, so you can enjoy sunsets here as well as cheese omelettes and coffee. It's run by a local journalist and a photographer, and often has interesting exhibits on display inside. Coffee comes from the espresso machine in the usual varieties, served with a home-made cookie. The menu also includes a nice iced hibiscus tea, chicken sesame salad, and good-sized pizzas and open sandwiches. Breakfast is good and served throughout the day. The owner has recently opened the Moon Peak Thali ten minutes down the road – the only place that serves Indian thalis and parathas in McLeod Ganj.

Namgyal Café

McLeod Ganj *Main Temple (98161-50562). Open 11am-9pm daily. $. No AmEx. Multi-cuisine.*
Overlooking the valley, on a lower level within the Main Temple complex, this is a pleasant haven for vegetarians visiting the temple and looking for a beverage and snack. The international nature of McLeod Ganj, and the temple complex, is demonstrated in the sheer variety of currencies of the banknotes posted all around the cash counter. Somewhat incongruously, the café is famous for its vegetarian pizzas, the best in town. There's also a range of Tibetan specialities including *momos* (dumplings) and *thukpa* (noodle soup).

Shop

McLeod Ganj is filled with little stores and street stalls selling all kinds of handicrafts, curios, touristy baubles and mountaineering equipment. Tibetan vendors put up street stalls each morning, and take them down each evening. Established stores are pricier, but have a wider range and often better quality and more contemporary designs on offer.

Every other shop in McLeod Ganj sells *thangkas*, ranging in price from a few hundred to several hundred thousand rupees. *Thangkas* tell stories, narrate biographies and can be a medium to express Buddhist ideals. Tibetans believe that apart from helping them meditate and worship, the creation and even the act of commissioning a *thangka* leads to an accumulation of karmic merit that brings good health, long life and prosperity. *Thangka* painters may spend years completing a single *thangka*.

Wherever you go you will find yourself being watched over by Buddhas, bodhisattvas (enlightened beings) or even a Green Tara – statues of brass or copper, often decorated with silver or gold. Trendy T-shirts, jerseys, scarves, bandanas, caps with colourful 'Free Tibet' designs, slogans and logos are available everywhere, and jewellery is also popular merchandise, from junk jewellery to real amber and turquoise.

Bookworm

McLeod Ganj *Hotel Bhagsu Road (01892-221-465). Open 9am-7pm Tue-Sun. No credit cards.*
Bookworm is a small, well-stocked bookstore owned and run by a famous McLeod Ganj resident: Tibetan activist, poet and writer Lhasang Tsering. There's a whole range of books on Tibet, from guidebooks to fiction, poetry and history. The shop also carries popular English thrillers and classics. Cheap secondhand books go for as little as Rs 10.

Eternal Creation

McLeod Ganj *Main Square, opposite Mcllo restaurant (98821-44156/workshop 01892-223-083/www.eternal creation.com). Open 10am-7pm Tue-Sun. No credit cards.*
This little boutique sells superbly tailored floral fashions for women, babies and children, and some accessories. Designs are from Australian designer Frances Carrington, who began this enterprise and a Himalayan workshop a decade ago. The brand has slowly become one of the largest private employers in the area and employs fair trade and labour practices. Eternal Creation's clothing is now sold in over 200 stores in Australia, Europe and Asia, but the prices here in McLeod Ganj are hard to beat.

Jewels of Tibet

McLeod Ganj *Jogibara Road, near Jimmy's Italian Kitchen (01892-221-240/98163-73772/yedon14@ yahoo.com). Open 9am-7pm Mon-Sat. No AmEx.*
A reliable jewellery store run by the young and enterprising Yeshi Dolma, who is also a member of the Tibetan parliament in exile. She sells a wide range of designs catering to different tastes, from traditional to contemporary. A few other items, such as singing bowls, are also available.

Norling Arts Shop

Norbulingka Institute *PO Sidhpur, near Lower Dharamsala (01892-246-402/www.norbulingka.org). Open 9am-5pm Mon-Sat. No AmEx.*
Inside the Norbulingka Institute, this well-designed store stocks the highest-quality Tibetan arts, crafts and artefacts, many of the pieces made by the institute's artists. If you want to buy a quality *thangka*, there is no better place than here. Books, handmade paper, Buddha statues, carved furniture, Tibetan carpets, fabrics, clothing, hand-stitched embroidery and boxes adorned with Tibetan art are also sold. The merchandise is quite expensive, but it is the best and you are supporting a legitimate enterprise when you buy here.

Tibetan Children's Village Handicrafts Store

McLeod Ganj *Temple Road (01892-220-618). Open 9am-7pm Tue-Sun. No AmEx.*

Many children from the Tibetan Children's Village School are trained to work on the simple but beautiful objects found in this store. This is your best bet to purchase some of their delightful creations at reasonable prices, as well as a wide variety of other Tibetan handicrafts. All proceeds go towards helping Tibetan children.

Arts

Tibetan Institute of Performing Arts

3km uphill from McLeod Ganj *Dharamkot Road (01892-221-478, 220-587/www.tibetanarts.org). Open 9am-4.30pm Mon-Sat.*

This institute, dedicated to the preservation of Tibetan performing arts, was set up by the Dalai Lama soon after he came to India. The institute's chief focus is the art of *lhamo* (traditional Tibetan opera), which visitors can experience at various events, including the nine-day annual Shoton Opera Festival. In addition, traditional Tibetan musical instruments like the *piwang* (fiddle), flute and *dranyen* (seven-stringed lute) are taught here, as is the art of creating garments, masks and props. The institute has a shop selling Tibetan music CDs, DVDs, postcards, books and beautiful Tibetan masks. Check the website for the performance schedule.

Stay

Accommodation is cheaper here than in many other Indian hill stations frequented by tourists. Whether you want to stay in the heart of town, or in the surrounding wooded area, there are plenty of delightful places to choose from. There is also a profusion of ultra-cheap backpacker hostels, both in McLeod Ganj and Dharamkot. Note, though, that there's little in the way of public transport and you must be willing to walk or hire a private taxi if you decide to stay away from the town's main streets.

Chonor House

McLeod Ganj *Temple Road, near Main Temple (01892 -221-468/94180-31468/www.norbulingka.org). $$. No AmEx.*

Run by the Norbulingka Institute, this is the first and most obvious choice for discerning travellers who want to be close to the Main Temple. It has a well-justified reputation as the best place to stay in town, not just from the point of view of location, but also for ambience, interiors and food. Note, though, that there is a small steep climb to the entrance (or you can access it from Hotel Bhagsu Road by a short dirt path). Richard Gere and Robert Thurman (Uma Thurman's father and a Tibetan Buddhism scholar) are regulars here, the former always preferring his favourite room, Kham, with its private balcony overlooking the Main Temple. Although it is one of the most expensive places to stay, it is still reasonably priced; with only 11 rooms, you need to book well in advance. Each of the rooms is different and individually decorated, from walls to carpet and bedspread; they showcase different themes or regions of Tibet and offer a glimpse into Tibetan art, craft and culture at its best. Best of all, the interior walls are covered in murals created by the master artists of the Norbulingka Institute.

Clouds End Villa

3km downhill from McLeod Ganj *Naoroji Road, above Hari Kothi, Lower Dharamsala (01892-224-904/ www.cloudsendvilla.com). $$. No credit cards.*

Clouds End Villa, a 15-minute drive towards Lower Dharamsala from McLeod Ganj, is a good option if you welcome some solitude and time away from the activities of the upper town. Set amid lush greenery, the property consists of a colonial-era bungalow with some later additions. There are ten spacious rooms with wooden flooring and ceilings and a large dining space that serves meals cooked to order, along with plenty of spaces to lounge around and relax in. It's not easy to get to or from the villa, except by taxi or other vehicle, unless you don't mind a stiff walk.

Glenmoor Cottages

1km uphill from McLeod Ganj *Upper Dharamsala (01892-221-010/021/www.glenmoorcottages.com). $$. No credit cards.*

Five idyllic cottages are hidden away in woods in a location that achieves a fine balance between tranquillity and proximity to the buzzing McLeod Ganj, which is just a short stroll down the hill. Owner Ajai Singh and his family have played host to a list of celebrities including Pierce Brosnan, Martin Scorsese, Richard Gere and Paul Simon. The cottages are built with local materials, have wooden floors and ceilings, and large windows. Set amid pine trees and manicured lawns, with garden chairs and hammocks, they are carefully spaced out to offer absolute privacy. The three smaller ones are at a lower level and have a double bedroom, attached bath, kitchenette and a small veranda; the larger cottages have the same facilities, though rooms are larger and there are split-level verandas overlooking pine forests.

Kashmir Cottage

2km downhill from McLeod Ganj *Kharadanda Road, Upper Dharamsala (01892-224-929/kascot55@ yahoo.co.in). $-$$. No credit cards.*

Kashmir Cottage has a peaceful setting, a couple of kilometres before you reach McLeod Ganj's main square (via the shorter, steeper route) from Lower Dharamsala. A winding road ahead of Men Tsee Khang, the Tibetan Medical and Astrology Institute, leads up to the property, which is surrounded by pleasant, simple gardens. The seven immaculately clean rooms are efficiently maintained and run by the family of the Dalai Lama's younger brother, Ngari Rinpoche. For the best views of the valley, get the cheapest rooms on the top; the two suites on the ground floor come with a sprawling garden and large airy rooms with plenty of sunlight. All are wonderfully quiet. The Cottage is popular with visitors to the nearby Institute.

Clockwise from top: Tibetan Children's Village Handicrafts Store; street stall; Norling Arts Shop.

Top: Glenmoor Cottages.
Bottom: Chonor House.

Norling Guest House

Norbulingka Institute *PO Sidhpur, Near Lower Dharamsala (01892-246-406/www.norbulingka.org). $. No AmEx.*

Set in a quiet corner of the Norbulingka Institute, a 45-minute drive from McLeod Ganj, this guesthouse successfully combines Tibetan architecture and interiors with modern design, to create a very comfortable and relaxing ambience. Rooms are set around plant-filled atrium. Black stone floors are offset with large windows that let in plenty of natural light. Everything is immaculate and visually pleasing, but the reception is often abandoned and you shouldn't expect too much in terms of room service and hotel-like facilities. The Norling Café serves a range of very good vegetarian food (you may need to order in advance). Service is slow, but in keeping with the whole atmosphere of the place: here, nothing is hurried or stressful.

Pema Thang Guest House

McLeod Ganj *Hotel Bhagsu Road (01892-221-871/ www.pemathang.net). $. No credit cards.*

A simple, comfortable guesthouse, Pema Thang doesn't compare to Chonor House in ambience, but it has a lovely location, far enough from the main streets to be peaceful and yet just a stone's throw away. And it's one third of the price. Run by the family of the Dalai Lama's former aide, it has one simple rule that guests must follow: if you intend to be out after 11pm, you need to inform the staff in advance. The café serves decent vegetarian meals at reasonable prices. Rooms are clean, with wooden floors and basic bathrooms. The ones on the top floor are best, with balconies and great views. Those on the ground floor are the least desirable. Whichever room you stay in, you will awake to the soothing chanting of prayers by the monks in the Main Temple.

Factfile

When to go

From March to early June McLeod Ganj experiences warm sunny days and pleasant clear evenings. It gets very crowded with tourists in May. Mid July to September is wet and it rains almost every day. October to February is cold, but visitors still come to McLeod Ganj, and it's a good time to avoid the crowds.

Getting there

Daily flights from Delhi to Dharamsala are operated by low-cost carrier Kingfisher Red, but check in advance about schedules; Gaggal airport is a 50-minute drive from McLeod Ganj. Direct, overnight, air-conditioned Volvo buses leave New Delhi's Inter State Bus Terminus for Dharamsala at 8pm every day for the gruelling 11- to 12-hour journey. Overnight trains take you from Delhi to Pathankot, a three-hour drive away; taxis at Pathankot charge Rs 2,000 to McLeod Ganj. A better option is to take one of two daily Shatabdi (fast) trains from Delhi to Amritsar; Dharamsala is a five-hour road trip from Amritsar by private taxi. Whatever option you take, your hotel in McLeod Ganj can organise a pick-up from Pathankot of Amritsar, or even Chandigarh, which is seven hours away.

For more information on travelling within India, *see p378* **Navigating India**.

Getting around

Walking is the principal means of getting around. However, Maruti van taxis are available at the taxi/bus stand, as well as auto-rickshaws that will take you to Dharamkot and around.

Tourist information

All the tourist information you need can usually be obtained from your hotel or a local travel agent.

The official tourist information office is near the Kunal Hotel (01892- 224-212, open 10am-6pm Mon-Sat), but it's of limited use as staff tend not to speak English.

Internet

Nyimon Cyber Café, Jogibara Road, near the Post Office (01892-221-882) is open from 10am to 8pm daily.

Coffee Talk, near the Main Temple entrance, offers free internet services to customers with their own laptops who order food over Rs 100.

Tips

● Most shops, markets and offices are closed all day on Monday. In general, McLeod Ganj shuts down early and starts early. This is not a party town.

● Foreigners intending to stay in Dharamsala for longer than 14 days, especially if they are taking part in courses and retreats, need to register personally at the Foreign Registration Office at the Superintendent of Police's Office in Lower Dharamsala.

● Most places of interest in and around McLeod Ganj are just a walk away and locals walk everywhere. Carry a comfortable pair of shoes, and rain gear if you're visiting in the monsoon season.

Wildlife

Kanha, Bandhavgarh & Panna

Wildlife and conservation in Central India.

Three wildlife parks – Bandhavgarh, Kanha and Panna – lie at the heart of Central India and are key to the country's tiger conservation efforts. Long avoided by tourists because of poor infrastructure, Madhya Pradesh state has finally awoken to its tourist potential, and is building decent roads to access its wonderful sites. The national parks' famed tigers may not reveal themselves to every passing safari jeep, but there is a profusion of wildlife within all three of these reserves. Peacocks routinely hold up traffic on their dirt roads, and families of langurs (black-faced monkeys) idly scratch themselves as they observe the visitors. Deer species like chital (spotted deer), nilgai (antelope) and barasingha (swamp deer) stand and stare as vehicles pass, and glimpses of an oriole or flycatcher are common.

Kanha, the land that inspired Rudyard Kipling's *The Jungle Book*, may have more tigers than the other parks, but you're more likely to spot one at Bandhavgarh, because it has a higher density of the beast. Panna, with its temples, attracts more local pilgrims than wildlife enthusiasts, but it's the place for spotting leopards, as well as crocodiles in the lovely Ken river.

A visit to these parks offers a chance to get close to nature: tree branches eat into cottage walls, monkeys tap at hotel windows, deer horns get stuck in fences. And you don't have to be a wildlife expert to enjoy the parks, either. The topography is unique, the forests throb with life, an elephant-back safari is thrilling and some resorts are so lovely you'll want to stay forever.

Clockwise from top left: Kanha Tiger Reserve/National Park; Bandhavgarh National Park (4); Panna National Park.

Explore

To get the best out of a visit to these national parks, plan to stay at least three days in each. Open-top jeep safaris are the principal means of exploring them, though walks with naturalists outside the park's perimeter can be just as exciting. Sunrise and afternoon to evening are the best times for wildlife sightings, though tigers are mostly spotted just after sunrise.

In **Bandhavgarh** and **Kanha**, park authority employees track the day's big cat sightings on elephants and relay information to the park offices by walkie-talkie. Registration at the park office gives you a token. If a tiger is spotted, and if your token number is called, you could get the chance to have an elephant-back safari to go deeper into the jungle to seek out the tiger.

Official wildlife guides are mandatory for every vehicle entering the park, even if you have a naturalist with you. The frenzy (created by drivers and guides) surrounding tiger-spotting can be somewhat off-putting. Ensure that your guide knows if you are interested in more than just tigers, or you will be sucked into a tiring game of racing around the park, rather than enjoying the diversity it offers. Naturalists accompanying you from your hotel work best when they know what guests are interested in, so if you're specifically keen on birds, reptiles – or you really want to concentrate on tiger-spotting – on a particular day, be sure to let them know in advance.

Most visitors pay for safaris through their resort as part of a package. All safari prices should include the complicated park entry fee, but do check to make sure. Fees are generally around Rs 25-Rs 40 for Indians, Rs 500 for others, with cameras, vehicles, guides and so on costing extra. Park entry times also vary according to the season but hotels and safari guides will know the most current times.

If you're visiting the park at **Panna**, it's also worth visiting the town, which is known for its many cenotaphs, two temples and nearby diamond mines.

BANDHAVGARH NATIONAL PARK

Bandhavgarh's high density of tigers means that the chances of sighting one on a safari are good – although by no means a foregone conclusion. A sign at the park's Tala Gate carries a picture of a tiger and reads something like: 'You may not have seen me but don't be disappointed. I have seen you.'

Roughly half the size of Kanha, Bandhavgarh's safari trails are shorter, allowing wildlife enthusiasts time to linger over interesting areas for longer. Besides the big cats, look out for fox, nilgai (antelope), chital (spotted deer), wild boar and over 250 species of bird, including an abundance of peacocks. Bandhavgarh's terrain is rugged and includes high cliffs and vast

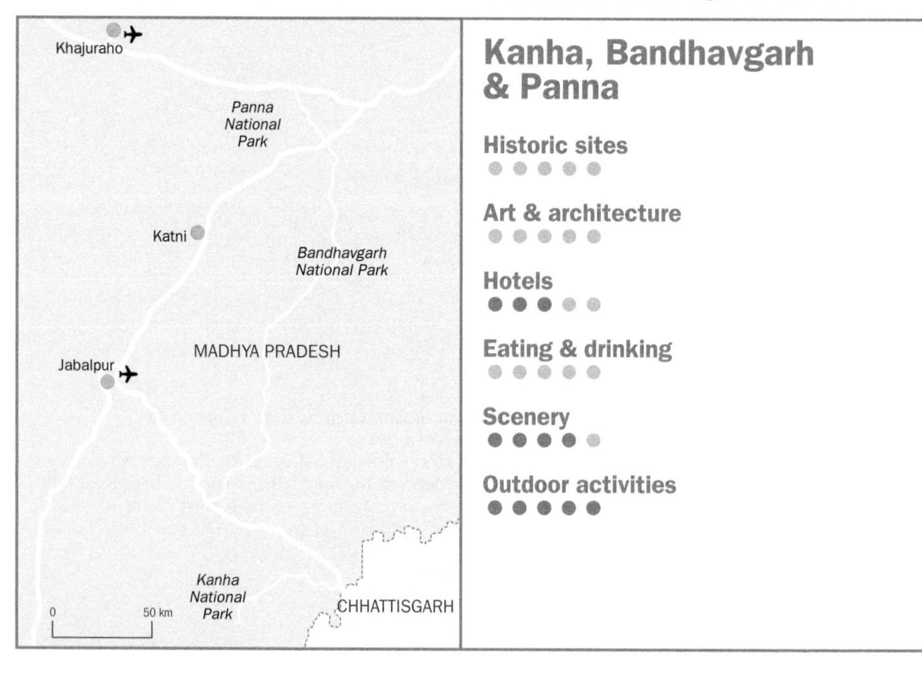

grasslands. Half- and full-day elephant-back safaris for up to three people (plus naturalist and park guide) are available at Bandhavgarh, though these need to be reserved through tour operators in advance (from Rs 15,000 per person) and cannot be booked at the park.

Located within park limits (but requiring a separate viewing tour) is Bandhavgarh Fort, on a massive plateau on top of a hill. Visit the fort in the evening to catch the sunset from a temple inside the ruins; alternatively, it's a good destination to head for with a picnic lunch and guide – resorts will be happy to arrange this.

Bandhavgarh National Park

Umaria District. Open Feb-June 6.30-9.30am, 4-6.30pm daily. Oct-Jan 7.30-10.30am, 3-5.30pm daily.

"Pass through the park's varied terrain to spot leopards, gaur (large wild buffalo), barking deer, barasingha (swamp deer), black buck and around 200 species of bird."

KANHA TIGER RESERVE/ NATIONAL PARK

At 940 square kilometres (363 square miles), Kanha is Madhya Pradesh state's largest national park, home to around 89 tigers, though this figure frequently drops as more and more tigers fall prey to the poaching that feeds the Chinese traditional medicine market. Enter through the Kisli or Mukki gates and pass through the park's varied terrain – sal and bamboo outcrops, open grasslands and ponds – to spot leopard, gaur (large wild buffalo), barking deer, barasingha (swamp deer), black buck and about 200 species of bird. The park's water sources are supplemented by pipe-fed ponds along the safari trails, ensuring both that animals survive the brutal summers and visitors get more sightings. There are films and wildlife dioramas at the little museum, and the Bahmni Dadar plateau is a good spot to catch the sunset.

Kanha Tiger Reserve/National Park

Capital District. Open Feb-June 5.30-11am, 3.30-7.30pm daily. Oct-Jan 6.30-11am, 2.30-6.30pm daily.

PANNA NATIONAL PARK

Though conveniently situated just 50 kilometres (31 miles) from the famous temple town of Khajuraho (*see p202*), Panna National Park gets fewer visitors than its more famous neighbours, mainly because of its small tiger population – the tigers that are here have been recently transferred from Bandhavgarh and Kanha.

However, Panna makes up for what it lacks in tigers with its scenery: the River Karnavati (popularly called the Ken) and its beautiful landscape of alternating thick teak forests and open grasslands lends a special appeal. The park's topography is stunning, especially after the monsoon, when you are likely to see gushing waterfalls and plenty of streams, which lure a variety of migratory birds. The long absence of tigers means the park is rich in a feline rival: the leopard. You will also have the chance to spot crocodiles as they slip into the river for a morning dip, glimpse paradise flycatchers flitting through trees, or spot sambar grazing along the Ken's banks.

You can take night safaris, boat rides and elephant safaris in Panna, as well as open-top jeep safaris. All jeep safaris (including night safaris) are organised by the resorts, and – unlike in Kanha and Bandhavgarh – are not controlled by park authorities. The park does organise hour-long boat rides during which you may spot a gharial, however.

Wildlife enthusiasts may also like to visit the nearby **Ken Gharial Sanctuary**, set up to protect this unique, now endangered, crocodile species that has long been hunted for its skin.

Panna National Park

Chattarpur District. Open Feb-June 5.30-11am, 3.30-7.30pm daily. Oct-Jan 6.30-11am, 2.30-6.30pm daily.

PANNA TOWN

The town of Panna is known for its many cenotaphs or *chhatris*, honouring long-forgotten royalty. The area where these are located is now a venue for street cricket. You will also find a couple of temples here: Baldeo Temple and Prannathji Temple, and the town's famous diamond mines (open 9am-1pm Mon-Sat).

Baldeo Temple

Panna Bazaar. Open 6-10am, 7-10pm daily. Admission free.

The story goes that Maharaja Rudra Pratap Singh, who ruled between 1870 and 1893, had been so impressed with European architecture on a trip abroad that he wanted to build a Hindu temple in European style when he returned. One look at Baldeo Temple reveals that his local architects lost the plot somewhat. Recently refurbished and repainted, the structure is a glorious mish-mash of assorted styles: barrack-like exterior walls, a Hindu-style courtyard, a colonial entranceway, classical arches, domes and Mughal-style curlicued arches. The priest holds a traditional *aarti* (ritual offering) under the chandeliers at seven every evening.

Prannathji Temple

Panna Bazaar. Open sunrise-sunset daily. Admission free.

The main shrine of the temple complex has beautiful murals depicting the life of Krishna on its outer walls. The domes of another temple display an unusual Islamic architectural influence when illuminated after sunset, and priestesses keep up a perpetual prayer reading cycle in one of the corridors. But it's the gold and silver altar inside the main shrine that will leave you speechless. It dazzles brighter than Panna's diamonds, which are said to be a boon gifted to the area by the resident deity.

Eat & Stay

Most accommodation is clustered around the entry gates to the national parks, while the newer luxury resorts are located five to seven kilometres away, allowing them to escape the touristy bustle. All three national parks have become much busier in the last few years, and many old-time lodge owners in Bandhavgarh and Kanha lament that each season brings at least five new competing properties. Many of the new resorts are in the parks' buffer zones, which means tales about tigers walking around just outside the reception area are as ubiquitous as a welcome drink and cold towel. Resorts are closed when the parks are closed, between July and September. There are no walk-in restaurants anywhere, so jungle lodge packages usually include Indian or Western meals, a safari, the services of an in-house naturalist and access to the hotel's collection of books and films. You may be charged extra for use of additional facilities like a gym or spa. Water is scarce in the summer months so you may find a pool closed and hotels requesting guests to conserve. Most resorts will accept credit cards for advance payment for rooms or packages, but may not be able to accept credit cards at the resort itself.

The Baagh

Kanha National Park *Gudma Village, near Mukki Gate (07637-296-340, 93034-91445/ www.thebaagh.com). $$. No credit cards.*

An additional letter 'a' is all that separates the Hindi words for garden and tiger, which is probably why the owners of Rajasthan's Garden hotel, the Bagh, named their luxury Kanha resort the Baagh. This three-year-old property has 24 three-room cottages, a dining hall that looks like a Raj-era officer's mess, a badminton court, spa and swimming pool. Don't judge the rooms by the low-roofed mud-walled reception area; they are quite spacious and come with private patios, marble bathtubs and solar heaters. Pick the suite – with private staircase and sunken bath – if you really want to live it up, and ask for your evening drinks to be served at the gazebo by the pool as you take in the sunset.

Chitvan

Kanha National Park *Samnapur Village, near Mukki Gate (93505-19798/98112-00094/www.chitvan.com). $$$$. No credit cards.*

About 3.5 kilometres from Kanha's Mukki Gate, Chitvan is accessible only via a very bumpy dirt road, but its isolation is part of its charm. The luxury cottages, complete with open-air showers and big picture windows opening out to the grassy outdoors, are suave and stylish without detracting from the rustic surroundings. Dinner is served by the pool in summer and inside what looks like a two-level ski lodge in cooler months. A vegetable patch for iceberg lettuce, courgettes and other hard-to-get foreign greens allows the menu to stretch further than hotels that source from the local market. The majority of the staff are local tribal, and Chitvan engages local kids to perform folk dances and offers cash incentives for them to stay in school. Service is thoughtful: the packed safari breakfast comes considerately accompanied with blankets to keep guests warm at dawn, and foot reflexology massages are available on call.

"A rickety bridge leads you over a crocodile-infested stream towards the rooms, which come with a terrace and sunken-in shower."

Jungle Mantra

Bandhavgarh National Park *Rancha Village, near Tala Gate (07627-280-547/94253-31207/ www.junglemantra.com). $$$. No credit cards.*

To reach Jungle Mantra, follow signs to King's Lodge, which is adjacent to this resort. Smack in the middle of the park's buffer zone, with a pond within its boundaries, Jungle Mantra gets more than its fair share of big cat sightings and wandering deer. The three-year-old property has simple air-cooled cottages furnished in cane, bamboo and wrought-iron furniture, and roomy bathrooms. Shailin Ramji, who gave up a job in finance in the UK to set up the lodge with his wife Rhea, is keen on employing local help, including in the kitchen. The restaurant serves up delicious Western fare; don't miss the stuffed chicken and fruit pie if they're available. Ramji is also an avid photographer and birder and great company on a safari.

Ken River Lodge

Panna National Park *Madla Village (98102-53436/ 98100-24711/www.kenriverlodge.com). $$. No credit cards.*

Top: Mahua Kothi (3). Bottom left: Pashan Garh (2). Bottom right: Tuli Tiger Resort.

The flooding banks of the Ken river have washed the lodge's cottages away three times in the last decade, but the owners have rebuilt each time, and thank heavens for that. Ken River Lodge's 20 mud cottages offer somewhat more affordable accommodation in Panna. The lodge has the kind of homely, informal feel that is immediately welcoming, helped by the fact that the property is also home to 24 cats, 11 dogs, eight bears and one nilgai, with jackals, hyenas and hogs often dropping in from the jungle next door. A rickety bridge leads you over a crocodile-infested stream towards the rooms, which come with a terrace and sunken-in shower. Have your drinks out on the raised-level bar (good for spotting wildlife). One of Ken River Lodge's USPs is being able to enjoy a beer as peacocks dance on the river's edge only a few metres away. Tribal dances are arranged in the evenings.

King's Lodge

Bandhavgarh National Park *Rancha Village, near Tala Gate (011-2588-5709/9802-53436/ www.kingslodge.in). $$$.*

All dark wood and stone, King's Lodge's 18 cottages, dining area and watchtower look more like an Indian version of a Scottish castle than a wildlife retreat. All rooms are the same size and clustered to accommodate large groups. There's a pool room and a small library of wildlife books to keep guests entertained between safaris. In addition, the lodge has bicycles for hire and nature walks are organised by an in-house naturalist. Walking tours of the park's perimeter to spot birds, flora and insects are among the more popular.

"Harmless creepy crawlies are permanent residents of the 17 simple rooms, lizards idly amble along ledges in reception and leopard sightings are common."

Kipling Camp

Kanha National Park *Mocha Village, Mandla District, near Kisli Gate (07649-277-218/ www.kiplingcamp.com). $$.*

Set up in 1982 by wildlife conservationists Bob and Anne Wright, Kanha's oldest lodge offers no-frills accommodation for serious wildlife buffs. Situated within the park's buffer zone, the camp intrudes into the jungle as little as possible. Beds of leaves are cleared for narrow dirt paths, harmless creepy crawlies are permanent residents of the 17 simple rooms, lizards idly amble along reception ledges and leopard sightings are common. Kipling's resident elephant, the very friendly Tara, allows visitors to bathe her in the afternoons, and Kim, the resident Labrador, follows you around and offers the evening's entertainment. Choose Indian meals unless you like plain, boiled and rather bland Western dishes. And make sure you get head naturalist Rishin Roy on your safari; it's hard to find a better guide in Kanha.

Mahua Kothi

Bandhavgarh National Park *Rancha Village, near Tala Gate (07627-265-416/022-6601-1825/ www.tajsafaris.com). $$$$.*

One of the Taj group's four national park lodges, in collaboration with &beyond (formerly CC Africa), Mahua Kothi is the most stylish and luxurious lodging in all Bandhavgarh. Hidden from view, the resort's 12 sienna-coloured cottages, with private porch areas, allow privacy for guests as well as the possibility of appreciating the wilderness while dining on penne arrabbiata, cucumber and apple soup, fish curry, lemon rice and the like. Thoughtful touches are everywhere – an umbrella stand near alfresco areas, little bottles of squash and ice boxes, along with *chaupad* (a traditional Ludo-like board game) in every room, to name a few. If you want to splurge on a hotel, this might be the place to do it. Mahua Kothi has the best safari vehicles in Bandhavgarh and a good team of naturalists, offering different tours for birders, tiger fans and general nature lovers, so guests get exactly the kind of outing they want. Follow your safari ride with a treat from the massage menu or an afternoon dip in the large courtyard pool.

Nature Heritage Resort

Bandhavgarh National Park *181 Tala (07627-265-351/94253-31202/www.nature heritageresort.com). $.*

Nature Heritage Resort offers a reasonably priced option for those who like their wilderness in small, controlled doses. The 20 rooms have a log-cabin appeal, with much of the decor done in dark wood lit by amber lights. There's a landscaped garden, log fences, cane furniture and front porches that offer a view of either the garden or the forest, but no spa or pool. Guests can access wildlife reports and films from the well-stocked library. Upgrade to a luxury room, and you'll have lovely views of the property and the jungle beyond from the attached balcony.

Pashan Garh

Panna National Park *Madla Village (022-6601-1825/ 07932-292-010/www.tajsafaris.com). $$$$.*

The newest of the Taj group's four luxury lodges in Madhya Pradesh, Pashan Garh is by far its most stunning property. Sitting on 22 acres of buffer zone land formerly belonging to local royalty, it looks like a super-luxury, upmarket version of traditional stone housing, with air-conditioning, private sit-out and outdoor pavilion, and little touches so characteristic of Taj hospitality. Exquisite furnishings make wide use of rich brown leather: it covers everything from the headboards to the boxes that hold toiletries, stationery, cool drinks and gym equipment in each of the 12 rooms. While the spa was not ready at the time of writing, in-room massages were available. The place relies largely on local produce for its food and employs locals, including head naturalist Ratna Singh, who helps people make sense of the jungle around them, while roaming in state-of-the-art safari vehicles. Pashan Garh encourages guests to get involved in local development by sponsoring $10 school kits for local kids. Blow on the emergency whistle if you smell trouble; there's one in every room.

Shergarh

Kanha National Park *Village Bahmni, Tehsil Baihar, District Balaghat (90981-87346/www.shergarh.com).* $$$.

Eco-conscious couple Jehan and Katie Bhujwala run this small but charming resort in a 20-acre tract of regenerated land, centred around a watering hole. Verandahs front each of the six tents. These are spacious, well maintained and comfortable, with smart, concrete bathrooms and tiled roofs. Service is extremely personalised and hands-on and guests tuck into home-cooked meals served outdoors at lunchtime and in the dining room at dinner (warmed by a log fire in winter). Hot water bottles are put in your bed at night; the tents can get pretty cold in winter. The owners are committed to the welfare of the local community and encourage guests to explore the local area, beyond the wildlife safaris.

Tuli Tiger Resort

Kanha National Park *Mocha Village, Mandla District, near Kisli Gate (07649-277-211/ www.tuligroup.com).* $$$.

Tuli is certainly among the swankiest of Kanha's resorts. Tiger territories are mapped out on the reception walls, tiger numbers are chalked on a blackboard, brass ram heads decorate the backs of chairs. Decor takes a sophisticated rustic approach, with earthy colours, organic shapes, and lots of wood. Eight luxury tents (better than the rooms) offer modern plumbing, air-conditioning, bathtubs, bar, mood lighting and television. Tuli rents gear so guests can fish in the pond; it also has two spa rooms, two restaurants and an audiovisual room for slide shows and films.

Factfile

When to go

October to April is the best time to visit, though most resorts remain open until mid June. It gets uncomfortably hot during the summer (Mar-May), when afternoon temperatures can hit 40°C, but hotel rates are lower during this time. Summer is also the best time to spot animals, since they tend to stay close to the limited water sources in the hot months. Parks are closed from July to September, as are resorts.

Getting there

A direct flight from Delhi can bring you to Jabalpur, the nearest airport, a 165km/103-mile, four- to five-hour drive away from Kanha. Gondia Junction is the nearest railway station for Kanha, while Katni is nearest to Bandhavgarh.

If you are travelling from Mumbai, fly to Nagpur; Kanha is 260km/162 miles or a seven-hour drive away. From Kanha, Bandhavgarh is 250km/155 miles (seven hours) to the north. Panna lies 250km/155 miles (six to seven hours) north-west of Bandhavgarh. Panna is just 50km/31 miles from the famous temple town of Khajuraho.

For more on travel within India, *see p378* **Navigating India**.

Getting around

Most hotels offer pick-ups from the airport or railway station for a fee. They also tend to have their own safari vehicles and many also have in-house naturalists to accompany guests into the parks. If you plan to travel from one park to another, you can hire a car at one hotel to drop you to your next destination.

Tourist information

Madhya Pradesh State Tourism Development Corporation Limited (07649-277-242/www.mptourism.com) has a counter at the Kisli Gate inside Kanha National Park, but you'll be lucky if you get someone to answer your call. Open Feb-June 5.30-11am, 3.30-7.30pm daily. Oct-Jan 6.30-11am, 2.30-6.30pm daily.

There's also a **Kanha Tourist information** helpline (07649-277-2227) and a **Bandhavgarh Tourism** office (07627-265-366). Park hotels and resorts are usually the best source of tourist information.

Internet

Internet access is close to impossible in these parts. At best, some of the most expensive hotels may have a connection in their office that they would probably allow a guest to use in an emergency.

Note also that mobile phone connectivity is non-existent in most areas right near the parks. Some hotels have patchy reception; the best reception can be found in market areas or near a busy town.

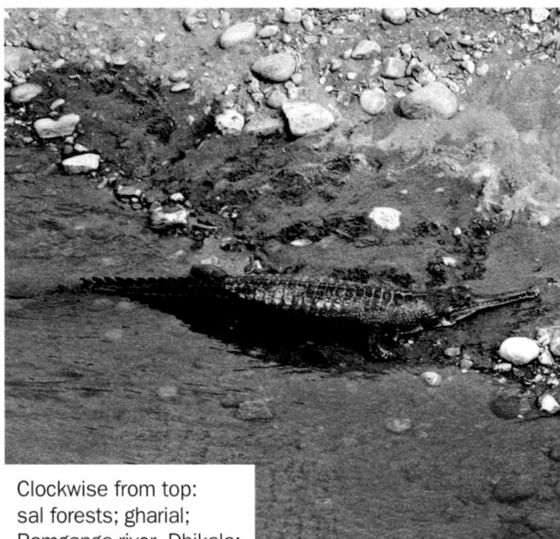

Clockwise from top:
sal forests; gharial;
Ramganga river, Dhikala;
elephant-back safari.

Corbett

Tiger country.

Jim Corbett Tiger Reserve, usually just known as Corbett, in the northern hill state of Uttarkhand, was India's first national park. On any given day you can find wild elephants scattered across the park's lands, enjoying the golden sunlight. Herds of deer and hog feed on the grass, jackals walk the dirt tracks and wild boar dig for roots. But danger lurks in the glades, where tigers wait silently and patiently for an opportune moment to break cover and seize their prey. The elusive Bengal tiger is Corbett's main attraction, and if you chance upon one of these magnificent beasts here, it is usually a genuine wild moment. Exploring the depths of these jungles on elephant-back, the truly lucky may even witness a face-off between a tiger and their safari elephant.

Located in the soft, rolling Shivalik Hills, the park sits between the outer Himalayan mountains and the swathe of moist grasslands (the Terai region) that runs parallel to this range. This strategic geographical location creates a remarkable landscape of hills, verdant valleys, sharp ridges, rivers and streams and expansive grasslands. The park encompasses a huge area of about 1,300 square kilometres (502 square miles) and includes three distinct wildlife reserves: the Corbett National Park, the Sonanadi Wildlife Sanctuary and the Kalagarh Reserve Forest.

Corbett isn't all about the tiger; it also provides a habitat for an amazing diversity of wildlife: leopard, sloth bear, wild elephant, sambar, chital, barking deer, jackal and – because of the nature of the habitat – the largest specimens of wild pig to be found anywhere. Reptiles are abundant, with two varieties of crocodile, as well as pythons and king cobras. As many as 580 bird species can be spotted, including those that pass through Corbett on their migratory path.

Explore

The legend of Jim Corbett – the famous hunter turned conservationist – has an enduring legacy in the jungle he loved. Born in the nearby town of Nainital, Jim was five when he first fired a rifle, but changed course later in life to kill only man-eating tigers and leopards. By the time his famous work *Man Eating Leopard of Rudraprayag* was published in 1948, he had transformed into an ardent conservationist who worked hard to bring protected status to the park.

Considering Corbett has the highest density of tigers in the world (studies indicate one tiger every five kilometres), it may seem surprising that it's not as easy to see one here as in Ranthambore or Bandhavgarh. But spotting one here gives far more in the way of an adrenalin buzz than some of the packaged tiger sightings that are experienced in other parks.

Corbett is divided into five zones, Bijrani, Dhikala, Jhirna, Domunda and Sonanadi, each requiring entry through a separate gate. At Dhikala and Jhirna there are watchtowers from where visitors can scour the landscape for wildlife. You need a permit to enter the reserve and must be accompanied by a 'nature guide'; permits can be obtained at the park office in Ramnagar (open 8am-1pm, 2-4pm daily). For day visits you can also get a permit at the entry gate (admission Rs 30 Indians, Rs 200 others, Rs 100 vehicle charges, Rs 250 accompanying guide). Only a handful of the park administration's nature guides are good, most are just average, but they make sure you don't lose your way or flout the rules (though few speak more than passable English). Note that guides remain compulsory even if you are accompanied by a naturalist from your lodgings.

The park is open from 7am until 5pm from November to February, and an extra hour earlier and later in the warmer months (March to June). Most visitors save themselves the trouble of figuring out its complicated logistics by booking safaris directly with their lodge in advance. This is particularly advisable for the very popular elephant safaris in the peak winter season.

Besides Jeep safaris and elephant-back safaris, the park also offers opportunities for fishing the golden mahseer (as well as goonch, trout and kalabasu fish) on the Ramganga and Kosi rivers: the Mahseer Conservation Project allows restricted catch-and-release fishing.

DHIKALA AREA

Every wildlife park has picture-perfect landscape that remains forever etched in the memory. For the Jim Corbett Tiger Reserve, it has to be the verdant Dhikala grasslands or *chaur*. Set against the blue waters of the Ramganga Reservoir, the dark green expanse is ringed by mountains in the north and tall, thick sal forests with cream-coloured flowers in the south. Wild elephants roam the grasslands in herds, while the usually

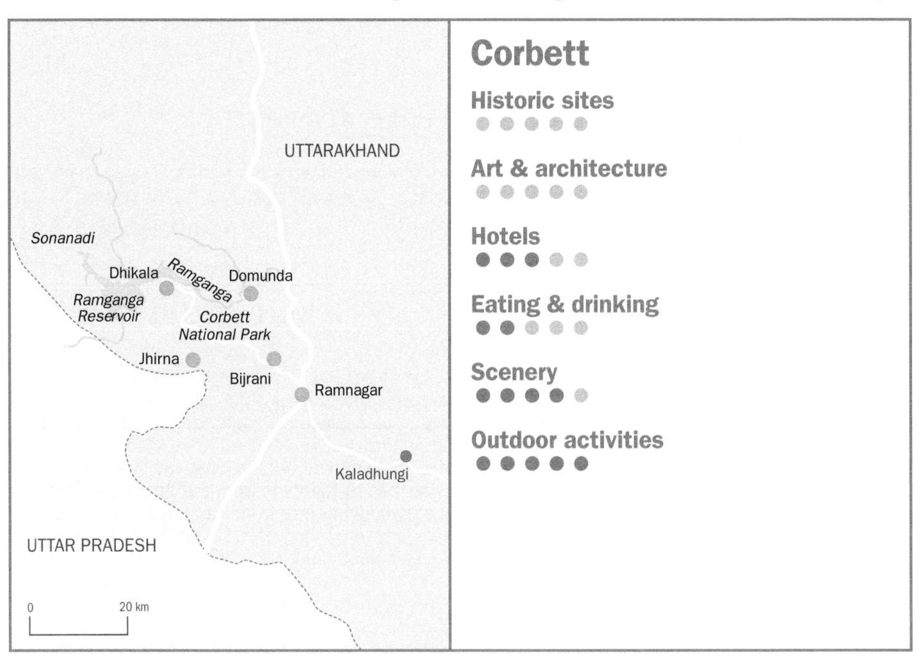

solitary tigers hide in the glades around, stalking the park's abundant sambar population.

Access to the Dhikala range is from the Dhangarhi Gate, 18 kilometres (11 miles) north-east of Ramnagar. The great part about this area is that you get to stay inside the park – and even better, only those with reservations to stay are allowed in. The Dhikala Forest Lodge & Complex – with rooms, library, restaurant and an elephant-ride service – provides most of theaccommodation. There is also a smattering of other Forest Rest Houses (FRHs), which you can book from the office in Ramnagar (*see p304*). These are at Kanda, Sultan, Gairal, Saraptuli and Khinanauli.

To the immediate west of the Dhikala Complex runs a famous dirt track called Thandi Sarak (Cool Road) that separates the grasslands from the sal forests; this is a good place to start looking for tigers. To the south-east, another track, Sambar Road, hugs the Ramganga river all the way down south to Khinanauli. It's a scenic road and as the name suggests, teeming with deer and other species, which, again, makes it a great place to watch for tigers. There are two ways to travel inside the park: Jeep safari or elephant safari. Elephants are available from the Dhikala Complex and will soon be available from Khinanauli too.

From Khinanauli, all along the Ramganga right up to Gairal, there are various vantage points to see wildlife next to the river. For a spectacular view of the river, stop at a point called High Bank on the road from Dhangarhi Gate to the Dhikala Complex. Here you can find the endangered golden mahseer. However, the major attraction of the Ramganga river has to be the large population of gharials (a unique species of crocodilian) and muggers (crocodiles) – that you see basking on the banks like prehistoric creatures. A sign at Dhikala puts everything in perspective: 'Swimming is prohibited in the Ramganga. Survivors will be prosecuted.'

Cross the Ramganga on two rickety wooden bridges at Khinanauli and you'll reach Phulai Chaur. This is another large area of grassland, interspersed with thick forests set against the rolling hills – again, ideal country for both tiger and elephant. The area is also good for birding: it's common to see pairs of Great Indian hornbills rolling in the mud of the dirt track or drongos flitting from tree to tree. It was in this area that the British ornithologist David Hunt, in 1985, excited about something he saw, stepped out of his Jeep, walked into the foliage and startled a tigress with cubs. He was killed instantly. Since then the park authorities have banned tourists from walking inside the park.

The Phulai Chaur dirt track rolls on for a few kilometres more before it ends in a finger-like piece of land that rolls out almost like a pier into the Ramganga Reservoir. Stop here to survey the rich waterfowl – cormorants, darters, herons, storks, lapwings, grebe and geese.

KANDA

From the Phulai Chaur road, a twisty rock and dirt track forks away up into the hills. This leads to Kanda Ridge, part of the Dhikala area and the highest point in Corbett at 1,043 metres (3,422 feet). The ridge provides stunning views of the Dhikala Chaur and the Ramganga Reservoir. Kanda has an old Forest Rest House that can be booked through the Ramnagar park office (*see p304*). The hilly area sees a lot of leopard activity and the lower slopes are known to have sloth bears. Birdwatchers may spot Himalayan birds like fire-capped tits, blue-winged minlas, laughing thrushes and khalij pheasants.

SONANADI

Sonanadi (Golden River) lies on the northern side of the tiger reserve – a quieter, lesser-known area, with fewer tourists and less infrastructure. But this, and the fact that you need a four-wheel drive to get through the forest, probably adds to its appeal. Access is from Vatanwasa Gate and the only place to stay inside (reached after three river crossings) is the Halduparao Forest Rest House, which sits magnificently on a cliff overlooking the Palain river. The forest is thick and there aren't any open grasslands around, making tiger sightings a little rare. But the charm of the area lies in its ruggedness and the fact that you are allowed to take short walks in the jungle here. Ask the forest guards for routes and for a small fee they may even be willing to accompany you. Because Sonanadi lies smack in the middle of their migratory route, wild elephants abound; huddling around a fire at Halduparao at night, listening to their trumpeting, is an added attraction.

BIJRANI & JHIRNA

Bijrani (on the reserve's south side) and Jhirna (on the south-east side) cater to the large number of tourists who come to stay on 'resort mile', a few kilometres west of Ramnagar. Most of the hotels here lie on a stretch of land called Garjia, cheek-by-jowl to the park's buffer area. This enables the resorts' managers to take liberties that are not allowed inside the park. Guests can be taken for walks inside the buffer area; you can camp, ride horses or even swim and fish in the nearby Kosi river. To enter the Bijrani and Jhirna areas you need to get day permits from Ramnagar. Since the park administration caps the number of vehicles entering these areas, it's necessary to book a long way in advance.

Access to Bijrani is from the Amdanda Gate, just two kilometres from Ramnagar. The area has less water compared to Dhikala, and hence looks scrubby, but there are frequent tiger and elephant sightings and occasionally a sloth bear is spotted. The Bijrani Forest Rest House provides accommodation inside the park. Elephant rides from the FRH are also available.

Like Bijrani, Jhirna is dry and its forest is scrubby. The area was dotted with villages as recently as 1994, but these have been relocated outside the park. Today, the jungle has bounced back, and with it the wildlife: tigers, elephants and sloth bears are frequently seen. The area is especially good for birding. Jhirna has the distinction of being the only area of the park that is open throughout the year.

Eat & Stay

Corbett is one of few parks that allows visitors to stay inside the national park area, in simple, rustic Forest Rest Houses (FRHs). Outside the core park area there are numerous resorts clustered on a strip near Garjia. If you opt to stay here, on 'resort mile', you won't experience the adventure of staying within the park but you won't have to rough it either. Besides this strip, there is a variety of other accommodation in different parts of the periphery of the reserve forest, where you get a wilderness setting – and amenities too. Finally, there are lodges much further afield in areas like Kaladhungi, which are a good distance from the actual park, but surrounded by superb reserve forests.

Built at the turn of the last century, the old colonial Forest Rest Houses that dot the Corbett landscape are perhaps the best places to stay to experience the jungle up close. The architecture is simple – a large living and dining room in the middle, bedrooms on either side and a huge verandah that runs along the front of the building. Though the fittings have become more comfortable over the years, they are at best functional.

They have the unique advantage of being right in the middle of the jungle: it's a memorable experience to settle yourself into an easy chair on the veranda and watch the darkness descend over it. Some of these FRHs – Khinanauli, for instance – have grasslands extending right up to the building, which means you can watch wild elephants pass or herds of deer fill up the compound as you lounge around sipping your drink. Note that you have to bring all your provisions with you at all FRHs except for Dhikala Forest Lodge and Garail, where you will find simple meals served without fanfare. In other lodges, the FRH caretaker usually offers to cook for a fee.

Booking the FRHs isn't easy, since everybody wants them. You have to contact the park administration's Ramnagar office (05947-253-977, 251-489, www.corbettnationalpark.in) at least one month in advance and be able to courier the charges via a bank draft or banker's cheque (in rupees). Bookings are accepted up to three months in advance, but payment can only be made one month before a proposed trip.

Facilities at each FRH are different, and rates vary from Rs 200 for a dorm room bed to Rs 3,000 for a private double room.

All accommodation – except FRHs – include meals in their rates as there are virtually no walk-in restaurants in the area. Most serve set meals and many will lay on a multi-cuisine buffet spread if there are more than a handful of guests.

Camp Corbett

25km E of Reserve *Kaladhungi, Corbett Nagar, (05942-242-126/www.cornwall-online.co.uk/camp-corbett). $$. No credit cards.*

Camp Corbett is far from any other resort, and an hour from any of the park's gates – but it is able to offer a very special experience. It's surrounded by reserve forest, with plenty of jungle trails that you can use without restrictions, and is a hotspot for birdwatchers. Jim Corbett wrote of the area's unmatched birdlife, and – as Camp Corbett's owners, the Anands, will point out – some 350 species have been spotted within a five-kilometre radius of their lodgings. Mrs Anand is a warm and friendly hostess who has been running this place with her husband since the 1980s. The property's 15 comfortable cottages have thatched roofs that provide warmth in the cold weather and keep the sun at bay in the warmer months, and solar panels for heating water. From the central *gol-ghar* (roundhouse) to the jungle sit-outs, the possibilities for relaxing are numerous, as are the activity options. The river is close by, and its rock pools are fabulous for a quiet dip on a sunny afternoon. There's no noisy music or loud guests who want to jam in the jungle (something you're likely to encounter at the big resorts near the park). All in all, an unpretentious, friendly place with a lot of charm.

Camp Forktail Creek

6km N of Dhangarhi Gate *Bhakrakot village, District Almora (05947-287-804/www.campforktailcreek.com). $$. No credit cards.*

There's an element of getting back to nature at Forktail Creek, where guests go without electricity and running water. The last half kilometre of track that takes you to the camp is an indication of what to expect: it's an uphill drive on a dirt road only accessible by 4X4. Ritish Suri and Minakshi Pandey have created a serene space, with a huge collection of books and a bunch of serious naturalists on hand. It's a hospitable and friendly set-up where the love of wildlife and the outdoors is primary, visible and genuine. The lodge provides the luxury of an authentic wildlife experience, but if luxuries like bathtubs and room service are important, then definitely look elsewhere. That's not to say that the place isn't comfortable, but if you're looking for somewhere that shuts out the jungle at the end of the day, this is definitely not it. Guests tend to be pretty active; the owners can organise multi-day safaris into the reserve, with stays in FRHs, the kind of trip not usually organised by tour operators or hotels. If they really must, guests can briefly check their email.

Corbett Hideaway

2km S of Dhangarhi Gate *Dhikala Zero, Garjia (05947-284-132/284-134/www.corbetthideaway.com). $$-$$$.*

Kosi River.

Top & middle: Hideaway River Lodge. Bottom: Corbett Hideaway.

Corbett Hideaway is one of the oldest and most well-maintained resorts around the periphery of the Corbett National Park, sprawled over extensive grounds on the bank of the River Kosi. Fifty-two luxury air-conditioned cottages are scattered among manicured lawns. The saffron-earthy look of the older cottages, all with verandas and cosy sitting areas with fireplaces, makes them more atmospheric (and expensive), and they have more space and privacy than the newer ones. They may suffer from more dampness in the wet season, though, as they are closer to the river. This resort probably offers the widest range of food and drink in the region, with facilities ranging from a grill restaurant (Jim's Grill) to a multi-cuisine restaurant (Gurney House), which includes a lovely alfresco dining space overlooking the Kosi. Service is laid-back and tends to be slow, so patience will help make your jungle trip a pleasant one.

Hideaway River Lodge

10km from Durgadevi gate *Jamun, Corbett National Park (05947-284-132, 284134/www.corbetthideaway.com). $$$.*

Deep within the forest, a tiger's roar could be your morning wakeup call at the Hideaway River Lodge. Run by the Mahseer Conservation Project, the lodge has a splendid location. For the serious wildlife enthusiast, this property – with no air-conditioning, electricity or cell phone signal – is perfect. It is on the periphery of the reserve forest, and close to the Ramganga river. Accommodation is in the form of thatched-roof 'cottage tents', each with attached bath and private veranda, protected with solar-powered electric fencing. There's running hot water (at fixed times), 'fine dining' (by forest standards), and the staff are a genial lot who provide excellent service. The Hideaway overlooks dense grasslands, and morning and evening safaris are organised by both Jeep and elephant.

Jim's Jungle Retreat

2km from Jhirna gate *Dhela village (93597-92915/011-6563-7980/www.jimsjungleretreat.com). $$$. No credit cards.*

This property has a superb location on the periphery of the reserve forest area, far from other resorts. Guests stay either in thatched cottages with private porches or spacious air-conditioned tents with attached baths – it's all quite simple, but comfortable. Each morning, the Retreat arranges great nature walks and every evening there's a showing of a video on local conservation efforts. There's a pool to keep your afternoon occupied – and cool. This resort's best asset is the highly personalised service provided by the excellent team, particularly the friendly manager and resident naturalist.

Factfile

When to go

The best time to visit Corbett is between 17 November and 15 June. Most of the park is closed between 16 June and 14 November, when monsoon rains cause river levels to rise and roads to get washed away.

Getting there

Delhi is 300km (186 miles) and around a seven-hour drive away. There's also a convenient overnight train from Delhi to Ramnagar (the nearest railway station and town). Ramnagar is 2km from the Amdanda gate and 51km (32 miles) from the Dhikala Gate.

For more on travel within India, *see p378* **Navigating India**.

Getting around

Either drive your own vehicle or hire a private taxi or Jeep in Ramnagar to travel inside the park. No fuel is available beyond Ramnagar.

Tourist information

The main park reception office is at Ramnagar (05947-251-489/www.corbettnationalpark.in). It is open 8.30am-1pm, 2-4pm daily from December to May, and 10am-noon, 1-5pm daily from June to November.

The office at the Jhirna Gate is open all year round from 10am to 4pm daily. There's also a visitor's centre at the park's Dhangarhi Gate, 18km (11 miles) from Ramnagar.

Tips

- **Corbett is a popular park** as it is easily accessible from Delhi. Book safaris and accommodation well in advance, or risk being disappointed.

- **When out on an early morning safari**, the open Jeeps can get pretty cold and windy, so go prepared with plenty of blankets and warm clothing.

- **Don't expect mobile phones to work** in most places and internet facilities are rare.

- **Carry cash** as very few places accept credit cards.

- **All accommodation** without exception (and this includes the upmarket Corbett Hideaway) have a problem with dampness, in varying degrees. This is the nature of the habitat.

Periyar National Park

Jungle retreat of the elusive Bengal tiger; home to many other species.

In the Cardamom Hills of Kerala state, a large, dense jungle is home to the Periyar National Park. Within this landscape of undulating hills, rivers, lakes, coarse elephant grass and lofty tropical trees lives India's most elusive and endangered animal, the Bengal tiger. At night, the bars at the hotels in the nearby village of Thekkady abound with stories of half-glimpsed whiskers and enormous footprints, but the truth is that tiger sightings are extremely rare these days. But if you are willing to endure a longish hike and some rough terrain in this superb wilderness, you're likely to spot at least a herd of wild elephants, if not bison, giant Malabar squirrels and perhaps a Malabar grey hornbill (Periyar is also home to 320 species of bird).

Periyar's wildlife conservation is conducted by local people. This community-based eco-tourism means that tourists get the benefit of local expertise, and the valuable revenue earned is ploughed back into the community. Most of the trackers and guides you will encounter once made their living through illegal operations in the forests. Today, they are an integral part of its conservation, and its chief protectors.

Though most activity in this thickly wooded area is centred around the jungle and the animals, Thekkady is also famed for its spices, and some spice plantations are open to the public, allowing visitors to experience the melding of the scents of peppermint, cardamom, nutmeg and cinnamon with the darker smells of the forest.

Clockwise from top: bullock cart ride; Elephant Camp; Periyar National Park (3).

Explore

Kumily is the nearest town to the park; from here it's four kilometres to the village of **Thekkady** and the entrance to Periyar National Park. Half of the 777-square-kilometre (300-square-mile) protected forest area here forms the Periyar National Park. It's a fantastic park, but not one to visit if your priority is to spot tigers, because chances are that you won't. But for tranquillity of setting and gorgeous natural environment, it's hard to beat. Outdoor enthusiasts will love the Periyar Tiger Trail, a hike through deep woods with excellent trackers.

The area around Thekkady produces excellent cardamom, cinnamon, pepper, nutmeg and cloves, and spice plantations are its other draw. There are several that are open to visitors, but only a few will also sell you what they grow. A polite and knowledgeable guide will accompany you and point out various herbs, spices and medicinal plants, patiently explaining what each one does. Most hotels organise spice garden visits. The area around Kumily (especially near Spring Valley) has several plantations, including Deepa World (www.deepaspiceworld.com) and Abraham's spice garden (www.abrahamspice.com).

THEKKADY

Park activities are run by the office of the Deputy Director (Project Tiger), Periyar Tiger Reserve (04869-222-027, www.periyartigerreserve.org). Admission to the park must be paid each time you enter (adults Rs 25 Indians, Rs 300 others; under-12s Rs 5 Indians, Rs 105 others). Activities cost extra, and no credit cards are accepted.

Bamboo Rafting

Trip 8am-5pm daily. Cost Rs 1,000 per person, minimum 10 people. No credit cards.

Riding on what at first glance appears to be a flimsy craft along waters in a wildllife-filled jungle may not sound sane. But, heading out into the morning mist, you'll discover it's not only safe, but a wonderful way to experience the jungle. The trip is an all-day activity. Setting off from the forest department office in Thekkady at 8am, four guides and an armed guard lead the group into the forest, past swarms of butterflies and insects, to Periyar Lake. The guides are almost all drawn from two relocated tribes in the area and they are intimately familiar with the jungle and animals. The rafting lasts for three hours; because it's quiet, the chances of spotting a herd of bison or elephants stopping by the banks to drink are higher than if you were on a motor boat.

Boat Rides

Kerala Tourism Development Corporation boat: upper deck Rs 150, lower deck Rs 75. Forest department boat: upper deck Rs 75, lower deck Rs 40. First ride 7am. Last ride 4pm. No credit cards.

Boat rides last about two hours, and given their generally raucous nature, it's unlikely that you'll spot anything more than a stray bison too well fed to clamber up the embankment and disappear into the forest. Because the animals are most likely to be spotted early in the morning, the first ride is the

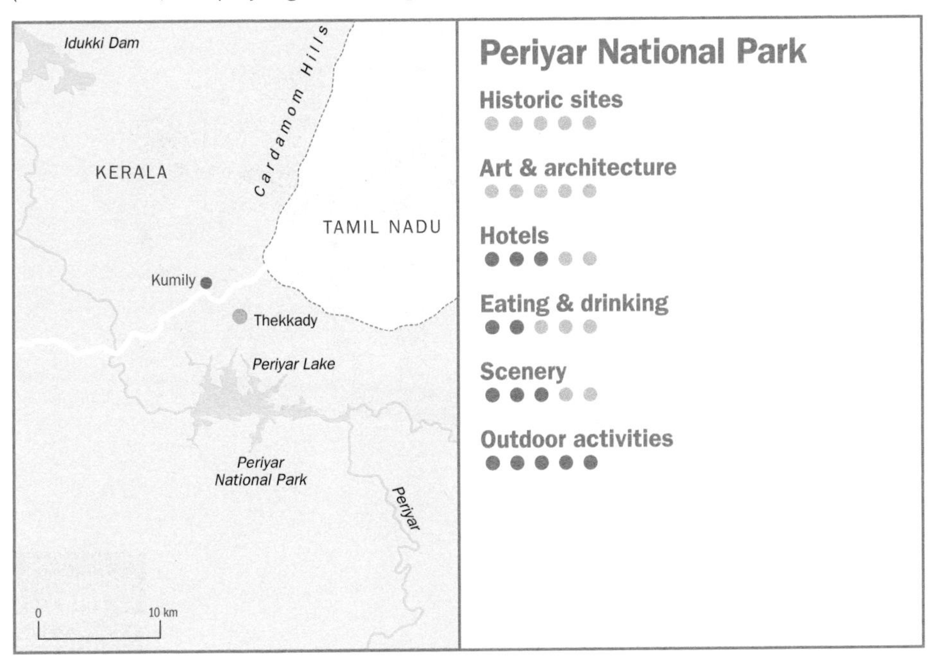

best one to take. To avoid long waits, ask your hotel to book tickets in advance. At the time of writing boat rides had been cancelled due to a tragic accident in 2009, but are likely to restart with better facilities and safety standards in 2010.

Border Hiking

Hike 8am-5pm daily. Cost Rs 750 per person, minimum 5 people. No credit cards.

This hike is fashioned to inform visitors about conservation, rather than simply being an opportunity for wildlife spotting: chances are you'll only see bison and elephants. A group of at least five walkers is required and – like bamboo rafting – the border hike is an all-day activity, starting at the forest department office at 8am. Two guides and an armed guard accompany the party into the jungle; the group will later climb hills, reaching heights of up to 1,300m (4,265ft). The guides carry simple vegetarian food. They're friendly and chatty, and dispense useful information and advice. For instance, they advise wearing specially fashioned 'leech socks' and will get you to dust your feet with tobacco powder to keep the hungry creatures at bay.

Bullock Cart Rides

Rides 6am-9am daily. Cost Rs 750 per person, minimum 5 people. No credit cards.

Three-hour bullock cart rides are a great way to intersperse all that jungle walking with some down time. A cart takes you into the area's villages, giving you the chance to see how the people of Thekkady live, and to interact with them. Your accompanying guide will be from a group of former sandalwood smugglers, now reformed. This resourceful gent will explain farming techniques and the history of the place, and will gladly answer questions. He also brings along breakfast for all. Proceeds from the rides go towards efforts at rehabilitating the local communities.

Periyar Tiger Trail

04869-224-571. Only for fit walkers, aged 15-65. No credit cards.

Periyar's best experience. The tiger trail, which takes either two days (one night, Rs 3,000) or three days (two nights, Rs 5,000), allows visitors to track the path of the tiger. If you are really lucky you might even spot one of the 40 or so that are said to live here, though, realistically, the chances of this happening are slim to none. However, visitors are likely to encounter Nilgiri langurs, lion-tailed macaques, barking deer and some of the 1,966 species of flower that grow here. The two-day trek begins at 9am, and ends just after noon the next day, taking hikers through 30km (19 miles) of dense jungle. Accommodation is in tents. Five guides and two guards accompany the group; they carry guns, as well as walkie-talkies, all the camping gear and food supplies. Drawn from the local pool of reformed poachers, they have fascinating tales to tell of their past lives of hunting and hiding from the law.

Elephant Camp

Thekkady Elephant Camp, Anavachal Road (04869-322-444/www.elephantcamp.in). Open 8am-6.30pm daily. 30min ride & photos Rs 350; 1hr ride with an elephant bath & photos Rs 1,000; 1.5hr ride with timber hauling, elephant bath & photos Rs 1,500. No credit cards.

On the main street outside the reserve you are likely to see more domesticated elephants than motorised transport. Apart from serving as timber-movers, elephants – being sacred to Hindus – are raised and housed in almost all of Kerala's temples. Head to the Elephant Camp in Periyar to spend a generous amount of time with these splendid animals. The camp offers a range of activities, from half-hour rides to feeding, bathing and watching them haul timber. The well-trained beasts wait patiently as you climb on their backs and pose for pictures, and will bid goodbye by benevolently patting you on the head with their trunk.

Jungle Treks

Treks 7-10am, 10am-1pm, 12-5pm daily. Rs 100 per person, minimum 5 people. No credit cards.

If you don't want to spend a whole day in the jungle but would still like to explore, three-hour treks are ideal. You will be accompanied by a trained guide, and though the chances of spotting any of the larger animals on your four-kilometre walk are slim, it can still be a very instructional and memorable experience; ask your guide to take you up one of the hills, as the views are spectacular.

Eat & Stay

Most of the hotels in Thekkady are on the main stretch of road leading to the reserve from Kumily. They generally don't have air-conditioning and at most times of year you'll not need it; in winter temperatures dip to around 10°C. All hotels have in-house restaurants where guests, and those staying elsewhere, can eat. Eating choices are limited to the hotels; all the places reviewed below offer good meals. Hotels make all arrangements for visits to the jungle or villages nearby.

Ambadi

Thekkady (04869-222-193/www.hotelambadi.com). $. No AmEx.

Despite being the oldest – Ambadi opened for business in 1982 – this is one of the better-maintained properties in Thekkady. It was designed by Laurie Baker, known for his eco-conscious Kerala-style homes, which use locally procured stone, tiles and brick. The hotel has 43 well-equipped rooms (deluxe rooms have huge bathrooms and a balcony). To add to its inherent charm, it's one of the cheapest hotels in the area, and excellent value for money. But while the rooms are great, the service doesn't always match: the in-house restaurant serves great meals at decent prices, but service is slow.

The Elephant Court

Thekkady (04869-224-697/www.theelephantcourt.com). $$$. No AmEx.

After Spice Village (*see p315*), this is easily the most luxurious and well-maintained resort in Thekkady. Once past its imposing façade with large columns, you'll find the patio rooms – the hotel has 52 – are spacious and inviting. Each has a wooden balcony of the kind unique to Kerala, large closet spaces and spotless bathrooms. Outside is a large

Clockwise from top left: Muthoot Cardamom County; Deepa World; Spice Village; the Elephant Court.

curvy pool and overlooking it is Pebbles, a Mediterranean restaurant. Service is good and staff usually go out of their way to secure you that hard-to-get ticket for a bamboo rafting trip or find you a guide.

KTDC Lake Palace

Thekkady (04869-223-887/www.lakepalacethe kkady.com). $$$-$$$$. No AmEx.

The only way you can stay inside the park is if you book into the Tourism Board's KTDC Lake Palace, a former royal hunting lodge that is superbly located on Periyar Lake, and can only be reached by boat. Lovely verandas, old-world charm and utter tranquillity greet you, but don't expect too much in terms of services and amenities. The six rooms are very charming, with period furniture and great views. They get booked up early, though, especially in high season. If you're really keen to stay here, you need to plan ahead.

Muthoot Cardamom County

Thekkady (04869-224-501/www.muthoothotels.com). $$. No AmEx.

Cardamom County has largeish rooms, a pleasant pool and an in-house Ayurveda centre. The hotel doesn't have large gardens, but makes up for it by the fact that rooms are perched one on top of the other, allowing excellent views of the surrounding greenery. Standard doubles have glass doors that open out to the courtyard. Rooms don't have air-conditioning, but they are comfortable; service and food is good.

Spice Village

Thekkady (04869-224-514/www.cghearth.com). $$.

Set on a ridge, this resort recreates a traditional Kerala village with great attention to detail. There are no fans or TVs and each of the 52 huts uses elephant grass as roofing. The cottages are all spacious and cosy, and the grounds are filled with fragrant plants. All the vegetables you eat are grown in-house. The Tiffin Room's expansive buffet usually contains fresh river fish, wild chicken, roast mutton, curries, local 'red' rice, *appams* (bowl-shaped rice-batter crêpes) and stew (peppery, coconut-based broth with veggies). Meals are usually preceded by a cooking demonstration. Follow with a visit to the Woodhouse Bar, it's walls covered with items of memorabilia. The long, narrow veranda is perfect for listening to the sounds of the jungle while sipping a drink.

Treetop

Thekkady (04869-223-286/www.hoteltreetop.com). $$.

While Treetop offers just about all the services that the other hotels in the area do, it has one thing that the rest don't – it is closest to park gates. While this may not seem significant, considering that the stretch on which these hotels sit is barely a kilometre long, many find staying here is a wise choice. Because the reserve is popular, and because getting on the boats or into the jungle require formalities, cars line up waiting to get in before the gates are open. If you're staying at Treetop, all you have to do is step outside your hotel. Rooms are bright and the service is perfectly competent.

Wildernest

Thekkady (04869-224-030/www.wildernest-kerala.com). $$. No AmEx.

With just ten rooms, this is one of the smallest hotels in Thekkady. It's not luxurious, and the rooms, though large, are quite sparsely furnished. However, if you're looking for a good budget option, this is one of two hotels to consider – the other being Ambadi (*see p313*). Each room here is different, and most have either a small garden or a balcony overlooking the dense bamboo groves nearby. Kuruvees, the company that owns this hotel, places great emphasis on conservation, and the hotel is built entirely of local stone.

Factfile

When to go

The winter months, between October and January, are the best time to visit.

Getting there

The two closest airports to Thekkady are in Madurai (137km/85 miles) and Kochi (190km/118 miles). Hotels can arrange for transport to and from the airport.

For more on travel, *see p378* **Navigating India**.

Getting around

Because Thekkady is in a wooded and remote part of Kerala, you'll do well to retain the services of the taxi that brings you here. However, if you intend to stay for longer than three days, you can also ask your hotel to arrange for transport to be available for you for the duration of your visit.

Tourist information

All park-related information can be obtained from Deputy Director (Project Tiger), Periyar Tiger Reserve, Thekkady (04869-222-027, www.periyartigerreserve.org). The office is open 8am-5pm daily.

Tips

- The area is heavy with mosquitoes, so take plenty of repellent and apply it well before the sun sets.

- Night temperatures tend to dip to 10°C, so pack warm clothes.

- Though you are not required to tip the guides, it is a good idea to do so at the end of hikes, rides or raft trips, as they invariably go well beyond the call of duty.

Alluring Escapes

Clockwise from top: Querim Beach from Fort Tiracol; Palolem; Anjuna Beach; Vagator; watching a bullfight at Benaulim.

Stunning beaches and a laid-back allure.

Goa is different. Here, the familiar subcontinental bustle and jostling give way to a measured languor and broad smiles. This is where the crowded cityscapes of urban India are replaced by coconut groves, and diesel fumes fade under the perfume of cashew blossoms and ripening mango. The blare of traffic yields to birdsong and the insistent whisper of sea on sand. Goa's landscape is remarkably varied, ranging from the thickly forested Western Ghats mountain range through lush river valleys to the famous beaches.

The former Portuguese colony (it only became part of India in 1961, 14 years after the rest of the nation achieved independence from the British) is India's smallest state by a considerable margin, but its charms are anything but pocket-sized, and exert a powerful allure. It retains much of a distinctive post-colonial Portuguese character. And though it is no longer the untouched paradise discovered by the flower children of the 1960s – packed as it is with India's burgeoning middle class, British package tourists and nu-rave neo-hippies – Goa remains pleasantly peaceful and relatively unspoiled, at least away from the main tourist areas. To its Indian visitors Goa is famously summed up by the Konkai word *sussegad*, meaning laid-back or relaxed.

Explore

Goa can be divided into **North** and **South Goa**, with the capital **Panjim** and **Old Goa** in the middle, both on the left bank of the River Mandovi. In the Mandovi river near Old Goa are three lovely islands: **Chorao**, **Vashi** and **Diwar**; they are connected to the mainland only by old-fashioned ferries that transport people and vehicles. The settlements and villages on the islands still have much of the essence of old Goa about them.

Chorao is also home to the small Salim Ali Bird Sanctuary, which is within the mangroves and best explored in a dugout. Nature reserves and sanctuaries cover a fifth of Goa's land, large stretches of which are unspoiled jungle filled with a wide variety of wildlife. Although the state's sanctuaries are open to visitors, most lack basic tourist facilities like trained guides or visitor centres. Cotigoa Wildlife Sanctuary (along the NH-17 to Karwar) is perhaps the only other accessible one, 20 minutes from Palolem. Its mixed deciduous forests are home to gaur, langur and macaque monkeys, wild boar, porcupines, leopards, jackals and a few sloth bears.

NORTH GOA

Goan tourism began here, at the far end of what was once a pristine 6.5-kilometre stretch of broad golden sand lined with rolling dunes and backed by coconut plantations. Long before strict coastal development laws were enacted, a sprawling five-star hotel complex was built amid the crumbling ruins of a 17th-century Portuguese fortress. The Fort Aguada Beach Resort threw open the floodgates to mass tourism when it started operations in 1972. By the late '90s the beach had become lined elbow-to-elbow with beach shacks and a warren of hotels, shopping centres, pubs, restaurants and supermarkets. The plateau on the **Sinquerim headland**, near the modern, squat Aguada Lighthouse, offers one of the best ocean views in Goa, with the wide mouths of the **Mandovi** and **Zuari rivers** on one side, and glorious beach on the other. However, since it was grounded in 2000, the ore-carrier ship *River Princess* has cut the beach to a tiny sliver of its former self because of the erosion it has caused.

Candolim, once a deserted expanse of banyan trees and soaring palm trees, is now mass tourism's ground zero in Goa. It's a maze of lanes and by-ways lined with hundreds of guesthouses, shops and restaurants and choked with traffic in peak season.

Long before tourists washed up on Goan shores, **Calangute** was a seafront idyll for genteel Goan families from all over North Goa and Panjim. Through the hot summer months of April and May, they retired here to simple rented accommodation and borrowed villas. All that is long gone: today Calangute's broad sands are as golden as ever

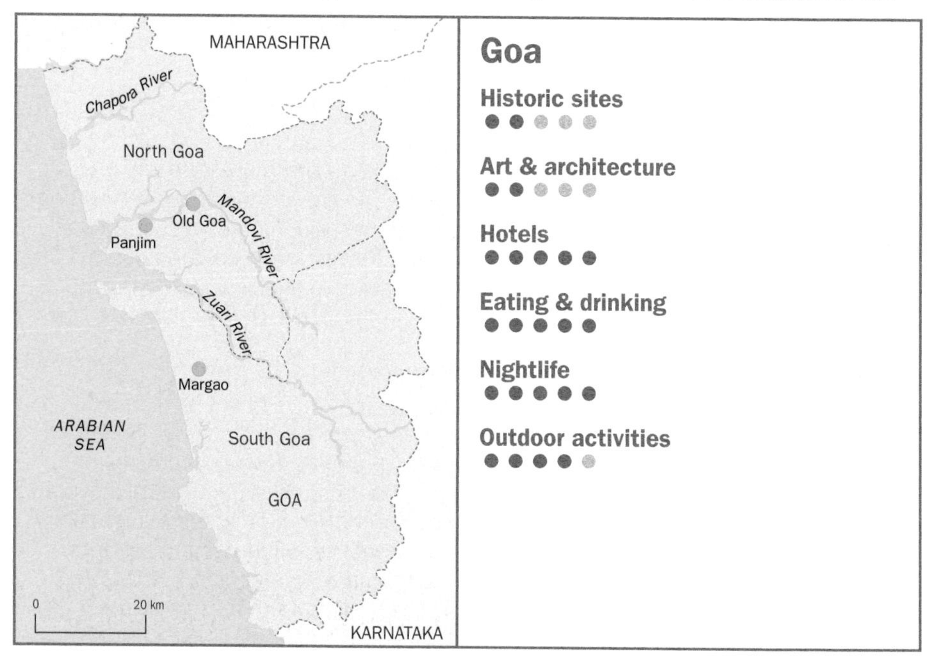

but they've been swamped, with thousands of Indian visitors rubbing elbows with Scandinavians and Brits, and a beach lined with paragliders, jet skis, speedboats and tightly packed sunbeds.

"Baga is now one of the most famous party hotspots in India, with lots of bars."

It's hard to tell where Calangute ends and **Baga** begins. Baga is now one of the most famous party hotspots in India, with lots of bars. Slightly quieter is Baga Creek, across a concrete bridge, where a long line of some of Goa's best restaurants operate out of converted old houses just metres from the riverbank. Like Calangute, Baga is nightlife central: the beach at both is crammed with shacks serving drinks until late, and the streets behind are lined with hole-in-the wall bars.

Anjuna is where the first tie-dyed '60s refugees headed for in search of freedom, sunshine and cheap drugs. But it is also home to writers and artists who simply like the vibe. Anjuna's famous flea market has changed since the early hippie days of the 1960s and '70s, when hashish was sold just like today's vendors hawk cheap T-shirts and wooden knick-knacks. Now tens of thousands converge on the flea market every Wednesday from October to April. The market sprawls over a piece of land by the beach, with hundreds of stalls selling everything from tie-dye bikinis to chillums, sitars and cushion covers.

As Anjuna steadily turns more mainstream and family-friendly, the hard core of trance music pilgrims, dropouts and committed stoners has shifted further north to the beaches and headland in the shadow of the rugged **Chapora Fort**. The fortress is crumbling to bits and overrun with vegetation, but offers magnificent views, with the Arabian Sea on one side and the harbour at the mouth of the Chapora river on the other. All this makes Chapora Fort one of the best sunset spots in Goa. In recent years, the winding palm-lined lanes of **Chapora** and the beaches of 'little' and 'big' **Vagator** have become home to a hard-edged subculture of Russians, Israelis, Italians and other Europeans. The atmosphere can be a little off-putting, with hundreds of foreigners jammed into pocket-size tavernas and chai shops, openly smoking chillums under the watchful presence of slightly menacing local minders.

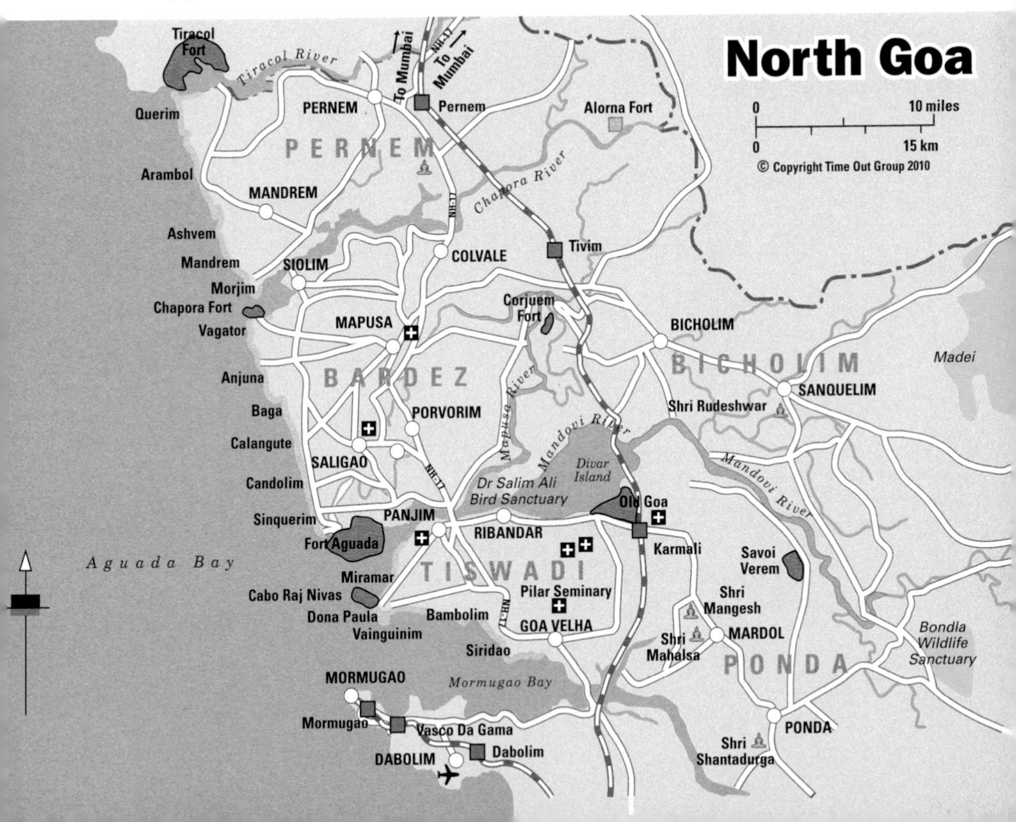

Across the long Siolim Bridge into Pernem district, the landscape shifts into deep countryside. Mass tourism didn't make it here until the bridge was built in 2002, although a few travellers made it to the strip of beach starting at **Morjim** and stretching north into **Ashvem**. But now that it's just a brisk 20-minute drive from Vagator, more development is on the way. The only thing holding back the hordes is the breeding habits of the protected migratory Olive Ridley turtles.

Mandrem still offers the secluded beach experience that first brought travellers to Goa, with friendly locals, communal football games on the beach and total quiet by late evening. Many of the kilometres of broad sand heading north towards Arambol are bound by a narrow river running parallel to the ocean, and there is little development here. **Arambol** is the largest coastal village in Pernem district, with a wide beach clustered with shacks. These days it can host several thousand visitors a day in high season (November to March) and has become part of the well-beaten track that so many once came here to avoid.

From Arambol, the coastal road cuts across country, climbing to the top of a rugged plateau and then cutting through jungle back towards the shoreline and the pristine Tiracol river. **Keri** (Querim), a long sliver of shining sand, is untouched by development. You can spend some hours here without seeing another soul. High on the headland, **Fort Tiracol** (now a heritage hotel, *see* p343) stands sentinel over Goa's northern border.

Finally, a half-hour drive inland from the beaches is **Mapusa**, the administrative and transport hub of North Goa. Mapusa can safely be avoided, although the Friday market is lively.

Temples north of Ponda

By the turn of the 17th century the Portuguese conquistadors had destroyed every Hindu temple they could find in Goa, with one particularly zealous officer, Diogo Rodrigues, tearing down over 280 temples across 58 villages in 1567. However, some precious idols were spirited away by loyal devotees, who stole across the rivers towards Ponda, a redoubt that didn't come under Portuguese rule until the 18th century, by which time their religious fervour had waned. There, nestled in thickly forested valleys, new temples went up to house the idols, with the result that, today, Ponda is home to some of Goa's most important Hindu sites.

The most famous of all of Ponda's temples is Shri Mangesh Temple (Priol, north-west of Ponda on the NH-4, open 7am-6.30pm daily). Its resident *shivalingam* (a clay phallus that represents Lord Shiva) is housed in a temple of Mughal type domes, baroque flourishes adapted from Goa churches, and an impressive octagonal tower that can be seen for miles.

A few miles away is the Shri Mahalsa Temple (Mardol, north-west of Ponda off NH-4, open 7am-6pm daily). At the end of a marble courtyard, there's a beautiful water tank fed by a freshwater spring, lined with coconut palms and traditional ghats used for ritual bathing (and doing the laundry).

South-west of Ponda, right on the edge of unbroken jungle is Goa's largest temple devoted to Shri Shantadurga, the goddess of Peace (an incarnation of Durga, Lord Shiva's consort), who remains one of Goa's most popular deities and is even venerated by Catholics. The temple was built by the Marathas in 1738, and is influenced by Goan church architecture.

"The architecture in Panjim is low rise, Latinate, with plenty of green spaces, and the riverfront setting ensures a pleasant and breezy atmosphere."

But if you can only visit one temple in Goa, it should be Tambdi Surla (11km north of Molem, 30 mins from Ponda along NH-4, open 6am-4pm daily), a 12th-century survivor that escaped the Portuguese because of its remote, near inaccessible location. Hewn from massive slabs of basalt that must have been carried across the mountains from the Deccan region beyond, it's a stunning and mysterious relic of the Kadamba era, the dynasty that ruled Goa until the 14th century.

PANJIM

Panjim retains an old-fashioned character that feels quite different from any other state capital in India. The architecture is low rise, Latinate, with plenty of green spaces, and the riverfront setting ensures a pleasant and breezy atmosphere. By the 1820s, Panjim had become the bustling administrative centre of the Portuguese Estado da India. Beautiful buildings from this period still crowd many of the old neighbourhoods and give the city its character. In recent years many of these architectural jewels have been restored.

Panjim is best explored on foot. Wander along the Mandovi riverfront; the riverfront road links the district of Sao Tome to the rest of Panjim,

Grandee designs

Just like their fellow Iberians, the Spanish colonists in Latin America, the Portuguese administrators of Goa managed their territorial holdings on the lines of the ancient Roman system of latifunda – huge landed estates parcelled out to trusted supporters of the regime. Important native collaborators, staunch mestiço allies, and loyal compatriots who wished to settle permanently were granted vast estates that functioned as fiefdoms, with all authority ceded directly by fiat. The hybrid aristocrats, called grandees, served as an instant class of intermediary rulers, and as the Portuguese court's interest switched to its colonies in Brazil, they steadily gained in power and influence even beyond Goa to the rest of the Lusophone colonial holdings.

In South Goa, particularly in the rich agricultural lands of Salcete, this ambitious cadre of landowners celebrated their flourishing fortunes by constructing grand, luxurious mansions. The front rooms were designed for spectacular entertainment on the European model, with ballrooms and raised stages for orchestras, and imposing dining rooms for lavish banquets and receptions that were imagined to be exactly like those in faraway Europe.

After Goa's liberation in 1961, land reform took back these vast agricultural holdings and dismantled the feudal system that supported the grand estates. Many of the palacios survive in various states of disrepair, with absentee owners now in Portugal or Canada. Of the surviving grand mansions, the gorgeous Figueiredo Mansion (House No. 376, Loutolim, donations accepted), a 15-minute drive from Margao, is the most beautiful home open to visitors. In 2008, the formidable and aristocratic Maria de Lourdes de Albuquerque inherited this magnificent, period-perfect 19th-century mansion built by her grandfather in a particularly fortunate location in South Goa. The house retains much of its former grandeur, with magnificent collections of antique furniture and porcelain. One wing, the Heritage Inn (0832-277-7028), is open for paying guests. Or you can sample a taste of the grandee way of life with a full Indo-Portuguese meal (minimum six people) in the formal dining room, complete with liveried service and century-old family crockery.

More imposing still is the spectacular Menezes-Braganza House in old Chandor (25 minutes drive from Margao, 0832-278-4201, open 10am-5pm Mon-Sat, admission Rs 100). Here gargantuan chandeliers dominate an opulent salon with marble walls and floors, filled with museum-quality antique furniture and Chinese porcelain. The east wing contains a famous private chapel, containing a sacred relic – a sliver of St Francis Xavier's fingernail, encrusted with gold and diamonds.

A great view into the ethos that produced these mansions is available at the 200-year-old Palacio do Deao (30 minutes' drive from Margao, opposite Holy Cross Church, Quepem, 98231-75639, www.palaciododeao.com, open 10am-6pm Mon-Sat, admission free), on the banks of the Kushavati River in Quepem. Built by a clergyman from Braga, Portugal, it lay in ruins until a young Goan couple, Celia and Ruben Vasco da Gama, agreed to take over its upkeep from Church authorities. Celia and Ruben keep the house open to visitors, and the highlight of each visit is a traditional South Goan meal in an attractive covered courtyard behind the house (approx Rs 250 per head).

A great place to learn more about these houses and the unique, distinctively hybrid Indo-Portuguese architecture is the excellent Houses of Goa Museum (Opposite Nisha's Play School, Torda, Salvador-do-Mundo, 0832-241-0711, Open 10am-7.30pm Tue-Sun, admission Rs 100), established by one of India's most prominent architects, Gerard da Cunha.

and then to Campal and Miramar. There's a pleasant waterfront walkway that runs from the quayside, where numerous tourist charters are berthed. Near here, the waterfront is dominated by Idalcao Palace, also known as the Old Secretariat. This mansion was built as a summer palace in the early 16th century by the Bijapuri ruler Yusuf Adil Shah. Plans are under way to convert it into a museum.

Panjim's commercial centre is dominated by the baroque Church of Our Lady of Immaculate Conception, near the municipal garden. The large and impressive church, sitting at the top of criss-crossing whitewashed stairways, has become an instantly recognisable symbol of the city. The church looms over the road leading to Altinho Hill, with the Garcia da Orta Garden on one side. Along the Dada Vaidya Road, which hugs Altinho Hill, is the Mahalaxmi Temple, the first Hindu temple to be allowed in the Portuguese territory after the Inquisition.

In Panjim's old Latin Quarter and heritage district, Fontainhas, a labyrinth of ochre and magenta buildings, pocket-sized balconies and tiny plazas, strict development laws now preserve hidden gems. Nearby, the landmark San Sebastian Chapel houses the large wooden crucifix that once towered over bloody deliberations of the Inquisition in Old Goa. The collection of altars and paintings here is one of the best in Goa, gathered by refugees who fled the plagues that decimated Old Goa throughout the 17th century. On the other side of the concrete walkway that crosses the Ourem river, a short walk leads to the ultimately missable Goa State Archaeological Museum.

A leisurely amble through Fontainhas towards the Mandovi riverfront brings you to the delightful 31st January Road (named for the date on which the Portuguese republican revolution erupted in 1910), which is lined on both sides with colonial-era buildings, many adorned with public shrines. In the evenings, these icons of Mary and ornate crosses are often visited by groups of hymn-singing supplicants, a village tradition that has survived the shift to the city.

Church of Our Lady of Immaculate Conception

Church Square, Emidio Gracia Road, near Municipal Garden. Open 7am-6pm daily.

This church was a symbol of Portuguese power when it was built in 1541, with gilded and ornate interiors; it was later expanded many times. It hosts one of the most popular Goan feasts in December, the Feast of Our Lady of the Immaculate Conception, when the nearby square is lit with candles.

OLD GOA

The original colonial capital, now known simply as Old Goa, is an area of empty avenues and ancient churches. It's a few kilometres from modern Panjim, linked by a centuries-old road that passes through some of the state's earliest colonial architecture at Ribandar.
A European-style metropolis whose grand architecture reflected its tremendous power, wealth and prestige, it was known as Goa Dourada or 'Golden Goa', and made a fortune in spices and slaves. Dominating the centre were churches, cathedrals, monasteries and convents built by Franciscans, Dominicans, Augustinians and other religious orders. Plague outbreaks in the 17th century forced residents to flee. Today, only the soaring architecture remains.

"The last of the Medicis, Cosimo II, the Grand Duke of Tuscany, financed the opulent altar that now holds the remains of St Francis Xavier."

On the crest of the city's tallest hill sits the Chapel of Our Lady of the Mount, one of the earliest Portuguese buildings in Goa. The early 16th-century chapel has been restored and hosts a classical music festival every March. Come here at sunrise to enjoy a magical view of slanting sunlight slowly illuminating the churches' whitewashed façades in the distance below.

Perched on the slope of Holy Hill is the fortress-like Convent of Santa Monica, the largest convent in Asia. Access is restricted, but if you ask nicely, you might be allowed into the private chapel at the rear. One wing, open to the public, houses the Museum of Christian Art (0832-228-5299, open 9am-5.30pm daily), a beautiful if indifferently curated collection of intricate chalices and other ritual objects, and some Christian paintings.

Nearby is the Royal Chapel of St Anthony, another mid 16th-century church that fell into decrepitude and was restored in 1960. Just behind is the detailed Chapel of Our Lady of the Rosary, one of the first buildings erected by the Portuguese in Goa. Down the hill along Rua das Naus de Omurz is the World Heritage Site precinct of the Basilica of Bom Jesus, Goa's most famous church and the resting place of the body of St Francis Xavier, the Jesuit missionary to Goa. Once each decade, his body is put on public display at Se Cathedral (open 7am-6pm daily), across the central square from the basilica. This impressive cathedral remains the largest church in Asia, despite one of its towers collapsing after being struck by lightning in the 18th century. Its typically Corinthian interior includes a barrel-vaulted ceiling, two long side aisles and a masterpiece of a gilded altar.

Across the road, towards the riverfront from Se Cathedral, sits another baroque architectural jewel, the Convent and Church of St Cajetan. Further on, new arrivals to the colonies first set eyes on the fabled Goa Dourada through the granite-faced, dilapidated Arch of the Viceroys. This stone gateway was built by the great grandson of Vasco de Gama, who became viceroy of Goa at the end of the 16th century and promptly erected this tribute to his ancestor. It was the main entrance to the city and the symbolic spot where Portuguese supreme commanders of the Indies handed responsibility to their successors.

Basilica of Bom Jesus

Rua das Naus de Ormuz, opposite Se Cathedral. Open 7am-6pm daily.

Goa's most well-known church, and one whose façade and layout show no local influences – it has a clearly Italianate look. The last of the Medicis, Cosimo II, the Grand Duke of Tuscany, financed the opulent altar that now holds the body of St Francis Xavier. It was sculpted by the Florentine artist Giovanni Batista Foggini, who took ten years to carve the intricate scenes from Xavier's life. Inside, in a silver casket, lies the 'incorruptible' body, whose face can be seen through a glass window. The body has become an object of pilgrimage that draws hundreds of thousands to a solemn exposition held once every decade, the last one in 2004.

Convent & Church of St Cajetan

Rua Direita, near the Arch of the Viceroys. Open 7am-6pm daily.

Built by a team of Italian friars dispatched to India by Pope Urban III, this domed church is shaped like a Greek cross and supposedly modelled on St Peter's in Rome. The altar is an exuberant work of art, with angels and cherubs rising to a gilded crown. In the crypt, sealed caskets hold the remains of senior Portuguese officials who never made it home.

SOUTH GOA

The original charms of India's sunshine state are better showcased in South Goa. It's bigger, less developed, with far more imposing colonial architecture, and the best beaches. For 24 kilometres (15 miles) uninterrupted white sands stretch from Cansaulim to Mobor. In the interior are the jungles of Cotigoa Wildlife Sanctuary (20 minutes from Palolem), and the lush agricultural hinterland of Quepem. Rich farmlands and a billion dollars in annual mining income have so far kept South Goa from racing to replicate North Goa's party strip, and luckily the south has so far been relatively untouched by mass-market package tourism.

However, the South Goa's idyllic and unspoiled character is increasingly coming under threat from proposed development. Construction companies and real estate entrepreneurs have snapped up stretches of land all the way down to the Karnataka border, and though it will probably take years to become as hectic as the north, large-scale development looks inevitable. But until that happens, much of the south offers a glimpse of older Goa, where farmers work the same fields and orchards that their families have tended for centuries. Spectacular rococo and baroque churches gleam with whitewash and sit amid emerald paddy fields. Old colonial-era houses are still meticulously maintained, and locals retain the gracious culture and beautiful manners that still count in Goa.

"South of Mobor, a winding coastal road seesaws through valleys cut with rice terraces and coconut and areca nut palm groves."

The hidden cove-like beach of **Bogmalo** is popular with visitors who want no-frills sun and sand holidays without the crowds of the north strip. Goans also come here to party when other beaches get too crowded, and there's a long line of bars trailing up Bogmalo Beach. South of Bogmalo, the beach turns to rock for a few kilometres before descending on to a 15-kilometre (nine-mile) stretch of white sand beach running from **Cansaulim** to **Betalbatim** and beyond through **Utorda** and **Majorda**. Much like North Goa, the entire beach is lined with palm-thatched restaurant-bar beach shacks, backed by thick coconut palms yielding to acres of well-tended paddy fields.

Like Calangute, its spiritual doppelgänger in the north, poor old **Colva** gets a bad rap. Part of the reason is that, just like Calangute, it was once a favoured getaway for the landed elite during the summer months, and has now been taken over by tourists from neighbouring states. But Colva has a broad expanse of sand, and plenty of room for everyone. Unlike Calangute and Baga, there are no deckchairs hogging the sand, and relatively few vendors hawking rugs and massages. Also, it's still a working beach: dozens of fishing boats depart each day from here before dawn.

Less than twenty years ago, **Benaulim** was deserted, used mainly by resident fishermen whose decorated wooden boats still line the sand. But tourism is steadily taking over as Benaulim's main trade, as visitors branch out from the behemoth Taj Exotica resort to a range of new hotels. Just beyond Benaulim village, the hill is crested by the Church of St. John the Baptist (open for mass at 8am daily). Built at the turn of the 16th century, it's a pretty example of Goa's classic neo-Roman church architecture. Like other coastal villages of South Goa, Benaulim displays much enthusiasm for *dhirio* (bullfighting), which is now banned, but continues nonetheless.

The beachfront continues straight down to **Mobor**, trailing through giant five-star complexes around Varca, and the package-tourist destination of **Cavelossim**. The beaches are beautiful but the fishing villages here have never been prosperous and there's little to do outside hotels.

South of Mobor, a winding coastal road seesaws through valleys cut with rice terraces and coconut and areca nut palm groves. On the way, the road forks right to the Cabo de Rama fortress overlooking the sea from a dramatic headland. Leaving the cape, the road to Palolem cuts through cashew plantations and paddy fields until another right turn leading to **Agonda**. Agonda remains one of Goa's best beaches, a small stretch of tranquillity that has escaped major tourist development thanks to strong and organised local opposition. It's perfect for lazy beach days, and from October to April there are a few temporary shacks offering food and drinks.

The old coastal road is the most enchanting way to arrive in **Palolem**. It is a beach of dreams and picture postcards. Once a distant point, well off the beaten track, today Palolem has become the choice for party-minded young backpackers and independent travellers. Around 50 shacks line the bay like beads in a necklace, many of them run by expat foreigners – it's now easy to find wood-fired pizzas, home-made houmous and English breakfasts. A leisurely 15-minute amble down the rocky coastline is **Patnem**, an escape from the crowds of Palolem. And beyond it, over the crest of another hill, is **Canacona**, with yet another sprawling five-star resort.

OUTDOOR ACTIVITIES

Goa is a good place for water-based outdoor activities and water sports including windsurfing, parasailing, waterskiing, sports fishing, kayaking, yachting and even some snorkelling. Every large resort and almost every major beach has some water sport facilities.

Numerous private operators conduct river cruises with interesting themes: spotting dolphins or crocodiles, for example.

Querim Beach.

Bags packed, milk cancelled, house raised on stilts.

You've packed the suntan lotion, the snorkel set, the stay-pressed shirts. Just one more thing left to do – your bit for climate change. In some of the world's poorest countries, changing weather patterns are destroying lives.

You can help people to deal with the extreme effects of climate change. Raising houses in flood-prone regions is just one life-saving solution.

Climate change costs lives.
Give £5 and let's sort it *Here & Now*

www.oxfam.org.uk/climate-change

Oxfam is a registered charity in England and Wales (No.202918) and Scotland (SCO039042). Oxfam GB is a member of Oxfam International.

Be Humankind **Oxfam**

H20 (98221-79986) at Vasco's Baina Beach, 15 minutes north of Bogmalo, offers a range of water sports. The highlight here is an underwater walk 3.7 metres below the surface in a giant fish-bowl helmet (Rs 1,500 for 20 minutes). At Thunder Waves (on the beach near Fort Aguada, 98221-76986) Morgan D'Souza offers dolphin trips, parasailing and jet-skiing.

While Goa isn't known for its dive scene or dive locations, you can do a PADI-certified dive course at Dive Goa in Dona Paola (O Pescador Resort, 93250-30110, 0832-246-5737, Oct-May only).

Eat

In high season (November to February), Goa's restaurant scene is the most vibrant and diverse on the subcontinent. Hundreds of temporary eating establishments and beach shacks spring up to take advantage of the roaring tourist trade – many run by visiting chefs from around the world. From April to September, however, many restaurants are closed. For outstanding Goan meals, make a trip to South Goa's old mansions. At Palacio do Deao (*see p324*), Celia Vasco da Gama cooks perfect Goan meat and fish dishes, and complex, fragrant curries. You'll need to give 24 hours' notice. Old Heritage Inn (part of the Figueiredo Mansion, 0832-277-7028, *see p324*) is a remarkable setting in which to enjoy the superlative Luso-Indian cooking of Maria de Lourdes Figueiredo de Albuquerque. She caters lunches (24 hours' notice, minimum six people) that feature her spectacular cooking from old family recipes, as well as dishes learnt in her decades in Mozambique and Lisbon.

Avanti Restaurant

Panjim *Rua de Ourem (0832-242-7179/98221-67005). Open 11am-3pm, 7-11pm Mon-Sat. $. No credit cards. Goan.*

With a first-floor balcony overlooking Panjim's Latin Quarter, it is a constant surprise that this restaurant has not been seized upon by the backpacker bibles. Not that Michael and Ovita D'Souza are complaining. Avanti has, over 25 years, become a cherished local favourite and is crowded at mealtimes with Goans in search of old-fashioned home cooking in a deeply traditional vein. This food is hard to beat, especially the roast tongue, aromatic vindaloos and tender beef chilli fry. The shark *ambotik*, its rich red curry soured with *kokum*, is the best in the state. This place is tremendous value for money too.

Bean Me Up

North Goa *House No.1639/2 Deulvaddo, Anjuna-Vagator (0832-227-3479). Open noon-4pm, 7-11pm Mon-Fri, Sun. $$. No AmEx. Vegetarian fusion.*

More a mini-conglomerate than mere restaurant, this North Goa institution has rooms, massages, a deli, boutique and children's area. But all that plays second fiddle to the food, which is serious vegetarian fare. There's world-class handmade tofu and *tempeh*, fabulous salads and a variety of fresh fruit and vegetable drinks. Dedicated carnivores can try 'wheat meat', which is really *seitan*. All this is the lovingly tended kingdom of a veteran of the Goa Freak era, transplanted New Yorker (and Goldie Hawn lookalike) Lisa Camps, who has lived in Anjuna for almost 30 years. Take a minute to chat; she and her partner Richard Chabin are the best source of information on what's worth checking out on these unruly fringes of the tourist scene.

Bocado de Cardenales

South Goa *251 Colomb, Canacona (99210-37069). Open 1-10pm Mon, Wed-Sun. $$. No credit cards. Spanish.*

It is quite surreal to experience a genuine Spanish restaurant hidden away on a tiny bay, where the authentic tapas menu is presented by a moustachioed Catalonian. Start with a plateful of *patatas bravas*, the classic tapas of fried potatoes in spicy sauce, mouth-watering *abondigas*, meatballs in gravy, garlic prawns, and the superb spinach gratinata topped with locally made smoked mozzarella. Main courses are generous and cooked with equal zest, like the Mediterranean classic *calamari negros*, or black squid, cooked in its own ink.

"There are lots of expertly made and presented nouveau Asian items like the inside-out sushi rolls, crispy pork-belly *pomelo* salad, and lemongrass-and-ginger crème brûlée."

Bomra's Restaurant

North Goa *Souza Vaddo, opposite Kamal Retreat, Fort Aguada Road, Candolim (98221-49633/34857). Open noon-2.30pm, 6.30-11.30pm daily. $$. No credit cards. Burmese.*

The location is undistinguished, the decor unremarkable, but then the 'Modern Burmese and Kachin cooking' arrives, and the meal is a complete knockout. Chef Bawmra Jap, a native Kachin, was trained in London's hothouse restaurant environment, and his expertise shows in the imagination and verve with which he reinvents this distinctive regional soul food. Outstanding dishes include Kachin chicken marinated in aromatic herbs, layered with plump shitake mushrooms, and cooked in a banana leaf; or home-made Shan tofu served with tamarind soya sauce. There are lots of expertly made and presented nouveau Asian items like

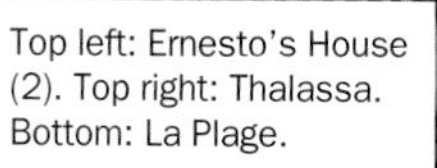

Top left: Ernesto's House (2). Top right: Thalassa. Bottom: La Plage.

Goan cuisine: all in the mix

'Please Sir, My God of Death,
Don't make it my turn today, not today,
There's fish curry for dinner'
- Bakibab Borkar, Goan poet

It tells you a lot about Goans that a common way of asking 'How are you?' in Konkani, the local language, is '*Nisteak kitem aslem*?', which translates as: 'What fish did you have today?' Food, and particularly seafood, is a Goan obsession, and the Goan cuisine in general is far removed from North Indian staples like butter chicken and biryani.

What Goans eat today would almost be unrecognisable to a 16th-century Goan. The cuisine was transformed by the arrival of Portuguese colonists, who brought with them a cornucopia of culinary treasures harvested from previous colonial adventures: chillies, tomatoes, potatoes, pumpkins, fruits such as guavas, pineapples and chikoos, and cashews; not to mention Iberian garlic sausages and *garrafãos* of vinegar, wine and olive oil.

As Portuguese influence took hold in Goa so did the Portuguese diet, edging out the traditional cuisine of Saraswat dishes from the Konkan region. The ubiquitous *vindaloo* (which tastes nothing like what the British know as vindaloo) is a corruption of *vinoo e alhoos*, a garlicky Portuguese wine vinegar marinade. *Chouriço*, those chubby links of spiced pork, are a Goan version of Iberian chorizo sausage. And *Sorpotel* started off as *sarablho*, a Portuguese stew of pork and offal. The bright red *sorpotel* (pictured) is now customarily served with *sannas*, steamed savoury rice cakes similar to *idlis*. The Portuguese also introduced influences they had picked up on their journeys to South-east Asia, Africa and South America: prawn *balchao* from Myanmar and chicken *cafreal* from Mozambique.

Saraswat touches were added back into the mix as a new Goan cuisine evolved – turmeric, cumin, cinnamon and cloves found their way into Portuguese *assados* or roasts, coconut and semolina showed up in *bolos* (cakes), and the local taste for strong spices led to versions of Portuguese dishes with so much chilli and vinegar that they would have been intolerable to the colonisers' palates.

Today, the staple Goan dish remains fish curry with rice, the exact ingredients of which vary widely from region to region, village to village, and even house to house. For most of the year, Goans tuck into prized estuarine shrimp and tiger prawns, mussels, langoustines, lobsters, pomfrets, kingfish, river perch and shark.

During the monsoon season, deep-sea fishing is banned to allow stocks to replenish, and Goans take to eating the *muddasho* (lady fish), a slender fish that is known for its buttery taste.

Other distinctive speciality Goan curries include the mild *caldine*, a children's favourite often made with eggs or vegetables, and the complex, vinegary *xacuti*, usually made with chicken, goat or beef.

The original Saraswat cuisine did survive as what is known as Gomantak cooking: thick-grained, nutty, reddish parboiled rice eaten with fish or shellfish that has been curried or fried. It's accompanied by mildly spiced seasonal vegetables, all flavoured with dark palm sugar (jaggery) and tamarind, with lashings of coconut in every form. Mud vessels and wood fires traditionally gave the food its characteristic smoky aroma, which is best captured in a steaming bowl of *canjee* (rice gruel), served with a wicked piece of mango pickle.

Always leave room for dessert, an area where Goan cuisine truly excels. Again, the Portuguese influence is in evidence. Along with *bebinca*, a layered cake made with dozens of egg yolks, comes *bolo sans rival*, a cake made with the leftover whites. Many sweet dishes are heavy on coconut, including the *batika* cake and the festival favourite *pattoyos*, a steamed coconut and jaggery dessert that comes wrapped in a segment of banana leaf.

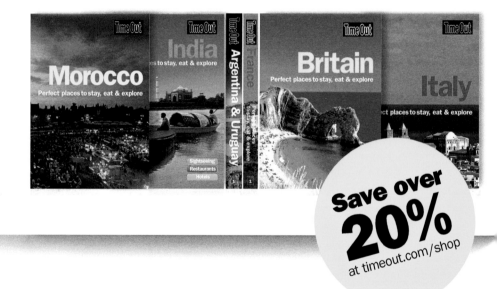

the inside-out sushi rolls, crispy pork-belly *pomelo* salad, and lemongrass-and-ginger crème brûlée. But it's the expert interpretations of the chef's home cuisine that really set this restaurant apart; little wonder Bomra's is being called the best Burmese restaurant outside Myanmar.

Café Chocolatti

North Goa *Near Whispering Palms Hotel, 409A Fort Aguada Road, Candolim (0832-247-9340/ 93261-12006). Open 9.30am-7pm Mon-Sat. $$. No credit cards. Café.*

You can breakfast all day at Ricardo and Nazneen Rebelo's pleasant and spotlessly clean café set under the trees of their front garden on a prime patch of Candolim's main drag. Stop by for the bountiful salads, refreshingly simple yet brilliant paninis, and fresh-baked biscuits and cakes. There are lots of great takeaway goodies, including addictive home-made chilli-chocolate truffles and chunky chocolate-chip cookies.

"Chef Vasco Silveira served in the Portuguese forces in Angola, and his cooking evokes the Lusophone arc that stretches from Mozambique to Macau."

Ernesto's House

Panjim *6/49 Mala, below Maruti Temple (0832-325-6213/98230-15921). Open 11am-3pm, 6.30-11pm daily. $$. No credit cards.*

Scions of old Panjim, Ernesto and Vasco Alvares, run this restaurant that opened in 2009 in a restored 160-year-old Goan villa in the Portuguese heritage precinct of Mala. The location is marvellous. Along with Fontainhas next door, Mala forms an integral part of India's only Latin Quarter. Besides the location, draws are the vibrant atmosphere fostered by Ernesto, in charge of front of house, and – of course – the food. It is chef Vasco, a man-mountain ironically called Vasquito (little Vasco), who delivers epic meals to your table. Try his signature filet mignon with blue cheese sauce, the famous barbecued ribs, or the zesty Zambezi chicken made with coconut cream and piri piri chillies. Save room for Vasquito's peerless *serradura* (sawdust pudding).

Horseshoe

Panjim *Rua de Ourem (0832-243-1788/564-4044). Open noon-2.30pm, 7-10.30pm Mon-Sat. $$. No AmEx. Portuguese.*

Chef Vasco Silveira is an ex-commando, who served with the Portuguese forces in Angola. His cooking evokes the Lusophone arc that stretches from Mozambique to Macau; you can watch him at work through the glass wall behind the bar. Both food and ambience are excellent. The mussels and tiny Goa sausage starters are famous. Don't miss out on the best *bacalhao* (cod) in any restaurant in Goa, or the grandmother-style mild chicken *guisado* curry. For pudding there's the aptly named *bolo sans rival* (cake).

Lila Café

North Goa *Baga Creek (0832-227-9843). Open 9am-6pm Mon, Wed-Sun. $$. No credit cards. Café/German.*

Smoked water buffalo ham, anyone? It's one of the home-made specialities at this bright, spacious German-run restaurant, which is easily among the most successful establishments in North Goa. Lila has a fanatically loyal multinational clientele that keeps coming back for its fresh-baked croissants, inventive pâtés, spätzle, goulash, superb fresh juices, excellent coffee and desserts. The same people come back to the same table to eat the same thing all through the season, but there's enough space for everyone at this unpretentious landmark.

La Plage

North Goa *Ashvem Beach (98221-21712). Open 8.30am-10pm daily. $$. No credit cards. French.*

Creative bistro-style French food, discreetly impeccable service, stunning location and real value for money make this restaurant – set in a windswept stand of coconut palms – so popular. Cooking is spirited and satisfying. Don't hold back with the delightful tapas, which include chicken liver pâté, a wonderfully succulent ceviche of raw kingfish marinated in lime and coconut milk, and platters of silken, gleaming beef carpaccio. Main courses are consistent and desserts refreshingly simple and delicious, as are the zesty gazpacho-style tomato cocktails and cucumber lassis.

Thalassa

North Goa *Near Nine Bar, Small Vagator Beach (98500-33537/ww.myspace.com/thalassagoa). Open 4pm-midnight daily. $$. No credit cards. Greek.*

This excellent Greek restaurant perched on a cliff above Vagator Beach is Goa's most recent runaway success story. It is run by Mariketty, a warm, hospitable native of Corfu, who relocated to India a few years ago. Mariketty creates Greek fare with aplomb. Deep-fried home-made feta cheese is addictive, and the *kleftiko*, a traditional Greek stew, with tender chunks of lamb, chicken, beef or vegetables topped with melted gobs of feta, is awesome too. Mouth-watering wraps of *souvlaki*, skewered meat or vegetables, are made with home-made pita bread topped with tzatziki and salad. Delicious, but not Greek, is the blueberry cheesecake.

Shop

Goa is famous for its flea markets. Anjuna flea market (*see p320*) is one of the most famous, but if you visit just one flea market it should be Arpora's rocking Saturday-night market, also known as Ingo's Bazaar (www.ingosbazaar.com), which features lots of live bands alongside the shopping stalls. Also on Saturday night is the flea market at Mackie's on Baga Beach.

Over the last five years there's been a profusion of home decor stores springing up in Goa, many of them in old colonial Portuguese mansions. Most sell exquisite pieces, but note that prices at some stores are pretty unearthly.

Everybody should take home some of Goa's most famous nuts, the cashew. Available virtually everywhere, shelled and unshelled, roasted, fried, salted, spiced and more, they sell for approximately Rs 300 per kilo.

One of Goa's most popular shopping centres is Acron Arcade (Fort Aguada Road, Candolim, open 10am-10pm daily). Downstairs, half the building is devoted to home decor from Yamini, an Indian chain selling handmade furnishings. The arcade also has a variety of men's and women's designer-label stores, along with leather accessories boutiques like Hidesign and body-care stores like Forest Essentials and Shahnaz Husain.

Literati Bookshop & Café

North Goa *E/1-282 Gaura Vaddo, Calangute (0832-227-7740/98226-82566/www.literati-goa.com). Open 10am-6.30pm Mon-Sat. No AmEx.*

Diviya Kapur's Literati is Goa's best bookstore café and hangout of India's A-list writers when they are on holiday. Situated in a beautiful 100-year-old villa, it has comfortable sofas to lounge on while perusing new and second-hand books. The back room and garden are often the venue for book readings, lectures and other events.

Paperworks

Panjim *Pinto Arcade, D Bandodkar Marg, Campal (0832-242-5841). Open 10am-5pm Mon-Sat. No AmEx.*

Exquisite handmade paper crafts that are locally produced are sold here at throwaway prices. There are notebooks, frames, notelets and cards, decorative gift boxes, wrapping paper, lampshades and more.

Sotohaus

North Goa *1266F Anna Vaddo, Candolim (0832-248-9983/www.sotodecor.com). Open 11am-6pm Mon-Sat. No AmEx.*

Sonia Weder and Thomas Schnider are a talented Swiss couple whose store offers beautifully made objets d'art, lamps, tables and other furniture. Besides metal, many pieces are made using banana, elephant-ear and papaya leaves, driftwood and even shed snake skins, all under thick layers of lacquer.

Velha Goa

Panjim *4/191 Rua de Ourem, Fontainhas (0832-242-6628/www.velhagoa.com). Open 9.30am-1pm, 3-7.30pm Mon-Sat. No AmEx.*

Velha sells *azulejos*, hand-painted tiles made in the Iberian tradition. They come in a variety of designs, colours and sizes, including some that feature Goan windows and others with Moorish design influences. Aslo in stock are ceramic bowls, coasters and frames for mirrors or pictures. At the nearby studio, you can watch artisans at work painting the tiles.

Wendell Rodricks Design Space

Panjim *Near Francis Luis Gomes Garden, Fontainhas (0832-223-8177/242-0604/www.wendellrodricks.com). Open 10am-6.30pm Mon-Sat. No AmEx.*

Feni for your thoughts

The French have their wine, the Greeks have their ouzo, the Germans their beer, but Goans have feni – and they don't really need anything else, thank you very much. Every April and May, the heavy scent of fermenting cashew drifts across the countryside and traditional stills fire up to make the year's batch of this deeply loved drink – a drink as synonymous with Goa as beaches and fish-curry-rice.

Feni (pronounced fey-nee) is a clear, powerful spirit that comes in two varieties: cashew and coconut. Coconut feni (also known as palm feni) is made all year round, mostly in South Goa, but is considered by purists to be an inferior version of the 'original' cashew feni, which can only be made after the cashew fruit harvest in March. The fruits are crushed and the juice left to ferment. The resulting liquid is then heated in large copper or earthen pots over firewood and the distillate collected through a coiled pipe. The first distillate is weak and makes a drink called urrak; it takes two or three distillations to make proper, strong feni, which is around 40 per cent alcohol.

Connoisseurs insist that good feni can be as smooth and nuanced as the finest single malt whiskies. It's by far the state's most popular drink, available at hole-in-the-wall taverns everywhere. These establishments serve homemade varieties poured from jerry cans or unlabelled plastic bottles. However, there are also lots of big-name brands, like Big Boss, that you can buy in wine shops. Drink it neat, with a squeeze of lime, a pinch of salt, or with lemonade. It's also fabulous in fruit cocktails. Watch out though – it has a kick like a gaur.

Clockwise from top left: Anjuna flea market; Basilica of Bom Jesus; Palolem.

Clockwise from top left: Park Hyatt Goa Resort & Spa; Rockheart; Siolim House; Park Hyatt Goa Resort & Spa; Siolim House.

Elegant couture by Goa's most celebrated designer and favourite of the Bollywood set. Come here if you like the cool, minimalist designs and clean lines that he's so famous for. Some antiques, jewellery, cosmetics and books are also on sale.

Nightlife

Goa's nightlife is legendary and somewhat notorious. There's a huge variety of clubs and bars, especially in the tourist hotspots, and it's common for tourists staying in the south to head out to North Goa to party. Most of Goa's nightclubs are closed off-season (April to mid October) and many have an entry cover charge that varies according to the season and day of the week.

Café Del Mar

South Goa *Palolem Beach (98232-76520). Open 24hrs daily. No credit cards.*
The most popular of Palolem's beach shacks is this sprawling, deeply laid-back wood and bamboo den serving hookah pipes, cocktails and snacks to a pounding soundtrack.

Cavala

North Goa *Saunta Vaddo, Baga (0832-227-6090). Open 9am-midnight daily. No AmEx.*
This old Baga hotel offers a warm welcome to a friendly (and older) crowd of locals, expats and regular returnees, with live music and retro nights, most often on Friday and Saturday evenings.

Club Tito's & Mambo's

North Goa *Tito's Lane, Baga (0832-227-9895). Open 7pm-3.30am daily. No AmEx.*
Tito's is possibly Goa's most famous nightclub. It's a lively and popular place catering for everyone who wants to party and have a good time; it is also quite the celebrity haunt. Mambo's, a few doors down, is a pub run by the same management, but with a more relaxed vibe; music here is a mix of hip hop and house, with some country thrown in. The whole lane is a series of establishments run by the same people.

Curlies, Café Looda & Shore Bar

North Goa *South Anjuna Beach (Curlies 98221-68628/Café Looda 0832-652-9323/Shore Bar no phone). Open 10pm-1am daily. No credit cards.*
Both Curlies and Café Looda are beach-shack restaurants that turn into lively beachside nightspots after sunset, with Curlies going heavy on trance and ambient sounds for its stoner patrons. The Shore Bar, a few minutes' walk up the beach north of Café Looda, hosts regular trance nights from 6pm to 11pm.

Nine Bar

North Goa *Above Little Vagator Beach (no phone). Open 6-10pm daily.*
Evenings kick off at Nine Bar, a mini-version of Paradiso (*see below*), with a clifftop view and a packed house of Indian and European party people warming up to some intense trance and psychedelic music. Things finish early here to and the crowd moves on to the next venue for the rest of the night.

Paradiso

North Goa *Anjuna (93261-00013). Open 10pm-5am daily. No AmEx.*
A huge club built on a series of psychedelically painted terraces overlooking the sea. Paradiso attracts some of India's best DJs, and when it's packed the energy level is hard to beat, pumped up by non-stop trance beats and the rhythm of the waves.

"The property extends over an undulating beachfront, full of mature coconut palms and frangipani trees, and you can hear the surf pounding just metres away."

Shiro Beach

North Goa *Candolim (0832-645-1718). Open 11am-1am daily. No credit cards.*
This is the Goa version of a popular Mumbai club and restaurant. It occupies a prime stretch of beachside land and draws a loyal crowd of well-heeled visitors to its high-ceilinged, dimly lit circular interiors with three huge white statues and fine outside deck area.

Stay

India's favourite holiday destination has hotel rooms to suit every budget and preference, from the no-frills bamboo huts of Palolem to the ultra-exclusive beachside villas of North Goa. Most of the huge resort complexes with extensive secluded beaches tend to be located in South Goa, the only five-star hotels in the north being the legendary Fort Aguada Beach Resort and Taj Holiday Village in Sinquerim (for both, see www.tajhotels.com). As well as exclusive villas, North Goa also tends to have lots of rooms-to-hire in family homes, beach-shack style accommodation and no-frills hotels. It is also worth considering a few atmospheric

Park Hyatt Goa Resort & Spa.

options that aren't very close to the beach, but are otherwise perfect for a holiday.

Those looking for week-long stays in true luxury at exclusive beachside villas in North Goa should consider the following options. Aashyana Lakhanpal (Escrivao Vaddo, Candolim, 0832-248-9225, www.aashyanalakhanpal.com, $$$$) is the converted holiday home of art-collecting industrialist Ajay Lakhanpal. It's an expansive modernist property, with a main villa and attached *casinhas* (cottages), filled with contemporary Indian art. The location is stunning, despite being surrounded on three sides by runaway concrete mayhem: it's on a huge plot, with one of the best swimming pools in Goa and a lovely private access route to the very best part of Candolim Beach.

On the same stretch of beach is Rockheart (14/A Annavaddo, Candolim, 98193-27284, www.rockheartgoa.com, $$$$). The original charms of Goa are still intact at this gorgeous three-bedroom villa. The property extends over undulating beachfront, full of mature coconut palms and frangipani trees, and you can hear the surf pounding just metres away as you relax in one of the thoughtfully placed hammocks. Though close to the main tourism strip, it feels like another world altogether.

> **"Each elegantly decorated room has a landscape theme – mountains, grasslands and so on; the best is the circular aquamarine room with octopus motif."**

Fort Tiracol Hotel

North Goa *Tiracol Pernem (0236-622-7631/ www.nilaya.com/tiracol.htm). $$-$$$.*

This gem has just seven rooms in an incredibly romantic location at the top of an old fortress perched high on a cliff: you can lose yourself in the sweeping views of the river and Querim Beach far below. Though run by the same couple that owns the new age celeb-magnet boutique hotel Nilaya Hermitage (www.nilaya.com), this property involves minimal fuss, with the emphasis on seclusion and the fantastic views from every window, including the bathrooms. A promenade inside the fort walls is lined with *charpoys* and tables for alfresco dining. Rooms have fans (there's no air-conditioning). The chapel in the courtyard is still used by Tiracol villagers three times a week for mass, and tourists visiting the fort can sometimes be a bit of a disturbance. Otherwise, Fort Tiracol is isolated, but there's a speedboat on hand to take you to the busier beaches to the south.

Panchavatti

North Goa *Corjuem Island (98225-80632/ www.islaingoa.com). $$$. No AmEx.*

Panchavatti is the eye-popping, sprawling hacienda on Corjuem Island that is the highly individualistic creation of Loulou Van Damme, a yoga-loving Belgian who has lived in India for many years. Her design sensibility evokes Morocco and the Mediterranean as much as India; the overall effect is somehow extraordinarily well suited to Goa. The vast property has many charms, including a wooden *machan* (viewing platform) overlooking the river, a kitchen garden and a satisfyingly deep cold-water pool. Loulou's spectacular cuisine has earned her fanatical loyalty from an international clientele.

Panjim People's

Panjim *E-212, 31st January Road, Fontainhas (0832-222-6523/243-5628/www.panjiminn.com). $$. No AmEx.*

In the lovely, sprawling colonial district of Fontainhas are three properties converted into hotels with the creative vision of owner Ajit Sukhijia. The best and most interesting of these is Panjim People's. The 120-year-old former schoolhouse has just four huge rooms, each with a pretty mosaic-tiled bathroom, antique beds, planter's chairs and original artwork.

Park Hyatt Goa Resort & Spa

South Goa *Arossim Beach, Cansaulim (0832-272-1234/www.park.hyatt.com). $$$.*

The Park Hyatt is probably the best of Goa's huge luxury hotels. The village-style resort is set in 45-acres of lush greenery, and the beautifully maintained gardens lead to some of South Goa's best beachfronts. The gigantic multi-level pool is connected by water slides and lined with sunloungers. Rooms are spacious, with outdoor seating. They overlook the grounds and beach beyond, have walk-in closets and humungous bathrooms with sunken tubs, and all the amenities you'd expect from a five-star hotel. The Park Hyatt is popular with families (kids are fabulously well looked after) and food is standard five-star fare, so if you're looking for quiet seclusion or fine dining you may not find it here. The hotel's award-winning Sereno Spa adds to the appeal.

Pousada Tauma

North Goa *Porba Vaddo, Bardez, Calangute (0832-227-9061/www.pousada-tauma.com). $$$.*

Step away from one of the busiest, noisiest junctions in all of tourist-crazed Calangute, into the calm beauty of this pioneering boutique hotel, lovingly created by owner Neville Proenca. A foliage-festooned gateway leads to a series of laterite cottages arranged around a pretty central swimming pool. Each elegantly decorated room has a landscape theme – mountains, grasslands and so on; the best is the circular aquamarine room with octopus motif. There's also a simple but enchanting restaurant, the Copper Bowl, set in a laterite colonnade and serving outstanding Goan food.

Siolim House

North Goa *Wadi, Siolim (0832-227-2138/ www.siolimhouse.com). $$. No AmEx.*
This 300-year-old Portuguese manor house was a wreck when Varun Sood bought it 12 years ago. Now lovingly restored – with wooden floors, high ceilings, antique furniture, a courtyard and swimming pool – it's a hotel that hates being called a hotel. Siolim provides visitors with an opportunity to luxuriate in atmospheric seclusion even though you're in the heart of one of Goa's most culturally significant villages, and also just a short taxi ride away from the edgy, happening beaches of North Goa's burgeoning neo-hippie scene.

Wildernest

North Goa *Off Sankhali, Chorla ghats (98814-02665/ www.wildernest-goa.com). $$. No AmEx.*
In an obscure corner of Goa is a natural paradise, its continued survival the result of a few nature-lovers' efforts to prevent the area from becoming an open cast mine. Far from the beach resorts of Goa, this little slice of heaven makes for a wonderful two-day escape to a true wilderness location, with trekking, birdwatching and serene silences, broken only by the call of the abundant birdlife. Accommodation is in cottages and huts. Valley Cottages are probably the best, with stunning vistas from their balconies and spacious bathrooms with huge bay windows. There's excellent food, representing the cuisines of three states, good service from staff who are keen to please, and a cool spring-fed infinity pool. The hotel will arrange a free pick-up from anywhere in Goa if you are staying for two nights. This is the jungle, so expect insects and carry repellent.

Factfile

When to go

October to February, when the weather is mild and pleasant, is the best time to visit Goa. Summer months, from March to June, are hot and very humid. The monsoon is a good time to go if you want peace and quiet but most of the nicer restaurants are closed and you cannot swim in the sea.

Getting there

Numerous direct flights make the short hop from Mumbai to Goa every day. Dabolim airport is 29km (18 miles) from Panjim, where you can get prepaid taxis. Trains chug into Goa from Mumbai some five times a day (journey time 9-12 hours); the major stops are Tivim for North Goa, Karmali for Panjim and Margao for South Goa. Goa is also very well connected by tourist and luxury buses from most major cities; overnight buses from Mumbai take 12 hours to cover the 590km (367-mile) distance.

For more on travel, *see p378* **Navigating India**.

Getting around

Taxis and cars with a driver are easily available for hire, but it's best to hire them for the whole day at a fixed rate. Self-driven (bicycles or mopeds) and motorcycle taxis (called 'pilots') are an innovative option for singles and couples.

Tourist information

The Directorate of Tourism is in Panjim (Rua de Ourem, 0832-222-6515), open 9.30am-1.15pm, 2-5.45pm Mon-Sat.

Internet

Sify Iway internet cafés are located all over North Goa and at least one other café can be found close to every major tourist area in the rest of the state.

Tips

● There are a few cases of drowning every year in Goa. Visitors are encouraged to be cautious when swimming in unfamiliar waters and to heed the safety signs. Although the Goa administration has engaged lifeguards to encourage beach safety, these facilities are currently rudimentary and obviously the whole 105km (65-mile) shoreline (with its 65km/40 miles of sandy beaches) cannot be monitored.

● Don't walk on secluded beaches alone at night. And, in general, only travel through lonely areas at night with reliable company.

● Drugs and raves, though immensely popular in certain areas of Goa, are against the law. So if you are caught, there is always a possibility that you could be prosecuted to set an example to others.

● You need an international licence to rent motorbikes in Goa. Only gearless bikes don't require a licence.

● Goa's three-day carnival, with Latin-flavoured bacchanalia and an afternoon parade of floats, is held in Panjim in February.

Kerala Backwaters

Emerald waterways and palm-fringed tranquillity.

Kerala's tropical backwaters have long been a meeting place for the world's major religions and ideologies, as well as for the melding of fresh and salt water. Yet they remain peaceful, gentle and slow. Here, women wash their clothes on the banks while men wait patiently behind fishing lines. Flotillas of ducks drift by, followed, perhaps, by a backwater bus full of lively children on their way to school. Vast expanses of calm, green waters end in a coconut tree-fringed horizon. Further inland from the lakes and lagoons, narrow canals lead into an even more unhurried world, without roads and cars, where every village home has a boat moored at its doorstep. This is the heart of Kerala: part Venetian, part tropical and entirely charming. This network of canals, rivers, lakes and lagoons, opening into the Arabian Sea, is an idyllic backdrop for an introduction to Kerala, her people, their food, and many other pleasant surprises.

All kinds of boats criss-cross the backwaters: narrow fishing boats fitted with storm lanterns to attract fish at night; government ferries carrying people and cars; and *kettuvallams*, the ubiquitous Kerala houseboat, composed of wooden planks tied together using coir ropes, and traditionally used to transport rice from the paddy fields to the coastal ports. Over 500 such barges, now remodelled as houseboats for tourists, are as much of an attraction of the backwaters as the teeming bird and animal life and the scenery. They are the most comfortable way to take in those emerald waters, coconut trees and paddy fields, villages, churches, mosques, temples and the odd Che Guevara cardboard cut-out.

Clockwise from top: Marari Beach Resort; Mararikulam; Spice Coast Cruises.

Explore

The backwaters are an interconnected network of inlets and five large lakes, linked by canals and over 40 rivers. About 900 kilometres (560 miles) of the 1,900 kilometres (1,180 miles) of waterways are navigable by boat. The backwaters stretch from **Kochi** in central Kerala to **Kollam** in the south, 72 kilometres (45 miles) short of the state's capital Thiruvananthapuram (Trivandrum).

The tiny, sleepy village of **Mararikulam** is 43 kilometres (27 miles) south of Kochi on the Malabar coast. **Alappuzha** (or Alleppey) town, capital of the district of the same name, is ten kilometres south of Mararikulam. Alappuzha is at the southern end of the massive **Vembanad Lake**, which spreads over 260 square kilometres (100 square miles). **Kumarakom** lies on the eastern shore of Vembanad Lake, and the bustling centre of **Kottayam** is 12 kilometres east of it, in the Meenachil river basin.

Kerala's backwaters do not have a significant number of historical sites or architectural wonders that lend themselves to regular sightseeing. Those who hire a boat for a day may well walk away unsatisfied, with few picture-postcard memories and fewer insights into Keralan life. Longer stays, overnight cruises and a leisurely exploration of the canals in the interior are more rewarding. To really experience this destination, you need to float the day away gently, eat vast quantities of fish and interact with local people.

While going by boat is obviously the way to explore the backwaters, having your own private boat – and the luxury of time – means you can stop on a whim to watch an elephant being bathed, or pull over at a narrow sandbar separating two lagoons and join the locals in their second favourite indulgence after communism – a football game.

CHURCHES, MOSQUES & TEMPLES

Kerala's religious amity is fabled. Many of the world's major religions arrived in Kerala very early and have peacefully co-existed since, even liberally taking on customs from each other. In the backwaters you are never too far from a historic church, mosque or temple. The Church of St Mary's in Champakulam, believed to be one of the seven established by St Thomas the Apostle, is one of India's oldest. Prayers and offerings made at the large St George Forane Church, built in 1810 in Edathua on the banks of the River Pampa, are believed to help devotees of all faiths recover from mental illness. The Sri Krishna Temple at Ambalappuzha, built in AD 790, typifies Kerala's temple architecture style and is famous for its *palpayasam*, a sweet pudding made of rice and milk that is offered to devotees as *prasadam* (blessed offering). Both the mosques, East and West Jama Masjid, in Alappuzha were established centuries ago.

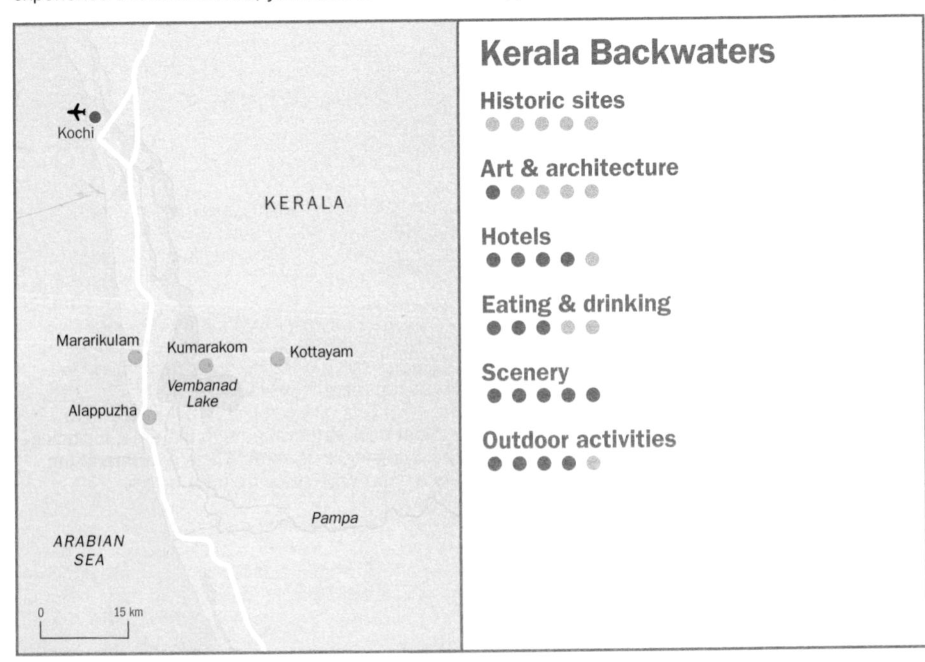

However, few temples in Kerala are open to non-Hindus, so check on individual temple policy before planning a visit.

TODDY SHOPS

Toddy or palm wine, or *kallu* as the locals call their favourite intoxicant, is a cultural hallmark of Kerala. Signboards marking toddy shops are a familiar sight throughout Kerala. Toddy is fermented sap collected from the flower clusters of toddy palms, which are cut to release the sap slowly into a clay pot. The liquid that accumulates in the pots is collected every day by toddy tappers, who supply the shops. Toddy is sometimes allowed to ferment for a day before being served. Apart from toddy (Rs 50 for a litre), these shops regularly dish up good food – fried and curried beef, chicken, crab, fish, frogs, mussels and prawns – all with a very generous helping of spice; it's recommended only for intrepid stomachs. Typically, the waiters note orders in chalk on the walls behind the predominantly male patrons, who come for the animated atmosphere as well as the toddy and food. Toddy can range from being sweet when freshly tapped, to sour when allowed to ferment.

BOAT RACES

Vallam kalli, or boat races, are a local custom dating back to the 16th century and a major tourist draw of the backwaters, especially in the area around Alappuzha. Most feature the *chundam valli* or snake boat, a 30-metre (98-foot) wooden boat with its rear section rising above the water to resemble a snake's hood. Traditionally, a snake boat is commanded by a captain, accompanied by three or four helmsmen and more than 100 oarsmen who row keeping in rhythm with a group of 25 singers. Typically, as many as 50 snake boats compete in a race that lasts for a few kilometres. The boat race season begins in June or July and continues until September. Major races include the Champakulam Moolam Boat Race (in the River Pampa, in June or July), the Jawaharlal Nehru Memorial Trophy Boat Race (Punnamada Lake, on the second Saturday of August) and the Aranmula Boat Race (also in the River Pamba, in August or September).

ALAPPUZHA

The historic and charming town of **Alappuzha** (Alleppey) is an ideal starting point for a backwater journey. It is dissected by numerous canals, backwaters and lagoons, which caused the English viceroy Lord Curzon to famously describe this sleepy area as the Venice of the East. Alappuzha town itself is wonderful to explore on foot, with many quaint side streets, colonial-era factories and warehouses, and shops selling curios and the salvaged remains of old homes; much of the town is only accessible on foot or bicycle. It is also the hub for most backwater tour operators, offering all kinds of pre-designed tourist packages, as well as the option of customised backwater experiences. Boat Jetty Road near the main bus stop in Alappuzha town is where most backwater tours launch from.

BACKWATER BOATS

The District Tourism Promotion Council (Boat Jetty Road, 0477-225-3308, www.dtpcalappuzha.com, open 9.30am-7.30pm, Mon-Sat) offers daily backwater tours. The Kuttanad Boat Cruise (Rs 300 for four hours) is a round-trip from Alappuzha to Kumarakom, including a stop in R-Block – man-made islands for paddy cultivation that are around 1.5 metres below sea level and hedged in by mud walls, similar to the dykes of the Netherlands. Expect to be bundled with plenty of others; the boat ride doesn't kick off until a minimum number of tourists turn up. DTPC also has luxury boats and speedboats for hire on an hourly or daily basis.

The Alleppey Tourism Development Co-operative (opposite Boat Jetty, 0477-226-4462, www.atdcalleppey.com, open 7.30am-8.30pm daily) books backwater cruises with private companies. Here tourists can book a houseboat for a day's cruise or a prolonged backwater adventure. Alternatively, visitors may make reservations through their hotel or approach a houseboat/boat cruise operator directly.

KOTTAYAM

Squeezed in between the Westerns Ghats, a mountain range to the east, and the backwaters to the west, is **Kottayam**. This little place made headlines in 1989 as the first Indian town to achieve 100 per cent literacy. Kottayam is an important commercial centre for trading spices and rubber, and is also renowned for inter-religious co-existence and amity. One of India's oldest mosques, the Juma Masjid in Thazhathangady, on the outskirts of Kottayam, has been here for some 1,000 years. Not too far away, in the heart of town, is the Thirunakkara Mahadeva Temple, a 16th-century Hindu temple dedicated to Lord Shiva. Apart from Islam and Hinduism, Christianity and the Syrian-Christian community in particular have flourished here.

Most backwater retreats in the area, including the charming backwater village of **Kumarakom**, are a short drive away from Kottayam.

Kumarakom Bird Sanctuary

Located in six hectares of wetlands on the eastern banks of Vembanad Lake, the small Kumarakom Bird Sanctuary is home to numerous local birds such as the egret, heron and various other waterfowl; it is also visited by Siberian cranes, teal and flycatchers in the migratory season. It is best

Clockwise from top left: Mararikulam; Marari Beach Resort (2); Coconut Lagoon; nutmeg.

explored by boat in the early morning, between June and August, while most migratory birds tend to come between November and February.

CANAL CRUISES

A backwater odyssey is incomplete without a cruise through the man-made canals that bisect villages in the interiors. These canals are narrow and shallow, and canopied by coconut trees; the only way to get to most of the village homes on their banks is by boat. The canals are also a rich ecosystem, abundantly filled with fish, water snakes, monitor lizards, water lilies and lotuses.

Many tour operators near Kottayam town offer canal cruises, including Tourist Land (0484-237-7880, www.vacationinkerala.com), which offers a day-long trip through the village canals near Vaikom in the Kottayam district. Its one-day package, Gramam (Rs 700 per head, including a traditional Keralan lunch), takes visitors through verdant and tranquil countryside and throws in a village tour as well, where you can watch people busy at work in the local industries – coir rope making and coconut processing.

MARARIKULAM

Mararikulam is a sleepy fishing village ten kilometres north of Alappuzha. Its main claim to fame is the wonderful Marari Beach, a verdant stretch of sand opening out to the Arabian Sea. The water here is seldom rough and generally safe for swimming. The Mararikulam Temple, dedicated to Lord Shiva, is the most important religious centre in the village, and there are a few other churches and mosques in the vicinity. However, rest and relaxation tend to be the primary endeavour for most tourists.

TUK TUK TOURS

For those who prefer terra firma, the backwaters can also be explored by auto-rickshaw or bicycle. Some ingenious auto-rickshaw drivers even offer package tours around the backwaters. Marari Tuk Tuk Tours (92497-06181), a collective of auto-rickshaw drivers in Mararikulam, can arrange a village tour (Rs 250 for two hours), an Alappuzha city tour (Rs 300 for one hour) or visits to temples and churches in the vicinity. Auto-rickshaw drivers often double up as valuable guides to the backwaters, and with a little persuasion will even let you drive their rickshaws a short way.

Eat & Stay

The large number and range of homestays, hotels, houseboats and resorts all along the backwaters mean a lot of options for visitors, each providing a different kind of experience – from a fishing village on a picturesque beach to a serene island accessible only by boat. Those planning long stays should ideally split their time between two or more types of accommodation. *Kettuvallams* or houseboats are surely the best way to soak in the backwater experience. And with over 500 registered *kettuvallams*, the choice may be wide, but the decision on which houseboat to go with is surprisingly easy. Ask what kind of boats you are going to be on (*see p353* Spice Coast Cruises) and where you will dock for the night and try to stay far from the crowds. Many operators tend to dock at just one spot at night, turning a particular area into a noisy marketplace, loud with the sound of dozens of generators.

Eating in the backwaters is limited to what your accommodation provides. All the larger resorts and hotels put on a multi-cuisine buffet, while smaller hotels and homestays usually serve a variety of Keralan cuisine, often with the chilli content toned down, in thali or buffet style.

A Beach Symphony

Mararikulam *(0478-286-5578/97442-97123/ www.abeachsymphony.com). $$$. No AmEx.*
Christel and Jan Arynn had been in the hospitality business for over a decade and a half before they moved to Kerala after a memorable holiday a few years ago. The boutique homestay they run offers the best access to Marari Beach on this pristine stretch. All four cottages here are traditional Keralan homes, carefully restored in distinct styles with European and even Moroccan flourishes. The large cottages each have a veranda with lounge chairs facing the sea, where all meals are served. The kitchen cooks up tasty Keralan fare and special care is taken to incorporate the personal tastes of visitors and not to repeat dishes for long-staying guests. Bathrooms are expansive affairs with an open-air shower in the middle of a fairly large courtyard. Spend languorous afternoons listening to the waves lapping the beach as you relax in one of the many hammocks strung between coconut trees.

Coconut Lagoon

Kumarakom *(0481-252-4491/www.cghearth.com). $$$$.*
A boat picks up guests from the main road and drops them off at the lobby, where warm smiles, a coconut drink and a flautist welcome them. At Coconut Lagoon, Vechoor cows (an endangered species of miniature cow) mow the lawns, the fish sanctuary has over 40 varieties of fish and tortoises, and the butterfly garden is perfect for whiling away a morning. On the complimentary sunset cruise on Vembanad Lake, the in-house naturalist points out birds returning to roost at the Kumarakom Bird Sanctuary nearby. Dinner is typically a lavish buffet including both Western and authentic Keralan fare. All 50 rooms here are reassembled from stately *therawads* (ancestral homes of the landed gentry) from around Kerala, and have terracotta floors, large open-air bathrooms and verandas right beside the many canals that criss-cross the resort. You can attend a yoga session, a cooking demo or a lecture on Ayurveda. Or just

laze on one of the many benches facing Vembanad Lake at the fringes of the resort. Whatever you choose to do, or not do here, will be entirely enjoyable. If, however, you're looking for something quiet and less commercial, opt for the Malabar House's smaller operations, like the *Discovery* (*see below*).

Discovery

Alappuzha *(0484-221-6666/www.malabarhouse.com). $$$$.*

The Malabar House group offers a slightly different version of the traditional Kerala houseboat with the *Discovery*, with contemporary features including a sundeck and an air-conditioned suite. The super-efficient crew takes visitors through lakes, rivers and channels on a two- or three-day cruise. The non-polluting boat is quiet, and one of the most eco-friendly options available; it also takes guests through some of the less-travelled and touristy parts of the backwaters.

Two other fantastic options offered by the same group are the lovely restored bungalows at **Privacy** (on Vembanad Lake) and **Serenity** (east of Kottayam).

Kumarakom Lake Resort

Kumarakom *(0481-252-4900/4501/ www.klresort.com). $$$$.*

Spread over acres of lush green land on the banks of Vembanad Lake, this luxurious resort has great views of the backwaters and a heritage feel. Its 66 rooms are built in Keralan style, with tiled roofs, terracotta and wooden floors, traditional temple murals adorning walls, and bathrooms with open-air shower areas. A 200m-long (655ft) meandering swimming pool runs alongside 26 rooms, while the others either have their own private pools or easy access to the infinity pool that stretches into Vembanad Lake. The Ayurveda spa, Ayurmana, and the Kerala cuisine restaurant, Etukettu, are both reconstructed piece-by-piece from traditional homes that were over two centuries old.

Marari Beach Resort

Mararikulam *(0478-286-3801/www.cghearth.com). $$$$.*

This is the earliest of Mararikulam's resorts. The architecture of the 62 cottages at Marari Beach is modelled on the huts of the local fishermen. Each has large, airy, elegant rooms with generous views of the beach, while the bathrooms have open-air shower areas canopied by coconut trees. Splash around in the Arabian Sea, watch the local fishermen return home each morning after a night at sea, explore the local village on a bicycle, or join an early morning *kalaripayattu* (an ancient local martial art) class. Like most other CGH Earth properties, Marari Beach is devoted to eco-tourism and is home to many native plants and trees, a biogas plant, an organic garden, a sewage treatment plant, a vermi-compost cell and a solid-waste management plant. Marari Beach might be a large resort, but it's charming nevertheless, and pays its dues to both the local ecology and the community.

Olavipe Homestay

35km S of Kochi *Olavipe Village, Poochakkal (0478-252-2255/www.olavipe.com). $$$. No credit cards.*

The Thekkanatt House, a graceful mansion commissioned in 1890, has been home to six generations of the Parayil family. Built on a small, idyllic island in the Kaithappuzha backwaters, this grand old home has changed little over the last century, and there's history waiting to be discovered in every nook and corner. In the four large guest rooms common sense replaces mod cons. A high roof and generous windows allow a gentle breeze from the backwaters to blow through. Air-conditioners and televisions are strict no-nos and guests are encouraged to get out and explore the village nearby, take a boat to the mainland, join the locals for a game of cricket, watch the butterflies in the front yard, or laze with a book on one of the cool stone benches overlooking the Parayil farms. Almost everything on the dinner table comes from the Parayil farms, the village or the backwaters. Breakfast, lunch and dinner are all cooked in traditional Keralan style, and are a community affair with hosts Anthony Tharakan and his wife Rema joining guests at a dinner table full of animated conversation.

Philipkutty's Farm

Kumarakom *Pallivathukal, Ambika Market PO, Vechoor (04829-276-529/98950-75130/www.philip kuttysfarm.com). $$$. No credit cards.*

Set on a sprawling island in the middle of Vembanad Lake, amid paddy fields and coconut groves, Philipkutty's Farm offers panoramic views of the backwaters and a truly agrarian experience. At the centre of the farm is a grand house surrounded by six large guest cottages. Each has understated decor, a spacious bathroom and stunning lake views. Accessible only by boat, Philipkutty's is delightfully removed from the bustle of the mainland. Here you can take a boat to watch the sunset, read a book by the lakeside, visit the vast family farm, explore the nearby village, or have family matriarch and fiercely competent cook Aniamma Philip, known as 'mummy' to the entire island and to guests, teach you a thing or two about Syrian-Christian cuisine.

Pooppally's Heritage Homestay

Alappuzha *Nedumudy (0477-276-2034/329-0800/ www.pooppallys.com). $$. No credit cards.*

When Everest conqueror Sir Edmund Hillary stayed with the Pooppallys many years ago, he described their home as a gracious old house with timeless charm. Built in 1895, the house is surrounded by paddy fields and a garden of cardamom, pepper, cinnamon, nutmeg, mango and guava on one side, and the holy River Pampa on the other. The five wooden cottages are all river-facing, and were built entirely using parts salvaged from old Keralan homes. From the comfort of your veranda, you can watch backwater buses and country boats float by, or get into one yourself. Host Paul Pooppally will gladly arrange for a country boat that you can take out yourself into the gentle river, or hire a boatman to go along with you. A short walk along the riverside will take you to the Nedumudy Bhagavathy Temple. Paul's daughter-in-law, Lisa Joseph, conducts cooking classes.

Punnamada Serena Spa Resort

Alappuzha *Punnamada (0477-223-3690/ www.punnamada.com). $$. No AmEx.*

Punnamada Serena Spa Resort is just a few metres away from the starting point of the annual Nehru Trophy Boat Race. Lake villas have verandas overlooking Vembanad

Ayurveda: Kerala's ancient medicine

Ayurveda is the world's oldest continually practised system of medicine, estimated to be well over 2,500 years old. The earliest known texts on Ayurveda describe – in detail – human anatomy, illnesses, medicinal plants and medicinal preparations from mineral and animal sources. Modern-day Ayurveda is based on these ancient texts. It has now found acceptance all over the world as a complementary and alternative medicine, as well as a short-term rejuvenation and wellness treatment.

According to Ayurveda, the balancing of energies is the basis of good health. It lays equal stress on body, mind and spirit – and on the prevention of disease – as it does on cures and treatments. Traditional Ayurveda uses lifestyle changes, diet control, herbs, massage, aromatherapy, colour therapy, cleansing techniques, yoga and meditation for stress relief, rejuvenation, beauty treatments and skin conditions – as well as treatments for orthopaedic problems, insomnia and even 'demonic possession'.

Though Ayurveda is practised all over India, and the world, Kerala is its spiritual home. Kerala has many traditional Ayurvedic treatment centres, and almost all resorts, hotels and homestays in the backwaters either have an Ayurvedic spa with a doctor on call or can arrange for one. Treatments for specific ailments last anywhere between 14 and 21 days, while more chronic conditions often require more time; treatment is accompanied by a prescribed vegetarian diet and is considered to be most effective during the monsoons. Practitioners recommend that to get full health benefits from this holistic system, individuals either go to a certified Ayurvedic hospital or a recognised private facility.

The **Kottakkal Arya Vaidya Sala** (AVS, Kottakkal, Malappuram District, 0483-280-8000, www.aryavaidyasala.com) is one such institution. It has three hospitals as well as medicine manufacturing units and research labs. It cultivates its own medicinal plants and regularly publishes Ayurvedic periodicals and books.

Kalari Kovilakom (Kollengode, Palakkad, 04923-263-737, www.kalarikovilakom.com) is a 19th-century palace, now run by the CGH Earth group, and offers 14-, 21- and 28-day Ayurveda packages, all of which are customised to patients' individual needs. There are ten traditional treatment rooms, a beauty therapy centre, gardens with herbs, a well-stocked library and a yoga and meditation hall.

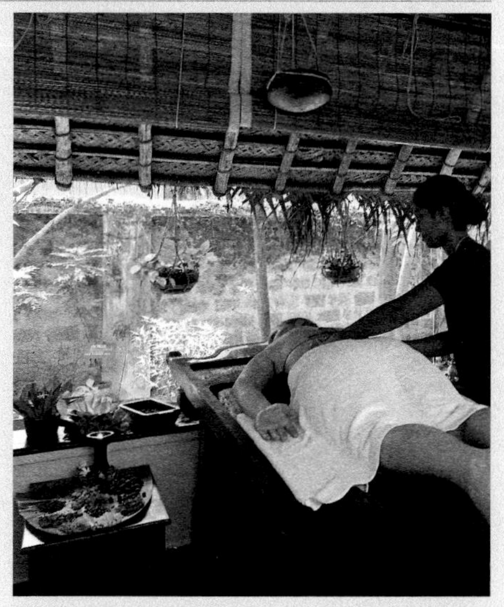

For those with less time, who simply want to experience some of the rejuvenating and general wellness benefits of Ayurveda, there are plenty of great options. At **Coconut Lagoon** (*see p349*), for instance, all consultations begin with a physical examination and general questions on lifestyle and diet. The doctors may then prescribe a detoxification programme or a series of rejuvenating treatments including herbal face packs for wrinkles and massages for general relaxation. **Pooppally's Heritage Homestay** (*see left*) has a room reserved for Ayurvedic treatments, with a traditional massage bed; an Ayurvedic practitioner is available on call. At the **Olavipe Homestay** (*see left*), guests may request a consultation with the Ayurvedic doctor in the village nearby, and the resident chef cooks up the prescribed vegetarian diet to go along with the Ayurvedic treatments. The CGH Earth's beach property, **Marari Beach Resort** (*see left*), has plenty of opportunities for pampering at its Ayurvedic centre, which has Green Leaf certification – a recognition of excellence given by the government of Kerala. This centre can also deal with more difficult, chronic conditions: qualified Ayurvedic doctors will diagnose and prescribe a course of treatment that can be pursued even after you return home. The resort even has its own pharmacy, with medicines and preparations made using herbs grown in a special garden at the resort.

Clockwise from top:
Kumarakom Lake Resort;
A Beach Symphony;
Marari Beach Resort;
Coconut Lagoon.

Lake; the rest face the pool. Rooms are elegant, with large four-poster beds, intricate woodwork, traditional roofs and a television – rare in the backwaters. Choola, the multi-cuisine restaurant, has a few tables on the lawns beside the lake, ideal for devouring the special duck roast, cooked in a rich, spicy gravy, while a raft of live ducks swims by.

Raheem Residency

Alappuzha *Beach Road (0477-223-9767/0767/ www.raheemresidency.com). $$$. No AmEx.*

One brief stretch of road separates the wonderful Raheem Residency from Alappuzha's unspoilt beach. This spacious bungalow was originally built by an Englishman in 1868, and has been home to the Raheems, a merchant family from Gujarat, for nearly a century. It has played gracious host to all manner of dignitaries, including Mahatma Gandhi and Jawaharlal Nehru. It is a delightful mish-mash of different architectural styles – colonial, Mughal and Keralan – and has been passionately restored by its current owners. Rooms are named after members of the family. Each is unique and filled with antiques, and the luxurious bathrooms inspire you to linger. There's a large living room with plush sofas and high ceilings, and a well-stocked library at the heart of the bungalow. One end opens out to a small courtyard with an apple tree and a pool, imported from France. Chakara is the rooftop restaurant, where traditional Keralan cuisine rules; it serves a fantastic Alleppey fish curry. Harbour, the bar next door, is run by the same management, offering residents the option to soak in the sea breeze along with a beer.

Spice Coast Cruises

Kottayam *Puthenangadi Boat Jetty (0478-258-2615/ www.cghearth.com). $$$$.*

Spice Coast Cruises, another CGH Earth enterprise, runs some of the more elegant houseboats on the backwaters, and these one- or two-bedroom barges have none of the irrational frills that mar many other houseboat experiences, such as a television with dish antenna that needs to be realigned with every turn the houseboat makes. Some other *kettuvallams* have garish upper decks that maintain a lofty distance between you and both the boat's crew and backwater life. On Spice Coast Cruises' *kettuvallams*, the vantage position is a comfortable divan with bolsters right behind the boat's captain. From here you can take in the sun, the breeze, the picturesque waterscape and learn more about the backwater way of life from the boat's crew, who are all locals, familiar with almost every nook in this riverine world. The crew will gladly point out ancient churches, temples and other attractions along the way, and even pull over so you can have a closer look, or stop at a toddy shop if you want to try the local favourite. At dusk, the houseboat drops anchor in the middle of Vembanad Lake, as opposed to other houseboats, whose operators prefer to stop closer to the banks. Here, under a starry night sky, Keralan life plays out at its charming best, as the call to prayer from a nearby mosque mingles with the sounds of temple festivities and the occasional plop of a fish. Meals are cooked by the crew on the boat, and feature fresh catch from the backwaters – large prawns and pearl spot fish, cooked the way you like it.

Factfile

When to go

The end of September to March is the coolest time of year to visit the backwaters, when Kerala is at its greenest. On the other hand, most visitors come during this time, so the backwaters can get a little crowded. Great hotel and houseboat deals can be struck during the summer and monsoon months, except when the snake boat races are on.

Getting there

Alappuzha is easily accessible by road from Kochi, which is also the nearest airport. It's also well connected by rail to cities like Kochi, Chennai and Bangalore.

For more on travel within India, *see p378* **Navigating India**.

Getting around

Regular government ferries ply routes between Alappuzha and other towns in the backwaters such as Kottayam, through lakes, rivers and canals, with stops in villages and islands on the way. Check with the Government Ferry Services office on Boat Jetty Road in Alappuzha for individual destinations and timings (0477-225-2015, open 5am-9.15pm daily). These backwater buses are the cheapest way to get around the waterways (Rs 20 for a three-hour journey) and are also a great way to mingle with the always-friendly Keralan locals. However, if you want the opportunity for unplanned stops so you can linger in a beautiful sunset, or to travel at your own pace, hire a boat or private taxi.

Tourist information

The District Tourism Promotion Council office is at the Boat Jetty in Alappuzha (0477-225-3308/ 1796, www.dtpcalappuzha.com), open 9.30am-7.30pm Mon-Sat.

Internet

Kottayam and Alappuzha towns have rather unreliable internet cafés, and most large hotels/resorts have internet access or are Wi-Fi enabled.

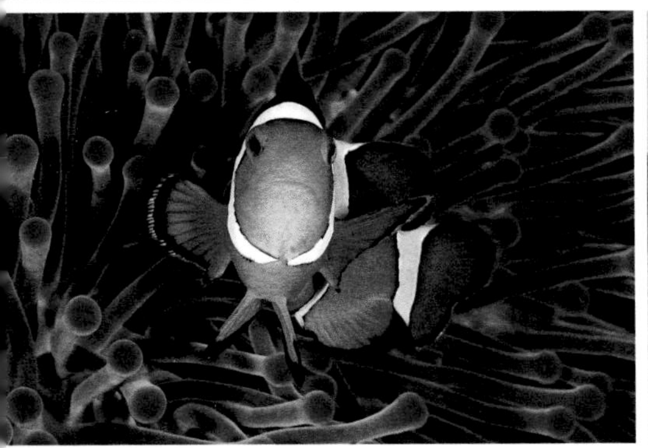

Top & bottom left: Havelock Beach No.5. Middle right: Havelock Island. Bottom right: Ross Island.

The Andaman Islands

Beautiful beaches; bitter history.

Hawaiian-American pop singer Jack Johnson was so entranced by the star-studded Andaman sky that he wrote a song about it named 'Hole to Heaven'. Besides pollutant-free skies and luxuriant tropical forests, the Andamans promise crystal-clear waters, golden sands, a dazzling array of marine life, the possibility of aquatic adventures, and long, uninterrupted silences. After the clangour and congestion of mainland India, the pristine, sparsely populated beaches make it easy to forget you're still in India. And, in fact, the territory is actually closer to Myanmar than to the Indian mainland.

Life here moves at a slow pace. Internet connections aren't quite as speedy, mobile phone networks are scratchy, and travelling between the islands involves long waits for ferries. But this change of pace is sought after by discerning travellers, who come to the Andamans to slow down, listen and observe – or to dive, snorkel, kayak or trek.

The islands' isolation made them a convenient location for a penal colony for the British colonial government, which dispatched thousands of Indian prisoners here. To Indians, the islands are still remembered as the dreaded Kala Pani – the Black Waters. It's a name that rang true metaphorically, but it's a terribly inaccurate description of the limpid, azure waters of the Andaman Sea.

Explore

The Andaman and Nicobar archipelago consists of 572 islands, the majority of them uninhabited, spread 780 kilometres (485 miles) north to south in the Andaman Sea. The Andamans is the larger cluster, with around 550 islands. The Nicobar Islands are completely closed to tourists. The isolated islands were once home to various indigenous groups, but contact with mainlanders drove many tribes to extinction. Only a few groups survive, among them the Jarawas, Onges, Sentinelese and Shompens. Most live on remote islands and visitors are warned against trying to make contact with them.

Travellers on a short trip can reasonably expect to visit only **Port Blair**, the territory's capital, located on the **South Andaman Island**, and **Havelock**, 54 kilometres (34 miles) to the north-east, a resort island a two-hour ferry ride away. Visiting other parts requires more time, and facilities are thinner, but there's much to enjoy and a trip of at least five days is recommended.

PORT BLAIR

Built on a small peninsula, this quiet town, the administrative capital of the Andaman and Nicobar Islands, was named for Archibald Blair, who conducted a survey of the islands for the East India Company in 1789. The remoteness of the Andamans made them a perfect location for a penal colony and the first prisoners were shipped here soon after Blair's expedition. Though malaria forced the British to abandon the colony in 1796, the penal settlement was re-established in 1858, shortly after the First Indian War of Independence. Conditions were harsh and convicts were put to work clearing the forests and building roads and houses.

Port Blair has enough attractions to keep visitors occupied for a couple of days. Most museums and sights are less than 15 minutes' drive from each other, but bear in mind that the steep hills the town is built on make getting around on foot arduous. The Aberdeen Bazaar is where you'll find most of the shops, along with ATMs and internet cafés. Tiny Chatham Island, with its saw mill, is at the peninsula's northern tip, linked by a bridge. As you work your way back from there, you can call in at the Samudrika Naval Museum and the Anthropological Museum.

The Fisheries Museum and the Cellular Jail are a short distance from each other on the north-eastern shore of Port Blair, near Aberdeen Jetty, from where boats leave for **Ross Island**. Harbour cruises leave the jetty every evening at 3pm and, take visitors around the bay for a two-hour trip, briefly stopping at **Viper Island**.

Anthropological Museum

Phoenix Bay (03192-232-291). Open 9am-1pm, 2-4.30pm Mon-Wed, Fri-Sun. Admission Rs 10; Rs 20 camera.

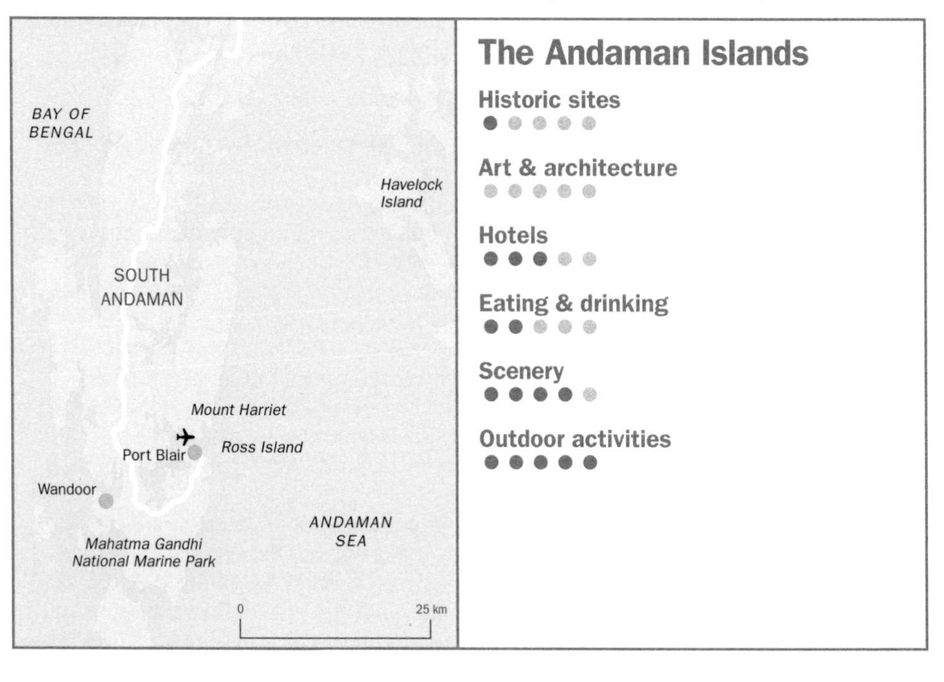

The aboriginal groups that inhabited the Andamans have not had a fair exchange in their encounter with the outside world. Most of these groups – the Jarawas, Onges, Shompens and Sentinelese among them – were hunter-gatherers, who lacked immunity to the diseases introduced by settlers. With the exception of the Nicobarese, who are thought to number around 30,000, most of the other groups are estimated to comprise fewer than 300 people. The Sentinelese of North Sentinel Island have been the most successful in keeping outsiders away, often greeting potential visitors with a hail of arrows. Nonetheless, it is estimated that they number under 250. The best place to learn about these native peoples and their ways of life is through the panels and artefacts at the Anthropological Museum. Displays include a mock-up of a Sentinelese hut, flint tools and weapons. There's a comprehensive introduction to the islands, and the museum shop has a small set of books on local tribes, in addition to shell souvenirs and postcards.

Cellular Jail

GB Pant Road (03192-230-117). Open 8.45am-12.30pm, 1.30-4.15pm (last entrance, museum closes at 5pm) Tue-Sun. Entry Rs 5; camera Rs 10; video camera Rs 50. Sound-and-light show 6pm Hindi, 7.15pm English daily (subject to weather conditions). Tickets Rs 20.

Construction of the Cellular Jail, with 696 dank cells housed in seven wings stretching out from a central tower like the spokes of a wheel, began in 1896. Over the next few decades, several freedom fighters were held here, often in solitary confinement. Only three wings of the jail still stand. In 1969, the well-preserved remaining section was declared a National Memorial. A small museum has life-size clay models of prisoners wearing fetters and chains spreadeagled over metal frames to be whipped, to show the barbarity with which inmates were treated. Carefully tended lawns stand between the wings and a shed on the grounds preserves the old gallows. Every evening, a moving sound-and-light show, with voices of famous Indian actors Om Puri and Naseeruddin Shah, tells stories of the jail and its inmates.

Chatham Saw Mill

Chatham Island (03192-232-778). Open 6.30am-3pm Mon-Sat. Admission Rs 10.

This is where you can see tree trunks the size of a small house being reduced to thin planks in a matter of minutes. Said to be one of the oldest saw mills in Asia, it was established in 1883 and most of its products are used locally. The complex is full of giant, buzzing machinery. Look for the bobbing logs being seasoned in the inlet by the edge of the mill. There's a small museum with samples of local tree species, including teak and paduk. Nearby stands a memorial to the prisoners brought to the islands after the First Indian War of Independence.

Corbyn's Cove

This stretch of beach, seven kilometres south-east of Aberdeen Bazaar, is Port Blair's favourite weekend spot. It's clean and, best of all, almost empty on weekdays. Peer into the World War II-era bunkers at each end of the beach. They're a reminder that the Andamans were the only part of India that the Japanese managed to occupy for any significant period during the war.

Fisheries Museum

Near Rajiv Gandhi Water Sports Complex (03192-231-848). Open 9am-1pm, 2-4.45pm Tue-Sun; closed every 2nd Sat. Admission Rs 5. Photography not permitted.

A 75cm giant clam weighing 105kg (231lb) greets visitors at the entrance to this museum. The aquarium section has such intriguingly named species as guitar fish and scorpion fish, while display cases are filled with fossils, the sting of a stingray and other piscine pieces. It's worth popping in for a visit on your way to (or from) Ross Island.

Mount Harriet National Park

Admission Rs 10.

The 365m (198ft) peak of Mount Harriet is the highest point on South Andaman Island and offers a commanding view of the outer islands. It's a 55km (34-mile) road trip from Port Blair, though the journey can be shortened to 15km (nine miles) if you take a ferry some of the way. Mount Harriet is a serene tropical woodland area that is perfect for short treks and picnics. Birdwatchers, mountain bikers and other nature trail enthusiasts will find this a pleasant, uncrowded place to spend the day.

"Today, many of the buildings have tall trees growing out of them, their roots spreading across the walls like giant webs."

Rajiv Gandhi Water Sports Complex

Aberdeen Jetty (03192-246-229). Open 10am-1pm, 2-5pm daily.

A rather ill-equipped facility, this complex gives visitors the opportunity to try their hand at jet-skiing (Rs 550 per person for ten minutes), paddle boating (Rs 20 for 30 minutes) and rowing (Rs 20 for 30 minutes). Most of the courses involve shuttling between the concrete pylons of the pier, which isn't very thrilling.

Ross Island

Ferries from Abderdeen Jetty 8.30am, 10.30am, 12.30pm Mon, Tue, Thur-Sun. Tickets Rs 75. Admission to Ross Island Rs 20.

This tiny island, a short journey from Port Blair, was where British administrators built their homes, away from the town. They attempted to recreate some of the comforts of home, constructing comfortable bungalows, a stately church with stained-glass windows, tennis courts and a bakery that was famed for its cakes and croissants. Perhaps

Clockwise from top left: Wandoor Beach; Havelock Beach No.7; Corbyn's Cove; Ross Island (2).

a little hyperbolically, they referred to their haven as 'the Paris of the East'. But the settlement was abandoned after an earthquake in June 1941 and never rebuilt because the Japanese occupied the Andamans the next year. Today, many of the buildings have tall trees growing out of them, their roots spreading across the walls like giant webs. Herds of spotted deer wander amid the ruins. The building that housed the bakery has since been restored and a slightly amateurish movie about Ross Island in its heyday is screened at 9.30am and 11.30am.

Samudrika Naval Maritime Museum

Delanipur (03192-232-871). Open 9am-noon, 2-5pm Tue-Sun. Admission Rs 10.

The Andaman and Nicobar Islands are home to 407 types of crustacean, 750 species of fish and 941 species of mollusc. You can see samples of some of these preserved in glass jars and displayed in showcases in this museum, run by the Indian Navy. Don't miss the nine-metre skeleton of a blue whale that washed ashore in the Nicobars in 1991.

WANDOOR

Wandoor Beach, 29 kilometres (18 miles) from Port Blair, presents those seeking solitude with the opportunity to have a beach almost to themselves during the week. But the main reason to come here is to take the early morning boat trips to the coral reefs off the islands of Red Skin and Jolly Buoy in the Mahatma Gandhi Marine National Park. Boats leave the little jetty about 200 metres from Wandoor beach at 10am from Tuesday to Sunday and return by 2.30pm (Rs 450). You'd do well to carry snacks and water. Snorkelling equipment is available to rent on the islands, as are glass-bottomed boats. As well as the underwater world, there's extensive birdlife to be seen.

HAVELOCK ISLAND

Havelock Island, 54 kilometres (34 miles) and a two-and-a-half-hour ferry ride from Port Blair, is the most visited location in the Andaman Islands after Port Blair, but it's still far from being crowded. Something of a diver's paradise, it also has stretches of empty beaches that are miraculously clear of the plastic debris that characterises much of the mainland coast. Blue, breathtakingly clear waters allow you to wade out to your chin and still see your toes.

Since it's a relatively little-visited destination, many of the beaches don't have names and are blandly referred to by numbers. Most hotels are clustered on the road between Beach No.3, which has a little market selling basic supplies, and Beach No.5. The most beautiful beach, most travellers acknowledge, is Beach No.7, also known as Radhanagar Beach. It is on the edge of a stretch of lush tropical forest and, at the far end, has a placid lagoon in which it's possible to float the day away on your back, gazing at the clouds above.

OUTDOOR ACTIVITIES

Havelock Island has numerous opportunities for nature walks, game fishing, snorkelling and scuba diving. Snorkellers and divers can see coral in orange, red, pink and yellow, along with turtles, rays and scores of species of colourful fish. Popular snorkelling sites include Elephant Beach, an easy spot for beginners, and South Button Island, with its barracudas, eels and angelfish. As well as these sites, divers speak well of the coral reefs of Dixon's Pinnacle, and the Lighthouse, which is suitable for night dives. Many shops in the main market have signs advertising angling and snorkelling expeditions for visitors, but if you're planning to go scuba diving, it's best to chose a well-known and reputable operator, such as those listed below. Most dive operators also have room on their boats for snorkellers.

Andaman Bubbles (Vijaynagar/Beach No.5, 03192-82140, 98452-36747, www.andamanbubbles.com) is run by a friendly Brit named Jez. It conducts several courses that meet standards set by PADI, from a one-day Discover Scuba Diving course (Rs 4,500) to Open Water Diver courses (Rs 18,000). Group size is limited to five and the outfit prides itself on its quality equipment.

A basic Discover Scuba Diving course at the PADI facility of Barefoot Scuba (Beach No.3, Barefoot Scuba Dive Resort, 94742-63120, www.diveandamans.com) costs Rs 4,500, while a three- to five-day Open Water Diver course is Rs 16,000. Snorkelling trips start from Rs 500.

At Barefoot Eco Tours (Havelock Jetty, 03192-282-151, www.wildandamans.com) half-day snorkelling trips start at Rs 1,200 per person (for four people) or Rs 2,000 (for two people). The company also runs kayaking excursions with prices from Rs 1,500, as well as treks, camping expeditions and guided birdwatching tours.

DIVEIndia (Beach No.5, 03192-214-247, www.diveindia.com) offers trips to the largest number of diving spots on the islands and conducts the broadest array of diving courses in Asia. It prides itself on constantly discovering new sites. Instructors are warm, with the ability to calm even the most nervous first-timer. An introductory diving course costs Rs 4,000, while the PADI Open Water course, which involves four dives, is Rs 18,000. Packages include full board at Island Vinnie's (*see p364*).

Havelock Tourist Services (Havelock Market, Beach No.3, 03192-282-163, 99321-90012, 99332-10052, www.havelocktourism.com) is run by the always-helpful Qutubuddin. It conducts sport fishing trips, snorkelling expeditions and boat rides and arranges treks. If you visit his shop, make sure to buy a scoop of his wife's delicious home-made ice-cream. He also has several internet stations.

Eat

Gourmets be warned: you're not likely to eat the best meal of your life in the Andamans, or even discover a local delicacy. Most produce – with the exception of fish – is shipped in from mainland India. And because the tourist industry is still in its fledgling stages, the food, though perfectly acceptable, is rarely exceptional. Most restaurants, especially on Havelock Island, are attached to hotels and resorts.

Annapurna Cafeteria

Port Blair *Aberdeen Bazaar No.71, Mahatma Gandhi Road (03192-234-199). Open 6.30am-10pm daily. $. No credit cards. South Indian.*

Funky lamps suspended from the ceiling are the only concession this air-conditioned vegetarian restaurant makes to decor. The focus is firmly on the food, which is served warm and quickly. The thalis are in great demand, as are the South Indian *idlis* and dosas, which are available in the morning.

Barefoot Restaurant

Havelock Island *Radhanagar/Beach No.7 (03192-220-191/www.barefootindia.com). Open 6am-10pm daily. $$. No AmEx. Multi-cuisine.*

If you've got a pasta itch, this is the best place to scratch it. The restaurant, attached to the Barefoot Resort, offers Western dishes at big-city prices. There are also Thai dishes, a healthy selection of seafood and thalis. Tables are on a large wooden deck, with an area that allows you to sprawl on the floor if you prefer to eat semi-prone: the restaurant encourages leisurely eating. It also serves a range of Indian wines.

Blackbeard's Bistro

Havelock Island *Vijaynagar/Beach No.5 (03192-282-170/www.emerald-gecko.com). Open 7-10am, noon-2pm, 7-9pm daily. $$. No credit cards. Multi-cuisine.*

The menu changes daily at Blackbeard's Bistro, attached to the Emerald Gecko resort, depending on what the manager has found in the market that morning. As a result, the food is fresh and often delicious. The restaurant prides itself on its Bengali fish dishes, made with hand-ground spices, coconut milk and mustard oil. But the Western dishes are also well made. Try the roast chicken, if it's on the menu when you visit, and leave room for dessert. In season, there's most often a musician performing at dinner time.

Corbyn's Delight

Port Blair *Corbyn's Cove (03192-229-311/www.sarovarhotels.com). Open 7-10.30am, 12.30-2.30pm, 7.30-10.30pm daily. $$. Multi-cuisine.*

This restaurant, attached to the Peerless Sarovar Portico Hotel, is housed in a large, airy white room with aqua-blue niches on one wall. It's all very tropical, with rattan lamp shades and cane furniture. The menu offers a range of Indian restaurant fare, from chow mein to veg au gratin and *paneer makhani*. There's also a buffet and, judging by how quickly diners refill their plates, they clearly approve of the chefs' efforts.

Gita Restaurant

Havelock Island *Havelock Bazaar (no phone). Open 7am-8pm daily. $-$$. No credit cards. Multi-cuisine.*

This roadside eaterie serves the kind of dishes that only seem to exist on the backpacker trail: honey-banana pancakes, doughnuts with Nutella and the like. But in addition to the omelette sandwiches and vegetarian thalis, Gita's menu has a small section featuring dishes the owner has been taught to make by homesick Israeli tourists. The Israeli salad is quite good, we were assured, as is the chicken shawarma.

Light House Residency

Port Blair *Aberdeen Bazaar No 11, Mahatma Gandhi Road (03192-238-918). Open 11am-11pm daily. $$. No credit cards. East Asian/Indian.*

The air-conditioned Light House Residency, at the end of the busy Aberdeen Bazaar, is housed in a building that seems rather delicate: each time someone pulls the door open, the windows rattle alarmingly. But the food is decent, especially the various kebabs, naans and rotis. Bangkok natives might have trouble recognising the dishes from the Thai section of the menu, and the Chinese dishes have been indigenised perfectly to suit the local palate.

"The first thing you notice as you enter this restaurant is a glass case filled with lobsters the size of your forearm, luscious fish and succulent crabs."

Mandalay

Port Blair *Marine Hill (03192-234-101/www.fortunehotels.in). Open 7.30-10.30am, 12.30-2.30pm, 7.30-10.30pm daily. $$. Multi-cuisine.*

Despite its name, the Mandalay restaurant at Fortune Resort Bay Island does not serve Burmese food. Instead, its menu lists Indian, Chinese and Western standards, which appear in a buffet on most days as well as on the à la carte menu. It's all quite competent, but it's the view from the deck of the lighthouse across the bay that is really the main attraction.

New Light House Restaurant

Port Blair *Marina Park, 1 MS Road (03192-237-356). Open 11am-10.30pm daily. $$. No credit cards. Multi-cuisine.*

Top: Corbyn's Delight. Middle: Blackbeard's Bistro. Bottom left: Red Snapper. Bottom right: Mandalay.

Top & middle right: Sea Princess Beach Resort. Bottom right: Fortune Resort Bay Island. Left: Barefoot Resort (2).

The first thing you notice as you enter this restaurant is a glass case filled with lobsters the size of your forearm, along with luscious fish and succulent crabs. All around, local families tuck in happily and noisily. The menu is varied and includes dishes such as chicken in Macau sauce, prawns in plum sauce, *mutter paneer* and spicy chicken Chettinad. The rooftop gazebo seems to be the preserve of groups of locals, mostly men, dawdling over bottles of beer and tucking into kebabs as they look out at the swimming pool opposite.

Red Snapper Restaurant

Havelock Island *Vijaynagar/Beach No.5 (03192-282-472/www.wildorchidandaman.com). Open 7.30-10am, 12.30-2pm, 6-9pm daily. $$. No credit cards. Multi-cuisine.*
On a wide wooden deck perched on stilts at the Wild Orchid resort, the Red Snapper cooks up dishes from around the world. Expect to find excellent Burmese garlic fish, red snapper fillet in lemon butter and herb sauce and Bengali fish fry. There are cocktails and beer, and the lemon cheesecake is superb.

The Waves

Port Blair *Corbyn's Cove (no phone). Open 11am-11pm daily. $. No credit cards. Multi-cuisine.*
Each weekend, the gazebos at this beachside restaurant fill up with local men steadily knocking back bottles of beer as they work their way through the tandoori seafood and kebabs on the menu. There are also Indian and Indian-Chinese staples. But it's the location, right by the ocean, that gives this establishment its cachet.

Stay

Much of the accommodation in the Andamans is only a couple of steps up from basic, but both Port Blair and Havelock Island have options that cater to those who don't want to rough it. Visitors to other islands shouldn't expect anything approaching luxury, however. Prices shoot up in high season (November to April).

Barefoot Resort

Havelock Island *Radhanagar/Beach No.7 (03192-220-191/044-2434-1001/www.barefootindia.com). $$. No AmEx.*
Situated on an isolated stretch of the already remote Beach No.7, Barefoot gives its guests convenient access to an expanse of sand that some travellers (and *Time* magazine) have described as the best beach in Asia. The spacious cottages, with thatched domes and walls, have large balconies with broad wooden benches and the air is filled with the cries of parakeets, bulbuls and blue jays. Dense tropical trees keep the temperature cool, so you won't miss an air-conditioner. Thoughtful touches include a brass pot of water at the steps of each cottage so guests can wash their feet when returning from the beach and an umbrella in case of an unexpected burst of tropical rain. The hotel organises nature walks, kayaking trips, diving courses and provides massage facilities too. The star member of staff is an elephant called Rajan, who spends much of its time in the jungle nearby, but can be persuaded to swim in the ocean with guests – for a fee of Rs 10,900. Visitors have spoken highly of the excellent beachside Italian restaurant run by an Italian couple, though they were away at the start of the 2009 season.

Emerald Gecko

Havelock Island *Vijaynagar/Beach No.5 (03192-282-170/www.emerald-gecko.com). $-$$. No credit cards.*
The thatched-roof bamboo huts at Emerald Gecko are delightfully basic, in keeping with the establishment's desire to be viewed as an eco-tourism destination. Huts have a small downstairs area with a bench for your luggage and a spartan bathroom (some have only partial roofs and coconut trees shooting out of the shower area). A steep ladder leads to the upstairs section, which has a bed with mosquito net, a writing table and a snug balcony with comfortable sofa. The front wall is little more than a bamboo curtain, which rolls up to reveal an ocean panorama. Staff are friendly (ask them about fishing and snorkelling trips) and the limited facilities are balanced out by the relatively low prices.

Fortune Resort Bay Island

Port Blair *Marine Hill (03192-234-101/www.fortunehotels.in). $$.*
This hotel winds down the side of a hill like a luxuriant creeper and offers superb views of Port Blair. Designed by India's most famous architect, Charles Correa, the resort has large porticos and airy corridors, all perfectly oriented to catch the ocean breezes. Statues, bas-reliefs and paintings of members of the local Jarawa and Onge tribal groups stare out from quiet corners. The rooms are comfortable, with standard amenities, but only eight of them have sea views. The in-house Nico Bar serves decent cocktails and its large wooden deck is a welcoming spot to idle away an evening. There's also a small pool. Ask about package deals if you book ahead.

Hotel Sentinel

Port Blair *Phoenix Bay (03192-244-914/www.hotelsentinelandamans.com). $$.*
With furniture made from local red padauk wood, Hotel Sentinel's rooms are spacious and spotless. Sitting in the heart of Port Blair but located amid a profusion of trees that filter out traffic sounds, the hotel is popular with guests on their way to and from Havelock Island. There's Wi-Fi in the lobby, a multi-cuisine restaurant, a bar and Kerala Ayurvedic massage treatments.

Hotel Sinclairs Bayview

Port Blair *South Point (03192-227-824/www.sinclairshotels.com). $$.*
Sinclairs Bayview is especially popular with Indian tourists and prides itself on the fact that most of its rooms have sea views. They all have soft beds, a television, coffee pot and a dressing table. There's a bar with billiards table, a little restaurant with an alfresco section, a pool and, at the edge of the garden, a World War II-era concrete bunker.

Island Vinnie's

Havelock Island *Vijaynagar/Beach No.3 (03192-214-247/www.islandvinnie.com). $.*

Most of Island Vinnie's nine 'tented cabanas' seem to be occupied by divers doing courses at the DIVEIndia centre attached to the establishment, but they're also popular with civilians who aren't overly bothered about having a solid roof over their heads at night. That said, the canvas tents here aren't that rudimentary. They're built on concrete plinths, have large beds with mosquito nets, plug points and a tiled bathroom with hot running water. The beach outside is snapshot perfect. This establishment was set up by Vandit Kalia (aka Vinnie) but is run by Prita Namjoshi, who spent several years in New York working in advertising, before putting down roots in the Andamans. Both make every guest feel welcome (even those who don't share their passion for diving). Inquire about the movie nights and about the menu at the Full Moon Café, which was planning to shift into these premises at the time of writing.

Megapode Camping Resort

Port Blair *Corbyn's Cove, near Science Centre (03192-227-113/www.aniidco.nic.in). $. Open Nov-Apr only. No credit cards.*

Sprouting out of the top of a hill like a sci-fi lunar colony, the white domes that form the Megapode Camping Resort are an interesting option for travellers with a taste for the slightly bizarre. Despite looking like mutant mushrooms, these half-spheres have most amenities that a not-too-demanding guest would need: colour TV, air-conditioning, a sanitary bathroom and a peek at the ocean from the porthole windows. The camp is four kilometres from the town centre, but you don't have to travel all that way to get a meal: the facility has a restaurant that serves basic Indian and Chinese dishes and stocks beer too.

Megapode Nest

Port Blair *Horticultural Road, Hadoo (03192-232-380/www.aniidco.nic.in). $.*

Before this old colonial complex was converted into a hotel, it was the official guesthouse for visiting judges and administrators. This explains its stunning hilltop location, with a view over a large section of Port Blair and the harbour, and its gracious, Raj-era wooden-framed buildings. The three-star hotel has 33 rooms; there are also ten cottages situated in the lovely gardens, amid the manicured lawns and the wrought-iron furniture, colourful flowerbeds and casuarina trees. The wood-panelled bedrooms are well furnished, with television sets and broad wooden writing tables.

Peerless Sarovar Portico

Port Blair *Corbyn's Cove (03192-229-311/www.sarovarhotels.com). $$. No AmEx.*

Enjoy a peaceful night accompanied only by the murmur of the waves and the song of the crickets, then watch a spectacular sunrise over the Bay of Bengal from the vantage point of your balcony. Aquamarine-themed rooms even have balcony railings reflecting the colour of the waters lapping up on the beach just beyond. This peaceful resort is actually just an eight-kilometre drive from the centre of Port Blair. Rooms have LCD television sets and the hotel has relatively quick internet service, so you're only as isolated from the world as you want to be. The hotel is set in a large garden with ashoka trees, coconut palms, hibiscus bushes and a vast lawn. Though Corbyn's Cove is a popular weekend spot for Port Blair residents, the beach is almost deserted on weekdays.

Sea Princess Beach Resort

Wandoor *New Wandoor (03192-280-002/sresort@hotmail.com). $$. No AmEx.*

Rooms at this Wandoor hotel have large, comfortable beds, clean (though simple) bathrooms and a TV, but their best features, by far, are the large French windows and the little balconies with easy chairs that look out on to a thick grove of coconut trees, with the glimmer of the ocean nearby. There's a small pool, a bar amid a profusion of trees, and a lush garden with paths meandering between thickets of red hibiscus flowers. The stretch of beach right outside the hotel – dotted with giant trees uprooted during the 2004 tsunami – is somewhat rocky, but swimmers will find clear waters a little way to the right. In the evenings, residents gravitate to the large wooden decks to watch the stars come out and listen to the cicadas. The restaurant serves competent standard Indian fare. The Sea Princess is conveniently located for travellers who want to take the early morning boat out to the Mahatma Gandhi Marine National Park.

Silversand

Havelock Island *Vijaynagar/Beach No.5 (03192-282-493/www.silversandhavelock.com). $$. No credit cards on site.*

With 34 handsome wooden cottages set around a stretch of lawn, the beach-front hotel is a couple of steps up from the Wild Orchid on Beach No.5 (*see below*). It's among the few resorts to provide TVs in each room, in addition to fridges. The Indian food at its restaurant is said to be the best on Havelock Island, and its dive centre offers scuba courses, and arranges snorkelling and fishing trips.

Wild Orchid

Havelock Island *Vijaynagar/Beach No.5 (03192-282-472/ www.wildorchidandaman.com).$$. No credit cards on site.*

Inviting red hammocks hang outside each room at Wild Orchid, an indication of the casual comforts within. With thatched roofs and bark walls, the rooms have beds with mosquito nets, bamboo wardrobes with safes and clean, rudimentary bathrooms. Most guests, of course, will spend the bulk of their time on the porch and on the sparkling beach outside, where Rs 100 buys a deckchair for the day, a bottle of mineral water and a juicy coconut to keep you hydrated. The hotel conducts snorkelling and diving trips, beach tours, fishing expeditions and, after the sun goes down, hermit crab races. The guestbook is filled with comments praising Benny and Lynda, the couple who manage the place, for their warmth, but even when they aren't on the premises, the staff make sure guests don't notice their absence.

Factfile

When to go

November to April are the coolest months, with average temperatures between 23°C and 28°C. This is also the time you're most unlikely to encounter the monsoon. No matter when you visit, though, be prepared for short bursts of tropical rain.

The main monsoon season runs from mid May to September. Several festivals are held in the islands during October.

Getting there

Port Blair is connected by direct flights from Chennai and Kolkata. At the time of writing, services were operated by Kingfisher Red and Jet Airways/Jet Lite.

Ship services are also available from Chennai, Kolkata and Vishakapatnam, but they are infrequent and take between 50 and 60 hours. Details of operating companies and schedules are available on www.tourism.andaman.nic.in.

For more on travel within India, *see p378* **Navigating India**.

Getting around

In Port Blair, auto-rickshaws are easily available. Settle the price to your destination before getting in, to avoid nasty surprises later. Most hotels have private taxi services.

Ferries from Port Blair to Havelock take two to four hours; schedules vary by season. Once you reach Havelock Island, taxis are available to take you to your hotel. From your hotel, it's easy to negotiate the restaurants and resorts between Beach No.3 and No.5 on foot or by auto-rickshaw. Beach No.7 is furthest from the hotels, but it can be reached by a fairly frequent bus service.

Tourist information

Sightseeing tours and tourist information can be obtained from the office of the government's Directorate of Information, Publicity & Tourism at Kamaraj Road (03192-232-694, open 8.30am-5pm Mon-Fri, 8.30am-1pm Sat).

The Directorate's counter at the Andaman Teal House in Delanipur (03192-232-642, open 8.30am-5pm Mon-Fri, 8.30am-1pm Sat) accepts bookings for sightseeing tours to spots in and around Port Blair, such as Wandoor and Mount Harriet.

The government's tourism website is remarkably informative, and can be accessed at www.tourism.andaman.nic.in.

Internet

Networld Internet Café Aberdeen Bazaar. Open 9am-9.30pm Mon-Thur, Sat; 9-11am, 2-9pm Fri; 2-9pm Sun.

Tips

● **Foreigners require entry permits** to stay on the islands for up to 30 days, extendable by another 15 days with permission. Permits are issued by immigration authorities at Port Blair airport. Permits for foreigners arriving by ship are available at Indian missions overseas, the Foreigner's Registration Offices at Delhi, Mumbai, Chennai and Kolkata and the immigration authorities at the airports at Delhi, Mumbai, Chennai and Kolkata. Even after obtaining permits, some places on the islands are restricted to foreigners.

For a list of permissible destinations, see www.tourism.andaman.nic.in/entry.htm.

● **Book your hotels on the internet**. Phones tend to be erratic, especially on Havelock Island.

● **Take a little extra cash** along to Havelock. Credit card machines at hotels often break down and though there's an ATM on the island (on the road between the jetty and Beach No.3), it sometimes runs out of cash.

● **Ask your hotel to book your ferry** tickets, both outward and for the return journey to Port Blair. Tickets can be difficult to acquire, especially just before departure time.

● **Though the Andamans** are far to the east of the mainland, they use Indian Standard Time (five hours and 30 minutes ahead of GMT). This means that it gets dark quite early, often by around 5.30pm. Consequently, it's bright enough to set out on trips as early as 7am or even earlier.

● **Carry mosquito repellent** for trips to Havelock. Some parts of the island get a little bug-ridden just after dusk.

● **As anywhere, take care** when swimming in unfamiliar waters.

● **It's best to book a Port Blair hotel** for the night of your return from Havelock Island on your way back to the mainland. You'll need to stay in Port Blair the night before departure since flights for the mainland often leave early in the morning.

Pondicherry

France's best-kept legacy in India.

With its French-influenced architecture and fine fusion food, Pondicherry (now officially renamed Puducherry), the main town in the union territory also called Pondicherry, has a very distinctive Franco-Indian spirit. In fact, some parts of the town's French Quarter barely feel Indian. France's National Day is celebrated every 14 July; streets are called *rues*, and the white-on-blue street signs resemble those in Paris; local buildings are known by their French names, and most staff in government and commercial establishments speak French.

Europeans have been fascinated by Pondicherry since ancient times. Arikamedu, near the present-day town, traded with the Romans, and later colonists – Portuguese, Dutch, Danes, British and French – all wanted a piece of the action. However, it's the French who left the most indelible mark here, their influence remaining even after their departure in 1954. Today, with warm hospitality and its unique melded heritage, Pondicherry exudes a sense of the comfortable co-existence of cultures. A facelift is currently breathing new life into the historic buildings of the French Quarter, while heritage eco-hotels, swish boutiques and Western cuisine thrive.

A short distance from the town is the settlement of Auroville, the concrete result of a utopian vision for alternative living – another reminder of the territory's openness to assimilating other cultures.

Clockwise from top: Tamil Quarter; Goubert Avenue; Matrimandir.

Explore

While the territory of Pondicherry (which covers four scattered regions) is 480 square kilometres (185 square miles), the main section of the town of Pondicherry, covered in this chapter, is just 20 square kilometres (eight square miles). Most sites can be navigated on foot or by bicycle or moped.

Pondicherry's French Quarter (once called Ville Blanche), along the coast, was laid out in a geometric grid pattern with straight roads intersecting at right angles, making it very easy to navigate. Goubert Avenue (Beach Road) runs parallel to and along the coast. Until the early 1990s this was a beach, but the construction of the harbour restricted and eventually stopped the natural movement of sand to the beach, and a groyne (a barrier made of large boulders) was then built to protect the coastline. About half a kilometre inland from the coast, the Tamil Quarter largely continues the grid. It lies behind the French Quarter, to the west of a canal called Gingy Salai.

Most of Pondy's sites are concentrated in the French Quarter, which is dotted with grand mansions, still referred to by their French names, along with government buildings, a picturesque promenade and green parks. However, the Tamil Quarter is not without its charms. Streets marked off by heritage preservation society INTACH (*see p373* **The heritage keepers**) have restored Tamil homes, with their community porches, sunlit verandas, sloping roofs and filigreed fences.

FRENCH QUARTER

The Pondicherry Museum (0413-222-3950, open 9.40am-1pm, 2-5.30pm Tue-Sun, admission Rs 2) on Ranga Pillai Street, off Bharati Park in the heart of the French Quarter, houses remains from the ancient Arikamedu settlement that traded with Rome. There are also sculptures from the Pallava dynasty and rooms that recreate scenes of French life in Pondy. Other sections display precious and semi-precious stone collections and South Indian temple architecture. Sadly, it's all quite poorly maintained and has little labelling.

Nearby, the Police Headquarters, Town Hall and Raj Bhavan, all built by former colonists, are worth a glance for their inspired architecture. These government buildings surround Bharati Park (open 6am-9pm daily), with lush shady trees, pathways, benches, stone sculptures and children's play areas. The Pondicherry Museum displays an interesting story about how the park's central monument, Aayi Mandapam, got its name. Three blocks north of the park on Rue Saint Gilles is the Sri Aurobindo Ashram (0413-223-3649, open 8am-noon, 2-6pm daily, admission free, certain sections need a pass), the resting place of Sri Aurobindo, philosopher and spiritual thinker, and the Mother, follower of Sri Aurobindo and founder of Auroville. A bookstore inside sells guides to the ashram and Auroville.

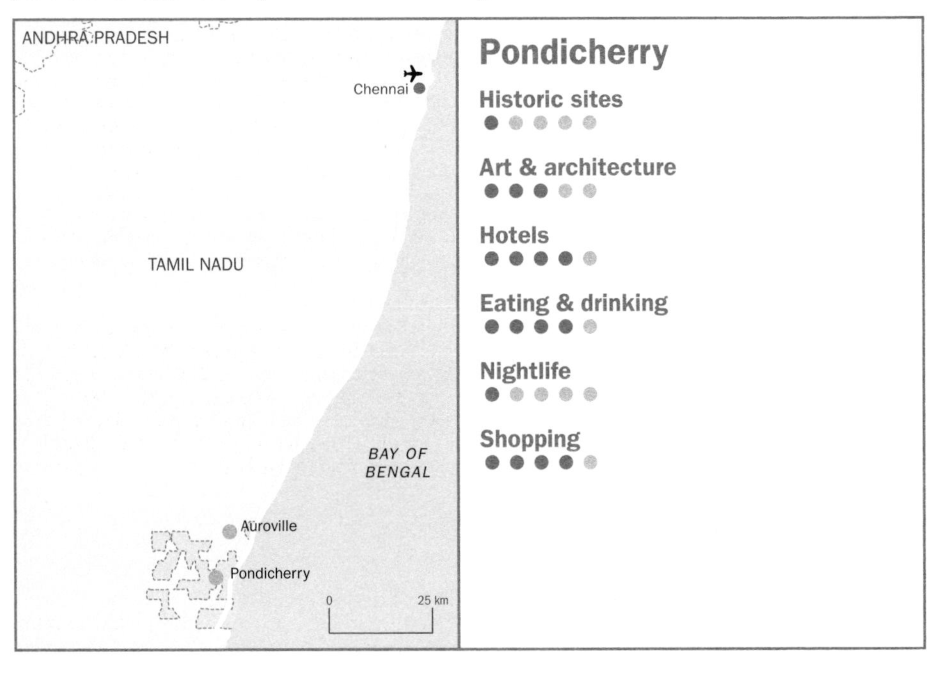

The major Tamil temple in the French Quarter, Manakula Vinayagar Koil, devoted to Lord Ganesha (0413-233-6544, open 5.30am-2.30pm, 4-9.30pm daily, admission Rs 2-10), is just south of the ashram. Apart from its typical colourful and ornate Tamil temple façade, it has murals depicting Lord Ganesha in various guises. Outside, real-life elephant Laxmi blesses devotees who make offerings to her, by placing the tip of her trunk on their heads. Further north, on the edge of town, the Aurobindo Handmade Paper Factory (0413-233-4763, open 8.40am-noon Mon-Sat, admission free, no photography) makes artfully designed, marble-finished paper from rag pulp. Visitors can make their own paper, or buy the products on sale from this ashram-owned enterprise.

The heritage trails to the north and south of Bharati Park show visitors much of the town's typical old architecture. Renovated façades add immense charm to Rue Romain Roland, Rue Labourdonnais, Rue Dumas, Rue de Bussy, Rue Suffren, Mission Street and Jawaharlal Nehru Street. For superb views of Pondy's skyline and seaside, visit Goubert Avenue (Beach Road). A four-metre statue of Gandhi marks the centre of this stretch, a big hit with both locals and visitors, with sunrise watchers coming here as early as 5.45am. The broad and well-maintained promenade is shut to vehicular traffic at sundown, making it a relaxing place to walk or cycle.

TAMIL QUARTER

Just off the busiest, most commercial streets of the Tamil Quarter is the Church of Our Lady of the Immaculate Conception on Mission Street, completed in 1791. Its neo-classical architecture is similar to that of other church structures in India at the time. The Sacred Heart Church is on Subbayah Salai, at the southern end of town, a few blocks from the Muslim neighbourhood around Rue Cazy. This church stands out for its Gothic influences and stained-glass interiors.

Best restored and preserved of the Tamil Quarter's streets are Rue de la Cathédrale, Rue Calve Subbraya Chetty to its south-west, and Rue Easwaran Dharmaraja Koil to its north-east. The INTACH office is housed in a traditional Tamil home within this neighbourhood and is worth a visit for more information on Pondy's architectural heritage (*see p373* **The heritage keepers**).

AUROVILLE

Auroville is a 25-kilometre (12-mile) scenic drive to the north-west of Pondicherry, in the state of Tamil Nadu. Auroville (the City of Dawn) is an experimental township, where people from around the world seek to live together in a green, peaceful and harmonious world. A 30-minute drive from Pondy, this utopian settlement (information booth open 8.30am-5.15pm daily) is the brainchild of the Mother, as the ashram's founder Mirra Alfassa is known. She was influenced by Sri Aurobindo's teachings and came to Pondicherry in 1914, staying here to develop a global village through socially relevant projects. The project has 80 settlements spread over 20 kilometres (12.5 miles), with approximately 1,200 inhabitants from India and abroad. The meditation chamber, Matrimandir, or Temple of the Divine Mother (free pass required from visitor's centre, open 10am-1pm, 2-4.30pm Mon-Sat, 10am-1pm Sun), a kilometre's walk from the entrance, is the spiritual centre of Auroville. It's topped by a golden ball, designed by Roger Anger, an avant-garde French architect and urban planner.

The township is open to day trippers, though advance permission is needed to visit some sections and the inner meditation chamber.

On the way to the Matrimandir is the Banyan Tree, the geographical centre of Auroville. This tree is said to be over 100 years old and has a diameter of over 50 metres (164 feet). Benches around the tree make this a good spot to rest, or linger and contemplate the township.

Just off Matrimandir is Savitri Bhavan (open 9am-noon, 2-5pm daily, admission free), a building named after Sri Aurobindo's epic poem. A statue of Sri Aurobindo stands outside; inside is a gallery with visual representations of this poem. Visitors can sign up for workshops or read Auroville-themed titles in the library.

Auroville's residents prefer not to think of their experimental township as a tourist attraction. However, there are some places where they don't mind sharing space with visitors; one such is the Solar Kitchen Coffee Shop (a kilometre south-east of Matrimandir, open daily), a terrace cafeteria where all food is prepared using solar power. It doesn't accept cash or serve day trippers, but guests who are staying in Auroville – who are entitled to a guest card, something like an internal credit card – can mingle and chat with Aurovillians without impinging on their privacy.

Visitor Centre

Just off entrance to the township, International Zone (0413-262-2239). Open 9am-1pm, 2-5.30pm daily. Information centre (0413-262-2373). Open 9am-1pm, 2-5.30pm Mon-Sat; 10am-noon, 2-5.30pm Sun.
The centre has information about Auroville and listings of accommodation for casual visitors and international guests who want to stay here.

Eat

When the French, Dutch and British set up shop here, they passed on their culinary influences. Perhaps the best example is the fusion of South

Indian and French cooking styles known as Creole cuisine (expect to find many versions of coq au vin, for instance). Inspiration has also been drawn from the Peninsula – fiery Chettinad flavours, Tamil Brahmin-inspired vegetarian savouries, Kerala's coconut-laced delicacies and Andhra's riotous curries.

Au Feu de Bois

French Quarter *36 Rue de Bussy/Lal Bahadur Shastri Street (0413-234-1821). Open noon-2pm, 6-10pm daily. $. No credit cards. Pizza.*

Pondicherry's sole wood-fired pizza place makes only three to four varieties, but it does them well. The dough is cooked just so, the crust is perfect, and the cheese home-made and sinful. This no-frills place was set up by a Frenchman, but its Tamil caretaker not only takes the orders, but is happy to discuss the art and science of pizza-making with diners.

Baker Street

French Quarter *123 Rue de Bussy/Lal Bahadur Shastri Street (0413-645-8888). Open 7am-8pm Tue-Sun. $. No AmEx. Western.*

Baker Street, as English as it sounds, is actually the ideal port of call for a homesick Frenchman. Baguettes, bagels, croissants, quiches line this bright, happy pâtisserie. Counter staff speak fluent French, and a crowded notice board is filled with information about what's going on in Pondy.

Le Café

French Quarter *Goubert Avenue, Beach Road (no phone). Open 8am-8pm daily. $$. No credit cards. Multi-cuisine.*

The only British building in the French Quarter, white-walled Le Café served as the Port Trust office before it was restored and converted into a seafront restaurant. Its biggest draw is the undiluted sea view, but the snacks are not bad either. Try the tangy, refreshingly chilled kombucha tea, made by fermenting tea using a mushroom culture. The downer is that its terrace seating remains closed most of the time. A tiny gift shop has reasonably priced Pondy souvenirs.

Carte Blanche

French Quarter *Hotel L'Orient, 17 Rue Romain Rolland (0413-2343067/www.neemranahotels.com). Open 7.30-10.30am, 12.30-2.30pm, 7-9.30pm daily. $$. No AmEx. Creole/Indian.*

The L'Orient hotel's charming garden restaurant is known to serve Pondy's best Creole cuisine. Try the steak with garlic butter, or a turmeric-infused creamy chicken in white curry. The beef and coconut curry with steamed rice and green salad and the succulent seafood platter served with greens are also good. The walls are lined with ancient maps of the Deccan Peninsula and the white wood and wrought-iron fittings add to the romantic atmosphere.

Le Club

French Quarter *Hotel de Pondicherry, 38 Rue Dumas, opposite Park Guesthouse (0413-233-9745/4210592). Open 7am-midnight daily. $$. No AmEx. French/Indian.*

The bar, with its elaborate drinks menu, dominates this *Gourmet*-magazine featured restaurant in the Hotel de Pondicherry. Breakfast features croque monsieur and crêpes; for dinner you'll get mint juleps and Malabar fish curry, with crème brûlée for dessert. Guests lingering on the rattan chairs swear that Le Club has the best cocktails in town. Get managing director Raj Malleappane to recommend signature cocktails and dishes. Saturday nights here have a real party atmosphere.

Coffee.com

Tamil Quarter *Dolphin House, 236 Mission Street (0413-4201245/www.coffeedotcom.net). Open 10.30am-8.30pm daily. $$. No AmEx. Café/Western.*

This relatively expensive internet café in a renovated loft is known as much for its high-speed internet as its pâtisserie. Its standard fare is quite a hit, though: coffee, tea, pasta, dessert and ice-cream. Wood-panelled walls, comfortable seating, plenty of reading material and movie nights make the café a popular hangout. There's a second branch at Rue Romain Rolland.

Hot Breads

French Quarter *Area No.42 Ambour Salai, Bharati Park (0413-222-7886). Open 7am-10pm daily. $. No credit cards. Café.*

Both sweet and savoury pastries are a hit at this cheery café off busy Ambour Salai. Jalapeno and chocolate puffs go well with flavoured sodas (try exotic lychee or caramel). Go early to be sure to find the full selection as pastries sell out early.

Satsanga

French Quarter *Near Law College, 32 Rue Labourdonnais (0413-222-5867). Open 8am-midnight daily. $$. No AmEx. Creole/Italian.*

For the meanest steak au poivre in Pondicherry, punters come to the L-shaped Satsanga, situated around a traditional Tamil home. Crowds at meal hours attest to the popularity of pancakes for breakfast, steak for lunch and risotto for dinner. Seating is available in the courtyard, or under the homely, tiled-roof interior with walls draped in Kanjeevaram silk saris. In keeping with the Pondy atmosphere, nobody is in any rush, so prepare for a long haul. Owner Pierre Elouard – who gave his restaurant the name Satsanga because it means togetherness – also organises music events in Chennai.

La Terasse

French Quarter *Near Beach Corner, 5 Subbiah Street (0413-222-0809). Open 8am-10pm daily. $. No credit cards. Pizza.*

Just off the seafront, this thatched-roof shack serves greasy Indian and Chinese food, but it's best known for its 17 kinds of pizza – ranging from margaritas to some with unconventional toppings such as aubergine, and even one loaded with pineapple, apple, grapes, tomato, onion and cheese (for those who like that sort of thing). ≈The decor, with plastic chairs, is not as creative as the food. The laid-back service means you can spend hours here with a book. The house dog keeps diners company.

Shop

There's plenty to buy in Pondicherry. Apart from the ashram boutiques selling paper products, incense and clothes, stores sell kitschy Indian accessories, handicrafts, designer garments, souvenirs and curios. The Tamil Quarter's busy streets have more conventional street markets and large stores, while in the lanes of the French Quarter cute boutiques with stylish storefronts tempt shoppers to spend more than they'd planned. Prices are similar to stores in big cities, but styles are unique. Auroville shops also tend to have branches in Pondicherry town.

Auroboutique

Tamil Quarter *12A Jawaharlal Nehru Street (0413-301-1340). Open 9.30am-1pm, 4-8pm Mon; Wed-Sun. No credit cards.*

Just by the ashram, this aromatic little shop sells Auroville products only: plenty of handmade incense sticks, paper, mobile phone holders, bookmarks, notebooks, candles and other gifts.

La Boutique d'Auroville

Tamil Quarter *38 Jawaharlal Nehru Street (0413-233-7264/www.auroville.com). Open 9.30am-1pm, 4-7pm Mon-Sat. No AmEx.*

This iconic 24-year-old Auroville store is packed with paper goods from the Handmade Paper Factory. Despite the high prices, the tastefully made clothes, bags, shoes, pottery, diaries, picture frames and bodycare products still tempt discerning buyers. There is also a branch of the boutique in Auroville.

Casablanca

Tamil Quarter *165, Mission Street (0413-233-6495/ www.hidesign.com). Open 10am-10pm daily.*

This two-level store is owned by Hidesign, the leather goods company. Pondicherry's most popular department store, it naturally has a massive leather section, but prices are better than at the main Hidesign stores. This is the place to buy both international goods and handicrafts, with Levi's jeans stocked alongside Auroville cotton pants. It's swish, loud and different from its comparatively conservative neighbours.

Cluny Embroidery Centre

French Quarter *46 Rue Romain Rolland, opposite Hotel L'Orient (no phone). Open 9am-1pm, 2-5pm Tue-Sat. No credit cards.*

Past a large wooden door in the French Quarter, with a quaint knocker, lies an open courtyard. In the rooms beyond, 40 local women work, creating exquisite pieces of embroidery. This centre, an apostolate of St Joseph of Cluny run by sisters from around the world, trains and employs the women. Sister Therese emphasises that the centre is only interested in genuine buyers and not window-shoppers.

Cre'art

French Quarter *First Floor, 53 Rue Suffren (0413-420-0258). Open 10am-7.30pm daily.*

Western kitsch meets Indian pulp fiction. With rooms devoted to clothes and accessories, kidswear, gifts and home accessories, it takes hours to explore the whole stock. Zany artefacts and Andy Warhol-inspired artwork can be bought at good prices. Tsunamika, the doll made by survivors of the 2004 tsunami, recycled paper products, silk pouches and more make this the ideal stop for gift-buying.

Focus Books

Tamil Quarter *204 Mission Street/Cathedral Street (0413-234-5513). Open 9.30am-1.30pm, 3.30-9pm Mon-Sat.*

Pondicherry's largest bookstore has a browser-friendly format and a large selection of fiction and non-fiction. Owner D Michael Anthony, who opened this store simply because he loves books, also owns Hôtel du Parc (*see p373*).

Geethanjali

French Quarter *20 Rue de Bussy (0413-420-0392/ geethanjalipondicherry@gmail.com). Open 9am-8.30pm daily. No AmEx.*

With four-poster beds, chairs, doorknobs, huge animal sculptures, figurines, dressers, carvings, pillars, free-standing doors and medicine chests from Madurai, Kozhikode, Rajasthan and Thanjavur, Geethanjali's three rooms resemble an overcrowded home. But the metal, wood, stone and glass objects are so pretty, the lush courtyard – with potted plants, petal-filled pools and decorative floor patterns – and warm staff so welcoming, that spending time and money here is a pleasure.

Kalki

Tamil Quarter *134 Mission Street/Cathedral Street); also at Visitor's Centre, Auroville (0413-233-9166/262-3450). Open 9.30am-8.30pm daily.*

Owned by scented-products company Maroma Auroville India, and garment manufacturer Aromode, Kalki sells merchandise that is anything but standard souvenir stuff. Here you'll find bags that defy geometry, flowing silk garments in deep colours, Indo-chic dresses and aromatic collectibles such as candles, incense and scented skincare products. Most items are one of a kind, handmade by artisans.

Kasha ki Asha

Tamil Quarter *23 Rue Surcouf (0413-222-2963/ www.kasha-ki-asha.com). Open 8am-9pm Mon-Sat.*

An American-owned enterprise, Kasha attempts to recreate a traditional ethnic Indian store. Each room is draped with wares: hand-woven fabrics, footwear, garments and accessories sourced from craftsmen and artisans across India. Its rooftop café is famous for coffees, croissants and cakes.

Nirvana Boutique

French Quarter *53B Rue Suffren, opposite Alliance Française (0413-420-9610/www.nirvana-boutique.com). Open 10am-1pm, 2-7pm daily. No credit cards.*

Nirvana's billboards, perched on trees and street corners across the neighbourhood, sport yesteryear's buxom acting-

The heritage keepers

One of Pondicherry's most iconic buildings (and its only remaining British one) is Le Café, the seafront restaurant on Goubert Avenue. It's a striking example of the success of the conservation work that is going on in Pondicherry. After the building suffered several disfigurements and ugly extensions, the Indian National Trust for Art and Cultural Heritage (INTACH) took it over and has restored it to its former glory, complete with white walls and arches. INTACH's work can also be seen at Neemrana's Hotel de L'Orient, now one of Pondy's top heritage hotels, and proof that heritage conservation and restoration don't necessarily require large amounts of rebuilding, nor mean that renovated buildings can't be put to practical use.

INTACH's Pondicherry office is located in a beautiful example of its own work. The 150-year-old building is one of the few surviving Franco-Tamil houses in Pondicherry. The ground floor exhibits unique elements of Tamil architecture, including the *thinnai* (veranda with masonry benches for visitors) and *thalvaram* (street veranda with lean-to roof over wooden posts), while the first floor has French influences, namely pilasters, masonry columns with capitals, arched windows and plaster decorations.

INTACH is an all-India organisation, but its Pondicherry chapter is one of the most active and successful. The group has restoration plans for all the old government buildings in town, as well as the whole stretch of Beach Road. It also offers a consultancy service to architects and owners to help them restore traditional elements to structures that have lost their original French and Tamil appearance. At the same time, INTACH is concerned with ensuring that restored buildings are adapted for modern use. To this end, it also works on modernising old buildings, making sure they meet contemporary needs without compromising the period aesthetic.

Preserving the distinctive nature of Franco-Tamil architecture has been crucial to the group's mission. 'Initially people thought we were anti-development,' said Ashok Panda, co-convener of INTACH in Pondicherry. 'But then they slowly realised that the only thing that distinguishes Pondicherry from Tamil Nadu is its heritage and its culture.'

'Before' and 'after' photos on the group's website (www.intachpondicherry.org) show the dramatic transformations of previously decrepit buildings that had lost all their French design elements of wooden shutters, white cornices and pilaster, with only minor adjustments to the interiors made to improve functionality.

On the Tamil side, the beautifully maintained *thinnais*, *thalvarams*, parapets and sunshades on Cazy Street and INTACH's home street of Rue Sri Aurobindo are the result of the organisation's extraordinary efforts.

A visit to INTACH's office goes a long way in helping to understand Pondicherry's unique history, culture and Franco-Tamil architecture.

INTACH

Tamil Quarter 62 Rue Sri Aurobindo (0413-222-5991/222-7324). Open 9am-1pm, 2-6pm Mon-Fri; 9am-1pm Sat.

dancing queen Vyjanthimala as a mascot. No handmade paper, incense or Auroville influences here; expect technicolour totes, vanity pouches, change purses, flashy jewellery, gypsy skirts, lampshades and stationery. Everything is infused with an element of Indian pop art, while T-shirts and messenger bags in the back room sport prints from old Royal Enfield bike ads.

Stay

Pondicherry's most appealing hotels are in restored buildings. The most location to find a touch of colonial grandeur is the French Quarter, but in recent years, the Tamil Quarter's heritage district has seen some beautifully restored Tamil homes converted into hotels as well. It is also possible to stay in Auroville; there are retreats within the township. The ashram also has several well-priced guesthouses in Pondicherry town.

For those looking for a fantastic – and quaint and quirky – seaside experience, the Dune, 12 kilometres north of Pondicherry along the East Coast Road in Tamil Nadu, is the place to go.

Calvé WelcomHeritage

Tamil Quarter *38 Vysial Street (0413-222-3788/ www.calve.in). $$. No AmEx.*

Once the home of a Chettiyar family, this is a wonderful example of 1850s architecture. With its tall columns, fine woodwork, handmade tiles, and internal courtyards with a functioning well, the hotel exudes character. The walls of the 11 air-conditioned rooms are done in Chettinad plaster using crushed eggshells. This keeps the interior surprisingly cool even in summer. Verandas and hallways have dowry urns and vintage gramophones, and some bathrooms come with copper bathtubs. Duplex rooms aren't quite as large as they sound, with a ladder-like staircase leading to an upstairs bed.

Dune Eco Beach Village

12km N of Pondicherry *Via Pondicherry University Pudhukuppam Keelputhupet (0413-265-5751/www.the dunehotel.com). $$-$$$$. No AmEx.*

Rooms are 'nature-cooled' and some of their doors could have been salvaged from an old temple. Decor includes colourful glass bangles and Rajasthani puppets. More distant shacks come with a bicycle so you can make your way around the property. Most of the food is organically grown in-house. Part tasteful luxury and part eco-friendly, Dune is all heart. With four bungalows, 30 villas and 20 rooms on a 30-acre coast-front property, this ever-popular beach village could have been a big-muscle hotel that shouldered the locals aside. Instead it works with and respects the fishing village nearby. It also has two fusion food restaurants and a spa.

Le Dupleix

French Quarter *5 Rue de la Caserne (0413-222-6001/ www.nivalink.com/ledupleix/index.html). $$$. No AmEx.*

Built in the 18th century for the mayor of Pondicherry, Le Dupleix has been restored to create a 14-room hotel, combining old French colonial heritage with contemporary design and comfort. Internal hallways are glass and metal, overlooking a garden restaurant that serves delectable Creole cuisine. Glass steps set over a waterfall lead to rooms and sitting areas upstairs. The well-furnished rooms, with four-poster beds and ornate wood-carved ceilings, are atmospherically lit. Suites are large and luxurious, and most rooms include a modern bathroom with bathtub.

The French Villa

French Quarter *51 Rue Suffren (0413-420-1545/ www.thefrenchvilla.in). $. No AmEx.*

Rooms at this airy and well-appointed guesthouse come with air-conditioning, hot water and cable television. Be warned, though, that en suites are not fully walled and have neither doors nor curtains. Ask to look around first, since identically priced rooms are quite different. The French Villa is on a leafy street in a neighbourhood packed with restaurants and plenty of 18th-century French colonial architecture. Café XO is its pleasant multi-cuisine eaterie.

Hotel de L'Orient

French Quarter *17 Rue Romain Rolland (0413-234-3068/www.neemranahotels.com). $$.*

The Neemrana brand of heritage hotels comes with certain expectations and L'Orient meets them all. This restored French mansion has 16 rooms, each named after a former French-occupied territory and each uniquely decorated. Karikal (with a private veranda) is palatial, while Satara, with an open-plan bathroom, diaphanous drapes around the bed and tall wooden windows, is compact. Larger suites have beds so high that they need wooden steps to get on them. Throughout, South Indian teak furniture, high ceilings, 18th-century maps and French memorabilia combine to create a period decor. There are no wall clocks, no fluorescent lighting and no room service – all part of the chain's endeavour not to seem like a hotel. The in-house store has a fine collection of home accessories and antique silver jewellery.

Hôtel du Parc

French Quarter *Opposite Manakula Vinayakar Temple, 5 Jawaharalal Nehru Salai (0413-222-6591/ www.hotelduparc.co.in). $$. No AmEx.*

Hôtel Du Parc wins on two counts: restoration and location. Just a short stroll from Bharati Park and many of the French Quarter's sights, eating and shopping, it was once the residence of Pondicherry's first governor, Joseph François Dupleix. The rooms are sparingly but uniquely done out; the bright mustard walls, turquoise fittings and white accents could be straight out of Provence, although the down side is that rooms have no views. Dining and other activities are set around the central courtyard with a 300-year-old mango tree. Internet and movies on demand keep guests connected.

Hotel de Pondicherry

French Quarter *opposite Park Guest House, 38 Rue Dumas (0413-222-7409/www.nathanswebworld.com/ projects/hotelde). $-$$. No AmEx.*

Set in a tropical garden, Hotel de Pondicherry is a restored 19th-century townhouse. Traditionally furnished French rooms have little bursts of colour and the semi-walled-off

Clockwise from top left: Coffee.com; Carte Blanche; Geethanjali; Cre'art.

Clockwise from top left: Hotel de L'Orient; The Promenade; Le Dupleix; Maison Perumal.

bathrooms, without doors, conceal only what's absolutely necessary. Rooms are named after figures from Pondy's history, with decor to match; so Pichaya, named after a Pondicherry artist, has an apt set of curtains, paintings and furniture. The hotel's three restaurants are its biggest draw.

Maison Perumal

Tamil Quarter *44 Perumal Koil Street (0413-222-7519/www.cghearth.com). $$.*
This property, restored by INTACH (*see p373*), has maintained all the elements that make a traditional home so warm, welcoming and environmentally friendly. The ten-room hotel and its *thalvaram* (street veranda with lean-to roof over wooden posts), *thinnai* (sit-out veranda with masonry bench) and *mutram* (inner courtyard) are managed impeccably by staff in traditional Tamil dress. The airiness and abundance of natural light create an instant feeling of comfort and well-being. Meals, with fixed daily menus, are served in the courtyard, and the Creole and Chettinad cuisine is irresistible; specials include a grilled seafood platter and lacy *appams* (bowl-shaped rice-batter crêpes) with stew.

The Promenade

French Quarter *23 Goubert Avenue (0413-222-7750/www.sarovarhotels.com). $$.*
Unlike many French Quarter properties, this five-star hotel, with just eight sea-facing rooms, doesn't have a traditional feel and could be a five-star hotel anywhere. Rooms have a bit more character than the lobbies and hallways, and the abundance of leather attests to the fact that it is owned by leather company Hidesign. It does, however, have great views of the old lighthouse next door and ample opportunities for people-watching along the seafront. As you'd expect, it has modern fittings and amenities, with a large swimming pool, 24-hour restaurant and a bar.

Villa Helena

French Quarter *14 Rue Suffren (0413-222-6789/villahelena@satyam.net.in). $. No AmEx.*
A large wooden door opens on to a quiet courtyard thick with foliage. Visitors walk through several hallways before they find the reception, making it feel as if you're trespassing in a grand 100-year-old home. Villa Helena's columns, arches and beams are all white, but the five rooms have lively bursts of colour. Each of the rooms – two on the terrace and three on the ground level – are individually decorated, and Japanese prints adorn the walls. This is a place for peace and quiet, and sprightly French owner Roselyn wants everyone – regulars and new guests – to be happy in this set-up, where visitors feel more like houseguests than hotel clients.

Factfile

When to go

December to March and August to October are the best times to visit. The high season is in December and January, when hotels get full. Excellent off-season rates are available to counter the unbearably humid summers when daytime temperatures can soar to 45°C.

Getting there

Chennai is the nearest airport, and there are direct flights from Mumbai, Delhi and Bangalore. From there a car and driver can get you to Pondicherry, 135km (84 miles) from Chennai airport, in three and a half hours.

For more on travel within India, *see p378* **Navigating India**.

Getting around

Most hotels offer transfers to and from Chennai airport, for a fee. Traffic-free streets mean that walking or using a bicycle or two-wheeler (moped) are the best ways to explore Pondicherry. Hotels can arrange for two-wheelers (on submission of valid documents), as well as auto-rickshaws or cars with driver to take you about town. On pleasant days, it's worth wandering around on foot.

Tourist information

Puducherry Tourism 40 Goubert Avenue/Beach Road (0413-233-9497/http://tourism.pondicherry.gov.in). Open 9am-6pm Mon-Sat.

Internet

It's easy to find internet cafés across Pondicherry and Auroville. Coffee.com (236 Mission Street) is the most sought-after for its high-speed access. Wi Corner (1 Cazy Street) is another popular café.

Tips

- Bicycles can be hired for as little as Rs 40 a day from many of the shops around town. Bikes are a very convenient way of getting around Pondicherry, and cycling means you avoid spending hours walking through areas you have already visited. If you are not cycling, carry a pair of good walking shoes. However, many hotels and shops around the ashram area will require you to take off your footwear, so plan accordingly.

- Many establishments take a siesta break from about 1pm to 4pm. It also gets warmer at this time of day, so find a cool place to hang out or give in to the siesta culture.

Navigating India

Getting from one destination to the other in India is often easiest by air. However, trains are a fascinating way to see the country – try to include at least one train journey in your itinerary. Within a destination, a car with driver is usually the most comfortable and least stressful way to get around, and is affordable for most visitors.

BY AIR

INTERNATIONAL

Almost every major airline operates flights into India from destinations around the world. Most fly direct to Mumbai or Delhi, and some also to Amritsar, Kochi, Kolkata, Bengaluru/Bangalore, Hyderabad, Chennai and Trivandrum.

DOMESTIC

Most of India's tourist destinations are well connected by domestic flights, though smaller places will require a flight change at a nearby hub. There are numerous domestic airlines, including several budget carriers. **Jet Airways** (www.jetairways.com) and **Kingfisher Airlines** (www.flykingfisher.com) are the top two domestic airlines in terms of network as well as good aircraft and service. Both now also operate low-cost no-frills airlines: **Jet Lite** (www.jetlite.com) and **Jet Konnect** (www.jetkonnects.in) from Jet Airways and **Kingfisher Red** (www.flykingfisher.com) from Kingfisher.

Air India (www.indian-airlines.nic.in) is the only other major airline with as wide a network, but this state-owned carrier, while functional, falls short of its two rivals in terms of convenience. Air India also operates budget flights under the banner of **Air India Express** (www.airindiaexpress.com).

Domestic air travel in India has become cheaper and more convenient than ever before. In addition to the budget airlines mentioned above, **Spice Jet** (www.spicejet.com), **Indigo** (www.goindigo.in) and **Go Air** (www.goair.in) are recommended; for flights in South India **Paramount Airways** (www.paramountairways.com) is also an option.

BOOKING ADVICE

When purchasing a domestic ticket, any change in itinerary translates to a cancellation, even if you are rebooking on another flight from the same airline. Try and buy flights that incur the least cost for a cancellation (usually a minimum of Rs 750); often the lowest fares are non-refundable, while paying only slightly more gets you a more flexible deal.

You can either book tickets directly with the airline or through a travel agent. For a convenient one-stop shop for all airfares try www.ixigo.com.

CHECK-IN

Check-in is a minimum of one hour before departure for a domestic flight and three hours before departure for an international one.

BY TRAIN

India's massive rail network covers almost everywhere in the country, and an Indian train journey is a fascinating experience.

Long-distance trains are those that provide sleeping facilities. Short-distance trains run during the day and over shorter distances, and these mostly only have seats.

The railway website (www.indianrail.gov.in) provides all the availability information a traveller needs, but is not easy to navigate and doesn't offer ticket sales. Availability information is also available at online travel website cleartrip.com.

BOOKING ADVICE

Booking tickets in advance is essential. The previously complicated ticket booking procedure has now become greatly simplified with online booking available through various Indian travel websites. Cleartrip.com and makemytrip.com are both reliable places to book (for a small fee – cleartrip.com charges Rs 100). The government-sponsored booking website is www.irctc.co.in.

Note that most large cities have multiple railway stations so ensure you book your journey to and from the correct one.

Foreign tourist quota

You cannot just arrive at the station and expect to get a seat on any train. Booking opens 90 days ahead of travel and seats/berths on popular routes like Mumbai–Goa are often booked well in advance in peak season (Nov-Mar). However, a small 'foreign tourist quota' of seats is held back for foreign travellers. These must be bought from the special foreign tourist reservation offices or counters at stations like CST Mumbai (first-floor booking hall) or New Delhi station (first floor) and are not available online. A passport is required as proof of foreign nationality. US dollars, British pounds and euros are accepted, but you can also pay in rupees if you show a foreign exchange receipt or ATM slip. For more information and other city locations where you can book under this quota see www.indianrail.gov.in/intert.html.

Indrail pass

If you're doing a lot of travelling, you can also buy an Indrail pass (from the same counter as the foreigners' quota tickets), which offers unlimited rail travel across India for up to 90 days.

Classes of service

Long-distance trains can have some or all of the following classes depending on the route: **AC first class (1A)** is the highest and most expensive, with fares comparable to airfare. Passengers have a door or a sleeping compartment (shared with at least one other person) that can be locked. Then comes the **AC 2 (2A)** and **AC 3 (3A)** tiers. All three of these classes have air-conditioning, tinted windows and padded berths; sheets and pillows are provided, doors are secured at night and attendants are available. The difference between them is mainly the number of berths in each section, with 1A having the least (two) and 3A the most (eight). Some trains also have a non air-conditioned first class **(FC)**. Sleeper **(SL)** class, which is the cheapest, is not air-conditioned, the berth is usually a wooden bench, there are no attendants and pretty much anyone can and does walk through the cabins; often passengers without reservations will also crowd these sections.

Trains travelling shorter distances have some or both of these classes: **AC chair car (CC)** and **second seating (SS)**; the former is air-conditioned and has relatively comfortable, individual seats that recline, while the latter can be anything from a wooden bench to a narrow padded bench shared by three people. Note that the lowest fare class train compartments can sometimes be unbelievably crowded with people filling the aisles and every possible floor space.

LOCAL TRAINS/METROS

Mumbai, Kolkata and Delhi have local train networks, all extremely crowded, though cheap and efficient. Tickets can be purchased at any of the stations. Those planning a lot of local travel may find a local train pass a worthwhile purchase.

TOY TRAINS

India has four 19th-century narrow-gauge trains still in operation, the first three of which are on the UNESCO World Heritage list. These are the **Darjeeling Himalayan Railway**, the **Kalka Shimla Railway** (Himachal Pradesh), **Nilgiri Mountain Railway** (Tamil Nadu) and the **Matheran Hill Railway** (near Mumbai). Journeys may have to be booked through a travel agent.

LUXURY TRAINS

There are several luxury trains that require you to make no effort beyond one booking (online or through various general sales agents or online agents; try www.royalindiatrainjourneys.com). You will travel like erstwhile Indian royalty, and be prepared to be waited on hand and foot.

India's first and most famous luxury train is the **Palace on Wheels** (www.rtdc.in), which plies a route that starts and ends in Delhi. It weaves through Rajasthan's key destinations (Jaipur, Sawai Madhopur, Chittorgarh, Udaipur, Jaisalmer, Jodhpur, Bharatpur) and includes a trip to the Taj Mahal. Even more luxurious is the new, all-suite **Royal Rajasthan on Wheels** (www.royalpalaceonwheels.com), which visits the same destinations. A less expensive version of these journeys is provided by **Heritage on Wheels** (www.heritageonwheels.org.in), which operates a route over four days, travelling to Bikaner and Shekhawati in Rajasthan; or you can take the shorter though less interesting two-day journey aboard the *Fairy Queen*, the world's oldest working steam locomotive.

Another train, the **Deccan Odyssey** (www.maharashtratourism.gov.in) journeys from Mumbai down the western coast to Goa, returning to Mumbai via Aurangabad (alternative routes also available). The **Golden Chariot** (www.thegoldenchariot.co.in) offers a similar luxurious experience in South India. Its week-long trip starts in Bengaluru/Bangalore and the train winds its way through historical sites, temples, a national park, the World Heritage Sites at Hampi and its surrounding area, and Goa.

There are a range of tariffs and travel classes on these trains. The Palace on Wheels departs every Wednesday (Jan-Apr, Sept-Dec). Other luxury trains run on variable timetables; check at www.indianrail.gov.in or with a reliable sales agent listed on the website.

BY BUS/COACH

While bus travel in India has improved in recent years, it is best considered only if you can't get a plane or train reservation or are on a budget. Newer buses, known as 'Volvo buses', are the best option, although they don't have toilets.

There are sleeper buses on popular routes like the 14-hour Mumbai–Goa trip, with reclining seats (see www.paulotravels.com). The Delhi–Jaipur route (six hours) has good buses, as does the Chennai–Pondicherry route (three hours). The overnight Goa–Hampi bus is also popular.

Be forewarned that 'video coaches' blare Bollywood films almost non-stop. And unless you don't mind travelling in an overcrowded, suspension-less bus with innumerable stops, don't travel on the dusty state transport buses.

Some routes can be booked online at www.redbus.in, www.travelyaari.com and www.ixigo.com.

BY CAR

India's notoriously bad roads have improved a lot in the last five years, and roads in Madhya

Pradesh to access the national parks of Kanha, Bandhavgarh and Panna have recently been completely redone. However, many rural roads remain terrible by Western standards, and those in cities such as Mumbai seem to be eternal works-in-progress, so expect plenty of potholes, especially during or just after the monsoon.

CAR HIRE

Hiring a care and driver (private taxi) is the best way of travelling between sites at most destinations, even with the abysmal state of the roads. Rental rates vary depending on the size and model of the car, whether it's air-conditioned or not, and whether the car will be used within the city or 'outstation' (outside the city limits). Prices range from Rs 6 to Rs 20 per kilometre, with a minimum charge of 200 to 250 kilometres per day. For those on a budget, the compact Indica (from Tata Motors) is invariably the cheapest car available. For longer drives, an SUV is better. In 2010 the most popular was the Innova (a Toyota), costing between Rs 8 and Rs 14 per kilometre.

In general, when booking through a travel agent, it's best to clarify all details in advance. Ask how many hours per day the car is for, whether there is a charge for a minimum number of kilometres per day, whether the driver's day or overnight charge (excluding tip) is included, and whether tolls, parking fees and taxes are covered. Get the full picture, and ask if there are any other hidden costs. Some agents will be open to negotiating a better price. Most hotels will also be happy to help with car hire; expect charges to be commensurate with the hotel's price.

It's very difficult to find self-drive hire cars in India, though Avis (www.avis.co.in) does offer them in some cities and you will also find them in Goa (although operators there are often not licensed to provide them). However, driving in India is not for the faint-hearted and we don't advise it: traffic is chaotic, rules are barely followed and road signs often non-existent. Also note that self-drive and chauffeur-driven cars cost almost the same. In addition to Avis, most of the tour companies listed below can also arrange car hire.

TAXIS

Most hotels offer pick-ups from the airport. At major airports you can usually hire a pre-paid taxi from a counter near the exit, which saves you the trouble of haggling. From airports and stations, drivers routinely overcharge, demand inflated 'luggage charges' and offer sob stories about having to spend days in line waiting for a fare.

Taxis in cities should run on meters but they often don't. Where they do, you usually pay the fare based on a chart that drivers must have in their cab by law, where, for instance, Re 1 on the meter is equivalent to Rs 14 and so on. This is unless the taxi has a digital meter, which will give you the correct fare upfront. In Mumbai, all taxis run on a meter and you should refuse to get in one that claims otherwise. In Delhi, fix the fare to your destination before you sit in any cab, which may not even have a meter.

AUTO-RICKSHAWS

These three-wheeled vehicles are found all over the country and are an efficient (although bone-jarring) way of getting around. In many cities and towns they run on meters, which must be read against a fare chart (as with taxis, *see above*). However, in Delhi, Goa and many other towns and cities, they don't have meters so you should fix your fare before getting in.

TOUR COMPANIES/CAR HIRE

All-India
Cox & Kings (www.coxandkings.co.in)
SITA Travels (www.sita.in, www.distantfrontiers.in)
TCI India (www.tcindia.com)

Online travel companies
www.cleartrip.com
www.makemytrip.com
www.travelocity.co.in

Amritsar
Om Auro Travels (0183-222-2182, 98729-81276)

Darjeeling, Kalimpong & Sikkim
Clubside Tours & Travels Pvt Ltd (0354–2254-646/www.clubside.in)

Delhi & North India
Marico Tours (011-2616-5403)
LPTI (011-4165-3100/www.lpti.co.in)

Goa
Vailankanni Auto Hires/Goa Cabs (0832-329-0584, 98221-01598/www.goacabs.com)

Hampi
Hamsa Tours & Travels (08394-228-101/www.malligihotels.com)

Jaipur, Jodhpur & Udaipur
Rajasthan Tours 'N' Travels (0294-329-5415/www.taxiwale.com)

Kanha, Bandhavgarh & Panna; Khajuraho, Orchha & Gwalior
Gulmohar Holidays (0751-407-4678, 98930-55864)
Chadha Travels (0761-322-178/320)

Kochi, Kerala Backwaters & Periyar
Kerala Adventures (0471-243-3398/www.keralaadventure.com)

Ladakh
Rimo Expeditions (0124-2806-027/www.rimoexpeditions.com)
Mountain Trails (011-6466-3444, 98100-42647/www.mountaintrails.in)

Pondicherry
Udaya Tourist Cabs (0143-222-3326/www.pondicherryudayatour.com)

Spiti
Spiti Ecosphere (98994-92417, 94182-07750/www.spitiecosphere.com)

Need to know

ACCOMMODATION

By and large, hotel rooms tend to be expensive for comparable facilities elsewhere in the world. In some places, like Delhi, there is a shortage of hotel rooms. Whenever you book a room make sure you ask what the total price including taxes is, as many hotels and restaurants add a hefty luxury tax to your bill.

HERITAGE HOTELS

Forts, palaces and historic buildings all over the country have been converted into hotels. Many great 'heritage' properties are included in this guide and hundreds more exist. Unfortunately, there is no definition or control over what gets labelled as a heritage hotel. Many are wonderful places, but as with old buildings anywhere, have problems with plumbing, steep staircases, ventilation and so on. Even some reputable hotel brands have heritage properties that are badly maintained. Ask plenty of questions to find out what kind of room you are getting before you book.

HOMESTAYS

These are rooms in a family's home rented out to tourists. They're extremely popular in Kerala (www.keralahomestaysonline.com, www.homestaykerala.com and hundreds of individual websites), and increasingly so in many other parts of the country (www.mahindrahomestays.com, www.comforthomestay.com), including the capital Delhi and the Himalayas (see www.himalayan-homestays.com). While they allow tourists to live and engage with local people, there is a huge variation in quality and facilities available, with no official minimum standards, inspection or governing body.

CONSULATES, EMBASSIES & HIGH COMMISSIONS

All foreign embassies are in Delhi. However some countries have consulates or high commissions in Mumbai, Kolkata and Chennai. Most consular and embassy offices are only open during weekday office hours so keep your country's toll-free emergency services number handy (*see p382*).

Australian High Commission 1/50 G Shantipath, Chanakyapuri, New Delhi 110021 (011-4139-9900/www.india.embassy.gov.au).

High Commission of Canada 7/8 Shantipath, Chanakyapuri, New Delhi 110021 (011-4178-2000).

Consulate General of Canada Fort House, Sixth Floor, 221 Dr DN Road, Fort, Mumbai 400001 (022-6749-4444).

Embassy of Ireland 230 Jor Bagh, New Delhi 110003 (011-2462-6733/www.irelandinindia.com).

New Zealand High Commission Sir Edmund Hillary Marg, Chanakyapuri, New Delhi 110021 (011-2688-3170/www.nzembassy.com).

New Zealand Honorary Consul Aashiana, First Floor, 5 Altamount Road, Mumbai 400026 (022-2352-0022).

South African High Commission B18 Vasant Marg, Vasant Vihar, New Delhi 110057 (011-2614-9411).

South African Consulate Gandhi Mansion, 20 Altamount Road, Mumbai 400026 (011-2389-3725).

British High Commission Chanakyapuri, New Delhi 110021 (011-2419-2100/www.ukindia.com).

British Deputy High Commission Naman Chambers, C/32 G Block Bandra Kurla Complex, Bandra (East) Mumbai 400051 (022-6650-2222).

US Embassy Shantipath, Chanakyapuri, New Delhi 110021 (011-2419-8000/www.newdelhi.usembassy.gov).

US Consulate Lincoln House, 78 Bhulabhai Desai Road, Mumbai 400026 (022-2363-2611/www.mumbai.usconsulate.gov).

CULTURE & ETIQUETTE

- Indians are usually warm and hospitable towards foreign visitors, have an interest in their opinions, and will think nothing of asking personal questions. The concept of personal space is different from that in the West, and you may find yourself backing up as someone talking to you inches closer and closer. Indians also like to feed (and overfeed) guests in their homes; you may have to cover your plate with your hands to get the flow of food to stop. In big, crowded cities, however, no one wastes time on niceties, while in smaller places people may be shy of greeting strangers. That said, don't be surprised if children point and giggle or adults come and say hello in the streets. To put an end to unwanted attention without seeming rude you can greet and then indicate with your body language (or by looking away) that the conversation is over.
- You may be surprised at the cursory, sometimes rude, way in which Indians deal with servants, waiting staff and other people working in service jobs – 'pleases' and 'thank yous' are not very common.

- Shaking hands is a common greeting, but Indians also touch their palms together in front of the chest and greet with 'namaste' or 'namaskar'. Less common in larger cities, it's a more appropriate way to greet elders and women from traditional families. Mainstream society does not look fondly on the idea of a man greeting a woman who is not his wife with a kiss, even on the cheeks, although many from the upper class have no problem with it. Stick to shaking hands and namastes if in doubt.
- Dress in the big cities is fairly liberal and you will see women dressed in a variety of styles. Dress for the occasion: if you're going to a nightclub or a posh restaurant then a tight skirt or a skimpy top is fine, but if you're going for a bus ride or a walk through a crowded bazaar then dress more modestly if you don't want to be the focus of a thousand stares. When visiting religious sites, both men and women should cover their arms and legs and, depending on the site, sometimes also remove shoes and cover the head. *See also p385* **Women**.
- Punctuality is not a great Indian virtue and you can often expect to be kept waiting, even in business contexts. Anticipate from the outset that tasks are likely to take longer than normal and go with the flow.
- On trains, buses and in traffic, Indians tend to jostle and push. Queuing does happen at railway stations and banks, but it's not universal – just as on the road, the biggest and fastest gets to the front first. No point in getting angry, though you are well within your rights to tell off those who try to squeeze into a queue.
- Don't believe every tale and story a guide tells you. Many like to weave tales of intrigue and over-the-top explanations are common; enjoy them with a pinch of salt.
- Many Indians find it hard to say no, particularly to a visitor. For instance, someone may send you in the wrong direction rather than say they don't know where the place you've asked for is. To know the difference will involve some amount of reading of body language and guess work. Or you may be told 'I will try' or 'let's see', which, frankly, could go either way. In government and bureaucratic contexts, however, saying 'no' is no problem; it's the 'yes' that's hard to come by. Indians sometimes indicate the affirmative with a head wobble that is neither the firm nod of a 'yes' nor the firm shake of the head that Westerners understand as 'no'. Recheck by asking.
- Although you will see men holding hands and being physically close, don't assume they are gay. Homosexuality, though as widespread as anywhere in the world, is frowned upon.
- Racism towards people of African origin is not uncommon. From stares and nightclubs refusing entry to locals assuming black people are drug dealers, it can take a variety of forms.

DRUGS

Cannabis and other recreational drugs are illegal in India, and penalties for possession are severe, with prison terms of up to ten years. But that hasn't hampered a widespread drug culture across social classes. You're likely to be approached by dealers peddling everything from hash and heroin to cocaine.

ELECTRICITY

In India electricity runs on 220-240 volts. Sockets vary greatly, but usually take round two-pronged Indian-style plugs. Most hotels will be able to provide you with a plug adaptor, but you'll rarely find a transformer to use with 110 volt US appliances. Electricity supply cannot be taken for granted anywhere in India. Mumbai is the only city in India with uninterrupted power supply. Power cuts are common everywhere else, though most hotels will have a generator for backup.

EMERGENCIES

The general emergency number for the **police** in Delhi and many other cities is 100, but it's not guaranteed that you will get through, or that you will get help. In Mumbai, call 1090 or the Tourism Police at 022-2262-1855.

If you have a **medical emergency** your best bet is to call an ambulance or head to the nearest large hospital of repute (some are listed below). Approach your hotel concierge or hosts for help.

Some 24-hour emergency helpline numbers that you can call from India:

Australia Consular Emergency Centre +61 2 6261 3305.
Canada Operations Centre for Foreign Affairs +1 613 996 8885.
South Africa Consular Services Operations Room +27 12 351 1000.
UK Consular Assistance Team +44 20 7008 1500.
US Overseas Citizens Services +1 202 501-4444.

FOOD GLOSSARY

abondigas meatballs in gravy
achaar or pickle; vegetables or unripe fruit pickled in fiery seasoning and oil
aloo/alu parathas flat bread stuffed with potato
alu/aloo tikkis potato patties
appam bowl-shaped rice batter crêpe
bhaji vegetable; also a generic term for cooked, spiced vegetable dish
bhajia deep-fried, chickpea-flour-dipped vegetable snack
bhuna gosht browned, spiced lamb or goat
biryani/biriyani pilaf usually with meat, fish, eggs or vegetables
chana/chole/chola chickpeas

chaat savoury snacks, typically served at road-side stalls
chapati thin, unleavened wholewheat flatbread
chicken tawa chicken cooked on a flat iron griddle
chingri malai coconut milk-based prawn curry
churi/choori naan sweetish naan with cashews and raisins
dahi batata puri tiny puris filled with potato, chutneys and yoghurt; chaat dish
dahl lentils
dosa savoury rice and black lentil batter crêpes or pancakes
dum pukht style of slow cooking after sealing the pot with dough
garam doodh hot (usually flavoured) milk
gassi thick coconut-based curry
ghee clarified butter
ghewar crunchy honeycomb cake from Jaipur
gulab churma sweet wheat dumplings with rose petals
gulab jamuns fried milk and flour dumplings soaked in sugar syrup
gosht mutton
idli savoury, steamed lentil and rice cakes
jhinga or **jheenga** prawns
kulfi Indian ice-cream
lachha parathas multilayered Indian bread
lassi sweetened whipped yoghurt drink
machli or **machchi** fish
malai cream
masalas spices
mutter paneer peas with cubed cottage cheese
mishti doi Bengali sweetened yoghurt
misi roti wholewheat flour and lentil chapati
mithai variety of Indian confectionery (also called sweetmeats)
murg/murgh/murgi chicken
mutton usually goat meat
naan tandoor-baked, leavened white flour flatbread
paan betel leaf with condiments
palak spinach
paneer pressed, dry cottage cheese
paneer korma cottage cheese cooked in gravy
paneer makhani cottage cheese in a buttery gravy
paneer palak cottage cheese with spinach
paneer tikka cottage cheese patty
pao bhaji potato or curried mixed vegetables with bread
paratha/parantha/parotta griddle-cooked flaky or stuffed flatbread
phirni rice pudding
pulao pilaf
puri/poori deep-fried puffed bread
rabri sweet, flavoured thickened milk dessert
raita blended yoghurt salad
rasam thin, soupy and peppery dal
rotis or **chapatis** thin, unleavened flatbread
sambar/sambhar dahl and vegetable stew; a South Indian staple
shahi tukda a rich bread pudding
sheermal saffron-flavoured sweetish flatbread
shammi kebab small patty of ground, spiced mutton or beef
tandoor clay oven (tandoori: cooked in a tandoor)
thali platter of multiple dishes served in small bowls with rice and flatbreads

FRAUDS & SCAMS

At some point during your stay you are likely to be accosted by street touts with fraudulent schemes, cons or scams, so stay alert. Agents offering travel services will profess legitimacy by claiming to represent a government body or one licensed by them. Don't make arrangements or go to hotels or shops with agents and touts soliciting you on the street/airport/station.

In Rajasthan and many other tourist hubs, taxi drivers may try to persuade you to shop at stores where they get hefty commissions, which of course governs the price you will pay. Try to shop independently from your driver or guide and ask your hotel for recommendations if necessary.

Taxi drivers and other service providers have been known to distract visitors, switch the Rs 500 note they just handed over for a Rs 100 one, and claim that's what you gave them. When handing over larger notes in cash, make a point of audibly announcing the denomination.

Don't pay for a service or object you haven't asked for, or get fooled into paying exorbitant rates for obvious rubbish. If in doubt, always ask. For instance, a person who decides to accompany you while walking around a tourist site may start up a conversation and offer information about the place; it's not too rude to ask if there will be a request for money at the end of the walk.

Most scammers play on your politeness and sense of guilt. Don't be afraid to be rude or say a firm 'no' if someone is bothering you. If that doesn't work, you'll have to learn to ignore those who are persistent. You could also try and get other Indian tourists, who are not being bothered, involved, and ask them to tell the offenders to go away. You'll be surprised at how well this sometimes works; but don't expect people to come to your rescue unless you ask nicely.

HEALTH & MEDICAL CARE

Though no vaccinations are absolutely required for entry to India (with the exception of yellow fever if you have been in certain countries in Africa and South America), doctors in many countries advise them. Check with your doctor at least three months before travel. The most common vaccinations recommended are against hepatitis A/B, typhoid and diptheria. You may also be recommended anti-malarial pills during your stay. If you're planning a long visit or trips to far-flung rural areas you may require additional vaccinations, such as rabies, tuberculosis, yellow fever and Japanese encephalitis.

MALARIA & DENGUE

Malaria is a potentially fatal disease spread by bites from infected mosquitoes. Thousands of people are infected with malaria in India each year, with the riskiest period being the monsoon (June-Sept). The typical incubation period is one week to one month, but travellers can fall sick up to a year after being infected. Symptoms include fever, body aches, chills, sweating, exhaustion, headaches, nausea and vomiting. The onset of malaria can be difficult to spot because the initial symptoms are flu-like, and the disease must be diagnosed by a blood test. Consult a doctor immediately if you develop malaria-like symptoms. Both the UK foreign office and the US state department advise travellers to India to protect themselves against infection with anti-malarial drugs. Note that there are some chloroquine-resistant strains of malaria present in India.

You can also protect yourself by using an insect repellent containing diethyltoluamide (DEET). A gel/cream called Odomos is widely available; keep windows closed at night and cover your arms and legs. Pyrethroid coils (mosquito coils) to burn are readily available, as are repellents that can be plugged into electrical sockets (Good Knight Activ+ is particularly effective), though all these can cause minor throat or other irritations. Mosquitoes can bite through thin clothing, but you can spray a permethrine insecticide on your clothes, which offers protection for up to two weeks.

Dengue fever is also caused by mosquitoes. Although fatal in fewer than one per cent of cases, it is a very unpleasant disease causing fever, headaches and severe muscle pain. Try to avoid bites using the precautions described above.

WATER

Tap water is not drinkable anywhere in India, so drink branded bottled water. Always check the seal of bottles, as these are sometimes refilled with tap water by unscrupulous vendors. In some places, such as Spiti and Ladakh, reputable NGOs provide reliable and safe water that you can use to fill your own bottle, which is a good option to reduce plastic waste.

Avoid salads unless they've been washed with boiled water or potassium permanganate ($KMnO_4$) and decline ice that hasn't been made with boiled or bottled water. The cylindrical ice with a hole running through it that is served at fancier restaurants is factory-made and generally safe.

HEALTH INSURANCE

All visitors should buy health insurance before arriving in India. If you need to be hospitalised, expect to be charged a security deposit until your insurance payment comes through.

PHARMACIES

Called chemists or medical shops, pharmacies are everywhere and even prescription drugs are often sold over the counter. They are not manned by qualified pharmacists.

HOSPITALS

Delhi All India Institute of Medical Sciences (011-2658-8500); Fortis Flt Lt Rajan Dhall Hospital (011-4277-6222); Indraprastha Apollo Hospital (011-26925-858); Max Healthcare Hospital (011-2651-5050).
Mumbai Bombay Hospital (022-2206-7676); Breach Candy Hospital (022-2367-1888); Hinduja Hospital (022-2445-2575); Kokilaben Ambani Hospital (022-3099-9999); Lilavati Hospital (022-2643-8281).

HOLIDAYS

Museums and other government-related establishments are sometimes closed on state or central government holidays. Government offices are also usually closed on Sunday and often on Saturday; some are open on the first and third Saturday of the month. India has three national holidays: **Republic Day** 26 January, **Independence Day** 15 August and **Mahatma Gandhi Jayanti** (birthday) 2 October. Other common holidays are **Holi** (Feb/Mar), **Christmas** (25 Dec) and **Diwali** (Oct/Nov). Depending on which part of the country you are in, there will be additional state holidays, usually associated with a festival.

LANGUAGE

There are 22 national languages in India, plus 844 dialects and sub-dialects. Although Hindi (not Hindu, which refers to a person who follows Hinduism) is the official language of the government, it is not spoken everywhere, particularly not in the southern states of Andhra Pradesh, Tamil Nadu, Karnataka and Kerala.

That said, it's not very difficult to get by with English. However, don't assume that because someone says a few words in English, they understand everything you are saying.

Indians have added their own flavour and twists to the language. You'll often hear a 'no?' tagged on to the end of a question, and Indians are also particularly adept at malapropisms, euphemisms, using double adjectives (small, small) or adverbs for emphasis, inserting words like 'simply', 'only', 'itself' into sentences and using the present continuous tense.

There are plenty of English words that are used differently in India. A 'hotel' often refers to a restaurant; 'issues' can refer to children, as in 'how many issues do you have?' or problems as in 'no issues' in response to a request. A spouse is referred to as your 'better half', and you may

come across phrases and expressions that leave you flummoxed. Depending on your perceived age, be prepared to be called brother, sister, uncle, auntie, or madam by everyone from auto-rickshaw drivers to college students. Some examples of idiomatic expressions:
Where are you putting up? Where are you staying?
What's your good name? What's your name?
Time-pass While away the time.
Pre-pone Bring forward; opposite of postpone.
Please revert back please respond or confirm.
Do the needful Take care of (it).

MONEY

The currency is the Indian rupee (short form Rs, although one rupee is written Re 1), which comprises 100 paise (p). Coins commonly come in Re 1, Rs 2 and Rs 5 denominations, though 25p, 50p and Rs 10 are also available. Paper money comes in denominations of Rs 5, Rs 10, Rs 20, Rs 50, Rs 100, Rs 500 and Rs 1,000. Change your money at established banks. Avoid money-changers offering black market rates – it's illegal and they are frequently scammers looking to short-change their victims.

ATMS

You'll find ATMs are everywhere in large cities, though you need to check in advance with your bank whether your card will work in India and what fee it will charge. They dispense rupees only. In smaller towns, national parks and in the upper Himalayas, you're likely to need cash. Many ATMs are guarded by watchmen, but exercise basic caution and discretion.

CREDIT CARDS

Credit cards are widely accepted in most large cities, though some establishments levy a charge. MasterCard (MC) and Visa (V) are most frequently accepted; American Express is less popular and only a few venues accept Diners Club (DC) cards. Hotels, restaurants and shops that do not accept American Express cards are mentioned in the chapters; where nothing is indicated, all cards are accepted.

To report a lost or stolen credit card call the company that issued it or these 24-hour helplines: American Express +1 715-343-7977; MasterCard 000-800-100-1087; Visa 000-800-100-1219.

TRAVELLERS CHEQUES

These are not usually accepted by restaurants and shops, though most hotels will take them.

POVERTY & CHARITY

No matter what you read or hear about India's booming economy, on the ground you will encounter the reality of hunger, poverty and suffering. Beggars and people who live in the street are everywhere, and you will constantly be accosted for money. In most cities, giving to one beggar invariably draws a dozen others to your side within seconds. On the other hand, you will see and meet people in genuine distress and you will have to decide what to do. Some worthwhile options to consider are to buy a needy person food instead of giving them money. Still better, perhaps, is to donate to a respected charity (and there are many) doing good work among the needy. Worthwhile charities include the Aseema (022-2640-7248), ASHA Foundation (www.ashaf.org), Deepalaya (www.deepalaya.org), Family Home (022-2413-0721), HelpAge India (www.helpageindia.org), Maharogi Sewa Samiti (mss.niya.org), Meljol (www.meljol.net), Mobile Crèches (www.mobilecreches.org), Pankhudi (080-2568-1076), Plan India (www.planindia.org), Prerana (www.preranaatc.com) and Salaam Baalak Trust (www.salaambaalaktrust.com).

SAFETY & SECURITY

India is a relatively safe country in which to travel. Muggings, robberies and serious crimes against tourists are rare, but they do occur and northern cities are generally more dodgy than the rest of the country. Take all the normal, obvious precautions, particularly when alone and at night. Pickpockets operate in crowded areas everywhere. Don't leave your luggage unattended anywhere in public. Some tourists have been drugged and robbed in India, so exercise extreme caution when accepting food or drink from strangers. Look up your country's travel advice before you begin your journey. *See also p383* **Frauds & scams**.

SHOPPING

Shopping is a challenge. Bazaars and even some established shops are open to bargaining and most will quote a price based on what they think you will pay. You could start with half the quoted price, though that's not a hard and fast rule. Make comparisons and don't feel embarrassed to come back to a store after making enquiries elsewhere. While bargaining is a given, take into consideration the situation and concede that a few rupees here and there may not be worth the haggle. Government-owned shops and many recommended in this guide sell quality wares at 'fixed' prices, which means no bargaining.

TELEPHONES & COMMUNICATION

Payphones and phone kiosks can be found on main streets all over India and can be used to make reasonably priced calls anywhere. Landlines in many towns and even cities are notorious for being out of order; mobiles are generally more reliable. There are internet cafés throughout the country, but don't expect fast connections.

CODES

India's country code is 91. Each city or town also has an area code, called the STD code, which starts with '0': Delhi is 011, Mumbai 022. Mobile phone numbers are usually ten digits and begin with a 9.

DIALLING WITHIN INDIA

When dialling from within the country keep the '0' in the STD code. You do not need to dial the STD code of the city when dialling a number within the same town or city. If using a mobile phone, however, you do need the STD code, even if calling from the same city.

DIALLING FROM OUTSIDE INDIA

Start with the international access code of your country, followed by the country code 91, drop the '0' before the area code and then dial the number. To dial a mobile number, dial the international access code, country code, and drop any zeros before the number.

MOBILE PHONES

Pre-paid SIM cards that fit into GSM phones are easily available. For security reasons, you need to provide passport-size photos, photocopies of your passport and other documentation before you can buy one. These SIM cards are easily rechargeable at kiosks and shops. Make sure you have a roaming facility unless you plan to stay in one place. There are innumerable service providers with varying coverage, though Vodafone, Idea, Loop, Aircel, BSNL, Tata Indicom and Reliance Infocom are the largest.

TIME

There is only one time zone in India and there is no daylight savings time. Indian Standard Time (IST) is GMT plus five and a half hours.

TIPPING

In restaurants, generally leave ten per cent. Hotel bellboys get tipped based on the standard of the hotel and how much luggage you have (anything from Rs 10 to Rs 50 or more is appropriate). In general, taxis and auto-rickshaws don't expect a tip, but it's always appreciated. For drivers of hired cars, a tip of Rs 150-Rs 200 per day is fair, unless you feel your driver deserves more.

It's hard to escape the system of tipping (or baksheesh). You will be accosted for baksheesh for just about every service and often for nothing at all, only because you are wealthier than the person requesting the tip. In the latter situation, learn to say 'no' and move on.

TOILETS

There are two kinds of toilet in India – the Western-style toilet and the Indian 'squat' toilet (a hole in the ground that usually has raised ribbed spaces to put your feet). Squat toilets take a bit of getting used to, but the absence of a seat makes them more hygienic. Traditionally, water and not toilet paper is used, so it's advisable to carry your own. Public toilets in most places, including many restaurants, and especially at railway and bus stations, are poorly maintained; or they just don't exist. Most major stores and shopping malls usually keep their toilets clean; alternatively, head to the nearest hotel.

VISAS & IMMIGRATION

All foreign visitors require a visa except for citizens of Nepal, Bhutan and the Maldives. There is no provision for granting visas upon arrival and you should apply to the Indian embassy or high commission in your home country. Visitors planning to stay more than 180 days must register with the Foreigners' Regional Registration Office in one of the big cities within 14 days of arrival. They are usually issued a six-month, multiple-entry visa but you can currently re-enter only after a gap of two months. Visa extensions are sometimes possible through the same office. In some places, such as Dharamsala and Goa, visitors on extended stays are advised to register at the local police station. Special Inner Line Permits are required to visit certain areas of Sikkim, Ladakh and the Andaman Islands, among other places.

WOMEN

While women in many Indian cities are independent, assertive and strongly represented in senior jobs, in most of the rest of the country they play a secondary role in a patriarchal society. Despite all those Bollywood posters of skimpily clad women, conservative dress is the norm – short skirts and tight tops are generally reserved for the upper classes, although jeans and T-shirts are the city college student's uniform.

Foreign women are likely to be objects of curiosity, and occasionally of lascivious attention, and it's best to avoid revealing clothing. Some Indian men have the idea that Western women are more open to casual sex than their Indian counterparts, so be careful about the kind of signals you send out.

Cat-calls, sexual harassment and worse by men is often referred to as 'eve-teasing', and is common. Although rapes and other sexual crimes are not common, they do occur.

Festivals & Events

Most festivals in India are religious in nature, and many religions practised in India follow lunar calendars so dates may change every year. Some may even move from one month to another.

JANUARY

All-India
Makar Sankranti/Pongal
Marks the sun entering Capricorn. Celebrated differently throughout India. In some states it's a kite-flying festival. In Tamil Nadu it's the start of the new year.

Allahabad & other North Indian towns
Maha Kumbh Mela
Hindu pilgrimage festival that involves bathing in holy rivers (next is 27 Jan-25 Feb 2013).

Magh Mela
Annual version of the Kumbh mela.

Jaipur
Jaipur Literature Festival
Asia's leading literary festival.
www.jaipurliteraturefestival.org

Kolkata
Dover Lane Music Festival
Indian classical music.

North India
Basant Panchami
Celebrates the coming of spring; dedicated to goddess Saraswati.

Port Blair
Island Tourism Festival
Two weeks of music, dance, arts and crafts and watersports events (end Dec-Feb).

FEBRUARY

Agra
Taj Mahotsav
Ten-day crafts and culture fest (8-27 Feb).
www.tajmahotsav.org.

Goa
Carnival
Three days of celebration, with music, floats and revelry.

Jaisalmer, Rajasthan
Desert Festival
Three days of music, puppet shows and dance.
www.jaisalmer.org

Khajuraho
Khajuraho Dance Festival
Classical Indian dance performances at the cave temples.

Mumbai
Elephanta Festival
Illuminated caves, folk dances and local cuisine.

Kala Ghoda Arts Festival
Nine-day festival of arts and heritage.
www.kalaghodassociation.com

Nagaur, Rajasthan
Nagaur Sufi Music Festival
Sufi and sacred music.
http://nagaursufifestival.org

MARCH

All-India
Holi
Also called Festival of Colours. Bonfires are lit the night before and people celebrate the onset of spring by throwing coloured powder and water.

Mahashivrati
Birthday of Shiva.

Muharram
Marks the martyrdom of Hazrat Imam Hussein.

Jaipur
Elephant Festival
Celebrated at the time of Holi, with folk dances and processions of bedecked elephants, elephant races, polo matches and tug-of-war.

Rajasthan, especially Jaipur and Udaipur
Gangaur Fair
Women honour the goddess Gauri/Parvati. Singing, dancing and colourful street processions.

APRIL/MAY

Amritsar, Punjab
Baisakhi
Harvest and religious festival.

Dharamsala

Buddha Purnima
Birthday of the Buddha.

Kerala

Temple festivals
Tributes to a temple's presiding god (at Thrissur and other locations in Kerala).

JUNE/JULY

Jaipur, Rajasthan & North India

Teej
Celebrates the advent of the monsoon with processions, stalls, fairs and dance.

Ladakh

Hemis Festival
Birthday of Guru Padmasambhava.

AUGUST/SEPTEMBER

All-India

Eid-ul-Fitr/Ramzan Id
End of Ramzan (Ramadan).

Ganesh Chaturthi
Birthday of Lord Ganesha. Celebrations are particularly huge in Mumbai.

Janmashtami
Krishna's birthday, celebrated in various ways. In Mumbai, human pyramids are formed to reach a pot of yoghurt hung up high.

Nag Panchami
Festival of snake worship. Most prominent in West Bengal, Maharashtra, Kerala.

Jodhpur

Marwar Festival
Local folk music and dance.

Kerala

Onam
Harvest festival; celebrations include processions and dance.

Nehru Trophy Boat Race
Snake boat race at Punnamada Lake, Alappuzha (second Sat in Aug).
www.nehrutrophy.nic.in).

OCTOBER/NOVEMBER

All-India

Bakri Id
Muslim Feast of the Sacrifice.

Diwali/Deepavali
Hindu festival of lights.

Navratri
Nine-day cultural celebration of worship and traditional dance, culminating in Dusserah.

Dusserah
Hindu festival celebrating the victory of good over evil.

Delhi

19th Commonwealth Games
3-14 Oct 2010.
www.cwgdelhi2010.org

Ananya
Classical dance at the Purana Qila.

Qutb Festival of Dance & Music
Classical music and dance at the Qutb Complex.

Delhi, Varanasi, other North Indian towns

Ramlila Mela
Celebrates the return of the Hindu god Rama from exile, with enactments of scenes from the *Ramayana*.

Hampi

Hampi Festival
Traditional music and dance.

Jodhpur

Rajasthan International Folk Festival
Features artists from Rajasthan and the world.
www.jodphurfolkfestival.org

Lucknow

Lucknow Festival
Lucknavi culture and cuisine.

Pushkar, Rajasthan

Pushkar Fair
Camel and cattle fair

Varanasi

Ganga Mahotsav
Five-day festival of classical music and dance.

DECEMBER

Goa

St Francis Day
Honours the death of St Francis Xavier (3 Dec).

Kochi

Kochi/Cochin Carnival
New year revelry.

Itineraries

How long do you need to see India? Many argue that two weeks is the very least you need to make a trip to India worthwhile, but much depends on what you are looking for. You can certainly have a pleasant, leisurely holiday in one destination in a week, or hurry around two, or even three, places. But of course it'll take a lot longer to sample and savour a wider selection of the myriad sites, cultures, terrains and cuisines that India has to offer. This is an enormous country. Distances between places are great, and transport and tourist infrastructure limited. Even if you're here for months you'll have to accept the fact that you'll only get to experience a small taste of India.

But it's perfectly possible for that taste to be highly rewarding. We've formulated the suggested itineraries – for one week and two (or three) weeks – on the basis of the kind of traveller you are: one who wants to pack in as much as possible, or the kind who prefers to take in India at a comfortable, relaxed pace.

Bear in mind that this guide is organised in a way that assists you with mixing and matching destinations to create your own itinerary, depending on your interests. So, for maximum variety, you might include an architectural gem, a big city, small city, wildlife park and/or one of our four alluring escapes, based on how much time you have. At the end of the book, we have also given some tips and additional destination combination suggestions to help you in your planning.

For more on arranging travel, *see p378* **Navigating India**.

Leisurely one week

Many of the destinations in this book would be suitable for a relaxing week's visit. All of the alluring escapes, for example, are comfortable destinations for a week-long sojourn: **Goa**, **Kerala Backwaters**, **Pondicherry** and the **Andaman Islands**.

Alternatively, you could cover one city (Mumbai or Delhi) and one additional destination. If you take in **Mumbai**, you could add on a trip to either **Aurangabad**, **Ajanta & Ellora** or a Rajasthan city – **Udaipur** or **Jaipur**. All are a short flight (1-1.5hrs) away.

If you begin in **Delhi**, you can take the overnight Ranikhet Express train to Ramnagar to visit **Corbett National Park** (alternatively, it's 7hrs by car) or fly to historic **Lucknow** (1hr) or the Hindu religious centre of **Varanasi** (1.5hrs).

Whirlwind one week

The most popular route for travellers with only a week in India is to visit what's known as the Golden Triangle: **Delhi**, **Agra** and **Jaipur** (all 4-6hrs apart by road). However, there are many other interesting options if you're willing to forgo the Taj Mahal (at Agra).

For a southern variation you could start in **Mumbai**, take a flight south to the temples of **Madurai** (via Chennai, 5 hrs), and make an adventurous two-day detour by road either to the Palani Hills (*see p197*) or the once-French coastal town of **Pondicherry** (6hr overnight train to Villupuram).

For those who'd like to experience North and South India, and get a sense of both the history and the natural beauty of each, a two-day trip to Delhi could be combined with a journey south to the **Kerala Backwaters** (3.5hr flight to Kochi, then 2hrs by car), Goa (2.5hr flight), or Pondicherry (2.5hr flight to Chennai then 2hrs by road).

Leisurely two weeks

Lots more options are open to you if you have two weeks to spend in India, even if you want to figure in plenty of down time into your stay. If you want to see something of North India you could begin with a few days in **Delhi**. Then fly to **Udaipur** (1.5hrs) for four days, taking in outlying attractions like the Ranakpur temples (*see p93*) and Kumbhalgarh Fort (*see p95*). A road trip can then take you to **Jodhpur**, stopping overnight at one of the region's famous heritage hotels en route, and getting a taste of rural Rajasthan. After a few days in Jodhpur, fly back to Delhi (2hrs), then travel onward by road to **Agra** (4hrs) or take the overnight train (10hrs). Spend a night (or more) in Agra before returning to Delhi to wind up your trip.

Another option is to go east. After two days of British Raj-era architecture and Bengali cuisine in **Kolkata**, fly to Bagdogra (1hr) and then travel by car to the eastern Himalayas to spend at least a week, visiting the Himalayan kingdom of **Sikkim** (4hrs), and possibly taking in **Darjeeling** and **Kalimpong** as well.

South India's temples are unforgettable, both for their elaborate architecture and decorative carving and for the insight they provide into local religious life and culture. The Meenakshi temple at **Madurai** is one of the most outstanding; a visit here can be combined with side trips to Karaikudi (*see p195*) and the Cardamom or Palani Hills (*see p197*). Take a flight from **Mumbai** to Madurai (via Chennai, 5 hrs). From Madurai, venture west by car to **Periyar** (3hrs) and then beyond to the **Kerala Backwaters** (4hrs from Periyar); alternatively, fly from Madurai to Bengaluru/Bangalore (1hr) and take the overnight train to **Hampi**. Return by air to Mumbai the same way (via Bengaluru), to finish your trip.

Another option is to start with a few days in **Mumbai** and then fly to **Kochi** (2hrs). Spend three days there and then take in a two-day wildlife experience at **Periyar** (4hrs by car) followed by a week enjoying both the beaches and backwaters of **Kerala** (4hrs by car), where you can indulge in some Ayurvedic spa treatments and rejuvenation therapies.

Whirlwind two weeks or relaxed three weeks

There's an almost endless range of variations possible if you want to pack as much as you can into a two-week trip. A good option is to arrive in **Mumbai** and fly first to the lake city of **Udaipur** (1.5hr) in Rajasthan, then to **Jaipur** (1hr), and then to **Delhi** (1hr), spending two days in each city. From Delhi make a day trip to **Agra** (4hrs by car), including a visit to Fatehpur Sikri (*see p163*). The next morning take the Swarna Shatabdi train from Delhi to **Amritsar** (6hrs, or 1.5hrs by air) to visit the Golden Temple and then drive to **McLeod Ganj/Dharamsala** (5hrs) the same night. Spend three days in Little Tibet experiencing Buddhist culture and walks on mountain trails, before returning back to Delhi via Amritsar.

Those keen on getting a varied cultural experience and sampling some of India's great architectural gems can take a train from **Delhi** to **Gwalior** (3-4hrs) and then explore **Orchha** and **Khajuraho** over six days by road, allowing time for travel and rest. From Khajuraho fly to **Varanasi** (40mins) for two days and then back to Delhi (1.5hrs). You'll still have time for a quick day trip or overnighter to **Agra** to see the Taj. Alternatively, drop one of these and spend three days in one of Central India's wildlife parks; **Panna** is just 50 kilometres (2hrs drive) from Khajuraho and **Bandhavgarh** is seven hours away.

A hectic South India tour could take you from **Mumbai** to **Madurai** by air via Chennai (5hrs). From Madurai, travel by road to **Periyar** (3hrs) and then onward to **Kochi** (4hrs) for a few days, followed by the **Kerala Backwaters** (2hrs) for four. Fly from Kochi back to Mumbai (2hrs), where you can spend a day or two exploring the city before heading home.

Energetic travellers wishing to combine both North and South India can begin in **Delhi**, visit **Agra** for the day (4hrs drive), then return to Delhi to fly to **Lucknow** (1hr) or **Varanasi** (1.5hrs) for a few days, returning the same way. Then fly south to Chennai (2.5hrs), from where you can take an overnight train or flight (10hrs train, 1hr flight) to **Madurai**. A few days later take a car (8hrs) or train to **Pondicherry** (6hrs to Villupuram) to spend the rest of your holiday either exploring Pondicherry's quaint French Quarter or relaxing at a nearby beach resort.

Other suggested destination combinations

Of course, there are numerous other possible destination combinations, and several of our suggested itineraries can be mixed and matched to create your own. Destinations that fit well together include:

Goa and **Hampi & Around**
Madurai and **Andaman Islands**
Khajuraho and **Bandhavgarh**
Agra and **Lucknow**
Varanasi and **Kolkata**
Amritsar and **McLeod Ganj/Dharamsala**
Kochi and **Periyar** and/or **Kerala Backwaters**
Mumbai and **Aurangabad, Ajanta & Ellora**
Jodhpur and **Udaipur**
Lucknow and **Varanasi**
Kolkata and **Darjeeling, Kalimpong & Sikkim**
Pondicherry and **Madurai**

Itinerary planning tips and advice

- Make sure your itinerary leaves enough time for you to explore and relax.
- Given the distances in India, you will spend a proportion of your holiday getting from one place to another. Make sure you factor in enough time for this – half a day at least for each change, even for a shorter journey or a flight.
- Many popular or small hotels are full in peak season (Nov-Feb), so booking these in advance is advisable.
- Make proximity to each other or good air connections a factor when choosing places to visit.
- Be prepared for the fact that different regions of India are culturally vastly different. You may find that North India (excluding the Himalayas) people who benefit from the tourist trade are generally more pushy (sometimes even aggressive) compared to their counterparts in the south.
- Mountain destinations (Ladakh, Spiti or Darjeeling, Kalimpong & Sikkim) are best visited by those who have at least ten days to spare. While it's not unknown for tourists with only a week in India to fly in and out of Leh in Ladakh, we don't recommend it. It takes a minimum of two days to acclimatise to the altitude, and before you have warmed up, it will be time to leave.
- Finally, always remember that in India you must expect the unexpected, in the form of delays, cancellations, miscellaneous unforeseen events, and various road- and weather-related problems and setbacks. Take them in your stride.

Advertisers' Index

Please refer to relevant sections for contact details

Introduction

The Great Cities

Mumbai

Delhi

Urban Gems

Jaipur

Alluring Escapes

Pondicherry

Husainabad Imambara, Lucknow.

Index

A

B

C

D

E

K

L

M